MANAGING CULTURAL DIFFERENCES

THIRD EDITION

THE M©©SERIES
MANAGING CULTURAL DIFFERENCES

Series Editors: Philip R. Harris and Robert T. Moran

---

* An *Instructor's Guide* is available. For details write Gulf Publishing, Book Division, P.O. Box 2608, Houston, Texas 77252-2608.

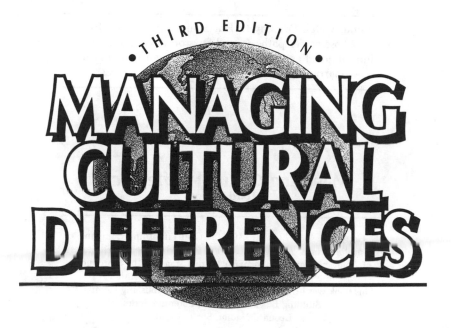

THIRD EDITION

MANAGING CULTURAL DIFFERENCES

Philip R. Harris
Robert T. Moran

Gulf Publishing Company
Houston, London, Paris, Zurich, Tokyo

To our wives, Dorothy L. Harris and Virgilia M. Moran,
whose career paths crossed ours on foreign soil and
international assignments, and who taught us so much in
marriage about managing cultural differences!

Managing Cultural Differences
Third Edition

Gulf Publishing Company
P.O. Box 2608
Houston, Texas 77252-2608

10 9 8 7 6 5 4 3

Library of Congress Cataloging-in-Publication Data
Harris, Philip R. (Philip Robert), 1926-
    Managing cultural differences/Philip R. Harris,
Robert T. Moran.
    —3rd ed.
        p. cm.
    Includes bibliographical references.
    ISBN 0-88415-078-X
    1. International business enterprises—Management.
    2. Acculturation. 3. Cross-cultural studies. I. Moran, Robert T.,
    1938- .   II. Title.
HD62.4.H37 1990
658.1′8—dc20   90-35354
                                                                    CIP

Contents

Unit I—Cultural Impacts on Global Management

Unit II—Cultural Impacts on International Business

Unit III—Cultural Specifics and Business/Service Abroad

Unit IV—Management Resources for Global Professionals

Foreword

At first glance, a book titled *Managing Cultural Differences* leads one to anticipate that this is, indeed, an oxymoron. Management and cultural differences just seem to not go together well.

Phil Harris and Bob Moran have taken on the heroic task of teaching us that through understanding of cultural differences, it is possible to facilitate the process of accomplishing goals and objectives. Their third edition of the popular book called *Managing Cultural Differences* is, indeed, a work that will stand the test of time.

For most managers who are now confronted with the international "context" the role that culture plays in affecting performance and opportunities is a secondary subject that is often handled through general observations and frequenting indigenous restaurants. Harris and Moran remind us that culture is like an iceberg—only part of it is seen, but most of it is not. It is this underbelly of cultural difference that forms the backbone of this text. I am particularly taken with the focus on the difference between coping with cultural differences and actually trying to manage this process. The authors use excellent case vignettes to show how one institution achieves their objectives in the international context, while another stumbles around never quite understanding why "things don't work in Bolivia!"

Too often, those of us who are charged with managing institutions forget that whatever culture exists, it is not static. It is equally true that when one is doing business with a Japanese corporation today, it is not the same as having done business with that same firm ten years ago. Too many of our intellectuals have given readers the impression that cultures can be described in a static state. The tendency to over-simplify, such as the observations on "Japanese management style," have frozen managers' impressions of how to deal in complex cultures. Perhaps the most classic example of this situation is in the current "restructuring" of the Soviet Union, and the recognition by the rest of the world that Russians are a collection of many, diverse cultures.

The first-time reader of this text should focus on several key elements that are unique to managing cultural differences. Moran and Harris have done an excellent job of provoking thought about the role that technology has played in forcing the globalization process upon us. They focus well on the role that the cliché of effective communication plays in this globalization process. The best reward for a first-time reader is that the authors don't simply speculate about communication; they actually let you work through a classic example of how communication works in a cross-cultural circumstance. Their pragmatic view of communication is best illustrated by the chapter on negotiation style. Here, they even provide a test that allows an individual to self-examine their own capabilities.

After completing the text, you should come away with the knowledge that it is possible to look at the future of a globalized industrial state with confidence that complexity can be overcome with knowledge and intelligent focusing on the principles of managing cultural change.

Roy A. Herberger, Jr., Ph.D.
President
American Graduate School
of International Management
Glendale, Arizona

Editor's Preface

We are fortunate. Drs. Harris and Moran have written a third edition of their important book. Too often, a new edition of a book is essentially the previous edition with some minor changes and updating. That is not the case with this new *Managing Cultural Differences*. The authors have done a great deal to increase its relevancy and timeliness. The first edition received an enthusiastic response and the authors used it in many of their workshops and seminars. They received feedback from participants and readers that has served to make this edition an even more important contribution than its predecessor.

Every day we find increasing evidence of the importance of understanding ourselves and others if we are to survive and live in the world. This applies to the economic level, as well as the social and political levels.

Within the U.S., there is an increasing concern about the impact of culture within organizations. This is healthy, although some people are blind to the realities of that impact. Though Drs. Harris and Moran are dealing with international factors, there is much material here that can help us to understand differing cultural norms within a U.S. organization.

As with previous editions, the authors have provided us with an amazing amount of insight and detail without overburdening us. The topic is difficult, but their presentation makes it easy, interesting reading. Their inclusion of incidents and examples highlights the theories and concepts spread throughout the book.

This book obviously has much to contribute to anybody engaged in international and cross-cultural activities. Likewise, it has a great deal to offer to anybody who is involved in the economic life of our country. The list of foreign companies operating in the U.S. continues to grow. We now have combinations of foreign and domestic companies that ten years earlier would have been almost inconceivable.

Indeed, the "global manager" can be operating in the U.S. as well as in some foreign country. It is no longer the location that distinguishes among managers but rather the range of different foreign nationals with whom they interact.

This is a book to be read first from cover to cover. Then, parts of it can be used frequently for reference and updating. You will find yourself returning to specific segments, exercises, and resources as the need arises. Do not hesitate to do so for there is much of value in this book that cannot possibly be absorbed in only one reading.

Leonard Nadler
Professor Emeritus, George Washington University
Series Editor, Building Blocks of Human Potential

Preface

In the past ten years the first and second editions of *Managing Cultural Differences* not only became popular with world managers and professionals, but were adopted as textbooks in more than 100 colleges and universities. Extra printings along the way confirmed the growing need for and interest in developing intercultural awareness and skills. Now at the beginning of a new decade—the last of the 20th century—we find ourselves compelled to provide still another edition. Why the need for a 1990s version of *Managing Cultural Differences?* First and foremost, are the accelerating and breathtaking changes within world culture that force revision of our content. Who could have predicted that since the last edition three years ago such radical changes would occur in the European Economic Community, the Eastern Bloc countries, and the People's Republic of China? Secondly, our expanding readership has sent to us remarkable input and insight, some of which shall be shared with you in these pages. We especially appreciate the endorsements not only from organizations worldwide, but from cities like Indianapolis, whose mayor wrote that *MCD* helped the city in planning for the Pan American Games which they hosted, as well as with other international initiatives of that municipality. We are grateful, too, to others who report that *MCD* provides managers with the tools to understand people and to develop cooperation, and that the book serves as a guide to the nuances of foreign management, which helps readers to avoid the cultural reefs that sink international business. That kind of encouragement prompts us to update our material.

Thus, this third edition has several new features and serves as a springboard for others, including:

- Timely additions that are culturally relevant, such as the section on *maquiladora* plants along the U.S.-Mexican border.
- Supplementary services to assist trainers, professors, and managers, including an *Instructor's Guide* and now the *Directory of Multicultural Resources* on floppy disk, so that the latest information in this area will be available to readers.
- A series of *MCD*-related books that focus on such topics as joint ventures, marketing, finance, and health services.

This third edition of *Managing Cultural Differences* is a result of the wide acceptance and utility of its previous editions in such fields as international business, communication, and training. Management's growing awareness of the pervasive influence of culture upon employee behavior, customer relations, work, and productivity has encouraged many others to study and describe the impact of intercultural management and relocation challenges. Increasing numbers of executives and educators are now accepting our basic premise that learning for greater cultural understanding and competency should be an essential part of all management and professional development, especially in business and professional schools. Therefore, with your encouragement, the authors now launch another completely revised version of our text aimed at advancing the tenets of effective cross-cultural management even further.

Managing Cultural Differences, Third Edition reflects the original edition's intent, but enhances the message with extensive new input. The material is reorganized and presented in a more integrated and relevant way for the benefit of our worldwide audience. It is structured around the *global manager,* an innovative concept on the cutting edge of international management that can prepare the reader to cope with a rapidly changing business environment. Simply put, the "global manager" exercises leadership at home or abroad, in private or public sector, in profit-making or non-profit organizations. A manager knows how to get things done; a leader has vision to look beyond the moment and to know what thing to do. Thus, this edition is filled with ideas and insights that broaden the manager or technician's horizons, while offering pragmatic means for improving performance effectiveness within or across borders. The book is in tune with the megatrend toward globalization, whether in the economy or marketplace, in communication or transportation, in management or the professions, in human services or militarization. Our purpose is not simply to help you better cope with cultural differences, but to facilitate cultural synergy or cooperative results through you.

For reader convenience, the material has been organized into four major parts. The first seven chapters are intended to increase your comprehension of the cultural impacts on management. Specifically, we examine the emerging role of the global manager as a cosmopolitan, communicator, negotiator, creator of synergy, leader in change, and influencer of organizational, work, and team cultures. The second unit explores in the next five chapters the cultural impacts on international business. Cross-cultural effectiveness is analyzed particularly in terms of the international assignment, business protocol, family relocation, and technology transfer. Special attention is devoted in this regard to means and methods of human resource development, collaboration, and networking among professionals and technicians. Six of the chapters in the third unit are entirely devoted to matters of culture specifics for those engaged in international business or service. How to do business with intercultural sensitivity and skill is reviewed for major world regions—North America, Latin

America, Asia, Europe, Middle East, India, and Africa. The concluding chapter pulls together the volume's themes and deals with high performance in new market opportunities.

The book is a balance of theory and models, as well as research results and practical guidelines. It contains many critical incidents, case studies, self-assessment tools, figures, and tables. The final unit embodies management resources for global professionals with instruments for data-gathering and analysis. The book concludes with a comprehensive bibliography, alphabetically arranged and keyed to the publishing dates of pertinent references in the chapters, and author and subject indexes to facilitate referencing and further research.

ACKNOWLEDGMENTS

Writing *Managing Cultural Differences* was not only a synergistic effort by the authors, but required the cooperation of many colleagues and clients. Whenever possible we have tried to acknowledge them in the text proper, as well as in the reference section. However, we are especially appreciative of the work of our editors, William J. Lowe and Timothy W. Calk of Gulf Publishing Company, as well as the series editor, Leonard Nadler of George Washington University. In particular, we would like to express our gratitude to these professionals for their very special contributions: the late Wolfgang Fassbender, Diebold Europe; Orville L. Freeman, Business International Corporation; Dorothy L. Harris, United States International University; the late John M. Hoffman, Family Relocation Services; the late June Inglima, United States Customs Service; the late Hank E. Koehn, Trimtabs Consulting Group; Krishna Kumar, University of Michigan; George W. Renwick, Renwick Associates of Scottsdale; Walter A. Schratz, Westinghouse Education Foundation; and V. Lynn Tyler, Brigham Young University.
George W. Renwick, Renwick Associates of Scottsdale; Walter A. Schratz, Westinghouse Education Foundation; Thomas C. Stevens, J.I. Case and Company; and V. Lynn Tyler, Brigham Young University.

In addition to many helpful members of our family and friends, we would be remiss not to pay particular tribute to these clients who helped us to test out our ideas and methods of cross-cultural training: ARAMCO; American Management Associations; Association of Venezuelian Executives; Chase Manhattan Bank; The Diebold Group; Esso Eastern, N. A.; *International Management* (London); Management Centre Europe; Philips, N. V. (Netherlands); Westinghouse Electric/Learning Corporations; United Nations *Development Forum* (Geneva); United States Navy and Customs Service; University of Strathclyde (Scotland); University of Sophia (Tokyo).

And finally, we wish to thank the following people for permitting us to use portions of their research: Nancy Baldwin, Maria Brightbill, Terry Finnegan,

Terry Frosini, Per Karlsson, Ricardo McFalls, Ales Roubinek, Sherry Schmulling, Carol Sussman, Farid Elashmawi, Israel Unterman, Rajesh Kumar, and Kazuo Takaiwa.

Philip R. Harris, Ph.D.
Harris International, Ltd.
LaJolla, California

Robert T. Moran, Ph.D.
American Graduate School
of International Management
Glendale, Arizona

Unit I
Cultural Impacts on Global Management

Change agents who are involved with international development of organizations want not only to improve them for the moment, but also to facilitate a far-reaching and long-lasting transformation of organizational life. For this to happen, our organizations must be seen and understood as cultural entities, determined, to a considerable extent, by behavioral norms that make up the "organizational unconsciousness." Once we are aware of the crucial norms, they can be consciously and systematically changed and supported, creating a long-lasting transformation that has ramifications for the larger society (Allen and Kraft 1984).

1
Managers as Cosmopolitans

For organizations to flourish, let alone survive in the decade of the 1990s, their perspective must be global. John S. McClenhen, Senior International Editor of *Industry Week* reports ". . . in order to capitalize on the globalization of commerce . . . American managers will have to think beyond the borders of the United States."

Time Magazine on October 9, 1989, from the perspective of foreign companies and individuals coming to the United States, put it this way, "I came, I saw, I blundered . . . for bosses from abroad, the U.S. is tougher than it looks."

If you can appreciate the significance of the following statements, you are probably concerned about managing cultural differences and creating cultural synergy:

1. Japanese culture promotes a tremendous sense of identity and group belonging. Creating ambiguity is almost a social obligation and unconscious process that often leads foreigners to draw false conclusions based on Japanese appearances.
2. In Saudi Arabia, the protocol is to use the first meeting for social acquaintance, warm-up, or trust building, and not as a time to conduct serious business.
3. Westinghouse has been in the midst of transforming its organizational culture, so that it may become more productive and profitable.
4. High technology and fast-growth companies are often harbingers of a new work culture.
5. In matters of recruitment and selection, Asian managers often rely on family and friends whom they can trust or have obligations to, while Western managers use more objective measures of competency.
6. When doing business in Indonesia, handshaking with either sex is perfectly acceptable, but using the left hand for this purpose is strictly "taboo"; in other cultures, handshakes are avoided, and some form of bow is preferred.
7. Los Angeles is increasingly becoming a capital Third World market with its diverse multicultural and multilingual population. Spanish and Korean are the second and third largest foreign-language groups. Cultural

3

themes greatly influence the success or failure of a product or service. For example, the Hispanic attitude toward fatalism reduces the appeal of product guarantees and warranties, and focusing on the family enhances product appeal.

8. The Business Council for International Understanding estimates that international personnel who go abroad without cross-cultural preparation have a failure rate ranging from 33–66% in contrast to less than 2% of those who had the benefit of such training.

9. Cultural competencies improve performance within international organizations and conferences, as was demonstrated at Intelevent '85 on the French Riveria. In attendance at this world conference on telecommunications were 300 senior executives and government officials from more than 20 countries who examined issues of international competition in their industry, joint ventures, and the increasing importance to trade of the Pacific and Indian basins.

10. John Hoff spent twenty years as a successful expatriate executive in Latin America. Upon his reentry into the U.S.A., he had severe difficulties adjusting. His company discharged him and he had to start up a new business on his own; his wife divorced him; within five years of his return, he committed suicide. Transitional experiences, often triggered by some traumatic event, usually imply a change in lifestyle and require adaptations in one's cultural responses.

Each of these "critical incidents" involved unique cultural situations. The summaries are authentic situations that provide a rationale not only for this book, but for why managers and other professionals must be more cross-culturally effective. It is our thesis that all management or professional development requires some intercultural learning and skill. Furthermore, we must learn to move beyond the mere coping with the cultural differences among the Earth's inhabitants, and create more synergy among them.

Since this book's first edition in 1979, this has not only been confirmed, but the consciousness of business and government leaders has risen relative to the importance of cultural factors on our behavior. Whether one is concerned about the supervisors of minority employees, the acquisition of a U.S. firm by a foreign owner, the joint venture or merger of two corporations, increasing tourism, world trade, or international economic cooperation, culture will impact the relationships and the operations. Whether our readers are executives or technicians, physicians or attorneys, educators or social workers, hospital or service administrators, military or public servants, or students preparing for such roles, the message of these pages is relevant. To intelligently comprehend world reports and news, we must read and listen with cultural sensitivity. In 1985, for example, there were two massive air disasters in the areas near Tokyo and Dallas. The Japanese apologized, negotiated, and settled claims. American management scrambled for legal advice, solicited attorney offers, and ended up with multiple suits. Why the difference in approach and what can we learn from the cultural responses to a similar event? Thurow and others (1985) at M.I.T. are now examining the Japanese view of the global management challenges.

We use the term "global managers" to encompass all of us whose responsibilities require us to deal with people and human culture. At the end of this chapter we have summarized a dozen reasons for acquiring cross-cultural understanding and skills that are in harmony with this introduction. But first, let us begin with the "big picture" of what is happening globally to managers and professionals. When cultural changes are seen in this larger context, strategic planning becomes more feasible (Kaynak 1984).

GLOBAL TRANSFORMATIONS

Too many corporate and government leaders are operating upon "old pictures" of the cosmos and human nature, including the nature of work, the worker, and the management process itself. Executives in transnational enterprises should join the common struggle for a world cultural rebirth, and assist in conjuring up the new visions that will energize or motivate the human family.

Psychiatrist Robert Jay Lifton put the matter succinctly:

> In times of severe historical dislocation, social institutions and symbols—whether having to do with worship, work, learning, punishment, or pleasure—lose their power and psychological legitimacy. We still live by them, but they no longer live in us. Or rather, we live a half-life with one another (Lifton 1974).

Dr. Lifton reminds us that the essence of human growth occurs when old routines break down and are replaced by larger spheres of change. Communal resymbolization then occurs in all aspects of human existence. The leaders help formulate more relevant life-enhancing imagery for the culture, and even the counter-culture forces effect the reconceptualizations by which we live. Just as the individual goes through passages in the life process and is challenged to renewal by transitional experiences, so too our collective selves. It is a continuing search for meaning that causes the phenomenon of passing over and coming back to one's own culture with new insights and life-styles. Whereas in the past such transformation was caused by great innovators, today many people participate in the resymbolization task. It is the authors' thesis that transnational managers, because of their knowledge and experience, are in an unusual position to join in the process of renewal. Their role in global enterprises offers an opportunity for re-creation of cultural assumptions, norms, and practices on a planetary scale.

Willis Harman of the Stanford Research Institute (SRI) reminds us that we can no longer view our world or culture in terms of industrial-age paradigms, which influence our perceptions, values, and behavior. Thus, today's leaders are challenged to create new models of management systems and organizations that better suit our superindustrial stage of development. For that to happen, managers and other professionals must become more innovative and cosmopolitan. In both his book and audio cassettes on *Global Mind Change*, Dr. Harman (1988) maintains that fundamental changes in societies result when people change their minds. That is, perennial wisdom is altered—whether unconscious belief or conscious reality—by a transformation of acceptable knowledge.

To grow beyond cultural limitations means to become truly cosmopolitan, as the dictionary defines it, "to belong to the world; not limited to just one part of the political, social, commercial, or intellectual sphere; free from local, provincial, or national ideas, prejudices, or attachments." Literally, a cosmopolitan is one who functions effectively *anywhere* in the world. For a successful transition to the twenty-first century, which is the thesis of this book, we should all become more cosmopolitan human beings, especially if one is in a leadership position.

On January 2, 1989, *Time* magazine named the Endangered Earth as "Planet of the Year." It devoted that whole issue to planetary happenings and concerns, featuring the constructive contributions that cosmopolitans could make to preserving of the Earth and its inhabitants. The recommendations included—

- Recognizing the value of genetic diversity and of species' preservation.
- Establishing global zoning plans to balance preservation and development.
- Making environmental review an integral part of financial lending provisions, so as to protect habitats.
- Increasing taxes on pollutants, as well as funding into research for alternative energy sources and tree planting.
- Encouraging recycling of wastes, banning waste ocean dumping and export, raising costs of garbage collection and toxic-waste removal so that its production will be curbed and research on it will be expanded.
- Promoting a North-South dialogue, so rich nations will help poor nations to curb population, improve their food production and environment, and cooperate in joint ventures to enhance the quality of human life on this planet.

GLOBAL LEADERSHIP AND MANAGERS

One of the transformations underway is in the role of manager. As Peter Drucker has consistently observed, the art and science of management is in its own revolution, and all of the assumptions on which management practice was based during the preceding Industrial Age are now becoming obsolete. Thinking managers alter not only their images of their role, but their managerial style and activities. One example is the way we now view "international" functions. As the vice president of AT&T, George Serpan admitted there is a need to reorient managers beyond just selling in the U.S.A., especially if trade imbalances are to be rectified. Louis Gerstner, vice-chairman of American Express, confessed that his company is revamping its management training because the artificial split between domestic and international training assumes international managers work in either a domestic or international environment, but not both. Today we operate in a world market that demands a more culturally sensitive management.

The invasion of foreign competition into the home turf, and the need to trade more effectively overseas has forced North American executives to become more culturally sensitive. Some companies are investing in university programs to educate global managers. The Estee Lauder firm contributed $10 million toward this goal at the University of Pennsylvania to establish an Institute of Management and International Studies. Their president, Leonard Lauder, stated bluntly that unless American management can learn to compete on a global scale, the country's position as a major industrial power will decline.

So the leading business schools, which until recently neglected international and intercultural education, are now rushing to include this perspective in their curriculum. Managing people from different cultures whether at home or abroad is suddenly receiving tremendous attention with business students, as well as those in education or human resource development. Although the market for cross-cultural training in industry and government has generally been premature and soft, it now is gaining strength.

Louis Korn, CEO of a leading executive search firm, said:

> Tomorrow's executives must possess a broad understanding of history, of culture, of technology, and of human relations. They must be as comfortable with cash management, as with history, anthropology, sociology, mathematics, and with the physical and natural sciences.

To that latter list of academic studies, we would add psychology and communications. But Korn wisely added that businesses should develop executive training and promotion practices that reward those who are forward-looking, can deal with different cultures, can manage the results of technological change, and can take the longer view.

A 1989 survey report of 1,500 top managers worldwide revealed that U.S. executives were too parochial and insular in their perspectives (*Los Angeles Times*, January 15, 1989, p. 5/6). Conducted by Korn/Ferry International executive recruiters and designed by Columbia University's business school, the findings faulted American managers for minimizing learning foreign languages and cultures, while other multinational executives placed a high priority on multiculturalism. The study indicates that U.S. managerial attitudes toward international business and communications point to a continuation of America's lagging competitiveness. The research projected economic conditions to the year 2000, revealing an expected shortage of talented executives prepared to run global businesses. The following extract from *The Economist* (June 17, 1989, p. 80) gives some of the highlights in this comparitive management analysis:

Myopic High-Fliers

WHAT does it take to get to the top of a big corporation? Brains, luck and ambition certainly help. But much also depends on the priorities of the big company in question. A recent survey by Korn/Ferry, a headhunter, and Columbia Business School found intriguing variations in what is expected of future chief executives. Americans will read them and weep.

Contrary to recent experience, American bosses think that foreign competition will pose much less of a threat in the twenty-first century than will domestic rivals. Thus today's American chief executives do not expect their successors to need much international experience. Instead they are grooming high-fliers with experience in marketing and finance. And they are hoping to add some grasp of production technology to the skills of tomorrow's chief executives, because they reckon their firms will in future compete hardest on price.

Japanese and Europeans, in contrast, expect international competition to be intense. Europeans expect more than half of their revenues to come from foreign markets. So international experience will be crucial for tomorrow's Japanese and European bosses. Instead of competing on price, Japanese and Europeans expect to compete on product quality and innovation. Predictably, the Japanese stress products the most. They want chief executives with technical and R&D skills, not marketing. Given the difference in emphasis, whose products do you expect to be buying in ten years?

Other global leaders in this industry mentioned how telecommunications and information processing is becoming the hub of senior management activity. George Pebereau, CEO of France's Compagnie Generale d'Electricite, spoke of market changes in worldwide distribution that are more appropriate to developing countries, particularly in Southeast Asia. Bjorn Svedberg, president of Sweden's LM Ericsson Telephone Company, called for corporate collaboration in the field of electronic systems, so that joint ventures would be facilitated to promote R&D, production, and sales. The same synergistic input came from Marisa Bellisario, managing director and chief executive officer of Italtel, who remarked that cooperation among European companies is the prerequisite to opening up their market in the EEC and elsewhere. From Japan to the U.K., the key executives were repeating some of the same basic themes.

A "global manager" is cosmopolitan, effective as an intercultural communicator and negotiator, creates cultural synergy, and leads cultural change, especially at work, in organizations and on project teams. This type of leader can be found in any human system or industry, in any career or profession. In the home culture, for instance, this attitude is translated into actions that ensure that minorities, immigrants, and refugees are afforded equal opportunity in the workplace; that foreign visitors and colleagues are made welcome; and that organizational cultures are made relevant to people needs, thereby enhancing human performance and productivity. When relocated within his or her own country, the global manager not only adapts readily to the new circumstances and life-style in the region, but helps other employees to make this acculturation. However, when abroad in a host culture, the person with this perspective seeks to integrate sensitively into the alien scene, while advancing the corporate and common good through respect of native heritage or custom.

It is a philosophy that has been confirmed by practitioners in many vocational fields as making good sense, both for people and business. Perhaps, this can best be comprehended in terms of "concepts," which, like paradigms or models, are general categorizations—intellectual hooks around which many ideas and activities can be hung or grouped. The following ten concepts contain the underlying message of this book, the essence for leadership and excellence in human, and most especially international, affairs, and should be incorporated into the development of global managers:

1. Cosmopolitan
2. Intercultural communication
3. Cultural sensitivity
4. Acculturation
5. Effective intercultural performance
6. Cultural management influences
7. Changing international business
8. Cultural synergy
9. Work culture
10. World culture

Many of these concepts would be useful when incorporated into the curriculum of a school of law, medicine, or human service; most of them would be valuable in university programs in education or international studies; all of them would be vital for contemporary schools of business and management.

Knowledge and application of these concepts have direct relevance to increase the effectiveness of multinational managers, international lawyers, economic and community development specialists, engineers and technicians, public health officials, and a host of other careers. Because of this, and their significance for the remaining chapters, we offer these explanations of the ten concepts so critical to the global manager's successful performance:

The Concept of the Cosmopolitan—being a sensitive, innovative, and participative leader, capable of operating comfortably in a global or pluralistic environment. This is a multinational, multicultural organization representative who can manage accelerating change and differences in his or her own life. The cosmopolitan manager is open and flexible in approaching others, can cope with situations and people quite different from his background, and is willing to alter personal attitudes and perceptions.

The Concept of Intercultural Communication—recognizing what is involved in one's image of self and role; of personal needs, values, standards, expectations; all of which are culturally conditioned. Such a person understands the impact of cultural factors on behavioral communication, and is willing to revise and expand such images as part of the process of growth. Furthermore, he or she is aware of such differences in others participating in human interaction, especially with persons from a foreign culture. As a manager, therefore, this individual would seek to get into the "world" of the receiver, and improve cross-cultural communication skills, both verbal and nonverbal. Not only does such a leader seek to learn appropriate foreign languages, but is cognizant that even when people speak the same language, cultural differences can alter communication symbols and meanings.

The Concept of Cultural Sensitivity—integrating the characteristics of culture in general, with experiences in specific organizational, minority, or foreign cultures. Such a leader acquires knowledge about cultural influences on behavior; cultural patterns, themes, or universals; diversity of macrocultures and microcultures. As a cosmopolitan manager, this individual can translate such cultural awareness into effective relationships with those who are culturally different.

The Concept of Acculturation—effectively adjusting and adapting to a specific culture, whether that be a subculture within one's own country or abroad. Such a person comprehends what is involved in self and group identity, and is alert to the impact of culture shock or differences upon one's sense of identity. Therefore, when operating in a strange culture or dealing with employees from different cultural backgrounds, this manager develops skills for adjusting and avoiding enthnocentrism.

The Concept of Cultural Management Influences—appreciating the influences of cultural conditioning on the management of information and human/natural resources. One's native culture affects the way a manager views every critical factor in the management process, from decision-making and problem-solving to supervision and appraisal. The cosmopolitan manager is aware that what is acceptable for leaders to do in one's culture, may be unacceptable and cause strife in another culture. Such an individual tries to adapt modern principles of administration to the indigenous circumstances, or educate the local populous to contemporary management practice and expectations.

The Concept of Effective Intercultural Performance—applying cultural theory and insight to specific cross-cultural situations that affect people's performance on the job. The multinational manager must understand the peculiarities of a people that influence productivity at work. Such a leader makes provisions for foreign deployment, overseas adjustment and culture shock, re-entry of expatriates, international report reading, changing organizational environment, and overcoming cultural handicaps and limitations.

The Concept of Changing International Business—coping with the interdependence of business activity throughout the world, as well as the subculture of the managerial group in all nations of similar ideology (e.g., capitalistic or communist nations). In the private sector, there is an emerging universal acceptance of some business technology—computers, management information systems, reporting procedures, accounting practices. Yet, the cosmopolitan manager is sophisticated enough to appreciate the effect of cultural differences on standard business practice, especially in terms of profits, organizational loyalty, and such common activities as reward/punishment of employees. The multinational or world corporation manager is also aware of acceptable, universal business principles and procedures.

The Concept of Cultural Synergy—building upon the very differences in the world's people for mutual growth and accomplishment by cooperation. Cultural synergy through collaboration emphasizes similarities and common concerns, integrating differences to enrich human activities and systems. By combining the best in varied cultures and seeking the widest input, multiple effects and complex solutions can result. Synergy is separate parts functioning together to create a greater whole and to achieve a common goal. For such aggregate action to occur, leaders require a new set of cross-cultural skills.

The Concept of Work Culture—applying the general characteristics of culture to the specifics of how people work at a point in time and place. In the macro sense, work can be analyzed in terms human stages of development—

the work cultures of hunter, farmer, factory worker, and knowledge worker. In the micro sense, work cultures can be studied in terms of specific industries, organizations, or professional groups. Currently, we are in transition to a new metaindustrial work culture, and global leaders have an opportunity to influence the outcome.

The Concept of World Culture—understanding that while various characteristics of human culture have always been universal, a unique world culture is emerging. Advances in mass media, transportation, and travel are breaking down the traditional barriers among groups of peoples and their differing cultures, so that a homogenization process is underway. Global managers are alert to serving this commonality in human needs and markets with strategies that are transnational.

Core Concept of Culture

When the ten previous concepts are combined with the powerful concept of culture, we have the makings of a global manager. Culture is a distinctly human capacity for adapting to circumstances and transmitting this coping skill and knowledge to subsequent generations.

However, it was only in the past decade that executives and scholars really began to appreciate how culture impacts behavior, morale, and productivity at work. Popular business journals and books raised management awareness that culture implies values and patterns that influence company attitudes and actions. Corporate culture affects how an organization copes with competition and change, whether in terms of technology, economics, or people. The work culture stimulates or constricts the energies of personnel, whether through slogans and myths, totems or taboos. Now management is more cognizant of its customs and traditions, rules and regulations, policies and procedures—such components of cultures are being used to make work more enjoyable, to increase productivity, and to meet consumer need and competitive challenge. Chapters 2, 7, 8, and 9 examine this further.

Culture gives people a *sense* of who they are, of belonging, of how they should behave, and of what they should be doing. Therefore, education and training of global leaders must include formal learning in the various cultural dimensions considered in this chapter and volume. It should begin with students who are preparing for business and the professions; extend to the inservice training of those in the government agencies, religion and the military; include those in international trade associations and supranational organizations, like the UN, NATO, WHO, and the EEC; and especially involve those in the voluntary service agencies from Peace Corps and International Executive Service Corps to foundation staffs, such as the Ford Foundation.

Even when there are apparent similarities of peoples in geographic regions, cultural differences may require alteration of strategic market planning. North American companies and unions discovered this in Canada when they tried to treat their operations there as mere U.S. extensions. Europeans realized this in Bolivia and Argentina where a common cultural heritage is altered by political and social conditions. Global planning not only requires an effective international management information systems, but input from a variety of locals at different levels of sophistication.

The cultural differences in the nature of managerial work is evident from recent research comparing the behavior of chief executives from various countries. Robert Doktor, a professor at the University of Hawaii, contrasted Japanese CEO's with their American counterparts and discovered significant differences in the way each group thinks and solves problems (Harris 1984). The Japanese interviewed, for instance, spent most of their time with their people, giving to them more time—they tended to engage in fewer work activities, but for a longer duration than their Western colleagues. Doktor concluded that Japanese CEO's go about problem solving in a more planned and orderly manner indicative of left hemispheric dominance, fulfilling their role in ways quite opposite to what other researchers discovered about American executives.

Cross-cultural management research can act as counterbalance to popular fads that advocate indiscriminate adoption of management practices that are successful in other countries. The president of the Work in America Institute, a New York-based work research organization, has wisely warned (Rosow 1982):

> American companies searching for quality have been jumping on the Japanese bandwagon without investigating whether Japanese management and work methods suit the American culture.

While global managers are open to management innovations from abroad and scan the international business environment, they also realize that cultural factors may hamper the supposed panacea from working in the home environment. Oversimplification can lead to dangerous assumptions, so international leaders need cultural sensitivity in their analysis of world literature and trends in management and commerce. Perceptions can be expanded and vision enlarged by acquiring learning from many fields, including the behavioral sciences. For example, global leaders may benefit from the insights that come from anthropological research regarding the character of human nature, the relationship of people to nature, the temporal focus of life, the modality of human activity, and the relationship of person to person. Chapter 10 discusses such issues in the context of business protocol.

Terpstra and David (1985) recommend that people in business be triply socialized—to their own culture, into its business culture, and into the corporate culture. When we operate in the global marketplace, by implication, we must also be informed about these three dimensions of the "other," whether that be a customer, competitor, venture partner, supplier, or government official. When we operate beyond our own borders, the best strategies and plans for marketing and sales, importing or exporting, can go astray if one ignores the cultural differences and does not sense the opportunities for cultural synergy. That is why this unit explores the global manager's role as cross-cultural communicator, negotiator, synergizer, change maker, and leader (Moran 1990).

It would appear that comparative management research in the world marketplace has focused on comparing *differences* in various cultures. Perhaps the time has come to direct investigations toward cross-cultural *synergy*. There are numerous examples of cooperation and collaboration in international management and community development and this book cites some of them. But what is needed is systematic research on how this is accomplished and what the results are. Chapters 4, 10, 12, and 20 explore these issues.

Readers can assess their own potential for cross-cultural management by using Appendices A–D at the end of this book. Fortunately, many multinational corporation managers are already demonstrating their capabilities for global leadership. They are learning the international business environment (Rugman 1985), the multinational codes and guidelines (Kline 1985), the management of cross-border technology transfer (Amsalem 1984), and the intricacies of intercultural negotiations (Casse and Deol 1985, and Moran 1985).

GLOBAL TRADE AND ORGANIZATIONS

In the United States there are more than 3,500 multinational corporations (MNC's), 30,000 exporting manufacturers, 25,000 companies with overseas branches and affiliates, and 40,000 firms operating abroad on an ad-hoc basis. To rectify American trade imbalances, federal legislation came into effect in 1985 to encourage establishment of the Foreign Sales Corporation. According to Amsterdam consultant George Dittmar of VMD International Trading, the FSC is a U.S. corporation that maintains an office in an American overseas possession or in a foreign country that has IRS-approved exchange of tax information. Its board of directors must by law have one member who is not a U.S. citizen. Dr. Dittmar believes it is an unusual opportunity for American concerns not only to take advantage of the tax incentives, but to develop collaborative relations with foreign trading companies who can offer in-country consulting and support services.

At the same time, the Commerce Department reported that foreign investors spent more than $10 billion to gain entry or control in U.S. firms. In addition to the expansion of new operations by foreign companies in the United States, their takeover activity is increasing. The range goes from The Bank of Tokyo's takeover of California First Bank and Midlands Bank of London's takeover of Crocker National Bank to France's Societe Nationale Elf Acquitaine acquiring of Texasgulf and Canada's Seagram Company obtaining a 20% stake in the Du Pont Company.

Such developments in international business and trade represent a challenge for global leadership in the managing of cultural differences and synergy. A survey of these trading partnerships' management would likely bear out our contention that most expenditures were on legal and financial services, and comparatively little was invested in cross-cultural training of the personnel involved.

In this century national organizations have quietly evolved into international organizations. This trend is especially fortuitous for cosmopolitan managers seeking to exercise global leadership. Dr. Jack Craig of Canada's York University summarized the evolution of such organizations as follows:

Profile of Transnational Enterprises

Organizational Design

From *ethnocentric* with complex organization in home country; centralized decision-making in headquarters; evaluation and control of performance based on home standards; communication flow outward to subsidiaries in host countries which have simpler organizations; ownership and recruitment of key management largely of home nationality.

To *polycentric* with varied and independent organization; less headquarter authority and decision-making; evaluation and control determined locally; wide variations in performance management and standards depending on local cultures; limited communication to/from headquarters and among subsidiaries; ownership, key management and recruitment from host country.

To preferred *geocentric* with increasingly complex, interdependent organization: seeking collaborative approach between and among headquarters/subsidiaries; uses standards for evaluation and control that are both universal and local; international and local executives rewarded for reaching both local and worldwide objectives; ownership, key management and recruitment is cosmopolitan—develop the best person anywhere is the criterion.

Typology or Form of International Business Activity

From *profit-oriented* and investor-owned corporations with direct investments in foreign subsidiaries and joint ventures or consortia, to *mixed orientations* (government-owned to service-owned co-operatives).

The next stage of this evolution seems to be the conversion of multinational organizations into world or global corporations. Several writers anticipated the trend and wrote eloquently on the subject. Perhaps the issue was best highlighted by Barnett and Muller (1974):

> The global corporation is the first institution in human history dedicated to centralized planning on a world scale. Because its primary activ-

ity is to organize and to integrate economic activity around the world in such a way as to maximize global profit, it is an organic structure in which each part is expected to serve the whole. . . . The rise of such planetary enterprises is producing an organizational revolution as profound for modern man as the Industrial Revolution and the rise of the nation-state itself. . . . With their world view, the managers of global corporations are seeking to put into practice a theory of human organization that will profoundly alter the nation-state system around which society has been organized for over four hundred years.

The implications of this quotation are, of course, that business today should be considered in terms of a single marketplace in which national boundaries serve as convenient demarcations of cultural, ethnic, linguistic, and political entities, but do not necessarily define business or consumer requirements. That view is endorsed by presidents of world trade associations.

Foresight on this matter was expressed in a speech before the International Industrial Conference by Walter B. Wriston (1974):

The development of the world corporation into a truly multinational organization has produced a group of managers of many nationalities whose perception of the needs and wants of the human race know no boundaries. They really believe in One World. They understand with great clarity that the payrolls and jobs furnished by the world corporation exceed profits by a factor of twenty to one. They know that there can be no truly profitable markets where poverty is the rule of life. They are a group that recognizes no distinction because of color or sex, since they understand with the clarity born of experience that talent is the commodity in shortest supply in the world. They are managers who are against the partitioning of the world, not only upon a political or theoretical basis, but on the pragmatic ground that the planet has become too small and that the fate of all people has become too interwoven one with the other to engage in the old nationalistic games that have so long diluted the talent, misused the resources, and dissipated the energy of mankind.

The international managers in the great world corporations are exposed daily to a bewildering variety of value systems and a steadily rising tempo of nationalism in many of the nation-states of the world. From this experience is emerging the perception that the relationship of the world corporation to the various governments around the world is worthy of reexamination.

The role of the world corporation as an agent of change may well be even more important than its demonstrated capacity to raise living standards. The pressure to develop the economy of the world into a real community must come, in part, from an increasing number of multinational firms which see the world as a whole. "Today's world economy . . . ," Peter Drucker has said, "owes almost nothing to political imagination. It is coming into being despite political fragmentation." The world corporation has become a new weight in an old balance and must play a constructive role in moving the world toward the freer exchange of both ideas and the means of production so that the people of the world may one day enjoy the fruits of a truly global society.

Global Markets and Responsibilities

A decade later such prophetic observations were confirmed during a colloquium of industrial and academic leaders at the Harvard Business School. Under the heading "Multinational Vs. Globals," the conclusions were reported in *The Economist* (May 5, 1984). Essentially, it was that more industries are becoming global, and that to compete effectively corporations must shed their multinational form and go global, too. The conventional wisdom of doing in ternational business is being replaced, namely, that companies be decentralized so they can produce and sell for local markets, thus meeting host government requirements of MNCs that they fly the local flag and give local management autonomy from head offices.

But in the metaindustrial work culture, the tastes for consumer and capital goods or services are becoming more homogeneous—global. Coca-Cola markets a worldwide brand, Arthur Andersen offers a global accountacy, Universal Medical Supply sells disposable syringes internationally, and Pan has created a universal market for its unprocessed pet food. A global industry is seen as one in which a firm's competitive position is interdependent on what happens in other countries. So whether one produces semiconductors or automobiles, a global strategy that benefits by economies of scale is necessary. But global does not necessarily mean gigantic, for some multinationals are reorganizing into smaller global corporations devoted to different market segments or niches. Such economic and corporate activities are opportunities for global managers who can exercise cultural sensitivity and synergy.

Among the gurus of global marketing is Harold Levitt, a Harvard professor and editor of its *Harvard Business Review*. His writings to combat marketing myopia confirm the previous observations, emphasizing that worldwide consumer preferences are becoming more similar. Levitt points to advances in technology, especially within communication, transportation, and travel, as the driving forces in the globalization of tastes, structures, and wishes at a scale of magnitude previously unimagined.

A 1987 McNeil-Leher news program on Public Broadcasting Service about this trend cited the homogenization of world culture by pop culture. The globalization process has been accelerating in many fields from law and accounting to the stock market and athletics. Satellite television has greatly contributed to the latter, with a great melding of sports and entertainment. Baseball is played from Japan to the Soviet Union, Russian hockey players are being drafted by the National Hockey League, world-class tennis players emerge from the Eastern Bloc nations, and now a professional international football league is being planned to lead to "World Bowl" games. Sports and entertainment are big business, and they are going international. What a challenge for cross-cultural skills and synergy!

The new international economic order emerging has been well documented in *The Global Marketplaces*. Its author, Milton Moskowitz (1989) examines major players in this arena—102 of the most influential companies outside of America (previously he chronicled *The 100 Best Companies to Work for in America*). These are company portraits of enterprises reshaping the world, while coping with cultural diversity. The multinational corporations come from 20 countries, but two-thirds are based in Britain, Japan, France, West Germany and Italy (see Chapters 15 and 16). Their story may help to explain why so many U.S. corporations are going through an identity crisis of global proportion. A 1987 survey by Lippincott & Margulies Inc. of 100 senior American communication executives revealed that U.S. firms are inadequate in extending corporate images internationally (*Insight*, July 27, 1987, p. 44). Only a third of the U.S. firms polled believed international image-making was important, and these results may indicate why the others are ill-equipped to face global competition. Philip Hinson of the U.S. Chamber of Commerce states that smaller businesses "do not have a great deal of international awareness or a strong perception of their export potential."

There is a growing awareness and action relative to the expansion of corporate social responsibility. Lloyd B. Dennis, chairman of the social policy committee at United California Bank put it this way:

> There is something happening in the relationship between business and society. I believe that the most influential segment of the business community—certainly a large number of the Fortune 500 companies, the multinational corporations—has accepted the notion that business should, nay, must be more socially responsible. They are recognizing that it is important to combine maximizing profits with upgrading the quality of life. A key reason for this is that many corporate heads are finding . . . their peers who are attempting to solve social problems that in one way or another threaten profits are ahead, in many ways other than profits, than if those problems are ignored.

Global Managers for Cooperative Movement

In addition to corporations, transnational cooperatives are emerging that also call for the talent of cosmopolitans. Cooperatives are voluntary associations created for mutual economic assistance, which are usually owned by their members or patrons. They annually redistribute the earnings and are run by directors who usually come from among the members. A nineteenth century movement formulated in Britain and France, they are most suited to the superindustrial age where there is much emphasis on participatory democracy and involvement. Part of this ideology is articulated by the International Cooperative Alliances as follows:

> All cooperative organizations should actively collaborate in every practical way with every other such co-op organization at the local, national, and international levels.

The cooperative movement has grown steadily in the twentieth century, so that small entrepreneurs and consumer groups have banded for effective action in such diverse fields as agriculture and fishing, construction and energy distribution, merchandising and financing. The credit union is an example of a type of banking cooperative that has swept across the world. The synergistic approach has been applied to the needs for rural electric power to urban development. Many of society's problems—inadequate housing, high cost of food, health and child care services—can be realistically solved by formal establishment of a cooperative. For example, nine million Canadians belong to some form of cooperative, and that country hosts the Cooperative Future Directions Project (Scott Library, York University, 4700 Keele Street, Downsview, Ont. M3J 2R2, Canada).

Just as corporations had to move beyond national borders and cultures to solve complex, interdependent problems and meet the challenge of the world market, so too cooperatives have had to go multinational. The leading researcher on this is Dr. Jack Craig, who defines a multinational cooperative as a combination or federation of cooperatives that have joined together to provide international goods and services. Contrary to the profit oriented corporation, cooperative earnings are returned to members, or put in reserve to generate other benefits for members, or to help other groups in society set up autonomous cooperative ventures.

Dr. Craig's thesis is that cooperatives provide a technique for organizing economic activity on a global basis, and can provide developing countries with a means for multinational exchange of technology, information, and resources in the areas of insurance, credit, manufacturing, and consumer services (Craig 1976).

The cooperative movement has been a boon to developing countries, and promise to have their greatest expansion in Second and Third World nations. Obviously, there is a great need and opportunity within the world cooperative movement for global managers who can implement the ten concepts previously described, especially in doing business with Socialist or "post-Communist" countries.

Global Macroproject Management

As a final illustration of trends in global trade and organizations demanding cross-cultural competence, consider the issue of macroprojects. Many problems today are so complex, institutionally interdependent, and huge in scope as to require a combination of skills and commitments. A new kind of macro-management is desirable for many global projects that may involve a consortium of countries, companies, and capabilities. Among the latter, large-scale enterprises necessitate both experience and expertise that range from the financial, ecological and technical to the political, legal, and cultural. Such long-term projects at the level of $100 million plus require a new kind of global project manager.

In recent years some of the most prominent projects of this nature have occurred in the Third World (Murphy 1983). In *Macro: A Clear Vision of How Science and Technology Will Shape Our Future*, F. P. Davidson and J. S. Cox describe past, present, and potential projects of this dimension. As a result of his involvement in English Channel tunnel planning, Davidson confirmed personally to the authors that cross-cultural blunders have been hindering the completion of that U.K. linkage to the continent. (Perhaps the 1986 signing of an agreement to proceed with the project indicates increased cross-cultural awareness.) Frustrations in that experience stimulated his professional development efforts toward the founding of The American Society for Macro-Engineering (Polytechnic Institute, Brooklyn, New York 11202) and the Institute of Large Scale Programs (University of Texas, 2815 San Gabriel, Austin, Texas 78705).

It also may explain why major world corporations, like Bechtel, are similarly involved in such endeavors. In fact, Bechtel's global reach and macro projects may be the prime example of the trend under analysis. Here is a private U.S. company that is San Francisco-based but operates in 20 countries. This master builder has successfully completed American undertakings that include everything from the Hoover Dam and San Francisco-Oakland Bay Bridge to the trans-Alaska pipeline to the District of Columbia's Metro subway system. But among its international superprojects, none compare with its current Saudi Arabian endeavor of Jubail. Within 10 years, Bechtel expects to complete this $135 billion planned community on the salt flats of the Persian Gulf. With a sister-city of Yanbu, this is a project of moon-landing proportions—megastructures that will provide massive housing, petrochemical complexes, refineries, steel mill, industrial park, hospital, recreational facilities, airport, and civic administration for the 21st century. The construction brigade alone requires 500 contractors, a multilingual work force of 41,000 laborers from 39 countries. So far the macromanagement skills of Bechtel's engineers have kept the project on schedule and with minimal criticism.

This is another demonstration of the *new management* required to solve international problems of the metaindustrial work culture. With a world population approaching 5 billion people, the Earth's resources are being strained, eroded, and sometimes depleted. Innovative management and leadership on a global scale will be indispensible to provide the food, energy, housing, and infrastructure needed for the planet's inhabitants (Charnes and Cooper, 1984).

CROSS-CULTURAL LEARNING

Writing in *Developing Human Resources*, Leonard Nadler suggests that *training* be the focus of the job, while *education* be thought of with reference to the individual, and development be reserved for organizational concerns. Whether one is concerned with intercultural training, education, or development, employees need to learn about culture and cross-cultural communication if they are to work effectively with minorities within their own society or with foreigners encountered at home or abroad. For example, there has been a sudden increase in foreign investments in the United States—millions of Americans now work within the borders of their own country for foreign employers. They had better have some cultural sensitivity in this regard, or their career development could be jeopardized. Management information specialists design computer programs, but how aware are they of their own cultural bias in this regard, how alert are they to the cultural needs of the users? Those engaged in the import-export trade, depending on their understanding and skill in cross-cultural relations, can advance or hamper their sales and exchanges. All along the U.S.-Mexican borders, twin plants are emerging that provide for a flow of goods and services between the two countries, but how knowledgeable are the participants of intercultural factors that influence their business? Whether one works in the exchange of people in the public or private sector, personnel require preparation to facilitate such cross-cultural transfers (see Chapter 19).

For those executives impressed by "bottom-line" considerations only, factors like these should be included in strategic planning:

- One out of six U.S. manufacturing jobs is dependent on foreign trade, while four out of five new manufacturing jobs result from international commerce.
- Premature return of an employee and family sent on overseas assignment may cost the company between $50,000 to $200,000 when replacement expenses are included.
- Mistakes of corporate representatives because of language or intercultural incompetence can jeopardize millions of dollars in negotiations and purchases, sales and contracts, as well as undermine customer relations.

- Managerial failures to be culturally skillful at work can weaken both productivity and profitability, while driving up expenses because of slowdowns, strikes, sabotage, and legal suits against the company.

The price of providing employees with education and training for intercultural effectiveness is miniscule compared to the financial losses that can occur because of personnel "faux pas" in cross-cultural business relations. The "payback" on organizational investments in human resource development that includes this component can be enormous, ranging from improved morale and goodwill to increased sales and trade. So why do many business schools and companies continue to neglect language, culture, and other international studies?

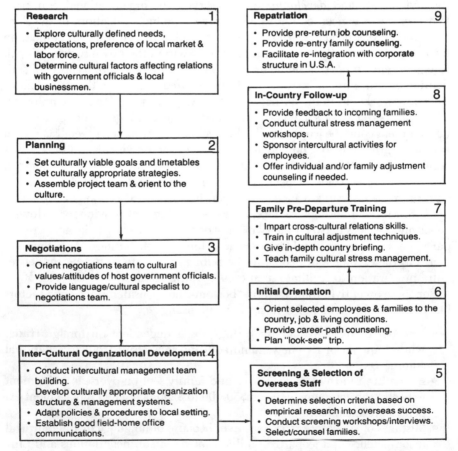

Figure 1-1. Major steps in a foreign deployment or domestic relocation program.

Cultural Strategies for Global Management

But it is the global organization or cooperative that has the most to benefit by comprehensive strategies to improve the human side of its international enterprise. Figure 1-1 provides an overview for relocation or business activities that are appropriate to a different region within one's own country or in a foreign nation. These culturally sensitive management efforts extend from research and planning, to negotiations and organization development, to recruitment and selection, to various development activities. The last five endeavors are depicted in terms of a foreign deployment situation.

Units I and II will provide more cultural specifics to enable managers to be more effective on a global scale. However, Chapter 8 analyzes the concept of culture in greater depth, especially in terms of relocation outside of one's home culture.

SUMMARY

Having a sense of culture and its related skills are unique human attributes. Culture is fundamentally a group problem-solving tool for daily coping in a particular environment. It enables people to create a distinctive world around themselves, to control their own destinies, and to grow in self-actualization. Sharing the legacy of diverse cultures advances our social, economic, technological, and human development on this planet. Culture can be analyzed in a macrocontext, such as in terms of national groups, or in a microsense, such as within a system or organization. Increasingly, we examine culture in a global sense, such as from the perspective of work, leadership, or markets.

Since all management is culturally conditioned, it stands to reason that there is much to be gained by including culture studies in all management or professional development. This is particularly relevant during the global transformation underway to an information society with a metaindustrial work culture. Culturally-skilled leaders are essential for the effective management of emerging global corporations, cooperatives, and projects, as well as for the furtherance of mutually beneficial world trade and exchange. In these undertakings, promotion of culture synergy by those who are truly global managers will help us to capitalize upon the differences in people, while ensuring their collaborative action.

Recall the critical cultural incidents at the chapter opening. In summary, here are parallel reasons why all managers should advance their culture learning, or why global organizations should include it in their human resource development strategies:

1. Culture gives people a sense of identity, whether in nations or corporations, especially in terms of the human behavior and values to be encouraged. Through it, for instance, organizational loyalty and performance can be improved, whether with majority, minority, or foreign employees.

2. Culture knowledge provides insight into people, so both managers and other professionals benefit when we understand both culture general and specifics to facilitate intercultural communication, client relations, and productivity. Thus, business protocol can be developed that is in tune with local character, codes, ideology, and standards.

3. Culture awareness and skill can be helpful in influencing organizational culture. Within global corporations, for example, their culture impacts performance on the job and with customers; furthermore, such entities as their subsidiaries, divisions, departments, or specializations have subcultures that can foster or undermine organizational goals and communications.

4. Culture concepts and characteristics are useful for the analysis of work culture, such as in context of the disappearing industrial and emerging metaindustrial work environments. Therefore, managers who comprehend cultural influences are better able to assess policies, procedures, and processes as to their appropriateness and relevance.

5. Culture insights and tools are helpful in the study of comparative management, so that we become less culture bound in our approach to leadership and management practice. For those who operate in the universal subculture of management, practitioners can become more effective in local negotiations and organizational relationships.

6. Culture competencies are essential for those in international business and trade. They not only help traders and technicians to avoid cultural blunders, but to create cultural synergy.

7. Culture astuteness enables us to comprehend the diversity of market needs, and to improve strategies with minority and ethnic groups at home, or foreign markets abroad. This would be especially meaningful for programs in the Pacific Basin or in Third World economies.

8. Culture perspicuity is applicable to all relocation experiences, whether domestic or international. This is valid for individual managers or technicians who are facing a geographic transfer, as well as for their families and subordinates involved in such cultural change.

9. Culture understanding and skill development should be built into all foreign deployment systems. Acculturation to alien environments can improve the overseas' experience and productivity, delimit culture shock, and facilitate re-entry into the home and organizational culture.

10. Culture capabilities can enhance one's participation in international organizations and meetings. This is true whether one merely attends a

conference abroad, is a delegate to a regional or foreign association, is a member in a world trade or professional enterprise, or is a meeting planner for transnational events.

11. Culture proficiency can facilitate one's coping with the trauma of transitional experiences, and enhance one's capabilities in transformational management.

Culture learning is a means for managers and other leaders to become more global and cosmopolitan in their outlook and behavior, as well as more effective and profitable in their practices.

Remember, the consensus is becoming "think globally, act locally."

2
Managers as Communicators

"*Verité en-deça des Pyrénées, erreur au delà.*"
"There are truths on this side of the Pyrénées which are falsehoods on the other."

—Blaise Pascal, *Pensées*

This quotation expresses in many ways the reason international managers must be skillful communicators. Perhaps the importance of international business communication can best be highlighted if we contrast some economic developments in the global marketplace, particularly as they affect the United States and its trade. Copeland and Griggs (1985) report:

- Some of the largest U.S. companies derive more than 35% of their revenues from their overseas operations.
- 80% of U.S. industry faces international competition, according to Robert Frederick, chairman of the National Foreign Trade Council.
- U.S. dominance in world agricultural trade has decreased since 1980.
- Mitsui U.S.A. is the U.S.'s fourth largest exporter.
- The U.S. is losing its advantage in the service exports, i.e., banking, etc.

TRADE PROBLEMS

At the same time U.S. government agencies are telling us that:

1. The U.S. percentages of world gross national product are declining.
2. The annual sales of 50 largest U.S. companies are not increasing as fast as 50 largest foreign companies.
3. We are importing more basic materials to meet production needs.
4. The overall competitive position of U.S. firms in international markets has declined over the past 10 years.
5. Illiteracy rate in Japan—7%; in U.S.—20%. High school dropout rate in Japan—6%; in U.S.—30%.

To clarify the issue further, consider the report, *What We Don't Know Can Hurt Us: The Shortfall in International Competence* (Commission on International Education, 1984) stated:

> "We Americans* no longer have the luxury of time and distance to justify our lack of concerted attention to the serious and dangerous lag—a shortfall in our international competence."

With our globally interdependent economy, it has become imperative to understand our world trade partners. But persons working internationally and participating in these intercultural experiences have learned that there are many problems when working or living in a foreign environment. Communication across cultural boundaries is difficult. Differences in customs, behavior, and values result in problems that can be managed only through effective cross-cultural communication and interaction. Persons of dissimilar backgrounds usually require more time than those of the same culture to become familiar with each other, to be willing to speak openly, to share sufficiently in common ideas, and to understand one another.

When people have misunderstandings or commit "errors" when working with persons from different cultures, they are often unaware of any problem. Cross-cultural *faux pas* result when we fail to recognize that persons of other cultural backgrounds have different goals, customs, thought patterns, and values from our own.

The personnel files of multinational corporations and government agencies are replete with documentation of intercultural communication misunderstandings. Some are not serious, while others result in organizational and personal tragedies. The individuals affected include company presidents, ambassadors, expatriate technicians and managers, spouses, and tourists. Usually, the cause of the more serious problems is that interpersonal work or social relations with the host nationals have gone sour, not because of personality factors, but because of ineffective communications and a misreading of the verbal and nonverbal communication signals.

CULTURAL DIFFERENCES AS RESOURCES

Managers, educators, and writers usually assume that cultural differences are barriers and impede communication and interaction. In order to overcome these barriers one should understand the differences between one's own culture and another's. For example, in the United States we value promptness. We generally make use of schedules and evaluate each other's behavior in these terms.

---

* The word "American" is used throughout the text with the realization that it can also refer to persons of Latin America and Canada. A more appropriate term perhaps is "United States national," but this becomes cumbersome and so we use the word "American." A North American commonly includes U.S. and Canadian citizens, while South American normally refers to the Latin countries south of the United States.

In some countries, to arrive late is the norm rather than the exception and it has a different meaning depending on how late one is, the circumstances of the meeting, and how well you know the person.

It is an assumption of this volume that cultural differences, if well managed, are *resources*, not necessarily handicaps. This statement may appear to be somewhat idealistic and contrary to the experiences of many international sojourners. However, if these persons were better prepared, trained, and briefed for their assignment, the situation in another culture can be quite positive.

A beginning point in the training and preparation is to consider the manager as an *intercultural communicator*. The words "manager" and "management" are difficult to define. They do not have exact counterparts in many languages and do not have the same meaning in any language. In the past a manager was defined as someone who is responsible for the work of other people, but the assumptions upon which management practice has been based for the past fifty years are now obsolete. Drucker (1977) stated that a "manager can be defined only by that person's function and by the contribution he or she is expected to make . . . the one contribution a manager is uniquely expected to make is to give vision and ability to perform." Kast and Rosenzweig (1985) state that managers are "those who convert the disorganized resources of man, machines, material, money, time, and space into a useful and effective enterprise." To convert "disorganized resources . . . into a useful and effective enterprise" one must be an effective communicator. However, an effective communicator working with American nationals in the United States is not necessarily an effective communicator working with Japanese or Saudi Arabians in the United States, Japan, or Saudi Arabia. But what about that magic word— communication? (See Asante and Gudykunst, 1989)

COMPREHENDING COMMUNICATION

Studies of what managers do each day indicate that 75% of their time is spent communicating. This includes writing, talking, and listening. In fact, all business ultimately comes down to transactions or interactions between individuals. The success of the transaction depends almost entirely on how well managers understand each other.

In my (Moran) experience of international consulting and conducting seminars in the United States and overseas for the past 20 years, I have heard businessmen and women make one consistent request of presenters (consultants, seminar leaders, speakers, and others) who have the possibility of influencing the way they manage and conduct business. They ask that the material presented to them be relevant and useful in their worlds (as opposed to academic, theoretical, and not particularly useful). Such is the goal of this book, which draws from the authors' own experiences, research, writings, as well as the work of others. So, if we are to better understand the global manager's role as a communicator, it is vital that we comprehend what is involved in the complex process of communication. As shown in the next section, it is a dynamic exchange of energy, ideas, information—even knowledge—between and among peoples. It is verbal and non-verbal and occurs at different levels—informal or formal, intellectual or emotional.

Most communication is manifest through symbols that differ in their meaning according to time, place, culture or person. Human interaction is characterized by a continuous updating of the meaning of these symbols. In the past twenty-five years, we have expanded our capacities for symbolic communication beyond what was accomplished in the previous twenty-five hundred years. The human species is extending its communication capabilities beyond print to that of electronic technology; in the process our whole thought pattern is being transformed.

Despite the technological wonders of satellite communications which helps to transform our planet into a global village, international relations require us to deal with one another on a person-to-person basis. For this to be effective interaction, we have to overcome language and stereotype barriers. This may require the mental elimination of terms like "foreigner" or "alien" and viewing the client or customer as an individual coming from a different country or culture.

AXIOMS OF COMMUNICATION

Every person is a versatile communicator. Language sets us apart from other creatures and seemingly is characteristic of the more developed brain. But humans have a wide range of communication skills that go beyond words to include gestures, signs, shapes, colors, sounds, smells, pictures, and many other communications symbols. The diversity of human culture in this regard may be demonstrated by the "artist" who may communicate both thought and feeling in paintings, sculpture, music, and dance. Through such media, the artist projects himself into people, things, and surroundings. He projects his way of thinking, his temperament and personality, his joys and sorrows into the world around him or one he creates. But technological man has vastly expanded his media facility or means for communicating.

Every person operates within his or her own private world or perceptual field. This is what is referred to as life space, and it applies to individuals as well as to organizations and nations. Every individual communicates a unique perspective of the world and reality. Every culture reflects that group of people's view of the world. From time to time, a true professional must check out whether one's view of the world or that of an organization synchronizes with the collective reality. This is particularly essential when "objective reality" is subject to the phenomenon of accelerating change. Cultural groups may have distorted views of world reality, as did China during the period of the Maoist "Cultural Revolution."

Every person projects himself into human communication. We communicate our image of self including our system of needs, values, and standards; our expectations, ideals, and perceptions of peoples, things, and situations. We project this collective image through body, bearing, appearance, tone of voice, and choice of words.

Every person is a medium or instrument of communication, not just a sender and receiver of messages. If a person is comfortable with himself and congruent, people usually respond positively. If one is uncomfortable with himself and incongruent, people will avoid him or respond negatively. The more aware the individual is of the forces at work within himself that affect behavior, the more able that person is to control his or her own life space.

Every generation perceives life differently. For example, the previous concepts of behavioral communication can be applied to a generation of people. The people of each generation project a unique image of "their" world at a certain point in time. This image reflects a generation's system of needs, values, standards, and ideals. The children of the "depression age" experienced life differently from today's children of affluence. As columnist Max Lerner pointed out (*Los Angeles Times,* February 1, 1970):

> All generations live in two worlds—an outer and an inner one. But each generation has its own inner universe—the subjective one, furnishing a window on the world through which it looks out at the outer universe. This inner world is formed early in the teens and twenties, perhaps thirties, and while it may continue to change in open-ended personalities, its basic frame remains much the same. My inner world was shaped by what happened in the 1920s, 30s and 40s; that of my son in the 1950s and 60s. We have different conditionings, hangups, life styles, and even vocabularies. Since the pace of social change which creates the gap is not slowing down, we shall have to learn with it, while making a creative leap of imagination to see the outer world through the inner window of the other generation.

If one expands upon Lerner's insight, related to adult and adolescent, the problem of communications between the generations and even cultures becomes more understandable. The supervisor of a young worker, for example, usually projects his or her generation's view of the world (past-oriented) and finds it difficult to facilitate communication by coming into the reality of the younger employee (future oriented).

Communication is at the heart of all organizational operations and international relations. It is the most important tool we have for getting things done. It is the basis for understanding, cooperation, and action. In fact, the very vitality and creativity of an organization or a nation depends upon the content and character of its communications. Yet, communication is both hero and villain—it transfers information, meets people's needs, and gets things done, but far too often it also distorts messages, develops frustration, and renders people and organizations ineffective.

The Communication Process

Communication is a process of circular interaction, which involves a sender, receiver, and message. Humans are versatile communicators; we can communicate with nature, animals, and other humans. In human interaction, the sender or receiver may be a person or a group of people. The message conveys meaning through the medium or symbol used to send it (the *how*), as well as in its content (the *what*). Since humans are such intelligent, symbol-making creatures, the message may be relayed verbally or nonverbally—words (oral or written), pictures, graphs, statistics, signs, gestures. Mankind's capacity to communicate ranges from smoke signals and the sound of drums to television and satellites. As a dynamic being, humans constantly invent new and improved ways of communicating, such as the computer or videophone. However, regardless of the communication symbol, a sender and receiver are normally involved.

Both sender and receiver occupy a unique field of experience, different for each and every person. Essentially, it is a private world of perception through which all experience is filtered, organized, and translated; it is what psychologists call the individual's life space. This consists of the person's *psychological environment* as it exists for him. Each and every person experiences life in a unique way and psychologically structures his own distinctive perceptual field. Among the factors that comprise one's field of experience are one's family, educational, cultural, religious, and social background. The individual's perceptual field affects the way he receives and dispenses all new information. It influences both the content and the media used in communicating.

An individual's self-image, needs, values, expectations, goals, standards, cultural norms, and perception have an effect on the way input is received and interpreted. Essentially, persons *selectively perceive* all new data, determining that which is relevant to, and consistent with, their own perceptual needs. Literally, two people can thus receive the same message and derive from it two entirely different meanings. They actually perceive the same object or information differently. Communication, then, is a complex process of linking up or sharing perceptual fields between sender and receiver. The effective communicator builds a bridge to the world of the receiver. When the sender is from one cultural group and the receiver from another, the human interaction is intercultural communication.

Once the sender conveys the message, the receiver analyzes the message in terms of his particular field of experience and pattern of ideas. Usually, he decodes the message, interprets it for meaning and encodes or sends back a response. Thus, communication is a circular process of interaction.

The communicator, whether as an individual from a cultural group or as a member of an organization, transmits many kinds of behavior. First, he communicates the intended message on both a verbal and nonverbal level. We also communicate unintended behavior, or subconscious behavior, on both a verbal and nonverbal level. In other words, communication at any level involves a whole complex of projections. There is a "silent language" being used also in the process of human interaction. It includes such aspects as tone of voice and inflection of words, gestures and facial expressions. Some of these factors that affect the real meaning and content of messages are referred to as "body language," that is, the positioning of various parts of the sender's physique conveys meaning. The person himself is both a medium and a message of communication and the way in which we communicate is vastly influenced by our cultural conditioning.

Global Communication Insights

Samovar and Porter (1976) define communication as "a dynamic process whereby human behavior, both verbal and nonverbal, is perceived and responded to."

For the manager working and communicating in a multicultural environment, we offer the following observations about the process of communication. These assumptions can also serve as practical guidelines for developing skills to become a more effective intercultural communicator.

No matter how hard one tries, one cannot avoid communicating. International managers may say they are restraining themselves and let the host nationals take the lead in negotiation situations in order to get a sense of what is happening. This may be an effective strategy. However, all behavior in human interaction has a message value and is communicating something to the persons present. While silent with words, body language is communicating. We communicate by our activity or our inactivity, by the color of our skin, as well as, the color of our clothes and by the gift we give or decide not to give. All behavior is communication because all behavior contains a message, whether intended or not.

Communication does not necessarily mean understanding. Even when two individuals agree that they are communicating or talking to each other, it does not mean that they have understood each other. Understanding occurs when the two individuals have the same interpretation of the symbols being used in the communication process whether the symbols be words or gestures. The American manager who gives a gift of yellow flowers in France or white flowers in Japan has communicated something but probably not that which was intended. In France yellow flowers suggest infidelity and white flowers in Japan are given at funerals to indicate sympathy.

Communication is irreversible. One cannot take back one's communication. It can be explained, clarified, restated, but it cannot be wiped out although we may sometimes wish that it could. Once we have communicated, it is part of our experience and it influences present and future meanings. The American manager who has sharply disagreed with a Saudi Arabian in the presence of others has committed an "impoliteness" in the Arab world that is difficult to remedy.

Communication occurs in a context. One cannot ignore the context of communication that occurs at a certain time, in some place, using certain media. Such factors have message value and give meaning to the communicators. For example, a business conversation with a French manager in France during an evening meal may be very inappropriate.

Communication is a dynamic process. Communication is not static and passive, but rather it is a continuous and active process without beginning or end. A communicator is not simply a sender or a receiver of messages but can be both at the same time.

These statements briefly outline several important characteristics of intercultural communication. Some are obvious, others not, but all, if internalized and understood would result in more effective communication. Each of us has been socialized in a unique environment. However, important aspects of the environment are shared and these constitute a particular culture. Culture poses communication problems because there are so many variables unknown to the communicators. As the cultural variables and differences increase, the number of communication misunderstandings increase. Those variables are further discussed in the remaining sections of this chapter.

CULTURAL FACTORS IN COMMUNICATION

Imagine yourself participating in the following cross-cultural situations that affect communication and understanding between two culturally different individuals. Then attempt to answer the questions posed before proceeding further:

- You are involved in a technical training program in China and one of your responsibilities is to rate persons under your supervision. You have socialized on several occasions and you and your family have spent some time with one of the Chinese you are supervising. The Chinese is an extremely friendly and hardworking individual, but had difficulty exercising the leadership expected of him. On the rating form you so indicated; and this was discussed with him by his supervisor. Subsequently, he came to you and asked how you could have said that about him. You indicated that you had an obligation to report deficiencies and areas to be improved upon to his supervisors. What cultural differences might cause misperceptions of performance appraisal and evaluation?

- You are negotiating a contract with a Japanese company and during the meetings there are times of silence on the part of the Japanese negotiating team. The negotiations, from your perspective as an American, appear to be proceeding at an unusually slow pace and even the simplest decisions or commitments appear to take an inordinate amount of time. You begin to push a little harder and your frustrations mount as you begin to hear statements from the Japanese such as, "it will take a little more time" and "this is quite difficult." What should you do? What is happening to the negotiating process? How do the Japanese negotiate?

- You are in Saudi Arabia attempting to finalize a contract with a group of Saudi businessmen. You are aware these people are inveterate negotiators, however, you find it difficult to maintain eye contact with your hosts during conversations. Further, their increasing physical proximity to you is becoming more uncomfortable. You also have noticed that a strong hand-grip while shaking hands is not returned. When invited to a banquet, because you are left-handed, you use your left hand while eating. Your negotiations are not successfully concluded. What may have been the reason for this? What cultural aspects are evidenced in this interaction, which if known, could improve your communication with your Arab clients?

- You are an American manager of a group of Puerto Rican workers in a New York factory. You resent the constant use of Spanish among your subordinates because you only speak English. You suspect your employees use their language as a means of criticizing and mocking you—they are often laughing and you wonder what it is all about. In bicultural/bilingual areas with large Hispanic populations, why should supervisors have some knowledge of Spanish? Why do your subordinates feel more comfortable in their native language? How could your company facilitate their instruction in the English language? Or should it?

- You are a female international executive who must negotiate in many countries. You are very competent, personable, and well groomed. How will you and your communications be received in (a) an organization or profession that is dominated by males; (b) an executive suite that is chauvinistic; (c) a country where women do not engage in business; (d) a culture where women are not held in high regard? What strategies can such a top manager use to overcome cultural barriers and prejudice?

These examples suggest a few of the many ways that culture can influence an individual in communicating. In the past, many American businessmen were not overly concerned with the ways that culture influenced individual or organizational behavior. However, because of serious and costly errors, many managers, executives, and technicians working in multicultural environments are now asking themselves questions such as:

1. What must I know about the social and business customs of country X?
2. What skills do I need to be effective as a negotiator in country Y?
3. What prejudices and stereotypes do I have about the people in country Z?
4. How will these influence my interaction?

The study of organizational behavior in management schools, which in the past was largely "culture bound," usually reflecting the U.S. viewpoint, is now being considered from a variety of perspectives that consider the cultural values and norms in the area being studied. This change in emphasis and orientation, although only a beginning, will result in more effective global negotiators and managers.

According to Edward T. Hall in his classic book *Beyond Culture*, the study of cultures and the consideration of ethnicities is especially important for Americans because they are generally intolerant of differences and have a tendency to consider something different as inferior. Many foreign assistance programs generate antipathy among indigenous peoples because of this. Consider this Iranian businessman's commentary:

> More than anything, I believe, Iranians' public demonstrations of anger are an expression of deep anxiety about the conflicts brought about by Westernization.
> Rather than being supportive and understanding of the dilemma, almost all the foreigners I knew in Iran (chiefly Americans) were not only ignorant of their hosts' ways but downright insulting. I cannot count the number of times I saw Americans ridicule and humiliate their Iranian coworkers. They were "farkles"—something less than human; their ancient customs were "hokey-pokey." I even knew of a fellow who rode his motorcycle through a mosque. The anti-Western sentiment that today has Iranians in the streets hardly comes as a surprise.

This same problem is seen in the U.S. in the relations between blacks and whites. Some Americans see blacks as underdeveloped whites. In fact, American black culture, as every culture, is rich, but until recently, was largely ignored. It behooves us as the new cosmopolitan manager or student of management to understand other cultures and effectively work with them.

In the classical anthropological sense, culture refers to the cumulative deposit of knowledge, beliefs, values, religion, customs, and mores acquired by a group of people and passed on from generation to generation.

Communication Keys—Context and Listening

In his various books, anthropologist Edward Hall makes a vital distinction between high and low context cultures, and how this matter of *context* impacts communications. A high context culture uses high context communications—that is, information is either in the physical context or internalized in the person. Japan and Saudi Arabia are examples of cultures engaged in high context communications, as are the Chinese and Spanish languages. On the other hand, a low context culture employs low context communications—most information is contained in explicit codes, such as words. North American cultures engage in low context communications, whether in Canada or the U.S.A., and English is a low context language.

Unless global managers are aware of the subtle differences, it could lead to communication misunderstandings when Japanese and American managers attempt to work together, or when Latin and North American managers seek to negotiate. The former is looking for meaning and understanding in what is not said—in the non-verbal communication or body language, in the silences and pauses, in relationships and empathy. The latter places emphasis on sending and receiving accurate messages directly, usually by being articulate with words. Japanese communicate by not stating things directly, while Americans usually do just the opposite—"spell it all out." Table 2-1 illustrates these cultural differences in context in terms of a managerial activity called performance appraisal. Contrast the differences in approach and communications for the American, Saudi, and Japanese managers. It helps to demonstrate the whole issue of comparative management within international business.

Another related consideration for global managers is the importance of *listening* so as to determine meaning in cross-cultural communication. North American education seems to emphasize articulation over the acquisition of listening skills, which are essential to international negotiations. Professor Lyman Steil of the University of Minnesota pioneered scientific research on listening and discovered that it is the communication competency that is used most, but taught least in the U.S.A. He summarized his findings in the following dramatic way:

Communication Skills

	Listening	Speaking	Reading	Writing
Learned	1st	2nd	3rd	4th
Used	Most	Next most	Next least	Least
(%−100)	−45%	−30%	−16%	−9%
Taught	Least	Next least	Next most	Most

Listening is perhaps the first skill learned because an infant must listen before it can speak or do a host of other things. Listening is certainly the first social skill acquired as the infant begins to react to environment. Unfortu-

Table 2-1
Cultural Variations:
Performance Appraisals*

Dimensions General	U.S. Low Context	Saudi Arabia High Context	Japan High Context
Objective of P.A.	Fairness, Employee development	Placement	Direction of company/employee development
Who does appraisal	Supervisor	Manager—may be several layers up—appraiser has to know employee well	Mentor and supervisor Appraiser has to know employee well
Authority of appraiser	Presumed in supervisory role or position	Reputation important (Prestige is determined by nationality, age, sex, family, tribe, title education)	Respect accorded by employee to supervisor or appraiser
	Supervisor takes slight lead	Authority of appraiser important—don't say "I don't know"	Done co-equally
How often	Once/year or periodically	Once year	Developmental appraisal once/month Evaluation appraisal—after first 12 years
Assumptions	Objective appraiser is fair	Subjective appraiser more important than objective Connections are important	Objective and subjective important Japanese can be trained in anything
Manner of communication and feedback	Criticism direct Criticisms may be in writing Objective/authentic	Criticisms subtle Older more likely to be direct Criticisms not given in writing	Criticisms subtle Criticisms given verbally Observe formalities
Rebuttals	U.S. will rebut appraisal	Saudi Arabians will rebut	Japanese would rarely rebut
Praise	Given individually	Given individually	Given to entire group
Motivators	Money and position strong motivators Career development	Loyalty to supv. strong motivator	Internal excellence strong motivator

* Adapted from report of the Association of Cross-Cultural Trainers in Industry, now Pacific Area Communicators of International Affairs, 16331 Underhill Lane, Huntington Beach, CA, 92647.

nately, this head start will normally be of no avail. Our skill at listening will not be developed or honed to its potential. Instead, it will degenerate into a habit, an unconscious response that will affect so much of our lives.

We learn to listen and talk before we read and write. Should we have difficulties with reading, writing, and talking, we will receive special assistance while at school. Why is listening not accorded the same attention, the same importance as speaking, reading, and writing?

Listening is a complex activity. The average person speaks around 12,000 sentences every day. The average person can speak at about 150 words per minute, while the listener's brain can absorb around 400 words per minute. What do we do with this spare capacity? Many of us do nothing. We become bored. A good listener is seldom bored. He uses this extra capacity to listen to the entire message and to more fully analyze the meanings behind the words.

Listening means different things to different people. It can mean different things to the same person in different situations. There are various types of listening behaviors:

1. *Hearing* is a physiological process by which sound waves are received by the ear and transmitted to the brain. This is not really listening in and of itself, though the two are often equated. Hearing is merely one step in the process.
2. *Information gathering* is a form of listening. Its purpose is the absorption of stated facts. Information gathering does not pertain to the interpretation of the facts and is indifferent as to the source.
3. *Cynical listening* is based upon the assumption that all communication is designed to take advantage of the listener. It is also referred to as defensive listening.
4. *Offensive listening* is the attempt to trap or trip up an opponent with his own words. A lawyer, when questioning a witness, listens for contradictions, irrelevancies, and weakness.
5. *Polite listening* is listening just enough to meet the minimum social requirements. Many people are not listening—they are just waiting their turn to speak and are perhaps rehearsing their lines. They are not really talking *to* each other, but *at* each other.
6. *Active listening* involves a listener with very definite reponsibilities. In active listening, the listener strives for complete and accurate understanding, for empathy, and to actively assist in working out problems.

The latter, active listening, is what our normal listening mode should be, but rarely is.

Listening is, above all, caring and a sharing of yourself. It is impossible for one to become an active listener without becoming involved with the speaker. Listening demonstrates the respect and concern that words alone cannot fully express. It has the unique power of diminishing the magnitude of problems. Having spoken to someone who listens, a person has the sense of already accomplishing something. Listening is, by definition, an action verb. Without it, our isolation grows and our own ability to open up and listen diminishes.

Listening fulfills another vital function as well. The listener provides feedback to the speaker concerning the latter's success in transmitting his message clearly. In doing this, the listener exerts great control over future messages that might or might not be sent. Feedback will influence the speaker's confidence, delivery, the content of the words, and every nonverbal facet of his attempt at communication.

Alexis de Tocqueville, the French statesman and writer, once commented that "Americans can talk about everything but cannot converse about anything."

Why did de Tocqueville find this to be so? Perhaps he realized that active listening is a process of thinking with people rather than thinking about them or for them. Such listening aims to bring about changes in people and to create an uncritical climate free from moralizing and evaluation. If we disagree with a message, we often block it—filtering it from our perception until very little of it gets through. We tend to hear what we want, or expect, to hear.

A good listener helps the speaker clarify or modify his ideas even as he expresses them, by responding with meaningful questions, comments, eye contact, gestures, and expressions. Silence is not golden except when one is actively being a good listener.

Levels of Culture and Human Interaction

Sharon Ruhly, modifying concepts presented by Hall in his now classic book, *The Silent Language* provides a system for analyzing different levels of culture that are called the technical, formal, and informal. This is a useful scheme for understanding cultural content and the amount of emotion attached to the content.

The *technical* level of culture, using the analogy that culture is like an iceberg (part of it is seen but most is not), is in full view and the technical aspects of a culture are learned in a student-teacher relationship. An example of a technical aspect of the American culture is the alphabet. There is little emotion attached to the technical level and there are few intercultural misunderstandings at this level, as the reason for a disagreement is usually quite easy to determine. Managers operate at the technical levels of culture when discussing the tolerance points of certain metals; however, when two managers are interacting over a period of time, it is difficult to remain exclusively at the technical level.

Continuing with the analogy of the cultural iceberg, the *formal* level of culture is partially above and partially below sea level. We learn aspects of our culture at the formal level usually by trial and error. We may be aware of the rules for a particular behavior, such as, the rituals of marriage, but we do not know why. The emotion at the formal level of culture is high and violations result in negative feelings about the violator even though the violation is often unintentional. The fact that the violated rule is local, i.e., an aspect of one culture and not another and therefore does not apply to everyone, is difficult to admit. A visiting business representative who uses a social occasion in France to discuss business with a French executive is violating a rule at the formal level of that culture.

The *informal* level of culture lies below "sea level" and actions and responses are automatic and almost unconscious. The rules of such behavior are usually not known although we realize that something is wrong. Informal rules are learned through a process called modeling. One example is the role behavior for males and females that persons are expected to follow in some cultures. Another concerns the appropriate time for Jane Smith, the American manager in France to begin calling her colleague, "Denise" instead of "Mademoiselle Drancourt." Emotion is usually intense at the informal level when a rule is broken and the relationship between the persons involved is affected. Violations are interpreted personally and calling a person by his first name too soon could be interpreted as overly friendly and offensive.

VARIABLES IN THE COMMUNICATION PROCESS

Samovar and Porter (1976) identify eight variables in the communication process whose values are determined to some extent by culture. Each variable influences our perceptions, which in turn influence the meanings we attribute to behavior. The manager seeking to work effectively in a multicultural environment should recognize these and learn the cultural specifics for the country or area to be visited (see Appendix A).

Attitudes are psychological states that predispose us to behave in certain ways. An undesirable attitude for managers working in a multicultural environment is ethnocentrism or self-reference criterion. This is the tendency to judge others by using one's own personal or cultural standards. For example, instead of attempting to understand the Japanese within their own cultural context, an ethnocentric person tries to understand them as similar to or different from Americans. As managers, it is vital to refrain from constantly making comparisons between our way of life and that of others when abroad. Rather, we should seek to understand other people in the context of their unique historical, political, economic, social, and cultural backgrounds. In that way it is possible to become more effective interactors with them. Stereotypes are sets of attitudes that cause us to attribute qualities or characteristics to a person on the basis of the group to which that individual belongs. Many studies of comparative management facilitate the development of stereotypes in that "management" is discussed largely in terms of the management system in the United States, and thus becomes the basis of comparison for management practices in other countries. An underlying assumption usually is that the American management system is the norm and other systems are compared to the United States.

Social organization of cultures is also a variable that influences one's perceptions. Michael Flack (1966) has made a useful distinction for managers in describing two societal compositions: the *geographic* society, which is composed of members of a nation, tribe, or religious sect; and the *role* society, which is composed of members of a profession or the elite of a group. Managers are members of the same role society, i.e., the business environment, but they are often members of different geographic societies. At one level communication between managers from two different cultures should be relatively smooth. On another level, significant differences in values, approach, pace, priorities, and other factors may cause difficulties.

Thought patterns or forms of reasoning may differ from culture to culture. The Aristotelian mode of reasoning prevalent in the West is not shared by people in Asia. What is reasonable, logical, and self-evident to an American manager may be unreasonable, illogical, and not self-evident to an Asian manager. We may often sound just as illogical to them as they do to us.

Roles in a society and expectations of a culture concerning role behavior affect communication. Behavior is usually incomprehensive because the rules concerning how a person in that position should act are unknown to us. The *meishi* or name card of the Japanese manager is important because it identifies his position in a company and therefore, the amount of respect that is appropriate. The length of time he has been in the company and his ability to make decisions are also known from his *meishi*.

Language skill in a host country is acknowledged as important by international managers, but many believe that a competent interpreter is all that is necessary. Sapir (1929) and Whorf (1952) hypothesized that language functions not simply as a method for reporting experiences, but also as a way of defining experiences for its speakers. Because culture and language are inseparably related, it is wise to rely heavily on competent interpreters to bridge cultural gaps.

Space is also a factor in the communication process. Americans believe that they own their bodies and they have a bubble around them that extends about two inches beyond their skin. If anyone breaks their bubble one must apologize and say "excuse me." The United States is a noncontact society. Many cultures, such as Latin American and Middle Easterner, are contact societies and require relatively close physical proximity to others during a conversation. Between males, touching is very common and handshakes are frequent and last throughout a litany of greetings.

Time sense also impacts upon human interaction. Americans perceive time in lineal-spatial terms in the sense that there is a past, a present, and a future. We are oriented to the future and in the process of preparing for it we save, waste, make up, or spend time. Zen treats time as a limitless pool in which certain things happen and then pass. North Americans are often confused by the Latin time sense when they do business in South America. Subsequent chapters will develop this further.

International Body Language

Many people believe that the language of gestures is universal.
Many people believe that one picture is worth a thousand words, the implication being that what we see is ever so much clearer than what is said.
Many people believe that communication means speaking and that misunderstandings only occur with speaking.
Many people believe that smiling and frowning and clapping are purely natural expressions.
Many people believe that the world is flat.

John C. Condon and Fathi Yousef, 1975

Do your actions really speak louder than your words? A classic study by Dr. Albert Mehrabian found the *total impact* of a message on a receiver is based on: 7% words used; 38% *how* the words are said—tone of voice, loudness, inflection and other paralinguistic qualities; 55% non-verbal: facial expressions, hand gestures, body position, and other forms of non-word expression.

Misunderstandings about intercultural non-verbal communication can result in problems for the international manager. What is non-verbal communication? It is interpreted in many ways but for our purposes, we mean:

1. *Sign language*—such as a gesture of a hitchhiker or the language of the deaf.
2. *Action language*—movements that are not exclusively used as signals, such as walking, nodding, or a pat on the back.
3. *Object language*—such as intentional or non-intentional display of material things, including the human body.

Non-verbal signals or gestures are used in all cultures, and all such gestures fall under three categories, two of which can create problems for the international traveler.

First, a gesture can mean something different to others than it does to you. For example, the A-OK gesture, as used in the United States, means that things are fine, great, or that something has been understood perfectly. But Brazilians interpret it as an *obscene gesture*, and to the Japanese it means money. A man might use the gesture to reinforce the fact that he is paying for a meal, or use it to show that a product or service is too expensive. For the French, it says "zilch," zero.

Second, a gesture can mean nothing to the person observing it. Scratching one's head or drawing in breath and saying "saa" are common Japanese responses to embarrassment. But Americans typically miss these cues because the gestures have no particular meaning in the United States.

Third, a gesture can mean basically the same to both people. In this case, meaning is accurately communicated and there are few possible misunderstandings.

Following are examples of gestures that are commonly misunderstood by persons from different cultures.

Hand and Arm Gestures

Most persons use their hands when speaking to punctuate the flow of conversation, to refer to objects or persons, to mimic or illustrate words or ideas. Often, gestures are used in place of words. Generally, Japanese speakers use fewer words and fewer gestures than American speakers; French use more of both and Italians much more.

In the United States, patting a small child on the head usually conveys affection, "good boy" or "good girl." But, in Malaysia and other Islamic countries, the head, considered the source of one's intellectual and spiritual powers, is sacred and should not be touched.

Australians signal "time to drink up" by folding three fingers of the hand against the palm, leaving the thumb and little finger sticking straight up and out. To older Malays, though, the thumb is a symbol of evil; the gesture can translate to mean "God is evil." In China, the same gesture means "six."

To get someone's attention or to summon a waiter or waitress is often a problem for international travelers. This task requires different gestures in different countries. For example, in restaurants in Anglo Saxon countries, including the United States: Call a waiter or waitress quietly ("Sir," "Miss," "Waiter") or raise a finger to catch their attention, or tilt one's head to one side. Do not snap your fingers.

On the Continent: Call louder for their attention, or clink a glass or cup with a spoon or your finger ring.

Africa: Knock on the table.

Middle East: Clap your hands in restaurants and elsewhere to get attention.

Columbia: With hand extended, palm down, move your index finger back and forth in a "scratching" motion.

Japan: Extend your arm slightly upward, palm down, and flutter your fingers.

Asia and South Pacific: Don't wave your index finger; it's considered uncouth, on the level of calling dogs.

Pakistan and the Philippines: Just say "pssssst!"

Spain and Latin America: Extend your hand, palm down, and rapidly open and close your fingers.

Singapore and Malaysia: To beckon a person, taxi, or waiter/waitress, extend your right hand palm down, keep your fingers together, fold your thumb across your palm or extend it, and wave your hand.

Eye Contact

In many Western societies, including the United States, a person who does not maintain "good eye contact" is regarded as being slightly suspicious, or a "shifty" character. Americans unconsciously associate people who avoid eye contact as unfriendly, insecure, untrustworthy, inattentive, and impersonal. However, in contrast, Japanese children are taught in school to direct their gaze at the region of their teacher's Adam's apple or tie knot, and, as adults, Japanese lower their eyes when speaking to a superior, a gesture of respect.

Latin American cultures as well as some African cultures, such as Nigeria, have longer looking time, but prolonged eye contact from an individual of lower status is considered disrespectful. In the U.S., it is considered rude to stare—regardless of who is looking at whom. In contrast, the polite Englishman is taught to pay strict attention to a speaker, to listen carefully, and to blink his eyes to let the speaker know he or she has been understood as well as heard. Americans signal interest and comprehension by bobbing their heads or grunting.

A widening of the eyes can also be interpreted differently, depending on circumstance and culture. Take, for instance, the case of an American and a Chinese discussing the terms of a proposed contract. Regardless of the language in which the transaction is carried out, the U.S. negotiator may interpret a Chinese person's widened eyes as an expression of astonishment instead of as a danger signal (its true meaning) of politely suppressed Oriental anger.

Arabs often look each other squarely in the eyes, as they believe "the eyes are the window to the soul," and knowing a person's heart and soul is important in order to work well together.

Other Gestures. In modern South China, a quick tongue protrusion and retraction signifies embarrassment and self-castigation, as at some social *faux pas* or misunderstanding.

While we're on the subject of *faux pas*, a belch after dinner in most of the world is considered rude, but in China it is both acceptable and a compliment. In France, Southern Germany, and Austria, a slight belch accompanied by an unembarrassed "pardon me" is in order. A "pardon me" is not required for belching in the Arab countries. A guest may also express pleasure at the meal by smacking the lips and clicking the tongue.

GUIDELINES FOR ENGLISH AND FOREIGN LANGUAGES

Much of the world's international business is conducted in English, because many Americans who participate in a large percentage of world trade speak only one language. Another reason is because the mother languages of the participants in international business is different and the language commonly understood is English (as is the case of Swedish traders in Saudi Arabia— the common language most likely is English.) Below are 20 propositions* for "internationalizing" the use of English:

1. Practice using the most common 3,000 words in English, that is, those words typically learned in the first two years of language study. Be particularly careful to avoid uncommon or esoteric words; for example, use "witty" rather than "jocose," or "effective" rather than "efficacious."
2. Restrict your use of English words to their most common meaning. Many words have multiple meanings, and non-native speakers are most likely to know the first or second most common meanings. For example, use "force" to mean "power" or "impetus" rather than "basic point." Other examples include using "to address" to mean "to send" (rather than "to consider") or using "impact" to mean "the force of a collision" (rather than "effect").
3. Whenever possible, select an action-specific verb (e.g., "ride the bus") rather than a general action verb (e.g., "take the bus"). Verbs to avoid include "do," "make," "get," "have," "be," and "go." For example, the verb "get" can have at least five meanings (buy, borrow, steal, rent, retrieve) in, "I'll get a car and meet you in an hour."
4. In general, select a word with few alternate meanings (e.g., "accurate"—1 meaning) rather than a word with many alternate meanings (e.g., "right"—27 meanings).
5. In choosing among alternate words, select a word with similar alternate meanings rather than a word with dissimilar alternate meanings. For example, "reprove" means to rebuke or to censure—both similar enough that a non-native speaker can guess the meaning accurately. In contrast, "correct" canmean either to make conform to a standard, to scold, or to cure, leaving room for ambiguity in interpretation by a non-native speaker.
6. Become aware of words whose primary meaning is restricted in some cultures. For example, outside of the United States, "check" most commonly means a financial instrument and is frequently spelled "cheque."

---

* From Riddle, D. I., & Lanham, Z. D., "Internationalizing Written Business English: 20 Propositions for Native English Speakers." *The Journal of Language for International Business*, 1985. Used with permission.

7. Become aware of alternate spellings that exist of commonly used words and the regions in which those spellings are used: for example, colour/color, organisation/organization, centre/center.

8. Resist creating new words by changing a word's part of speech from its most common usage; for example, avoid saying "a *warehousing* operation" or "*attachable* assets."

9. Avoid all but the few most common two-word verbs such as "to turn on/off (the lights)" or "to pick up" meaning "to grasp and lift."

10. Maximum punctuation should be used, e.g., commas that help clarify the meaning, but could technically be omitted, should be retained.

11. Redundancy and unnecessary quantification should be avoided as they are confusing to the non-native speaker who is trying to determine the meaning of the sentence. For example, factories cannot operate at greater than capacity—"peak capacity" is redundant.

12. Conform to basic grammar rules more strictly than is common in everyday conversation. Make sure that sentences express a complete thought, that pronouns and antecedents are used correctly, and that subordination is accurately expressed. For example, the sentence, "No security regulations shall be distributed to personnel that are out of date," needs to be rewritten as, "Do not distribute out-of-date security regulations to personnel."

13. Clarify the meaning of modal auxiliaries; for example, be sure that the reader will understand whether "should" means moral obligation, expectation, social obligation, or advice.

14. Avoid "word pictures," constructions that depend for their meaning on invoking a particular mental image (e.g., "run that by me," "wade through these figures," "slice of the free world pie"). A particular form of mental imagery likely to cause misunderstandings if taken literally is the use of absurd assumptions; for example, "suppose you were me" or "suppose there were no sales."

15. Avoid terms borrowed from sports (e.g., "struck out," "field that question," "touchdown," "can't get to first base," "ballpark figure"), the military (e.g., "run it up the flag pole," "run a tight ship"), or literature (e.g., "catch-22").

16. When writing to someone you do not know well, use their last name and keep the tone formal while expressing personal interest or concern. Initial sentences can express appreciation (e.g., "We are extremely grateful to your branch . . .") or personal connection (e.g., "Mr. Ramos has suggested . . ."). Closing phrases can express personal best wishes (e.g., "With warmest regards, I remain sincerely yours . . .").

17. Whenever the cultural background of the reader is known, try to adapt the tone of the written material to the manner in which such information (i.e., apology, suggestion, refusal, thanks, request, directive) is usually conveyed in that culture. For example, apologies may need to be

sweeping and unconditional (e.g., "My deepest apologies for any problems . . ."); refusals may need to be indirect (e.g., "Your proposal contains some interesting points that we need to study further . . .").

18. If possible, one should determine and reflect the cultural values of the reader on such dimensions as espousing controlling versus adapting to one's environment, emphasizing individual versus collective accomplishments, or focusing on quantitative versus qualitative changes. When in doubt, a variety of value orientations should be included: "I want to thank you [individual] and your department [collective]. . . ."

19. When the cultural background of the reader is known, try to capture the spoken flavor of the language in writing. For example, communications to Spanish-speakers would be more flowery and lengthy than those to German-speakers.

20. Whenever possible, either adopt the cultural reasoning style of your reader or present information in more than one format. For example, the following sentence contains both a general position statement and inductive reasoning: "Trust among business partners is essential; and our data show that our most successful joint ventures are those in which we invested initial time building a personal trusting relationship."

Besides these points, we recommend the following:

1. Oral presentations that involve intercultural communications should be made plainly, clearly, and slowly, making one point at a time. Use visual aids whenever possible.
2. Paraphrase in intercultural conversations, encouraging your counterpart to do the same with your input.
3. International business communications by telephone are helped when important issues are confirmed by telex, fax, or written reports.
4. International meetings are facilitated with a written summary, preferably in the language of the receiver or client.
   (Refer to "Meeting Management Planning Inventory," Harris, 1989).
5. Written brochures, proposals, and reports should be translated into the native language of the receiver or client.

This subject has become so significant that a major new journal is now available that deals with foreign language training, cultural briefings, and interpersonal communication skills (*International Business Communications*, MCB University Press, 62 Toller Lane, Bradford, UK BD8 9BY).

Although English is becoming a global language, bear in mind (a) many speak or listen in it as a second language and may have difficulties in comprehending compared to those for whom it is a native language; (b) American language is different from, though rooted in, British English, which is further modified as it is used in the British Commonwealth nations.

Foreign Language Competency

To survive and communicate, the average European speaks several languages. The typical Japanese, too, studies English as well as other languages. This is not true of most U.S. citizens who even when they study a foreign language, often lack fluency in it. A recent magazine feature used the headline, "American—the Deaf and Dumb Giant."

Victor Hao Li, president of the East-West Center, has one answer to the huge trade deficit of the United States with Japan. In an interview with the *Los Angeles Times* (March 14, 1988, p. 3), he started by comparing numbers— about 23,000 American college students were studying Japanese in 1986, while in that same year, 20 million Japanese were studying English. Li then asked, "Is it any wonder that American sellers have difficulty penetrating foreign markets? We do not speak the most important language of all for that purpose—the language of the customer. That is a national scandal." He believes that the contrast in culture contributes as much to the trade deficit as economic and political differences.

Recently, a management consulting firm conducted a survey of 256 U.S. international executives, of whom 75% were born in America and spent an average of 88 days on business annually outside of North America. Almost 60% of the respondents spend 2–4 months abroad each year, while 25% spend more than 4 months overseas annually. Sixty percent of these international executives have lived outside their country in the course of their business careers for a median of 3.3 years abroad. Yet, only 44% expressed fluency in another language than English. Since the question was not asked, one can only speculate on the degree of cross-cultural training that they had received in either their university education or from their companies. Such data not only underscores the need for human resource development, but points up the value of the recommendation of the President's Commission on Foreign Languages and International Studies. This government report (1979) specifically urged American business and labor to give more priority to foreign language and international studies training in their staff recruitment, as well as encouraging colleges and universities to include such studies in their business and labor offerings. Certainly anyone hoping to exert leadership in international business should have developed such competencies.

The President's Commission stated:

> Americans' incompetence in foreign languages is nothing short of scandalous, and it is becoming worse. Historically, to be sure, America's continental positions between vast oceans was a basis for linguistic as well as political isolation, but rocketry as well as communication satellites render such a moat mentality obsolete. While the use of English as a major international language of business, diplomacy, and science should be welcomed as a tool for understanding across national boundaries, this

cannot be safely considered a substitute for direct communications in the many areas and on innumerable occasions when knowledge of English cannot be expected. The fact remains that the overwhelming majority of the world's population neither understands nor speaks English; and for most of those who learn English as a foreign language, it remains precisely that.

So for those who would be competent in global communications, cultural awareness and specifics, even area studies, are not enough: some foreign language skills are most necessary. The Commission makes many recommendations for improving the situation in the U.S.A., including a greater use of America's ethnic and linguistic minorities as part of the remedy. The media are urged to play a more important role in developing a more internationally informed citizen. Perhaps they can counteract the findings of a recent study of U.S. college students in which the Educational Testing Service discovered half of the sample to be remarkably uninformed about international relations.

But there is one area of the Commission's report that is important to all readers, regardless of their national affiliation. It maintained that business and labor should give more priority to foreign languages and international studies in recruitment and training of staff, while colleges and universities are asked to make such training an integral part of their programs in business and labor studies. Furthermore, they suggested that professional education and training associations intensify their international efforts, especially ensuring that teacher and trainer education programs get such an emphasis.

Perhaps the Commission report did have the desired impact upon U.S. educators, students, and business. According to the *New York Times* (December 2, 1986), economic self-interest, among other factors, is prompting renewed interest in languages and foreign affairs, as indicated in these statistics:

- 70 colleges and universities added some foreign-language study to requirements for admission and graduation;
- 30 states have instituted language requirements in public schools;
- 45% of New York State's high school students now enroll in foreign language courses;
- 50% rise over the last five years is reported in Texas' enrollments in foreign-language studies.

Think of the cultural synergy that could be promoted if the millions of foreign students in many nations were not only given cultural and language training for the host country prior to their departure, but upon arrival in the nation they are visiting! This is especially valid in corporate foreign deployment programs. Bankers, for instance, being prepared for the world market, do not only need to know the banking laws and practices of the country to which they are being assigned, but should also receive training in its language and culture.

However, the severest lack of language skills seems to be among U.S. teachers and diplomats. There is a need to raise standards requiring such competencies, and increase the number of qualified teachers and foreign service officers with skills in languages other than English.

To further reduce misunderstanding in business and international relations, we often resort to interpreters of the foreign language. But translations are given in a cultural context, and the linguistic specialists themselves require cross-cultural training. International education and business can be facilitated by *competent* simultaneous interpretation. Linguistic Systems, Inc. of Cambridge, Massachusetts, U.S.A., reports that an international business conference can be held in 12 languages and with an audience of unlimited size. Since nine tenths of the planet's people do not speak English, communications through the oral/written word will require fast, accurate, technically precise, and culturally sensitive translations. New equipment for simultaneous interpreting, graphic presentations, and later reporting have done much to foster international cooperation. The mass global use of the computer creates a universal language of another type. Also, through the wizardry of electronic technology, forthcoming inventions will translate for us, which will further break down the barriers between and among the inhabitants of this global village. Pocket translators, which are now available are only the beginning.

ASSUMPTIONS OF UNIVERSALITY

The following material is from management training materials prepared in the United States to be used in other cultures. Only a short portion is used but it is suggested that the reader identify the cultural factors, that are *assumed to be universal* in this material. The issue is how adequate or appropriate is this communication training for international managers, especially with regard to written materials (see example on facing page).

The "Managing Climate" section is based on American assumptions and priorities and are often not compatible with the assumptions and priorities of many Middle Easterners. The material would make distressing demands upon Middle Eastern participants, because it prescribes a mold for the efficient communicator into which most Middle Easterners would not fit.

In the left column of the "Managing Climate" instrument (page 51) are behaviors that help build a trust climate, and on the right side are behaviors that can help preclude a trust climate. There are some problems with such assumptions:

1. It is stated that an open and natural expression of doubt, concern and feelings would facilitate a climate of trust. This may be so from a Western perspective, but it might become a barrier to effective communication in the Middle East. Middle Easterners are sensitive, especially when it

Managing Climate*

Behaviors that Help *Build* a Trust Climate

1. Express your doubts, concerns and feelings in an open, natural way. Encourge your subordinates to do so also.
2. When subordinates express their doubts, concerns and feelings, accept them supportively and discuss them thoroughly.
3. Set honesty as one standard that will not be compromised. Demand it from yourself and from your staff.
4. Be clear about our expectations when assigning work or eliciting opinions. Explain your reasons, wherever possible, behind requests and directions.
5. Encourage subordinates to look to you as a possible resource in accomplishing results, but develop and reinforce independence.
6. When something goes wrong, determine what happened, not "who did it."
7. Encourage active support and participation in corrective measures from those involved.
8. Share credit for successes; assume the bulk of responsibility for criticism of your unit.

Behaviors that Help *Preclude* a Trust Climate

1. Look on expressions of feelings and doubts as signs of weakness.
2. Be sarcastic, but cleverly so.
3. Let your subordinates know that you expect them to "stretch the truth" a little if it will make the organization look good.
4. Be secretive. Never let them really be sure what's on your mind. This keeps them on their toes.
5. Discourage subordinates from coming to you for help. After all, they should be "stem-winders" and "self-starters."
6. When something goes wrong, blow up, hit the ceiling, and look for the guilty party.
7. Gossip about and disparage others on the staff when they are not present. Overrespond to casual comments by others about your people.
8. Take credit for successes. Plan vendettas and other ploys to make other organizations look bad. Draw on subordinates for carrying these out. Always insist on plenty of documentation to protect yourself.

* Used with permission. Parts are omitted to preserve continuity. These sections are direct excerpts from the training materials of a multinational corporation whose name shall remain anonymous for obvious reasons of critique.

comes to the expression of doubt and concern in an open manner, in a non-familiar setting. Middle Easterners cherish honesty, but tact is extremely important when expressing doubt. This could be viewed as disagreement or disharmony, which might cloud the trust climate between persons. Middle Easterners are generally very temperamental, and therefore try to avoid arguments. Once there is an argument, it tends to be heated because each one in the discussion wants to be right.

2. The management style in the Middle East tends to be much more authoritative than in the United States. This is a cultural characteristic that can be explained by the following:

   - Governments in the Middle East generally are much more authoritative than governments in the West, with the absolute authority being vested in the hands of the ruling class.
   - The social structure—older persons are highly respected in the Middle East, and this stems from religious teachings.
   - The family structure—the father in a family in the Middle East is generally the most respected and authoritative person. He is the highest authority, and his children look up to him for guidance.
   - The manager in the Middle East enjoys his power and exercises his authority. Possessing power and authority in the Middle East is generally relished by those who possess it. To give into subordinates would be viewed by them as possessing weakness.

3. Although honesty is highly regarded in the Middle East, it is coupled with the concept of saving face and preserving one's honor. Middle Easterners are introverted and shy until a mutual trust is built, and at that time a person will share his concerns. The process of developing mutual trust takes a long time when compared with the establishment of relations in the United States. Honesty is also a word that has many meanings depending on the situation.

4. Clarity in expectations is extremely important. It is very difficult to read another person's mind, but stating clearly what another wants is Western. Another way would be to anticipate the needs or expectations of another (i.e., as Middle Easterners often do).

5. Encouragement of subordinates to look up to their superiors as a possible resource for accomplishing results. However, the people in the Middle East like to be independent, especially persons who are educated. If the superior is a foreigner, they probably would resent referring to him at all times for accomplishing tasks or results because it might make them feel inferior. The job might get done, but if not enough responsibility is given to the person from the Middle East, the trust climate would be stifled. They may also adapt the attitude of carelessness and simply do what is required from them without further incentive.

6. When things go wrong, it is sometimes necessary to tell someone that an error was made by someone in the organization, but this must be done very tactfully.

It is evident from the foregoing comments that the training material as presented is generally inappropriate for use in other cultures, in this case the Middle East, because it is based on American cultural assumptions and values. So, the following questions arise:

1. Is the material appropriate for international management training?
2. Is it appropriate for training Americans to communicate effectively with people in host cultures, such as in the Middle East?
3. Is the material appropriate for training Middle Eastern personnel to communicate with Americans? *Yes, if we assume that the Middle Easterners are willing, in order to communicate with Americans, to communicate like Americans.* But this is not usually the case.

Guidelines for Trainers

The following points are relevant for trainers working in the Middle East, and illustrate concepts described earlier in the chapter. Culture specifics are discussed later in the book.

1. The person with whom a Middle Easterner is working is more important than the mission, product, or job.
2. Quiet strength is a greater value than an obvious use of power.
3. Patience is a virtue.
4. Friendship and trust are prerequisites for any social or business transactions, and are slowly developed.
5. Confrontations or criticism in the presence of others should be avoided.
6. Middle Easterners love the spoken word, tend to ramble and don't get to the point quickly.
7. Middle Easterners are masters at flattery and appreciate compliments.
8. Middle Easterners find bluntness very disrespectful, which is why they usually respond in the most agreeable manner, regardless of truth.
9. Middle Easterners are very emotional people and are easily outraged by even slight provocations.
10. Middle Easterners are proud and their dignity is important to them.

SUMMARY

The most basic skill that international managers must cultivate is in intercultural communications. To facilitate our interactions with persons who do not share our values, assumptions, or learned ways of behaving requires new competencies and sensitivities, so that the very cultural differences become resources. The complexities of the communication process have been reviewed here from the perspectives of cross-cultural behaviors and factors; listening and foreign language skills levels and variables when interacting; body language; and gestures. Assumptions of communication universality were examined in the context of training materials used with multinational managers. We hope that readers are sufficiently convinced to give a high priority in international management or technical development to intercultural communications and acquisition of foreign language proficiency, for as Edward T. Hall and Mildred Hall observe in *Hidden Differences—Doing Business with the Japanese*:

> Each cultural world operates according to its own internal dynamic, its own principles, and its own laws—written and unwritten. . . . Any culture is primarily a system for creating, sending, storing, and processing information. Communication underlies everything. . . . Culture can be likened to an enormous, subtle, extraordinarily complex computer. It programs the actions and responses of every person, and these programs can be mastered by anyone wishing to make the system work.

3
Managers as Negotiators

Questionnaires sent to a number of large corporations recently asked what kinds of seminars or consultations they need most. The activity getting the highest support was negotiation skills with foreign governments and business (74%).

World traders have always demonstrated the ability to deal or bargain, even when a people's language and culture were quite different. Marco Polo and his family gave us a marked demonstration of this in the past, just as modern Arab traders do today as they jet around the world putting together business ventures. To negotiate also means bringing about a satisfactory settlement. Increasingly, global managers are appreciating the importance of this competency, either domestically or abroad. Whether it is a labor negotiation in the home culture or government contract in a host culture, executives in transnational enterprises appreciate the importance of this management skill.

To carry out its mission, an organization must be able to persuade not only its employees and customers, but the many publics on which it is dependent. For example, some writers and researchers of multinational corporations in the past few years have been introducing new relationships and new concepts to our thinking. One insight is the relationship between the viability of a multinational corporation (MNC)—i.e., the degree to which the financial objectives of the company have been or will be attained—and the "legitimacy" of an MNC—i.e., the perception of the corporation's stockholders that the institution deserves to exist. Indices of viability include profit, sales, market share, and return on investment. Legitimacy occurs when home and host governments believe that the MNC is essential for promoting social and economic well being of their countries. Legitimacy is confirmed *not* by management, but by external sources, and the future of many corporations depends on legitimacy as much as viability. In the past, an MNC was considered legitimate if it was viable; today it must demonstrate its legitimacy to groups with the power to affect its viability. Negotiation skill becomes a means to accomplish this.

William C. Turner, former U.S. Ambassador to the Organization for Economic Cooperation and Development, stated in a 1981 speech to the Menlo Group in San Francisco:

In some countries, government policy and administrative constraints may well now be as important a consideration in shaping the opportunities for corporate growth as traditional market factors, such as demand and competition. Under these conditions, the management of multinational corporations has found it increasingly necessary to develop new and improved means for both understanding and anticipating those external, nonmarket forces which will adversely impact their strategy, investment, and operations.

It also implies the practice of corporate diplomacy through synergistic negotiations.

Sometimes these negotiations are conducted in adversarial situations. In a *Newsweek* commentary (January 14, 1980) in reference to Iran, entitled "Why Sanctions Won't Work," Roger Fisher stated:

In pressing for economic sanctions against Iran, President Carter is making two classic errors of international relations: reacting rather than acting purposively, and ignoring the perceptions and legitimate interests of the other side. The cure to an international conflict is to understand our interests and those of our adversary, and then to find measures that will solve their problem in a way that solves ours. Punishing governments has not worked in the past and will not work now.

This chapter is about international business negotiations—negotiations that result in mutual benefit, and that are purposeful rather than reactive. As in the previous chapter, the goal is to be both conceptual, practical, and useful. Material for *Getting Your Yen's Worth: How to Negotiate with Japan, Inc.* (Moran 1985) is included to illustrate concepts and culture specific information about Japan.

NEGOTIATING ACROSS CULTURES

Negotiation is a process in which two or more entities come together to discuss common and conflicting interests in order to reach an agreement of mutual benefit. In international business negotiations, there are cultural dimensions in every aspect of the negotiations. In preparing for and analyzing a negotiation it is useful to review these dimensions and by study and observation determine one's counterparts attitude and orientation towards the selection of the negotiators, the values or priorities present, the outcome, and the movement. The following examples of variations from a number of cultures are taken from *The Cross-Cultural Dimension in International Negotiation* (Fisher 1981).

There are many differences in the negotiation process from culture to culture and they involve language, cultural conditioning, negotiating styles, approaches to problem solving, implicit assumptions, gestures and facial expressions, and the role of ceremony and formality. Specific variables of which an American negotiator should be aware are:

1. Cultural conditioning with regard to the way negotiators view the nature of the negotiation process itself. American negotiators are often frustrated because their counterparts do not enter in the expected give-and-take, which they typically experience in domestic or labor-management negotiations in the United States. We are frustrated when we do not experience this overseas.
2. The use of a "middle man." For many cultures, such as the Japanese, to openly disagree is not a pleasant experience and whenever there is a conflict in a negotiation situation, very often a go-between or a third person is used to assist in the negotiation process.
3. Trusting the other party. American negotiators usually begin a negotiating session by trusting the persons until proven otherwise. However, the French are more inclined to mistrust until faith and trust is proven by their counterparts.
4. Viewing the process as a problem-solving exercise whereby a number of fallback positions are carefully discussed prior to a session. However, other cultures do not view it as a problem-solving exercise and their first position is the only position they have discussed and the one they wish to present and have accepted.
5. The importance of protocol. Mexican negotiators are often selected for their skill at rhetoric and making distinguished performances. Negotiation is perceived from their perspective as a time to test Mexican honor and to determine the attitude of the American negotiators towards Mexicans.
6. Selection of the negotiation team. In the United States, persons are selected primarily on the basis of technical competence. However, in other societies one may be negotiating with people who do not have a high degree of technical competence, because the members of a negotiation team are selected on the basis of personal power or authority.
7. How the negotiating team views the decision-making process. In the United States, negotiators approach the negotiation session and the decisions that result from it by essentially saying, "anything is O.K. unless it has been restricted." However, their Soviet counterparts approach the same situation with, "nothing is permitted unless it is initiated by the state."
8. Decision-making. In Mexico, decisions are typically from a top-down position in an organization and these reflect the personalities of the individuals. And when Mexican negotiators work overseas, they prefer to work with high-level people and typically link issues with trade-offs (for example, conceding a point on narcotics control in exchange for freer vegetable importation into the United States).

For international negotiations to produce long-term synergy, and not just short-term solutions, managers and their representatives, such as attorneys, should be aware of the multicultural facets in the process underway. The negotiator must enter into the private world or cultural space of the other, while at the same time sharing his or her own perceptual field.

Dr. Glen Fisher in a paper prepared for the Foreign Service Institute of the Department of State asked, "Whether skill in international negotiation can be learned, or is it a product of personality and experience?" It is our belief that negotiating is a skill and it can be improved. It is the purpose of this section to suggest some of the cultural variables and what specific skills are required.

Pierre Casse, lecturer in the Economic Development Institute at the World Bank, stated that international negotiators need five skills. We have changed some of the wording on his list, but accept the skills he identifies as being necessary for the international negotiator. The skills are (Casse 1979):

1. To be able to see the world as other people see it and to understand others' behavior from their perspective.
2. To be able to demonstrate the advantages of what one's proposals offer so that the counterparts in the negotiation will be willing to change.
3. To be able to manage stress and cope with ambiguous situations as well as unpredictable demands.
4. To be able to express one's ideas so that people one negotiates with will accurately understand.
5. To be sensitive to the cultural background of the others and adjust the suggestions one makes to the existing constraints and limitations.

Israel Unterman, a professor at San Diego State University and a leading researcher on negotiation and cross-cultural communication proposes that intercultural negotiation skills are best taught by:

1. Preparing a flexible scenario in which a student or trainee devises a set of modified, strategic plans and approaches.
2. Using negotiating teams for practice in comprehending selective barriers and gateways to effective communication, such as culturally-influenced body language or behaviors.
3. Learning exercises in use of voice, word congruence, listening skills, coping with emotional responses and stress, and closing the negotiation with some kind of agreement.

Unterman advocates the case study method for teaching negotiation skills, and his ongoing research analyzes the differences among national teams and the cultural variations that influence the process and outcome of the negotiation and decision-making.

WHAT AMERICANS BRING TO THE NEGOTIATING PARTY

When people communicate with one another, they make certain assumptions about the process of perceiving, judging, thinking, and reasoning patterns of each other. They make these assumptions usually "out-of-awareness" or without realizing they are making them. Correct assumptions facilitate communication, but incorrect assumptions lead to misunderstandings and miscommunication often results.

The most common assumption that is made by persons who are communicating with one another is called *projective cognitive similarity*, that is, they assume that the other perceives, judges, thinks, and reasons the same way he does. Identical twins communicate with ease. Persons from the same culture but with a different education, age, background, and experience often find communication difficult. American managers communicating with managers from other cultures experience greater difficulties in communication than with managers from their own culture. However, in some regards American managers share more interests and terms with other members of the world managerial subculture than with their own workers or union leaders. The effects of our cultural conditioning are so pervasive that people whose experience has been limited to the rules of one culture have difficulty understanding communication based on another set of rules.

An excerpt from the diary of the captain of the U.S. ping-pong team during his visit to the People's Republic of China in 1971 illustrates this point (Kraemer 1973):

> I seemed to have some kind of a communication gap with many of the Chinese I met. I had a number of talks, for example, with our interpreter, but we sometimes had difficulty getting through to each other. He spoke excellent English, and I used very simple words, but he often apologized and said I should get a better interpreter because "I just don't understand what you are saying." I used words like "individual" and "unique." They are words he knows, but he couldn't relate them to the idea of doing what you want to do. "Do what I want to do?" one puzzled Chinese asked me. He looked terribly confused, as if to say, "How do you do that?" I guess in China you have to do what the chairman tells you to do and then everything is cool and happy.

Many comments can be made about his diary entry, but the most important is that the American's apparently simple question, "But what do you want to do?" implies certain assumptions about the cognitions of the Chinese interpreter. That is, that the Chinese interpreter understood and valued the idea of individual choice. However, this assumption was probably not valid, because individualism, as known and practiced in the United States, is not well understood or valued by the people of The People's Republic of China. The American was not able to see the outward cultural expression of the Chinese society and in order to do this, the American must fully comprehend the values and principles of his own culture.

In order to create cultural synergistic solutions to management problems or to transfer management techniques to another culture, a U.S. manager must identify and understand what is American about America, what common cultural traits are shared by Americans, and what values and assumptions are the foundation for their management practices. Mark Twain stated, "The only distinguishing characteristic of the American character that I've been able to discover is a fondness for ice water." There is much more.

Awareness of such cultural influences is essential for any manager who seeks to transfer management concepts or technology. Depending on the cultures, there may be an overlap of values in a specific area, and therefore, the problems related to transferring ideas will be minimal. However, in some instances the gap will be significant and cause serious problems.

John Graham and Roy Herberger (1983) suggest a combination of characteristics that American negotiators typically use. They are part of the cultural baggage such nationals bring to the negotiating table and, according to Graham and Herberger, typify the "American John Wayne" style of negotiating:

1. I can go it alone. Many U.S. executives seem to believe they can handle any negotiating situation by themselves, and they are outnumbered in most negotiating situations.
2. Just call me John. Americans value informality and equality in human relations. They try to make people feel comfortable by playing down status distinctions.
3. Pardon my French. Americans aren't very talented at speaking foreign languages.
4. Check with the home office. American negotiators get upset when halfway through a negotiation the other side says, "I'll have to check with the home office." The implication is that the decision makers are not present.
5. Get to the point. Americans don't like to beat around the bush and want to get to the heart of the matter quickly.
6. Lay your cards on the table. Americans expect honest information at the bargaining table.
7. Don't just sit there, speak up. Americans don't deal well with silence during negotiations.
8. Don't take no for an answer. Persistence is highly valued by Americans and is part of the deeply ingrained competitive spirit that manifests itself in every aspect of American life.
9. One thing at a time. Americans usually attack a complex negotiation task sequentially, that is, they separate the issues and settle them one at a time.

10. A deal is a deal. When Americans make an agreement and give their word, they expect to honor the agreement no matter what the circumstances.

11. I am what I am. Few Americans take pride in changing their minds, even in difficult circumstances.

FRAMEWORK FOR INTERNATIONAL BUSINESS NEGOTIATIONS

A successful negotiation is a "win-win situation" in which both parties gain. Many factors affect its outcome, such as how consistent the negotiator's acts are with the other party's values, the approach he uses, his attitude, the negotiating methods he employs, and the concern he exhibits for the other side's feelings and needs. Negotiation comprises all of these factors.

There are varied negotiation postures, bases from which to negotiate. One framework by Stephen Weiss and William Stripp (1985) maintains there are 12 variables in every negotiation with persons from other countries that impact the negotiation (and therefore can significantly influence the outcome either positively or negatively).

1. *Basic Conception of Negotiation Process.* In American business, negotiation has traditionally been, and in many places continues to be, construed as a competitive process of offers and counter-offers in which one party's gains are the other's losses. An alternative general model is joint problem-solving. Another possibility is a contingency view that admits the use of either problem-solving or bargaining, depending on the issue at hand. And one could see negotiation as primarily a debate. All four treat problems or issues explicitly.

2. *Negotiator Selection Criteria.* These criteria include negotiating experience, status (seniority, political affiliation, sex, ethnic ties, or kinship), knowledge of the subject, and personal attributes (e.g., affability, loyalty, and trustworthiness in the eyes of the principal.

3. *Significance of Type of Issue.* At least four types of issues (concerns) may call for negotiation or arise during it: substantive, relationship-based, procedural, and personal/internal. The first covers such matters as price and number of units to be sold; the second, compatibility of styles and mutual trust; the third, although related to the second, the type of structure/format of discussions concerning substantive and relationship-based issues (e.g., preconditions, agenda-setting); and the fourth, respect, reputation, and dissent within one's own negotiating team.

4. *Concern With Protocol.* Concern with protocol has to do with the importance placed on the existence of and adherence to rules for acceptable self-presentation and social behavior (the international courtesies of business, for example).

5. *Complexity of Communicative Context.* Complexity refers to the degree of reliance on nonverbal cues to convey and to interpret intentions and information in dialogue. These cues include distance (space), gaze, gestures, and silence, to name just a few.

6. *Nature of Persuasive Arguments.* One way or another, negotiation involves attempts to influence the other party, to be persuasive both in presenting one's own goals and in responding to others'.

7. *Role of Individuals' Aspirations.* The emphasis negotiators place on their individual goals and needs for recognition may also vary. Some take the attitude "to thine own self be true," while others "know their station in life" and closely align their own needs with the community good.

8. *Bases of Trust.* Negotiators can go with past record of trustworthiness (documented evidence, direct experience, professional reputation), intuition (status/visibility, knowledge/expertise), or the existence of external sanctions by which to regulate conduct (e.g., "bargaining in good faith") or enforce an agreement.

9. *Risk-Taking Propensity.* In negotiations, differences in avoidance of uncertainty show up in willingness to divulge critical information when counterparts' trustworthiness is questionable; openness to novel approaches to outstanding issues; willingness to go beyond superiors' directives and authorizations; responses to proposals with unknowns or contingencies; and the desired form of a final agreement.

10. *Value of Time.* For most Americans, "time is money." This attitude toward time is evinced in the importance attached to setting specific appointments in advance, the punctuality expected and observed in keeping appointments, and the urgency imputed to meeting deadlines.

11. *Decision-Making System.* This variable refers to the system by which negotiators reach decisions within their teams, and between their teams and the organization they represent.

12. *Form of Satisfactory Agreement.* The desired form of a negotiated agreement is based on many concerns and practices: trust, communication, credibility, salience of certain types of issues, commitment, enforceability and more.

With these twelve variables in mind, the international negotiator is now able to develop a profile of his negotiating counterparts.

Chapters in Unit Three will cover culture-specific information to assist the negotiator in developing profiles for various countries.

USING INTERPRETERS

There is a joke that goes,

Q: "What do you call a person who can speak two languages?"
A: "Bilingual."
Q: "How about three?"
A: "Trilingual."
Q: "Good, how about one?"
A: "Hmmm . . . American!"

The importance of an interpreter in business negotiations cannot be over-stressed. It is the interpreter who can assist with the accurate communication of ideas between the two teams. It is advisable to remember the following points concerning the use of interpreters:

1. Brief the interpreter in advance about the subject. (Select an interpreter knowledgeable about the product, if possible.)
2. Speak clearly and slowly.
3. Avoid little-known words, such as "arcane" or "heuristic."
4. Explain the major idea two or three different ways, as the point may be lost if discussed only once.
5. Do not talk more than a minute or two without giving the interpreter a chance to speak.
6. While talking, allow the interpreter time to make notes of what is being said.
7. Do not lose confidence if the interpreter uses a dictionary.
8. Permit the interpreter to spend as much time as needed in clarifying points whose meanings are obscure.
9. Do not interrupt the interpreter as he translates, as interrupting causes many misunderstandings.
10. Avoid long sentences, double negatives, or the use of negative wordings of a sentence when a positive form could be used.
11. Avoid superfluous words. Your point may be lost if wrapped up in generalities.
12. Try to be expressive and use gestures to support your verbal messages.
13. During meetings, write out the main points discussed. In this way both parties can double check their understanding.
14. After meetings, confirm in writing what has been agreed.
15. Don't expect an interpreter to work for over two hours without a rest period.

16. Consider using two interpreters if interpreting is to last a whole day or into the evening, so that when one tires the other can take over.
17. Don't be concerned if a speaker talks for five minutes and the interpreter covers it in half a minute.
18. Be understanding if it develops that the interpreter has made a mistake.
19. Ask the interpreter for advice if there are problems.

Recall also the problems pointed out in the last chapter when one is totally dependent upon a translator to communicate one's thought!

Translingua of San Diego, international communication consultants, warns that a company whose work is poorly translated into another language runs the risk of being laughed at, offending a customer, and in the end, losing a deal. They cite as an example Coca-Cola advertising when that soda was first introduced into the Asian market. The firm's name and product were translated into Chinese characters that sounded correct, but actually read, "Bite the wax tadpole." Pepsi-Cola had a comparable communication disaster when it moved into the Thai market using their American slogan, "Come alive, you're in the Pepsi generation." Only later did their managers discover that the real Thai translation said, "Pepsi brings your ancestors back from the dead."

SKILLS OF SUCCESSFUL NEGOTIATORS

The following is a summary of a research project that analyzed *actual* negotiations.* The researchers' methods allowed them to differentiate between skilled negotiators and average negotiators by using behavior analysis techniques as they observed the negotiations and recorded the discussion. They identified "successful" negotiators as those who—

1. Were rated as effective by both sides.
2. Had a "track-record" of significant success.
3. Had a low incidence of "implementation" failures.

A total of 48 negotiators were studied who met all of these three success criteria. They included union representatives (17), management representatives (12), contract negotiators (10), and others (9).

The 48 successful negotiators were studied over a total of 102 separate negotiating sessions. In the following description, the successful negotiators are called the "skilled" group. In comparison, the negotiators who either failed to meet the criteria or about whom no criterion data were available, were called the "average" group.

---

* *Behavior of Successful Negotiators*, Huthwaite Research Group Report, 1976, 1982.

During the Planning Process

Negotiation training emphasizes the importance of planning.

1. *Planning Time*—No significant difference was found between the total planning time that skilled and average negotiators claimed they spent prior to actual negotiation.
2. *Exploration of Options*—The skilled negotiator considers a wider range of outcomes or options for action, than the average negotiator.

   Skilled negotiator—5.1 outcomes or options per issue
   Average negotiator—2.6 outcomes or options per issue

3. *Common Ground*—The research showed that the skilled negotiators gave over three times as much attention to common ground areas as did average negotiators

   Skilled negotiators—38% of comments about areas of anticipated agreement or common ground
   Average negotiators—11% of comments about areas of anticipated agreement or common ground

4. *Long-Term or Short-Term?*—With the average negotiator, approximately one comment in 25 met the criteria of a long-term consideration, namely a comment that involved any factor extending beyond the immediate implementation of the issue under negotiation. The skilled negotiator, while showing twice as many long-term comments, still only averages 8.5% of his total recorded planning comment.
5. *Setting Limits*—The researchers asked negotiators about their objectives and recorded whether their replies referred to single-point objectives (e.g., "We aim to settle at 83") or to defined range (e.g., "We hope to get 85 but we would settle for a minimum of 77"). Skilled negotiators were significantly more likely to set upper and lower limits—to plan in terms of range. Average negotiators, in contrast, were more likely to plan their objectives around a fixed point.
6. *Sequence and Issue Planning*—The term "planning" frequently refers to a process of sequencing—putting a number of events, points, or potential occurrences into a time sequence. Critical path analysis and other forms of network planning are examples.

Typical sequence plan used by average negotiators

A then B then C then D
Issues are linked.

Typical issue plan used by skilled negotiators

          A

             B

  D

      C

        Issues are independent and not linked by sequence.

	Number of Mentions Implying Sequence in Planning
Skilled negotiators	2.1 per session
Average negotiators	4.9 per session

The clear advantage of issue planning over sequence planning is flexibility.

Face-To-Face Behavior

Skilled negotiators show marked differences in their face-to-face behavior, compared with average negotiators. They use certain types of behavior significantly more frequently while other types they tend to avoid.

1. *Irritators*—Certain words and phrases that are commonly used during negotiation have negligible value in persuading the other party, but do cause irritation. Probably the most frequent example of these is the term "generous offer" used by a negotiator to describe his own proposal.

	Use of Irritators Per Hour Face-To-Face Speaking Time
Skilled negotiators	2.3
Average negotiators	10.8

2. *Counter-Proposals*—During negotiation, one party frequently puts forward a proposal and the other party immediately responds with a counter-proposal. Researchers found that skilled negotiators made immediate counter-proposals much less frequently than average negotiators.

	Frequency of Counter-Proposals Per Hour of Face-To-Face Speaking Time
Skilled negotiators	1.7
Average negotiators	3.1

3. *Argument Dilution*—This way of thinking predisposes us to believe that there is some special merit in quantity. Having five reasons for doing something is considered more persuasive than having only one reason. We feel that the more we can put on our scale, the more likely we are to tip the balance of an argument in our favor.

	Average Number of Reasons Given By Negotiator to Back Each Argument/Case S/he Advanced
Skilled negotiators	1.8
Average negotiators	3.0

The researchers found that the opposite was true. The skilled negotiator used less reasons to back up each of his/her arguments.

4. *Reviewing the Negotiation*—The researchers asked negotiators how likely they were to spend time reviewing the negotiation afterwards Over two-thirds of the skilled negotiators claimed that they always set aside some time after a negotiation to review it and consider what they had learned. Just under half of average negotiators, in contrast, made the same claim.

This research is the best available that clearly indicates the *behavior* of skilled negotiators. These are the behaviors to imitate or avoid.

ETHICAL ISSUES AND NEGOTIATIONS

The negotiator, working in a multicultural environment, often experiences conflicting loyalties—loyalty to one's conscience, the laws of one's home country, the laws of the host country. The business practices at home and abroad, company codes of conduct are examples of different loyalties which may, at times, appear contradictory. The following mini-cases are based on actual situations. Read each, then decide your course of action and rationale.

Case 1: Purchasing Manager—Latin America*

You have recently taken over as purchasing manager in your company's manufacturing plant in Latin America. The head of a local firm visited you last week and tried to persuade you to buy ball bearings (an essential part of your product) from him, Roberto, instead of his competitor from whom you are currently buying them. He would charge the same price but promises very

---

* Written by George W. Renwick and Robert T. Moran (1982)

prompt delivery. Your plant runs on a very tight schedule and there have been some problems when the current supplier has not delivered on time. Roberto also indicated that this contract with you would be worth $10,000 to him. This would be paid to you, gratefully and privately, in such a way that no one would ever know about it.

You need some money very badly to cover family medical bills and your daughter's education. Such payments are legal and are often made in the country in which you are now living. After thinking about it, you realize that your predecessor, who was just promoted to a high position in the home office, probably received a payment from the current supplier. Your company's traditional Code of Conduct, however, clearly says personnel do not take such payments. You have checked out Roberto's firm; it is reputable and his ball bearings are of equal quality to those your company is now buying.

What, Specifically, Will You Do? Why?

Case 2: Sales Rep—Middle East

You are the sales representative for your construction company in the Middle East. The company has bid on a substantial project that it wants *very much* to get.

Yesterday, the cousin of the minister who will award the contract suggested that he might be of help. You are reasonably sure that, with his help, the chances of your getting the contract would increase. For his assistance, Ahmed expects $20,000. You would have to pay this in addition to the standard fees to your agent. If you do not make this payment to Ahmed, you are certain that he will go to your competition (who have won the last three contracts), and they *will* make the payment (and probably get this contract too).

Your company has no code of conduct yet, though a committee was formed some time ago to consider it. The government of your country, however, recently passed a Business Practices Act. The pertinent paragraph is somewhat vague, but this kind of payment would probably be judged in violation of the Act.

The person to whom you report, and those above him, do not want to become involved. The decision is yours to make.

What, Specifically, Will You Do? Why?

Case 3: Vice-President of International Sales—Hazardous Materials in West Africa

For only one year now, you have been the vice-president of international sales of a multinational firm that produces and markets chemicals. The minister of agriculture in a small developing country in west Africa has requested from you a series of large shipments, over the next five years, of a special insecticide that only your firm prepares. The minister believes that this chemical is the only one that will rid one of his crops of a new infestation that threatens to destroy it. (You know, however, that one other insecticide would be equally effective; it is produced in another country and has never been allowed in yours.)

Your insecticide, MIM, is highly toxic. After years of debate, your government has just passed a law forbidding its use in your country. There is evidence that dangerous amounts are easily ingested by humans through residue on vegetables, through animals that eat treated crops, and through the water supply. After careful thought, you tell the minister about this evidence. He still insists on using it, arguing that it is necessary and it will be used "intelligently." You are quite sure that, ten years from now, it will begin to damage the health of some of his people.

Both the president and the executive vice-president of your firm feel strongly that the order should be filled. They question the government's position, and they are very concerned about the large inventory of MIM on hand and the serious financial setback its prohibition will cause the company. They have made it clear, however, that the decision is up to you.

The company has a Code of Conduct, and your government has a Business Practices Act, but neither cover hazardous materials.

What, Specifically, Will You Do? Why?

NEGOTIATION STYLE

The "Negotiation Skills—Self-Assessment Exercise" on pages 70–74 gives feedback on a person's negotiating style, as well as information on how to recognize a style in one's negotiating counterparts and effective ways to respond to specific styles.

Beliaev, Mullen, and Punnett (1985) recently addressed the cultural environment of U.S.–U.S.S.R. trade negotiations. By using a questionnaire with executives from both countries, they discovered that American executives found their Soviet counterparts to be more lengthy, secretive, and tougher in such negotiations, while the Russians were found to have to consult more frequently with their government officials, introduced new demands during the course of the negotiations, and have less authority to make concessions. The investigators concluded that Westerners would benefit in their negotiations with Communists if they had greater cultural awareness, especially how their own values influence the negotiating process (e.g., American individuality, time consciousness, use of human resources, risk perception, and results orientation). They also identified the need for better understanding of Soviet licensing process and for avoiding ethnocentric judgments of Soviet actions.

(text continued on page 74)

Negotiation Skills
A Self-Assessment Exercise*

Please respond to this list of questions in terms of what you believe you do *when interacting with others.* Base your answers on your typical day-to-day activities. Be as frank as you can.

For each statement, please enter on the Score Sheet the number corresponding to your choice of the five possible responses given below:

1. If you have never (or very rarely) observed yourself doing what is described in the statement.
2. If you have observed yourself doing what is described in the statement *occasionally, but infrequently:* that is, less often than most other people who are involved in similar situations.
3. If you have observed yourself doing what is described in the statement about *an average amount:* that is, about as often as most other people who are involved in similar situations.
4. If you have observed yourself doing what is described in the statement *fairly frequently:* that is, somewhat more often than most other people who are involved in similar situations.
5. If you have observed yourself doing what is described in the statement *very frequently:* that is, considerably more than most other people who are involved in similar situations.

Please answer each question.

1. I focus on the entire situation or problem.
2. I evaluate the facts according to a set of personal values.
3. I am relatively unemotional.
4. I think that the facts speak for themselves in most situations.
5. I enjoy working on new problems.
6. I focus on what is going on between people when interacting.
7. I tend to analyze things very carefully.
8. I am neutral when arguing.
9. I work in bursts of energy with slack periods in between.
10. I am sensitive to other people's needs and feelings.
11. I hurt people's feelings without knowing it.
12. I am good at keeping track of what has been said in a discussion.
13. I put two and two together quickly.
14. I look for common ground and compromise.
15. I use logic to solve problems.
16. I know most of the details when discussing an issue.
17. I follow my inspirations of the moment.
18. I take strong stands on matters of principle.
19. I am good at using a step-by-step approach.
20. I clarify information for others.

*Adapted by Pierre Casse from Interactive Style Questionnaire (Situation Management Systems, Inc.) in *Training for the Cross-Cultural Mind,* SIETAR, Washington, D.C., 1979. Used with permission.

21. I get my facts a bit wrong.
22. I try to please people.
23. I am very systematic when making a point.
24. I relate facts to experience.
25. I am good at pinpointing essentials.
26. I enjoy harmony.
27. I weigh the pros and cons.
28. I am patient.
29. I project myself into the future.
30. I let my decisions be influenced by my personal likes and wishes.
31. I look for cause and effect.
32. I focus on what needs attention now.
33. When others become uncertain or discouraged, my enthusiasm carries them along.
34. I am sensitive to praise.
35. I make logical statements.
36. I rely on well tested ways to solve problems.
37. I keep switching from one idea to another.
38. I offer bargains.
39. I have my ideas very well thought out.
40. I am precise in my arguments.
41. I bring others to see the exciting possibilities in a situation.
42. I appeal to emotions and feelings to reach a "fair" deal.
43. I present well articulated arguments for the proposals I favor.
44. I do not trust inspiration.
45. I speak in a way which conveys a sense of excitement to others
46. I communicate what I am willing to give in return for what I get.
47. I put forward proposals or suggestions which make sense even if they are unpopular.
48. I am pragmatic.
49. I am imaginative and creative in analyzing a situation.
50. I put together very well-reasoned arguments.
51. I actively solicit others' opinions and suggestions.
52. I document my statements.
53. My enthusiasm is contagious.
54. I build upon others' ideas.
55. My proposals command the attention of others.
56. I like to use the inductive method (from facts to theories).
57. I can be emotional at times.
58. I use veiled or open threats to get others to comply.
59. When I disagree with someone, I skillfully point out the flaws in the others' arguments.
60. I am low-key in my reactions.
61. In trying to persuade others. I appeal to their need for sensations and novelty.
62. I make other people feel that they have something of value to contribute.
63. I put forth ideas which are incisive.
64. I face difficulties with realism.
65. I point out the positive potential in discouraging or difficult situations.

(continued on next page)

66. I show tolerance and understanding of others' feelings.
67. I use arguments relevant to the problem at hand.
68. I am perceived as a down-to-earth person.
69. I go beyond the facts.
70. I give people credit for their ideas and contributions.
71. I like to organize and plan.
72. I am skillful at bringing up pertinent facts.
73. I have a charismatic tone.
74. When disputes arise, I search for the areas of agreement.
75. I am consistent in my reactions.
76. I quickly notice what needs attention.
77. I withdraw when the excitement is over.
78. I appeal for harmony and cooperation.
79. I am cool when negotiating.
80. I work all the way through to reach a conclusion.

Score Sheet

Enter the score you assign each question (1, 2, 3, 4, or 5) in the space provided. *Please note:* The item numbers progress across the page from left to right. When you have all your scores, add them up *vertically* to attain four totals. Insert a "3" in any number space left blank.

1. _____	2. _____	3. _____	4. _____
5. _____	6. _____	7. _____	8. _____
9. _____	10. _____	11. _____	12. _____
13. _____	14. _____	15. _____	16. _____
17. _____	18. _____	19. _____	20. _____
21. _____	22. _____	23. _____	24. _____
25. _____	26. _____	27. _____	28. _____
29. _____	30. _____	31. _____	32. _____
33. _____	34. _____	35. _____	36. _____
37. _____	38. _____	39. _____	40. _____
41. _____	42. _____	43. _____	44. _____
45. _____	46. _____	47. _____	48. _____
49. _____	50. _____	51. _____	52. _____
53. _____	54. _____	55. _____	56. _____
57. _____	58. _____	59. _____	60. _____
61. _____	62. _____	63. _____	64. _____
65. _____	66. _____	67. _____	68. _____
69. _____	70. _____	71. _____	72. _____
73. _____	74. _____	75. _____	76. _____
77. _____	78. _____	79. _____	80. _____
IN: _____	NR: _____	AN: _____	FA: _____

Negotiation Style Profile

Enter now your four scores on the bar chart below. Construct your profile by connecting the four data points.

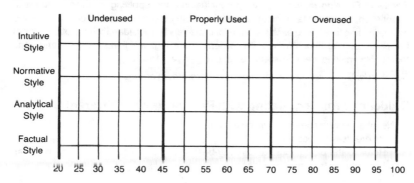

Description of Styles

Factual

Basic Assumption: "The facts speak for themselves."

Behavior: Pointing out facts in neutral way, keeping track of what has been said, reminding people of their statements, knowing most of the details of the discussed issue and sharing them with others, clarifying, relating facts to experience, being low-key in their reactions, looking for proof, documenting their statements.

Key Words: Meaning, define, explain, clarify, facts.

Intuitive

Basic Assumption: "Imagination can solve any problem."

Behavior: Making warm and enthusiastic statements, focusing on the entire situation or problem, pinpointing essentials, making projections into the future, being imaginative and creative in analyzing the situation, keeping switching from one subject to another, going beyond the facts, coming up with new ideas all the time, pushing and withdrawing from time to time, putting two and two together quickly, getting their facts a bit wrong sometimes, being deductive.

Key Words: Principles, essential, tomorrow, creative, idea.

Normative

Basic Assumption: "Negotiating is bargaining."

Behavior: Judging assessing and evaluating the facts according to a set of personal values, approving and disapproving, agreeing and disagreeing, using loaded works, offering bargains, proposing rewards, incentives, appealing to feelings and emotions to reach a "fair" deal, demanding, requiring, threatening, involving power, using status, authority, correlating, looking for compromise, making effective statements, focusing on people, their reactions, judging, attention to communication and group processes.

Key Words: Wrong, right, good, bad, like.

(continued on next page)

Analytical

Basic Assumption: "Logic leads to the right conclusions."

Behavior: Forming reasons, drawing conclusions and applying them to the case in negotiation, arguing in favor or against one's own or others' position, directing, breaking down, dividing, analyzing each situation for cause and effect, identifying relationships of the parts, putting things into logical order, organizing, weighing the pros and cons thoroughly, making identical statements, using linear reckoning.

Key Words: Because, then, consequently, therefore, in order to.

Guidelines for Negotiating with People Having Different Styles

1. Negotiating with someone having a *factual* style—
   - Be *precise* in presenting your facts.
   - Refer to the *past* (what has already been tried out, what has worked, what has been shown from past experiences . . .).
   - Be *indicative* (go from the facts to the principles.
   - Know your dossier (including the details).
   - Document what you say.
2. Negotiating with someone having an *intuitive* style—
   - Focus on the situation as a whole.
   - Project yourself into the future (look for opportunities).
   - Tap the imagination and creativity of your partner.
   - Be quick in reacting (jump from one idea to another).
   - Build upon the reaction of the other person.
3. Negotiating with someone having an *analytical* style—
   - Use logic when arguing.
   - Look for causes and effects.
   - Analyze the relationships between the various elements of the situation or problem at stake.
   - Be patient.
   - Analyze various options with their respective pros and cons.
4. Negotiating with someone having a *normative* style—
   - Establish a sound relationship right at the outset of the negotiation.
   - Show your interest in what the other person is saying.
   - Identify his or her values and adjust to them accordingly.
   - Be ready to compromise.
   - Appeal to your partner's feelings.

(text continued from page 69)

Getting It All Together in Negotiations

The cross-cultural negotiation process is where the global manager practices all the skills considered so essential for success in the overseas' assignment (Kohls, 1979). These include patience, tolerance for ambiguity, realistic expectations (toward goals and tasks to be achieved), and warm human relationships (like a sense of humor). In *Going International* Griggs and Copeland (1985) say negotiating with foreigners involves positioning one's proposals, making concessions (or not), selecting the right negotiation team, utilizing the art of persuasion, going behind the scenes presented or viewed, understanding international contracting, and walking away from bad deals.

In the film, *Doing Business in Japan: Negotiating a Contract*, Vision Associates illustrates the issues of intercultural commercial activity through the inability of both sides in the negotiations to comprehend and deal with their own cultural differences. The Americans do not appreciate the importance of little things like business cards in two languages, or big things like the structure of the Japanese corporation and what roles the titles really represent. The motion picture dramatically underscores the tendency during negotiations for both sides to sound out the other, yet be unclear about the respective positions to be pursued eventually in later discussions. The film examines other subtle issues involved in the negotiation, such as observing proper formalities, developing social relationships, behavior at social events, linguistic differences (when "yes" does not mean "yes"), group decision-making (*ringi* system), emotional sensitivity and obscuring, gift giving, saving face, and Japanese avoidance of contractual relations as known in the West.

Rajesh Kuman (1988) developed a theoretical framework for analyzing processes and outcomes of business negotiations. It is based on the notion of a "standard—a cognitive construct that defines the frame of reference for an individual." The model suggests that the use of different standards evokes different emotions in the negotiators which, in turn, influence the negotiations. Specifically, it proposes that Americans use an "ideal/own" standard for evaluation that is associated with emotional dejection and frustration. The Japanese, on the other hand, seem to employ an "ought/other" norm that produces agitation emotions. Much of this inferential action in intercultural negotiation appears to occur outside of the individual's conscious awareness. The study confirms the importance of role taking and empathetic skills in effective interaction.

John Graham, best known for studies of Japanese-American interactions (1984), was invited to the U.S.S.R. to teach negotiations. With increased Soviet interest in international trade, they wished to learn more about traders from other countries. Graham found a reverse situation in Russia compared to other cultures. With a shortage of goods, the seller seems to be "king"; goods have been allocated according to centralized planning, salaries have little to do with performance, and customer service is a new concept. Under the reform movement of President Mikhail S. Gorbachev, encouragement is given to supply-demand economics, and direct negotiations by state-owned enterprises, as well as bargaining with suppliers and customers, are growing within the huge country. Graham found his Moscow businessmen hungry for information about the West and anxious to improve their bargaining skills. He believes that the promotion of international trade is good for all parties involved and contribute to the cause of peace over weaponry.

The point is that many of the cross-cultural insights and proficiencies described throughout our subsequent chapters come together in the process of negotiating.

SUMMARY

Managers need skills as intercultural negotiators if they are to effectively manage international business relations, so as to get results that are mutually beneficial. However, managers from different cultures approach this negotiation process in unique ways. To obtain some synergy in this important managerial activity, this chapter analyzed some of the variations across cultures in this regard, as well as identified some of the skills to be enhanced. It provided a framework for more satisfying cross-cultural negotiations, tips for using interpreters, and research findings on what constitutes successful negotiation posture. To confront the ethical issues involved in the process, several critical incidents were offered for problem solving. Finally, the chapter presented the reader with the opportunity to assess his/her personal negotiating style.

4

Managers as Facilitators of Strategic Collaborations

Companies are just beginning to learn what nations have always known: in a complex, uncertain world filled with dangerous opponents, it is best not to go it alone.

Kenichi Ohmae, *Harvard Business Review*
March-April 1989

This chapter outlines some of the cultural elements in forming strategic alliances and creating opportunities for collaboration. These partnerships are often an economic necessity in today's world to assist in defraying enormous fixed costs required to succeed.

Multinational managers are required to meet, socialize, and negotiate with foreign businessmen and government officials on a regular basis. A requirement that is common to most of their activities is that the manager be able to communicate and work with persons who have grown up and who have been socialized in a different cultural environment. Customs, values, life styles, beliefs, management practices and most other important aspects of one's personal and professional life are therefore different. For the global manager to be effective, one must be aware of the many beliefs and values that underlie his or her country's business practices, management techniques, and strategies. These beliefs and values are so much a part of many managers' culture that they take them for granted and without challenge. They do not realize that many are culturally conditioned. Awareness of such values and assumptions is critical for managers who wish to transfer technology to another culture. This chapter will explore some of the beliefs, values, and assumptions that underlie U.S. management techniques and principles and contrast these with the values and assumptions underlying the management techniques of other cultures. Following this analysis, we shall suggest how an international manager, using the approach of cultural synergy, can integrate the contrasting values within the organization. Finally, we shall describe some of the skills required for a manager who wishes to transfer technology to others in a different culture and society.

CULTURAL SELF-AWARENESS

Table 4-1 identifies several U.S. values with possible alternatives. Examples of how the cultural system might influence management are also indicated in the third column.

The order of the values and the sequence is not important. They are not mutually exclusive nor comprehensive. The ideas will be useful for a manager who will be working in a multicultural environment in the U.S. or another country. They will also be helpful to any foreign manager who is trying to understand U.S. managers and U.S. management techniques.

The purpose is not only to compare cultural values affecting management practices in culture X with those in culture Y, but also to provide a basis whereby a manager might "synergistically" relate to managers trained in another cultural system and management practices developed in other cultures.

The aspects of the U.S. presented in Table 4-1 are from the author's (Moran) own experience and others' (Wallin 1976, Stewart 1976, Newman 1972, Kraemer 1973). Further discussion of American culture is in Chapter 15.

Table 4-1 illustrates how the cultural system or differences in attitude, values, assumptions, personal beliefs, interpersonal relationships, social and organizational structure affect the traditional management functions of decision-making, promotion, recruitment and development, organizing, planning, and motivation. Given these differences, and given their profound effect upon management's functions, the international manager is constantly faced with a complex challenge: how to accommodate (and even take advantage of) these differences within the organization; and how are the diverse people in the organization going to execute their essential functions? Examination of Table 4-1 in detail should increase American cultural self-awareness when interacting with global managers from other countries. (Appendices B and C can also assist in further self-understanding.)

MULTICULTURAL UNDERSTANDING

A European executive described the multicultural challenge this way: "I can't think of any situation in my 25 years of international experience when international business was made *easier* because managers from more than one country were participating."

Earlier this year, I (Moran) was invited to participate in a staff meeting of a large U.S. high-technology company. The president and his direct subordinates were present. After exchanging a few pleasantries, the president went to a blackboard, grabbed a stub of chalk, and with one bold gesture drew a horizontal line about three feet long. At one end of the line he wrote in large letters

Table 4-1
U.S. Values and Possible Alternatives

Aspects* of U.S. Culture	Alternative Aspect	Examples of Management Function Affected
The individual can influence the future (where there is a will there is a way).	Life follows a preordained course and human action is determined by the will of God.	Planning and scheduling
The individual can change and improve the environment.	People are intended to adjust to the physical environment rather than to alter it.	Organizational environment morale, and productivity
An individual should be realistic in his aspirations.	Ideals are to be pursued regardless of what is "reasonable."	Goal setting career development
We must work hard to accomplish our objectives (Puritan ethic).	Hard work is not the only prerequisite for success. Wisdom, luck and time are also required.	Motivation and reward system
Commitments should be honored (people will do what they say they will do).	A commitment may be superseded by a conflicting request or an agreement may only signify intention and have little or no relationship to the capacity of performance.	Negotiating and bargaining
One should effectively use one's time (time is money which can be saved or wasted).	Schedules are important but only in relation to other priorities.	Long and short range planning
A primary obligation of an employee is to the organization.	The individual employee has a primary obligation to his family and friends.	Loyalty, commitment, and motivation
The employer or employee can terminate their relationship.	Employment is for a lifetime.	Motivation and commitment to the company
A person can only work for one company at a time, (man cannot serve two masters).	Personal contributions to individuals who represent an enterprise are acceptable.	Ethical issues, conflict of interest
The best qualified persons should be given the positions available.	Family considerations, friendship, and other considerations should determine employment practices.	Employment, promotions, recruiting, selection, and reward
A person can be removed if he does not perform well.	The removal of a person from a position involves a great loss of prestige and will be rarely done.	Promotion
All levels of management are open to qualified individuals (an office boy can rise to become company president).	Education or family ties are the primary vehicles for mobility.	Employment practices and promotion

(table continued on next page)

Table 4-1 (Continued)
U.S. Values and Possible Alternatives

Aspects* of U.S. Culture	Alternative Aspect	Examples of Management Function Affected
Intuitive aspects of decision-making should be reduced and efforts should be devoted to gathering relevant information.	Decisions are expressions of wisdom by the person in authority and any questioning would imply a lack of confidence in his judgment.	Decision-making process
Data should be accurate.	Accurate data are not as highly valued.	Record-keeping
Company information should be available to anyone who needs it within the organization.	Withholding information to gain or maintain power is acceptable.	Organization communication, managerial style
Each person is expected to have an opinion and to express it freely even if his views do not agree with his colleagues.	Deference is to be given to persons in power or authority and to offer judgment that is not in support of the ideas of one's superiors is unthinkable.	Communications, organizational relations
A decision-maker is expected to consult persons who can contribute useful information to the area being considered.	Decisions may be made by those in authority and others need not be consulted.	Decision-making, leadership
Employees will work hard to improve their position in the company.	Personal ambition is frowned upon.	Selection and promotion
Competition stimulates high performance.	Competition leads to unbalances and leads to disharmony.	Career development and marketing
A person is expected to do whatever is necessary to get the job done (one must be willing to get one's hands dirty).	Various kinds of work are accorded low or high status and some work may be below one's "dignity" or place in the organization.	Assignment of tasks, performance, and organizational effectiveness
Change is considered an improvement and a dynamic reality.	Tradition is revered and the power of the ruling group is founded on the continuation of a stable structure.	Planning, morale and organization development
What works is important.	Symbols and the process are more important than the end point.	Communication, planning, quality control
Persons and systems are evaluated.	Persons are evaluated but in such a way that individuals not highly evaluated will not be embarrassed or caused to "lose face."	Rewards and promotion, performance evaluation and accountability

* *Aspect* here refers to a belief, value, attitude or assumption which is a part of culture in that it is shared by a large number of persons in any culture.

"GET OUT," and at the other end of the line, "MAKE THEM DO WHAT WE WANT." He then came to where I was standing, handed me the chalk and said, "You're an expert, give us your advice." I thought for a minute about the purpose of the meeting, namely, to discuss this company's relationship with a number of Japanese companies in which it has minority interests. Obviously, the president had reached a crossroads and wanted to make a choice. I went to the blackboard, and outlined a third alternative. I wrote, "LEARN TO WORK WITH THE JAPANESE."

It is our opinion that cultural diversity is viewed by many, and perhaps most, international managers as something to be overcome, or as a barrier. We believe diversity can and must become a resource if our business relationships are to survive. The creation of cultural synergy can be mutually beneficial.

Cultural Awareness of Others

To be effective in transnational activities takes astute awareness of both our home and host cultures. It can be costly in time, energy, and money if we are not tuned into the cultural proclivities of those with whom we seek to do business or to serve. Perhaps a few illustrations can point up the pitfalls and the possibilities:

- Before selling abroad, one must know more than the currency exchange and the target market, as Warren Cook and Stephen Kyle found out in May 1985. In planning to take their American Festival of Arts, Crafts & Music to Amsterdam, these Californians thought they had planned carefully. They had made several trips to Holland to scout out the site of the show and projected attendance of 35,000. What they failed to take into consideration was that their exhibition of 140 craftspeople took place on the Whitsun holiday weekend at a time when the weather was perfect for the shores of Haarlem—only 5,000 of the locals attended their festival. Also, the Dutch who were there were more interested in the blue-grass band that was playing than shopping, particularly because many of the items on display were used by Americans, not generally by the Dutch (e.g., toothbrush holders, porcelain coffee mugs). Yet, American Craft Enterprises reported earning $15 million at four exhibitions in Europe last year, while U.S. General Exhibitions sold $12 million worth of goods. With international shows, it helps to know local customs and to move beyond one's own culture to create synergy. (*Forbes*, July 29, 1985:135.)
- Since the Marshall Plan, the history of international development projects indicates that despite the spending of billions in the last four decades, world poverty has not been greatly reduced. Those in the foreign aid business have yet to formulate effective policies and programs that work for a wide range of cultures and ideologies. This is especially true in the Third World where 70% of the world's population subsists on only 20% of the

global income (Todaro 1979). Aid policy and technology transfer must be appropriate to the people, place, and circumstances. Community development requires contingency strategies so that the assistance and technology is compatible with a given culture. The training provided by development specialists cannot be alien to the indigenous trainees, but should consider the institutional, structural, ecological or cultural differences. Otherwise, we do not receive gratitude and cooperation, but resentment and resistance.

- Entrepreneurial activities overseas offer opportunities for investment growth, when they are culturally realistic and sensitive. Throughout the world, countries are offering incentives to foreigners to join local entrepreneurs in new ventures, particularly in high technologies. In developing nations from India and Pakistan to Malaysia and the Philippines, to Jamaica and Ireland, governments are offering generous funding, credit lines, tax holidays, and other attractions to lure First World venture capitalists and executives into joint enterprises with their business leaders. Even economically advanced nations, such as the United Kingdom, are doing the same for their less-developed regions by establishing "enterprise zones," such as in Scotland and Wales. But for synergy to occur, the global investor or entrepreneur must be cognizant of the local culture, economic conditions, and customs, such as will there be adequate power, supplies or trained native supervisory personnel? Many of the new agreements also require the foreign partners to provide the locals with adequate training so as to ensure the success of technological ventures.
- International joint ventures are the rage and an opportunity for cultural synergy. Pittsburg, California is the site of one daring bicultural endeavor to revitalize an old steel mill. State-of-the-art technology is transforming the facility into a factory where American workers process steel coils made by workers in South Korea. The $400 million project brings together USX and the Pohang Iron and Steel Company, replacing conflict with cooperation among the world's steel makers. And the change agent or catalyst for this alliance is a Fordham University professor and industry expert, Dr. William T. Hogan, S. J.

Learning *About* Other Management Cultures

To create opportunities for collaboration, international managers must learn not only the customs, courtesies, and business protocols of their counterparts from other countries, they must also understand the "national character," "management conceptions," and "mindsets" of these people. Dr. Geert Hofstede is a European who has helped identify important dimensions of national character.

In his book *Culture's Consequences* Hofstede identifies four dimensions of national culture (see also Chapter 13):

1. Power distance
2. Uncertainty avoidance
3. Individualism/collectivism
4. Masculinity/femininity

Power distance indicates "the extent to which a society accepts that power in institutions and organizations is distributed unequally."

The second dimension, *uncertainty avoidance*, indicates "the extent to which a society feels threatened by uncertain or ambiguous situations."

Individualism is the third dimension and refers to a "loosely knit social framework in a society in which people are supposed to take care of themselves and of their immediate families only." *Collectivism*, the opposite, occurs when there is a tight social framework in which people distinguish between in-groups and out-groups; they expect their in-group (relatives, clan, organizations) to look after them, and in exchange for that owe absolute loyalty to it."

The fourth dimension is *masculinity* with its opposite pole, *femininity*. This dimension expresses "the extent to which the dominant values in society are assertiveness, money and things, not caring for others, quality of life and people."

The most significant dimension related to leadership in Hofstede's study of 40 countries was the power dimension. On the basis of mean ratings of employees on a number of key questions he assigned an index value to each country.

Figure 4–1 shows the positions of the 40 countries on the power distance and uncertainty avoidance scales, and Figure 4–2 shows the countries' positions on the power distance and individualism scales.

The United States ranked fifteenth on power distance, ninth on uncertainty avoidance (both of these are below the average), fortieth on individualism (the most individualist country in the sample), and twenty-eighth on masculinity (above average) (Rhenman and Stromberg, 1970).

In Hofstede's study the United States ranked fifteenth out of 40 on the power distance dimension. If this had been higher, then the theories of leadership taught in the United States might have been expected to be more "Machiavellian." We might also ask how U.S. leaders are selected. Most are selected on the basis of competence, and it is the position of the person that provides the authority in the United States, which is, theoretically at least, an egalitarian society. In France, there is a higher power distance index score, and little concern with participative management, but a great concern with who has the power.

Even today, French industry and the managers who run it are a mixture of the old and the new. Anthony Rowley said of the French, "Behind the glittering technological triumph of the Concorde and the insolent innovation of the Citroen motorcars, the backward and fragmented structure of many parts of French industry still survives unharmed." France is still an industry of fam-

(text continued on page 85)

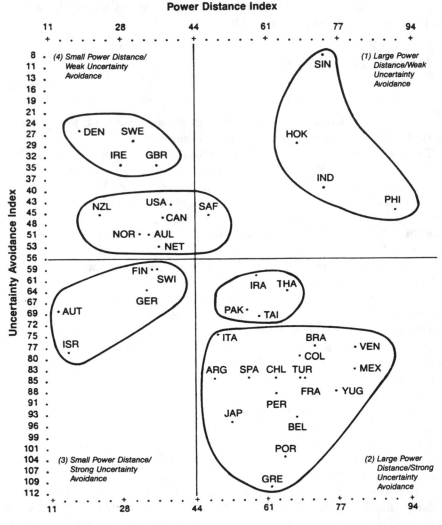

Figure 4-1. Position of 40 countries on the power distance and uncertainty avoidance scales (Hofstede 1984).

ARG	Argentina	FRA	France	JAP	Japan	SIN	Singapore
AUL	Australia	GBR	Great Britain	MEX	Mexico	SPA	Spain
AUT	Austria	GER	Germany (West)	NET	Netherlands	SWE	Sweden
BEL	Belgium	GRE	Greece	NOR	Norway	SWI	Switzerland
BRA	Brazil	HOK	Hong Kong	NZL	New Zealand	TAI	Taiwan
CAN	Canada	IND	India	PAK	Pakistan	THA	Thailand
CHL	Chile	IRA	Iran	PER	Peru	TUR	Turkey
COL	Colombia	IRE	Ireland	PHI	Philippines	USA	United States
DEN	Denmark	ISR	Israel	POR	Portugal	VEN	Venezuela
FIN	Finland	ITA	Italy	SAF	South Africa	YUG	Yugoslavia

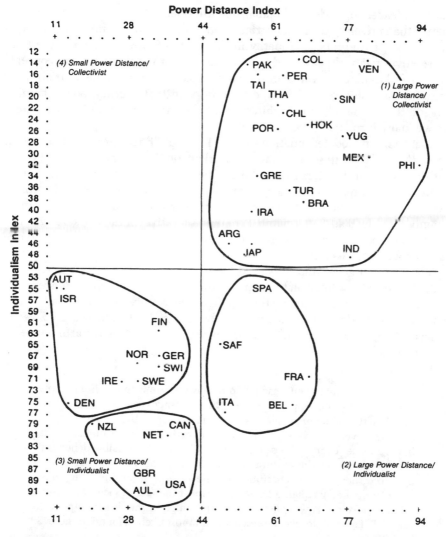

Figure 4-2. Positions of 40 countries on the power distance and individualism scales (Hofstede 1984).

ily empires with many paternalistic traditions. There is also a remnant of a feudalistic heritage that is deeply rooted within the French spirit, which could account for the very conservative and autocratic nature of their business methodology. (Specific aspects of the French national character are presented in detail in Chapter 16.)

Hofstede has shown that in countries with lower power distance scores than the United States, such as Sweden and Germany, there is considerable accep-

tance of leadership styles and management models that are even more participative than presently exist. Industrial democracy and codetermination is a style
that does not find much sympathy in the United States. Codetermination in
Germany is relatively new, and in labor relations it is a revolutionary concept.
It is also a large step towards greater worker participation in the decision-making and leadership roles of large corporations in that country. Some theorists
suggest that it could be the beginning of a reordering of the capitalistic system
as we know it today.

The German Codetermination Act of May 4, 1976 requires companies with
more than 2,000 employees to include workers on the supervisory board (similar to a board of directors in the United States), with the extent of the worker
representation on the supervisory boards depending on the number of employees in the corporation. If there are more than 2,000 employees, there are 20
members on the board, of whom 10 are representatives of the workers. Of these
10, six must come from the shop floor, three are elected by the unions, and one
is to be a senior executive.

The German government, backed by labor, is a supporter of the Act, but
must be careful not to alienate the powerful business community. Hofstede has
demonstrated that in Germany there is high uncertainty avoidance and, therefore, industrial democracy is brought about first by legislation. In Sweden
where uncertainty avoidance is low, industrial democracy was started with local experiments.

Hofstede continues,

> The crucial fact about leadership in any culture is that it is a comple-
> ment to subordinateship. The Power Distance Index scores . . . are in fact
> based on the values of people as *subordinates*, not on the values of superi-
> ors. Whatever a naïve literature on leadership may try to make us be-
> lieve, a leader cannot choose his style at will; what is feasible depends to
> a large extent on the cultural conditioning of his/her subordinates. I
> therefore show . . . a description of the type of subordinateship that,
> other things being equal, a leader can expect to meet in societies at three
> different levels of Power Distance, and to which his/her leadership has to
> respond. The middle level represents what most likely is found in the U.S.
> environment.

Where does this leave us as international managers? Perhaps we pick and
choose, and adopt what is appropriate in the home culture. The matter is
brought into focus as we examine a specific management system. The underlying assumptions regarding leadership in the United States are clearly seen in
the practice of management by objectives. This assumes that a subordinate is
independent enough to negotiate meaningfully with a superior (not too high of
a power distance), that both the superior and the subordinate are willing to
take risks (a low uncertainty avoidance) and that performance is important to
both (high masculinity).

Hofstede continues to demonstrate the importance of cross-cultural research:

Let us now take the case of Germany. This is also a below-average Power Distance country, so the dialogue element in MBO should present no problem. However, Germany scores considerably higher on Uncertainty Avoidance; consequently, the tendency towards accepting risk and ambiguity will not be present to the same extent. The idea of replacing the arbitrary authority of the boss by the impersonal authority of mutually agreed-upon objectives, however, fits the low Power Distance, high Uncertainty Avoidance cultural cluster very well. The objectives become the subordinates' "superego."

In a book of case studies about MBO in Germany, Ferguson states that "MBO has acquired a different flavor in the German-speaking area, not least because in these countries the societal and political pressure towards increasing the value of man in the organization on the right to codetermination has become quite clear. Thence, MBO has been transposed into Management by Joint Goal Setting (Führung durch Zielvereinbarung)." According to him, MBO fits the idealogical needs of the German-speaking countries of the moment. The case studies in Ferguson's book show elaborate formal systems with extensive ideological justification; the stress on team objectives is quite strong, which is in line with the lower Individualism in these countries.

The other case on which specific information is available is France. In France, MBO was first introduced in the early 1960s but it became extremely popular for a time after the 1968 students' revolt. People expected that this new technique would lead to the long overdue democratizing of organizations. Instead of DPO (Direction Par Objectifs), the French name for MBO became DPPO (Direction *Participative* Par Objectifs). So in France, too, societal developments affected the MBO system. However, DPPO remained in general as much a vain slogan as "Liberte, Egalite, Fraternite" (Freedom, Equality, Brotherhood) did after the 1789 revolt. Franck wrote in 1973 ". . . I think that the career of DPPO is terminated, or rather that is has never started, and it won't ever start as long as we continue in France our tendency to confound ideology and reality . . ." In a postscript to Franck's article, the editors of *Le Management* write: "French blue and white-collar workers, lower-level and higher-level managers, and 'patrons' all belong to the same cultural system which maintains dependency relations from level to level. Only the deviants really dislike this system. The hierarchical structure protects against anxiety; DPO, however, generates anxiety . . ."

The reason for the anxiety in the French cultural context is that MBO presupposes a depersonalized authority in the form of internalized objectives; but French people, from their early childhood onwards, are accustomed to large Power distances, to an authority that is highly personalized; in spite of all attempts to introduce Anglo-Saxon management methods, French superiors do not easily decentralize and do not stop short-circuiting intermediate hierarchical levels, and French subordinates do not expect them to. The development of the 1970s have severely discredited DPPO which probably does injustice to the cases where, starting from less exaggerated expectations, individual organizations or units in France have benefitted from it.

The consequences of Hofstede's conclusions are significant. Leadership, decision-making, teamwork, organization, motivation, and in fact everything managers do is learned. Because management functions are learned, they are based on assumptions about one's place in the world. Managers from other business systems are not "underdeveloped" American managers.

Peter Drucker has aptly observed that there are no underdeveloped countries, only undermanaged ones. Yet, how much of this Austrian management theorist's concepts are globally applicable? Some hold there is a managerial subculture around the world in which many "Druckerisms" are appropriate. In this international microculture, pragmatism is the norm, and managers borrow and adapt administrative techniques from everywhere if it helps them to meet objectives.

Learning *from* Other Management Cultures

The crow imitating the cormorant drowns in the water.

—Japanese proverb

The process of learning and applying management practice from one culture to another is a tricky one. In a superb journalistic presentation, the National Broadcasting Company produced a documentary (June 24, 1980) centered around the question, "If Japan Can . . . Why Can't We?" Viewers were shown the Japanese workers engaged in quality circle activities, and it was obvious that there was a high degree of cooperation between labor and management. The presentation confirmed the success of Japanese business.

In contrast, consider another media report just seven years prior to this television production, which highlighted an American work scene and focused on why one of the great U.S. automobile manufacturers got into serious economic difficulties:

> Two Chrysler assembly workers put a 13-hour stranglehold on the company's huge Jefferson Avenue plant Tuesday idling some 5,000 employees. The two men scaled over a 10-foot-high wire crib and pushed the control button, cutting off the electricity . . . Workers gave them a wire cable which they used to secure the crib. More workers gave them heavy chains and locks to further secure their positions. When the men finally came out at 7:11 p.m. they were given a hero's ride out of the plant.

> *Detroit Free Press*
> July 25–26, 1973

The NBC production examined very carefully some of the similarities and differences in the Japanese and U.S. management systems. The program posed a question: Can the United States, which has been on the top for so long, borrow from another business system?

It is our conviction that all persons and organizations can learn from others and adapt aspects of those systems to fit their own. Here is an example of what we might learn from the Japanese, based on one of the authors' (Moran) experience:

> I'd like to tell you how I first learned about Japanese management techniques. Between 1965 and 1968, I was the playing coach of the Seibu Railroad Ice Hockey Team, the best team in Japan. The owner of the team and the president of the company, Yoshiaki Tsutsumi (identified by *Fortune* magazine in 1989 as one of the world's 10 wealthiest people), decided to devote some of his time to developing ice hockey in Japan in preparation for the 1972 Winter Olympics, which had just been awarded to the city of Sapporo in northern Japan . . .
>
> In October 1968, shortly before leaving with a group of 25 Japanese hockey players for a one-month, 17-game series against Canadian amateur and semi-professional hockey teams throughout Canada, I was asked to attend a meeting with Mr. Tsutsumi. I was told the purpose of the meeting was to decide on the wardrobe for the players during their tour of Canada, which was to take place in January (Canada's coldest month).
>
> There were six persons at the meeting, including the owner/president, his secretary, three other staff persons, and myself. After exchanging pleasantries, we began the serious business of selecting what would go into each player's luggage bag.
>
> Department managers from the Seibu Department Store were waiting in an adjoining room with samples of the various possibilities. The meeting lasted over four hours. First, we decided on the outerwear—coats, hats, gloves, and overshoes. Then the formal and informal suits and sweaters, and finally the *underwear.* Yes, we even decided on the kind and number of undershorts that each player would be allocated. The person making these decisions was the president himself, Mr. Tsutsumi. Of course, many hundreds of hours were spent planning other aspects of the tour.
>
> Of the 17 games played in Canada, the Japanese team won 11, and from both Canadian and Japanese perspectives, the tour was a total success. On several occasions, during the pregame discussion and between-period pep talks, the fact that the company president was concerned about them to the extent of assisting with the selection of their wardrobe was mentioned. He also telephoned before and after each game and spoke to several of the players a number of times. In my opinion, this was an example of Japanese management in its purest form.
>
> What is the moral of this story? Is it that the owners of amateur and professional hockey teams (and perhaps baseball, football, and other teams as well) should select the underwear for their players? No, it isn't. But having worked and conducted communication and team-building

workshops for a professional hockey team in the National Hockey League, I certainly believe that a little more care on the part of the owners in *communicating* and working with the players might have done wonders for their morale and have had a positive impact on their ability to win hockey games.

Can the crow learn to imitate the cormorant? Can any management system borrow from another? In some cases, yes, and in others, no. Work environments in various countries are culturally different, but sometimes cultural synergy can be produced, as when Japanese copy successfully many American management practices.

In a front page feature on "Americans Watched as Executives," the *Los Angeles Times* (July 11, 1988, p. 1/14) examined American managers working for Japanese companies in the U.S. The article focussed on the Japanese representatives assigned to Americans to learn and help on the job, and described the cultural confusions that arose. The Americans perceived their international colleague as a "shadow," there only to grade them; they saw themselves in subordinate roles with no real power or future in a Japanese company whose heart, soul, and authority is 5,000 miles away in Tokyo. The Japanese found the Americans competent, but questioned their loyalty and dedication; the Americans' emphasis on salary and benefits was in glaring contrast to their own traditions. The Japanese needed the Americans' insights on U.S. society, government, and business practice, but the Americans felt insecure with the Japanese firm because they envisioned themselves only as "frontmen" unable to make the real decisions. The U.S. executives did not realize that for most Japanese, theirs was a temporary assignment here, a step in the career ladder within a parent company, but they must maintain work relationships with peers back home that may last a lifetime.

Such realities are not uncommon practices with MNCs in other countries, and as the Japanese multinational corporations mature, they are changing, depending more on locals and sharing authority with them. Both parties must appreciate they are part of an international management team whose members have different styles that can be merged for greater effectiveness.

BEYOND AWARENESS

Almost everything that appears in management literature is *comparative* in nature. A book compares, for example, managerial processes and interdepartmental relations in the United States and Germany. Or an article compares the career paths of Japanese and American managers. These kinds of cross-cultural studies are useful, and an excellent example is the work of Bernard Bass (1979) and his colleagues, who studied the attitudes and behavior of corporate executives in twelve nations. First, however, because our world is becoming more pluralistic and interdependent, it is vital, though difficult to study *interactions* between managers from more than one country.

Second, we should not assume that the U.S. management techniques are necessarily the best for American managers or for managers of other countries. American management techniques are based on American values and assumptions (for example, that we can influence and control the future to a high degree). Managers from other countries do not necessarily have such values and assumptions—at least they do not place as much emphasis or importance on them.

Third, improved individual and organizational performance is the purpose of most organizational change. This is generally accepted by managers. In attempting to implement changes that facilitate individual and organizational performance, one strategy that has not been sufficiently employed in the United States with any degree of consistency is that of studying other nations' management systems, and asking what we can learn from them.

Many managers feel that there's no need to do this. After all, they ask, "Hasn't the United States developed the most highly sophisticated system of management in the world? And don't the managers of the best foreign companies come to U.S. business schools for MBA degrees and executive management courses?" Yes, it may be true that many foreign managers come to the U.S. for training, but Americans can still learn from and borrow aspects of foreign management systems, which are superior in many ways.

CULTURAL SYNERGY

The following phrases, which have been taken from many sources, have been used to describe cultural synergy:

1. It represents a dynamic process.
2. It involves two, often opposing, views.
3. It involves empathy and sensitivity.
4. It means interpreting signals sent by others.
5. It involves adapting and learning.
6. It means combined action and working together.
7. Synergy involves joint action of discrete agencies in which the total effect is greater than the sum of their effects when acting independently.
8. It has the goal of creating an integrated solution.
9. It is sometimes related by the analogy that $2 + 2 = 5$ instead of 4, but given the various cross-cultural barriers, cultural synergy may be the equation $2 + 2 = 3$. If the cultural synergy sum is not negative, progress has been made.

10. For two prospective synergists to synergize effectively, true and complete understanding of the other organization and especially of the culture is necessary.
11. Cultural synergy does not signify compromise, yet in true synergy nothing is given up or lost.
12. Cultural synergy is not something people do, rather it is something that happens while people are doing something else that often has little to do with culture.
13. Cultural synergy exists only in relation to a practical set of circumstances, and it occurs by necessity when two or possibly more culturally different groups come to the mutual conclusion that they must unite their efforts to achieve their respective goals.

Cultural synergy can be approached in two different ways. One could be called the "Ugly Foreigner" approach. (We do not use "American" as Americans do not have exclusive rights to "ugliness.") This corresponds to Nancy J. Adler's "cultural dominance model" of management described in the next section.

The organization or nation providing the technology, capital, or resources has the power to impose its business or management system on another system. Previous and current histories of multinational corporations are replete with examples of the "Ugly Foreigner" approach.

At the other extreme is the "When in Rome, do as the Romans" management approach. Basic to this strategy is the parent organization's concern for the culture or business system in which it is operating. Every attempt is made to use local labor, management and organizational style; it is a polycentric approach. As Lee Camarigg (1980) states:

> The process of developing cultural synergy can be compared to the process two individuals go through when they marry. Though raised in unique cultures with unique values, they come together and develop their own new environment. This involves discussions about such things as housing and furniture (plant and facility), when meals will be served (scheduling), and how much money will be spent for what (budgeting). Besides the quantitatively measureable aspects of this new environment, there develops a style of living, relating, which is mutually agreed upon. Aspects of this new environment are composed of (1) consciously accepted values and mores, that are part of each individual's previous environment; (2) consciously agreed upon values and mores which require discussion and compromise either by one or both; (3) unconsciously agreed upon values and mores, which are aspects of one of the partners' environment and are accepted by the other without notice or compromise; and (4) unconsciously agreed upon values and mores that develop as one partner reacts to the other. These are the problematic aspects of a harmonious relationship.

The consciously accepted values and mores that were part of each individual's previous environment form the area of overlap. These are shared values and mores and are generally accepted mutually as valid. An example in the marriage scenario might be the religious practice of the couple. If both have been attending church regularly, in all probability, they will continue to do so. The same is true if they have not been attending regularly. It is doubtful that because of the marriage they will start.

Examples of Cultural Synergy

The basis for studying managers is not through comparisons, but through *interactions*. Aspects of North American or European managerial systems are not necessarily appropriate for managers of other geographic areas and may not even be the best for their own managers. Let's look at a few examples from both a practical and a theoretical perspective.

Model One: The Type Z Hybrid

William G. Ouchi and Alfred M. Jaeger (1978), identify characteristics of typical American organizations (Type A):

1. Short-term employment
2. Individual decision-making
3. Individual responsibility
4. Rapid evaluation and promotion
5. Explicit, formalized control
6. Specialzied career path
7. Segmented concern

and characteristics of typical Japanese (Type J) organizations:

1. Lifetime employment
2. Consensual decision-making
3. Collective responsibility
4. Slow evaluation and promotion
5. Implicit, formal control
6. Nonspecialized career path
7. Holistic concern

They then compare these organizations and relate them to their sociocultural roots. They conclude by presenting a hybrid organizational form (Type Z), which they suggest may be useful in the United States.

Each of the two types of organizational structures (American and Japanese) represent a natural outflow and adaptation to the environments to which they belong. However, several U.S. companies are now using aspects of Japanese management with great success.

Ouchi and Jaeger suggest the following characteristics for Type Z organization (modified American):

1. Long-term employment
2. Consensual decision-making
3. Individual responsibility
4. Slow evaluation and promotion
5. Implicit, informal control with explicit formalized measures
6. Moderately specialized career path
7. Holistic concern for individuals

Model Two: The GM Experience

In the early 1970s, a 55-year-old General Motors factory in Tarrytown, New York, was infamous for having one of the worst labor-relations and poorest quality records at GM (*Time* 1980). A turnaround grew out of the realization by local managers and union officials that disharmony threatened the plant's continued operation. Employees worried they'd lose their jobs so they began to work together to find better ways to build cars. Before this decision to work together, 7% of the workers were absent regularly and there were 2,000 outstanding employee grievances against management. The change came after GM management showed workers proposed changes at model changeover time in 1972 and asked for their comments. Many good ideas were presented. The plant supervisors also began holding regular meetings with workers to discuss employee complaints and ideas to improve efficiency. The benefits of these changes resulted in high-quality products, less than 30 workers' grievances outstanding, a less than 2.5% absentee rate, and declining work turnover.

Such changes were all integral parts of the Japanese management system, but they fit for the U.S. workers at Tarrytown. They are also in harmony with American management theory of more participative leadership. In 1985, under Chairman Roger Smith they were part of GM strategies for renewal or new plants, like the Saturn project.

Model Three: Adler's Dominance, Compromise, and Synergy Models

A professor at the University of Montreal, Nancy J. Adler theoretically distinguishes between a cultural dominance model of management, a cultural compromise model of management, and a cultural synergistic model (Adler, 1986). The cultural dominance model, described earlier as an "ugly foreigner" approach, is used when a company chooses to have one culture's style of management superimposed on the employees and clients of another culture. This model of management does not recognize or acknowledge the specific business or management styles of the nondominant culture. An example of the culture dominance model would be a U.S. organization that attempts to conduct business (marketing, advertising, or organization structure) in the same way in Paris as in Los Angeles.

The cultural compromise model uses management policies and practices that are similar between the cultures involved in the business association. The new international organization culture that is created using this model is limited to those areas in which the national cultures are similar, as might be the case in North America.

Concerning her third model, Adler states:

> The cultural synergy model is designed to create new international management policies and practices. The cultural synergy model recognizes the similarities and differences between the two or more nationalities that make up the international organization. The cultural synergy model builds a new international organization culture that is based on the national cultures of both employees and clients.

Model Four: MNC Orientations

David Heenan and Howard Perlmutter (1979) do not use the word "synergy," but list ethnocentric, polycentric, regiocentric, and geocentric as four orientations toward the subsidiaries in a multinational enterprise. *Ethnocentric* organizations use home-country personnel in key positions everywhere in the world, believing they are more intelligent and capable than foreign managers. *Polycentric* organizations leave the foreign managers alone (as long as the organization is profitable), because those managers know what is going on better than anyone else. *Regiocentric* organizations assign managers on a regional basis, such as a regional advertising campaign by French, British, and German managers with a European orientation. *Geocentric* organizations attempt to integrate diverse viewpoints through a global systems approach to decision-making. In this case, superiority is not equal to nationality, and all groups can contribute to the organization's effectiveness.

Heenan and Perlmutter observe:

> Multinational corporate planners are evidencing renewed interest in environmental scanning and assessing outside forces. External stakeholders, particularly government and labor, are given major attention in charting the future worldwide course of the firm. What emerges from this review is a transformed MNC—an institution prepared to modify policies which may be outdated (such as insistence on wholly owned foreign subsidiaries) in favor of strategies more compatible with the realities of the times. Consequently, mixed strategies on key decisions regarding ownership, staffing, and product development are adopted to accommodate varying stakeholder interests. . . .

The social architectural view of multinational organization development is based on the premise that the MNC is a purposeful system with its viability and legitimacy codetermined by internal and external stakeholders. As a rule, our suggested approach involves identifying the key stakeholders, examining the quality of relationships between stakeholders, and mobilizing their commitment to greater multi-nationalism. Our objective: to understand existing institutions and to help in some way to design new ones that can keep pace with the fundamental value changes that now influence the global industrial system.

These four demonstration models of cultural synergy are indications of wide-ranging possibilities for cooperation, a norm of the new work culture described in Chapter 7.

JAPANESE-AMERICAN MANAGEMENT SYNERGY

One of the most dramatic cases in point for East-West synergy lies in the interdependent relationship between Japan and the United States. Forty years ago, Julian Ely was part of the Allied military occupation of Japan. Today, this Los Angeles communications consultant, aware of the Japanese economic miracle and the American contribution to this rebirth, believes in the interlocking destinies of both nations. He is convinced that only through synergy can both peoples prosper by joint enterprises in both the public and private sectors. Ely (1986) examines the Japanese/American dynamic and the potential for mutual collaboration in the emerging Information Society, and envisions both as co-leaders in global free-enterprise that involves sharing human, technical, and financial resources, instead of destructive trade competition and protectionism. Such a partnership in joint ventures on this planet and in outer space could lead to a socio-economic transformation that benefits the world at large, as well as the two countries involved.

Some of the reasons for current Japanese success in production, distribution, and marketing has been the ability of this people to learn from advanced Western nations and then apply such appropriately to their own cultural situation. Nowhere is this more evident than in the field of management where Japanese executives borrowed ideas from the United States—some of which had been either discarded or not implemented fully by the Americans—then refined these for their own increase in productivity. Later, to their credit, some of these renewed techniques and practices would be re-exported profitability to North America. That such a synergistic strategy works is attested by the 300 Japanese-owned or controlled firms now operating in the U.S.A. By adapting their own and our methods to the U.S. workplace, Japanese companies have been able to overcome differences in culture and work attitudes. Despite difficulties with American unions and traditional management, the *U.S. News and World Report* (May 6, 1985:75), noted that Japanese managers abroad have pursued their concept of job flexibility, training employees for more than one job; have emphasized quality over quantity; have interacted daily on the plant floor with personnel and "rolled up their sleeves;" have drawn upon worker knowledge and resources to improve productivity; and have engaged in symbolic actions to remove barriers between labor and management. American managers now working for Japanese corporations are getting enthusiastic about their management style. The article cited quoted William Nelson, a vice-president for Kikkoman Foods: "I think our greatest advantage is the concern for the individual. Every company believes that it does care, but it seems to me that the Japanese carry it deeper. I know we do here."

The same feature reported on another American manager working for the joint GM-Toyota venture in California. Robert Hendry finds that the decentralized decision-making and notions of growth/earnings/profits are strengths of quality production that U.S. companies should emulate. And they are! Stunned by being outperformed in everything from silicon chips to car tire manufacturing, American executives from Westinghouse to Cencral Motors have been flocking to Japan to study their management "secrets." Now many American companies have started to adapt Japanese management style to their needs. This implementation of Japanese management techniques falls into two broad perspectives; one area concerns changing the overall corporate mindset or philosophy of management while the other focuses on specific management techniques. The larger arena focuses on philosophy and structure. Some American companies are instilling a company-wide quality consciousness whereby every worker is becoming a quality control technician.

Many American companies have also made significant changes in the more narrowly focused manufacturing techniques. Kanban manufacturing, quality control circles, and just-in-time (JIT) purchasing are finding their way more frequently into mainstream American industrial production. These techniques are not only narrower in focus, but also less culture-bound, more concrete, and easier to implement. They offer morale-boosting successes to fuel the subsequent implementation of the larger focus.

If one can see the connecting link between the two perspectives, one can understand that the key to Japanese management success. Successful adaptation of these methods inherently depends upon an organization's human element. Better utilization of the human resources of a firm is the Japanese secret. Hatvary and Pucik (1981) state:

> We believe the essence of management in large Japanese companies is a focus on human resources, which reflects an explicit preference for the maximum utilization of the firm's human resources, as well as an implicit understanding of how an organization ought to be managed.

All the suggestions we have concerning adoption of Japanese management techniques are based on the premise that upper management believes that both the manager and the worker's potential has been constricted in many instances by traditional American management practices. Boosting the morale, knowledge, responsibility, and therefore productivity of a corporation's workforce by using Japanese techniques can only be accomplished if employees realize that they have a growing role in the firm's processes, problems, and profits. With this, we offer the following Japanese strategies that can enhance American productivity and increase American firms' market share through better goods at lower prices.

However, the exchange of information and insight is not one way, but bicultural and tricultural, as these next two illustrations demonstrate:

- *Los Angeles — Tokyo communication traffic* is heavy, especially at night U.S. time when offices are closed and electronic exchanges are at their highest. Most of the data pours into California after midnight by fax, telex, voice mail, and other communication technologies to be processed by the locals in the morning when they come to work. The Japanese style of decision-making by consensus produces six times more communications than that of foreign affiliates. Moreover, Tokyo-based companies commonly have outposts in many countries with disparate time zones, further fueling the information volume that is costing them over $250 million annually for telecommunications. It is also another manifestation of two great economies that are intertwined, so that readers in both countries get the same news on the same day. If one hopes to do business with the Japanese, then learn about their cultural affinity for advanced communcations.
- *Tri-country collaboration* is evident in two nine-story buildings being built of stunning design on a platform over the Montparnasse train station in Paris. The construction is in cooperation with the French unit of Los Angeles-based, Kaufman and Broad Home Corporation, with financial partner, Groupement Foncier Francais and Japanese investor, Kowa Real Estate Co., Ltd. The 15-acre Atlantique Montparnasse development of $372 million is a landmark macroproject that involves an international consortium of some of the largest industrial and financial firms in Japan. It is a telling example of capital and competence flow across borders, resulting in real estate development on a global scale.

JIT Production

Many manufacturing experts have echoed the belief that the Japanese have "out-Taylored" us. This refers to Fredrick Taylor's classic time-and-motion studies, which have been the foundation for successful management of labor productivity in the manufacturing process. With the introduction of the just-in-time production system (JIT), the scientific management of manufacturing goods appears to have advanced by another quantum jump. The JIT system is centered on the notion that goods should be *pulled* through the factory by demands from the next work station, the next department, and in reality, from the marketplace (as opposed to the practice of management *pushing* a quantity of goods through the factory to the market). The key elements of the system were perfected by Toyota, where it is called Kanban manufacturing, after the cards used to signify parts orders from farther down the line. This system is now used by Toyota in their plant in Georgetown, Kentucky.

The most revolutionary factor of JIT production is its attack on basic economy of scale beliefs. In American factories, the correct economic order quantity is determined by balancing set-up costs with carrying costs. Excessive production incurs excessive carrying costs; limited production causes excessive labor costs in changing set-ups for manufacturing runs. But, this new Japanese system shows us that set-up costs are not fixed. Simplifying dies, machine controls, and fixtures can speed set-up time. American workers can easily throw into the rework box fifty defects out of a production run of one thousand pieces. Defects are to be expected in such large runs. But if a workstation receives only forty pieces and two are defective, they will immediately feel the pinch and inform the offending worker or station. Note that the defect ratio has not changed (5%), just the worker's perspective.

JIT production is a major evolution in the manufacturing process. Its essence is the constant, efficient production of small units of parts. To sum up, the major JIT productivity enhancements include less buffer stock, less scrap, less rework labor, lower inventory interest, less in-process storage space, less inventory handling equipment, and less inventory accounting.

In order to fully implement JIT production a firm's purchasing department must adopt JIT purchasing methods. Again, the Japanese tell us that we have been too cautious. Instead of supporting a handful of suppliers of a particular item "just-in-case" they are needed, manufacturers can determine which supplier is the most efficient and develop just-in-time purchasing ties with only this firm.

Close contractual and geographical *relations* also foster a synergistic and quality-enhancing atmosphere. A manager of an American subsidiary of a Japanese electrical machinery manufacturer stated in a JETRO publication (1980):

> Each time we received a delivery of unsatisfactory goods, we have returned them and made a detailed claim. In this way, we have gradually improved performance. What is most important after all is a positive attitude of fostering improvement.

Quality Control Circles

Another major element of Japanese management that is finding increasing acceptance in America is quality control circles (QCC), originated in the U.S., perfected in Japan, and reapplied here. Westinghouse's manager for quality and reliability assurance, Ralph Townsend (1981) highlights three potential problem areas for QCC implementation:

> Workers should be told in no uncertain terms that ideas for raising efficiency will not lead to layoffs. Bonuses, rare in Japan, should be used in the U.S. because workers expect rewards for outstanding performance and commitment. Finally, don't let this be just another crazy idea from the quality boys, get the bosses involved.

These three warnings correspond to three central features of OC circles. Worker loyalty and commitment is crucial to any quality buildup, fear of layoffs stemming from productivity gains will surely grind to a halt any attempt at developing QCC. Bonuses are a way for the firm to show workers that they really are a part of the team, returning a portion of the savings realized to the circle involved reinforces the unifying spirit. And, Townsend's last point concerning upper management involvement is voiced constantly by all QC experts and probably the single most important element of a QCC program.

The QC circles are also aided by line managers who have been specially chosen to teach problem-solving skills. These teacher-managers are of vital importance to a QCC program, so great care must be taken in choosing personnel for this job. And, this should be a temporary assignment, given real prestige by management, so that it is considered a step forward in the manager's career path. Training is both on-the-job and in the classroom for the QC circles.

The average Japanese worker receives five hundred days of training in his first ten years on the job. That is one day a week for ten years! Americans must learn to take a longer perspective. The concept of capital budget systems that demand early payback has become bankrupt in the face of competitors' staying power. We need to look at our factories afresh, as in the following example of a Japanese and a North American autoparts firm bidding on a new plant:

> The Japanese company bid $100 million for a plant with forty one of the required machines. The North American firm bid $300 million for a plant with thirty nine of the same machines! The difference was in plant layout; the Japanese firm required only 300,000 square feet, while the North American firm allocated 900,000 square feet. Less space means less inventory, less materials handling equipment, and less room for error.

Many American firms have already taken recovering steps toward corporate well-being through usage of Japanese and other foreign management techniques. And no industry has come farther faster than the U.S. auto industry.

Chrysler has dodged the bankruptcy bullet and saved millions of dollars of interest charges by repaying government-backed loans seven years early. But how can this be? American automakers were up against the ropes in the mid-1980s. Overall vehicle production had been nearly cut in half from the peak year. And still today, Michigan congressional representatives pander to their beleaguered constituencies by claiming that Japanese refusal to arbitrarily extend their voluntary restriction to free market access in the U.S. auto market is a second Pearl Harbor. Such comments fly in the face of the current booming market, the unprecedented industry profit forecasts, and the fantastic job American automakers have done in applying Japanese techniques to their operations.

First, let us examine the industry as it operated before this recent revitalization. In a 1980 *Los Angeles Times* article, Mr. Martin Douglas states:

> I am—or was—an American autoworker. I built General Motors cars for sixteen years. Then, in March, I was laid off indefinitely . . . The worker who performs a certain job 320 times a day, five days a week knows more about the specifics of his particular job than anyone else. Yet, in sixteen years, I have never been consulted or seen any other assembly line worker consulted on how to improve a job qualitatively or quantitatively . . . The autoworker can only build as good a car as he is instructed or permitted to . . . We on the line take our cue from those in the head office. If they don't really care about quality, they can't expect us to either.

More than sour grapes from a disgruntled ex-employee, comments of this type must have struck a raw nerve in auto industry management—some are getting the message that creating synergistic, rather than adversarial, relations with workers is the way to go.

It would be a mistake to think that Japanese management is perfect, for one can even learn from the mistakes of another country's managers. Magoroh Maruyama in an address to East-West Center alumni (June 27, 1985) listed a few failings of Japanese managers in general:

1. Inadequate communications with the locals when abroad, which creates an impression of secrecy.
2. Imposing upon visiting foreigners or locals overseas the Japanese business custom of evening socializing when the real informal management communications occur (the non-Japanese are not conditioned to these "drinking" parties).
3. Ethnocentric attitudes toward indigenous people as being "backward," needing to be taught to use our machines properly.
4. Problems overseas of adequate systems for servicing and repairing Japanese products.

The admirable aspect of Japanese managers, however, is that they continue to learn, to change, and to improve.

Magoroh Maruyama, a distinguished Asian professor, is doing research on alternative concepts of management. One of the basic differences identified by Dr. Maruyama between Eastern and Western management is the non-Aristotelean versus the Aristotelean logic underlying the two systems; this may cause confusion in intercultural interactions between their representatives. He also pointed out specific differences within Asian management. Table 4-2 summarizes Maruyama's insights and perhaps fosters synergy.

Table 4-2
Multicultural Management Concepts*

Asian and African	European and North American
Heterogeneity:	
May be source of mutually beneficial positive-sum, win-win atmosphere; harmony in diversity or dissimilar elements.	May be source of conflict, while homogeneity supposedly fosters peaceful equality; efficiency by organizing into like groups or categories.
Polyocular Vision:	
Objective truth is neither important nor useful; different individuals have different points of view and that "difference" enriches us with indispensable information; important to see same situation from varied views.	Belief in "objective" truth and differences are often attributed to error—monocular vision prevails; let us stick to where we agree and discard or avoid our disagreements; do not clutter thinking or problem-solving with too many viewpoints.
Decision-making by consensus aims at agreement that allows for future adjustment of benefits or inconveniences resulting from the choice.	Consensus is reaching the same opinion or conclusion so that a unanimous decision satisfies all and no adjustment is needed.
Job rotation's value is being able on a project to "think in one another's head" and to feel mentally connected; individuals in team or worker group then able to see same situation from different viewpoints.	Job rotation on a team is to prepare human substitutes when a worker is absent, or to relieve fatigue and monotony associated with doing same job.
Differing Philosophies/Constructs:	
Groups are for a network of interpersonal relations, for the individual to use to own advantage, as well as mutual benefit; self-sacrifice for the group is ultimately for one's own benefit; shared responsibility.	Group is a supra-individual entity in which the person sacrifices for the good of group or organization, for joint advantage or in the interests of others; individual responsibility to group.
New employees must establish relational identity with fellow workers and mutually grow—multi dimensional.	Each employee performs a specialized function that contributes to role identity—one dimensional.

* M. Maruyama, *Asia Pacific Journal of Management*, January 1984

SYNERGISTIC SKILLS FOR GLOBAL MANAGEMENT

Let us now consider the question of being an effective manager in an overseas assignment. In the cross-cultural management literature, there is a lack of precise statements or criteria concerning the factors that are related to cross-cultural adaptation and effectiveness. Paul Illman (1976) correctly states that "effective screening of candidates at home will often prevent failures abroad." He continues that personality, intolerance, the inability to adjust, and having a demeanor of superiority are main causes for failure, and technical skills, managerial skills, and human skills are the basis for success. Studies (Ruben 1983) have begun to identify the factors that are associated with "effectiveness" in a multicultural environment. They conceptualize the sojourner or overseas manager as a teacher possessing knowledge and skills that he wishes to share or transmit to others. As a teacher, one must have the knowledge and skills of inquiry or study, and be able to communicate these understandings to other persons in such a way that they will be able to accept and use them. Cross-cultural management effectiveness, therefore, involves job and intercultural communication competence. The latter involves participation and skills transfer. Consider the following case:

> Mr. Rose has recently accepted a position as a technical adviser in a country in the Middle East. His company has been working in that country for several years and has recently signed a five-year extension of a program that was originally conceived to take five years.
>
> Mr. Rose is looking forward to his assignment. He is technically qualified, highly motivated, and his work experiences and previous success convince him there will be few problems that he cannot handle satisfactorily.
>
> Shortly after arriving, however, he experiences frustrations and undue delays. He is working with Mr. Z., a host national, and together they have responsibilities for one aspect of the project. Working with Mr. Z. is not satisfying and Mr. Rose seriously begins to question the competence and training of Mr. Z.
>
> Mr. Rose tried to get to know Mr. Z. in an effort to determine ways of determining the problem, but his attempts were not successful.
>
> From his company in the United States, Mr. Rose is receiving telexes several times a day as the project had fallen considerably behind schedule. They also became a source of frustration for Mr. Rose and he began to feel in the middle of two forces pulling in the opposite direction. In his opinion, Mr. Z. and many of his colleagues were not highly proficient or motivated to accomplish the tasks. His superiors back home did not understand or accept his situation and pressured him to adhere more closely to the timetables set earlier.
>
> Mr. Rose made a decision that the only way he could get the job done was to do it himself. He gradually assumed more responsibility and

within a matter of two months the original timetable was being followed
more closely.

The important question, as a manager in a foreign country, is Mr. Rose succeeding or failing? If one considers Mr. Rose's role as "getting the job done"
then we could say that he was succeeding. However, if one takes the view that
he was also a coach or teacher, expected to communicate skills and transfer his
knowledge, he was not doing very well.

A most unfortunate consequence also related to the decision of Mr. Rose to
do it himself is the probable alienation of Mr. Z. and the almost certain reinforcement of the view that U.S. nationals in that country are often unfriendly,
insensitive, and are not really too interested in the welfare and development of
the country or the people.

Cross-cultural communication behaviors or skills can be learned, so a manager can function effectively with host nationals. We are making important distinctions between cognitive competency or awareness and behavioral competency at this time. Behavioral competency is the ability to demonstrate or use
the skills. Cognitive competency is the intellectual awareness or knowledge
base.

The following skills have been identified by Ruben's research as being associated with effectiveness in a multicultural environment in transferring knowledge. We shall refer to these skills as abilities. Most of these are common sense
but often not demonstrated by multinational managers or supervisors of minority employees in one's own culture:

Respect. The ability to express respect for others is an important part of effective relations in every country. All people like to believe and feel that others
respect them, their ideas and their accomplishments. However, it is difficult to
know how to communicate respect to persons from another culture. The following are questions that should be considered in the case of an overseas' manager working in another culture with persons from that culture. What is the
importance of age in communicating respect? What is the significance of manner of speaking? Do you speak only when spoken to? What gestures express respect? What kind of eye contact expresses respect? What constitutes "personal
questions" as an invasion of privacy and a lack of respect? These are only a few
of the many questions that could be generated relating to the important question, "How do I demonstrate that I respect the people I am working with?"

Tolerating Ambiguity. This refers to the ability to react to new, different,
and at times, unpredictable situations with little visible discomfort or irritation. Excessive discomfort often leads to frustration and hostility and this is not
conducive to effective interpersonal relationships with persons from other cultures. Learning to manage the feelings associated with ambiguity is a skill asso-

ciated with adaptation to a new environment and effectively working with managers who have a different set of values.

Relating to People. Many Western managers, concerned with getting the job done, are overly concerned with the task side of their jobs. In transferring skills and knowledge to persons in another culture, there is a requirement of getting the job done, but also the ability to get it done in such a way that people feel a part of the completed project and have benefited from being involved. Too much concern for getting the job done and neglect of "people maintenance" can lead to failure in transferring skills.

Being Nonjudgmental. Most people like to feel that what they say and do is not being judged by others without having the opportunity of fully explaining themselves. The ability to withhold judgment and remain objective until one has enough information requires an understanding of the other's point of view and is an important skill.

Personalizing One's Observations. As has been indicated previously, different people explain the world around them in different terms. A manager should realize that his or her knowledge and perceptions are valid only for self and not for the rest of the world. Thus, one would be able to personalize observations, be more tentative in conclusions and demonstrate a communication competence that what is "right" or "true" in one culture is not "right" or "true" in another. As one author said, "this is my way, what is your way? There is no 'the' way"—it is all relative.

Empathy. This is the ability to "put yourself in another's shoes." In this context, most people are attracted to and work well with managers who seem to be able to understand things from their point of view. Mr. Rose did not seem to have much empathy for Mr. Z.

Persistence. This is an important skill for effective cross-cultural functioning, for a variety of reasons. The multinational manager may not be successful the first time and he may not be able to get things done immediately, but with patience and perseverance, the task can be accomplished.

Such then are some of the qualities that global managers must cultivate in themselves if they propose to create cultural synergy. Imagine what could happen in international or diplomatic relations if these same attitudes prevailed. Some of the characteristics were advocated recently to improve Soviet-American relations by two synergistic scholars. Vadim Sobakin, a Moscow law professor, and Roger Fisher of Harvard Law School co-chaired a meeting of attorneys from both countries. For detente to occur between nations, they urged respectful attitudes marked by mutual understanding, effective intercultural communication, reliability, consultation, and building upon common concerns (*Los Angeles Times,* April 7, 1985:IV/5). Certainly these are the conditions that contribute to cultural synergy.

CHALLENGES IN INTERNATIONAL MANAGEMENT

We invite our readers to analyze the following material ("Cross-Cultural Management," *International Management,* March 1985) and complete the exercise with colleagues from other cultures in light of the chapter messages:

Trivial Pursuit™ is a board game that has sold millions of copies throughout the world. The game requires players to answer questions in a number of categories such as geography, entertainment, history, art and literature, science, and nature and sports. The category of the question is determined by a roll of the dice.

I would like to invite you, the reader, to play this game. You have rolled the dice and drawn the category "International Management." This is your question: "Which countries produce the most competent internationalists in business?"

If the question were in Trivial Pursuit™, it would be in the genius edition—a very difficult question. Two words in the question contribute to the difficulty—competent and internationalists. A standard dictionary provides this definition of competent: "well qualified, capable, fit." "Internationalist" is a little more murky. The dictionary definition is "a person who believes in internationalism." But what is internationalism? Again, with help from the dictionary: "The principle or policy of international cooperation for the common good."

Before giving my answer, I'd like to discuss the origin of the question and the process of arriving at the "correct" answer. The question was suggested by a friend of a friend. This means I really don't know whose question it is. But the suggester of the question thought the answer was Japan. My friend disagreed for the following reasons.

Japan indeed has a successful track record of best-selling products, including cars, electronic equipment and steel, among others. This is largely accomplished through Japanese businessmen who work for the nine giant Japanese trading companies—the *sogo shosha.* But the Japanese cheat in trade, he said. They have been found guilty of commercial piracy, bribery and falsifying documents. They also distort the international value of the yen, my friend said, so that some Japanese goods sell for less in other countries than in Tokyo. Moreover, they have exploited the open-door policy of some countries while vigorously pursuing a closed-door policy for themselves.

A Vote for the United States

Another businessman who was listening to this conversation said he thought the United States produced the most competent internationalists in business. The United States is the biggest economic entity in the history of the world, with dominant positions worldwide in computers, space, medicine, biology, and so on. Its competent internationalists in business make this possible.

This was overheard by a French manager, who said that Americans are naïve internationally. American businessmen, according to him, are the most ethnocentric of all businessmen (the dictionary definition is "one who judges others by using one's own personal or cultural standards").

Besides, he said, American businessmen have their priorities mixed up. They are too materialistic, too work-oriented, too time-motivated, and equate anything "new" with best. Americans also have the highest attrition rate (dictionary definition—"return early from an international assignment") of any country, said the French manager.

The question is indeed a tough one. At a recent meeting of American managers attending a seminar on international joint ventures, I posed the same question. It evoked considerable discussion but no agreement. One person suggested they vote and most hands were raised when Sweden was proposed. But Sweden, said one person who voted for another country, couldn't be the winning answer. Sweden is too small and the Swedish economy has declined sharply since the late 1970s because Swedish internationalists aren't aggressive enough.

At this point, another participant suggested the right answer was the Soviet Union. Most people laughed at this suggestion. I assume that meant disagreement.

Britain has had foreign operations for centuries. Maybe the British manager is the most competent internationalist. But when business travellers from several countries discussed this possibility while caught in Geneva International Airport recently during a snowstorm, no one thought Britain was the winning answer because Britain has lost so much in the international marketplace. Several businessmen from Britain were among those who participated in the discussion.

Since no agreement could be reached on the correct answer to my first question, I decided to rephrase it: What contribution to a multinational organization is made by managers of various nationalities?

Different Contributions

Hari Bedi, an Indian expatriate working for a large multinational company in Hong Kong, believes that Asian internationals use the 5 Cs of *continuity* (a sense of history and tradition), *commitment* (to the growth of the organization), *connections* (where social skills and social standing count), *compassion* (balancing scientific and political issues), and *cultural sensitivity* (a respect for other ways).

These qualities are among the contributions made by Asian managers to a multinational organization, he says. Western managers, according to Bedi, use the 5 Es: *expertise* (experience in managerial and technical theory), *ethos* (practical experience), *eagerness* (the enthusiasm of the entrepreneur), *esprit de corps* (a common identity), and *endorsement* (seeks unusual opportunities).

The answer is that the managers of every country contribute something to a multinational organization. The usefulness of that contribution depends on the situation. Competent internationalists (we're back to my first and discarded question) are able to recognize the contribution made by managers of various nationalities. They are also able to develop solutions to problems faced by multinational organizations by using these contributions *and* cultural diversity as a resource, rather than a barrier to be overcome.

The Beginning or the End of Cooperation

With international trade and foreign investments on a steady increase, particularly with Third World countries that have strong nationalistic tendencies, deep understanding of forces at work and skills to manage these forces will be keys to successful international management. Thus, organizational strategy of the future will account for differences in strength and direction. Human resources will be used to contribute the maximum to the organizational objectives, emphasizing the individual's special skills or values. The criteria applied in decision-making will increasingly consider differences of the cultural values, while at the same time will also make maximum use of them. Thus, the global manager's task is recognizing these differences and combining them in an optimal way. This must be accomplished within the contexts of the indigenous national and organizational cultures if synergy is to be achieved. The case for this position is well stated by Gary Wederspahn (1981):

> A heightened awareness of each other's cultural values enables co-workers of different nationalities to develop management strategies and plans to minimize potential conflicts and stress. But most importantly, it offers the possibility of helping them see differences as a source of *positive diversity* and enrichment of the management team that can enhance its overall effectiveness by turning cross-cultural stress into synergy.

SUMMARY

Cultural synergy is like a successful marriage. Two people, two organizations, or two nations come together for mutual benefit to develop a relationship that is different in quantity and quality and in productivity and reward, from the sum of their individual contributions. Even naive interpreters of world events and varied groups' relationships realize that short-term solutions and problems result from the dominance model of management or the ugly foreigner approach.

All relationships are about interactions that influence each other. It is expected this volume will provide a framework and strategies for solving problems and building relationships that are in the best sense of the word "synergis-tic." George W. Renwick (1980), in examining Australian and American differences, concludes:

> If these two people who differ on such fundamental points are to get on better with one another and work together with more satisfaction they can no longer assume they are similar to one another, they must begin to investigate their differences as well as their similarities and train them-selves to recognize and *take advantage* of both.

We call the "training" Renwick refers to as the ability to manage cultural synergy.

Cultural synergy can occur in the micro-management of a single enterprise or it can occur between and among human systems. The disappearing indus-trial paradigm in North America placed labor, management, and even govern-ment in competition and, often, in opposition to each other. The success of Ja-pan has demonstrated the obsolescence of that approach, because in Japan government and industry cooperate for the good of the whole country. We pro-pose that a synergistic "partnership" is necessary for survival in the future be-tween the public and private sectors among managers, workers, and consum-ers. The emerging role of global manager implies the application of synergistic skills. Chapter 12 will provide further insight on this theme.

5
Managers as Leaders in Cultural Change

The three concepts of culture, communication, and change are interconnected. Since culture is a human creation, it is subject to alteration, depending on time, place, or circumstance. It is our thesis that the role of the global manager requires the conscious exercise of leadership in cultural change.

COMMUNICATION AND CHANGE

Communication is a prime dynamic that determines the kind and rate of change in society. Mass communication and its technology is one factor contributing to the acceleration in the rate of change. Communication involves the establishing of relationships, while change causes an altering of such relationships. Communication is an energy exchange, whereas change requires the shifting of energy priorities. Change challenges leadership to deal more effectively with differences, which occur when the status quo has been unfrozen because of new inventions, new insights, new attitudes, new people.

When a computer is introduced into a corporation, there is a change in role relationships. When a management information system is introduced into an office, the data available for decision-making affects relationships. When a local company moves beyond its borders into the international marketplace, there is not only a transformation of attitudes, but policies, procedures, and even structures may change. When minority people are brought into the workforce in greater numbers, there is an altering of relationships with the majority personnel. When women are promoted into a management made up largely of males, female relationships with male supervisors are subtly influenced. All such actions provoke change in organizational culture. So too, when managers, sales persons or technicians, as well as their families, are deployed overseas for a lengthy assignment, there is a profound transposition in their relationships to their "world" and the "foreigners" in it.

The paradox of change, as Benjamin Disraeli reminded us, is that it is inevitable and constant. Furthermore, it is an event and a process. It also forces leaders to view it either as a problem or an opportunity. Today's managers operate in a world culture that has changed more rapidly and extensively than any other period in human history. To survive and develop, administrators need new skills to cope with change, as well as to build a new openness to it in their life-styles along with mechanisms for planned change in their systems.

This chapter views planned change in terms of three interactive cultures: (1) *cyberculture*—the urban, technological, superindustrial society that is emerging; (2) *organizational* culture—the base from which the cosmopolitan manager or professional operates; (3) *national* culture—the people and place in which one seeks to live and conduct business. Increasingly, that latter culture is different or foreign from the majority culture in which we were born and formed. The thesis here is that our behavior is influenced and we are changed by the impact of these three cultures upon us, especially as actors in leadership roles. But we need not passively react, for we have the means to temper or tamper with these interacting cultures. Specifically, modern management theory maintains that managers have a responsibility to be proactive agents of change. That is, we can initiate actions to correct obsolescence. Such innovative activity is not limited to one's corporation or agency, but extends into the community, wherever that may be. In a time when nation states seemingly falter, world corporations prosper. Skilled change agents are needed in this period in human development when politicians often feel impotent, as corporate executives exercise global influence.

Obviously, not all change is desirable. Critical choices have to be made about the overall wisdom of an alteration. Certainly, haphazard change is to be avoided. Because accelerating change is a reality of our world, change must be managed if it is not to cause disastrous dislocation in the life spaces of people and their organizations or societies. Perhaps the place to begin is for the reader to assess his or her attitudes toward change, as well as to consider *why* planned change is essential. It is a challenge to reeducate one's self and to reevaluate our psychological constructs—the way we read meaning into the events and experiences of our lives.

HUMAN FACTORS IN CHANGE

Each of us has a set of highly organized constructs around which we organize our "private" worlds. We construct a mental system for putting order, as we perceive it, into our worlds. This intellectual synthesis of sense perceptions relates to our images of self, family, role, organization, nation, and universe. These constructs then become anchors or reference points for our mental functioning and well being. Our unique construct systems exert a pushing/pulling effect upon all other ideas and experiences we encounter. They assign meaning quickly and almost automatically to the multiple sensations and perceptions that bombard us daily.

Not only do individuals have such unique sets of constructs through which they filter experience, but groups, organizations, and even nations develop such mental frameworks through which they too interpret information coming from their environment. The intense interactions of various segments of their populations form construct sets that enable them to achieve collective goals. In this way a group, organizational, or national "style" or type of behavior emerges. Through communication in such groupings, people share themselves and their individual perceptions converge into a type of "consensus" of what makes sense to them in a particular environment and circumstance. Culture, then, transmits these common, shared sets of perceptions and relationships. But since human interaction is dynamic, pressures for change in such constructs build up in both individuals and institutions. For example, when a manager from Grand Rapids, Michigan, is transferred for three years to Riyadh, Saudi Arabia, that person is challenged to change many of his or her constructs about life and people. The same may be said for the corporate culture which that individual's company attempts to transplant from Midwest America to the Middle East. These forces for change can be avoided, resisted, or incorporated into the person's or the organization's perceptual field. If the latter happens, then change becomes a catalyst for a restructuring of constructs and an opportunity for growth. In other words, the employee and the company can adapt and develop.

The fast pace of modern life, the demise of traditional values and supports intensify emotional stress and strain of change for human beings and their systems. Change can involve pain, whether it be the divorce of marital or business partners, the loss of job or loved one, a transfer within or outside one's country, the merger of two departments or two corporations. The cosmopolitan does not try to deny or minimize the negative impact of change upon people. Instead, such leaders attempt to help their personnel or their clients to plan for such change, to transform it, but at the very least to cope effectively with the challenge as a means for growth and improved quality of life.

Because culture provides conditioned control systems upon individuals and their institutions, the sensitive manager who operates abroad takes such powerful influences into consideration while attempting to introduce a new product or service, a new method or technology. In intercultural situations, we should be aware of the human factors involved with our proposed changes. Knowingly or unknowingly, we are agents of change in the life space of others with whom we relate. By exercising skill in planned change, we cannot only facilitate people's preparation and acceptance of change, but we may do it in such a way as to reduce stress and energy waste. Maximum two-way communication about the proposed change can create the necessary readiness for its eventual implementation. The presence of sudden changes can be defused. While proposing innovations, leaders can endeavor to reduce the uncomfortable threat feelings of those involved. Thus, negative reactions like apathy or sabotage, protest or revolt can be minimized.

It is important for modern management to appreciate that for most of human history, most of the globe's inhabitants were raised in hierarchical societies where personal choice and progress were limited, and one's place was immutable. For generations people survived by remaining within their prescribed roles, adapting to the pattern of thought, belief, and action of their local cultural group. Except for less developed countries, all this is changing in our cosmic village—mankind is in the midst of a mind-boggling transformation that offers seemingly unlimited choices and opportunities. We change our environment and are changed by it. We create technology, and we are physically and psychologically changed by it. In the process traditional customs, values, attitudes, and beliefs are disrupted. Yet, as our culture and social institutions change, we *learn* to change ever more effectively and our capacity for such learning is seemingly inexhaustible. Cosmopolitan leaders are in the forefront of this phenomenon and should be on the cutting edge of innovation, while mindful of the human dimensions involved.

One aspect for the exercise of international leadership is helping people to cope more effectively with varied life identity crises by the creation of new images. Such crises, which contribute to future and organizational shock, may be seen as a series of concentric circles, which begins with the individual as the inner circle and expands to roles, organizations, nations, and, finally, species.

Starting in the center with the *individual*, it is apparent that our various self-images are threatened by accelerating changes within various global cultures. Traditional human conceptions are breaking down under the impact of contemporary events. We are forced to conjure up new perceptions of ourselves, both individually and institutionally. The increasing gap between where technology is and where culture lags contributes to identity crises for many persons on this planet. We thought we knew who we are, but the old absolutes give way, and we are uncertain. We are people in transition, caught between disappearing and emerging cultures.

Not only is the self-concept for many in doubt or inadequate, but traditional *role* images in society are being undermined. What is a woman, a black, a teacher, a manager, a parent? We thought we knew, but again rapid change makes us unsure, causing us to redefine our roles. Nowhere, for instance, is such crisis more pronounced than with the Arab women today. Contrast the upper-class, educated Arab female in chic clothes who may jet around the world, with her Islamic sister in the peasant class—uninformed to a large extent and with a life wholly centered around her family and village. Both represent strikingly different roles in a Moslem world turned upside down.

Role Changes. For two decades, Cynthia Fuchs Epstein (1989) has researched the changing roles of men and women, discovering that gender differences are mostly in our minds and quite superficial. Her book, *Deceptive Distinctions: Sex, Gender and the Social Order*, contains behavioral science insights into how men and women live, work, and relate to each other. Epstein found that the differences are largely created and kept in place by social, not biological forces, and therefore, are subject to change. People should not permit themselves to be typecast and culture bound in their career aspirations. In advanced societies changes in this regard are rapid as workers move beyond traditional role concepts and fight for equality.

Similar representations may be made of *organizations*, because human systems—collections of people—also suffer identity crises. Caught between a disappearing bureaucracy and an emerging "ad-hocracy," the institution may experience down-turns in sales, poor morale, membership reductions, bankruptcy threats, obsolete product lines and services, and increasing frustration with unresponsive management. Organizations, then, are challenged to go through planned renewal and to reproject their public images.

So too with *nations*. When the social fabric unravels or wavers, there are national identities in crisis. Four such examples are the U.S., which lost "face" in Vietnam and had its diplomats seized as hostages in Iran; Great Britain, which lost its empire and nearly went bankrupt as a nation; Japan whose very economic and technological progress threatens its traditional culture and East Germany, which lost many citizens to the West in 1989–1990. Whether one goes to Canada, Pakistan, or China, the peoples of various countries seek to rediscover their collective selves in the post-national period.

In some lands, the struggle for national identity is epitomized in a name change, as from Congo to Zaire or Rhodesia to Zimbabwe. Elsewhere, as in the U.S.S.R.'s Baltic republics, the citizens seek greater ethnic identity and autonomy from centralized control. Whereas, in the People's Republic of China, the current turmoil centers around democratization and the totalitarian control of the Communist Party.

Finally, homo sapiens struggles with an identity crisis for the *species*. We thought we were earthbound, but now we have launched out into the universe. What are the limits of human potential? Is our real home out there? Cosmopolitan leaders can help in promoting synergy between past and future conceptions of ourselves, which so powerfully influence our behavior and accomplishments.

Management guru Peter Drucker (1989) peers ahead to the 21st century in *The New Realities*, and provides a disturbing perspective of the changes ongoing in society. He examines our altered perceptions of government's role, and thinks politicians are falling behind the new realities. For example, he presaged the "decolonization" of the Soviet empire, and anticipated the breakup of that huge country into European and Asian parts. So-called Western "leaders" fail to consider the revolutionary consequences of this and the declining presence of military power and massive armies. National economies, he says, are shaped increasingly by global events.

But Drucker really aims his sights on changes in the post-business society. He describes a world of knowledge workers in companies reorganized to be leaner and more specialized and in growing nonprofit and volunteer sectors. He stresses the need for new approaches to politics, economics, and management, and increased innovation in how we define problems and organize ourselves for work now and in the future.

William Christopher (1980) suggests that business itself has an identity problem in the emerging superindustrial age:

> If we have no concept of what we are as a business enterprise, our journey into the future will be haphazard . . . If our actions, adjustments, and reactions derive from a philosophy in tune with the world around us, we will find some kind of identity . . . that is consciously articulated and made central to every action taken everywhere in the organization. . . .

Christopher proposes that this search for a more relevant identity seek answers to such questions as, What business are we in? What are we as an organization? What should we become? The authors would add two more: Who are our customers? Where are our markets? Many corporations are afraid to enter into the world marketplace, cope with diverse customs or import/export regulations. Sony Corporation's Akio Morita once observed that the trouble American corporations have penetrating the Japanese market is partially of their own making. That is, the U.S. companies too often envision themselves only in terms of their domestic market, are too fearful of unfamiliar business environments, and do not commit themselves to long-term overseas investments.

Harvard business professors George Lodge and Richard Walton fear the United States is losing its capacity to compete in world markets (1989). They suggest that companies have two choices—they can leave the country and establish operations offshore where costs are lower and the production environment more inviting; or they can stay and change themselves and their environment. The latter implies both internal and external alterations toward new relationships that are cooperative, intimate, long-term, consensual, and flexible; and competitive units that shorten development time from product conceptualization to commercialization while achieving advantages through (a) R & D coalition of rivals; (b) partnership of manufacturers, suppliers, and customers to lower costs, improve products and processes; (c) consortium of capital and labor to achieve global competitiveness over the long-run; and (d) cooperation between business and government in new patterns of problem-solving, planning, and coordination. For this transition to occur, Lodge and Walton advise adoption of sound change models and strategies, economic incentives, education and training in new sociopolitical beliefs and attitudes, redefinition of institutional forms and role, and managerial competence in innovating.

Perhaps this discussion on human factors related to change can be taken from the realm of the abstract, and made more concrete in terms of global leadership by means of the case study on the following page.

Case Study:
Mitsubishi Changes Its Image and Strategies*

The Mitsubishi Corporation is an example of a human enterprise that has successfully been altering the way it envisions itself, and as a result, changing the culture of its operations and the way in which it communicates its strategies. The entity came into being over a hundred years ago as a general trading company. In 1870, this *Sogo Shosha* viewed itself as an organization to serve the needs of Japanese society through trade abroad, thus ending centuries of isolation and avoiding foreign domination. The organization was to be a buffer for indigeneous companies against foreign merchants through its controlled trade channels. Through it, Japanese businesses could acquire the raw materials and technologies from around the world, while gaining access to export markets.

Mitsubishi's mission and growth was interrupted by World War II, after which it was restructured and renewed. For thirty years in the postwar period, the firm contributed to helping Japan Inc. become Number One in world trade. By 1983, this leading general trading corporation had $65 billion in sales. Along the way, it had created a subsidary, "Mitsubishi International Corporation" (MIC) based in New York, which alone accounted for $12 billion of its corporate income. Yet in the mid '80s, the organization was going through another identity crisis and changing its image as a commission trader. If it was to continue its successful operating mode, sustain growth and profits into the next century, then it would have to embark on investing ventures that could dwarf past economic achievements!

The primary reason for this organizational change was brought on by new conditions in Japan where Mitsubishi's clients were now able to do their own overseas purchasing and marketing. Furthermore, other factors in the changing world economy warranted transformation of corporate strategies. Many company traditions, common within Japanese industry, were inhibiting Mitsubishi's growth and flexibility. Such resisting forces to change were rigid corporate formulas and policies—including the management of human resources from recruitment and selection, to compensation and promotion. Overly defined management systems for overseas operations, reluctance to appoint foreigners to leadership positions, and lack of new skills for discovering resources and technology were among the problems.

To survive and prosper, Mitsubishi and MIC initiated planned changes in this decade so that the organization might become a more effective global enterprise by being more proactive, rather than reactive. Beside giving subsidiaries more autonomy, Mitsubishi sought growth opportunities worldwide in knowledge, environmental, health and leisure industries, as well as in high-technology businesses and resource development. MIC, for instance, entered into more successful joint ventures with American companies, assisting the latter with its international trading expertise. MIC dispersed its operations around the United States. Most important, it provided greater opportunity for North Americans in its hiring and promotion policies, especially among locals with a high performance record for innovation and self-direction. A key ingredient in the changes was more and better HRD endeavors for both Americans and Japanese personnel. Americans can now

---

* The authors are indebted to the research of two St. John's University scholars, Miller and Sugiyama (1984) for the insights of this mini case.

be found in key management positions, and often spend some time at corporate headquarters in Tokyo. MIC's dedication seems to be toward personal growth opportunities for employees, "globalization," and "Americanization" in the positive sense of that term. One wonders if these changes extend to female personnel, given the historical role of Japanese women as "housewives-servants" and the cultural discrimination against women workers (40% of the Japanese workforce)?

The changes in Mitsubishi leadership are reflected in efforts to adapt new technologies for the creation of new products and services. Another illustration is the corporate commitment to synergistic agreements in its international activities, such as the Battelle Institute—in Japan, the company acts as Battelle's agent in fostering research on behalf of industry. Mitsubishi still faces many more challenges for change, but in the process, it is becoming a world corporation that is more flat and decentralized in structure, more entrepreneurual in management skills, more active in the practice of corporate social responsibility, more concerned about human resource development, and more committed to promoting exports in the countries in which it operates. Fundamentally, Mitsubishi ensures its success because it is willing continuously to alter its organizational culture and exercises leadership in implementing the new strategies.

CHANGE AND CULTURE

Culture is communicable knowledge for human coping within a particular environment that is passed on for the benefit of subsequent generations. Just as mankind is unique in its capacity for creating communication symbols, so too only our species develops culture as a means of adaptation to physical or biological surroundings. For millions of years our biological evolution was marked by slow and gradual change. This leisurely pace was also characteristic of cultural adaptations in general, while specific cultures operated in relative isolation with geographic limitations. Then in the past three centuries, as the human race moved into a period of psychosocial evolution, there has been acceleration in the rate of change. The first chapter provided an illustration on the history of human development that emphasized this speed-up in change, a compression in time itself. This astronomical acceleration has weakened the traditional folk wisdom for survival and advancement. The impact of rapid change, particularly in this century, has undermined many ancient local cultures. Will this breakdown of indigenous cultures contribute toward the emergence of a planetary culture?

Some cultural systems are more open and accepting of change, while others can only integrate it in a very gradual manner, to avoid violent reaction. Furthermore, the process of innovation differs by culture. The complexities of Western cultural living would appear to stimulate creativity without inordinate attention to details. On the other hand, change in Eastern culture, as in Third World nations, is often accompanied by painstaking concern for its effect on relationships, so there is a preference for bending the cultural bonds within the existing system to avoid radical alterations.

Cosmopolitan managers must function in the midst of paradoxes involved in social and cultural change. Despite the acceleration in the change rate in the last half of this century, the pace of change varies enormously in different cultures. Yet, no tribe or group is today too remote not to experience its influence. And despite the current disturbances caused by such swift alterations, there can be patterned continuity, such as what seemingly occurs in Japan or China today. While the mainstream of civilization plunges into the superindustrial stage of human development, there still exist living laboratories of mankind's past cultural stages. Enlightened peoples are seeking to preserve these microcultures as long as possible, rather than destroy them with "progress."

There are many forces causing change in the very processes of cultural development—innovation, diffusion, acculturation, and rapid creation and disposal of new institutions. With advances in mass communication and transportation, no human group is too remote to avoid such influences. It is indeed possible for some areas to overstep literacy and industrial stages into new forms of communication and technological civilization.

Another seeming paradox of cultural change is that innovations are more likely to occur in times of turmoil and transition such as we are going through; they seem to occur in cultures experiencing social and political uncertainties, in mild ferment, as contrasted to more stable or static societies. More and more, the world's people are coming to *value* change, and to be more futuristic, rather than past oriented. Many are convinced that mankind can create its own future.

Modernization, in any event, uproots traditional structures, institutions, and relationships. The universal patterns of change being described here are expanding the horizons of local peoples, and fostering the "planetization" of the human race. A final paradox is that the very agents of such change are themselves changed in the process. Witness what is happening to English culture as a result of the imperial forays throughout the "commonwealth" by the former British colonialists. The English were agents of civilizing change in many countries. Today the U.K. is in a state of ferment and social change brought about, in part, by the presence in Great Britain of their former or current commonwealth members!

At the executive and managerial levels of Japanese business, Western observers have noticed dramatic and subtle changes occurring, while Japanese capitalize on foreigners' stereotypes about themselves. They will even "act like Americans" if it will gain them competitive advantage. Japanese push rapidly into new markets, so now they are becoming "Europartners" to gain a foothold in the single EEC market. Currently in Japan, women are the catalysts for social and political change there, particularly with reference to their role in work and society.

DEVELOPING CHANGE STRATEGIES

International managers should be sources of innovation, yet skillful in managing change. The *Harvard Business Review* has defined the management of change as "innovation and creativity in the achieving of goals." Agents of change may apply their efforts, in this context, to altering personal, organizational, and cultural goals. With a multinational manager operating in diverse cultures and circumstances, for example, the very differences require appropriate adaptation of corporate objectives and procedures (Dyer, 1985). Similarly, such managers should review their personal and personnel aims in multicultural settings. Their revision might include a goal of learning to be comfortable or at home anywhere that person happens to be located, even if it means creative circumvention of local constraints. Innovators may respect the established system, while working to bend or beat it to make it more responsive to satisfying human need.

The *New York Times* once ran this interesting advertisement:

> WANTED—CHANGE AGENTS—Results-oriented individuals able to accurately and quickly resolve complex tangible and intangible problems. Energy and ambition necessary for success.

Within an organization or culture, what then would be the focus of such a change agent when employed? Probably, the initial concern would be to examine the change possibilities in six categories:

1. Structure (the system of authority, communication, roles, and work flow).
2. Technology (problem solving mechanisms, tools, and computers).
3. Tasks (activities accomplished, such as manufacturing, research, service).
4. Processes (techniques, methods, procedures, such as management information systems).
5. Environment (internal or external atmosphere).
6. People (personnel or human resources involved).

Having decided upon which category or combinations to focus one's energy for change, the leader might follow these steps:

1. Identify specific changes that appear desirable to improve effectiveness.
2. Create a readiness in the system for such change.
3. Facilitate the internalization of the innovation.
4. Reinforce the new equilibrium established through the change.

The skilled change maker is aware that any change introduced in one element of the previous chain affects the other factors (Kanter, 1983). The parts of complex systems are interdependent, so the innovator attempts to forecast the ripple effect. Change agents must take a multidimensional approach, considering legal, economic, and technological aspects of the change without ignoring its social, political, and personal implications. They also operate on certain assumptions:

1. People are capable of planning and controlling their own destinies within their own life space.
2. Behavioral change knowledge and technology should be incorporated into the planning process.
3. Human beings are already in the midst of profound cultural change.

The implication of the latter statement is that the people to be involved in the new change process may be suspicious of simplistic solutions as a result of the information/media blitz to which they have been exposed. They may already be suffering from information overload, experiencing a sense of powerlessness and loss of individuality; and they expect innovative and involving communication about the change. Essentially, the change maker may employ three change models to bring about a shift in the status quo:

1. *Power*, political or legal, physical or psychological—coercion to bring about change may be legitimate or illegitimate, depending on the purpose, the ingredients, and the method of application (legislative power may be used to promote equal employment opportunity or to prevent a disease epidemic, while the authority of role or competence may be called upon to overcome resistance to change).
2. *Rationale*—the appeal to reason and the common good, but this approach must face the fact that people are not always altruistic and self-interest may block acceptance of the proposed change, no matter how noble or worthwhile for the majority.
3. *Reeducative*—conditioning, training, and education become the means to not only create readiness for the change, but to provide the information and skills to implement it.

Each model has its strength and weaknesses, and sometimes the latter can be overcome in a combination of approaches.

The fields of planning, technological forecasting, and future studies provide change makers with new tools and processes for bringing about managed innovation. Through research, publications, conferences, and seminars, cosmopolitan leaders can hone their skills in planned change. Some multinational corporations have their own units engaging in such studies, sometimes sharing the results of their investigations (e.g., General Electric's report on *The Future of the Business Environment*).

Security Pacific Bank in California, for instance, has a vice-president in charge of future research. This executive searches out trends in life styles and indicators of alternative futures to determine their implications for banking policies, procedures, personnel, and customers. Others may seek assistance from "think tanks" like the Hudson, Stanford, or Rand research institutes.

Public agencies have begun to introduce futures studies into their professional development of personnel. For example, the Commission on Peace Officers Standards and Training (POST) in Sacramento, California, has designed their Command College around police becoming more proactive. Through their various workshops, executives in law enforcement learn about the changing work environment, developing a futures perspective for problem-solving, decision-making, and leadership. One of the external civilian faculty, Dr. Dorothy L. Harris, indicates each police administrator undertakes an independent study project to practice skills in environmental scanning, identification of emerging issues and trends, cross-impact analysis, data gathering methods, strategic and transition management. The reports examine alternative futures using relevance tests, scenarios, case studies, and other futures techniques.

Change specialists and futurists are emerging in many fields, such as strategic planning and management, or in traditional disciplines from architecture to anthropology. The Society for Applied Anthropology, for instance, has a Cultural Futures Research network and journal (Box 15200, Northern Arizona University, Flagstaff, AZ 86001, USA). A number of change products are also available from Knowledge Systems, Inc. (7777 W. Morris St., Indianapolis, IN 46231, USA) and the World Futures Society Bookstore (4916 Saint Elmo Ave., Bethesda, MD 20814, USA).

The how of planned change offers a variety of approaches. It can be as simple as "imagineering" at a staff meeting regarding the likely changes to become realities in a decade based on present trend indicators. Or it may be using the more elaborate Delphi technique, in which a questionnaire is developed with about a dozen likely situations that may occur in the future within a company or a culture. Members or experts may then be asked to rate on a percentage basis the probability of the event happening. Results are then tabulated and median percentages for each item determined. A report of results is circulated among participants, and they are asked to again rate the alternative possibilities after studying peer responses. The number of further administrations is up to the sponsor.

Perhaps one of the most practical methods of planned change for the purposes of this discussion is *force field analysis* developed by the late psychologist, Kurt Lewin. This conceptual model is based upon the understanding of "life space." Each individual lives in his or her own private world, just as employees function within a unique organizational space, and citizens within a distinctive national space. This invisible space is our perceptual *field*. There are many forces operating to influence human behavior—ideals and principles (e.g., profits or service); other people (boss, peers, family); and within ourselves (self image, needs, values, standards, ideals, or expectations that contribute to perception). Lewin's point is that the change maker must unfreeze the present equilibrium between two sets of *forces*—the driving forces for change and the resisting forces trying to maintain the status quo. For this he provides a method of *analysis* that will facilitate the establishment of a new equilibrium. One can use this technique to promote a change in self regarding diet, or to foster a change in an organization, or to lobby for a change in a nation. The United Nations can employ the method for furthering a UNESCO change on a world-wide basis, just as those in religious, educational, or criminal justice systems may affect planned change in their fields of endeavor.

Some of the steps to be taken in the process of force field analysis are:

1. *Describe the change.* In detail what exactly is planned in terms of the total system?
2. *Identify the change.* Is it a change in policy, structure, attitude, procedure, program, or combination of these?
3. *Self-analysis.* What is your relation to the change and what needs/motives are behind your efforts in this regard?
4. *Cultural analysis.* What is the present environment that requires this change and why will the organization or society (or the individual) benefit from this innovation? What are the likely related effects if this alteration is introduced? That is, the impact on the other interdependent elements in the socio-economic system.
5. *Inventory resources.* What material and human resources are present that would foster this change if mobilized and channeled? Who are the people likely to promote the change and provide leadership, so the instigator of the change may keep a long profile?
6. *Diagnosis of driving/resisting forces.* What is the number and strength of the forces, human and nonhuman, that would promote or resist this change? How can the driving forces be mobilized, enforced, and increased in order to change the current equilibrium between driving/restraining forces? How can the resisting forces be weakened, undermined, removed or isolated? In other words, what strategies can be used to increase the driving forces, and decrease the restraining forces, possibly by converting some of the latter into the former? Remember these forces may be physical or psychological, people or events/situations, nature or acts of god.
7. *Prepare the case.* Why should this change be instituted and what is its rationale? Do investigation, research and development on the case for human and financial investment in this change? Anticipate arguments against the change and develop counterarguments that may be included in this presentation, or held for use at the point of decision making. Include the cost savings and budget factors.
8. *Communicate the case.* What can be done initially to create a readiness for change by opening up the communication system to dialog on the proposed change? How can people who have to implement the change

be involved in the planning process for it? Who should get the complete case for the change, and on the basis of need to know, how can it be condensed in various versions that are appropriate to various levels in the system? Remember to use multi-, and even mass, media as appropriate, and to be alert to intercultural communication differences in the message transmission.

9. *Channel resistance.* In this tug of war between the pro/con change forces, have we allowed for creative dissent to cause modification or alteration of the change plan? Are we tailoring the case for change to meet the needs of individuals (e.g., for more information, ego support), as well as confronting those who have a vested or conflict of interest that causes them to oppose the change? Have we missed any strategies for gaining support among the reluctant?

10. *Project ahead.* If the goals of this change are understood and accepted, what are some of the probable outcomes to be expected? What alternative plans or strategies can be undertaken if the change is rejected or abandoned? What related changes might be promoted to strengthen this one? Will we be open to continuous changes upon the one being now sponsored? Should a pilot project be considered first?

11. *Action plans.* How can a final favorable decision be ensured? How can the plan for change be implemented. What is to be done, steps to be followed? Who is to do it? Where is it to be done? When is it to be done? Once the change is accepted and functioning, how can it be internalized and stabilized? That is, how can it be temporarily "frozen" into the system and reinforced?

12. *Evaluate change.* Is the change actually working effectively? Does it need further modification or alteration? Should it be replaced? Should action research or follow-up study be inaugurated? Realistic fact finding may be in order on the feasibility of the change after its inauguration, especially by those who are external consultants or had no part in fostering the change.

Cosmopolitan managers may find the following tips for fostering change especially helpful in intercultural situations. (They were prepared by Harris International, La Jolla, California.)

1. Include in the planning process everyone concerned about the change.
2. Avoid discrepancies between words and actions relative to the change.
3. Set realistic time frames for bringing about the change, neither too long nor short.
4. Integrate the activities involved in the change with available budget and resources.
5. Avoid overdependence on external or internal specialists.

6. Avoid data gaps between the change efforts at the top, middle and lower levels of the system.
7. Avoid forcing innovations into old structures incapable of handling them.
8. Avoid simplistic, cook-book solutions to the problems connected with change.
9. Realize that effective relations are a condition for change, not an end.
10. Apply change intervention strategies appropriately.
11. Identify personnel capable of diagnosing the need for change.
12. Capitalize on the pressures both from within and without the system for the change.
13. Wait for the right time when individuals or institutions are hurting enough to be ready for change.
14. Search the system at all levels for the leadership to effect the change.
15. Promote collaborative efforts between line and staff in planning and implementing the change.
16. Take calculated risks to inaugurate necessary change.
17. Maintain a realistic, long-term perspective relative to the change.
18. See to it that the system rewards people who cooperate in carrying out the change and in establishing a new norm.
19. Collect data on the situation to support the change and eventually evaluate it.
20. Set measurable objectives and targets relative to the change that are both tangible and immediate.

Introducing change in multicultural organizations is more difficult than in domestic organizations. Figure 5-1 suggests a way change agents can anticipate resistance to change and measure the degree of risk. It can be used in the following way. Suppose, there are five nationalities (national culture 1 = France, national culture 2 = U.S., etc.) working together in an organization and a decision was made that detailed performance appraisals were necessary to be implemented every six months for all employees. It was also assumed this decision was of high importance to the success of the organization. If the compatibility of this change was plotted on Figure 5-1 for working for that organization, the likelihood of success could be determined. In reality, often a change is compatible with one group but not another. The change agent then needs to consider the cultural underpinnings resisting the change, and make appropriate interventions.

To conclude this section, remember change is more acceptable when it is understood; is related to one's security; results from previously established principles; follows other successful changes; prior changes have been assimilated; new people, departments or programs are involved; personnel share in the planning and benefits; and people are trained for it.

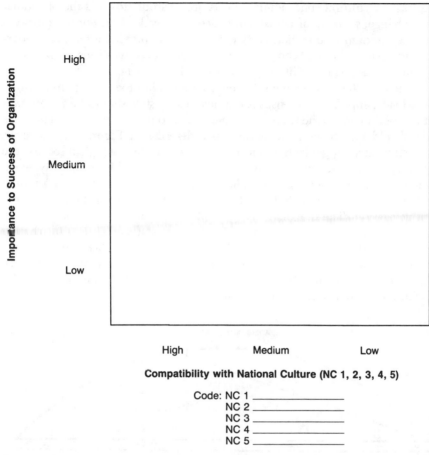

Figure 5-1. Instrument for plotting success/resistance to change in multicultural organizations.

LEADERSHIP AND CHANGE

Global leaders cope more effectively with change by means of strategic planning and management. One of the principal exponents in that emerging field is H. Igor Ansoff, a professor at United States International University. For world corporations, such as Mitsubishi, discontinuous change, he believes, can be costly both in terms of loss of profits and in reversing losses. Ansoff (1984) advocates a form of strategic response to change that is both decisive and planned. He concludes that behavioral resistance to change is a natural reaction because our culture and power are threatened. Therefore, effective leaders anticipate resistance, diagnose it, and then manage it.

Just as our cultural conditioning affects our attitudes toward the phenomenon of change, so too it influences our concepts of leadership. For our purposes here, the Random House Dictionary definition may provide a base for understanding—a leader is one who guides, directs, conducts, while leadership is the position or function or ability to influence or lead others.

For the past 30 years behavioral science research has focused upon the *function* of leadership. The consensus is that leadership style should be situational; that is, appropriate to the time, place, culture, and people involved. Thus, the leader should operate within a continuum as described in Figure 5-2. However, in a postindustrial organization within an advanced, technological society, the middle to right hand range of the continuum is preferable, especially when dealing with knowledge workers. The words in the center of the continuum highlight the dominant style in each leadership posture from telling to complete delegation. The diagonal line symbolizes the delicate balance between leader authority and group freedom. This balance shifts according to whether the authority is shared or centered in the ruling person or class. For example, an authoritarian leader dictates policy and tells the group members, whereas, in a group that has much freedom and authority is wholly shared, the leader abdicates total control in favor of total delegation.

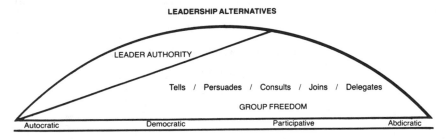

Figure 5-2. Leadership is situational and operates within a continuum of alternative styles, as conceptually illustrated here.

In modern, more democratic societies and organizations the trend is away from leadership centered in a single person, to members of a group contributing toward the leadership function by sharing talent and resources. The research of social scientists confirms that participation and involvement of members in the decision-making process can result in more effective and productive behavior. In terms of participative management this principle is expressed as follows: those who will be substantially affected by decisions should be involved in those decisions. But it takes a skillful and competent leader to implement such an ideal.

For the would-be synergistic leader or manager the implications of all this is that we must first reexamine our conception of human nature and the assumptions upon which we "manage" others. Then we must literally create social or organizational cultures that reinforce the natural tendencies toward industriousness, responsibility, and planning for change. This requires renewal of the values that influence leadership styles, so as to emphasize creativity, collaboration, teamwork, mutual concern, and service. Synergistic organizational or institutional forms encourage self-actualization. But throughout this process these new human systems must educate and train their members in new interpersonal and organizational skills, so that adherents can communicate and cooperate across cultures, and act together for mutual benefit. It also implies helping participants to conserve and develop human and natural resources for the common good. Finally, it means that leaders must acquire and practice a new synergistic form of power; namely, that of group initiative and cooperative action.

Cornelius Brevoord of the Graduate School of Management in Delft has translated these concepts into the context of the modern corporation. He suggests a Theory Z form of leadership, based on goal-setting, which structures and runs the organization. This is of creative benefit to its personnel and produces wealth in a socially and scientifically responsible manner. The new function of management, then, is to promote the right combination of the system's elements, that is, the interacting equal forces of people, goals, structures, and technology. Effective management enables the system to respond rapidly and adequately to a changing environment or society.

In the literature of education and training today, there is increasing emphasis on use of left/right brain learning activities. It appears that certain capacities are associated with either side of the cortex. Similarly, it is known that every person has qualities that are associated with both the female and male psyche. Holistic learning of males would include cultivation of those aspects commonly associated with the feminine character, and vice versa for the female. Furthermore, it has also been observed that one of the major problems with world leadership, whether political or corporate, is its male domination. Key decision makers tend to be chauvinistic and skewed toward the male perception of "reality" and the male approach to problem-solving. If we are to have synergistic leadership, male and female thinking and powers must be integrated. Perhaps the planet's persistent, unsolved problems—mass unemployment, hunger, violence, aggression, underutilization of human resources, etc.—exist partly because our attempts to manage them have been so lopsided. That is, over one half of the human race, women, are too frequently excluded from the decision-making process and the halls of power.

Human development will never achieve its potential as long as women are denied their right to share fully in the management of our social institutions. Some will argue that such a situation was only in the past, and characteristic of hunting and agricultural stages of the human condition. But even in this so-called age of enlightenment, there are industrial societies that consistently deny women an opportunity to fully participate in worklife, especially at the managerial levels. There are many factors throughout the world that constrain female leadership, but there are three that must be overcome if true synergy is to be achieved: (a) obsolete rural mindsets that restrict the role of women within a culture to that of wife and mother; (b) women's own inadequate self-images, which psychologically handicap them from greater self-fulfillment; and (c) male chauvinism, which underutilizes female talents or misuses women's competencies. Each of these constraints requires massive reeducation and attitude change, which is the objective of the universal women's liberation movement. Synergy is thwarted as long as beliefs, attitudes, and traditions in which distinctions are made of people's intrinsic worth on the basis of sex prevail. Whether aware of it or not, the sexist believes women are inferior and behaves accordingly. As with racism, it causes humankind to restrict development of its potential.

Consider the following*:

In 1984, approximately 300 women alumnae of the American Graduate School of International Management living abroad were contacted to discover their international pursuits and to determine how their sex and education affected their positions today. Of the 31 alumnae responding, all but three are living outside their native country. They are primarily in management and marketing positions from the Middle East to Asia to Europe. As different as their specific circumstances and professions are, their experiences are remarkably similar.

When asked how the culture in which they are working views women, the majority describe themselves and their professional positions as outside the cultural norms. A woman management consultant in West Germany says: "Most women in West Germany are considered in their proper place in society if they are either housewives or mothers."

A manager in strategic marketing finds that for Austrian women, "work is a temporary state until they marry and begin having children." Furthermore, she adds, "they accept this role 100% and do not fight it by applying for promotions."

Credibility Problems

In Asia, the situation is similar. A Citicorp executive responsible for recruiting and staff relations in Tokyo said women are "not expected to be serious about their jobs and so are given little responsibility." She adds: "It has been difficult to establish that I am in a responsible job and have authority to make decisions."

---

* Reprinted with permission from *International Management*, March 1986.

In Scotland, an applications and systems consultant with a computer firm says, "The United Kingdom and Scotland in particular are years behind the United States with regard to treating women as equals."

Considering these cultural attitudes, are women internationalists treated differently from host country nationals who are women? Most responded yes. They find that being a "foreigner" gives them a special status that preempts the place reserved for women. In the Dominican Republic, for example, one woman stated: "There is a consciousness of the fact that I am different because I come from a different culture."

Freedom in Japan

Being different in Japan is a definite plus. Western women have much more opportunity in Japan than host nationals. According to a supervisor with Kanda Institute of Language, "The Japanese people give a lot of freedom to foreigners." And that works to the advantage of working women from the West.

Most of the women international managers agree that their sex neither hinders nor helps their careers. As a project officer for the U.N. Food and Agriculture Organization in Chad sees it, her effectiveness has a greater impact on how she is viewed than the fact she is a woman.

However, given the growing involvement and importance of North American, European, Asian and Middle Eastern firms in international business and, therefore, the need for managers to have a sophisticated understanding of international business, it is incumbent upon firms to learn how best to utilize both their male and their female personnel. Perhaps we should focus on the skills required to get the job done.

Leaders who promote planned change in the work culture practice synergistic leadership, which

1. Emphasizes quality of life, rather than just quantity of goods/services.
2. Promotes concepts of interdependence and cooperation, rather than just competition.
3. Encourages work and technology in harmony with nature, rather than conquering it and avoiding ecological considerations.
4. Is conscious of corporate social responsibility and goals, rather than just technical efficiency and production.
5. Creates an organizational culture that encourages self-achievement and fulfillment through participation, rather than dogmatism and dependency.
6. Restates relevant traditional values such as personal integrity, work ethic, respect for other's property, individual responsibility, and social order.
7. Encourages the capacity for intuition, creativity, flexibility, openness, group sensitivity, and goal-oriented planning.

To exercise any leadership in complex systems in transition today is a challenge. The neat, orderly world of the past is gone, and traditional leadership approaches are inadequate. It is an illusion that the single leader or decision maker can make the difference, and this explains why so many people internationally are disillusioned with contemporary political "leaders." Now, only the combined brainpower of multiple executives or teams is most appropriate, so that many become involved with their unique resources and mobilized toward complex solutions (Harris, 1987).

Innovative managers assist people and their social institutions to build upon, yet to transcend, their cultural past. Anthropologist Edward Hall recalled that formerly one stayed relatively close to home so behaviors around us were fairly predictable. But today we constantly interact personally or through media with strangers, often at great distances from our home. Such extensions have widened our range of human contact and caused our "world" to shrink. Multicultural leaders not only have insights and skills for coping with such changed circumstances, but readily share them with their colleagues and systems. To be comfortable with changing cultural diversity and dissonance, we must literally move beyond the perceptions, imprints, and instructions of our own culture.

SUMMARY

Culture is a dynamic concept that changes, as does the way we communicate it. Those with the mindset and skills of a global manager exercise proactive leadership in altering both the macro and micro levels of culture. To cope effectively with accelerating change, cosmopolitan managers continuously revise their images of self, role, and organization, so that attitudes and behavior are modified accordingly.

Although our outlooks on change and leadership are culturally conditioned, global managers realize that the new work culture worldwide requires us not only to be open to change, but to build it into our social systems. Thus, we must stay relevant in meeting human needs by creating new markets, processes, products, and services. If we are to avoid culture lag, then innovative leaders must be involved in the *transformation* of their societies and workplaces, as well of management and organizations. The case study on Mitsubishi demonstrated how its organizational culture and strategies are being transformed from a general trading company to a diversified world corporation.

To deal with contemporary uncertainty and turbulence, organizational leaders use a variety of methods and techniques to plan change and foster strategic management that is futuristic. They are also mindful of the human side of rapid change, assisting members or employees to cope with the uprooting of traditional customs, careers, structures and procedures.

Leadership styles are situational, dependent to a degree on the people and culture at a point in time. Generally, the metaindustrial work culture calls for more participative, team-oriented management that responds rapidly and synergistically to the changing environment. In the emerging work culture, leadership opportunities are shared with competent knowledge workers, regardless of sex, race, religion, or nationality (Harris, 1989).

The challenge was most appropriately put to us in an address of Paul Doucet, director general of communications for the Canadian International Development Agency (1981):

> If, in the process of meeting people of other cultures, we do not change ourselves, we will not only have missed an opportunity for growth, personal and collective, but we will have become irrelevant in our own society.

The underlying assumption of this chapter is that global managers should be change makers, and this begins with one's self!

So, the cosmopolitan manager listens with a sensitive inner ear to catch the voices of the future thereby not missing the beat for the orderly direction of change. Through planning and research, such administrators promote a climate of renewal that avoids obsolescence. Attuned to the knowledge society, innovative leaders realize that ideas today have greater impact on people and their cultures than the invasion of armies. Thus, they seek to comprehend trends, to watch for signs of change, and to stay alert to innovative means for controlling it. These are the means for the *survival of the wisest* in the emerging cyberculture. To use them effectively is in the tradition of our innovative ancestors who climbed down from trees and walked upright, who formed tools and used tree branches as levers, who put fire to work and harnessed power, who substituted brain for brawn, who created automation and cybernation, who flew to the moon and back!

6
Managers as Influencers of Organizational Culture

Companies grow in many ways. However, when the growth is accomplished through acquisitions or joint ventures, there is a significant effect on the human resource function of the organization. There are "minefields" everywhere. The material in this chapter serves as a map around some of these.

If global managers are to be effective leaders, then we need not only understand the influence of culture upon organizations and its adherents, but utilize that culture to improve performance, productivity, and service. Organizations create culture; to be renewed and re-structured, they alter it. Culture explains the pattern of assumptions and behavior formulated by human systems in response to their environment, whether it is a nation with its macroculture, a local community with its needs and customs, a market with its consumers and suppliers, or an industry with its colleagues and competitors. The resulting organizational culture is a set of coping skills, adaptive strategies used by members in and out of the system. Organizational culture represents understandings and practices regarding the nature of people and the entity—whether it is a corporation, association, or government agency—about reality and truth, vocational activity, or work. Such organizational culture is manifested in values, attitudes, beliefs, myths, rituals, performance, artifacts, and myriad other ways.

COPING WITH ORGANIZATIONS' CULTURAL DIFFERENCES

What have these people in common?

- Sally has just graduated from college and is hired as a management trainee for a multinational corporation.
- Hari just received his MBA from an American university and is employed in his own country of Pakistan for a Middle Eastern Airline.
- Frank has been an American expatriate for six years and has been reassigned to corporate headquarters in Boise, Idaho.
- Mohammed, an Egyptian who was educated in Britain, is posted temporarily for additional training at a factory of his transnational employer in Fort Wayne, Indiana.

- Patricia, of New England Yankee stock, is transferred by her company, A.T.&T., to their offices in Macon, Georgia.
- Lee is leaving his native Korea to supervise a construction crew of his fellow nationals in Saudi Arabia where his company has a subcontract with the U.S. petroleum manufacturer.
- Brett is a senior vice-president with an Ohio company that has just been acquired by the nineteenth largest multinational corporation in the world.
- Alicia, a Hispanic high school graduate, has just been recruited under an Affirmative Action plan to work in a government law enforcement agency that has been dominated until now by white Anglo males.

Each of these individuals is faced with the problem of integration into an unfamiliar organizational culture. Perhaps, it would be better to think of it as the challenge of acculturation. They must learn the accepted cultural behavior in a unique organizational environment that will ensure their entry, acceptance, and effectiveness in that setting. Their approach to the different institutional contexts can facilitate their success or failure in the corporation or agency. Writing on "The Organization as a Microculture," Leonard Nadler, professor at George Washington University, reminds persons in situations such as were described previously that their own "cultural baggage" can impose limitations on their own creativity. One may have a "tunnel vision" based on past experience that hampers adequate adjustment and performance in the new scene. Whether one is a recruit in the organization, transferred within the company domestically or internationally, or an employee of a subsidiary owned by a larger entity, each must learn to cope with a unique subculture.

There are many dimensions to this concept of the organization as a microculture, which are influenced by the larger macroculture in which it operates. Everything the reader has learned previously in this text about culture in general, can be applied to organizational culture. The various ways to study a national or ethnic culture that are described in Chapter 8 are equally valid for the subculture of any human system that employs people for a specific purpose. Furthermore, there are related concepts, even synonyms, that amplify the subject under consideration, such as organizational environment, climate, or atmosphere. Each organization also has a distinctive psychological and even physical *space* that it occupies in a society or macroculture. The organization's culture is intertwined with its sense of space, and each influences the other. It carves out its own "territorial imperative" with reference to an industry and competitors.

Some corporations, for example, provide a psychological space that is unhurried and uncluttered, while others provide a situation that is stressful and crowded. The cultural behavior of the organization can be further manifested in the space allocations for executives and workers, for departments and divisions. Organizational space becomes a consideration in making many management decisions, such as the site for training programs, what public tours are to be shown, what areas are designated as "security" and entrance there is limited, what external structures and appearance communicate to a community. When planning change, the invisible space of the organization must be examined in terms of forces therein that influence employee behavior. Within the "private world" of a company or agency, one studies the driving forces, for example, that would facilitate the proposed change in the culture, as well as the resisting forces that would perpetuate the status quo. Institutions, like individuals, have their own perceptual fields or base from which they operate in the larger culture.

The organization's culture affects employee, supplier, and customer behavior, as well as community relationships. The reader would do well to consider these ideas in terms of one's own organizational culture, its client's or customer's organizational culture, as well as related organizational cultures (such as contractors, competitors, or government regulators). Furthermore, the issues of this chapter have implications regionally, nationally, and internationally. The corporate culture of Coca-Cola influences and is influenced by the regional culture wherein are located its headquarters and principal activities, Atlanta, Georgia. That same corporate culture interfaces with American culture in its domestic marketing, as well as when it produces and sells its soft drinks abroad, whether in China or Mexico. Coca-Cola's corporate culture has impacted upon the Mexican people, for instance, and it has adapted to the Spanish culture of the United States' adjoining neighbor on its southern border.

The organization's culture has a powerful impact on the worker's or member's morale and productivity. It even influences the organization's image of itself which, in turn, is communicated to its public. Those associated with the organization can either accept or reject its culture. If it is the former, then the member may conform or modify that culture. If it is the latter, then its personnel become frustrated or leave that organization.

Before concluding this section, it might be helpful to define organization and culture, so that the inter-relatedness of both concepts can be more fully appreciated.

An *organization* serves some human need—comfort or camaraderie, products or services, inspiration or education—through people who perform some function or work. The organization has been described as a collection of human objectives, expectations, and obligations. It structures human roles and relationships to attain its ends. (Reorganization, on the other hand, involves the severing of existing relationships, dissolution of existing structure, and the changing of organizational goals.)

Essentially, the organization is an energy exchange system. It transforms the input of natural or material energy, as well as human psychic and physical energy, into an output. To accomplish this, a system of feedback control is used, such as organizational communication: management information about budgets, productivity, human assets or personnel, and other facets of administration. The organization can be a government agency, a corporation, a trade or professional association, or a nonprofit entity. Whatever form this human enterprise takes, it acts as a lens to focus the energies of its people toward predetermined goals and objectives.

One who prefers a systems approach to viewing organizations is Dr. Raymond Forbes, director of organizational services of Northwest Airlines. Forbes defines an organization as an open, purposeful, social, and technological system that achieves its objectives by focusing energy extracted from its environment. He describes its characteristics as:

1. Purpose (mission or goal).
2. Structure (formal/informal allocation of responsibility/power).
3. Internal systems (support services of people/technology).
4. Human interchange (organizational communications).
5. Culture (known body of policy, rituals, rules, regulations, and procedures).
6. Human knowledge (the know-how of manufacturing, marketing, administration, rendering services).
7. Work itself (job content and performance).
8. Results (outcome or effects produced by organization).

However, it can be argued that many of these elements are actually part of the organizational culture. Forbes also provides useful explanations of related terms: "a system is a combination of component elements in dynamic interaction." He views the characteristics of an "open system" as (a) input and output flow of energy and matter; (b) development and maintenance of a steady state for input of new energy and matter that does not disturb the system's structure and order; (c) increased controls to meet increased complexity and differentiation of component elements; and (d) extensive transactions with the surrounding environment. In the post-industrial scene, organizational cultures should be open systems in which synergistic leadership will ensure ultrastability.

Culture is the way of living developed and transmitted by a group of human beings, consciously or unconsciously, to subsequent generations. More precisely, ideas, habits, attitudes, customs, and traditions become accepted and somewhat standardized in a particular group as an attempt to meet continuing needs. Culture is overt and covert coping ways or mechanisms that make a people unique in their adaptation to their environment and its changing conditions.

Organizations are actually *microcultures* that operate within the larger context of a national macroculture. Thus, an organizational culture may be the Mexican government, an American multinational or foundation, a British university or trust, the Roman Catholic Church, the Russian airline, Swedish Employers Federation, or the Association of Venezuelan Executives. Other transcultural organizations are synergistic in their structural make-up, such as

UNESCO, International Red Cross, Diebold Europe, Management Centre Europe, or OPEC.

Figure 6-1 illustrates many of the aspects of organizational culture.

There are aspects of an organization's culture that are formal, explicit, and overt, just as there are dimensions that are informal, implicit, and covert. Fundamentally, the organization viewed as an energy exchange system has inputs into the social system of information and resources. Physical and psychic energy pours into the organization, along with capital, to be transformed into output. In attempting to achieve its goals and mission, the organizational culture is further influenced by leadership practices, norms and standards, rules and regulations, attitudes and principles, ethics and values, policies and practices, structures and technologies, products (artifacts) and services, roles and relationships. To facilitate these activities, cultural mandates or traditions are

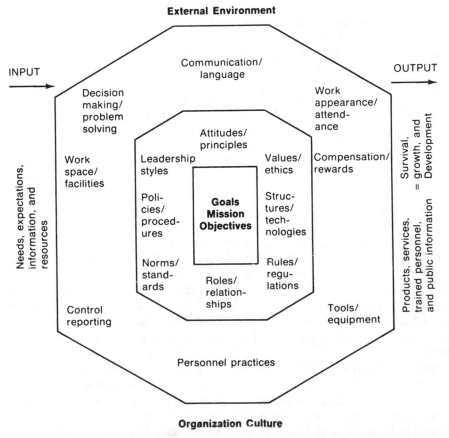

Figure 6-1. Conceptual illustration of the various aspects of organizational culture.

established concerning dress codes, work hours, work space and facilities, tools and equipment, communication procedures and special language, rewards and recognitions, as well as various personnel provisions. The resulting cultural behavior and activities are manifested in the outputs, such as products, services, personnel, or public information.

An organization as large as General Motors, for example, has many subcultures in the form of divisions for manufacturing, marketing, and other functions or models of cars. It may have many domestic and foreign subsidiaries that also have unique subcultures. The largest transnational corporations adapt themselves to the culture and circumstances in which they operate, while trying to retain that which gives them their distinctiveness and accomplishments. The GM culture is quite different from that of competitors within one's own country, such as Ford Motors, but it is especially different from a comparable company abroad, such as in Japan or Volvo in Sweden. The formal aspects of GM's culture are like the tip of an iceberg—its overt activities are written objectives, technological processes, raw materials, and manpower skills; the informal or covert elements involve attitudes and feelings, values and group norms that dominate the organization and affect both productivity and quality control. When General Motors, for example, opens a subsidiary plant in Juarez, Mexico, it developed a Mexican-American management team to create a plant culture appropriate to that community. It provided the Mexican and American managers, and their spouses with language and cultural training to enhance the success of the intercultural operation.

Today, General Motors has a corporate culture in transition (Harris 1985). It is transforming itself from an industrial to a metaindustrial work environment. This involves more than just acquisition of high technologies in the form of automation and robots. In the restructuring of its management, Chairman Roger Smith, acquired Electronic Data Systems of Dallas. He then proceeded to transfer all MIS/EDP functions and personnel into the new subsidiary. By this strategy, he created an organizational prototype for GM of the future, for EDS is a high-tech, entrepreneurial company of computer services whose output, work force, and management style is foreign to the industrial traditions of the auto giant. (See page 138 for a brief case study.)

Contemporary organizations, like General Motors, must cope with more than the cultural differences in companies or divisions that occur because of acquisitions, mergers, or foreign expansion. They also struggle to transform an industrial into a technological work culture centered around information processing and microelectronics (Harris 1983, 1985).

To assess the status of one's own system in this regard, an *Organizational Culture Survey Instrument* is included in Appendix D. It can also be used for human factor data gathering with colleagues in a company or agency, so that a profile for diagnostic purposes can be drawn from a compilation of the feedback data obtained from others. Analysis of findings from questionnaires or in-

Culture Shock: The EDS Merger*

General Motors employees are among the best paid and best cared for in American industry. Salaries are competitive, benefits topflight, bonuses abundant. Longtime executives say the princely perks instilled a feeling that the company was invulnerable and that promotion was inevitable.

But the acquisition of Electronic Data Services is shaking up the company. "For too long, there was a feeling that GM executives were protected, cradle to grave," says one division executive. "Now, we're starting to worry more about the health of the goose and not just the golden eggs it lays."

In the freewheeling computer industry, EDS is an oddity, run like a military school. The behavior of EDS founder H. Ross Perot strongly reinforces that image. When EDS employees in Iran were taken hostage, Perot financed a paramilitary team that rescued them from the country.

So when GM transferred its own 10,000 data-processing employees to the payroll of EDS, they suffered culture shock—at EDS, there are no beards, no tasseled shoes, no cocktails at lunch. Benefits are lower, too. Many of the transferred people revolted. Some 600 are expected to resign or retire. An additional 700 to 800 transferred workers are leading a campaign to join the United Auto Workers. The company has no unions, and EDS Senior Vice President Kenneth Riedlinger vowed to battle the organizing move, now before the National Labor Relations Board.

The no-nonsense, task-oriented attitude of EDS managers has Smith's enthusiastic backing, leading some GM executives to wonder aloud who took over whom. In fact, Smith and GM leaders want EDS to be a role model for the parent company. "EDS gets everyone involved," says Smith. Adds Riedlinger: "EDS is a little, bitty company compared to GM. We're used to moving quicker and freer. We're not used to dealing with a structure like GM."

One reason a "little, bitty" company can influence a giant parent company is that EDS knows computers, and computers will redefine the way cars are produced worldwide. Experts agree that the robots of today—welding seams, carrying heavy components, spraying paint—are but the infancy of a rapid evolution in manufacturing. GM is venturing into tomorrow's generation of robots, which "see" parts through visual sensors, literally learn from their mistakes and monitor thousands of product-quality tests at every point of car assembly.

"We are just at the beginning," declares Riedlinger. "Now, robots simply replicate the motions of a human being. In the future, masses of robotic and plant-floor devices will be controlled from a central data-processing system." GM is investing in companies with technological leads in robotics, machine vision and artificial intelligence. All such devices are run by computers.

Besides car production, though, EDS is influencing GM in business and management systems. Smith envisions the Saturn subsidiary as almost a "paperless" company, with little corporate protocol to inhibit creativity. Says EDS Chairman Perot: "Roger told me, 'If anybody shows up with a GM procedures manual, I want you to shoot him.' " EDS already is tightening GM's management controls. A new computer method of tracking health-care costs could save GM up to $200 million annually—about 10% of the $2-billion bill.

* Source: *U.S. News and World Report* (March 11, 1985, p. 56).
Postscript: Chairman Smith forced Perot off the GM board and has since retired.

ventories, then gives management the personnel's perceptions of corporate culture, and the directions for planned changes.

ANALYZING ORGANIZATIONAL CULTURE

Since an organization's culture is multidimensional, we need some means for analyzing its ways for coping. For example, suppose a professor or private sector manager was appointed to a federal agency. How does one understand the rites, customs, procedures, and survival habits of public service bureaucrats? Perhaps one is a consultant or contractor on assignment to Washington, D.C., and required to interface with civil service administrators. How does one quickly catch on to the folkways, the jargon, the myths, and the work traditions of the "Capitol tribes"? The same methods that anthropologists have devised to classify and comprehend a national or tribal culture can be applied to government or corporate culture.

Thus, application of such research to the federal bureaucracy helps us to understand these language peculiarities:

1. Turn nouns into verbs—to prioritize and strategize, for instance, emphasize action over meaning.
2. Translate everything into numbers—through quantification or statistics, decisions can be justified in the mumbo-jumbo of cost-benefits equations.
3. Use the art of ambiguity to smooth the political process—since everyone wants agreement at any cost, language is often not clear on purpose.
4. Expect internal memorandums to be used in protection of status power or turf—the magic ritual calls for privately circulating drafts to negotiate the contents or to legitimize what is already known and decided upon privately (this memo exchange can be a means for busy work and looking important).

Another feature of federal culture communicates one's GSA (Government Service Administration) rank and status through space. The size of an office, its facilities and furnishings, help to clarify one's importance and power—it is the stage where ranking bureaucrats perform and display their trophies of "accomplishments" and connections. Rites of passage in the huge system can be noted by the acquisition of name plates, business cards, and service awards until a career is finalized with a retirement pin and dinner.

Until recently, cultural anthropologists have failed to transfer their insights to modern corporations, associations, and agencies. Back in 1979, when the first edition of this volume was published, a chapter was devoted to organizational culture at a time when most management consultants ignored the topic. Then articles began to appear on corporate culture in both popular and academic business journals. Finally, a series of books have appeared on the subject from Kennedy and Deal (1982), Harris (1983 and 1985), and Schein (1985). In the latter volume, *Organizational Culture and Leadership*, the author examines minutely what culture is and does, how it begins and develops within human systems, and how it changes.

Wilkens (1989) examines a related concept, the developing and altering of corporate character, including the organization's unique internalized value and competitive skills. The issue of corporate transformation as a means of institutional revitalization has attracted the attention of both executives and consultants (Kilmann and Covin, 1987). Leaders are particularly concerned about creating high performing cultures within organizations (refer to Chapters 7 and 19).

John Sherwood (1988) makes a compelling case for high-performance, high-commitment *work cultures*, citing many progressive companies, such as General Electric, Proctor and Gamble, Digital Equipment, and Ford, which are innovating in the redesign of work and organizational structure. Sherwood maintains that personnel exhibit energy because work is challenging and significant; in such firms, continuous "learning" is emphasized and rewarded for quality performance. He recommends as a tool for this purpose design teams to redesign sociotechnical systems.

Sherwood believes that management will succeed in gaining a competitive advantage only when leaders change their views about people and the design of work, linking human and technical resources in a collaborative work *system*. He advocates many of the same approaches suggested in this text, underscoring that leaders inspire and articulate high performance.

One way of characterizing an organization's culture is in terms of ten major classifications. In the case study that follows the paradigm is presented in the context of a single global corporation. A description is provided for each of these ten dimensions, and then its application is also illustrated within this company. Deliberately, the enterprise selected does not have its headquarters located in the U.S.A., and offers culture contrasts for learning purposes.

The target company is Schlumberger, originally a French corporation that has moved beyond a single national identity. It has been called by Jacques de Fouchier as the single best company in the world, so it is a model for excellence. This noted financial analyst supports his evaluation by stock value growth from $35 a share to $75; a jump in the firm's annual profits from $27.1 million to $1 billion.

Although the case is lengthy, it will provide the reader not only with information on how to study organizational culture, but demonstrates how one social system is moving in the direction of the new work culture. It illustrates how the ten classifications in this model can be used when visiting a company or when reading about it.

The basis for this analysis of Schlumberger is a two-part article in *The New Yorker* by Ken Auletta (June 13, 1983). That writer later expanded his story into a significant book, *The Art of Corporate Success* (1984). In it, he describes the leader of one of the world's largest and most profitable corporations, Jean Riboud, 64, as an enigma who has adopted as Schlumberger's corporate credo, "strive for perfection." Riboud believes that, "If you want to innovate, to change an enterprise or society, then it takes people willing to do what's not expected." This is how corporate heros and myths are made!

Being a dynamic organization, Schlumberger has changed even since this case was written—the Fairchild division was sold and the corporation had to retrench due to the world market drop in oil sales and revenues.

This case has offered an extensive overview of cultural transformation in a distinguished transnational enterprise to illustrate the various characteristics to be analyzed. However, if Thomas Peters and Robert Waterman (1982) are right, the search for excellence can be abetted by studying the organizational cultures of the best-run companies.

(text continued on page 149)

Case Study in Corporate Culture: Schlumberger

I. Organizational Identity, Image, and Mission
(The way the enterprise sees and projects itself, particularly with reference to the nature of its business or its rationale for being.)

In a speech before the New York Society of Security Analysts, Schlumberger's CEO, Jean Riboud said the company has but one business:

> From the first day, Schlumberger's technology was to collect and to interpret data, basically physical parameters. It happened that the first data we collected, the first data we interpreted, were on an oil well, propelling us in the oil-field service. . . . Today, it is clear that there is a common thread, a common technology to all our undertakings. We are involved and committed to collect, to transmit, to compute, to analyze, to interpret data. It is the case in an oil well. . . . It is the case for the new parameters to enhance drilling efficiency and safety. It is the case for collecting and analyzing voltage measurements in the electricity-distribution system to operate fast protection devices. It is the case for the sophisticated Fairchild automatic text equipment.

Although a huge multinational corporation, it sees itself as a big family enterprise. It seeks to give its people something larger than themselves to believe in. It believes that it has the responsibility that religion used to have, namely, to strive to perform a service and measure itself against a higher standard than making profits, that is, seeking perfection. Again, Riboud:

> If I have one purpose today, it is to expand the concept of merging together into one enterprise, Europeans, Americans, and citizens of the Third World; to bring Asians, Africans, and Latin Americans so they feel

at home with their own culture, their own religion, and yet feel that Schlumberger is their family.

II. Organizational Space and Scope

(The way the group defines and delineates itself, both in terms of physical and psychological space in society or its macroculture. The boundaries by which it demarcates itself from other entities and its expectations of those associated with it. The territorial imperative related to an industry or its competitors. The scope is the extent of its activities as seen in departments, divisions, subsidiaries, acquisitions and joint ventures.)

Schlumberger, the parent multinational corporation, is incorporated for tax advantages in the Netherlands Antilles, and dominates the oil-field services industry. It has a near monopoly on the wireline business (70% of the world market) from which it derives 45% of its revenues and 70% of its profits. Its divisions include Wireline, Measurements & Control (⅓ annual income) which is Europe's number one manufacturer of electric meters. Its subsidiaries include Forex Neptune, the world's most profitable oil-drilling service; two well-testing companies—Johnston-Macco (U.S.A. and Canada) and Flopetrol (South America), also well run and profitable; Computer Aided Systems, a new enterprise that makes CAD/CAM systems (computer-aided designs and manufacturing); Applicon, a pioneer in automating design and drafting processes; and Fairchild Instruments in California, producer of tiny microprocessors. The latter holds the key to the production of smaller oil services equipment, more technical measurement, and reduced logging time as a means for the corporation to enter the field of artificial intelligence. It also has a joint venture in Dowell Schlumberger, a pumping and cementing company that is jointly owned with Dow Chemical.

> The company is not interested in financial acquisitions. We acquire companies only if the acquisition represents an expansion of our basic business.
>   Arthur Lindenauer, Executive Vice President, Schlumberger.

When it does consider a take-over, the policy is that it must be friendly. . . . While they operate globally, this premier corporation focuses on its principal business and industry, and all its other activities support or are compatible to that basic business thrust.

III. Organizational Attitudes, Beliefs, and Myths

(The dominant philosophy or belief system of an organization is an elusive element that is at the core of its success or failure. It is expressed in myriad ways, formally and informally, as well as consciously and unconsciously by its personnel, publications, and practices. Such ideals and principles impact employee behavior, and create driving themes like "profits," "innovate" or "service." Some of these attitudes and beliefs get translated into actions, real or imagined, called myths. Myths are traditional or legendary stories about corporate heros and events of exceptional character.)

Schlumberger is determined to stick to what it knows best. It avoids large debt burdens (in 1982, it had a cash pool of $2 billion, $300 million and long-term debt of only $462 million). Compare this long-term debt-to-equity ratio of 6.6% with that of the average American corporation's 38%! . . . It is cosmopolitan, moving beyond its French national identity to include Americans, other Europeans, and especially Third World nationals among its board, executives, and engineers. . . . Since it is in the oil-field service business, it does not own natural resources (oil) in any nation, but services those who do, nor does it engage in consumer advertising or government lobbying. . . . It believes in motivating people and forging consensus. . . . Although its founders and present chairman are socialists, the company is apolitical, avoiding politics, and identification with any one nationality. Yet Jean Riboud's convictions do form the basis of his management style—united Europe and world government and concern over the dangers of nationalism, opposition to privilege and ruling classes, the spread of democracy (especially within French culture), the development of the masses (especially in the Third World), equality over establishment, meaningful forms of capital gains or estate taxes, fiscal conservatism blended with a liberal's compassion and commitment to change. The beliefs and ideals of an executive leader also can influence followers!

Schlumberger's success has been partially attributed to the "pride-and-humility factor"—their engineers are unusually proud and self-confident, but their supervisors try to instill a sense of humility with admonitions like "don't act like King Kong" because they represent the leading company in their field. The company is concerned about "demotivated" people who do not give their best, and it promotes a "will to win" as central to its company spirit. In a speech, Riboud tried to define their corporate spirit:

> We are an exceptional crucible of many nations, of many cultures, of many visions. We are a totally decentralized organization. . . . We are a service company, at the service of our customers, having a faster response than anyone else. We believe in the profit process as a challenge, as a game, as a sport. We believe in a certain arrogance; the certainty that we are going to win because we are the best—an arrogance that is only tolerable because it is coupled with a great sense of intellectual humility—the fear of being wrong, the fear of not working hard enough.

IV. Organizational Values and Norms
(The needs of any enterprise to survive and develop lead to the setting of priorities as to what it values as important, as well as to standards of member behavior or job norms. Such measures of worth are positive or negative, written or unwritten, and powerfully influence employee behavior. Company maxims or value systems re-inforce established standards and expected performance for career growth. They are evident not only in policy statements and personnel manuals, but also in company logos, slogans and symbols.)

Managers are responsible for the fundamental motivation of Schlumberger people. . . . Moving people keeps the Schlumberger system alive; it keeps personnel on their toes. Transfers that are lateral or into a different aspect of the business keep people from feeling they know everything. . . . Schlumberger relies on research and technology, and seeks solutions to field problems there, not in law, finance or clever manipulation. . . . Talented people can be found anywhere in the world, and the company's responsibility is to develop such human resources. . . . Schlumberger relies on brains that cannot be nationalized (and usually avoids joint ventures as a result with governments—there is one exception, a venture with the Mexican government). . . . Commitment to decentralization causes it to value lean companies, especially with regard to central management and staffs—it is an entrepreneurial, not a managerial corporation. . . . The emphasis is equally on profitability and customer service. . . . Stay slim and discard products that do not capture a large share of the market. . . . Yet profits should be only one element in judging human performance. . . . This company is an extension of the personal values of its executive leadership—"humility, loyalty, preserving faith in an idea, serving people, being trusting, being open-minded to different cultures, being ambitious and competitive, and yet mindful of tradition" (Jean Riboud).

"It's easy to be the best. That's not enough. The goal is to strive for perfection" (Jean Riboud).

V. Organizational Communication and Language

(Human systems have unique interaction processes, lexicons, and jargons. As a whole, or within its subcultures, unique terminology, codes, acronyms may be in wide use. The cultural orientation may lean toward formality or informality in organizational communications (e.g., in the use of titles and rank). There is both verbal and non-verbal communication to be observed, as well as specific orientations (e.g., sexist or not). With the introduction of computers into organizations, management information systems should also be analyzed, as well as regional or subsidiary differences.

In the *New Yorker* articles, there were few direct references to communications within Schlumberger, so this consultant can only summarize by inference the actual situation. For example, as a multinational and multicultural conglomerate, it is obvious that a variety of languages are spoken by personnel in this company, but that French and English would be the dominant ones, except in Latin American operations where Spanish might be more in vogue (but in Brazil where it would be Portuguese). Since the company is dominated by engineers and places great emphasis on research, technical terminology should be prevalent, with a tendency to be concise and to quantify. Because organizations communicate shared values, Schlumberger representatives are likely to be authentic in their business interactions, leveling with customers to keep their good will. There is a likelihood, furthermore, that although the corporate values espouse equality, that there is sexism in the communication system. Schlumberger seems to suffer from culture lag when it comes to equal opportunity for women and blacks. Among its 2,200 field engineers in 1982, only 32 were women (partially because few women are found in oil camps). The company's male orientation is communicated in little ways, such as, at its Paris headquarters, the well-appointed men's rooms have fine linen towels, while the ladies' room has paper towels. Yet Riboud is making all kinds of efforts to have all nationalities represented in the company, and all kinds of skin color represented, according to his female secretary.

Its management information system is highly computerized with four major data processing centers. To overcome information bottlenecks from the field, well-log data are generated at every well site, and to improve speed of analysis and interpretation, the parent company is depending on its Fairchild subsidiary and artificial intelligence (a computer capable of reproducing the same knowledge base and reasoning process of inference, intuition, induction and deduction, as is used by a human expert). Again we turned to Schlumberger's chairman, Riboud:

This technological revolution—artificial intelligence—is as important for our future as the surge in oil exploration. It will force us to design new tools; it will change the capabilities of our services; it will multiply the effectiveness of our instruments.

It will change the order of magnitude of our business. Sensing artificial intelligence as a growth industry, Schlumberger jumped in early with investments and in 1982 introduced into the oil field a Dipmeter Adviser—connected to a computerized data base, it automatically performs the selected functions of an engineer. With such attitudes, it is easy to envision that Schlumberger will be in the forefront of new communication technology applications, such as teleconferencing and satellite communication.

VI. Organizational Processes and Learning

(Organizational culture can be examined in terms of the processes used by the enterprises for manufacturing, technology, reasoning, human relations and development. The range goes from the processing of information to the acquisition of knowledge, such as through education and training.)

Because Schlumberger does not sell or lease its equipment, but only provides technological services, its equipment is the most technologically advanced. Competition in the oil field hinges on technology, so the company innovates and remains a leader in high technology. Research and development get high corporate priority. It spends more money on wireline R&D than the total wireline profits of any of its competitors! (Compare that to the average American company, which in 1982 spent 3.8% of its revenues on research and development, while in that same year Schlumberger increased such investments to 5% of its revenue or $326 million—a rise of 36% in that year alone.) In addition to the artificial intelligence research at Fairchild and Applicon laboratories, this company invests in its knowledge workers (e.g., 30 Ph.D.'s in artificial intelligence research, plus considerable technical support staff, so that now it is one of six top corporations in this research field). The goal of its Computer Aided Systems is to develop a completely automated factory.

Schlumberger recruits worldwide (in 1981–82, 41% of its engineers came from developing countries), and it trains its multinational force of engineers at thirteen training sites with the latest of equipment. A third of the training instructors are from the Third World countries.

The process of goal setting reveals something about the culture. In the wireline division, the manager in Egypt has a thick book of his annual goals, set in the field and not in central headquarters. His superiors had specified their expectations in terms of profit margin gain, return on investment, share of the market, permissible lost time on the job, number of engineers to be recruited, and facilities to be completed in the next year. This division manager, in turn, gave the managers who reported to him specific sets of targets. It's a management by objectives system that works.

VII. Organizational Personnel—Recognitions, Rewards, and Heros

(The organization seeks and re-inforces a certain type of person. Recognition and rewards are bestowed for certain types of achievement, productivity, performance, experience. Commendations, citations, uniforms, pins, adornments are part of the multiple way to signify accomplishment, rank, and promotions. The compensations range from salary and bonuses, to ownership and profit-sharing, to incentive travel and varied fringe benefits. The perks for managers and sales personnel can be quite creative. The high performers often become the corporate heroes. The heroes personify the culture's values and act as behavior models. They range from the company's founders and outstanding entrepreneurs to its inventors and top researchers to its exceptional sales persons and creative deviants. The one thing they have in common is that they are all super achievers.)

Among the 79,000 Schlumberger employees, most are engineers and technicians. For the most part, these knowledge workers are multicultural, but the executive level is dominated by Europeans/Americans. Until recently, women tended to be transparent in the workforce, mainly in non-professional and non-managerial positions. Schlumberger engineers are usually sent fairly young into the field for an early taste of responsibility; they are rewarded for being aggressive and taking risks. Recruiting is very selective, promotions are from within—most executives started in the field. This company's people learn and mature very early and quickly, and they are known for their independence. They are urged to stay close to customers, have pride in the company, and be mobile or ready for transfers. Apparently, Schlumberger is inadequate in its foreign deployment services for employees—no provisions seem to be made for the wives' careers, or for countering their loneliness and culture shock when the husband is assigned to remote locations. However, there is usually good job security with a career for life, if one wants it. One of the rewards is intangible—knowing that you are among the best. . . .

The heros began with the founders of the company in 1926—two brothers, Marcel and Conrad Schlumberger. They transferred their personal values into their organizational creation, especially friendship and honesty. Conrad helped to engender the family spirit in the corporation by escorting personnel to the railroads when they left for overseas assignments, by knowing their families and children. The brothers emphasized human relations, communicated shared democratic values, and conveyed that their work mission was a "noble activity." They set policies to avoid conflict of interest with customers, and made it clear that with Schlumberger one started a calling, not just a career. "They were not just merchants, but missionaries," is the way one of their daughters describes them. When Jean Riboud took over as the top executive, he carried on these traditions and is known for similar qualities. Anne Schlumberger, one of the founder's daughters, states that "Riboud is loved because he is very friendly. It is love of people and interest in their life." A citizen of the world, a confidante of President Francois Mitterand, a devoted husband to his Indian wife, Krishna, and proud father of a son and three grandchildren, Jean has been an inspiration for 16 years as chief executive to Schlumberger personnel. Now he has moved up to chairman of the board, and appointed Michael Vaillaud president and CEO. At 51, Vaillaud is relatively new to the company where he served in both its electronics and oil-field services divisions, after a career as a diplomat. He has a relaxed manner, broad interests in history and the arts, and leads a team of exceptional executives, like American Thomas Roberts of Fairchild and Frenchman Euan Baird and Englishman Ian Strecker, both of the Wireline Division.

But the company spirit is not just top down, it also rises from the bottom. As the company grew, the culture was transmitted by its growing number of engineers. They would go through basic training together and become like a clan—working in remote areas together, sometimes for seven days a week for two-month stints, they became close as they ate, drank, showered, watched video cassettes, and vacationed *together.* For months, their only contacts were often only employees of Schlumberger or other oil companies. Thus, a certain spirit has been passed on in the corporate gene pool.

VIII. Organizational Rites, Rituals, and Feeding Habits

(The organization's culture transmits in many ways "the way we do things around here." The values, expectations, standards and procedures get ritualized and even celebrated. It is evident in meeting formats, writing styles, special events like retirement dinners, the hoopla that marks big achievements, the symbols of recognition and accomplishment, the chain of command, and even the incentive sales conventions at posh resorts. Food and feeding habits are also an important cultural manifestation, so organizations issue rules on length of lunch and coffee break—when employees may eat. They also may have policies on where they may eat (on the shop floor, cafeteria, executive dining rooms); what and how to eat (expense-account lunches with lavish menus, overtime or travel meal allowances, sales breakfast meetings, "brown bag" lunches for discussions, special menus in the cafeteria like inclusion of "soul food," etc.)

Schlumberger, we can presume, is favored with an international cuisine in its headquarter buildings and main plant, possibly with a flavor of French cooking. Out in the oil fields, we suspect it is hearty, plain, and healthy meals that are served the engineering personnel. One of its rites would be the management-by-objectives system that we have already described. Since it perceives itself as "one big family," it is probable that there are rituals to preserve this idea in far-flung operations, especially in new acquisitions. The friendly spirit is even engendered in acquisitions, which must not be hostile, and efforts are consciously made to instill the Schlumberger spirit even in non-oil services acquisitions. The global "moving around" phenomenon goes up even to the executive level through lateral transfers and consolidations. The spirit of seeking technological breakthroughs, of focusing upon research and development, extends throughout the whole enterprise and its acquisitions. But an astute, on-the-scenes observer at Schlumberger facilities would have no difficulty picking up the varied rites and rituals that set this multinational corporation apart from its competitors.

IX. Organizational Relationships

(Each culture has its unique attitudes toward various forms of relationships and sexuality. In human systems, organization charts and structures, role definitions, work segregation, security clearances, status supports and other such means affect organizational relations. Equal Employment Opportunity in some countries is an external force changing these cultures by opening the way for women and minorities to gain entry and to move up the organizational ladder. These attitudes and relationships have significant impact on work atmosphere and productivity, employee rapport and morale, career development and corporate loyalty. The "old boy" network is being expanded to include all types of networks that help people gain information and insight to advance on the job and up the organization.)

It has been well established above that Schlumberger is multicultural in its relationships and in the process of moving beyond its male orientation. Family kinships, knowledge worker networks, and the engineering fraternity are valued. Friendly relations among all levels of the organization would seem to predominate. But there are contradictions, as we have pointed out, such as with reference to the family emphasis—outside North America, the company discourages engineers who are married; the wives of Schlumberger employees find it difficult to pursue careers because of the frequent transfers, often to Muslim nations where dictates of tradition keep a woman at home. Customer relations are prized, and the emphasis is on service and honesty. Relations with peoples of developing nations are cultivated in the company spirit of equality. Man-machine relations are not feared, but encouraged through the use of automation, artificial intelligence and robots. Schlumberger representatives tend to be more cosmopolitan, and less ennthocentric, in their relationships, and very competitive; a high quality in human relations is espoused.

X. Organization Look, Style, and Reputation

(The appearance of an organization can be judged by its buildings and equipment, by the external vitality and dress of its employees, by its reports and publications, but mainly by its products and services. The psychological climate can be sensed in a corporation's creative environment or internal atmosphere, its flexibility and innovation, its practice of social responsibility, and its concern for human resource development. Its style can be seen in the way the enterprise operates—its rules and regulations, such as dress codes; its maintenance policies and practices; its sharing of power and encouragement of participation. One distinctive characteristic of all cultures is its sense of time and time consciousness, and this should be examined under this category. Finally, how do others outside the organization view this human system—customers, suppliers, investors, and all types of analysts.)

A review of the previous nine categories should provide a sufficient fix on the look and style of Schlumberger's corporate culture without repeating it here. For example, we know that it is a lean organization, technologically superior and innovative, win and success oriented, internationally-minded, and open to change. Schlumberger's time horizons are longer than most Western companies, and they are willing to wait for return on their investments. For example, when they took over the Compagnie des Compteurs in 1970, it took them seven years to transform it into a success. When Jean Riboud thinks of oil profits, he looks at the long term and he is optimistic, expecting Schlumberger to experience steady profit growth in a recessive economic cycle.

When it comes to reputation, we already have some insights from the previous sections about how others feel regarding this conglomerate. So let us to go the experts:

- In 1981, the *Institutional Investor's* John Wellemeyer said, "We particularly emphasize the appeal of Schlumberger. The stock price of this premier oil company will be the first to recover."
- Both competitors and Wall Street analysts are generally optimistic about Schlumberger's future. "They're a mighty fine company," said Marvin Gearhart. Eberstadt's Philip Mayer noted in 1982 that this company was "technologically better equipped and more sensitive to new market opportunities than I've seen it in ten years."

Perhaps, the best insight to the company reputation and future is the length of space an American magazine devoted to this enterprise, ending with this quotation from Chairman, Jean Riboud:

If we lose the drive, and fear searching for new technologies, or fear taking incredible gambles on new managers, or fear to heed the voices of other countries and cultures, then we become an establishment. (If that happened, Schlumberger may remain powerful and profitable, but ultimately it will decline.) . . . It's easy to be the best. That's not enough. The goal is to strive for perfection.

(text continued from page 141)

TRANSNATIONAL DIFFERENCES AND ORGANIZATIONAL CULTURES

Because the microculture is a reflection of the macroculture, it stands to reason that the location of an organization will be affected by the culture of the community that surrounds it. Even within a country, such as the United States or India, this would be a significant factor affecting worker behavior. There is an interaction continuously between the majority and minority cultures, each influencing the other. Thus, when a manager goes abroad, outside his or her native culture, the organizational culture which that person represents should adapt to local circumstances. Furthermore, the organizational cultures in the host country with whom the expatriate interfaces are quite unique manifestations of the indigenous culture. Should this person who is a foreigner in a strange land go to work for one of the local companies or government agencies as a consultant or even an employee, the individual should expect that things will be done quite differently from "back home" and that people in the native organization will behave very differently from colleagues in one's own country.

The state of technological, economic, and social development of a nation will also affect the organizational cultures. First World nations, for instance, may have more organizations using the emerging adhocracy model, while Third World countries might still use the industrial or traditional organizational modes. Typical managerial activities such as planning and innovating, organizing and controlling, recruiting and selecting, evaluating and rewarding/punishing, leading and relating, communicating, problem-solving and decision-making, negotiating and managing conflict, supervision, and training are all conducted within the context of the dominant local culture. Thus, that unique people's perception of their world and of human beings, their motivational orientation, their ways of associating, their value and activity emphasis, will be reflected in the social institutions they establish. A corporation or government agency mirrors the images and imprints of the indigenous population to various degrees.

Perhaps some examples of such cross-cultural differences in organizations and their workers will best illustrate this point that requires such sensitivity upon the part of visitors or expatriates. In a traditional Latin organization that is rapidly disappearing, the supervisor-subordinate relationships are such that an employee would never *directly* approach a foreman or manager to discuss a problem—in the old authoritarian mode, one does not question the boss. In Japan, where the GNP is beginning to match the United States, the corporation's first duty is to its employees, and it is not considered demeaning for the worker to identify with the organization that employs him or her. In Japanese industry, the adversary labor-management relationship is considered unhealthy and uneconomic, the survival of an elitest attitude from the industrial revolution. For the most part, corporate, not government, enterprises provide for employee welfare more efficiently and less bureaucratically. In fact, corporate elitism is frowned upon, and group harmony is accented. Interestingly enough, part of this new organizational culture in Japan resulted from the American occupation of their country. In Arab organizational cultures, personal relations and trust are paramount. Thus, Westerners who try to negotiate with Middle Eastern firms and their representatives, especially when attempting to act as a "middle man," do well when: (1) they are genuine and sympathetic while clarifying the options; (2) they present the possibilities so that everyone is a winner and saves "face"—maximize gains for each contestant, minimize risks and costs, and present opportunities for compromise; (3) they are a trust broker, so that the two parties can trust the "midwife" until they can learn to trust each other.

Every item in the last section on categories for analyzing organizational culture thus takes on an *intercultural* connotation. For instance, in the fifth classification, "Communication and Language," consider that a language is a means of communicating within a particular culture. There are approximately 3,000 different languages, and each represents a different perceptual world. Many nations may share an official language, such as English, but have a variety of versions of it, such as British or American. In India, the official language is Hindi, but English is a "link" language among fifteen major languages and innumerous dialects; organizations in that country may be expected to speak the official language, but only 30 % of the population do so, and personnel in many companies will probably speak the local language and all that it implies. Thus, in the matter of organizational communications, a social institution may reflect the nation's language homogeneity or heterogeneity.

To further illustrate this point, consider the cross-cultural implications of *time and time consciousness*. In some countries, company representatives may start a meeting within an hour of the time agreed upon, and the sequence of one's arrival at that staff conference may depend upon one's status in the organization, or one's age. The length of work days have great diversity in different cultures—in some starting and stopping is exact, and may be spelled out in a union contract, whereas in others it goes by the sunrise and sunset, or the heat of the day, or the seasons. The idea of coming late is very relative in macro-/microcultures—age, in some cultures, determines that older executives come last to business meetings. The time for training may depend on such cross-cultural factors as availability of people on their own, not company time; on the use of new educational technology; on new concepts of human resource development. The rhythm of life for a people is determined by their stage of human development; therefore for populations in the pre-industrial nations, time is shaped by the natural cycles of agriculture; whereas in industrialized nations, the artificial time of the clock and the assembly line regulate workers. In the superindustrial society, time becomes a scarce resource, while in underdeveloped nations time is abundant. Sociologist Daniel Bell reminds American "clock-watchers" that the computer with its nanoseconds is considered a time saver in organizational cultures of high technology. For some populatons, the rhythm of life is linear, but for others it is cyclical.

The culture of a work system must be adapted to the macroculture in which it operates. Yet organizational leaders everywhere can learn from each other, regardless of where in the world the entity functions.

The transnational corporation that moves beyond the culture of a single country and operates comfortably in the multicultures of many nations obviously will develop a unique microculture of its own. Its organization model and environment will reflect the synergy of the diverse macrocultures in which it functions, as well as the varying managerial approaches to business, government, and people. John Lutz, a principal in McKinsey and Company of New York, pointed up the pragmatic approach of multinational corporations in international business:

> How can management organize to deal with worldwide opportunities?
> First, worldwide enterprises organize themselves to carry out their inter-

national activities in different ways, *depending on their traditions*, the nature of their business, and the balance of centralized or decentralized decisions that stem from the particular marketplace they are serving.

Lutz further observed that to meet the challenge of geographic dispersion, organizational changes were necessary in terms of *corporate planning* regarding diversification of product line for world enterprise; in *finance*, where new systems for managing cash flow, as well as currency exchanges, to and from corporate headquarters; in *logistics*, relative to purchasing and traffic of material resources; in *personnel functions*, for the recruiting, development, transfer, promotion, and compensation of competent employees in all corners of the world regardless of nationality; in *public affairs*, so that actions are undertaken that integrate community concerns in both base and host country operations. Thus, far-flung business activities require a new organizational culture that is able to accommodate itself to cross-cultural realities.

The multinational entity becomes a conglomerate of organizational cultures. For example, through acquisitions and mergers, the mother corporation may develop a variety of overseas subsidiaries. The central base operation then impacts considerably upon the organizational culture of its affiliate, but that company abroad inputs and influences the headquarters' culture.

The multinational enterprise adapts to the larger culture in which it functions, depending on its experiences with the external environment. Vern Terpstra (1985) identifies five factors to be considered in international business:

Cultural Variability—the degree to which conditions within a macroculture are at a low or high, stable, or unstable rate. The more turbulent the macroculture, for instance, the more unpredictable are business operations. The internal structure and processes in that situation requiring rapid adjustment to change, would demand open channels of communication, decentralized decision-making, and predominance of local expertise.

Cultural Complexity—that is the issue of high and low context cultures to which we previously referred in Chapter 4. It requires a response from corporate leaders that considers the covert and overt approaches of the macroculture.

Cultural Hostility—the degree to which conditions locally are threatening to organizational goals, norms, values, et al. Depending upon how the transnational corporation is perceived, the indigenous environ may range from munificent to malevolent in terms of acceptability, cooperation, political climate, material and human resources, capital and good will. In response, the organizational culture may range from integration and collaboration to tightening up and finally being forced to leave.

Professor Terpstra maintains that the previous three dimensions occur within cultures, but that the next two can be observed among macrocultures.

Cultural Heterogeneity—the degree to which cultures are dissimilar or similar. It is easier for a transnational corporation to deal with a culture that is relatively homogeneous, or like the base culture (e.g., English-based multinationals would have an edge possibly in British Commonwealth nations). But when a culture is diverse and disparate, then it is difficult for the central headquarters to coordinate the behavior of subsidiaries and their employees. Management may have to be more differentiated, semiautonomous, and decentralized units may have to be established. Expatriates from the base culture may be more prone to culture shock on assignment in the host culture.

Cultural Interdependence—the degree of sensitivity of the culture to respond to conditions and developments in other cultures. This dimension may range from economic dependence on other nations for raw materials, supplies, and equipment, to adaptation and adoption of new technology and processes from other interacting cultures, to being subject to scrutiny in the host culture for attitudes and actions that occurred on the part of the corporation in another culture.

Thus, all such factors impact upon the multinational's organizational culture, influencing decisions, planning, information systems, and conflict resolution. Terpstra cites a variety of strategies that a transnational corporation can use to cope with the vagaries of international operations—environmental impact assessments, comparative and/or cluster analysis, cultural scanning and intelligence systems, computer simulations, social cost/benefit analysis, systems dynamics and modeling, social indicators/quality-of-life monitoring, risk analysis and scenario writing, trend extrapolation and technological forecasting, and establishment of external affairs units. For a multinational to be effective, synergy should occur between the host, base, and international business environments. It requires adaptations within the transnational organization's culture to factors of language and communication, law and politics, values and beliefs, education and training, technology and material resources, and local social organization.

Probably, the factor of greatest cross-cultural difference in organizations throughout the world is in the concept of management. Although there is a global sub-culture of management emerging, the previous five chapters have demonstrated the nuances or differences that each macroculture brings to the subject of leadership. Use of Appendix B, "Cross-Cultural Management," demonstrates this. For the truly global manager, there is much to be gained from mutual exchanges on this issue of organizational culture.

Is it any wonder that Peter Drucker suggested in a *Wall Street Journal* interview (June 4, 1980) that it is no longer a case of "what can we learn from

American management, but what can American managers learn from foreign management?" Here are a few of the trends abroad he suggested worth emulating:

1. Management demanding responsibility from workers down to the lowest level of the organization.
2. Customized employee fringe benefits based on individual need, which may include housing allowances, insurance options, etc.
3. A sense of marketing that means knowing what is of value to the customer, thinking in terms of market structures and specific markets, and aiming at global markets.
4. Marketing and management strategies based on innovation, replacing the old, outworked, or obsolete—many foreign business planning sessions start with the question, "What are the new things we are going to do?"
5. Separation of short from long-term expected results, permitting a second budget in corporations for expenditures over a long period of time.
6. Managers who perceive themselves as national assets and leaders responsible for development of proper policies in the national interests.

Drucker points out that many such overseas management trends may have originated in the United States, but were not put into practice here.

SYNERGY IN ORGANIZATIONAL CULTURE

Synergy is another dimension of organizational culture that takes on increasing importance as international business and government activities become more global in scope, more complex in practice, and more sophisticated in technology. In Chapter 1 we cited it as one of the characteristics of the global manager, expanding further on this vital quality in Chapter 4, that is, the need to create cultural synergy so that the enterprise values cooperation, collaboration, and team management. Promoting synergy in and through the organization is one of the characteristics of the new work culture.

To facilitate understanding of this key concept, imagine the following seven scenarios for which we will later provide examples of how synergistic relations can be fostered in acquisitions, relocation, structural change, personnel change, role change, consortium formation, and global consultation:

> • The chief executive officer of a large multinational corporation visits the facilities of a newly acquired subsidiary corporation to determine which of the parent company's policies, procedures, and personnel should be utilized in the merged firm, and which approaches or strategies should be retained. The assessment process will begin at lunch with the president of the acquired organization.

- A New England plant is being relocated to Alabama. Its employees have been given the opportunity to move to the South and join an enlarged workforce of local southerners. The plant manager is a technocrat from England who immigrated to the United States five years ago.
- A major retailer is in the midst of profound organizational change. A traditional enterprise with branches throughout the country, it is proud of its seventy-five years of customer service and the long employment records of its faithful employees. Declining sales, fierce competition, inflation impact, and like factors led to the election of a new chairman of the board. This administrator has brought in some very competent, modern managers, and together they have begun to shake up the whole "empire."
- A European conglomerate has purchased controlling rights of an American steel manufacturer. Key management positions have been filled with French, Italian, and German managers, and most of the competent American management has been retained. Plans are underway to improve operations and turn the company into a profitable venture.
- The management information systems (MIS) specialist is a relatively new position, surrounded by seeming magic and myth. But general managers are becoming less dependent upon the computer professionals in the data processing department. Now their own managers are more sophisticated at information processing, and all have access to their own microcomputers.
- Common Market partners are involved in a joint venture to produce an innovative airplane. It began with three major companies from three different countries, and eventually a fourth company/country entered into the agreement.
- A Canadian consulting firm agreed to assist a Mexican corporation in the use of advanced technology. It is part of a larger deal between the governments of both countries in which Mexican energy is to be supplied in return for Canadian expertise and equipment.

The common element in each of these scenarios is the opportunity to exercise leadership in cultural synergy. Differences in organizational cultures in these seven situations can either undermine the intended actions, or can be used to enhance goal achievement. Each cultural challenge will be addressed later in this chapter. But first, some further amplification on the world synergy seems to be in order.

Synergy, the dictionary assures us, is cooperative or combined action. It can occur when diverse or disparate groups of people work together. The objective is to increase effectiveness by sharing perceptions, insights, and knowledge. The complexity and shrinking of today's world literally forces people to *capitalize* on their differences. For example in each of the opening scenarios, the participants can either impose "their way" or organizational culture, upon the others, often to their mutual detriment, or they can be aware of each other's cultural strengths and biases, in terms of their national and organizational characters. But a better approach is to objectively evaluate what is of "value" in each of the existing enterprises, and build upon such foundations. The synergistic agents are sensitive to cultural differences and opportunities for *mutual* growth and development.

For example, a "high synergy corporation" would be one in which employees cooperated together for mutual advantage because the customs and traditions of that entity supported such behavior. In such a noncompetitive atmosphere the individual serves or works toward his/her own advantage and that of the group. Social and corporate obligations and responsibilities are put above personal desires or wishes. Personnel operate to ensure the mutual advantage from their common undertakings.

There are seven specific situations when synergy in organizational culture is most desirable. They are exemplified by the previous incidents, and they include:

Acquisition. Whenever a corporation acquires or merges with another entity domestically or internationally, synergy skill is required. For organizational effectiveness, there must be a synthesis of two distinct microcultures, not just an imposition by the more powerful company. This is particularly true in the case of a newly acquired subsidiary. The executives from the parent company can do much to facilitate the integration process if they will take time to analyze the subsidiary's culture by the ten parameters cited in the previous section. Furthermore, this merger of two organizational worlds and climates can be aided when management from the acquired firm shares its distinct culture with the other, helping them to understand policy, procedures, and processes, as well as corporate goals, attitudes, and strategies (Bing 1980). A week's "cultural awareness workshop" for the senior management of both organizations has many "bottom-line" implications and will foster more effective colleague relationships.

Relocation. Any time a company moves an existing facility and some of its personnel to another site, at home or abroad, synergistic efforts must be undertaken. People being up-rooted from a community where they are secure need assistance to integrate into the new setting, especially when there are significant geographic and cultural differences involved between the two locations. Such relocation services by the corporation must go beyond moving and new community information because employees require orientation to the realities and opportunities of the new cultural environment. "Culture shock" can be delimited within one's own country or overseas. Furthermore, the "locals" need assistance in accepting the new plant or office and its relocated employees. Popping a new enterprise into a small, unprepared community may not only offer jobs for the locals and improve their economy; it may also swamp their sewer and water facilities, and their educational and public services. Corporate management must cooperate with local officials so that the influx of people and money is planned and controlled. Further information on this issue is included in Chapters 8 and 9.

Structural/Environmental Change. When there is a major alteration within the organizational structure or environment, people should be prepared for the new shift in policy, procedure, product or service. Planned change strategies can be used to ready personnel for reorganization and renewal without abrupt distruption of the work climate. Sometimes the necessary changes are dictated by competition or growth. As of 1981, one hundred thirty American corporations reported growing at twice the normal growth rate of the past five years. Such rapid increases shortens planning time and sharpens the potential for conflict. The quickening of the work pace on understaffed operations can lead to greater resentment, exhaustion, and "burn out" on the part of employees. Pressure and stress can build up on the "fast track" even for managers. Involving personnel in cooperative efforts to regulate and control change or growth can counteract such system overload.

Personnel Change. Whenever the composition of a workforce shifts, planned endeavors are needed to integrate the "newcomers," while reducing the psychological threat to the "old-timers" and gaining their assistance in the effort. In addition to the hiring of large number of women or minorities into work environment, there might be an influx of migrant or refugee laborers.

Sometimes, Third Country nationals or foreign executives can cause the organization to become more heterogeneous and less homogeneous. However, these individuals may also enhance synergy. The *New York Times*, for example, recently published a feature on "foreign-born executives" who are successfully moving ahead within American corporations. As mature adults from different cultures and management backgrounds, these professionals have not only integrated into, but mastered the complexities of giant U.S. companies, even to the point of receiving major appointments in the federal government. This internationalization of big business is also an example of synergy in which the "authority of competence" is considered more important than the place of one's origin, or the person's skin color and sex. It requires a reeducation of locals as to the realities of the pluralistic or multicultural workplace, and of the valuable contributions of "foreigners." European business leaders not only bring unique perspectives and talents to their American corporations, but global insights for the international markets.

Role Change. The introduction of new technology into an organization usually means that personnel roles and relationships change. In the traditional industrial-age corporation, work disciplines, units, and departments were fairly stable and separate. But in complex, post-industrial organizations the divisions between line and staff are fluid and often nonexistent. The superindustrial "adhocracy" requires greater collaboration between specialists and general managers. Newly created disciplines, specializations, and some work units may be relatively temporary. Thus, new interpersonal skills are required that enable personnel to form quick, intense organizational relations of a cooperative, mission-oriented nature. This is evident in today's project/product teams and matrix management forms. More on this in the next chapter.

Consortium. If an organization or a state does not have the natural, material, or human resources to undertake something on its own, it must move outside its own orbit to seek partners who will join in the endeavor for mutual benefit. Synergy is required for a combination of institutions to pool their talent and capital for a successful operation. Project management, for instance, provides opportunities for diverse departments and activities within a single organization to come together to achieve desired objectives. This approach has brought together different companies from the same or several industries, from the same or many nations. The very complexities of the superindustrial society demands such collaboration, particularly in large-scale enterprises such as space exploration and research.

Global Consulting. Whenever a group of "experts" enter the organization culture of a client ostensibly to render help, synergistic skills are necessary. Knowingly or not, the representatives from a consulting group merge their organizational culture into the client's environment. When such assistance is rendered on an international scale, the intervention may also include two national cultures. Consultants should attempt to integrate themselves into the organizational space of their customers, and not impose the mind-set or systems of the advising group. If an American accounting firm institutes a general management consulting division and expands into the world market, their accounting and financial analysis may also be culturally based and even biased. For synergy to occur in the consultation of their American representative, their consultants should examine how the financial practices and systems in the host culture work. Determine then what approaches of modern "American" business accounting would be appropriate, especially since much of it is based on disappearing "Industrial Age" thinking.

These seven dimensions can be used as a model for better understanding synergy in organizational culture. Perhaps some specific examples of how such synergy occurs will make the point. The following illustrations are either drawn directly from the authors' consulting experience, or from published accounts.

During the previous industrial stage of human development, there was much concern about the formation of cartels, and antitrust legislation resulted to prevent corporate collusion. But economics have so radically changed that the very survival of some business enterprises is dependent upon the sharing of information and cooperation within the same industry. Destructive competition may be a relic of the past that some national industries can no longer afford. Archaic government regulations not only need to be revised, but new laws must be formulated that will facilitate corporate synergy, especially when business entities move beyond their own national borders. The following are examples of how some corporations have addressed their synergistic needs:

Multinational Acquisitions. Westinghouse Electric Corporation, Pittsburgh based, is one of the twenty largest corporations in the world. A subsidiary like Westinghouse Learning Corporation moves beyond education and acquires companies throughout the nation in school supplies, computer operations, and even bottling. Each of the firms taken over has its own particular organizational culture, sometimes reflected by the locality in which the subsidiary's headquarters are located. When Westinghouse Broadcasting moves beyond the acquisition of television and radio stations into housing and construction, the "Pittsburgh engineers" from the conglomerate's corporate headquarters are far afield and often into alien company environments. But when Westinghouse buys almost controlling interest in companies in Australia or Africa, the organizational culture is extended into "foreign cultures," which offer great challenges to the corporate executives back in the U.S.A. To promote synergy, this transnational enterprise brings managers from its subsidiaries and affiliates around the world to Pittsburgh for management development, which may range from computer seminars to cultural awareness workshops. Yet, so much more remains to be done in preparing cosmopolitan overseas representatives, especially among the legal staffs who are in the forefront of acquisitions and negotiations. Remember the message of Chapter 3?

Texacana Relocations. General Motors, Detroit based, established a twin plant relationship between its Mansfield, Ohio facility and a new assembly operation in Juarez, Mexico. The American management and their families were relocated to El Paso, Texas. From there the U.S. managers commute daily across the border to the Mexican plant where they train and consult with competent Mexican executives who are to take over total operations within several years. To promote transnational synergy and link the new enterprise with other nearby GM plants in Mexico, organization development specialists from the company arranged for language and culture training at American universities for the Mexican and American managers and their families. But how much help was provided to the transplanted "Ohioians" to adjust to life in a Texas border town? A broad spectrum of "relocation services" should be offered to employees, as well as their families, if new adjustments are to be facilitated, productivity maintained, and change opportunities utilized.

Parent/Subsidiary Change. TRW, Cleveland based, was a traditional industrial organization. Then it got into the space business through a subsidiary established in Redondo Beach, California. But TRW Systems was unable to operate like its parent company. Its personnel were largely knowledge workers, most with advanced degrees. Its product was not primarily intended for this planet. In fact, the problems connected with "getting a man on the moon" were so complex, that entirely new management forms and organizational models had to be created. Thus, TRW Systems pioneered matrix management in which a professional might report simultaneously to several managers. To deal with the organizational problems involved, behavioral scientists within the company organized "team building sessions" so that employees would learn to work together more effectively in this different organizational culture. Eventually, the OD specialists were brought back to Cleveland to show the parent corporation how they might undergo organizational renewal in a planned way—such changes do not come easily or quickly.

Refugee Influx. Coca Cola Bottling Company, Atlanta based, has plants all over Florida. In the past their employees were usually white southern males, until they began to bring in large numbers of female and black personnel. But all were still largely Americans. Then the Cuban refugees in the 1970s and '80s began to seek asylum in this southern state and went to work for the refreshment firm. Suddenly, the plant culture began to become multicultural and bilingual. Some of the new Hispanic employees were from a higher educational level than the American southerners, but not at the same financial level.

The challenge for synergy has stiffened with the influx of many exiled Haitians seeking employment with the soft drink firm. These black West Indians are of African heritage, speak Creole or French, and have come to America seeking a better way of life. They are in difficult economic straits, mainly possessing agricultural skills and limited education. With government assistance, the number of Cuban and Haitian workers is likely to increase in the Coke plants, so many of the native white and black Americans are somewhat disgruntled about the situation. Thus, personnel changes are causing swift organizational changes, and "preventative maintenance" is in use among the work force. Management takes steps to promote a more cooperative plant climate, so that career development for all enhances its human assets.

Role Challenges. N.V. Philips, Eindhoven (Netherlands) based, has a huge multinational enterprise that is linked together by sophisticated information and technical systems. From a small Dutch light bulb factory in 1891, it has expanded to a vast array of electronic productions: from cassettes and shavers to washing machines and television systems. A firm that struggled under Nazi occupation in the 1940s, it has emerged as a worldwide concern in 70 countries employing more than 380,000 people. Furthermore, it has accepted multinational responsibility in Third World countries for improving the communities in which it functions. To meet the synergistic needs of this superindustrial entity, Philips has formed a unit devoted to organizational renewal. Social researchers and internal consultants examine various aspects of work and organization in order to design more meaningful jobs, improve strategic planning, and prevent dissonance between information and control systems. In addition to such efforts to bring organizational culture in tune with contemporary work realities, industrial relations and international personnel have inaugurated sophisticated training in cultural awareness for expatriate managers. Since 1960, this Netherland conglomerate has been involved in work humanization programs. Even the roles of people on the assembly line have been changed by the establishment of autonomous work groups. As a result, Philips' internal studies indicated productivity doubled and worker job satisfaction increased. Role change for Philips and its people is a continuing process.

Airbus Consortium. Airbus Industrie, Europe based, is an exceptional example of how synergistic effort can overcome corporate, cultural, and national rivalries. It successfully produces the A300 and A310 wide-body jets which by 1980 had seized a fifth of the world's commercial-aircraft market. France and Germany each own 38% of the venture, while Britain has 20%. Two German firms merged to form Deutsche Airbus and make the fuselage and vertical tail. CASA of Spain owns 4% of the project and builds the horizontal tail. France's Aérospatiale produces the cockpit, part of the center fuselage, and assembles the aircraft into final form. Despite differences in management philosophy and practice, worker organization, and even languages, this fragile balance of interests converged and achieved its goals. This technological innovation even provides the option of either the British Rolls-Royce or an American Pratt & Whitney engine.

A variety of organizational problems had to be confronted in each of the national components, but the cooperative endeavor pushed ahead with great efficiency under a flow chart that spread over the map of Europe. Decentralized production makes it easier to increase output to meet growing demand, and when extra workers are needed, they are drawn from partner companies' other projects. Technocrats have jumped traditional barriers among people on the continent, and choose personnel not "on the color of their passports" but on their ability to do the job. Even the U.S. Eastern Airlines bought the craft because it was fuel-efficient and reliable. Moving toward a European family-style operation, Airbus Industrie has resurrected the civilian aircraft business on that continent through the principle of collaboration, and is now into producing a new generation of air carriers.

International Consulting. International Consultants Foundation, Washington and Stockholm based, provides a model for cooperation among professional consultants for their common benefit. Obviously, the major consulting firms have many resources to engage in a world practice. But independent consultants have limited resources, and only themselves to offer to their colleagues for professional development and support. Thus, an American and an Englishman combined their talents to formulate a network of consultants from a variety of disciplines who operate on a global basis. They have met annually in such diverse places as the Bahamas, Copenhagen, Washington, D.C., Calgary, and Dublin. From these conferences, proceedings are published on their insights, along with occasional monographs on special topics of interest to those in the consulting field. An annual registry of members provides a description of each consultant's competencies, and is used for joint marketing efforts. A periodic newsletter keeps members up-to-date on matters of concern. The executive board is multinational and multicultural, and the two key offices are rotated between Americans and Europeans.

When such international consultants collaborate on a global project, it represents the merger of national and organizational cultures. Similarly, synergy must then be sought with the client's organizational culture. Regardless of where the customer may be located in the international marketplace, the external consultant must enter into that organizational world and operate effectively within *that* space.

Whether an internal or external consultant, one must realize that behavioral science technology is largely a product of Western culture. Therefore, it has to be adapted or enhanced in different cultural settings. Many advanced technological innovations may or may not be appropriate in whole or part, depending on the local context.

At the national level, a Society of Professional Management Consultants promotes similar synergistic collaboration. SPMC is even encouraging local consultants roundtables (CONRO) as a form of networking. More on synergy among professionals and technicians in Chapter 12.

PEOPLE AND FUTURE ORGANIZATIONAL CULTURES

There has to be a fit between people and their organizational culture if synergy is to occur. In the future global managers will direct more effort toward promoting that match.

One strategy is to carefully search and select personnel who will be comfortable in a particular system, then acculturate them to a strong culture. Richard Pascale describes how many of the best-managed companies get recruits who adopt the corporate collection of shared values, beliefs, and practices as their own (*Fortune*, May 28, 1984). Once on board, there is a "socialization" process that ensures a unity in image and purpose. Great American corporations like IBM, Proctor & Gamble, Morgan Guaranty & Trust, according to this Stanford business professor, excel at this. Rigorous screening by line management, intensive simulation training, immersion of recruits into demanding programs, and promotions based on performance progress are among the methods employed. Each step in this career development involves quantifiable measure of performance. Proctor & Gamble, for instance, uses three factors to measure managers—building business volume and profit, and conducting planned change. IBM tracks adherence to its major values and policies, and has a mechanism for disciplining violators of corporate norms (a period in the penalty box, such as assignment to a less meaningful job in a less desirable location). There is also positive reinforcement by rewards, a powerful means for reinforcing corporate values and beliefs—who gets rewarded and why is related to performance. One of IBM's strong mechanisms for acculturation of employees is education and training. In 1988 alone, it invested $1.1 billion in human resource development and assessment. Because this union-free organization spends $350 a day for one trainee in a conventional classroom, it is moving rapidly toward promoting personnel learning, empowerment, and responsibility building by interactive self-study and tutored video models.

Such strong culture firms further ensure commitment with transcendental values. With IBM, it's a service philosophy that is overriding; with Delta Air Lines, it's family feeling and teamwork that focuses upon customers; with Digital Equipment, the emphasis is on innovation creating freedom with responsibility. These organizational cultures also reaffirm continually the company folklore on watershed events in their pasts and "how we do things around here." Behavior models among management display the same traits and become mentors to young protégés. Proctor & Gamble brand managers exhibit extraordinary consistency—they are usually analytical, energetic, and adept at motivating others. To better manage organizational energies, the strong culture offers a consistent set of implicit understandings that help in dealing with ambiguities of business politics and relationships. Pascale reminds us that cultural guidelines make organizational life less capricious, improve organizational communication and trust, and empower employees by supplying continuity and clarity, which then reduces anxiety.

Another strategy is to adapt the organization to its people, especially in terms of a particular place or time. It is not only plant and equipment that can rust and deteriorate. Within human systems, values and norms, policies and practices, leadership and technologies can also lag or become obsolete. That may call for planned renewal when the people and their productivity are being undermined by outdated or archaic approaches or processes. In the behavioral sciences, technologies have been created for such organization development (OD). Consultants, either internal or external, are used to solve people and structural problems, while facilitating planned change by management of the organization's culture. More recently, a new type of consultant is emerging who is concerned about promoting organizational transformation (OT). The emphasis is upon the practices of transformational leadership or new management; upon organizational vision and futuring regarding what the organization should become in the light of changing times and peoples.

Corporate culture is dynamic, and leaders should not underestimate the adaptive changes necessary for survival (Toffler 1985).

The new organizational culture should enable people to

1. Spend their lives on something worthwhile that will outlast them.
2. Live a life of consequence without stress and undue cultural restraints.
3. Preserve for tomorrow what we can use up today.
4. Value the work as much as we did the work ethic.
5. Accept differences and appreciate similarities.
6. Seize opportunities for personal and professional development, while overcoming the disadvantages to developing one's potential.

Relative to the people in tomorrow's organization, it is obvious that these will be largely knowledge/technical and service workers of multicultural backgrounds. Because managerial skills will be scarce and in demand, one can envision the development of a cadre of executives and administrators capable of being transferred across the traditional boundaries of nations, industries, and public/private sectors. Dr. Chris Argyris of Yale University believes that the organizational culture of the future will include personnel policies that:

1. Encourage employees to be authentic with one another and management.
2. Fully appreciate the value of human resources, as well as other factors that contribute to organization success.
3. Foster individual responsibility for career development.
4. Take a holistic approach to promoting organizational health.

Significantly, management consultants are beginning to appreciate that the informal culture of an organization has as much influence on corporate effectiveness as the formal structure of jobs authority, technical and financial procedures. Thus, the target now for planned change must be the organizational climate, along with the work attitudes and habits of employees. Organizations of the future will be excellent to the extent that they maximize their human energy assets, and minimize their human energy losses. They must be able to capitalize on ad hoc, unstructured relationships among people, to cope effectively with uncertainty and accelerating change, and to cooperate in multicultural environments.

Many scholars believe that we are now entering into the period of the "Third Industrial Revolution." Mechanization and computerization were the focus of the first and second industrial revolutions. But the current revolution, sometimes called metaindustrial, centers around the needs and aspirations of employees in the design and implementation of production and other work systems. Thus, the shift in these three work revolutions has been from products to things to people and information processing (Harris 1983 and 1985).

To humanize the workplace, Harvard professors Neal Herrick and Michael Maccoby (1981) propose the application of four principles:

1. *Security*—employees must be free from fear and anxiety concerning health and safety, income, and future employment.
2. *Equity*—employees should be compensated commensurate with their contributions to the value of the service or product.
3. *Individuation*—employees should have maximum autonomy in determining the rhythm of their work and in planning how it should be done.
4. *Democracy*—employees should, whenever possible, manage themselves, be involved in decision-making that affects their work, and accept greater responsibility in the work of the organization.

Efforts to improve the organizational culture based on such premises can be found throughout the world, especially in North America and western Europe. Managers, consultants, and researchers are cooperating in sharing their findings relative to quality of worklife and participation experiments.

Convergence of endeavors to "humanize the organizational environment or work culture" is happening on a universal scale and calls for more synergy on the part of corporate and government leaders.

Organizational Change in Transitional Economies

For the decade of the '90s, remarkable alterations are underway within organizations in the Second World of communist-run governments and the Third World of developing countries. The transition is from centralized planning of socialist economies to a free-market economy and political democracy. The trend is evident from Eastern Europe, such as in Hungary and Poland, to Africa in mildly socialist states, such as Tanzania. The impact of these changes is being felt even within the USSR and the PRC. As the macroculture shifts, so does the microculture of institutions. Thus, organizational cultures within these societies are experiencing profound transformations. Free enterprise within the private sector is being encouraged, while the public sector companies are being sold to investors of cooperatives.

The most dramatic example of this is in Germany within its two Western and Eastern states. As political unification moves ahead, economic integration progresses. West German corporations are acquiring or merging with DDR counterparts, such as in airlines, chemical, automotive, and media industries. Consider the executive challenges involved in integrating such disparate organizational cultures, one conditioned by capitalist and the other by communist systems! Imagine the differences in workers—one group attuned to participation, innovation, and profit motivation, and the other to totalitarianism, bureaucracy, and autocratic management.

SUMMARY

Those who would be global managers are able to understand and analyze the impact of culture on organizations. Furthermore, we should lead in influencing cultural change within our institutions or systems. When groups of people formulate an organization, its culture reflects that of the larger community, and impacts behavior both within and without the enterprise. The human and material energy exchanged through the organization is affected by culture, which may foster or undermine productivity and profits. Organizational culture may motivate or obstruct high performance.

Whether in a corporation, association, or government agency, culture is multifaceted and can be diagnosed in various ways, such as in terms of the subsystems that compose it. One model proposed in this chapter uses ten major classifications for analysis: (1) organizational identity or image and mission (its rationale); (2) organizational space and scope (its demarcations); (3) organizational attitudes, beliefs, and myths (its philosophy); (4) organizational values and norms (its priorities and standards); (5) organizational communication and languages (its media and message); (6) organizational processes and learnings (its operational mode); (7) organizational personnel and leadership (its recognitions and rewards for behavior models); (8) organizational rites, rituals and feeding habits (its customs and traditions); (9) organizational relationships (its roles and their interface); (10) organizational look, style and reputation (its appearance and public aura). This paradigm was then utilized to characterize the culture of a prominent global corporation in the energy field—Schlumberger.

When an organization's culture moves beyond national borders, it should adapt to the differences within a host macroculture. Transnational enterprises take on the coloration of multicultural operations and personnel. To create synergy in organizational culture requires new managerial skills. These were seen in the context of seven organization cultural opportunities for cooperation: (1) acquisitions or mergers; (2) relocation of facilities and/or personnel; (3) structural or environmental change; (4) personnel change; (5) role change; (6) formation of a consortium or joint venture; and (7) global consultation.

Finally, the future of organizational cultures was forecast, especially in terms of their fit to people and adaptations to new workplace realities.

Remember, organizational culture has been described as an *invisible giant* because it is so pervasive and powerful—it's simply "the way we do things around here." That *way* changes at various stages of the organization's development, especially when a corporation goes from domestic to international, from traditional to new management, or from manufacturing to service orientation. Organizational culture can be a bridge or barrier to change. When it's the latter, effective leadership alters the culture. Above all, the image projected to the world outside the organization must be in harmony with the reality of the internal culture.

7
Managers as Influencers
of Work and Team Cultures

Culture is like a diamond—hold the jewel to light, turn it, and we get another perspective. In considering how it impacts management, we can view it not only in terms of the organization, but also in the context of work in general, and teams or small groups in particular. Chapter 1 emphasized that a global manager understands the concept of work culture, and exercises leadership in altering it when the work environment is out of tune with reality. We cited the work cultures of the past that were created to meet human needs at different stages of development—hunting/tribal, agricultural/rural, and industrial/urban. Now we have the opportunity to influence the creation of a new work culture that is emerging—metaindustrial or technological. It has also been described as cybercultural and superindustrial.

TRANSFORMING THE WORK CULTURE

The end of the Second World War also hastened the demise of the industrial work culture centered around factories, the traditional manufacturing industries, the production of things, and bureaucratic work systems. With advances in communications, computers, microelectronics, and biotechnology, the workplace began to be revolutionized. **New management** strategies and styles became necessary, while organization models and designs were being changed. Two AT&T reports (Coleman 1980) correctly identified the shift to the Information Society, and the challenge to create structures and strategies suitable to the metaindustrial age. George Kozmetsky (1985) stated the issue succinctly:

> The first need in the 1980s for creative and innovative management is to understand that we are in a period of transformation, and not simply transition. Today's managerial and economic uncertainties will not simply disappear by expanding our high technology industries or revitalizing our basic industries. These are transitional processes.

Kozmetsky argues for a transformation of the culture through both social and technological innovation. As a co-founder of Teledyne, Inc. and former dean of University of Texas' school of business, he can appreciate how the **new technologies** are the principal driving forces of the emerging work culture. Table 7-1 illustrates his schemata of technology for now and tomorrow. As this research and resulting technology is transferred from one country to another, from the military to civilian market, from the government or university laboratory to industry or hospitals, a cross-cultural experience occurs. The Technology Transfer Society (#302, 7033 Sunset Blvd., Los Angeles, Ca. 90028), for instance, probes how to facilitate this transmission through interdisciplinary and synergistic approaches. *Leading-Edge Technologies* is a periodical that keeps a global manager abreast of new technical developments. Available three times a year, it is a joint venture of the KMPG Peat Marwick High Technology Practice and the University of Texas (c/o Institute of Constructive Capitalism, 2815 San Gabriel Ave., Austin, TX 78705, USA).

Work culture manifests patterns, explicit and implicit, of worker behavior related to their occupational efforts at a point in time and a stage of economic and human development. Such vocational achievement is communicated through symbols and embodied in artifacts, like computer chips, laser art, electronic banking and the other applications of modern technologies. We humans, as tool-creating beings, have also evolved in the sophistication and pervasiveness of our technology. The metaindustrial arts and sciences now dominate

Table 7-1
Technological Drivers of the New Work Culture

1. Microelectronics	Advanced chips, very high-speed integrated circuits (VHSIC); Advanced software applications; Personal computers; Distributed computing; Unique databases.
2. Medicine	Biotechnology; Psychotherapy; Transplantation; Birth control; Genetic Engineering; Medical electronics.
3. Materials	Special application designs; Photosynthesis; Supercold technology.
4. Industrial and scientific instruments	Robotics; Automated batch production; Control electronics.
5. Energy	Solar; Fusion; Coal technology; Satellite power stations; Geothermal; Biomass.
6. Defense technologies	Electronic warfare; Nuclear; Biological; Economic.
7. Agricultural technologies	Genetic modification and selection; Electrostatic spraying; Waste management; Nuclear radiation.
8. Water	Desalinization; Growth regulation; Conservation; Weather modification; Transportation.
9. Other	Airwaves and communication; Construction; Transportation.

* Reprinted with permission from *Transformational Management* by George Kozmetsky (Cambridge, MA: Ballinger/Harper & Row, 1985).

both our global culture and work environment. The very space technologies that permit our entry into the high frontier spin off the high technologies that alter and improve life on this planet.

It is impossible here to fully describe this new work culture, but Table 7-2 outlines this metaindustrial work scene in terms of eight classifications, comparable to some explained in the last chapter.

Table 7-2
The Metaindustrial Work Culture*

Components of Organizational Culture	Organizational Manifestations	Metaindustrial Organizational Illustrations
Rationale and Identity	Reasons for existing Self-image Beliefs, attitudes Philosophy Space, boundaries Strategies, structures	Profitable, quality service, transnational system Energy exchange system Promotion of innovation, synergy, excellence Corporate social responsibility Business computer or conceptual modeling; futuristic, long-term planning; goal- and results-oriented.
Purposes and Standards	Mission, goals Objectives Corporate assumptions Norms Priorities, schedules Performance criteria Personnel rules Codes of ethics	Multinational operations; Pacific Rim focus MBO system to link levels, operations Use of new technologies, including robotics, to facilitate mission Criteria of competence; creativity; tough-minded analysis High achievement; performance emphasis Rules customized, developed by implementers High standards, integrity; culturally sensitive behavior; commission, yes; bribery no
Look and Style	Corporate leadership style Policies, procedures Time sense Appearance, dress	Participative; consensus oriented Management of responsibility, accountability

(table continued on next page)

Table 7-2 (Continued)
The Metaindustrial Work Culture*

Components of Organizational Culture	Organizational Manifestations	Metaindustrial Organizational Illustrations

	Food, fitness habits
	Corporate environment
		24-hour operations;
		  long-term; futuristic
		Informal, casual appropriate
		Healthful diet; wellness
		  programs
		Dynamic, flexible,
		  stimulating environment

Processes and Activities	Operational practices,
	  projects
	Products, services
	Manufacturing, technology
	R&D
	Systems and program
	  emphasis
		Matrix, team management
		Knowledge, information
		  processing
		Microelectronic technologies
		Technical, human factor
		  research
		Interdisciplinary, software
		  creation

Communications and Information Systems	Formal, informal systems
	External, internal systems
	Management info systems
	  (MIS)
	Community, government
	  relations
	Specialized languages,
	  vocabularies, codes,
	  signals
		Functional, open, authentic,
		  circular
		Mass media, closed circuit
		  TV; feedback
		Centralized EDP,
		  decentralized minicomputer
		Synergistic partnerships
		Computerized languages,
		  security systems; nonverbal
		  awareness; multilevel
		  communications and
		  interactions

Human Resource and Personnel Patterns	Recruitment and selection
	Role and task assignments
	Career, professional
	  development
	Education, training
	Skills acquisition, learning
	Performance regulation,
	  control
	Human energy
	  conservation, utilization
		EEO, pluralistic; competency
		  criteria
		Broad, flexible; self-designed
		Investment in human assets
		Teleconferencing;
		  teleprocessing
		CAI, self-learning AV systems
		Results- and achievement-
		  oriented; monitoring by
		  individual and team
		Emphasis on actualizing
		  human potential

Interpersonal Relations	Organizational networks Personnel and contractor relations Client, customer relations	Global electronic connections Integrated, helful Consultative, facilltative Robotics interface

Table 7-2 (Continued)
The Metaindustrial Work Culture*

Components of Organizational Culture	Organizational Manifestations	Metaindustrial Organizational Illustrations
	Human-machine relations Intra-, inter-group, subsidiary relations Intercultural relations	Cooperative, collaborative Sensitive, skillful, interdependent
Recognition and Rewards	Quality of work life and morale Personnel needs and motivations Employee status and respect Intrinsic, extrinsic rewards Compensation plans Incentives, ownership	Increase employee control over work space Ego, self-fulfillment emphasis to energize Democratization, participation opportunities More autonomy, professionalization Tailor to individual needs, choices Profit sharing, stock options, formation of multinational operatives

* Extracted with permission from Harris, P. R. *New Worlds, New Ways, New Management* (Ann Arbor, MI: Masterco Press/AMACOM, 1983).

For the past forty years a wide range of behavioral scientists, in cooperation with executives and other organizational leaders, have been engaged in transforming the work environment from that of the industrial age toward the directions indicated in the above summary. Wayne Holtzman, a University of Texas psychology professor, highlighted one such research effort for the improvement of work life quality:

> A good example is the major program for organizational assessment developed at Michigan's Institute for Social Research. Supported by both the Ford Foundation and the U. S. Department of Commerce, this research program includes a number of quality-of-work-life projects representing an effort unprecedented in scope, magnitude, and sophistication. Work experiments of this type are generally carried out on factory workers who participate directly in the change program. Various experimental techniques are tried, such as forming autonomous work groups, rotating workers through different tasks to provide enrichment and variety, providing special training in interpersonal skills, giving a feedback of results as changes are implemented, altering the physical or technical setting in order to form whole task groups, and changing the reward system to reinforce group performance (Charnes and Cooper 1984).

This is typical of the efforts, especially of a small group nature, to help employees in the transition to the new work culture. But what about management?

The authors have sensed that high tech and fast growth work environments may be the harbingers of tomorrow's work culture. So consider the culture shock of smokestack managers who try to switch into the high tech environment. John Bussey did a feature on these adjustment problems for the *Wall Street Journal* (January 10, 1985). Trauma results because of work culture differences between industrial and metaindustrial businesses. The following items from Bussey's article illustrate the acculturation problems:

1. Smokestack industry gets hung up on the elegance of decisions versus the substance.
2. Managerial skills and attitudes acquired in basic industries do not always transfer into new technology jobs.
3. Long-term employment, continuity, and status is not normal in the high tech culture. It is a fast track world in which products become obsolete in months, and manufacturers may rapidly switch to totally new product lines.
4. The high tech work experience is like riding a roller coaster from boom to bust to boom again, in which career safety and security has been replaced by innovation and creative risk management with independence prized more than adherence to corporate policies—the work is both demanding but thrilling while life is lived on the edge.
5. The new work environment is both market and technology driven, requiring managers to be familiar with technology terminology, concepts and journals, while emphasizing informality in everything from dress to office appearance.

Such differences explain why one former chemical executive discovered that he could not fit into the culture of a Silicon Valley firm, and why others experience disorientation as they try to make the cross-over into the metaindustrial work scene. It is why we noted in our opening chapter that all management today, in a sense, is cross-cultural. It is why as consultants we are finding more demands for our services related to the transition into the new work culture, than the entry into a foreign culture abroad.

Our research has identified ten general characteristics of the emerging work culture (Harris 1985). Workers at all levels in the future will generally manifest or seek *more*:

1. Enhanced quality of work life.
2. Autonomy and control over their work space.
3. Organizational communication and information orientation.
4. Participation and involvement in the enterprise.
5. Creative organizational norms or standards.

6. High performance and improved productivity.
7. Emphasis on new technology utilization.
8. Emphasis on research and development.
9. Emphasis on entrepreneurialism/intrapreneurialism.
10. Informal and synergistic relationship.

In the context of the emerging work culture, let us examine a few of these trends in a little detail. Take the second and fourth items, the desire for more control and for more involvement. John Lawrence (*Los Angeles Times,* March 31, 1985) relates this to power sharing, which he thinks may transform the workplace. Even the language of business changes to accommodate this development—"informating," "self-managing," and "manufacturing professionals" (to replace production workers) are some examples of the new terminology. It is reflective of the movement toward more participative forms of organization, in which "commitment" replaces "control" as a management emphasis. The computer provides more information to more people at work, spreading out the decision-making and judgments (e.g., informating process). The net result in operations is that everyone, in a sense, becomes a manager and more self-managing.

Or consider item nine on the entrepreneurial spirit, which is not only more evident in the U.S.A. today, but in China and even within the U.S.S.R. Table 7-3 illustrates the differences between entrepreneurial and administrative cultures.

All of the entrepreneurial characteristics described in Table 7-3 are appropriate for the new, metaindustrial, work culture, whereas those listed for the administrative characteristics are more suited to the disappearing industrial work culture. Thus, the global manager is faced with a transition and must practice a form of transformational management that enhances the ten trends described.

Return to the second and last classifications—more autonomy and synergistic relations. Another major manifestation of these trends is in team management. Knowledge workers of today and tomorrow want to share in the managerial responsibilities of planning, problem-solving, and decision-making. They welcome intense, although at times temporary involvement and ad hoc relationships, such as are featured in the new matrix organization, or project/product team. Therefore, we will devote the remainder of this chapter to the subject of team culture and management.

Perhaps our rationale for this can be better understood by ending this section with two more mini cases:

- The Wang Company has been noted as a well managed, high flying and profitable firm whose corporate comportment is typical of the new work culture. Its core product has been word processing systems includ-

(text continued on page 176)

Table 7-3

The Entrepreneurial vs. Administrative Culture*

	Entrepreneurial Focus		Administrative Focus	
	Characteristics	Pressures	Characteristics	Pressures
Strategic Orientation	Driven by perception of opportunity	Diminishing opportunities; Rapidly changing technology, consumer economics, social values, and political rules	Driven by controlled resources	Social contracts; Performance measurement criteria; Planning systems and cycles
Commitment to Seize Opportunities	Revolutionary, with short duration	Action orientation; Narrow decision windows; Acceptance of reasonable risks; Few decision constituencies	Evolutionary, with long duration	Acknowledgment of multiple constituencies; Negotiation about strategic course; Risk reduction; Coordination with existing resource base
Commitment of Resources	Many stages, with minimal exposure at each stage	Lack of predictable resource needs; Lack of control over the environment; Social demands for appropriate use of resources; Foreign competition; Demands for more efficient resource use	A single stage, with complete commitment out of decision	Need to reduce risk; Incentive compensation; Turnover in managers; Capital budgeting systems; Formal planning systems

* Reprinted with permission, H. H. Stevenson and D. E. Gumpert, "The Heart of Entrepreneurship," *Harvard Business Review*, March–April, 1985:89.

Table 7-3 (Continued)
The Entrepreneurial vs. Administrative Culture*

	Entrepreneurial Focus		Administrative Focus	
	Characteristics	Pressures	Characteristics	Pressures
Control of Resources	Episodic use or rent of required resources	Increased resource specialization Long resource life compared with need Risk of obsolescence Risk inherent in the identified opportunity Inflexibility of permanent commitment to resources	Ownership of employment of required resources	Power status, and financial rewards. Coordination of activity Efficiency measures Inertia and cost of change Industry structures
Management Structure	Flat, with multiple informal networks	Coordination of key noncontrolled resources Challenge to hierarchy Employees' desire for independence	Hierarchy	Need for clearly defined authority and responsibility Organizational culture Reward systems Management theory

(text continued from page 173)

ing more than one terminal. But rapid changes in the high tech market now favor unified, computer-based office systems that encompass word processors, personal and microcomputers, telephone switchboards, and other new communication components. Among the reasons for Wang's having difficulties in meeting this challenge is that the corporation has had separate R & D teams for its word-processing and data-processing products. These teams did not interface with one another, and when it came time to integrate personnel from the two groups, they found it hard to communicate and cooperate with people there from their counterpart group. After having been king of their market corner, Wang is having to fight back to gain its former leadership.

(Los Angeles Times, February 23, 1985)

• For Honeywell's Aerospace and Defense Units, an interest in teamwork and participation grew from the desire of management to be progressive, as well as from the nature of the technology and the structures required for it. The value of collaboration and teamwork has long been understood in the aerospace industry, which pulls together functional specialists to work on complex projects. To accommodate these needs, the matrix organization was resorted to which provides dual or multiple roles for reporting purposes. Further participation was promoted through wide use of quality circles. The goal is to mobilize more people in problem-solving for improved task performance (R. M. Kanter in Kimberly and Quinn 1984).

Multicultural Workforce

The North American workforce is changing so dramatically that books and video series now address the topic of *valuing diversity* (Copeland Griggs Productions, 302 23rd Ave., San Francisco, CA 94121, USA; ODT Associates, P.O. Box 134, Amherst, MA 01004, USA; Crisp Publications, 95 1st St., Los Altos, CA 94022 USA). The diversity in the work environment ranges from the talent of individuals to a new range of problems. For some, the latter are expressions of "future shock"—the inability to cope with too-rapid changes, leading in turn to various kinds of substance abuse from drugs to alcohol. The globalization of health problems and disease is most evident in new toxic pollutants on the job to the current plague of acquired immune deficiency, resulting in new training programs and visual aids for managers (e.g., *AIDS in the Workplace*, Films Inc., 5547 North Ravenswood Ave., Chicago, IL 60640-9979, USA).

Perhaps this kaleidoscopic workforce is manifested most in high tech and health care industries. In the U.S., for instance, a shortage of qualified engineers, scientists, mathematicians, nurses, and other technicians has brought about an influx of such professionals from abroad. Other social forces contribute to diversification in the corporate world, ranging from cycles of immigration and more working women to equal opportunity and affirmative action legislation. The results are seen in:

- Inhouse training for managers in cultural differences, how to communicate with employees who have English as a second language, how to avoid sexism and bias in work relations.
- Organizational policy and emphasis on the worth of individuals and capitalizing on their unique strengths, regardless of their age, gender, race, religion or origin.
- Removal of hidden obstacles or "glass ceilings" that prevent women, minorities, and foreigners from advancing within the organization.
- Marketing strategies aimed at multicultural, diverse consumers or customers. (Epstein, 1989; Glover and Shames, 1989; Lauffer, 1985; Morrison et al., 1987, 1988).

The need for such positive approaches can be confirmed by sociologist, John P. Fernandez, who for the past sixteen years has questioned over 17,000 employees of two dozen of the largest American corporations regarding racial and sexual prejudice at work (*Los Angeles Times*, April 17, 1988, p. 5). Two-thirds saw evidence of sex discrimination on their jobs, while 60% saw signs of racism. Such undesirable behavior grew more intense as women and minorities advanced into management. Is it any wonder that consultants dealing with such difficulties predict that by the year 2000, white males will have to become bicultural, while managers who haven't learned to manage diversity will be considered incompetent?

SYNERGY IN TEAM MANAGEMENT

In this post-industrial period of human development, traditional organizational models and managerial styles are gradually being replaced. They are inadequate and unproductive with the new knowledge workers. Therefore, a major transition is underway in social systems from "disappearing bureaucracies" to "emerging ad hocracies." In these turbulent times, leaders facilitate the transcendence from past to futuristic operations by promoting matrix or team management approaches. Whether the strategy is called a project, task force, product or business systems team, or ad hoc planning committee, work is organized around a "temporary" group that involves permanent (functional) and impermanent lines of authority. Such endeavors at organizational alteration and design are bridges from the way we have been doing work to the way we will be conducting human enterprise in the decades ahead. Today's microelectronic and semiconductor companies often result from the synergy of entrepreneurial teams.

The dictionary defines a "team" as a number of persons associated in some joint action, while "teamwork" is described as cooperative or coordinated effort on the part of persons working together. Dr. William Dyer (1987) notes that "teams are collections of people who must rely upon group collaboration if each member is to experience the optimum of success and goal achievement."

The Society of Advanced Management explains "management" as a science and an art:

> Management as a science is organized knowledge—concepts, theory, principles and techniques—underlying the practice of managing; as an art, it is application of organized knowledge to realities in a situation with a blend or compromise to obtain practical results.

Changing technology and markets have stimulated the team approach to management, as well as awareness of the interdependence of organizational components. Furthermore, the complexity of society, and the human systems devised to meet continuing and new needs, requires a pooling of resources and talents. Inflation, resource scarcity, reduced personnel levels, budget cuts, and similar constraints have underscored the demands for better coordination and synergy in the use of "brainpower." Professors Stanley Davis and Paul Lawrence (1977) have cited three conditions for the growth of matrix organizational approaches, and have summarized the situation fostering a multiple command structure, system, and behavior:

> *First condition: outside pressure for dual focus.* The very size of some tasks, which customers, governments, or society require of the organization, forces new divisions of labor and authority.
>
> *Second condition: pressure for high information-processing.* The nature of work that is "too big" for traditional approaches also requires innovative, high-speed communication networks that keep all informed who have the "need-to-know" about work progress. An enriched information-processing capacity is essential in decentralized organizations where interdependence increases the communication load.
>
> *Third condition: pressure for shared resources.* Large-scale projects demand both human economies and high performance. The pressure builds for fully utilizing scarce human resources to meet high quality standards. Matrix management permits redeployment of expensive, highly specialized talent, as well as of costly capital resources and physical facilities.

In effect, the matrix or team management model causes a new organizational culture to be formulated. As noted previously, high technology corporations are indicative of this change, with project teams consisting of a variety of skilled specialists from management information systems, accounting, and new technologies. Obsolete business separations give way to synergistic, functional arrangements among those employed in manufacturing, marketing, and administration; line and staff activities overlap and often merge.

Synergy through team efforts can occur within a single enterprise, or among different organizations that formerly competed or rarely mixed. The trend is evident among companies, agencies, and associations, as well as between the private and public sectors. Davis and Lawrence maintain that matrix management is moving beyond industry to insurance, banking, accounting, law, securities, retailing, construction, education, and health and human services. This is happening, in addition to the previously mentioned conditions, because of pressures created by geography, functions or services, and/or distinguishable clients. The computer has been the most powerful tool in making team management feasible, and it has fostered a revolution in organizational culture. Figure 7-1 offers a model of matrix organizational structure, and a summary of when and why a matrix management approach is recommended is shown on page 180.

Regionalism has also promoted team management strategies. Governmental entities find that problems of planning, economics, ecology, conservation, and even population control are too big for local solutions. Only by the integration of overlapping jurisdictions and efforts can the public sector meet the challenges of the superindustrial age. Thus, there is a remarkable growth in the establishment of interagency task forces in planning, training, or criminal justice activities. For effective macro problem-solving in complex societies, regional commissions are sometimes formed in which local governmental power is delegated to a more comprehensive organization, bringing together a technical support staff with representatives of each local government.

Regardless of the type of organization, team management calls for new skills if personnel potential is to be fully realized. Although the team is composed of knowledgeable people, they must learn new ways of relating and working together to solve cross-functional problems and to attain synergy. Experienced

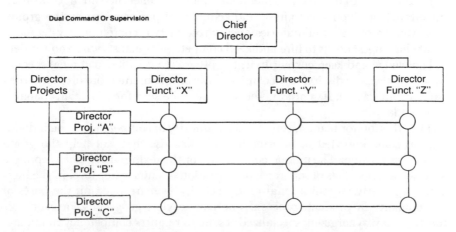

Figure 7-1. Model of matrix organizational structure.

Use Matrix Management* . . .

When—
- *Rapid technological advancements*
- Need for *timely decisions*
- Vast quantity of data
- Increased volume of new products and services
- Need for simultaneous dual decision making
- Strong constraints on financial and/or human resources

Why—
- Flexible adaptive system
- Provides timely, balanced decision making
- Permits rapid management response to changing market and technology
- Trains managers for ambiguity, complexity, and executive positions
- Synergizes, motivates, and focuses human energy

---

* Courtesy of Hughes Aircraft Company, Dr. Jack Baugh.

employees of hierarchical organizations have been conditioned to traditional organizational culture, so synergy in teams must be *created* (Casse 1982). Furthermore, the issue is not just how the team can function more synergistically, but how it integrates with the overall organization or society that it supposedly serves.

CREATING A TEAM CULTURE

For any team to be effective, members should be concerned about coordinating efforts, productive activities, and economical performance by the group. Jack Morton of Bell Laboratories once wrote of two contemporary management challenges: one is to hire and keep competent specialists who know a field of knowledge and keep current in it; the other is to get these technical specialists coupled across disciplines because today's problems are more often interdisciplinary in nature. Essentially, the same may be said for any team management endeavor.

The criterion for team selection is the *authority of competence*—the individual has some knowledge, information, or expertise that can help the group achieve its mission. The unique competence of the team participant becomes a new norm, regardless of sex, race, organizational seniority, or level in the hierarchy. Formerly, organizational group activity was arranged on the bases of commonality in product, process, function, service, geography, or even customer. Today, synergizing specialized resources requires competency in managing small- or large-scale projects, and expertise in time and conflict management. Because a technician may serve on two or more projects, while based in an existing functional area, three managers may have to share that human resource by creating integrative mechanisms that ensure the common organizational good.

Increasingly, team management is employed when the organization's activities are less repetitive and predictable. Such an approach increases the need for liaison, management by exception, and sharing of authority and information. All this is contrary to traditional organizational cultures. Management in transition today challenges organizations to improve information processing, enhance integration of realistic schedules, and share decision-making, subject to continuing revision and change.

Furthermore, there is a fundamental shift in the way power is exercised. Interfunctional product teams, for example, involve a delicate balance of power among peer specialists. Because joint decisions are to be made, each member must be sensitive to the others if the contributions of all are to lead to the team's success. The product manager's task is to facilitate collaboration across functional lines. For many this will necessitate an "attitude change." In America, there is much discussion about "reindustrialization," which demands cooperation rather than confrontation in the triple relationship between business, labor, and government. The attempts to resolve the U.S. automobile industry's crisis illustrate how essential such synergistic problem-solving is. Rather than considering each other natural enemies, these three elements must compromise and collaborate if each is to succeed. Even where a functional approach to business is still in force, labor and management can develop team relations. In Japan, to cite one illustration, quality-control circles made up of workers and supervisors meet regularly to discuss how to improve product quality.

Peter Drucker (1985) reminds us that "top management strategies are not mechanical; they are above all cultural." Thus, when an organization opts for team or matrix management, it implies a change in its ways of acting and thinking. Team management means the creation of shared values and assumptions. Thus, team members can begin to identify with one another and develop expectations of predictable behavior. But people are products of national cultures. So, while some form of team management may be characteristic of advanced technological societies, it will reflect a country's macroculture. Thus, the German *vorstand* is a board-like group with collegial decision-making and coordination among top managers. The French, on the other hand, are averse to absolutist power and omnipotent authority, so their organizations separate authority from responsibility so as to simultaneously protect individual and collective actions. Modern matrix management typically reflects American culture, and is less popular with the British, who place more emphasis on form and ordered regularity.

Because the authors are products of Canadian and United States cultures, this book reflects a North American approach. Therefore, the following observations on what is considered desirable in a team culture might be questioned in whole or part by readers from other national backgrounds. In any event, for purposes of discussion, here are eighteen guidelines that we think also facilitate team success:

1. Tolerance of ambiguity, uncertainty, and seeming lack of structure.
2. Taking interest in each member's achievement, as well as the group's.
3. Ability to give and accept feedback in a nondefensive manner.
4. Openness to change, innovation, and creative problem-solving.
5. Creation of a team atmosphere that is informal, relaxed, comfortable, and nonjudgmental.
6. Capacity to establish intense, short-term member relations, and to disconnect for the next project.
7. Seeking group participation, consensus, and decisions.
8. Concern to keep group communication on target and schedule, while permitting disagreement and valuing effective listening.
9 .Urging a spirit of constructive criticism, and authentic, nonevaluative feedback.
10. Encouraging members to express feelings and to be concerned about group morale/maintenance.
11. Clarifying roles, relationships, assignments, and responsibilities.
12. Sharing leadership functions within group, and utilizing total member resources.
13. Pausing periodically from task pursuits to reexamine and reevaluate team progress and communications.
14. Fostering trust, confidence, and commitment within the group.
15. Being sensitive to the team's linking function with other work units.
16. Fostering a norm that members will be supportive and respectful of one another, and realistic in their expectations of each other.
17. Promoting an approach that is goal-directed, divides the labor fairly, and synchronizes effort.
18. Setting high performance standards for the group.

Each team experience is different, and organizations should encourage such uniqueness, just as in a department and division. Yet at the same time, coordination and integration of team effort with other units and the whole enterprise is essential if the sum is to be greater than its parts. When team cultures contain the elements previously outlined, and are reflective of the whole organizational environment, then they become closely knitted and productive. The more team participation is provided, and the more employees *included* in team decision-making, the healthier and more relevant will that human system become.

The teams may be part of the formal organization structure as in the case of matrix management. However, some traditional hierarchies are slow and difficult to change. Then collateral organizations of informal teams may be formulated as a secondary mode of problem-solving. This unofficial, parallel organizational arrangement is a change strategy to use with problems that are intractable in the formal system. Such an approach is especially useful to middle managers because it gives them visibility and experience in group action on high-priority, organization-wide problems that are persistent and often neglected by the traditional organization, which concentrates on structured problems of authority and production.

Team management is suitable for knowledge problems that require high-quality, creative solutions with rapid processing and high output. When complex, modern problems are *less* structured, quantifiable, definable, and past experience is unreliable, then team managment is necessary.

A CASE FOR TEAM EFFECTIVENESS

Team and matrix management seemingly came to the fore with space industry, and the NASA goal to put a man on the moon. One of the successful pioneers in such approaches is TRW Systems in Redondo Beach, California, U.S.A. We are indebted to its former vice-president and now an independent consultant, Sheldon A. Davis, for the elements of the following case constructed from his writings and interviews.

Davis defines "work culture" as the habitual patterns of communication between departments and individuals, especially with regard to the perception of each other's roles, behavior, and attitudes. He envisions "organization development" as a long-term program of systematic attention to modify and improve that work culture. Davis sees "team building" as a key OD tool to assist people whose jobs are interrelated to examine how effectively they function as a team, to identify barriers to their collaboration, and to mutually undertake means that eliminate or reduce such obstacles. The focus is upon work behavior and how it influences job performance of the individual and other team members. Consider this case for team development: *

> A major aerospace firm had a number of projects underway that required the services of highly specialized employees. Such personnel were to be assigned to one or more projects on a part-time basis from their regular departmental locations. At first, line managers were reluctant to share their "man-power" with project managers because of conflicting loyalties, especially that the ad hoc groups would claim too much time of this talented employee. Frankly, the line supervisors distrusted the PM's

---

* Refer to film and Leader's Guide on *Team Building*, BNA Films, 9410 Decoverly Hall Road, Rockville, MD. 20850. Other recent films are "Team Building: No One Works Alone" and "Group Productivity" from CRC Films, 2223 Faraday, Ste.F, Carlsbad, CA 92008.

ability to consider the interests of other units in the organization equally with their own needs.

Top management insisted that this project management approach was an essential first step to a major reorganization. From occasional task force utilization, the corporation intended to move in the direction of matrix management. That meant introducing a multiple command system where one competent worker might report to two or more bosses. The company was developing a support program for this purpose, including a new computerized, management information system. The old organization chart was to give way to a "matrix" type illustration of diverse reporting relationships that included both permanent and temporary management authority.

To help the temporary project teams work more effectively the personnel department was introducing a new organization development program that included team building sessions. One laboratory manager resented taking his people off their jobs for such "navel gazing." But the project managers who had temporary authority over some of the same employees countered, "It's not just important to get the job done, but occasionally to examine *how* it is done and *how* we are collaborating. That's what team building is all about, plus improving the interface between the teams and the functional units."

The lab manager retorted, "We need to coordinate our activities and perform economically. If this team building will help to accomplish that, then *maybe* it will have some pay-off to replace the time my people will lose from their jobs." The PM responded, "My project is only a minimum core group for overall planning, budgeting, coordination, and systems engineering. We depend on your department's expertise for the design and technical work. Eventually this matrix approach will help us all get maximum utilization of scarce, technical resources. It will help us to magnify the impact of our human assets!"

"But you and I, plus the other PM's, are all competing for the same resources and manpower," the lab manager continued. "There is going to have to be a lot of trade-off on the part of all of us with managerial responsibilities, and we are not used to working like this. I can see us at cross-purposes with much conflict."

"Well," the PM remarked, "I understand that Personnel also plans some intergroup team building so that we learn new skills for this purpose. They maintain that the conflict can be managed and utilized for the common good, and that we can learn cross-functional collaboration for complex space productions. Team building is supposed to give us an opportunity to develop linking or coupling relations to avoid waste of our energies."

The lab supervisor sighed, "Those sessions better work, then, or this place is going to be in one big mess. Engineers and scientists are no-nonsense characters, not used to that human relations stuff. One value I do suspect that will come from such training is that technical types will learn some people skills that might eventually help to make them better managers when they get into supervision."

IMPROVING TEAM PERFORMANCE

Just like the organization in general, we might have an image of the team as an "energy exchange system." When the group functions, human psychic and physical energy is used effectively. Team interaction is an energy exchange. As the group seeks to achieve its goals, members energize or motivate themselves and one another by their example. Team planning and changes become projections on energy use and its alteration. Every aspect of the group process can be analyzed in terms of this human energy paradigm. The key issue, then, is how the team manages its energies most productively, and avoids underutilizing or even wasting the group energies. There are ways that members can analyze their functions and performance in projects, task forces, or product teams.

Team behavior can be examined from the viewpoint of task functions, which initiate, give or seek information, clarify or elaborate on member ideas, and summarize or synthesize. It can also be seen from the angle of group maintenance or morale building, such as encouraging, expressing group feeling, harmonizing, compromising, and "gate-keeping" on communication channels.

Such data-gathering can be useful periodically to improve the group's effectiveness. Not only can the information help the person to change his or her team behavior, but when such data are combined into a visual profile, they offer a diagnosis of team health from time to time. It is recommended that teams pause on occasion for self-examination of their progress. Sometimes a third-person facilitator, such as an internal or external consultant, can be most helpful in this regard. When the group's analysis of its maturity is summarized on a newsprint tablet or overhead slide, or even in a typed summary report, the team can then view the total assessment and discuss its implications for effective energy use.

Team participation is an intensive learning experience. When members voluntarily involve themselves and fully participate, personal and professional growth is fostered. The team is like a laboratory of the larger organizational world in which it operates. Although a temporary experience, it is an opportunity for individual and team development. Each participant shares self and insights from the basis of unique life and organizational experiences. Synergy occurs when the members listen to each other and enter into the private worlds of the others. Total team perception and wisdom then become more than the sum of the parts. To promote maximum self-actualization and energize the group's potential, the following eight ground rules for greater team effectiveness are recommended. Remember, these suggestions come from the authors' cultural perspectives:

1. Be *experimental*—in this learning experience test new styles of leadership and communication, different kinds of behavior and attitudes, new patterns of personal participation and relationships, joint problem-solving efforts.

2. Be *authentic*—level in your communication; tell it like it is in your feedback; care about team members, even enough to confront them, rather than play games.
3. Be *sensitive*—express your feelings, and be conscious of the other person's feelings; emphatically respond and reflect on the sender's real meaning, not just his or her words. Be aware of the whole range of non-verbal communication and cues.
4. Be *spontaneous*—respond creatively to the here and now data produced in the group; to the person as he or she now reveals self. (Avoid being strategic or manipulative, or engrossed in the previous there and then.) Warmly receive the sharing of another and thereby be confirmed yourself.
5. Be *helpful*—accept the other's perception of self and the situation; avoid imposing your system, values, or opinions upon the other. A helping relationship means that the other must perceive your assistance as being helpful. This will occur when you help that person discover new dimensions for self; to appreciate the need to break through his own barriers. By sharing yourself, you permit another team member to enlarge and revise his own psychological construct (namely, the way that person reads meaning into his life experiences).
6. Be *open*—consider other viewpoints and possibilities, rather than being closed-minded or locked into your own previous conceptions. Evaluate and check feedback from others to arrive at your own determination. Be flexible, not rigid in responding to new ideas and different perceptions.
7. Be *time conscious*—the team meetings are limited in time availability for accomplishing a specific task. Avoid taking up too much "air time" or diverting the group from its mission. Be willing to listen, but when others stray from the subject, bring the group back on target.
8. Exercise *group leadership*—team participation is an opportunity to practice the whole range of leadership skills, whether as an initiator or follower. The participative team is a leaderless group, in the sense that there is no authoritarian leader. The leadership is shared and group centered. Each is permitted to do "his or her thing," which will contribute most to group progress (from promoting the accomplishment of a task, to the maintenance of group morale).

William W. Hines, a utility training manager, describes five goals for increasing team effectiveness:

1. Look at how well team members communicate as a group.
2. Observe how they problem solve.

3. Help them better understand their own defined corporate objectives.
4. Assist the team in developing skills to manage and handle interpersonal conflict better.
5. Aid them in developing closer and more collaborative relationships.

Hines proposes several types of team meetings to evaluate how the group is functioning: (a) feedback sessions with the facilitator on the results of individual interviews with members; (b) creative problem-solving or "brainstorming" meetings on obstacles to team effectiveness; and (c) weekly team building meetings to deal with identified interpersonal and work problems (usually about two hours in length).

In the process of human resource development, behavioral science consultants have created several methods and techniques for team development. The regular team-building session is considered an ongoing process to alter the way an integrated unit works together, and essentially is a change strategy. William G. Dyer of Brigham Young University (1987) suggests that team-building be viewed as a cycle consisting of "problem identification, data-gathering by and among members, diagnosis and evaluation of the data, problem-solving and planning on the findings, implementation of the action plans, and then assessment of the results."

The following experience of one of the authors (Harris) illustrates the origin and purpose of team-building within a traditional bureaucracy:

> The top management of a very large fire and emergency department for a major California county were alarmed. The first-line managers, called "battalion chiefs," were considering turning their professional association into a union. To counteract the identification of these chiefs with rank and file employees and to strengthen their image of themselves as *managers*, the key administrators decided to initiate a management development institute for the battalion chiefs, each of whom might command upwards to a thousand employees during a major emergency.
>
> I designed a behavioral science program for this purpose, but built into the training some features of organization development. That data-gathering by means of instruments and group process produced information that was compiled into a report for upper management. The principal problem was a breakdown in communication between middle and upper level management, and it was perceived that the latter lacked synergy— they did not work well among themselves as an executive group and communicated confusion downward. Management accepted one of my recommendations and opted for team-building sessions for themselves.
>
> The two-day session was held at a fire camp away from the command headquarters. Top management first examined in depth the implication

of their subordinates' feedback. Then more data-gathering was done among the chief engineers as to how they saw themselves as a team, their roles, and their relationships. This consultant and a colleague not only provided some input on how they might become a more effective administrative group, but helped these public service executives to examine the "pay-off" functions of their own jobs. After two more off-site sessions, we compiled a report on the team-building findings and recommendations. As a result of this, the key management group inaugurated their own plan to maintain the progress attained and confront the issues that hampered their working as a team. In other words, they committed themselves to action for internal improvement of their performance as a work unit, and strove to become behavior models for the next level of supervision.

Research in project and matrix management has demonstrated that organizations that take time for team-building usually increase their productivity. It is one of many innovative managerial technologies for organization development, which have ranged from sensitivity training and career development programs to job enrichment and videotaping of top performers in problem-solving sessions.

Team development should focus upon the nature of work performed, the relationships of team members who must do the work, and the way in which their work together is structured. In addition to diagnosis and data-gathering, team-building helps organizational associates to confront as a group their problems, challenges, processes, and behavior. The emphasis is upon such questions as:

- What is it like to work here?
- What kinds of things help or hinder us in working together?
- What is our job and our responsibilities?
- What are our expectations of this team and each other?
- What changes could be made to improve performance?
- What does each group member need to do differently?
- What can this unit do to work more cooperatively?
- How do other teams or work units perceive us, and vice versa?
- What commitments is each member willing to make to increase our effectiveness?

Team-building is an opportunity for participants to practice skills in data collection and analysis, human relations and feedback, negotiation and compromise, conflict management, and problem-solving. It is a chance for group introspection on "hang-ups" that affect job performance, the quality of staff meetings, the hidden agendas that undermine progress, the blocked feelings that hold back effort, the attitudes and actions that sidetrack the team. It is a synergistic system for developing organizational collaboration among knowledge workers or technical specialists. The overriding issue it confronts is "trust" and the degree to which it exists among team members and with other work units. In complex organizations in which people are so interdependent, high trust levels ensure achievement.

Gordon F. Shea (1984) maintains that trust should be considered a resource to be cultivated by managers. As president of Prime Systems in the Washington-Baltimore area, he assists clients to utilize trust as a social-survival mechanism that allows us to cooperate for mutual benefit. Team cultures can be created that foster trust and the risk-taking related to trusting others, and means can be installed to measure its progress in the group.

Because team-building strategies are still emerging, one can only review how they have been used. Dr. W. Warner Burke, editor of *Organization Dynamics*, described these five uses:

> *Start-ups*—team-building with a new group, such as plant management of a facility before it opens, or prior to the inauguration of a business systems planning group, or when several departments are relocated into a new facility.
> *Interpersonal relationships*—team-building sessions, usually off-site, for an intensive period together for analysis of ongoing team relations.
> *Content problems*—team meetings on everyday work and decision-making for effective team performance, often held on-site for short periods of time with an external facilitator. Consultation is offered on team maintenance issues, task process, norms and values.
> *Training*—team input sessions with an OD practitioner to provide education on group decision-making and communication, problem-solving skills, interface with other teams, etc.
> *Long-range planning*—team sessions on forecasting, budget planning, member replacement, impact of technological/organizational changes on the team.

Typically, an internal or external facilitator provides process consultation on how the team operates, pursues its tasks, makes its decisions, shares its leadership, sets its standards and procedures, confronts and utilizes conflict, and communicates with one another and other organizational units.

Obviously, team-building must be supplemented with technical training in project or matrix management operation. In workshops on project management, the author (Harris, 1988) provides input on the interpersonal dynamics of ad hoc groups while a colleague offers training on the technical processes for managing the project. The latter instructs workshop participants on the project management system, organization, and objectives; and project planning, scheduling, control, appraisal, and review.

The aim of both dimensions of this management development is to promote understanding of both organizational relations and human motivation on the one hand, while teaching skills for managing temporary teams of talented people. The end purpose is to understand who is going to do what and when. Team development, as Sheldon Davis reminds us, counteracts *reverse synergy*—when people cancel each 'other out by not hearing, not building or working together, putting each other down, or blocking the contribution of human potential.

The following articles* illustrate synergistic aspects and activities:

Dr. William Dyer, an American expert on group dynamics, describes teams as "collections of people who must rely upon group collaboration if each member is to experience the optimum of success and goal achievement."

Synergy, or accomplishing more than the sum of the parts through team efforts, can occur within a single enterprise or among different organizations that formerly competed or rarely mixed. The need for synergy is becoming evident in public as well as private sector companies, agencies and associations.

Regardless of the type of organization, team management calls for new skills if the potential is to be fully realized. Although the team is made up of technically competent people, they must learn new ways of relating and working together to solve problems and to attain results.

Hence, synergy in teams must be learned. Furthermore, the issue is not just how the team can function more synergistically, but how it can integrate more effectively with the overall goals of the organization.

Team Effectiveness

The contexts or situations in which multicultural teams made of members from two or more cultures must function are now many and varied. A few years ago it would have been difficult to find examples of multicultural teams. But today the list of multicultural organizations with employees from different cultures working together is almost endless.

Examples include a multicultural team of graduate students completing the requirements for a marketing class at a U.S. or European business school; a team of Japanese and U.S. employees implementing the Toyota producing system at the Japanese carmaker's plant in Georgetown, Kentucky; German and U.S. chemists working together in Mobay Corp., a U.S. subsidiary of Bayer AG; employees from many nationalities working together at IBM Europe's Paris headquarters; professionals at all levels from more than 50 countries working for Aramco in Dhahran, Saudi Arabia.

Not surprisingly, the majority of people who work in multicultural teams or in multicultural organizations find it more difficult than working in homogeneous groups where everyone is from the same culture. However, a model can be used to predict the effectiveness of any multicultural team or organi-

* Reprinted with permission from *International Management*, December 1988.

zation. The actual effectiveness of the team or organization is a function of the potential, or synergy, which is possible, less the losses from the problems that inevitably arise from the process of working together.

A survey of managers from two large multicultural organizations illustrates this point. When asked to list the advantages of cultural diversity in their organizations, they stressed the following: an opportunity to share experiences and technology; a better approach to global competitors; access to a larger pool of international managers; ability to manufacture products at the most profitable location; a chance to improve cross-cultural understanding; and the opportunity to learn different viewpoints about the same issue.

The list of advantages proved to be fairly easy to generate. However, when the same people were asked to list the disadvantages of working in a culturally diverse organization, they completed the task in less than half the time it took to list the advantages.

Personality Conflicts

Among others, they listed the following disadvantages: poor communications because of different languages; problems due to different managerial styles; more complex decision-making processes; reduced promotional opportunities; greater complexity in getting things done; more personality conflicts; prejudice and stereotyping of personnel.

Airbus: An Exceptional Multicultural Success

As Europe moves closer to economic integration, the role of cross-border alliances in the success of the EC's Internal Market programme becomes more vital. Removing Europe's remaining physical, technical and fiscal barriers will open the way for even more of these transnational mergers.

But centuries-old cultural barriers will continue to remain, posing many hard questions, such as:

Will managers, technicians and executives from France, Germany, Spain, Italy and other EC countries possess the skills and attitudes to work in multicultural environments?

Will a true "Euromanager" ever evolve?

If not, what will be the consequences for the lofty ideal of a borderless Europe?

Insights into some of these issues are provided by a recent study of transnational projects in the European aerospace industry. Not surprisingly, Christian Koenig, the French professor responsible for the study, ranks the Franco-British Concorde project a notable failure, while citing the four-nation Airbus project as one of the great success stories of collaborative relationships.

It is fair to say that the Concorde project and Airbus Industrie began with equal potential to draw synergy from diverse groups working together. Why then should one fail and the other succeed?

The foremost reason Concorde was not successful—apart from the oil price rises of the early 1970s—was that problems at the top prevented management from ever tackling the serious disruptions that occur when diverse groups work together.

From the start, Concorde's top management was mired in external and internal politics. Decisions were invariably made at ministerial level, and managers did not have the power and authority to give the organization the leadership it needed. Moreover, there was a consistent lack of coordination and cooperation between the government partners and industry on either side of the channel.

In contrast, at Airbus, professionals are in charge and have the power to make and implement decisions. From the standpoint of organizational structure, Airbus is far more decentralized. Its decision-making process is relatively short. Unlike Concorde, Airbus is flexible and adapts easily and responds quickly to changes in the external environment.

In addition, the roles of Airbus's British, French, West German and Spanish partners are all clearly defined, and there are reinforcing mechanisms to keep them together. Top management assists in the integration process but is also sensitive to the roles of the various partners. Executives and technicians from each of the four nations have goals and targets that help transcend the cultural factor. There is a tremendous spirit of teamwork at Airbus and pride among employees in their work.

To successfully produce widebody jets that have seized a significant share of the world's commercial aircraft market, Airbus has had to overcome vast differences in languages, management philosophies and styles, work organizations and huge logistical problems. It has pushed ahead with great efficiency using flow charts that spread over the map of Europe.

As a result, not only has the consortium resurrected the civilian aircraft industry in Europe through the principle of collaboration. With its sensitive and skillful management of cultural diversity, it has set up a model for post-1992 European transnational cooperative ventures, and clearly demonstrated the benefits that can accrue from international alliances.

---

* Reprinted with permission from *International Management*, February 1989.

Further insight on this subject matter is offered in Chapter 12 on synergy among professionals and technicians.

TEAM CULTURE CHARACTERISTICS

If the organization's culture emphasizes employee participation through team management, the group microcultures are likely to reflect that system's macroculture. Thus, collaborative management should be evident not only within an individual team, but in intergroup relations. There is an implicit assumption that the work team culture exerts a significant influence on individual member behavior (French and Bell 1984). As a team member, one functions beyond the individual level, becoming representative of the group "persona." Those who serve in two or more interlocking groups are expected to act as linking pins in the accomplishment of organizational mission through these separate but interdependent entities.

Everything that anthropologists would examine in the culture of people in a national or organizational group can be analyzed in the miniature environment of the team. That can range from the group's beliefs and attitudes, to procedures and practices, to priorities and technologies. The team atmosphere, task orientation or processes, communication patterns, role clarification or negotiation, conflict resolution, decision making, action planning, intragroup and intergroup relations—all can be scrutinized for better diagnosis of the group's dynamics. When a global manager or consultant engages in such analysis, the team can be helped to become more effective in the use of its energies.

Whether it is a family group (a permanent work unit) or a special group (temporarily constituted for a particular purpose), each individual contributes uniquely from his or her own experience and talents. The team's resources can be strengthened when intercultural differences are used for synergy, rather than allowed to become a cause for divisiveness. The differences of perception that arise from varied academic or training backgrounds, work expertise and experiences, ethnic and national origins can enrich the group's basis for creative problem-solving and achievement. The team's culture can be the means for capitalizing on such, so that all members accomplish something together. A strong team culture enhances group communications and permits confrontation, so as to stimulate group growth and cohesion. Then, as a team identity is strengthened, group morale, cameraderie, and "esprit de corps" are also improved.

In this final section, we will adapt the paradigm offered in the last chapter for analysis of organizational culture. However, in applying the ten dimensions of that model to team culture, we will employ the explanations of those classifications from Chapter 6's summary. At the same time, an anecdote from a team experience illustrates the concept. (From a case study by the author on an office automation (OA) task force established to introduce new technologies, Harris, "Future Work III," *Personnel Journal*, August 1985.)

1. *Team Rationale* (members are aware of their charter, have clarified their goals/targets, and developed a sense of identification with the group and its mission). . . . The OA Task Force had been established by the CEO to facilitate implementation of the corporate plan for introducing office automation throughout the company. The eight members had defined their objectives, set their priorities, and decided upon three more stages beyond conception—*initiation* of the strategic and tactical plans for automation; *contagion* management by integrating pilot projects into mainstream operations as use of the new technologies becomes more widespread; *consolidation* of advances made by the changes, and integrating them into the organization's total information system.

2. *Team Demarcations* (members develop their group physical and psychological space, while limiting the scope of team operations). . . . The OA Task Force got office space and support services alotted to it in the

EDP (electronic data processing) department. This strategy was used to bring office automation into the whole MIS (management information systems) operation. They decided to focus their efforts on computer and communication technologies, and to exclude all robotic applications to the office. They recommended that another task force be set up for this purpose when necessary.

3. *Its Philosophy* (member attitudes, beliefs, and myths about team mission). . . . OA team members viewed automation as a necessity if productivity was to be enhanced, costs contained, and if information was to be truly valued as a resource.

4. *Its Priorities and Standards* (member values and norms). . . . OA task force first sought standardization of hardware and software to be utilized for automating offices, seeking to identify and coordinate the interface of existing micro or personal computers. Early on, they decided that the new equipment would be used to accomplish their own team tasks, and that all members would document their own experiences in "debugging" the new systems. As they introduce this technology to the workforce, they would informally and with humor share their own personal experiences ("horror stories") in transitioning to the new equipment. In effect, they would become OA behavior models.

5. *Its Media and Message* (team communications and languages). . . . Team members cultivated a relaxed, informal, and open system of communication among themselves, which they transmitted throughout organization as they attempted to win over the larger organization to the new technologies. Because technicians can become mechanical and mysterious in their own jargon, the OA members decided to personalize and demystify the changeover. They held informal meetings for those suffering from cyberphobia (fear of technology) or cyberphrenia (addicts of technology), training the former in computer languages, acronyms, and new terminology like "informating" (making data and information more broadly available).

6. *Its Operational Mode* (team organizational processes and ways of learning). . . . The team did force field analysis of the driving and resisting forces related to the introduction of the change to automation. They then set about to strengthen the driving forces, and to weaken the restraining forces. Early on the OA Task Forces decided upon "power sharing" among themselves, and a strategy to empower office managers and staffs through the effective use of the new technology. They established an "electronic bulletin board" for sharing data about office automation among themselves, when with other personnel involved. They used teleconferencing to link together corporate offices nationwide so that the total system shared in the excitement and struggle related to the changeover.

7. *Its Recognitions, Rewards, and Heroes* (behavior re-inforced within and without the team relative to personnel). . . . The OA team established an "OA Award" for the member who had accomplished the most in the previous month toward fostering task force objectives. Then they extended similar recognition to the high performers in company offices who had achieved the most in adapting to the new technology. They convinced the CEO to institutionalize this into an annual picnic outing in which he personally presented a home "PC" to the three biggest heroes in the battle of automation. They also started a cartoon contest, first among themselves and later companywide, for the funniest drawings or illustrations on the traumas of OA transition; winners received extra software kits and had their works published in the corporate newspaper.

8. *Its Customs and Traditions* (organizational rites, rituals, and feeding habits). The OA team members adopted a quiet, underused courtyard at corporate headquarters for their meetings. There they held "court" with "bag lunches" for weekly brainstorming on how they could advance the OA cause. They coined a slogan, "Become a self manager through office tech" and spread it throughout their "Fortune 500" corporation. Their idea was that office automation enabled more to share in management responsibilities, like making judgments and decisions. They started wearing pins with "computer power" boldly spelled out, until they began giving them as prizes to those who had advanced the most in performance of their electronic work stations.

9. *Its Roles and Their Interface* (organizational relationships). . . . When the OA Task Force met for the first time, they noted that there were not enough women included, so they asked the CEO to confirm their choice of a few more females to balance their team. They then picked the most able secretaries in the firm for this purpose. No one person was given the secretarial responsibility on the team; they shared such work by using their computers as word processors. The team set as one of its targets the examination of how automation changed roles and relationships. They focused upon the alteration of the role of managers and their secretaries.

10. *Its Appearance and Aura* (team look, style, and reputation). . . . During the course of their short organizational life, the OA team developed a reputation as an innovative, action oriented group who were concerned about the human aspects of office automation. As people become more comfortable with the new technologies, they were grateful to the task force members whose efforts facilitated their transition into the new work environment and away from a linear work approach.

These ten descriptions demonstrate how a team's culture may be systematically analyzed. These classifications may be adapted by observers for any type of team environment from assembly line workers to a community development group, as well as for any functional subdivision within an organization. (For further information on office automation in the new work culture, refer to Chapter Two, *Management in Transition* by P. R. Harris, San Francisco, CA: Jossey-Bass, 1985.)

In examining a team's culture, it is also possible to modify the Likert (1967) questions on six major categories of management. An effective metaindustrial team would be characterized in this way:

1. *Leadership*—Is substantial or complete confidence shown in team members? Are they free to discuss pertinent ideas, and is each one's contributions sought and used fully?
2. *Motivation*—Are the predominant motivators involvement, recognition and rewards? Does each member feel equally responsible for mission achievement, and do all engage in cooperative effort?
3. *Communications*—Is the information flow within the team circular and shared equally? Is the upward and intergroup communication as authentic and accurate as it is within the team? How sensitive and aware are members of their colleague's problems and concerns?
4. *Decisions*—Are members fully involved in decisions within the group, and is consensus sought when feasible?
5. *Goals*—Does the setting of team goals involve a group action, and is resistance confronted and channeled into agreement?
6. *Control*—Are team review and control functions shared? Are data gathered by the group used for self-guidance and problem-solving? Are cliques undermining team energies?

We realize that a group is not automatically a team, and that team building may be in order to improve the group's performance. Casse (1982) suggests that the synergistic process within teams must be organized, promoted, and managed. He believes that team synergy results when members go beyond their individual capabilities—beyond what each is used to being and doing. Together the team then may produce something new, unique, and superior to that of any one member. For this to happen, he suggests that multicultural managers, such as of a project or team, require *self understanding*, as to their own cultural influences and limitations; *understanding of others* exercised by respect and empathy to each member, while avoiding attributions, judgments, and stereotyping; *interacting* in such a way as to effectively communicate, relate, listen, observe, adjust and learn from exchanging; while cultivating *other skills* involving toleration of ambiguity, persistence and patience, as well as assertiveness in presenting self. If a team culture exemplifies such qualities, then members as a group would be better able to realize their potential and achieve their objectives.

Team Culture Diagnosis

Data-gathering instruments can be purchased or created to help team members and management understand individual behavior within the team or group. Four such instruments include the Individual Behavior Analysis, which assists in diagnosis of interpersonal performance within a work unit or team; the Team Performance Survey, which can be used in team building sessions to evaluate a group's progress and problems; the Team Synergy Analysis, a self-assessment of synergistic skills in group situations; and the Group Maturity Analysis, for assessing member behavior that facilitates group accomplishment. These evaluation instruments can also be used by external observers of a team's culture and interactions. (These instruments can be obtained in quantity from Management Research Systems/Talico, Inc., Ste. 5, 2320 S. Third St., Jacksonville, FL 32250, U.S.A.)

Indrei Ratiu, a founding partner of Paris-based Intercultural Management Associates, has suggested the following criteria for evaluating the effectiveness of a multicultural team *(International Consulting News,* April 1987):

- Do members work together with a common purpose (something that is spelled out and felt by all to be worth fighting for)?
- Has the team developed a common language or procedure (a common way of doing things, a process for holding meetings)?
- Does the team build on what works (learning to identify the positive actions before being overwhelmed by negatives)?
- Does the team attempt to spell out things within the limits of the cultural differences involved (delimit the mystery level by directness and openness regardless of cultural origins of participants)?
- Do the members recognize the impact of their own cultural programming on individual and group behavior (deal with, not avoid the differences in order to create synergy)?
- Does the team have fun (within successful multicultural groups, the cultural differences become a source of continuing surprise, discovery, and amusement rather than irritation or frustration)?

SUMMARY

The transformation of work underway calls for a new management and metaindustrial organization. Propelled by a changed economy featuring new technologies and a global market, the very culture of work is being altered. Personnel seek an enhanced quality of work life featuring more autonomy, participation, information, and creative norms. The knowledge worker expects more emphasis on high performance, technology utilization, R&D, entrepreneurialism, and relationships that are both informal and synergistic.

The metaindustrial work scene involves complexity, and demands high output and fast growth from those who enjoy the "privilege" of working for income. Team management makes it possible to achieve and maintain this in a work culture that emphasizes information processing and service. Although the new technologies can facilitate the operations of such teams, it is an understanding of group dynamics that enables us to exercise team leadership and to promote better intergroup relations. Team experiences today challenge participants to revise and expand self and role images, especially if the work is to become more meaningful and if we are to benefit from organizational relationships. To produce synergistic team actions requires the acquisition and practice of new skills. A case for team building was made through several organizational illustrations of what is meant by team effectiveness, and eight guidelines were offered that can ensure this.

Finally, a model was again presented for analyzing culture, this time in the context of teams. Additional discussion of international project teams is found in Chapter 12.

In conclusion, we again remind our readers that the issue of both work and teams is culturally relative. Some cultures are not team oriented, and more individualistic; each macroculture has its own style of team management when the approach is introduced. However, global managers will increasingly employ some form of team approach in the emerging work culture.

Unit II
Cultural Impacts on International Business

The multicultural manager is someone who has to handle things, ideas, and people belonging to a different cultural environment. He or she can work either in a multinational corporation, an international organization, an institution located in a foreign country, or even in local, regional, or national organizations in which people do not share the same patterns of thinking, feeling, and behaving. . . . Thus, traditional management training must be adjusted to the new requirements of the managerial functions. Management activities related to planning, organizing, leading, and controlling have to be approached from a cross-cultural perspective if private and public organizations want to keep up their productivity (economic, social, and cultural) inside and outside to the countries or cultures they belong. The challenge for the intercultural trainer is to see how critical managerial processes—such as communication, problem-solving, decision-making, performance appraisal—can be (a) transplanted from one culture to another with the necessary adjustments, and (b) presented to managers of any kind of organization, so that they can put their own actions into an intercultural perspective and learn from them.*

---

* Excerpt from *Training for the Multicultural Manager* by Pierre Casse of the World Bank (1982).

8
Managing for Cross-Cultural Effectiveness

In a sense, all life is an intercultural experience. It begins in our struggle between our left and right brain qualities, the male-female side of our person alities—the yin and the yang. As Pierre Casse (1980) reminded us, culture shock may occur with each contradiction or confrontation between various values, beliefs, and assumptions. The issue here is how effectively we cope with cultural differences, and how able we are in creating synergy. The achievement of that desired result can be hastened by acquisition of knowledge and skills.

Human migration, particularly, has been a catalyst challenging us to deal with cross-cultural matters. The force of circumstances—economic, social, political, religious, whatever—causes groups of people to leave their home culture and to enter into an alien environment. Then the process of coping and acculturation begins, whether we are called nomads, refugees, immigrants, migrant or foreign workers, international traders or performers, even tourists or astronauts. The scope of this challenge is evident every time we pick up a newspaper, and read of intercultural efforts like these:

- 60,000 Hmong refugees have resettled in Fresno Valley, and thousands more of these Laotian tribesmen are expected to seek out this California haven. American allies in the Vietnam War, this aboriginal people coming from the hunting and primitive agricultural stages of development find it very hard to adjust to a modern urban, technological culture. However, the principal of Wolters Elementary School reports that "the kids are soaring—they study hard, pick up English quickly and even do better in math," but he worries about them becoming Americanized too quickly and losing too much of their own culture. . . .
- Every year more than 20,000 people from more than 120 countries come to the United States to learn our technology and management systems. Sponsored by United Nations agencies, their own governments or companies, or U.S. aid programs, they come for seminars and courses that can range from weeks to years. Such international trainees are usually mature, educated, and well traveled, but many return frustrated and highly dissatisfied from their intercultural experience here. According to a director of such international programs for the U.S. De-

partment of Agriculture Graduate School, the difficulties can be traced to two causes: lack of adequate cross-cultural learning prior to departure and upon arrival in North America, and cultural insensitivity on the part of HRD professionals here relative to the trainees' needs and the relevancy of training content. . . .

• Thousands of entertainers and athletes now travel around the world on professional overseas tours. Many of them experience severe cross-cultural problems that undermine their performance, and may even result in their being incarcerated in a jail or hospital. To help, the Los Angeles Olympic Committee in 1984 provided their staff with intercultural training to improve their effectiveness with international visitors. The United States Sports Academy in Mobile, Alabama, has also inaugurated a prescreening strategy to try and predict success of applicants for assignments abroad.

• The trade shift from the Atlantic to the Pacific stimulates a greater exchange of Asian and Pan American peoples. Recognizing this new reality, the California Department of Education is funding projects for staff development in intercultural communication. The Chinatown Resources Development Center in San Francisco (94108) has developed a directory and library of resources on the subject for interested educators.

• Business women increasingly must cope with cross-cultural handicaps as they operate in the global market. *Savvy*, a national magazine for female managers, published a "Foreign Handbook" (April 1984) to give readers tips on working abroad. These clues ranged from taxes on overseas' earnings to dealing with discrimination on the job in Japan (from Japanese females, not males). It not only reported on where to get intercultural training, but success stories of Western women functioning effectively in Asia and the Middle East.

• Technical consultants and international project managers are too often woefully ignorant of cultural differences. To remedy this somewhat, *Worldwide Projects*, a publication for the multinational community involved in the design, construction, and financing of international projects have been carrying features with cross-cultural information. A recent editorial (February/March 1985) by the Saudia Arabian deputy minister of communications warned on transplanting transportation standards from one culture to another. Since they employ consultants from North America and Europe, as well as other countries, the problems of differing standards for road design and construction was solved by communicating their in-country standards and expectations, suitable to their climate, circumstances, and people. The minister challenge is for those in government who are responsible for effectively utilizing and managing advisors from abroad.

• Those in the travel industry are finally awakening to the importance of cross-cultural competencies for those involved in agency operations.

The *Travel Agent* recently carried an article (Harris/August 27, 1984) that called for cultural understanding and skills by would-be travel professionals who wish to improve client services both at home and abroad. Then guidance can be provided by agents to enable their customers not only to avoid "faux pas" with foreigners, but actually to enjoy the differences in the world's peoples.

The common element in these incidents is improving human performance through education, training, or communication about cultural differences. They illustrate diverse cross-cultural opportunities. The vocational dimensions of our lives offer so many intercultural challenges for increasing effectiveness. They range from being the only black on an engineering staff, or the only Hispanic on a college business faculty, or the oldest president in the nation's history, to being the one female in the executive suite, or the one bank financial analyst in a wheelchair, or the one male nurse in a pediatrics hospital. Today, as Auren Uris and Jane Bensahel remind us (*Los Angeles Times*, January 12, 1981), lifestyle, age, sexual orientation, ethnicity, and all sorts of other facets of cultural preference can mark us as "different." Differences do not necessarily mean barriers; they can become bridges to understanding and enrichment of our lives. Perhaps the greatest difference facing the mass of the world's workers will be the transition from the industrial to metaindustrial way of life (Harris 1985).

Management increasingly is responding to the needs of both a multicultural workforce and market. Jan Gaston of Lingua-Tech in Menlo Park, California, specializes in language education with Silicon Valley executives. This not only involves teaching Americans how to speak foreign languages and understand their cultural context, such as Japanese and Chinese, but also foreign scientists and technicians now working in high tech firms on the West Coast who need more comprehension in English and our American culture. Gaston believes that many of the fast growth companies are only beginning to appreciate the importance of interculture issues and idiosyncracies, especially frustrating in the engineering arena when communication can be hampered by a lack of language skill or because of cultural misunderstanding.

To illustrate how global managers are improving organizational effectiveness in this regard, consider the following three mini cases:

- Exxon Research and Engineering Company has a specially designed program to equip supervisors with skills for managing and making full use of the talents of a culturally diverse work force. The training focuses upon equal employment opportunities and affirmative action, especially for women and minorities. It involves such persons as resources in the training, and uses a case study approach for this purpose.

- U.S. Customs Service in its Los Angeles and Chicago regions adopted a strategy that all customs officials should be professional intercultural communicators. To increase skills in that regard, the agency not only introduced more foreign language training, but a series of Managing Cultural Differences Workshops conducted by this author. The aim was to improve communication with foreign visitors, as well as with minorities both in the workforce and among the traveling public. This three-day session used multimedia, customized case studies, and group dynamics to raise the consciousness level of participants, and improve their cross-cultural effectiveness as public servants.

• Digital Equipment Corporation developed a guidebook and a course for their high tech employees going overseas on company assignments. Authored and conducted by Dr. James Catoline, the program is called *Managing Across Cultures*. It is centered around four major themes— adjusting in a different culture; the effects of cultural values on business and communication; assessing readiness for foreign deployment; and reentry or returning home. It involves a job analysis tool, and administration of a pre-departure questionnaire that looks at the overseas' situation in terms of work, family, and personal needs.

Unit I, Chapters 1–7, provided a general overview of culture as it affects global managers. We have examined culture's impacts on our perceptions and the need to be more cosmopolitan. We have reviewed how the concept of culture can be employed to improve communications, negotiations, synergy, and planning for change. We have applied cultural paradigms to our organizations and teams. Since repetition is the mother of learning, we will repeat many of these cultural insights but in another context. In Unit II, we focus upon international business and the global marketplace, so that we may be more comfortable anywhere on this planet and improve our effectiveness as actors on the world's stage. This chapter, and the next, analyze why and how we may increase our cultural awareness and skills. Other chapters in the unit concentrate on issues of technology transfer, intercultural training, and synergy among practitioners.

CAPITALIZING ON CULTURAL UNIQUENESS

Our very way of thinking is culturally conditioned. Eastern cultures analyze in ideograms or visualizations, whereas Western cultures tend to use concepts. Because a concept is a general notion or idea that combines the characteristics known about a subject, it provides a framework for thinking or analyzing a particular topic or experience. For example, here are actual excerpts from news stories, which can be analyzed in a particular conceptual context:

Princeton, N.J.—Girls have a hard time assuming leadership roles because there are few woman leaders to model themselves after and society treats such females as deviants, report researchers from the Education Testing Service. . . . In classroom discussions, boys' ideas are traditionally given greater weight than girls, and teachers seldom assign females to classroom leadership roles. Such sex stereotypes need to be reversed the researchers maintain.

Quinhagak, Alaska—Natives in rural Alaska are caught in a grinding collision between two worlds, modern and traditional. Increasingly they fear that their subsistence-centered life style, the basis of their culture, will be crushed by the advancing technological society. Subsistence for such Eskimos goes beyond the definition proposed in Congress: "The customary and traditional uses in Alaska of wild, renewable resources for direct personal or family consumption as food, clothing, shelter, fuel, tools, transportation." For the native subsistence is more than support, it is really an entire way of life. It is not just food for the stomach, it is food for the soul.

Tokyo, Japan—The executives of McDonald's hamburger restaurant realized when they went into business here eight years ago that they had to adapt to Japanese attitudes rather than merely replicate their American operations. Therefore, the first McDonald's was set up in a prestigious location in order to impress the Japanese, who would have considered it a second-class enterprise had it been started in the suburbs. McDonald's efforts here have been successful because they sought to understand Japanese behavior, and coped effectively with Japan's different way of doing things.

New York, N.Y.—The American businessman overseas often operates under demanding conditions. He suffers the hardship of giving up cold martinis for warm beer as one way to integrate into the English business community. He must keep his mind on business during the rounds of Geisha houses as a prelude to concluding a deal in Japan. And if he operates in Spain, he must brace himself for the rigors of 11 p.m. dinners and negotiations that may continue into the small hours of the morning!

What, then, do all these press accounts have in common that can make these commentaries more meaningful? Obviously, the concept of *culture*. It is a very useful tool for understanding human behavior around the globe, as well as within our own country.

Insights about this concept come largely from the behavioral sciences of sociology, psychology, and anthropology, which study and inform us about how people behave, why they behave as they do, and what the relationship is between human behavior and the environment. Each of us tends to view other people's behavior in the context of our own background, that is, we look at others from the perspective of our own "little world" and are thus subjective. Cultural anthropology is particularly helpful in balancing our perspective by providing objective ways for analyzing and appreciating cultural similarities and dissimilarities. For example, in our society poverty is considered a handicap and a condition to be overcome; whereas in other parts of the world poverty is taken for granted, or even is seen by some as a special blessing.

In essence, human beings create culture or their social environment, as an adaptation to their physical or biological environment. Customs, practices, and traditions for survival and development are thus passed along from generation to generation among a particular people. In time, the group or race become unconscious of the origin of this fund of wisdom. Subsequent generations are conditioned to accept such "truths" about life around them, certain taboos and values are established, and in many ways people are informed of the "accepted" behavior for living in that society. Culture influences and is influenced by every facet of human activity.

Individuals are strongly inclined to accept and belive what their culture tells them. We are affected by the common lore of the community in which we are raised and reside, regardless of the objective validity of this input and imprint. We tend to ignore or block out that which is contrary to the cultural "truth" or conflicts with our beliefs. This is often the basis for prejudice among members of other groups, for refusing to change when cherished notions are challenged. It can become a real problem when a culture and its way of thinking lag behind new discoveries and realities. Scientific and technological advances, for instance, have outrun common cultural teachings for masses of people. This is one of the byproducts of the acceleration of change, and results in a culture gap.

Culture helps us to make sense out of that part of the planet or space inhabited by us. The place is foreign only to strangers, not to those who inhabit it. Culture facilitates living by providing ready-made solutions to problems, by establishing patterns of relations, and ways for preserving group cohesion and consensus. There are many roadmaps, or different approaches for analyzing and categorizing a culture to make it more understandable and less threatening.

CHARACTERISTICS OF CULTURE

Culture provides a people with identity. The next paradigm can be a means for understanding either a macroculture or a microculture. The ten categories, among others, can be used for studying any group of people, whether the global manager is visiting a new plant in the rural South of the United States or a high tech twin plant in Taiwan.

Sense of Self and Space. The comfort one has with self can be expressed differently by culture. Self-identity and appreciation can be manifested by humble bearing in one place, while another calls for macho behavior; independence and creativity are countered in other cultures by group cooperation and conformity. Representatives of some cultures, such as Americans, have a sense of space that requires more distance between the individual and others, while Latins and Vietnamese want to get much closer, almost familiar. Some cultures are very structured and formal, while others are more flexible and informal. Some cultures are very closed and determine one's place very precisely, while others are more open and changing. Each culture validates self in a unique way.

Communication and Language. The communication system, verbal and nonverbal, distinguishes one group from another. Apart from the multitude of "foreign" languages, some nations have fifteen or more major spoken languages (within one language group there are dialects, accents, slang, jargon, and other such variations). Furthermore, the meanings given to gestures, for example, often differ by culture. So, while body language may be universal, its manifestation differs by locality. Subcultures, such as the military, have terminology and signals that cut across national boundaries (such as a salute, or the rank system).

Dress and Appearance. This includes the outward garments and adornments, or lack thereof, as well as body decorations that tend to be distinctive by culture. We have been aware of the Japanese kimono, the African headdress, the Englishman's bowler and umbrella, the Polynesian sarong, and the American Indian headband. Some tribes smear their faces for battle, while some women use cosmetics to manifest beauty. Many subcultures wear distinctive clothing—the "organization-man" look of business, the jeans of the youth culture throughout the world, and uniforms that segregate everyone from students to police. In the military microculture, customs and regulations determine the dress of the day, length of hair, equipment to be worn, and so forth. In colonial times, the U.S. Marines wore long hair, dressed in pantaloons, and carried muskets—yes, many aspects of culture eventually do change!

Food and Feeding Habits. The manner in which food is selected, prepared, presented, and eaten often differs by culture. One man's pet is another person's delicacy—dog, anyone? Americans love beef, yet it is forbidden to Hindus, while the forbidden food in Moslem and Jewish culture is normally pork, eaten extensively by the Chinese and others. In large cosmopolitan cities, restaurants often cater to diverse diets and offer "national" dishes to meet varying cultural tastes. Feeding habits also differ, and the range goes from hands and chop sticks to full sets of cutlery. Even when cultures use a utensil such as a fork, one can distinguish a European from an American by which hand holds the implement. Subcultures, too, can be analyzed from this perspective, such as the executive's dining room, the soldier's mess, the worker's hero or submarine sandwich, or the ladies' tea room, and the vegetarian's restaurant.

Time and Time Consciousness. Sense of time differs by culture, so that some are exact and others are relative. Generally, Germans are precise about the clock, while many Latins are more casual—"mañana." In some cultures, promptness is determined by age or status, thus, in some countries, subordinates are expected on time at staff meetings, but the boss is the last to arrive. Some subcultures, like the military, have their own time system of twenty-four hours—one p.m. civilian time becomes 1300 hours in military time. In such cultures, promptness is rewarded, and in battles, the watches are synchronized. Yet, there are natives in some other cultures who do not bother with hours or minutes, but manage their days by sunrise and sunset.

Time, in the sense of seasons of the year, varies by culture. Some areas of the world think in terms of winter, spring, summer, and fall, but for others the more meaningful designations may be rainy or dry seasons. In the United States, for example, the East and Midwest may be very conscious of the four seasons, while those in the West or Southwest tend to ignore such designations—Californians are more concerned with rainy months and mud slides, or dry months and forest fires.

In the new technological work culture, many industries, such as in power and communications, operate on a round-the-clock schedule. This is of concern to chronobiologists who specialize in research on the body's internal clock by analysis of body temperature, chemical composition of blood serum and urine, sleepiness and peak periods of feeling good. Drastic changes in time, such as can be brought on by shift work, can undermine both performance and personal life, leading to serious accidents on the job.

Relationships. Cultures fix human and organizational relationships by age, sex, status, and degree of kindred, as well as by wealth, power, and wisdom. The family unit is the most common expression of this characteristic, and the arrangement may go from small to large—in a Hindu household, the joint family includes under one roof, mother, father, children, parents, uncles, aunts, and cousins. In fact, one's physical location in such houses may also be determined—males on one side, females on the other. There are some places in which the accepted marriage relationship is monogamy, while in other cultures it may be polygamy or polyandry (one wife, several husbands). In some cultures, the authoritarian figure in the family is the head male, and this fixed relationship is then extended from home to community, and explains why some societies prefer to have a dictator head up the national family. Relationships between and among people vary by category—in some cultures, the elderly are honored, whereas in others they are ignored; in some cultures, women must wear veils and appear deferential, while in others the female is considered the equal, if not the superior of the male.

The military subculture has a classic determination of relationships by rank or protocol, such as the relationships between officers and enlisted personnel. Even off duty, when on base, the recreational facilities are segregated for officers, noncommissioned, and enlisted personnel. The formalization of relationships is evident in some religious subcultures with titles such as "reverend," "guru," "pastor," "rabbi," or "bishop."

Values and Norms. The need systems of cultures vary, as do the priorities they attach to certain behavior in the group. Those operating on a survival level value the gathering of food, adequate covering and shelter; while those with high security needs value material things, money, job titles, as well as law and order. America is a country in the midst of a values revolution as the children of the depression days give way to the children of affluence who are concerned for higher values, like the quality of life, self-fulfillment, and meaning in experiences. It is interesting to note that in some Pacific Island cultures, the greater one's status becomes, the more one is expected to give away or share.

In any event, from its value system, a culture sets norms of behavior for that society. These acceptable standards for membership may range from the work ethic or pleasure to absolute obedience or permissiveness for children; from rigid submission of the wife to her husband to women's total liberation. As anthropologist Ina Brown reminds us, "People in different cultures are pleased, concerned, annoyed, or embarrassed about different things because they perceive situations in terms of different sets of premises." Because conventions are learned, some cultures demand honesty with members of one's own group, but accept a more relaxed standard with strangers. Some of these conventions are expressed in gift-giving; rituals for birth, death, and marriage; guidelines for privacy, showing respect or deference, expressing good manners, etc.

Beliefs and Attitudes. Possibly the most difficult classification is ascertaining the major belief themes of a people, and how this and other factors influence their attitudes toward themselves, others, and what happens in their world. People in all cultures seem to have a concern for the supernatural that is evident in their religions and religious practices. Primitive cultures, for example, have a belief in spiritual beings labeled by us as "animism." In the history of human development there has been an evolution in our spiritual sense until today many moderns use terms like "cosmic consciousness" to indiciate their belief in the transcendental powers. Between these two extremes in the spiritual continuum, religious traditions in various cultures consciously or unconsciously influence our attitudes toward life, death, and the hereafter. Western culture seems to be largely influenced by the Judeo-Christian-Islamic traditions, while Eastern or Oriental cultures seem to have been dominated by Buddhism, Confucianism, Taoism, and Hinduism. Religion, to a degree, expresses the philosophy of a people about important facets of life—it is influenced by culture and vice versa.

The position of women in a society is often the manifestation of such beliefs—in some societies the female is enshrined, in others she is treated like an equal, and in still others she is subservient to the male and treated like chattel.

A people's religious belief system is somewhat dependent on their stage of human development: tribesmen and primitives tend to be superstitious and the practice of voodoo is illustrative of this; some religions are deeply locked into the agricultural stage of development, while many so-called advanced technological people seem to be more irreligious, substituting a belief in science for faith in traditional religions and their practices.

Mental Process and Learning. Some cultures emphasize one aspect of brain development over another, so that one may observe striking differences in the way people think and learn. Anthropologist Edward Hall maintains that the mind is internalized culture, and the process involves how people organize and process information. Life in a particular locale defines the rewards and punishment for learning or not learning certain information or in a certain way, and this is confirmed and reinforced by the culture there. For example, Germans stress logic, while the Japanese and the Navajo reject the Western idea of logic. Logic for a Hopi Indian is based on preserving the integrity of their social system and all the relationships connected with it. Some cultures favor abstract thinking and conceptualization, while others prefer rote memory and learning. What seems to be universal is that each culture has a reasoning process, but then each manifests the process in its own distinctive way.

Work Habits and Practices (e.g., Rewards and Recognitions). Another dimension for examining a group's culture is their attitudes toward work, the dominant types of work, the division of work, and the work habits or practices, such as promotions or rewards. Work has been defined as exertion or effort directed to produce or accomplish something. There are a variety of terms related to the concept, such as labor, toil, undertaking, employment, as well as career, profession, occupation, and job. Some cultures espouse a work ethic in which all members are expected to engage in a desirable and worthwhile activity. In other societies this is broadly defined, so that cultural pursuits in music and arts or sports are included. For some cultures, the worthiness of the activity is narrowly measured in terms of income produced, or the worth of the individual is assessed in terms of job status. In the past, or where a religious view of work still prevails, work is viewed as an act of service to God and people, and is expressed in a moral commitment to the job or quality of effort. In Japan, the cultural loyalty to family is transferred to the organization that employs the person and the quality of one's performance—it is expressed in work group participation, communication, and consensus.

Work within a country can be analyzed as to the dominant vocational activity of the majority. Thus, in the context of stages of human development, a people can be characterized primarily as hunters, farmers, factory or knowledge/service workers. Most economically advanced societies are in transition from an industrial work culture to a metaindustrial or technological type of work. Prior to this century, work required considerable expenditure of physical energy; today more emotional and mental energy is necessary because the nature and tools of work have changed (such as from the availability of new technologies in the form of automation and robots). The attitude change is away from work as subsistence, and the distinctions between work and play are eroding. New conceptions of work are evolving so that it is seen as more than earning a living, and the shift in work is away from material production to non-material goods, like information processing and service. The emphasis is upon quality of work life—the "worth ethic" now considers an employee's worth beyond the job.

The manner in which work is divided in a culture can also be evaluated. From the feudal ages through the industrial age, whether in the military, trading companies, or industrial corporation, the bureaucratic culture was expressed in a hierarchy. The pyramid organization that resulted was divided by level and functions, each with its own head. The trend is away from this form of defined, individualistic activities toward teams, work sharing, and other new norms of an emerging work culture. (Work policies, procedures, customs, and traditions can also be studied as indicated in Chapters 6 and 7.)

Another way of observing a culture is to note the manner and method for proffering praise for good and brave deeds, length of service, or some other types of accomplishment, ranging from war bonnets and belts of scalps to testimonial dinners and expense accounts, to commendations and medals.

These ten general classifications are a simple model for assessing a particular culture. It does not include every aspect of culture, nor is it the only way to analyze culture. This approach, and others described in subsequent chapters, enable managers to examine a people systemically. Our breakdown into ten categories is a convenient beginning for cultural understanding that can be used as one travels around the world and visits different cultures, or the model can be used to study the microcultures within a majority national culture. Just remember that all aspects of culture are interrelated, and to change one part is to change the whole. There is a danger in trying to compartmentalize a complex concept like culture, yet retaining a sense of its whole.

SYSTEMS APPROACH TO CULTURE

Because there are many different anthropological approaches to cultural analysis, some readers may prefer to use this coordinated systems approach as an alternative. A system, in this sense, refers to an ordered assemblage or combination of correlated parts which form a unitary whole (Miller 1978).

Kinship System—the family relationships and way a people reproduce, train, and socialize their children. The typical American family is nuclear and a rather independent unit; in other countries, there may be an extended family that consists of several generations held together through the male line (patrilineal) or through the female line (matrilineal). Such families have a powerful influence on child rearing, and often on nation building. The multinational manager needs to appreciate the significance of this influence to supervise effectively minority workers like blacks or chicanos in the United States, or to deal in the world marketplace with businessmen from Vietnam or China. Family influences and loyalties can affect job performance or business negotiations.

Educational System—how young or new members of a society are provided with information, knowledge, skills, and values. If one is opening up a factory in India, for instance, the training plan had better include the rote method of education, whereas in some advanced societies the expectations would be for sophisticated, educational technology. Educational systems may be formal and informal within any culture.

Economic System—the manner in which the society produces and distributes its goods and services. The Japanese economic system is an extension of the family and is so group oriented that many foreigners view it as "Japan, Inc." Today, while much of the world is divided into capitalistic or socialistic economic blocks, it is evident that regional economic cooperatives are merging to cross national and ideological boundaries. Macroeconomics is the study of such systems.

Political System—the dominant means of governance for maintaining order and exercising power or authority. Some cultures are still in a tribal stage where chiefs rule, others in the Middle East have a ruling royal family with an operating king as headman, while still others in the First, Second, Third, or Fourth Worlds prefer democracy or communism, or some medium between these political extremes. Although world society seems to be evolving beyond the nation-state, the cosmopolitan manager is forced to understand and deal with governments as they presently are structured with all their diversity, and even regressiveness.

Religious System—the means for providing meaning and motivation beyond the material aspects of life, that is, the spiritual side of a culture or its approach to the supernatural. The significance of this has been alluded to earlier under "Beliefs and Attitudes." This transcending system may lift a people to great heights of accomplishment, as is witnessed in the pyramids of Egypt and the Renaissance of Europe, or it may lock them into a static past. It is possible to project the history and future of India, for instance, in terms of the impact of its belief in reincarnation, which is enshrined in its major religion. Diverse national cultures can be somewhat unified under a shared religious belief in Islam or Christianity, for example.

Association System—the network of social groupings that people form. These may range from fraternal and secret societies to professional/trade associations and the Mafia. Some cultures are very group oriented and create formal and informal associations for every conceivable type of activity. Other societies are individualistic and avoid such organizing.

Health System—the way a culture prevents and cures disease or illness, or cares for victims of disasters or accidents. The concepts of health and wholeness, well being and medical problems differ by culture. Some countries have witch doctors and herb medications, others like India have few government-sponsored social services, while Britain has a system of socialized medicine. The U.S.A. is in the midst of a major transition in its health care and delivery system, and there is increasing emphasis on holistic health and Eastern treatments.

Recreational System—the ways in which a people socialize, or use their leisure time. What may be considered play in one culture may be viewed as work in another, and vice versa. In some cultures "sport" has considerable political implications, in others it is solely for enjoyment, while in still others, it is big business. Certain types of entertainment, such as a form of folk dancing, seem to cut across cultures.

These systems are the principal ones that might be examined by a person trying to better understand a particular culture. They offer an orderly approach to the study of major or minority cultural groupings. For business persons hoping to succeed in a foreign culture, such information and insight could make the difference between profit and loss.

Obviously, there are many other systems that could be analyzed within a culture, such as work or management systems. Hay Associates of Philadelphia, a Pennsylvania management consulting group, advises its clients that what may be effective in home operations in attracting, motivating, and retaining managerial talent may not work in subsidiaries abroad. For purposes of human resource management, they suggest examination of overseas' enterprises in the context of three microcultures or systems of organization—the *bureaucratic*, the *technical*, and the *managerial*. Table 8-1 provides a summary of the Hay model in terms of structure, job designs, decision-making, control, compensation plans, job security and career development. It can be used for systematic analysis and assessment for human resource management of foreign entities. Global managers might apply the paradigm for examination of employee values and motivations abroad, for in-country evaluation of the effectiveness of multinational personnel policies and programs, local management's readiness for change. The Hay consultants have found the model useful for understanding the cultural leanings of overseas subsidiaries, so that American human resource practices could be adapted.

Table 8-1*
Managing Human Resources in Different Cultures

	In the Bureaucratic Culture	In the Technical Culture	In the Managerial Culture
Structuring the Organization	Establish rational and detailed organization chart to be communicated throughout the organization.	Develop, organize and obtain consensus or interrelationships among functions.	Keep organization minimal and adaptive to changes.
Designing Jobs	Formalize and standardize job descriptions. Put emphasis on tasks to be performed.	Formalize relationships as accountabilities will be most often shared. Put emphasis on processes to be adopted.	Be flexible and formalize accountabilities. Put emphasis on end results to be accomplished.
Delegating Decision-Making Authority	Extremely limited delegation and freedom are required.	Decision-making must be mostly controlled.	High degree of delegation and freedom is supported.
Controlling and Assessing Performance	Need for a heavy system of administrative checks and balances to measure how tasks are performed. Emphasis is on compliance with standards and norms.	Effective cost accounting system is required to measure efficiency. Emphasis is on qualitative criteria.	Sophisticated control system is required to measure end results. Emphasis is on quantitative criteria.
External Competitiveness	Usually minimal.	Median.	High.
Internal Equity	Must be absolute and normative. Must integrate seniority and diplomas.	Limited. Must reflect balance of power among functions.	Fair Must reflect job value and performance.
Incentive Components	None	Limited	High
Benefits	Highly formalized and common throughout the organization.	Formalized and personalized.	Informal and personalized.
Providing Job Security	Must be absolute.	Fair	Minimal

* From Management Memo #316, May 7, 1979, Hay Associates, 229 South 18th St., Philadelphia, Pennsylvania 19103, U.S.A. Reprinted with permission.

Table 8-1 (Continued)
Managing Human Resources in Different Cultures

	In the Bureaucratic Culture	In the Technical Culture	In the Managerial Culture
Career Development	Strict and objective rules and procedures must be established for promotions and career developments.	Develop bridges between functions to improve organizational integration.	Reward high performers through rapid promotions.

The Bureaucratic Culture. Typical of protectionist and developing countries (France, Japan), this culture is also most frequently found in companies operating in protected and stable markets. It is characterized by an impersonal style and absolute reliance on standards, norms and rigid procedures. Best supported by a strictly pyramidal and centralized hierarchy with very little internal competition, this is truly the place for the "organization man."

The Managerial Culture. Typical of trading countries early open to free competition (The Netherlands, Switzerland), this culture is most frequently encountered in companies operating in highly competitive and innovative industries. It is characterized by a truly managerial style and clearly performance oriented. Supported by a flexible and adaptive organization, it is the reign of the business manager.

The Technical Culture. Typical of countries with a long tradition of technical expertise (Germany, U.K.), this culture is also most commonly found in companies operating in well-established and traditional industries. It has a somewhat paternalistic style and relies heavily on technical know-how. Supported by a heavy functionalized organization, functional "warlords" attempt to build empires around their know-how, leading to fierce interdepartmental competition. Recognition and ultimate power at the top goes to the technician.

KEY CULTURAL TERMINOLOGY

The specialists who make a formal study of culture use terms that may be helpful to the layperson trying to comprehend the significance of this phenomena in business or international life.

Patterns and Themes

Some cultural anthropologists, like Ruth Benedict, try to search for a single *integrative pattern* to describe a particular culture. Thus, the Pueblo Indians may be designated as "apollonian"—people who stick to the "middle of the road" and avoid excess or conflict in their valuing of existence. The pinpointing of a consistent pattern of thought and action in a culture is difficult, so other scholars prefer to seek a *summative theme*. This is a position, declared or implied, that simulates activity and controls behavior; it is usually tacitly approved or openly promoted in the society. One can note that in most Asian cultures there is a "fatalism" theme, while in the American business subculture the theme is profits or the "bottom line."

Explicit and Implicit

Some aspects of culture are overt, while others are covert. Anthropologist Clyde Kluckhohn reminds us that each different way of life makes assumptions about the ends or purposes of human existence, about what to expect from each other and the gods, about what constitutes fulfillment or frustration. Some of this is *explicit* in the lore of the folk, and may be manifest in law, regulations, customs, or traditions. Other aspects are *implicit* in the culture, and one must infer such tacit premises by observing consistent trends in word and deed. The distinction between public and hidden culture points up that much of our daily activity is governed by patterns and themes of which we may be only dimly aware, or totally unaware of their origin or meaning. Such culturally governed behavior facilitates the routine of daily living, so that one may perform in a society many actions without thinking about it. This cultural conditioning provides the freedom to devote conscious thinking to new and creative pursuits. It is startling to realize that some of our behavior is not entirely free or consciously willed by us. At times this can be a national problem, such as when a society finally realizes that implicit in its culture is a form of racism, which requires both legislation and reeducation in equal employment opportunity and affirmative action to rectify.

Micro- or Subcultures

Within a larger society, group, or nation sharing a common majority or macroculture, there may be subgroupings of people possessing characteristic traits that set them apart and distinguish them from the others. These *subcultures* may be described in group classification by age, class, sex, race or some other entity that differentiates this micro- from the macroculture. Youth, or more specifically teenagers, share certain cultural traits, as do Blacks, Jews, or other ethnic groups. Occupationally, there are many microcultures, such as white- or blue-collar workers, police or the military, college students or surfers, the underworld or drug culture.

Universals and Diversity

The paradox of culture is the commonalities that exist in the midst of its diffusion or even confusion. There are generalizations that may be made about all cultures that are referred to as *universals*: age-grading, body adornments, calendar, courtship, divisions of labor, education, ethics, food taboos, incest and inheritance rules, language, marriage, mourning, mythology, numerals, penal sanctions, property rights, supernatural beliefs, status differentiation, tool making and trade, visiting, and weaning, etc. Thus, certain activities occur across cultures, but their manifestation may be unique in a particular society. And that brings us to the opposite concept of cultural *diversity*. Some form of sports or humor or music may be common to all peoples, but the way in which it is accomplished is distinctive in various cultural groupings.

The close relationship between human behavior and culture was underscored by Leslie White when he commented, "Instead of explaining cultural differences among peoples by saying one culture is phlegmatic, taciturn, unimaginative, and prosaic, we might view these behaviors as differences in cultural traditions that stimulate a respective population."

Rational/Irrational/Nonrational Behavior

Among the many definitions of culture, consider it as historically created designs for living that may be rational, irrational, and nonrational. *Rational* behavior in a culture is based on what that group considers as reasonable for achieving its goals. *Irrational* behavior deviates from the accepted norms of a society and may result from deep frustration of an individual in trying to satisfy needs; it would appear to be done without reason and possibly largely as an emotional response. *Nonrational* behavior is neither based on reason, nor is it against reasonable expectations—it is dictated by one's own culture or subculture. A great deal of behavior is of this type, and we are unaware of why we do it, why we believe what we do, or that we may be biased or prejudiced from the perspective of those outside our cultural group. How often and when to take a bath frequently is a cultural dictate, just as what food constitutes breakfast. What is rational in one culture may be irrational in another, and vice versa. Some societies send political dissidents to mental institutions for what is considered irrational behavior.

Tradition

This is a very important aspect of culture that may be expressed in unwritten customs, taboos, and sanctions. Tradition can program a people as to what is proper behavior and procedures relative to food, dress, and certain types of people, what to value, avoid, or deemphasize. As the song on the subject of "Tradition" from the musical, *Fiddler on the Roof*, extols:

> Because of our traditions, we keep our sanity. . . . Tradition tells us how to sleep, how to work, how to wear clothes. . . . How did it get started? I don't know—it's a tradition. . . . Because of our traditions, everyone knows who he is and what God expects of him!

Traditions provide a people with a "mindset" and have a powerful influence on their moral system for evaluating what is right or wrong, good or bad, desirable or not. Traditions express a particular culture, giving its members a sense of belonging and uniqueness. But whether one is talking of a tribal or national culture, a military or religious subculture, traditions should be reexamined regularly for their relevance and validity. Because of accelerating change, traditions must be revised or adapted to fit the changed condition of a technological age in the midst of creating a world culture.

CULTURAL UNDERSTANDING AND SENSITIVITY

The cosmopolitan manager, sensitive to cultural differences, appreciates a people's distinctiveness, and seeks to make allowances for such factors when communicating with representatives of that cultural group. He or she avoids trying to impose one's own cultural attitudes and approaches upon these "foreigners." Thus, by respecting the cultural differences of others, we will not be labeled as "ethnocentric." *The Random House Dictionary* defines ethnocentrism as

> Belief in the inherent superiority of one's own group and culture; it may be accompanied by feelings of contempt for those others who do not belong; it tends to look down upon those considered as foreign; it views and measures alien cultures and groups in terms of one's own culture.

Through cross-cultural experiences, we become more broadminded and tolerant of cultural "peculiarities." When this is coupled with some formal study of the concept of culture, we not only gain new insights for improving our human relations, but we become aware of the impact of our native culture upon us. Cultural understanding may minimize the impact of culture shock, and maximize intercultural experiences. For the manager it represents a new body of knowledge or a tool to increase professional development and organizational effectiveness with employees, customers, and other people encountered in the course of daily business. Certainly, it should teach us that culture and behavior are relative, and that we should be more tentative, and less absolute, in our human interactions.

To manage cultural differences more effectively, the first step in the process is increasing one's general cultural awareness. One must understand the concept of culture and its characteristics before a manager can fully benefit by the study of cultural specifics and a foreign language.

If global managers are to practice civility and avoid indiscretions while operating in the world marketplace, we must know and observe international etiquette. A gentleman or woman is a person who never intentionally inflicts pain. In observing local cultural and social customs, sensitive leaders avoid using the name of God in Islamic countries, never call a Muslim a Mohammedan; pronounce national and individual names correctly; adhere to in-country preferences for titles, dress, distance, and other formalities or informalities.

SUMMARY

Developing cultural awareness and understanding in global managers has been the central thrust of this discussion. Wide-ranging applications of such insights at home and abroad were provided to emphasize how human performance could be improved by these means. To increase our effectiveness in international interactions, the concept of culture and its characteristics were examined in some depth. Several approaches for examining any macro- or microculture were offered. One provided ten general classifications for this purpose.

A systems strategy for studying a culture was also reviewed, including a model for managing human resources in three different types of work culture—bureaucratic, technical, and managerial. Business leaders were invited to expand their vocabulary and insights by adopting some of the terminology employed by cultural anthropologists. It is hoped a groundwork was laid for better cultural comprehension that will lead to better appreciation of the chapters to follow on international business exchanges.

9
Managing Transitions and Foreign Deployment

Early researchers in cross-cultural studies were concerned primarily with the change experienced when a person leaves his home culture to go abroad. Today, the emergence of a global economy and market is moving nations into growing interdependence, facilitating the cross-border flow of people, ideas, and information. Mass media and transportation, particularly satellite technology, have literally turned this planet into a village, and its diverse inhabitants are becoming more comfortable with one another.

We have been intimating that the trauma of transition not only involves going overseas, but increasingly will focus upon our coping capacity with the new work culture. Paul Strassman (1985), a Xerox vice-president, for instance lectures and writes on the theme, "The Transformation of Work in the Information Age":

> It is the task of our leadership to rethink the values of our industrial culture and to devise new organizations, new roles for people, new economic relationships, and new ways for communicating. A service-based economy that maximizes the value of its people is just ahead of us.

COPING WITH TRANSITIONAL CHALLENGES

Increasingly we interact with people who are very different from us, or with situations that are very unfamiliar to us. Even when we share a common nationality, we may have to deal with citizens who are indeed "foreign" to us in their thinking, attitudes, vocabulary, and background. Or we find ourselves encountering conditions that are totally unexpected and cause us to be very uncomfortable.

It is not just an issue of going abroad to a strange land that calls for innovative coping, but we may have challenges within our environment to move beyond our upbringing or local cultural conditioning. Such *transitional experiences* urge us to go forward and succeed in a new unknown, or to regress back into the safe past. Depending on how we answer such challenging opportunities, growth or disruption may follow. Such experiences happen to minority or foreign students who enter college, white supervisors of minority workers; prison parolees, returning veterans; married couples who divorce, families who move from one geographic area to another location within a nation; those who change careers in midlife or have major alterations in their roles; and to multinational managers and technicians going overseas (Harris, 1985).

To get a sense of transitional experience that can cause cultural shock, consider the following scenarios:

First World to Third World. You board a jet for a year's assignment abroad in a country radically different from your own, in which you will be perceived as "the foreigner." You leave a so-called advanced nation—an urban technological society—and in a matter of hours find yourself in an ancient, agricultural land. The mass of people live as rural peasants in villages, with a scattering of immensely populated cities. You have been raised in a Western culture in the Judeo-Christian tradition, but your hosts are in Eastern culture, from a Hindu-Moslem tradition with a bewildering variety of minor religions (from Parsi, who leave their dead on high places for the vultures to consume, to Jains, who will not kill any living thing including flies and insects). Depending on your host's religious affiliation, beef or pork are forbidden foods, so poultry and fish will be your main diet. You must now cope with an Oriental mindset; an Asian sense of time, place, and face. The population is multicultural and multiracial, speaking fifteen different languages and over five hundred dialects. Suddenly, you are aware that beneath a veneer of modernity, you realize that what you once read about in the Bible or history, is now real—bullock carts, sacred animals, dung used for building material, widows throwing themselves upon their husband's funeral pyre, and poverty like you did not know still existed. All the things you took for granted in your "developed" country are not available—from radio or television at any hour, to filing cabinets and electric appliances, to convenience packaging and frozen foods. All your reference points and groups are off. Simple actions at home become horrendous operations here. Now make the most of this opportunity and enjoy your visit!

Majority to Minority Culture. Your company transfers you and your family to a section of your country where you feel like an "immigrant." From the Northeast you come to this Sunbelt that is so different and unique. In fact, your boss suggests you enroll in Rice University to take a course entitled, "Living Texas." She says it will help you and your family to get introduced to the myths and mannerisms of Texans, so you will not be so culturally isolated among these boisterous, unusual natives. It teaches newcomers how to adapt to this former republic, rather than have you try to recreate the environment you just left. You are considered "people from the outside" in this land of rapid growth and petropower, which Easterners tend to stereotype as a center of rightism, repression, and racism. It is a state of contrasts from huge ranches and high technology to Bible-belt mentality and laws. So you sign up for the course that covers everything from "Talking Texas" and Texas cooking to the Mexican side of the Texas revolution and Texas folk heroes. If you can adapt, you will probably fall in love with these friendly people, their jalapeño lollipops and chili pepper dishes and even discover their diverse ethnic mixture and the "Austin sound" of music.

Mainland to Island Mentality. You are an American of Puerto Rican descent, one of many thousands born or reared on the U.S. mainland. As a second-generation "Neorican," you decide to go back to the Commonwealth for college. You are enrolled in the Catholic University of Ponce, but you are having trouble assimilating to the land of your ancestors. As an ex-New Yorker, you learn you have no edge in getting a part-time job because of your better education. Yes, you are resented in an economy with an average 20% unemployment. When you get a position, you get paid less than NYC; high-paying jobs are scarce. Furthermore, you realize that you also speak Spanish poorly in comparison with the natives, and in this culture you are perceived as an "outsider." As one of more than a million Neoricans here, you are seen as a group to be more independent and aggressive—you think, act, and talk *differently*. Some of you have not been able to adjust and so returned to the States. You are somewhat ridiculed by the locals because you are unfair competition for scarce jobs among a growing population, you speak "Spanglish" (a mixture of English and Spanish), you have odd cultural traits, and you come from a "drug culture" (metropolitan New York). Furthermore, when you do speak English well, your fellow students and workers think you are "showing off!" In fact, although you had a normal, happy home life on the mainland, here you have to fight an *image* of Neoricans as "drug addicts, immoral, overly aggressive, and undereducated." Although you avoid politics, you are accused by your presence of helping to speed up the cause of statehood. Yet, you love the climate, the beaches, the life-style, and the people. You know that upon graduation, your temporary job with the airline can be turned into a permanent one as a customer representative. So you decide to plant roots and join "Neoricans in Puerto Rico, Inc."

These three incidents are real transitional experiences. Having indepth, intercultural encounters can be stimulating or psychologically disturbing, depending on your preparation for them and your approach to them. The process of adjustment or acculturation to a new living environment or a different kind of people takes time, usually some months, for we have to learn new skills for responding and adapting to the unfamiliar. The stranger the environment or indigenous population, the longer it may take the "foreigner" to adapt and the more that individual may be "thrown off" by the situation. When abroad, the extent of the trauma depends on whether one lives on the economy, or in a military/diplomatic/corporate compound with his or her own kind. The experience of coping with human differences around this globe can be renewing or devastating.

In the musical *Fiddler on the Roof*, Tevye, the father of the family, sings a wonderful tune entitled, "Tradition," which provides two helpful insights into this issue of transitional experiences. He observes, "Because of our traditions, we have kept our balance for many years. Because of our traditions, everyone of us knows who he is and what God expects of him." When we are in a place where the traditions and customs are foreign and unexpected, we may lose our balance and become unsure of ourselves. The same thing can happen within our own society when change happens so rapidly that all the old traditions, the cues we live by, are suddenly undermined and irrelevant. Stress and frustrations can build up when we go outside our own culture, or even within our own society when it is in the midst of a profound transition, as it is in the last part of the twentieth century. Under such circumstances our very sense of self becomes threatened.

Transitional experiences offer us two alternatives—to cope or to "cop out." We can learn to comprehend, survive in, and grow through immersion in a different culture. The positive result can be further self development and movement toward a higher level of personal awareness and growth. Whenever we leave home for the unfamiliar, it involves basic changes in habits, relationships, and sources of satisfaction. Inherent in cultural change is the opportunity to leave behind, perhaps temporarily, one set of relationships and living patterns, and to enrich one's life by experimenting with new ones. Implicit in the personal conflict and discontinuity produced by such experiences is the possible transcendence from environment or family support to self support. Intercultural situations of psychological, social, or cultural stress also stimulate us to review and redefine our lives; to see our own country and people in a new perspective. Or, we may reject the changes or new culture and possibly lose a growth opportunity (Furnham and Bochner, 1987).

CULTURE SHOCK

Grammatically, the term should be "cultural shock," but popularly it is known as culture shock. The phenomenon may, and often does, occur during a major transitional experience. But, what is it exactly? Perhaps a few quotations may help us to get a fix on the concept.

Dr. Kalervo Oberg, an anthropologist, referred to culture shock as a generalized trauma one experiences in a new and different culture because of having to learn and cope with a vast array of new cultural cues and expectations, while discovering that your old ones probably do not fit or work. More precisely he notes:

> Culture shock is precipitated by the anxiety that results from losing all our familiar signs and symbols of social intercourse. These signs or cues

include the thousand and one ways in which we orient ourselves to the situations of daily life: how to give orders, how to make purchases, when and when not to respond. Now these cues which may be words, gestures, facial expressions, customs, or norms are acquired by all of us in the course of growing up and are as much a part of our culture, as the language we speak or the beliefs we accept. All of us depend for our peace of mind and efficiency on hundreds of these cues, most of which we are not consciously aware.

As modern managers become more cosmopolitan in their attitudes and lifestyles, the impact of culture shock may be lessened. Research is underway to try and identify those individuals who are more prone to suffer from this malady, especially severe when one must live for a long time in another culture. Professor W. J. Redden (1975), developed a *Culture Shock Inventory* for this purpose. His premise is that:

> Culture shock is a psychological disorientation caused by misunderstanding or not understanding the cues from another culture. It arises from such things as lack of knowledge, limited prior experience, and personal rigidity.

Therefore, he assesses persons going on foreign deployment on eight measures:

1. Western Ethnocentrism—the degree to which the Western value system is seen as appropriate for other parts of the world.
2. Intercultural Experience—the degree of direct experience with people from other countries, through working, traveling, and conversing; also learned skills, such as language and culture studies.
3. Cognitive Flex—the degree of openness to new ideas, beliefs, experiences, and the ability of the individual to accept these.
4. Behavioral Flex—the degree to which one's own behavior is open to change or alteration; the ability to experiment with new styles.
5. Cultural Knowledge: Specific—the degree of awareness and understanding of various customs, beliefs, and patterns of behavior in a specific other culture.
6. Cultural Knowledge: General—the degree of awareness, sensitivity, and understanding of various beliefs and institutions in other cultures.
7. Culture Behavior—the degree of awareness and understanding of patterns of cultural differences and human behavior.
8. Interpersonal Sensitivity—the degree of awareness and understanding of verbal and nonverbal human behavior.

These categories are interesting for they provide clues to the kind of personality to be cultivated if a professional or manager is to successfully cope in the international arena.

Psychologists Judith Meyers and Collen Kelley have developed the "Cross-Cultural Adaptability Inventory" (1989). This 50-item questionnaire, which can be completed in about twenty minutes, measures four dimensions associated with effectively adapting and adjusting to another culture. They are emotional resilience, flexibility or openness, perceptual acuity, and personal autonomy. These factors consistently appear in the literature on intercultural competence, but, to date, no norms or comparative data are available. However, as an instrument used in a training program, it is very helpful. (For information contact: Judith E. Meyers, Ph.D., 1125½ Torrey Pines Road, La Jolla, CA 92037 USA)

Studies have shown that children are more adaptable to new cultural challenges, while spouses, usually wives, are more prone to experience cultural shock—its impact is lessened on their partner immersed in the foreign business experience. However, upon return to the home culture, the manager, professional, or technician is likely to confront "reentry shock."

When in a strange culture, our concerns that may disturb or frustrate, may be real or imagined. Those in culture shock manifest obvious *symptoms* such as excessive concern over cleanliness, feeling that what is new and strange is "dirty"; this may be seen with reference to water, food, dishes, and bedding, or it might be evident in excessive fear of servants and shopkeepers relative to the disease they might bear. Other indications of the person in such trauma are feelings of helplessness and confusion, growing dependence on long-term residents of one's own nationality, constant irritations over delays and minor frustrations, as well as undue concern for being cheated, robbed, or injured. Some become mildly hypochondriac, expressing overconcern for minor pains and skin eruptions—it may even get to the point of real psychosomatic illnesses. Often, such individuals postpone learning the local language and customs, dwelling instead on their loneliness and longing for back home, to be with one's own and to talk to people who "make sense." However, persons who seek international assignments as a means of escaping "back-home problems" with career, marriage, drugs or alcoholism will probably only exacerbate personal problems that might be better resolved in one's native culture.

Culture shock is neither good or bad, necessary or unnecessary. It is a reality that many people face when in strange and unexpected situations. Individuals should seek to minimize the dysfunctional effects and maximize the opportunities of another cultural experience. World corporations, government agencies, and international foundations, should try to reduce culture shock in order to be more cost effective, to promote the employee's productivity abroad, or to improve client and customer relations with host nationals. What can be done to facilitate acculturation when business or pleasure take one for an extensive stay in another country or continent? Such answers are equally valid for foreign students brought to another country for study or training, as well as to bicultural exchanges or third country nationals who are brought to one's homeland for business or public service.

Organizations responsible for sending others abroad should be careful in their recruitment and selection of their own nationals for foreign service. Surveys have shown that those who adjust and work well in international assignments are usually well-integrated personalities with qualities such as, flexibility, personal stability, social maturity, and social inventiveness. Cosmopolitans either have fewer prejudices, or are at least aware of their own biases, and can be more tolerant of the objects of their bias. Such candidates for overseas work are not given to grandiose or unrealistic expectations, irrational concepts of self or others, nor do they have tendencies toward excessive depression, discouragement, criticism, or hostility.

On the other hand, one should also be realistic about the difficulties that may be experienced when living abroad. Intestinal disorders and exotic diseases *are real*, and may not always be avoided by innoculations or new antiobiotics. In some countries, water, power, transportation, and housing shortages *are real*, and one's physical comfort may be seriously inconvenienced. In other nations at various stages of development, political instability, tribal wars, ethnic feuds, and social breakdown may make such places undesirable, for a time, in which to accept or seek an assignment. Real difficulties can arise from not knowing how to communicate in a land that is foreign to a person, or in trying to cope with strange climates or customs. But we are born with the ability to learn, to adapt, to survive, to enjoy. After all, human beings do create culture, so the shocks caused by such differences are not unbearable or without value. The intercultural experience can be most satisfying, contributing much to personal and professional advancement. One can discover neighbors everywhere, and develop friends in the world community.

Consultant Martha Sinetar uses the term *relo shock* to describe the confusion, lethargy, "blues," or other ailments that may accompany domestic relocation of job and residence. To meet the challenge of personal growth and adaptation involved, she recommends (1986):

- Let go of the past and get enthusiastically excited about a new experience, rather than be overwhelmed by fear of the unknown.
- Transform angry and negative feelings into positive emotions and planning for the new opportunity.
- Reinforce your own self-confidence and the self-esteem of family members so you can indeed cope with and capitalize on the transfer.
- Visualize your ideal move by scrutinizing your motives and values and then commit to the relocation.
- Know and establish your stability zones by instituting in the new location those familiar habits and routines that make you feel at home, giving sense and permanence to your new life.

The phenomenon and process of culture shock has applications to other life crises. The descriptions and information provided in the previous section have transfer value for the person going through a divorce, or recovering from near-death illness. For example, there is the matter of *role shock*. Each of us choses or is assigned or is conditioned to a variety of roles in society and its organizations—son or daughter, parent or child, husband or wife, teacher or engineer, manager or union organizer, man or woman. In these positions, people have expectations of us and we have expectations of them, and such expectations often differ for a role in different cultures. A woman, for instance, may do in one culture what is forbidden in another. In some societies, senior citizens are revered, while in others they are ignored. In some places, youth regards teachers with awe, while in others they treat them as inferiors or "buddies."

But that role perception is subject to change, even accelerated change, as many are experiencing today within their own culture. The person who has a particular understanding of what a manager is and does, may be upset when he or she finally achieves that role and finds it to be changed, so that one's traditional views of the function are suddenly obsolete. It can be very disconcerting, and the shock may be severe or long lasting. Role shock can lead to identity crisis if one's life is tightly linked to a job or role. A cross-cultural assignment can accentuate role shock. Many technicians sent abroad find themselves in totally different role requirements than back home—for example, they may be asked to do less themselves, and to devote more time to training, consulting, and supervising.

When individuals return from foreign deployment, possibly having experienced long times as expatriates, there is another form of reverse culture shock that can be faced. Having perceived their own culture from abroad, more objectively, one can have a more severe and sustained jolt through *reentry shock*. Robert Maddox, writing in *Personnel*, maintains that the problem is growing in the multinational marketplace, and that managers need special counsel to assist their reintegration into their native country and parent organization. Some returning "expats" feel a subtle downgrading and loss of prestige and benefits. Others bewail the loss of servants and higher social contacts, as well as other overseas "perks." Many feel uncomfortable for six months or more in their native land, frustrated with their old company, bored with their narrow-minded colleagues. They seem out of touch with what has happened in the country or corporation, and no longer seem to fit in. The phenomenon can be temporary and the person assisted with reorientation programs. But for some, culture and reentry shocks can be the means for major choices and transitions to a new locale, new job or career, and new life-style. Other "expats" never make the necessary adjustment, and live as strangers in their own homelands.

So many people are saying, "stop the world, I want to get off"; many are succumbing to escapisms like alcoholism, drug addiction, terrorism, or hedonism. Many who cannot "shift their gears" to the new culture and life-style, who cannot make the transition to a different society of the future, will not make it into the twenty-first century, either figuratively or literally. It is our contention that people who are more cosmopolitan, have experienced culture shock, have profited from opportunities to deal with human differences, are, as a result, likely to cope more effectively with future shock. As human society moves beyond industrialism and creates a new civilization, people need to become more anticipatory, as well as participatory in the decisions that shape their future. By adapting and planning change, we can ease the trauma of transition! One can begin the process by completing the *So You're Going Abroad Survey* (Appendix A).

FOSTERING ACCULTURATION

Stress or tension is no respecter of time, place, or persons. In today's "pressure-cooker" world, some tension is almost normal, so modern persons must learn to defuse stress, reduce tension to controllable levels, and to alleviate pressures. Otherwise, insecurity, instability, and insomnia take over.

Characteristic of American culture is the drive for success, and a low tolerance for failure. When such nationals go abroad, they often find it more difficult to evaluate progress and measure their success. This frustrates them, leading to greater anxiety, sometimes to hostility, and eventually to reduced productivity. What, then, can be done to better manage the expected stress and strain of intercultural living and working? Meditation, biofeedback, and exercise are certainly preferable to tranquilizers.

Writing in *Mental Hygiene* some years ago about "Family Adaptation Overseas," H. David and D. Elkind pointed out that stable, healthy family relationships abroad can make the difference between success and failure in the foreign assignment. Families trained to interact in mutually supportive ways can provide themselves with their own resources for adjustment in an alien environment. In other words, an innovative family community can provide the ego support that may not, at first, seem evident in the second culture. But suppose a manager, technician, or professional is sent abroad without family for some length of time? Here are ten tips that anyone may employ to deflate the stress and tension of culture shock wherever and whenever it may be confronted:

Be Culturally Prepared. Forewarned is forearmed. Individual or group study and training are possible to understand cultural factors in general, as well as cultural specifics. The public libraries will provide a variety of material about a particular culture and nationality, if one has the motivation to read beforehand about the people with whom he or she will soon be living. The public health service can also advise about required innoculations, dietary clues, and other sanitary data about the land of one's hosts. Before departure, the person scheduled for overseas service can experiment with the food or restaurants representative of the second culture. Furthermore, one might establish contact in his or her homeland with foreign students or visitors from the area to which one is going. A "Directory of Intercultural Resources" is presented at the end of this book in Appendix E.

Learn Local Communication Complexities. By all means, study the language of the place to which one is assigned should it be different from one's native tongue. At least, learn some of the basics that will help in exchanging greetings and shopping. In addition to courses and books on the subject, audio tapes, cassettes, and records can advance one's communication skills in the second culture before and after departure. Sometimes a class can be attended or a tutor obtained for additional language study upon arrival. This is important to ascertain the nonverbal communication system in the country, such as the significant gestures, signs, and symbols. Published guides of culture specifics can be most helpful to learn expected courtesies, typical customs, and other niceties that improve intercultural relationships. Not only does the new foreigner need a local dictionary, but also must learn what newspapers and magazines will provide the best insight into this people.

Mix with the Host Nationals. Socialization with people from the nation to which one intends going is essential, both before departure and upon arrival. Those met in one's home culture may provide introductions to relatives and friends in their native land. Try and live on the economy. But if one is forced into living within a company or military colony of one's own kind, then avoid the "compound mentality." Immerse oneself in the host culture. Join in, whenever feasible, the artistic and community functions, the carnivals and rites, the international fraternal or professional organizations. Offer to teach students or business people one's language in exchange for knowledge of their language; share skills from skiing to tennis and it will be the means for making new international friends.

Be Creative and Experimental. Dare to risk, try, and learn, and perhaps even to fail, which also can lead to wisdom. Truly, nothing ventured, nothing gained. It takes social imagination to leap across cultural gaps, and to put oneself in the other's private world. Innovations abroad may mean taking risks to get around barriers of bureaucracy and communication in order to lessen social distance. This principle extends from experimenting with the local food to keeping a diary as an escape to record one's adventures and frustrations. Tours, hobbies, and a variety of cultural pursuits can produce positive results in a strange land. In a sense, one needs to be open and existential to the many opportunities that may present themselves while abroad to know more about the locals who are seemingly so different.

Be Culturally Sensitive. Be aware of the special customs and traditions which, if followed by a visitor, will make one more acceptable. Certainly, avoid stereotyping the natives, criticizing their local practices and procedures, while using the standard of one's own country for comparison purposes. Recognize that in some cultures, such as in Asia and the Middle East, saving face and not giving offense may be considered very important. It takes great sensitivity to make such fine distinctions, so that one senses when the natives are merely being polite or gracious rather than hurt us with a "no." Americans, for instance, are quite pragmatic and like to organize. It may be a real challenge, then, for such persons to relax and endeavor to get into a different rhythm of the place and people they are visiting. Appendix C provides a useful "Intercultural Relations Inventory" for contrasting home/host cultures.

Recognize Complexities in Host Cultures. Counteract the tendency to make quick, simplistic assessments of situations. Most complex societies comprise different ethnic or religious groups, stratified into social classes or castes, differentiated by regions or geographical factors, separated into rural and urban settlements. Each of these may have distinct subcultural characteristics over which is superimposed an official language, national institutions, and peculiar customs or history that tie this people together. Thus, avoid pat generalizations and quick assumptions—the particular people you meet there may not be representative of the majority culture. Instead, be tentative in one's conclusions, realizing one's point of contact is a limited sample, within a multifaceted society.

Perceive Self as a Culture Bearer. That is, each person bears his or her own culture, and distortions, when going abroad. Thus, one views everything in the host culture through the unique filter of one's own cultural background. The cause of disturbances in one's experience in a foreign land may be in the visitor's upbringing or culture, or in lack of understanding of the second culture. If the visitor comes from a culture that is impersonal, then that person can expect to be startled in a culture in which "personalism" is esteemed. So too, if one is raised in democratic traditions, that individual may be jolted in a society that values the authority of the head male in the family and extends this reverence to national leaders.

Be Patient, Understanding, and Accepting of Self and Hosts. In strange situations, one must be more tolerant and flexible. In the unfamiliar environment, an attitude of healthy curiosity, of willingness to bear inconveniences, of patience when answers or solutions are not forthcoming or difficult to obtain, is valuable to maintain mental balance. Such patience must be extended from self to other compatriots who struggle with cultural adjustment, to the locals who may function at a different pace. Time can be a great healer and work wonders in foreign cultural encounters that may vex and irritate.

Be Most Realistic in Expectations. Avoid overestimating oneself, one's hosts, or the cross-cultural experience. Disappointments can be lessened if one scales down expectations and needs as appropriate for the local scene. Thus, one may be pleasantly surprised when things happen beyond one's expectations. This is most sound advice when one moves from the First World to the Third or Fourth Worlds. It applies to everything from airline schedules to renting rooms. Multinational managers, especially, must be careful in new cultures not to set unreasonable work expectations for themselves or their subordinates until both are more acclimated. At least, make allowances for jet fatigue before mounting the parapets!

Accept the Challenge of Intercultural Experiences. Anticipate, savor, and confront the psychological challenge to adapt and change as a result of a new cross-cultural opportunity. Be prepared to alter one's habits, attitudes, values, tastes, relationships, or sources of satisfaction. Such flexibility can become a means for personal growth, and the transnational experience can be more fulfilling. Of course, a deep interest and commitment to one's work—professionalism—can be marvelous therapy in intercultural situations, counteracting isolation and strangeness when living outside one's culture.

Programs to foster acculturation can be designed for every transitional situation likely to cause a shock or trauma. Sullivan/Lullin Associates of San Diego, California (92108), for instance, have created workshops and handbooks to ease executive and/or employee relocation, whether it involves a job or a plant change. The aim is not only to streamline the entry process, but to keep productivity levels up during the transition. Such professional endeavors deal with wide ranging transitional issues from disengagement from one's present assignment, to spouse re-employment, to managing the family move. However, for purposes of illustration the following section concentrates on the principal deployment challenge—to a foreign culture.

Many domestic and international freight forwarders and real estate companies are getting into the business of relocation services, both at home and abroad. One such enterprise that is particularly sensitive to the cross-cultural factors involved is Dean Worldwide of Huntington Beach, California (92647).

Airlines have many helpful brochures on the area to which you may be traveling or aids to facilitate your trip. Continental Airlines (P.O. Box 4607, Houston, TX 77210-4607, USA), for instance, provides a packet on how to control jet lag, including a time zone planner. The U.S. Government Printing Office (Washington, DC 20402-9342) offers an annual catalog of revelant publications such as foreign area studies of various countries, or pocket guides to Japan, Korea, United Kingdom, Low Countries (Belgium, Luxembourg, and The Netherlands), and even Puerto Rico. The Council on International Educational Exchange (205 East 42nd St., New York, NY 10017, USA) has useful monographs, such as the annual *Student Travel Catalog* of questions and answers on work, study, and travel abroad.

A FOREIGN DEPLOYMENT SYSTEM

In today's global village there is a vast migration of people from one nation to another to study and work for days, months, or years. Some corporations have a corps of international employees who get transferred from country to country, remaining away from their native land, except for short vacations or business trips, literally for decades. Many citizens leave their motherland to seek employment abroad, or are invited by a foreign government.

The need for immediate and vast transfers of knowledge and technology from developed to less developed societies is immense. It has been spurred by the discoveries of tremendous natural resources, especially gas and oil, in Third World countries. The superindustrial nations need the natural resources and raw materials of less developed countries to refine and manufacture, as well as to supply energy to their own affluent consumers. Preindustrial nations usually have human or natural resources, but need the brain power and technology of the advanced countries to capitalize on their own assets. Therefore, human intercultural exchanges and international business will increase as world culture and homogenization progresses.

The issue, then, is can these transcultural interchanges be facilitated for the benefit of both the expatriate and the indigenous population, as well as for the enhancement of both home and host cultures? For this reason, there should be a foreign deployment policy and system.

Any organization—government, corporation, or association—has a responsibility to carefully select and prepare representatives being sent abroad. Obviously, any enterprise that undertakes an international operation would ensure that their representative is technically qualified to perform in the new environment. But is the individual psychologically suitable and ready to function normally in the strange culture? If not, employee effectiveness and productivity, international goodwill, and customer relations can be undermined. The focus of this section is on why organizations should assume responsibility for their overseas representatives, and how to provide adequate intercultural preparation and support before, during, and after foreign deployment.

There is strong economic, as well as social, case for investment in a deployment system. The cost of cross-cultural preparation and support services overseas is miniscule in comparison to the organizational expenses incurred when an employee and his or her family return prematurely from an international assignment. Based on place and circumstances, researchers estimate that the costs can range from $50,000 to $200,000. That does not include the thousands—sometimes millions—of dollars lost in contracts or because of overseas representatives' protocol blunders. A few thousand dollars invested in foreign deployment services really can have ROI (return on investment). Too many companies choose the wrong people to go abroad, prepare them inadequately for the cross-cultural experience, and treat the spouse or family as chattel.

For expatriate managers and technicians it is no longer big salaries, exotic travel, sunshine, and servants. The reality now is that the "foreign" manager is expected to mix with the nationals and know local customs, to treat local subordinates with respect and modify corporate culture to fit the local character. There are also new dangers in many countries that range from terrorism and kidnappings of executives in the Third World, to urban crime and substance abuse that plague dependents in First World nations. If not prepared for the stress and strains of the intercultural experience, a manager may join in expanding these statistics—a Business International Corporation survey showed that one in three American expatriates fails to complete the full tour of duty, while European expatriates' failure rate is only one in seven.

Several key questions must be asked to determine if an organization needs a foreign deployment policy system. Does the company, agency, or association experience—

1. A costly premature return rate for many employees and their families when assigned outside the country?
2. Continuing complaints from its foreign service personnel regarding problems of cross-cultural adjustment, especially in their interactions with host nationals?
3. Lowered morale, productivity, and cost effective utilization because of personnel problems of a personal and intercultural nature while abroad?
4. Undue concern about employee, customer, public, or government relations at the foreign site operations?
5. Readjustment problems when overseas personnel return to the home culture and corporation?

If the answer to any or all of these inquiries is positive, and the organization wants better results from its international personnel, then the organization must focus on:

1. Choosing and training the foreign deployment staff—those individuals responsible for recruiting, training, and processing employees for assignments abroad.
2. Selecting, developing, and preparing personnel for foreign transfer, or to work domestically in international business activities.
3. Facilitating the acculturation of foreign personnel coming to the parent company culture, such as the United States, for orientation, training, consultation, or temporary duty (This refers especially to overseas representatives of subsidiaries abroad, or licensees who come to corporate headquarters on short-term visits.)
4. Applying the insights and programs developed for foreign deployment to domestic operations where appropriate. That is, redesign of policies and

systems for internal transfer within the parent culture, as well as in the recruitment, selection, development, and supervision of minority employees.

Figure 9-1 provides an overview of the foreign deployment cycle.

Host culture integration

Steps 6 to 10

6 7 8 9 10

5

11

4

Entry process

Steps 1 to 5

3   **Individual Team or Family**   12   Steps 11 to 13   Reentry process

2

13

1

15   14

Steps 14 and 15

Home culture reintegration

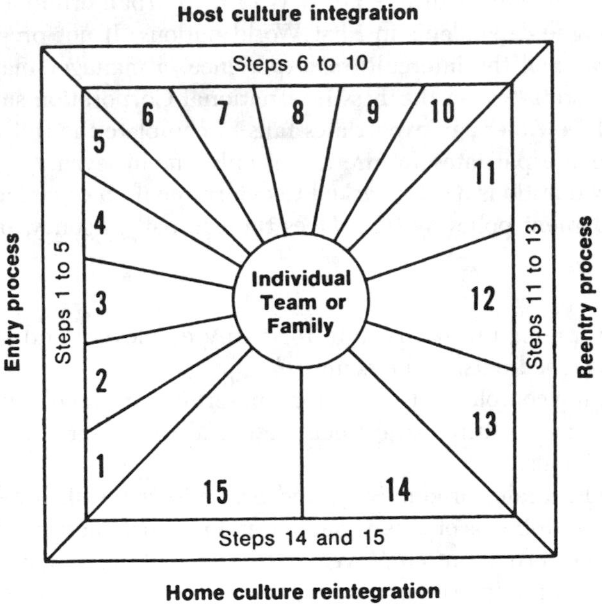

1. Selection and preparation of F.D. staff
2. Recruitment of overseas candidates
3. Selection of personnel for foreign service
4. General cultural or area training
5. Specific culture and language training
6. Departure and travel
7. Onsite orientation and briefings

8. Culture shock/adjustment
9. Overseas monitoring and support services
10. Acculturation-making host friends
11. Withdrawal, psychologically anticipating going home
12. Exit-transition, travel home or visit other countries
13. Reentry shock
14. Readjustment
15. Reassignment in parent organization

Figure 9-1. Foreign deployment cycle one might follow when entering and exiting another culture.

Recommended Deployment Steps

As Figure 9-1 indicates, there are fifteen steps that an individual might take when going through the major stages of entry to and exit from a second and different culture. The entry process begins with the sponsoring organization

making a careful selection and preparation of the foreign deployment staff—
recruiters, processors, and trainers. The second step is recruitment of candidates who are suitable for assignment abroad. The third step involves selection
of the best personnel for foreign service, which might include assessment, interviews, simulations, and evaluation of personal data gained from personnel records, tests, and instrumentation.

In preparing these individuals, and possibly their families, the fourth step is
general cultural awareness training or geographic area studies (e.g., Asia, Europe, Africa). The process of host culture integration begins at home with the
fifth step of culture specific and language training. It might include contacts
with nationals of the second culture.

The sixth step is departure preparations and travel to the new culture. After
arrival, the seventh step is orientation and briefings on the indigenous population and society, as well as on the organizational culture to which an individual
is assigned.

The eighth step is initial culture shock to a greater or lesser degree, and the
inevitable adjustments to the differences in the strange culture. The tenth step
is acculturation—adapting to the second culture, making progress living there,
developing acquaintances and even friends among the locals.

The next stage is the reentry process to the native land. It begins abroad with
the eleventh step—psychological withdrawal from the host culture and people.
The twelfth step is exiting, including the transition afforded by travel. It
should be planned to permit visiting other countries and cultures for a gradual
transfer back to the homeland.

The last stage of home culture reintegration involves three final steps. Step
thirteen is reentry shock, most prevalent among managers as they experience
the changes in their organization and society since they left. Step fourteen is
gradual readjustment to the changed situation, which may take up to six
months or a year. The last step is reassignment to a post in the parent organization, a looking back with satisfaction at the personal and professional growth
that occurred during the overseas assignment, and the impact of that learning
on the individual's career development.

All of these steps should be considered by the organization that is responsible
for sending people abroad. They should become facets of the system that must
be established for the purposes of foreign deployment. It is a continuing cycle
for the exchange of people, and for effective intercultural relations.

Organizations can undertake certain policies and actions to facilitate the adjustment and performance of employees abroad. Policies may state that no pets
may be taken overseas, or a bonus may be given for staying an extra year.
Among the actions that a corporation or agency can take to improve foreign
adjustment are:

1. Form an information network on the local culture/situation among
   multinational representatives who have served or are in the host area.

2. Rotate assignments of employees without families to permit them more home visits.
3. Allow two workers to share overseas tasks, so that one can be rotated home regularly.
4. Develop country or area manuals for employees to supplement the standard commercial publications.
5. Screen out early in recruitment, selection, and training, the nonadjusters (those with allergy, drinking, marital problems, etc.).
6. Use media reports of the overseas work scene in training to encourage or discourage personnel preparing for deployment.
7. Avoid making statements in training that are contrary to onsite experience.
8. Counterbalance the stress and strain of cultural adjustment with the opportunity for an enriching personal and professional experience.
9. Allocate housing abroad on a numbered, first-come, first serve basis.
10. Create a program or center for expatriate family support services, particularly for adolescent dependents.

Such pragmatic deployment strategies can do much to foster employee integration into the strange culture, as well as to help them get control of their new job situation.

Now because of a trade shift to the Pacific Basin, more personnel are being sent to the Far East, so culture specifics are very important (Chapter 15). Though fewer North Americans may be traveling to the Middle East for business, what can we *learn* from our experience there? Remember Iran in the days of the Shah—some say that the unacceptable behavior of foreigners involved in technology transfer contributed to the rise of religious fundamentalism and the present isolationist policies in that country. There were many companies that developed intelligent programs to acculturate their people to the Persian culture and avoid being offensive. Yet, back in the 1970s, Gus Lanzo, Director of Career Education and Development for the Grumman Aerospace Corporation, estimated a $100,000 per person loss for premature return of their personnel from Iran. This figure includes travel, housing assistance in home and host culture, training, and replacement expenses.

The necessity for an effective relocation system is not limited to the private sector, but applies equally to public agencies that send employees abroad, whether on short- or long-term assignments. Within the government this applies to more than the State Department, and includes entities that extend from the Department of Commerce to the Federal Aviation Administration. The military has always provided some, but inadequate amounts of cross-cultural and foreign language preparation for its overseas personnel. When security lapses became evident among the embassy guards of the U.S. Marine Corps, the media became incensed. One editorial lamented, "Marines Mirror a Cultural Failure" (*Insight*, May 4, 1987, p. 64), but nowhere in the article did the writer cite the failure by the State Department or Corps to provide adequate cultural training for the young, unsophisticated Marine guards, often from rural, minority, or otherwise educationally and socially limited backgrounds, assigned to alien situations.

Behavioral scientists have now begun to investigate the whole phenomenon of people living and working in isolated and confined environments (Harrison, Clearwater and McKay, 1990; Connors, Harrison, and Akins, 1985). The latter range from offshore oil rigs and polar research stations to undersea submarines and space stations. At the University of California Space Institute, Harris (1988/90) is applying the same strategies suggested in this chapter to extraterrestrial living. The research focuses upon development of space personnel deployment systems for the orbital environment and at a Moon or Mars base (O'Neill, 1989).

COMPONENTS OF A RELOCATION SYSTEM

Stage One—Employee Assessment

The first major component in a relocation or foreign deployment system involves evaluating individuals who are sent abroad and evaluating the organizational program responsible for the transfer and reentry process. From the perspective of the organizations' responsibilities, a complete foreign deployment system should:

1. Ascertain the adaptability of key personnel for foreign service, including their ability to deal with the host nationals effectively.
2. Summarize a psychological evaluation of the candidate's skills in human relations within an intercultural context, as well as the candidate's ability for coping with changes and differences; the candidate's susceptibility to severe culture shock.
3. Identify specific physical and intellectual barriers to successful adjustment in the foreign environment, if possible, to correct any deficiencies.
4. Highlight any specific technical or management factors that need strengthening before the cross-cultural assignment.
5. Find out any family problems or situations with dependents that would undermine employee effectiveness abroad.
6. Provide this assessment for top and middle management personnel on a priority basis, then supervisors and foremen, and finally technical and hourly employees.
7. Determine the suitability of any employee, even those on temporary assignment out of country, such as short business trips.
8. Provide a special review of individual suitability for foreign deployment in remote sites with limited input and support services.

9. Adapt the process to meet the needs of foreign nationals brought on assignment to domestic operations, or for Third World nationals (TCNs) brought to the foreign work site.
10. Interview candidates for foreign deployment with questions by psychologists and international personnel specialists.
11. Provide group meetings for candidates, possibly including employees who have returned from the foreign site, or host country nationals, to study interactions and determine suitability of prospects.
12. Use instruments for data gathering about the candidates' attitudes and competencies regarding change, intercultural knowledge and relations, and communication skills—these may involve commercial or home-made questionnaires, inventories, checklists e.g., culture shock tests. There are some samples of such instruments at the end of the book in the Appendices A-D
13. Use one-way mirrors, video or audio tape, closed circuit television, simulation games, and other educational or personnel technology as a basis for observation.

The overseas assessment process might further investigate:

14. The tasks or activities the candidate might engage in, and the candidates' ability to accomplish them.
15. The people with whom the individual will interact and the individual's ability to deal with representatives of the indigenous population.
16. The extent to which the official position requires social interactions with host and third country nationals, as well as expatriates, and the capacity of the candidate to deal with such variety of human relationships.
17. Whether the work can be handled by an individual or requires team collaboration, especially with persons outside the company, if the work is to be done in a remote location, and how the candidate is likely to cope with the situation.
18. The language skills required (English or a foreign language) and the capacity of the candidate to meet them (how skillful must the candidate be in speaking the foreign language).
19. The situational environment of the foreign assignment, and the likelihood of this particular candidate to cope effectively under these circumstances. For example, is the culture like or very unlike the home culture, does it require the individual to operate in a manner quite different from a similar position in the home environment?
20. Whether the individual is provincial in outlook, or has that person demonstrated prior interests in things foreign—how cosmopolitan in attitude is the candidate, and what is the individual's experience outside the home culture?

21. Whether the candidate possesses a realistic concept of life overseas—job requirements, incongruities, opportunities, and frustrations—and if the candidate has previously visited the job site, what reactions did the candidate have?
25. The candidate's ability to operate autonomously, to deal with differences, and to cope with discontinuity.
26. Hypothetical situations, critical incidents, or case studies that approximate the new assignment and how the candidate responded, especially when there was job or social friction.
27. How the person envisions the absence of several years from the homeland while on foreign assignment. (Is the individual realistic on how it will affect and change his or her personal life and that of dependents, as well as impact on career development and life plans?)
28. How the candidate would be rated on overall assignment suitability relative to knowledge of the demands to be made upon him or her by the foreign job and society.

The assessment process should provide the candidate with factual information about the host country and assignment. Having seen films, slides, or videotapes of the onsite situation, and having discussed the salary adjustment, housing provisions, tax problems, and other such realities, the candidate should be given the opportunity to choose. This may result in the candidate refusing the foreign assignment.

The assessment center techniques used in some large companies may be modified to assist with recruitment and selection of overseas personnel. Or, if an Office of International Personnel does not exist, the organization may have to use an external resource, such as an international executive/management/technical search firm, or hire "job shoppers." Some organizations use a selection review board made up of their own employees or members, qualified volunteers, and people who have served in the target culture. Existing specialists in corporate health and personnel services can provide valuable data if the candidate is already an employee, or they may assist with the testing of those who come from outside.

The qualities described as the outcome of cross-cultural training in Chapter 11 could also be the criteria for selecting candidates for overseas service—empathy, openness, persistence, sensitivity to intercultural factors, respect for others, role flexibility, tolerance for ambiguity, and two-way communication skill. Research indicates that possession of these characteristics is correlated to adaptation and effectiveness outside an individual's home culture.

Paul W. Russell, Jr. (1978) reviewed the literature for the past two decades on what factors are associated with successful international corporate assignments. His "Dimension of Overseas Success in Industry" is found on page 240.

Dimensions of Overseas Success in Industry

(Asterisks indicate most desirable characteristics of foreign deployment candidates.)

1. Technical Competence/resourcefulness
   *Technical skill/competence
   Resourcefulness
   Imagination/creativity
   Demonstrated ability to produce
      results with limited resources
   Comprehension of complex relationships

2. Adaptability/emotional stability
   *Adaptability/flexibility
   Youthfulness
   Maturity
   Patience
   Perseverance
   *Emotional stability
   Variety of outside interests
   Ability to handle responsibility
   Feeling of self-worth/dignity
   Capacity for growth

3. Acceptability of Assignment to Candidate and Family
   *Desire to serve overseas
   Willingness of spouse to
      live abroad/family status
   Belief in mission/job
   Stable marriage/family life
   *Adaptability of spouse/family
   *Previous experience abroad
   *Motivation
   Willingness to take chances
   Willingness to travel
   (Negative trait: overly strong ties with family in home country)

4. Planning, Organization, and Utilizing Resources
   *Organization ability
   Self-sufficient as manager
   Ability to build social institutions
   Management skills
   Administrative skills

5. Interpersonal Relationships/Getting Along with Others
   *Diplomacy and tact
   Consideration for others
   Human Relations skills
   Commands respect
   *Ability to train others
   Desire to help others
   Ability to get things done through others
   Sense for politics of situations

6. Potential for Growth in the Company/Organization
   *Successful domestic record
   *Promotability
   Organizational Experience
   Industriousness
   *Educational qualifications
   *Mental alertness
   Intellectual
   Dependability
7. Host Language Ability
   *Language ability in native tongue
8. Cultural Empathy
   *Cultural empathy/sensitivity
   *Interest in host culture
   Respects host nationals
   Understands own culture
   Open-minded
   Area expertise
   *Ability to get along with hosts
   *Tolerant of others' views
   Sensitive to others' attitudes
   Understands host culture
   Not ethnocentric/prejudiced
   Objective
9. Physical Attributes
   *Good health
   Sex gender acceptability
   Physical appearance
10. Miscellaneous
    *Character
    Generalist skills
    Independence on job
    Social acceptability
    *Leadershp
    Friendliness
    Initiative/energy

From P. W. Russell (1978)

Some organizations try to circumvent the selection problem by hiring for overseas assignment personnel with successful international experience and language skills, or host and third country nationals. Obviously, to assure effectiveness, some type of evaluation process should be utilized even in choosing such persons.

Two Israeli scholars, Yoram Zeira and Ehud Harari (1977), found that these indigenous people had morale problems centering around blocked promotions, transfer anxieties, income gaps, unfamiliarity with host culture, adaptability difficulties, avoidance of long-range projects abroad, inappropriate leadership styles, and inability to participate in decision-making and screening management information. Furthermore, investigations indicated that third country nationals with high potential and·a desire for promotion are not always anxious to serve abroad, especially after one or two international transfers. Zeira and Harari discovered that variegated international experience is not necessarily translated into managerial behavior compatible with local environmental needs and headquarter expectations. They believe that no multinational staffing policy is free of serious dysfunctional aspects, but means must be sought to diminish such effects.

The final aspect of the assessment cycle after the individual evaluation is corporate. That is, periodic objective assessment of the current status and practice in selection, orientation, training, and onsite assistance provided to employees who are transferred outside the home country of the organization. There might be an advantage in having external consultants study how effectively the program/system prepares personnel to deal with intercultural differences related to both management and life styles. For example, a large international construction firm had an elaborate department and plan for human resource development of employees sent abroad. When the corporation president arrived onsite in Saudi Arabia, he was besieged by workers and their families with personal and personnel problems. Obviously, the deployment program was not working. He fired the vice-president of human resource development on his return to the United States.

The corporate assessment process might include a survey of employees overseas regarding their special needs and problems related to foreign assignment, and how well their orientation program helped them to cope with the onsite reality; or the investigation might be limited to expatriates who have returned home.

As previously indicated, some evaluation would be in order for the staff involved in recruitment, selection, and training of overseas personnel as to their appropriateness for these tasks, and the validity of their assumptions and practices.

If a corporation or agency is not using an external consulting group to conduct its relocation services, then internal organizational resources should be developed before the next stage in the deployment process can occur. For example, a corporate library or data bank on cultural specifics would have to be developed for each overseas' location in which the company operates. In a large multinational organization, both management and employees would have access to this information on a "need-to-know basis." Thus, suppose a technician had been selected for a specific foreign site and was to be transferred there in six months. Here are some of the activities that person might engage in:

1. Consult the organizational data bank for relevant cross-cultural information about the country and culture to be entered (e.g., input on housing,

education, customs, food, etc.). Be prepared while on foreign deployment to make personal notes for additional contributions to this computer bank upon return from abroad.

2. Consult the organizational directory of returned employees from the country to which assigned. Prepare to contact and interview some of these fellow workers for personal insights on their experiences in the host culture.

3. Consult the organizational data bank on resources to be contacted at home and onsite that would enable employees and dependents to become more effective in the new cross-cultural opportunity (e.g., language training possibilities, geographic area studies and economic information, universities and research centers with required specialists and information).

4. Consult the organizational library for international personnel to review pertinent books, periodicals, and brochures, as well as any self-instructional media programs.

5. Keep a personal reference notebook for significant data gathered relative to the search undertaken in this phase.

6. Check the organizational data bank, manuals, or files on company policies for overseas employees (e.g., conditions of employment, compensation, termination, grievances and discipline, paid sick leaves, vacation, leaves of absence, insurance and disability, relocation allowances to and from site, travel time, legal liabilities, educational and local travel opportunities, continuation of employee benefits abroad—credit unions, employee assistance, company publications onsite).

7. Seek necessary immunizations and medical aid from organizational health services.

A checklist for some of these items, entitled "So You're Going Abroad," is provided in Appendix A.

The most up-to-date studies on selection are reported in the *International Journal of Intercultural Relations*, Special Issue, "Intercultural Communication Competence," Pergamon Press, Volume 13, Number 3, 1989.

Stage Two—Employee Orientation

Prior to departure overseas, the second component in a foreign deployment system is some type of self-learning/training in culture general and specifics. In the *general* program for increasing cultural awareness, several alternatives are possible, and are described in detail in Chapters 9, 10, and 11. These orientation programs are intended for an organization's managers, technicians, sales and marketing personnel engaged in international business, executives, and their families.

The content includes learning modules on cross-cultural communications and change, understanding culture and its influence on behavior, culture shock and cross-cultural relations, improving organizational relations and intercultural effectiveness. Additional topics include transnational management of responsibility; intercultural performance appraisal; intercultural concepts of productivity, leadership, and conflict management; and the changing role of multinational managers. Essentially, it is in-service training in comparative management.

Still another approach to replace or supplement formal group instruction is individualized learning packages for the employee and the employee's family. This is a programmed learning and media instructional system on cultural differences in general, and for the specific country to be visited. For example, simulations, slide/cassette, and videotaped presentations on cultural awareness are combined into a standardized presentation that serves those assigned abroad singly or in small groups where group training is not feasible. Such a self-instructional program could be utilized at home with one's family. It might also serve as a preparation for classroom instruction. The best single source of training aids in this area is the Intercultural Press (P.O. Box 768, Yarmouth, ME 04096, USA). Two recommended newsletters are *Intercultural News Network* (16331 Underhill Lane, Huntington Beach, CA 92647, USA) and *Training & Culture* (GilDean Group, 1375 Lake City Way, NE #105, Seattle, WA 98125, USA).

Specific area programs can be developed for orientation purposes. That is, a cultural briefing program for personnel assigned to a particular geographical area or country that is foreign to them. Thus, the Middle East could be a subject of area study with particular emphasis on Saudi Arabia and Iran. A learning program of twelve or more hours can be designed that consists of videotape or film cassettes inserted into a teaching machine, and a discussion guide or self-instructional manual for individual study. The same material could be projected on a large screen for use in group training situations. Chapter 11 reviews several methods that organizational trainers can use in this orientation.

Obviously, no foreign deployment orientation is complete without adequate language and technical training to fit the employee properly for an overseas assignment. However, the focus here is on cultural training and preparation. Foreign student advisors in various American universities can be a helpful resource to those planning orientation programs for employees abroad. They may not only assist with student speakers for country specific information, but they design orientation programs for foreign students coming into the United States. Many of their techniques and approaches can be adapted to corporate cross-cultural programs, and the National Association of Foreign Student Advisors can be very useful in this regard. The East-West Center in Hawaii, a federal institution, has many programs and publications worthy of consideration by cross-cultural trainers.

Most multinational organizations are now including the spouse in the cross-cultural training. Because wives, in particular, seem most affected and challenged by culture shock, it not only helps their adjustment abroad to include them in the training, but provides them with insights to share with dependents. It also helps them understand their husband's problems in the foreign work situation. In the past decade the number of women managers going overseas has been increasing. There has been little research yet on the issue of what is happening to the male spouse of those who are married, or how those who are mothers cope abroad with responsibilities for children (Ramsey, 1987).

Consensus of experienced trainers is that cross-cultural orientation should be flexible, experiential, individualized, participative, and integrated with home and onsite situations.

When the pre-departure training takes up the issue of stereotyping others, it is also valuable to consider their images of "typical" Americans. In Southern California, there is an Association of Cross-Cultural Trainers in Business. At one of their network meetings, Scott Mitchell of Los Angeles summarized the foreigners' stereotypes of Americans: outgoing, friendly, informal, loud, rude, arrogant, hard working, have-all-the-answers, not status conscious, disrespectful of authority, ignorant of other countries and their cultures, generous, always in a hurry, etc. Much learning could be promoted among U.S.A. citizens scheduled to go abroad on assignment by small group discussions of how to counteract that stereotype.

Perhaps a few specific corporate practices in overseas orientation may best make the point. The Fairchild Company approach to training employees includes:

1. Examining the other culture/country with emphasis on proper attitudes, tools, and skills to be effective there.
2. A means for developing realistic expectations about the assignment and the foreign country.
3. An opportunity to experience and test the mindset and coping skills necessary for effectiveness abroad.
4. An intensive learning period to acquire information about intercultural communications, cultural adaptation, area studies, and specifics of processing, moving, and transporting personal effects.

The Grumman Aerospace Corporation has established policies for international assignment covering certain personnel needs, not unlike those proposed here: recruiting; selection procedures; training; housing allowances; medical services; educational facilities and allowances; tax allowances; transportation allowances; travel arrangements; overseas salary compensation; and pets. Their planning for employee deployment abroad includes: (a) defining scope of tasks overseas; (b) personnel planning and scheduling; (c) site preparation; (d) recruiting and selection; (e) personnel preparation; (f) administration of physical moves. The cultural orientation includes the employee family and takes from three to six months on the average. In addition, simultaneous planning, training, and scheduling onsite is offered to local nationals who will be working with the Americans. The Grumman Aerospace Corporation believes the essential elements of indoctrination to prevent culture shock encompass these aspects of a target country: geography; climate; history; religion; social customs; schools; politics; law; language; working conditions; and the standard of living.

Morrison Knudsen International has ascertained that the ten most important concerns of expatriate employees are: base pay; overseas salary living allowances; information on housing, food, and medical care abroad; married versus single status overseas; foreign premium/differential; work conditions onsite; and skill and leadership ability of project supervisors.

The last model is more comprehensive and is from Bechtel Corporation. The policy manual, *Corporate Orientation for International Assignments*, considers all facets of selection, training, and orientation of employees for service abroad, and uses multimedia, guest specialists, group participation, and resource materials that are accurate and current. (Bechtel produces a series of booklets on specific countries and cultures for employees.) The goal is to standardize the plan so that any corporate office may use the training aids. The orientation policy is quite explicit. Four major areas covered by corporate trainers and processors are:

1. Cross-cultural (culture, customs, and people of the area to which assigned).
2. Job orientation (specifics of project scope and organization, employee position and responsibilities, company formalities and procedures, supervisory responsibilities, review of the local work situation relative to manpower training needs, safety, labor relations, and local employees onsite).
3. Area specifics (employee/family concerns, medical care, insurance and benefits, compensation and employment conditions, taxes and housing, transfer of household and personal effects, local schools and education allowances, local facilities for transportation, rest/recreation/vacation opportunities).
4. Human relations (especially for management level, this deals with local government, U.S. representatives abroad, clients and their needs, roles with Bechtel employees and dependents onsite).

Among the recent trends in cross-cultural orientation of personnel is learning that is both competency and computer-based (Harris, ed., 1984). Mumford (1975) describes the research of McBer and Company of Cambridge, Massachusetts. Conducted for the U.S. Navy, it identified the competencies required of human resource specialists engaged in training for the Naval Overseas Duty Support Program. Fifteen basic skills emerged from interviews with successful performers. These were grouped in five clusters—achievement characteristics (self-confidence, concern for quality and standards, initiative, results oriented, planning and organizing skills); diagnostic ability (conceptualizing, learning from mistakes, nonverbal sensitivity); influence ability (including political awareness, organizational communication, and marketing skills); intercultural awareness (nonjudgmental attitudes toward other cultures and skill in intercultural interaction); teaching skills (oriented toward trainees and experiential learning.)

In the same proceedings on "Computer-based Learning" Reynolds made the case for computer-assisted instruction, especially in newly industrialized countries. It seems that we have not begun to tap the power of the computer for cross-cultural training in foreign languages, storage, and retrieval of intercultural information, especially regarding culture specifics and testing on international competencies.

Earlier we proposed that organizations that regularly send personnel abroad should develop a resource library or computer data bank with information on both culture general and specifics for the areas in which they operate. Now we would like to summarize current thinking on this second stage of foreign deployment in the form of four recommendations for orienting employees. Those with international personnel responsibilities should either provide the context for the following or supervise the overseas candidates in learning this prior to departure abroad:

Phase One—General Culture/Area Orientation

1. Become culturally aware of the factors that make a culture unique, and the characteristics of the home culture that influence employee behavior abroad.
2. Seek local cross-cultural experience and engage in intercultural communication with microcultures within the homeland, so as to sensitize self to cultural differences and how to cope with them.
3. Encourage spouses to develop programs and experiments that foster more cosmopolitan attitudes in the family, and counteract ethnocentrism— cook national dishes of other countries, attend cultural weeks or exhibits of foreign or ethnic groups, socialize with people from a different cultural or racial background, try folk dress or dances of other people.
4. Read, understand, and practice the corporate policies on equal employment opportunity and affirmative action.

Phase Two—Language Orientation

1. Undertake 60 to 80 hours of formal training in the language of the host country to which assigned.
2. Supplement classroom experience with 132 to 180 hours of self-instruction in the language—listen to audio cassettes or records in the foreign

tongue, read newspapers, magazines, or books in the new language, speak to others who have this language skill, listen to music in the language.

3. Build a 500 word survival vocabulary.
4. Develop specialized vocabularies—on the job, with the maid, in the marketplace, etc.
5. Seek further education in the language before departure, but most certainly, upon arrival in the country of assignment.
6. Practice the language at every opportunity, especially with family members.
7. Use audio or videocassettes before departure and abroad to increase proficiency in the target language.

Chapter 2 discussed the global manager's role as a communicator and made a case for including foreign language skills. It cited the need for such competency based on the 1979 report of The President's Commission on Foreign Language and International Studies. A case for investment in such language and intercultural training can be made for furthering international trade and correcting U.S. imbalances in that regard. It would seem to be a necessity in the professional development of those in the global travel, transportation, communication, and construction industries. There are those who would argue against investing in foreign language training. They maintain that English is becoming the principal language of world business.

Indeed, 345 million people use English as their first language, and another 400 million as their second. It is the medium for sharing 80% of the information stored around the world in computers, the international airlines industry, and other aspects of commerce or diplomacy. But English is the native tongue for only twelve nations, though it is widely spoken or understood in 90 other countries. However, there are 4.8 billion people on this planet, and to communicate effectively with them and to penetrate their markets, global managers and technicians will need fluency in more than English. For example, Chinese is spoken by a billion people, and those business leaders hoping to succeed in that emerging Asian market, need to acquire a minimum of fifty words in that language.

Phase Three—Culture Specific Orientation: Training and Learning

1. Learn about the specific culture of the country to which assigned, preferably during the six months prior to departure. Gather data about the size of the country and its population (demographic facts), the customs, mores, values, taboos, history, social systems, and communication pat-

terns. Learn what is necessary regarding the host culture's family, educational, political, and social system; history and laws; regulations and taxes; food and housing; recreational and travel prospects. Understand and prepare for "culture shock."

2. Check out specific company policies for the assigned country, relative to allowances for transportation, housing, education, expense accounts, and provisions for salaries, taxes, and other fringe benefits including medical service and emergency leave.

3. Find out and obtain necessary transfer documents (passports, visas, etc.), and learn customs policies and regulations, as well as currency restrictions, for entry and exit of both assigned country and the native land.

4. Interview fellow employees who have returned from the host country. Get practical information about banking, shopping, currency, climate, mail, and law enforcement.

5. Read travel books and other information about the country and culture, especially that provided by the sponsoring organization.

Phase Four—Job Orientation: Information Gathering

1. Obtain information about the overseas job environment and organization; the clients and contractors; key personnel; the work schedule and hours; hiring status and contract monitoring; job drawings, specifics, or other papers; purchasing and field procurement; project procedures and progress reports; quality control and job-site security; and labor relations, especially with third world nationals and host country nationals.

2. Learn of the local population's attitude toward the project to which assigned, especially the government officials. Know what customs and restrictions to observe relative to the job.

3. Arrange for necessary technical training to assure high performance abroad.

Strategies of foreign deployment should encompass the staff engaged in recruiting, selecting, and training; the employee and dependents assigned abroad; and the host culture managers who are responsible for organizational personnel in the strange environment. The focus should be on the opportunities afforded by the international assignment for personal growth, professional exchange and development, and effective representation of country and corporation.

As a result of his Peace Corps training endeavors on behalf of Denver's Center for Research and Education, Dr. Albert R. Wight suggested the Experiential Learning Model for cross-cultural orientation (see Figure 9-2). In reviewing the research literature, Dr. Wight confirms that innovative, experienced-based training models are needed to adequately prepare trainees to live and work effectively in another culture. The design of such programs must be structured to achieve increased participant involvement in and responsibility for the learning process. The orientation should be trainee-centered, especially on problem solving, in contrast to the memorization of facts.

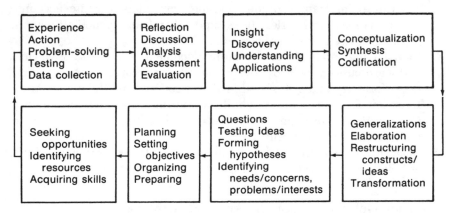

Figure 9-2. Cross-cultural orientation can be achieved by means of an experiential learning module, such as this one developed by Dr. Albert Wight.

Stage Three—On-site Support and Monitoring

An effective foreign deployment system should include human resource support services, as well as a method for continuous monitoring of the worker's performance. Now that employees have been recruited, selected, trained, and transported abroad, the personnel responsibility should be to: (a) facilitate their integration into the strange work environment and host culture, (b) evaluate their needs and performance, and (c) encourage morale and career development. Toward the end of the person's tour of duty, the office of international personnel should assist in an orderly transition to the home culture and the domestic organization.

As a follow-up to the predeparture training, some type of orientation and briefing should occur regarding the local situation soon after the family arrives in the foreign country. Back home there might have been a lack of readiness to listen to details about the job and new community. Now that the expatriates are faced with the daily realities of coping in a strange country, there may be a greater willingness to use helpful hints. Also, the family may have many questions that they wish to ask of those with experience on the scene.

Within a week to three months after arrival, this on-site accultural program should get underway. Volunteers are likely to come from workers' families, as well as the foreign community to assist in this "indoctrination." The consulate staff may provide resource professionals for this purpose. In any event, the on-site orientation should be pragmatic, and meet the needs of the expatriate family. It should demonstrate that the company cares about its people. It should aid the new worker or family to (a) resolve immediate living problems; (b) meet the challenge of the host culture and the opportunities it offers for travel, personal growth, and intercultural exchange; (c) attempt to reduce the culture shock, and to grow from that experience; (d) provide communication links to the local community and the home organization. Much of this can be accomplished in a systematic, informal, friendly, group setting.

Janet June Reinhart, formerly in charge of relocation services for Dean Worldwide in Huntington Beach, California, advocates the keeping of a journal of one's cross-cultural learning experiences abroad. These notes can range from tips on shopping to real estate locations and their desirabilities. This information can be invaluable when shared with one's colleagues or placed into the company's data bank on overseas' sites. Writing in her company's newsletter on adjusting to the international life-style, she shared experiences that ranged from exchange rates to women's being allowed to drive cars. Here is a sampling of Reinhart's comments to illustrate how other corporations might utilize employees' insights from their experience with different cultures:

> Communication is another area of adjustment—not just the language, but the TV, telephone and newspaper (TV that doesn't come on until four o'clock in the afternoon, news reports that are not entertaining, editorials that don't cover the latest issues in U.S. government, and telephones that are disconnected because the last tenant hadn't paid his bill and you haven't done it for him).
>
> Methods of banking, paying bills, going to the movies, driving a car, buying insurance, heating your house, buying the Christmas tree, baking cakes, a husband who works long and sporadic hours are others of an endless list of everyday events that are habitual and familiar chores that can become uncomfortable, annoying and disconcerting when the system and method and timing have to be relearned or newly integrated into what was once a smooth, organized lifestyle.

Three formal steps that the organization's human resource development staff might take abroad are:

1. *An adjustment survey*—Using a paper/pen instrument (questionnaire, checklist, inventory) approximately three to six months after arrival, request that the employee supply feedback on the foreign deployment situation. That person, possibly with the aid of other family members, should carefully fill out the form so as to identify their special needs, problems, and advantages found in the alien culture. An envelope may be provided to return the information directly to an external consulting firm or to cor-

porate personnel officials in the home culture. Greater cooperation and authenticity might be forthcoming if on-site management does not have access to the individual responses. If third-party anonymity is desirable, then the external resource might be used to collect and analyze the data. A second administration of the inquiry form might be considered twelve or eighteen months after arrival, or just prior to completing the assignment.

2. *Data analysis and reporting*—The information is analyzed from two viewpoints: individual need, and foreign deployment policies and practices. The material would be analyzed for the identification of problems and the recommendation of solutions. Reporting enables back-home management to monitor its foreign deployment system, while onsite management can improve the quality of working life for the expatriated employees. As group data are compiled and stored in a computer, a profile is drawn on overseas employee needs and concerns relative to foreign deployment at a particular location. This collection of significant information is then used in future orientation and training programs for planning. Data stored from deployment groups over a period of years provide insight into the requirements of overseas personnel in a geographic area, such as the Middle East. The results from such inquiry studies, whether used on a short- or long-term basis, have preventative value relative to problems of cultural adjustment, and lead to considerable savings in financial and human terms.

3. *Organizational communications*—To counteract alienation, loneliness, and feelings of being "cut off," a corporation, association, or agency must establish communications links with its representatives abroad. Newsletters, and other company publications are only a first step in this regard. The corporate office of international personnel could regularly send video or audio cassettes to expatriates and their families. In addition to internal news and communication items that keep overseas' employees up-to-date, morale-booster messages from key officials could be incorporated into this informational system. More importantly, the cassette media could be used to continue the cross-cultural training undertaken in the predeparture and onsite briefing sessions. It can also be used for professional development of employees in technical matters. The taped lessons would be for re-inforcement of previous learning, and ego building at the foreign location. The program aims to "plug in" the worker to domestic company operations, and build confidence in the employee relative to the importance of the overseas assignment. The cassettes can be played in the home for family discussion, or with small groups of employees in a training session with the onsite supervisor.

Part of the on-site support service should include further language training, whether in formal or informal group learning situations. Tutors, or home study cassettes, tapes, or records and closed circuit television can be valuable media for this purpose. Local nationals might be employed for this language and cultural instruction.

Gus Lanzo of Grumman Aerospace Corporation believes that the success of overseas sales efforts is very dependent on the caliber of predeparture and in-country training of personnel. His company's follow-up efforts range from meeting the family at the overseas destination to providing temporary and permanent accommodations, and information on available schooling, transportation, and communication. In remote areas, the corporation takes on the responsibility of providing such things as a bus service, a motor pool, telex, news bulletins, and even school and shopping systems.

Ideally, at least six months before completion of the foreign assignment, the employee should be getting assistance relative to departure, transition, and reintegration into the native land and domestic work environment. Grumman's program considers these practical needs of the returning family: (a) transportation to the airport; (b) stopover vacation enroute based on length of overseas duty; (c) interim housing, if necessary, while the family is "settling in" to the United States; (d) financial adjustments to reward successful foreign performance; and (e) guidance on new job assignments within or without the company. The whole Grumman foreign deployment policy is to give recognition, stature, and status to the program and the personnel involved.

Snodgrass and Zachlod (1977/78) point out some special problems that those assigned outside the United States experience:

> . . . Termination of participation by Americans in any bi-national situation is more related to unsatisfactory family adjustments than unsatisfactory work relationships. There may be a single pivotal factor which accounts for an unsuccessful adjustment, e.g., the wife's inability to adapt to a role other than a domestic housewife, or women who have previously enjoyed a career and suddenly find themselves without meaningful identity. Other studies have found that the problem of American identity becomes quite serious after the third or fourth year for the children and parents. This problem is compounded when they are forced to return to the States, or when teenagers go home to college and university work. . . . Families trained to interact in mutually supportive ways can provide themselves with resources for adjustment in the alien environment.

Onsite support services cannot be just for the first year abroad, or take for granted that the adjustment is satisfactory if the family manifests no overt problems in the first two years of a five-year tour of duty overseas. There must be a continuing follow-up and undergirding of the foreign deployment program with reinforcement inputs, "hotline" alerts and counseling, and other innovative means to reduce family stress and strain. A positive, preventative program can be launched to reduce dependents' anxiety when one parent's assignments require extensive travel. The same approach is required when a parent is like an itinerant because of frequent absence such as occurs in offshore drilling jobs.

Corporate leadership is required to help the overseas employees and their families develop a sense of community, organizing to supply necessary services to their offspring. For instance, it is obvious that many American teenagers need help finding outlets for their energies when overseas, especially when the social supports (rapports, fashion, and dating opportunities) are severely restricted or nonexistent in a remote location. Creative parents and corporate personnel can join with local resources to provide American adolescents with a place to belong to and activities they enjoy.

Furthermore, more emphasis should be given to mental health services in both the selection and support of overseas personnel. Researchers recommend an overseas counselor for family adjustment problems, supportive assistance from American community service organizations (e.g., Rotary), improved psychological screening by American businesses sending personnel overseas, and increased orientation and training in personal security against acts of terrorism, such as kidnappings or thefts. Reorientation services to American school and college requirements should be provided for adolescents returning to the United States. It is interesting to note that the problems of a Japanese family returning to their homeland are often exacerbated after a long tour abroad, and the children find it most difficult to reintegrate into the closed school and employment systems in Japan. One solution the Japanese are pursuing, like the Americans before them, is to open their own schools and colleges overseas for their expatriate dependent children—the curriculum and language is that of the homeland, and the institutions are open to the local students. Obviously, organizations that disrupt normal family life by a foreign deployment assignment have some responsibility to facilitate the tour of duty abroad and the return to the homeland.

A total system of transcultural personnel services should offer counseling and community services to expatriate families. Frequently, a group of organizations in the same industry, or multinational contractors working on the same project or in the same region can best meet this objective. For example, thirty companies in the petroleum field have banded together in the informal Overseas Industrial Relations Discussion Group to deal with common concerns in foreign deployment. Similarly, giant corporations in overseas construction and engineering have formed the International Occupational Program Association. IOPA is a structured vehicle for confronting the alcohol, emotional, and related family problems within employee populations overseas.

Stage Four—Reentry Program

The last component in the foreign deployment system involves reintegrating the expatriate into the home society and domestic organization. For a person who has been abroad for sometime, the homeland and the organizational culture have changed in the meantime. The reentry process begins overseas with the psychological withdrawal of the expatriate faced with returning home. The organization provides services to facilitate the employee's exit from the foreign assignment—travel and transition assistance. Upon return, reentry shock may occur for six months or more, as the person struggles to readjust to the lifestyle and tempo of the changed home and organizational cultures. Apart from the challenge of reestablishing home and family life is the issue of reassignment in the parent company or agency. Again, the previous section on transitional experience applies to this situation.

For many expatriates, it is a time of crises and trauma, the last stage of the culture shock process. The experience abroad for those who are sensitive and who got involved in the host culture was profound. It causes many people to reexamine their lives, values, attitudes· to assess how they became what they are. It prompts others to want to change their life-style. The reentry home becomes the opportunity to carry out these aspirations. Individuals are not satisfied to return to old neighborhoods, old friends, or the same job or company affiliation. Many wish to apply the new self-insights, and to seek new ways of personal growth. The organization that sent them abroad in the first place should be empathetic to this reality, and be prepared to deal with it.

The problem is exacerbated when internal political turmoil in the host nation suddenly forces an employee and family to return home. In the last decades, experiences of Americans in Vietnam and Iran provide "horror stories" of expatriates forced to abandon jobs, personal savings, and belongings because of a change in the foreign government. Harrassed, exhausted, frightened families may be air lifted back to the United States. One wonders about the degree of responsibility their sponsoring organizations assumed for their integration into the U.S., as well as for financial losses.

Robert Maddox (1971) first raised the issue of the quality of managers sent to foreign subsidiaries, and his insights are still valid regarding the trend of sending the organization's most competent personnel abroad because, among other reasons, it costs 2 1/2 times what the same manager costs the company at home, and 4 1/2 times what it costs to employ a local national counterpart. The policy, he noted, is to assign managers who are on their way up in the organization. After a few years in the international operation, they are brought back to the home office with a more cosmopolitan viewpoint, and knowledge of world business realities. However, Maddox discovered through interviews with multinational corporation executives that the major problem in this regard is "reentry."

Sometimes the problem is accentuated by small-minded domestic management that downgrades the managers brought home to the United States. Because of high salaries, bonuses, servants, and other benefits overseas, some expatriates are discontented with the lowered expectations and compensation at home. For some, there is a distinct change in the level of social life; they do not have the social privileges and contacts, the perks and emoluments of the foreign situation. They may return to the life of a middle manager in middle-class suburbia without movement in prestigious circles and involvement with high-level government officials. Often, their role in the domestic organization is less exalted, and the scope of their decision-making authority is restricted. Furthermore, the returned manager is somewhat out of touch with American culture, for their native society is different from when they left. This difficulty is found in the public, as well as the private, sector—missionaries, government officials, Peace Corps volunteers, and other such persons subject to lengthy assignments abroad are prone to reentry shock and all that it implies. It is an old syndrome—"How are you going to keep them down on the farm after they have seen Paris!"

The foreign deployment system is incomplete unless it helps returning employees to fit into the home culture and organization. The system may involve group counseling with personnel specialists, psychologists, and former expatriates. Ideally, the family should be included in the discussion whether they have been abroad or not. For some, the personal crises are so severe that intensive individual psychological counseling is in order.

An annotated "bibliography on cross-cultural reentry" has been compiled by Clyde N. Austin of Abilene Christian University (1983), and it is widely used.

To capitalize on human corporate assets, the organization should further close the deployment loop with special assistance, such as financial aid to obtain a home mortgage, or outplacement advisement because a position is no longer available in the home organization or the person wishes a change of affiliation and career. For a few, it may be legal assistance because a divorce is inevitable. In such ways the sponsoring organization fulfills its responsibility toward the overseas employee reassigned home.

However, expatriates coming back from an overseas assignment are a valuable resource. The corporation can learn much from their cross-cultural experience. The information can be used to improve the whole foreign deployment process. Some possibilities to consider are:

1. Data gathering from all employees who return from either temporary or longer relocations abroad. A standardized questionnaire or interview procedure can be developed and the results stored in a computer for future use. Separate records can be kept on those in the premature return group. Interview with high performers abroad might be videotaped.
2. Data analysis and application of the information obtained from employees upon reentry would be carried out by the office of international personnel or external consultants. Findings would be studied for ways to improve recruitment and selection of personnel for overseas assignment;

employee training programs for foreign deployment; management policies and practices at foreign sites; consumer, customer, public, and employee relations in target countries; and relocation assistance for the returning expatriate employees.

3. Consultation with foreign deployment specialists and policy changes should follow as a result of the findings. The results have implications for corporate manpower policy and practice, especially relative to cost reductions and effectiveness of the international business operations.

4. Human resource development programs in multinational organizations should benefit from these procedures, and special undertakings may be stimulated by the findings and recommendations of specialists' reports on the foreign deployment situation. For example, some of the data may have lateral application to domestic management practice or development, particularly with minority personnel. It may be helpful in understanding company reports that come to headquarters from international subsidiaries. It may prompt a systematic inventory of skills in the international work force, encourage the design of an international or in-country performances review and appraisal system, show the need for an International Managerial Replacement Planning System, foster the development of strategies for the interim utilization of expatriate technicians and managers before their next overseas assignment, and bring to management's attention the need for a system that brings host or third country nationals into the domestic operation.

Rosalie Tung (1988) examines the issue of managing personnel abroad in her book, *The New Expatriates*. To bolster the contention that human resource management (HRM) is the key to successful international operations, she surveyed current programs at training institutes (UK's Center for International Briefings at Farnham Castle, as well as Japan's Institute for International Assignment and Japanese American Conversation Institute). In addition, she analyzed the expatriate policies and practices within British, Italian, Swiss, and German multinationals and two transnational corporations (an MNC owned by people of different nationalities with two or more parent headquarters, such as Unilever). Tung, a professor at Canada's Simon Fraser University, concluded that European and Japanese multinationals have lower failure rates with "expats" because they are more international or global in their orientation, and select and train people who are more adept at living and working in a foreign environment. Multinational organizations must provide a cross-cultural component in the human resource development of not only those they send abroad, but also with the company's local host nationals who must learn to work effectively with internationals.

SUMMARY

Life is filled with turning points, crises that can be turned into challenges for personal and professional growth. Such transitional experiences are characteristic of going abroad and the passage from the industrial to metaindustrial work culture. The trauma experienced in this adjustment process can take many forms, whether it is called culture or re-entry shock, role or organization shock, or even future shock. Essentially, cross-cultural transitions threaten our sense of identity, whether the cause be serious illness, death of a loved one, divorce, major job or organizational change, relocation into a strange environment, or a new role brought on by altered circumstances. Such transitions force us to rethink and reevaluate the way we read meaning into our private worlds. They are opportunities to learn, to grow, and to transform our lifestyle, management, or leadership.

This chapter reviewed transitional models that illustrate both the negative and positive stages of adjustment. Organizations can assist personnel to delimit such shocks to their systems by coaching, counseling, and training. The stress and anxiety that results need not lead to severe disorientation, depression, and unhealthy behavior. Withdrawal, alienation, and hostility can be countered by increasing awareness and information, providing enjoyable intercultural experiences, as well as facilitating integration into the unfamiliar situation.

When considered in the context of sending employees overseas on assignment, the return on organizational investment in cross-cultural preparation and continuing support services can be considerable. We recommend that sponsoring multinational corporations or agencies institute a *foreign deployment system*. A variety of helpful strategies could be employed during the four major stages of the relocation processes—(1) assessment of competent personnel to be deployed abroad, including recruitment and selection; (2) predeparture orientation, including culture and foreign language training, preferably with family groups; (3) on-site monitoring, evaluating, and supportive services; (4) reentry program that begins when in the foreign environ and facilitates the readjustment to the home macro and microcultures. This enlightened approach to transnational activities cannot only reduce premature return costs and much unhappiness among expatriates and overseas' customers, it can improve performance, productivity, and profitability in the world market (Tung, 1988).

Global managers ensure that transitional experiences beyond one's traditional culture or background contribute to a heightened sense of self, rather than permitting them to deeply threaten the ego. Such cosmopolitans act to promote intercultural contacts that are more satisfying because the people involved are better able to communicate, to perceive and deal effectively with differences, and to enter into interpersonal relationships. Through such successful coping, we reaffirm our own uniqueness in relation to others, especially those who appear alien and strange upon initial encounter.

10
Managing Business Protocol and Technology Transfer

World trade is considered by many to be the human race's best chance to maintain global peace and prosperity. Luis Aranda, a business professor at Arizona State University, maintains the potential for substantial international commerce is largely untapped, citing trillions of unearned dollars based on figures in the *Statistical Abstract of the United States*. In his study of the Arizona World Trade Association, Aranda discovered that the members surveyed were mainly in the export business, while a third were in imports, but only a fifth of the respondents provided some management development for international business (*Training and Development Journal*, April 1986, pp. 71–73). To improve trade and lower deficits in the global marketplace, Aranda advocates more than training in managing change, interpersonal skills, and cultural difference. He believes companies with universities and associations should be providing employees with:

- *Technical knowledge* for penetrating foreign markets (e.g., introducing new products in foreign markets, licensing patents and dealing with nontariff barriers abroad, identifying potential export opportunities.)
- *Comparative management* for dealing with foreign business and government (e.g., comparison of regional management practices, cross-cultural negotiating skills, current international business issues and trends; refer to Nath, 1987).

Because the general management culture within any country or area reflects its surrounding ethnic background, those who would do business outside their own nation require insight about the host culture. There are numerous information resources for gaining such insight (see *Managing Cultural Differences' Directory of Intercultural Resources* database, Gulf Publishing Company, 3301 Allen Parkway, Houston, TX 77019, USA).

Dr. Farid Elashmawi of Tech Trans offers special programs in "Training for Global Success" that range from intercultural communications to joint ventures. It is in the latter field that he thinks intercultural competence is most needed. The Parker Pen Company (P.O. Box 1616, Janesville, Wis. 53547) has available survey results from 200 executives as to "do's and don't's " for Americans who wish to flourish in the international market. Among don't's: don't use slang, colloquialisms, and regional expressions; avoid bad language, off-color remarks, and sexual symbolisms; do not interrupt clients or rush to bluff your way through something you do not understand. The positive strategies urged in this report have already been covered in our previous chapters.

Another cultural dimension requiring caution is the legal system in various countries. One can cross the border from the U.S. whose legal practices are rooted in English Common Law in which "you are innocent until proven guilty," and cross over into Mexico still guided by the Napoleonic Code where if accused, "you are guilty until you prove your innocence."

Human and legal rights differ by nation. Gene LaPere wrote *Never Pass This Way Again* in which she described her ordeal caused by a persistent street peddler in Pamukkale, Turkey. To get rid of the pesky salesman, she paid $20 for three dirty marble heads that turned out to be ancient Roman sculpture from nearby ruins. Detained by customs officials, she was accused of smuggling antiquities, and faced Turkish law based again on the Napoleonic Code. The harrowing experience ended by an unauthorized escape. Robert L. Pisanti, attorney with the Philadelphia-based International Legal Defense Counsel, says up to 3,000 Americans are arrested annually in foreign countries and warns that U.S. constitutional guarantees and passports are meaningless when abroad, and that one had best know and observe the laws of the foreign country in which you visit or do business (*Insight*, March 7, 1988, p. 35).

MIND YOUR WORLD MANNERS

There are principles of intercultural etiquette that should be observed by all foreign travelers or with foreign visitors, but especially by those in leadership positions within business, professions, or government. Etiquette and protocol are tied up with ritual and ceremony, form and tradition, rank and class—they carry more weight in older nations than in younger, more equalitarian democracies. Breaches in this regard reveal one as ill-bred, ignorant, or racist—such as asking:

- A woman from India about the red beauty mark (tikka or kumkum) on her forehead.
- An Asian, if he or she is Japanese, Chinese, Vietnamese or what.
- An African-American female with braided cornrows about washing her hair.
- A native American-Indian to share his or her spirituality and ritual.

When it comes to international business, a breach of etiquette or protocol can result in a loss of contract, even when the host is polite about the intercultural failure. Or thoughtful observation of such procedures can also lead to millions in new business, as a Citibank representative discovered when he presented his Arab host with a transmitter gadget for tracking birds. This may explain why the New York-based International Protocol Officers Association, established in 1985, already has 300 members. Its founder, Sondra Snowdon (1986) has written a book *The Global Edge* to facilitate participation in the niceties of the world marketplace. (Also refer to DeMonte 1988; Rowland, 1985; Reardon, 1981.)

One illustration is the matter of business cards with English on one side, and the language of the host culture containing the same information on the reverse side. In Japan, that card or "meishi" is an indispensable business tool that connotes rank and credentials, as well as legitimizes an introduction. In that culture, the exchange of business cards is an important formality with a ritual of its own—it establishes a relationship, expresses individuality, and promotes corporate image. To a Japanese manager who has spent his entire work life with one company, it provides a form of identity, an expression of social and business self, a place in hierarchy. Some cards now contain pictures, computer chips, bar-code readers, or are produced in metal. Mitsubishi has a solid gold card that is now sold at $50 each (¥6,000), while Mitsui's bar code can be downloaded into a computer or the card can be read by a telephone device that automatically dials the number on it. Koraro Uteji of Aerpia, Tokyo, invented an audible business card with a magnetic tape on the back that will "speak" when run through a reader (*The Economist*, Dec. 24, 1988, p. 60). Given the customs of Nippon, outsiders there learn not to toss business cards on a table, not to stuff them in wallets to be sat upon, not to offer a cheap or soiled card, and not to list the title of "attorney or lawyer" if in the legal profession (find a substitute designation). Yes, there are a variety of ways to show aplomb and good manners abroad.

Interculturally insensitive behavior and bad manners are equally inappropriate in the domestic scene, especially at the workplace. In multicultural California, for instance, 35% of the population is of Mexican heritage, 25% of Asian background, and only 20% of European origin. Cultural sensitivity applies everywhere! Remember, no one person is representative or an "encyclopedia" of their group's history and culture.

THE NEED FOR APPROPRIATE PROTOCOL

Since the early 1970s, the U.S. balance-of-payments deficits forced the dropping of the fixed exchange rate system and the value of the dollar declined. The idea of the finite nature of resources and the limits-to-growth gained attention. The concepts of pluralism and the interdependence of all countries became evident.

By the mid 1970s, international business was heavily politicized with government regulations at both ends. It became a multi-actor era in which the business interests, the two (or more) governments, as well as regional and international interest groups, determined to a large extent risk and the profits of any business venture.

In this environment international marketers and managers require new skills. The new "technocrats" are young, well-educated, and possess a strong sense of nationalism, which shows itself in a variety of ways. These technocrats are dedicated to the task of building their economies and like their counterparts in the United States and other countries, they are somewhat anti-establishment and skeptical about the contribution derived by their country from the presence of multinational corporations (MNC's). As a result of this evolution, MNC's have a more delicate relationship with their external environments than they have had previously.

Managers must, therefore, be capable of effectively *communicating their goals* across cultural boundaries to the external stakeholders of their firms. They must understand how their host national counterparts perceive them in order to establish goals that are considered legitimate in today's international business environment. Managers must not only understand how to communicate, emphasize, and relate to their host national counterparts, but must also be aware of the underlying value structures that give rise to the particular type of organization to which the host national belongs, be it a government body, trade union, customer group, or supply organization. Only then will the expatriate manager be able to understand and assess whether the MNC can or should be perceived as legitimate by his or her host organizations. The global manager must skillfully manage the protocol of conducting business in other cultures as well as transfer technology when required. The material in this chapter will assist in this process.

THE CULTURAL MANAGEMENT SYSTEM

International managers function within four basic intermeshing systems of management philosophy and practice: the technical system, the economic system, the political system, and the cultural system. The first three systems are relatively easy to quantify. For example, the use of government statistics, trade association and industry figures, and other quantifiable items are readily available in most countries including lesser developed economies. The cultural system has received the least consideration, because it tends to be abstract and its influence on management is difficult to specifically describe.

The *macro-environmental* approach in cross-cultural management attempts to identify the impact of education, politics, law, etc. on management practices and effectiveness. The assumption is that management practices depend on these external variables and the differences among organizations in various countries can be explained as a result of differences in environmental conditions. This approach is useful. However, it is incomplete, because it seems to imply that the individual passively adapts to his environment, and gives the manager little credit for influencing the environment.

Our approach will be *behavioral* in the sense that we will attempt to explain behavioral differences in managers and organizations as a function of cultural influences. The assumption is that a manager's attitudes, values, beliefs and needs are determined at least in part by his or her culture. Management practices and theories will, therefore, vary from culture to culture. Taking the behavioral approach allows us to respond to our previous question: What are the determinants of human behavior? Or, how can I understand why a manager is acting in a particular way?

In the global manager's attempt to understand one's self, as well as to comprehend and predict the behavior of others, he or she uses a multilayered frame of explanation. If one knows the culture of the other person, then it is possible to make tentative predictions about the person's behavior. Furthermore, if one knows the other person's social roles and personality, one can predict behavior with a greater degree of accuracy.

It is impossible to study in detail every culture, and to make comparisons with similarities and differences from our own native culture, but we can present a conceptual framework for making comparisons. It is based on the concept of national character or basic personality concept as developed by Dr. Abram Kardiner and Dr. Ralph Linton (1981). The concept rests on the following premises:

1. That an individual's early experiences exert a lasting effect on his personality.
2. That similar early experiences tend to produce similar personality configurations in the people who experience them.
3. That the childrearing practices and socialization techniques of a society are culturally patterned and tend to be similar (although not identical) for the various families within the culture.
4. That these practices and techniques differ from culture to culture.

A wealth of evidence has been provided by anthropologists, sociologists, psychologists, and others to support these premises. Therefore, it follows that:

1. Members of any culture have many elements of early experience in common.
2. They also have many elements of personality in common.
3. Since the early experience of individuals differs from one culture to another, the personality characteristics and values differ from culture to culture.

The *basic personality* of a culture is the personality configuration shared by most members of the culture, as a result of early experiences that they have in common. This does not mean that behavior patterns of all members of a culture are similar. There is a wide range of individual differences, but there are many aspects that most of the people share to varying degrees. In Unit 3, unique cultural aspects of several areas of the world are discussed.

These local customs and practices can serve as guidelines for managers who must determine appropriate and inappropriate ways of interacting. They illustrate geographic themes and patterns that can be identified to facilitate international business.

As in previous chapters, the nontechnical aspects of business are considered. These pragmatic observations, subject to change with time, circumstances, and the personalities involved, are proposed as hints for facilitating international business. As Edward T. Hall (1976) says:

> Deep cultural undercurrents structure life in subtle but highly consistent ways that are not consciously formulated. Like the invisible jet streams in the skies that determine the course of a storm, these hidden currents shape our lives; yet their influence is only beginning to be identified.

In this chapter we will propose two conceptual frameworks or models for understanding the behavior of foreigners and, in particular, the behavior of managers from other cultures. The frameworks help a manager determine "what went wrong" when there is a problem or a misunderstanding, but more importantly, they show how to predict with some degree of reliability the impact of his or her behavior on persons whose value systems, way of life, and management philosophy may be very different from his or her own. This helps the multinational manager understand the behavior of the other colleagues, and use the appropriate protocol and transfer of technology.

THE ANTHROPOLOGICAL FRAMEWORK

This section draws largely on the work of Florence Kluckhohn and Fred Strodtbeck (1961), Stephen H. Rhinesmith (1971), Joseph J. DiStefano (1972), and Edward C. Stewart (1976).

Before considering a model for understanding management behavior in different cultures, several working definitions would be useful. A *formal organization* is a system of consciously coordinated activities or the forces of two or more persons who interact to attain personal and common objectives. The work of the manager is to coordinate human and nonhuman resources in order to accomplish the objectives of the organization. Typical management functions involve planning, organizing, recruiting, selecting, rewarding, leading, communicating, relating, problem-solving, decision-making, conflict managing, negotiating, controlling, training, evaluating, and innovating activities.

A *value* is a conception of an individual or group of individuals that is either "implicit or explicit of the desirable, which influences the selection from available modes, means, and ends of action." The concept of value is important because managers from the same culture tend to have similar values, and these value systems influence their interpersonal relationship and their performance of leadership activities.

There are five crucial and common questions applicable to man ("man" is used here in the generic sense, including male and female):

1. What is the character of innate human nature?
2. What is the relationship of man to nature?
3. What is the temporal focus of life?
4. What is the modality of man's activity?
5. What is the relationship of man to man?

The range of solutions to these questions is illustrated in the matrix in Table 10-1. The matrix suggests that, for each culture, there is a preferred way of responding to each question from among the alternatives presented. Underlying these preferences are values, which are ideas about what is right and wrong, good and bad. Values not only influence our behavior, but provide us with a focus for understanding our own behavior as well as the behavior of persons from different cultures.

What Is the Character of Innate Human Nature?

Table 10-1 is a three-way classification for the sake of illustration, and undoubtedly further distinctions can be made. In the United States most agree that the influence of Puritan ancestors is strong and many believe that human nature is basically evil but perfectible. Control and discipline are required to achieve goodness. Others in the United States now seem to believe that man is a mixture of good and evil. There is no evidence of a society that is committed to the definition of human nature as immutably good.

What Is the Relationship of Man to Nature?

Most North Americans believe that man is master of nature. The harmony orientation can be observed in Japanese, Chinese, and many American Indian tribes including the Navajo and Hopi. Accepting the inevitable and the subjugation of man to nature is evident in societies that place a high belief in fate.

Table 10-1*
Cultural Influences on Life Issues

Cultural Approaches	A	B	C
What is the character of human nature?	Man is evil†	Man is a mixture of good and evil†	Man is good†
What is the relationship of man to nature?	Man is subject to nature	Man is in harmony with nature	Man is master of nature
What is the temporal focus of life?	To the past	To the present	To the future
What is the modality of man's activities?	A spontaneous expression in impulse and desires	Activity that emphasizes as a goal the development of all aspects of the self	Activity that is motivated primarily toward measurable accomplishments
What is the relationship of man to man?	Lineal—group goals are primary and an important goal is continuity through time	Collateral—group goals are primary. Well-regulated continuity of group relationships through time are not critical	Individual—the individual goals are most important

* Exhibit modified from Kluckhohn and Strodtbeck, p. 11ff.
† This assumes that human nature is either mutable or immutable.

What Is the Temporal Focus of Life?

The solutions to this question (past, present, and future) are present in all societies but the ordering of one over another is what distinguishes the societies. Most middle class North Americans are oriented to the future, whereas peasants in many societies focus on the "now" more than the past or the future, and the Chinese orientation, as well as other cultures, is very much to the past.

What Is the Modality of Man's Activity?

The spontaneous expression of impulses stresses the release and indulgence of existing desires. An example is the behavior of people in Brazil at Mardi Gras. Activities that emphasize the development of all aspects of a person can be seen in Eastern culture and among an increasing number of "holistic" Westerners. The "doing" or activity oriented towards accomplishments is most familiar to North Americans and managers in particular.

What Is the Relationship of Man to Man?

This question may be restated, "Whose welfare is primary?" Most North Americans possess an individual orientation, so the individual's welfare is most important. The extended families of many cultures would be an example of the collateral group when the welfare of the group supercedes the welfare of the individual members. The English aristocracy would be an example of a lineal group orientation where the welfare of the group is important and the social class continues through time.

We have identified the questions and defined the solutions with several examples from a variety of cultures. The framework will be useful if managers are able to apply it to some of the problems they experience when working with persons from different cultures. Other examples are presented in Table 10-2.

Having covered this material, the question for managers is how can it be used? The conceptual scheme can be used to anticipate problems before they occur or to analyze problems once they exist. (The questionnaire included in Appendix B is useful in anticipating and analyzing cross-cultural management problems.)

Table 10-2
Managerial Examples of Basic Questions

What is the character of innate human nature?

Example of management problems affected by question:	*What kind of control system is necessary?*		
Examples reflecting the range of solutions to management problems:	If man is evil, elaborate controls are necessary.	If man is neither good nor evil, a system to avoid temptation is necessary.	If man is basically good, managers need a control system to gather information necessary for decision-making only.

What is the relationship of man to nature?

Example of management problem affected by question:	*How will methods of controlling the birth rate be accepted?*		
Examples reflecting the range of solutions:	Subjection to nature—no methods will be accepted. If one is to become pregnant it will happen.	Harmony with nature.	Master of nature. Any method will be okay if medically safe.

What is the temporal focus of life?

Example of management problem affected by question:	*What goals should the organization have?*		
Examples reflecting range of solutions:	Past—the goals of the past are sufficient.	Present—the goals should reflect the present demands.	Future—the goals should be directed towards trends and the situation of the future.

(table continued on next page)

Table 10-2 (Continued)
Managerial Examples of Basic Questions

What is the modality of man's activity?

Example of management problem affected by question:	*What motivates people to work?*		
Examples reflecting the range of solutions	Work only as much as is necessary for the day.	A balance between work and nonwork.	Work to accomplish and to demonstrate hard work and competence.

What is the relationship of man to man?

Example of management problem affected by question:	*How are people selected for employment?*		
Examples reflecting range of solutions:	Hire a close relative.	Hire a relative or friend of someone in the organization.	Hire the best person.

What is the organization's responsibility to nature and the community?

Example of management problem affected by question:	*What is the extent of corporate social responsibility?*		
Example reflecting range of solutions:	Control all exploitation of nature and regulate society completely.	Within reason balance ecological and economic policies; gradual implementation of environmental controls.	Individual's right to the good life, so supply the means for unhampered employment.

Suppose your assignment as a manager is to investigate the cultural differences in manufacturing and accounting management technology in a Latin American country. North American management theory is based on the premise that each person in the organization performs his tasks in a way that promotes the organization. Helping or hiring one's friends or relatives is subordinate to achieving organizational objectives. To reduce the number of cultural errors, a manager can examine the different solutions to all management questions that are being considered. Where differences exist, the manager can determine, in advance, when to modify a management practice to fit the situation. The manager can also know where the difference exists and will be able to intervene at that point rather than another area. The major benefit of this approach is to begin with a conceptual framework and deduce from it where specific problems might occur. This is accomplished by an awareness of the areas of difference between the two cultures at an abstract level and then generating specific and concrete management problems that might occur or have occurred as a result of the differences. If the framework is used as suggested, it will help managers avoid quick and erroneous conclusions about the causes and solutions to cross-cultural management problems. It will also assist in determining the appropriate social or business protocol (Loft 1973).

ATTRIBUTION THEORY FROM SOCIAL PSYCHOLOGY

At a recent orientation session conducted for executives, managers, and their families from several European countries in the midwest, a couple from the Netherlands related the following incident. Shortly after arriving in the United States for a two-year assignment, they were invited to a barbecue by the international vice-president of their company. They arrived and within ten minutes, in their own words, "they had been insulted so often they were ready to go home." What had happened? First, from the perspective of the couple from the Netherlands; they had been invited to a meal by the international vice-president. Their expectation was that they would be the only couple present. Second, when they were introduced to the other guests many of the American women did not shake hands and "some of them shook hands with their left hand." Also, some of the men did not stand. They were incensed and "highly insulted." From the perspective of the Americans, however, the purpose of the barbecue was to provide an opportunity for the newly-arrived expatriates from the Netherlands to meet several others in the company as well as a few people from the neighborhood. The American women may have extended their left hand as a friendly or warm gesture that is sometimes seen in the midwestern United States. But the important fact is that the couple from the Netherlands felt insulted and the purpose of the event from the point of view of the Americans was not accomplished.

Harry C. Triandis (1975) cites the following situation of a similar nature. In many cultures, servants and domestic help do most of the tasks around a home, including the cleaning of shoes. In the United States, such employees usually do not clean shoes as part of their responsibilities. If Mr. Kato, a Japanese businessman, were a house guest of Mr. Smith, an American businessman, and asked the "cleaning person" to shine his shoes there could be a problem. It is, or at least could be, an inappropriate request. However, the crucial question is, what *attributions* does the cleaning person make concerning Mr. Kato's request? There are probably two possibilities. One is that he or she could say Mr. Kato is ignorant of American customs and in this case the person would not be too disturbed. The cleaning person could respond in a variety of ways, including telling the Japanese guest of the American custom, ignoring the request, and speaking to his or her employer. However, if the cleaning person *attributes* Mr. Kato's request to a personal consideration (he is arrogant) then there will be a serious problem in their interpersonal relationship. If a person from one culture is offended by a person from another culture and one believes it is because of culture ignorance, this is usually forgiven. If one "attributes" the offense or "error" to arrogance there will be serious problems.

Attribution theory is concerned with how people explain things that happen. It is a way of explaining to ourselves why things happen in the world. It helps to answer such questions as:

1. Why did Mr. Kato ask the cleaning person to shine his shoes?
2. Why did I pass or fail an examination?
3. Why can't Molly read?
4. Why has the Soviet Union agreed to on-site nuclear inspection?

There are many ways of perceiving the world and given the almost limitless possibilities, we must subconsciously and habitually "screen" and organize the stimuli.

We also interpret behavior in terms of behaviors appropriate for a role. The couple from the Netherlands expected to be the only persons invited to the barbecue and once there, expected other guests to use their right hand and to stand when being introduced. Mr. Kato expected that it would be acceptable to ask the cleaning person to shine his shoes. From the perspective of the cleaning person, this is not acceptable. When each one's expectations were not realized they attributed motives to the "offender" based on their cultural construct.

Attribution theory helps to explain what happens and is applicable to cross-cultural management situations for the following reasons:

1. *All behavior is rational and logical from the perspective of the behaver.*
   At a recent seminar involving Japanese and American businessmen, an American asked a Japanese what was most difficult for him in the United States. The Japanese replied that "the most difficult part of my life here is to understand Americans. They are so irrational and illogical." The Americans present listened, and were both amused and surprised.
2. *Persons from different cultures perceive and organize their environment in different ways, so that it becomes meaningful to them.*

To be effective in working with people from different cultures requires that we make *isomorphic attributions* of the situation, i.e., we put ourselves "in the other person's shoes." Isomorphic attributions result in a positive evaluation of the other person because they help us to better understand the other's behavior (verbal or nonverbal).

The following example is quoted from Harry C. Triandis (1975); it actually is taken from the files of a Greek psychiatrist. As background information it is important to remember that Greeks perceive supervisory roles as more authoritarian than Americans who prefer participatory decision-making. Read the verbal conversation first, then the attributions being made by the American and the Greek.

Verbal Conversation*	**Attribution†**
American: How long will it take you to finish this report?	American: I asked him to participate.
	Greek: His behavior makes no sense. He is the boss. Why doesn't he *tell* me?
Greek: I do not know. How long should it take?	American: He refuses to take responsibility.
	Greek: I asked him for an order.
American: You are in the best position to analyze time requirements.	American: I press him to take responsibility for own actions.
	Greek: What nonsense! I better give him an answer.
Greek: 10 days.	American: He lacks the ability to estimate time; this time estimate is totally inadequate.
American: Take 15. Is it agreed you will do it in 15 days?	American: I offer a contract.
	Greek: These are my orders: 15 days.

In fact the report needed 30 days of regular work. So the Greek worked day and night, but at the end of the 15th day, he still needed one more day's work.

Verbal Conversation	**Attribution**
American: Where is the report?	American: I am making sure he fulfills his contract.
	Greek: He is asking for the report.
Greek: It will be ready tomorrow.	Both attribute that it is not ready.
American: But we had agreed it would be ready today.	American: I must teach him to fulfill a contract.
	Greek: The stupid, incompetent boss! Not only did he give me wrong orders, but he does not even appreciate that I did a 30-day job in 16 days.
The Greek hands in his resignation.	The American is surprised.
	Greek: I can't work for such a man.

---

* This is the spoken dialogue between the American and the Greek. It could be tape recorded, written, or videotaped. It can be measured.

† The "attributions" made by the American and the Greek are not externalized and cannot be recorded.

This illustrates that at almost every place in an intercultural conversation, the statement of one person leads to an intimation that does not match the attribution of the other. These are extreme examples of non-isomorphic attributions, and they are working to the detriment of the relationship.

The intercultural skill of making isomorphic attributions is vital to appropriate protocol and effective technology transfer.

PROBLEM-SOLVING ACROSS CULTURES

Understanding intercultural conflicts is not easy. Solving them is difficult and many do not even try. Likert (1976) wrote:

> The strategies and principles used by a society and all its organizations for dealing with disagreements and conflict reflect the basic values and philosophy of that society.

The following is a five-step method of problem solving across cultures:

1. Describe the problem as understood in both cultures.
2. Analyze the problem from two cultural perspectives.
3. Identify the basis for the problem from both viewpoints.
4. Solve the problem through synergistic strategies.
5. Determine if the solution is working multiculturally.

The case study that follows illustrates these steps.

(text continued on page 275)

Anatomy of a Cross-Cultural Problem

Description of the Problem

Perhaps one of the most difficult problems encountered by American businessmen and their respective families while conducting business and residing in Great Britain, is the apparent inability of the British to accomplish anything with speed or efficiency. Some foreigners in the U.K. believe this problem is inherent within British society and also manifests itself in the management structure of an English firm. Some American businessmen are continually frustrated by the seemingly slow and inhibited method of business procedure in Great Britain. Many examples can be cited whereby the newly arrived American executive has rushed into his British colleague's office in London full of zestful ambition to get the project underway, only to be quickly stumped by the tranquility, self-restraint, and perhaps, a seeming indifferent nature of the British associate.

---

* This worksheet was completed by Christine Reddy, an English graduate student of the American Graduate School of International Management, September 1980.

American families living in Britain complain of the inordinate amount of time required by various service industries to respond to a request to perform the task at hand. For instance, should one require a plumber or an electrician, it is quite likely that the customer may have to wait twenty-four hours, and when the expert finally does arrive, he typically takes a longer time than one would deem necessary in the U.S. to carry out the job.

Analysis of the Problem

From the U.S. Perspective—

From the American perspective, the British are criticized as being too soft and gentlemanly, lacking in aggression and self-discipline. Further, they are too comfortable with their heritage and current situation. Thus, they do not have an appetite for change and innovation.

Americans sometimes feel that the British do not have enough formal business education and that they are business amateurs in a specialist's world. Consequently, Americans may believe the British do not have either the capability to fully engage in rugged competition, nor do they have enough dedication to the profit motive.

As a result, Americans may conclude that the average British worker is basically lazy, unmotivated and ineffectual. Some British employees have an external image of incompetence and unenthusiasm. Therefore, Americans perceive the British laborer as apathetic relative to how quickly he tackles a job, or indeed, whether is it accomplished at all between the necessary breaks for tea.

From the British Perspective—

The British worker does not understand the constant need for rush that is so typical of his American counterpart. He or she views the American as being impatient, brash, overly aggressive, and forever striving to prove himself to his superiors.

The Britisher lives in a more relaxed and slow-paced environment, a characteristic that is attractive to foreigners. With centuries of European civilization behind them English people take life in stride. They do not see an overwhelming necessity to attack immediately a management problem or service call in the same way that his American peers do. While the British realize they must become more efficient and productive if they are to promote a healthier economy, they do not feel it is necessary to sacrifice their more casual and restrained nature, or quality of life, in favor of improved service and competitiveness.

Identification of Basis of the Problem (Analysis of values, etc.)

From the U.S. Perspective—

An American executive would, perhaps, summarize the basis of the problem of doing business with Great Britain as being a lack of aggression on the part of his British associate. An amusing comparison between the more assertive American attitude and the rather quiet and comfortable English approach is demonstrated by the anecdote of the American shoe salesman who was sent to Africa to sell shoes. A British salesman was also sent by his company in order to survey the potential market. Upon the arrival of the Englishman, he immediately sent a wire back to his home office in Northampton and said, "Nobody wears shoes here. Coming back at once." The American sent a telegram saying, "Nobody wears shoes here. Send two million shoes."

The American has been raised on the values of hard work, individual achievement, and success and evidence abounds of his constant quest to do better. Children are raised to believe that through applied effort and determination, one can climb further up the social ladder, get a better education, make more money, and marry someone successful. Consequently, it is imbedded in the American spirit to take every advantage for opportunity and achievement, and devote oneself to the classic American dream—to earn a small fortune through hard work and a determination, to succeed, and then retire and live comfortably from the profits.

Directly related to the American value of success is the belief that a person is individually responsible for one's own fate and has to rely on one's own resourcefulness. Consequently, in order to survive, flourish, and achieve, the American spirit is full of drive and competitiveness. These two factors of the American character have been paramount to the success of American industry.

From the British Perspective—

Perhaps the most interesting contrast from the British point of view is the difference between how the two parties view business in general. In American society the industrialists were often admired for their wealth and power, whereas in Great Britain the industrialist lacked status. One

must remember that because of the rigid class structure and restricted system of education, work did not inspire the same ambitions, social mobility, or status paths that it did in America. Work was previously disdained by all classes. There was a tendency for members of the upper elite to live a leisured life and they often looked upon the concept of work as being "beneath them." And the lower class, or the laborers, worked because of their economic and social dependence. Thus, because the British labor force was polarized by those people who had to work and those who did not, the education system was not concerned with promoting management or business education.

Another virtue of the British that is closely allied to work, but that is at odds with the American view, is that of competitiveness. In England, the competitive spirit is traditionally more likely to be on behalf of one's group, team, or nation against another. The difference between the American individualistic spirit of competitiveness and the British communal orientation also points to the basis of the problem encountered by American executives operating overseas.

While the British are characterized by their lack of aggression, they feel that it stems from a rational need to keep things under control. As a result, the British are well-known for affecting a certain docility and appearing aloof.

The British belief in self-restraint and the unflappable spirit is in direct opposition to the American brand of aggressiveness, but they believe these characteristics, rather than being detrimental to Great Britain, have been greatly responsible for peace and order within that country.

Problem-Solving Across Cultures

The expatriate managers should be aware, prior to their arrival in England of the different customs and traditions, beliefs and values systems of their host nation so they may understand what problems they can expect to encounter beforehand. Perhaps, by emphasizing the myraid differences found between the two cultures, the visitor would use more patience and understanding in dealing with their hosts. Many Americans believe that because the two countries share a common language, they also share a common culture. However, the problem described is a perfect example of how two cultures may operate in opposition to each other. Therefore, it is imperative that an American executive preparing to do business in Great Britain be made aware of the cultural nuances of the British in order that he may operate effectively within that environment.

Assessment of Implementation

Again, because the problem described does not relate to a specific confrontation, but is rather a direct result of the differences between two cultural groups, this step would be difficult to oversee. The American expatriate who has been, we hope, well-versed in the ways and mores of his British hosts, would be responsible for employing cultural sensitivity in all of his or her actions and should refrain from attempting to use an American ethnocentric approach in dealing with the British.

To determine the effects of a foreign deployment or cross-cultural indoctrination program, after a few months onsite survey, the feelings and attitudes of the American expatriate and his British colleagues to see whether or not they are both satisfied with their cross-cultural dealings with each other. Although good trade relations might indicate that the American and British executives are communicating effectively, oftentimes one must look much deeper, because in many cases cultural misunderstandings are not verbally stated, but rather remain under the surface where they do the most harm.

Bribery

One of the universal, negative aspects of human behavior is corruption. Truth and honesty are noble ideals, but they are also relative to the beholder. As global managers operate transnationally, they are faced with a situation that in one country is lawful or accepted practice, and elsewhere is illegal. Bribes, for example, may be common ways of doing business to ensure service in the host culture, but quite illegal in the home culture. Although we have mentioned this issue elsewhere in this text, in a chapter on business protocol, we thought the reprinting of this following interview is the best we could offer our readers on the matter.

A Conversation With John Noonan* —

"Hard-Core Bribery Will Go the Way of Slavery"

John Noonan, a leading legal scholar and philosopher, is professor of law at the University of California at Berkeley. His books include historical studies of contraception, divorce and usury. His new work, Bribes, *chronicles the history of bribery from Biblical days to the present time.*

"The Concept Has Roots in Religion"

The concept of bribery dates back to ancient Egypt and Israel and has its roots in religion. In these ancient societies there was at least one type of powerful person you were not supposed to go to with a gift: The judge hearing your case. The judge was the representative of the divine, so you didn't deal with him as though it were a market transaction.

In the later Roman Empire there was some attempt to generalize from judges to other public figures who were not supposed to receive money for their decisions. During this time there was no real enforcement; bribery was realized more as a moral idea than an effective legal norm. Over the ages the bribery ethic came to be enforced, though in the United States you only begin to get serious enforcement against high officials—cabinet officers, federal judges—in this century.

"A Desire to Have Public Purity"

Since the 1960s there has been a quantum jump in bribery prosecutions in America. At one level, that can be explained by centralization of federal power: Just as many other things have come to Washington, so has enforcement of bribery laws.

The usual restraint on prosecuting bribery at the local level has been that everybody is to some extent a part of the system, so they are constrained from being too harsh on others who work in it. But the federal system doesn't have those constraints; it comes down hard on the locals. It can smash a whole system of local corruption, and in many parts of the country it has done just that.

Another more speculative explanation is that the jump in enforcement goes hand in hand with a perceptible decline in the desire to enforce sexual morals that began in the '60s. My speculation is that there's a desire to have public purity somewhere—and, if not in our sexual life, then with our public officials. It's interesting that a common language covers both sexual and public virtue. For example, the judge who sells out is considered a prostitute.

"Defining Bribery Is Not Easy"

The push against bribery in the past two decades has produced much legislation, including the Racketeer Influenced and Corrupt Organizations Act and the Foreign Corrupt Practices Act. The latter is unique in the history of the world because it makes bribing someone else's government a crime. What's also unusual is that it applies to the bribe giver rather than the bribe taker.

Defining bribery is not always easy, because many actions fall into a gray area. The cash bribe is the hard-core thing. But once you move away from that you always have questions. If you work at the Pentagon as a procurement official on a weapons system and the contractor hires you to work for him, did he do so because you're a wonderful, efficient administrator or because you gave him a contract? The same holds in political appointments. Did you give a relative of a congressman a job in exchange for a vote or because of his or her administrative skills? It's hard to work out a standard that would be enforceable criminally in such matters.

The Western Ideal Is Accepted "Universally"

Bribery today is universally condemned. The Western ideal has been accepted everywhere, though in many places adherence may be more rhetorical than real.

Eventually I think hard-core bribery will wither away, though gray areas will remain. I suppose that reflects faith in rationality. Bribery is now seen as a bad thing for government, which has become more public—thanks in part to the media. The perception of bribery as an evil, the publicity given it and now the great stress on purity in public office are pushing to eliminate hard-core bribery. It will go the way of slavery.

As indicated earlier, the perception of bribery is culturally relative. In some countries, the same action might be considered a tip (to ensure promptness or service), especially when dealing with a bureaucracy. Among government officials in many lands the ethical dilemma has also been labeled, "influence peddling." Here there is a fine line between legal and illegal or even immoral behavior. In a recent scandal at the U.S. Department of Housing and Urban Development, political influence was used to obtain favorable treatment and contracts from the federal government. Part of the problem was in the people involved, part in the faulty legislation under which they operated, and part was in the system and management procedures. However, the spread of questionable and inappropriate behavior in both business and government within so-called advanced countries has led to a demand by the public for more character education in the schools, especially university courses in ethics at business and professional schools.

APPROPRIATE TECHNOLOGY TRANSFER

Perhaps the message in this chapter can best be focused by a discussion of technology transfer. Since culture involves the transmission of both knowledge and experience, the arena of technology is one of its most practical manifestations. Technology represents that branch of knowledge dealing with industrial arts, applied science, and engineering—the material objects and artifacts of civilization. When technology results in concepts, inventions, processes, production methods, and mechanisms that are transferred from its place of origin elsewhere, it becomes a *cross-cultural* phenomenon. Seurat (1979) who has written a realistic treatise on technology transfer describes this human characteristic as "the capacity to store and transmit to people the accumulated experience of others." When it is done properly, human progress and prosperity are advanced, but if improperly, then human life and property may suffer. A laudable goal is to improve the standard of living for those who are to benefit from the transfer.

Technology involves much more than the sale of licenses, franchises, and other forms of agreements for sharing the technology. It may include the transmission of a scientific theory, an engineering capability, or management system—everything from drawings, plans, and manufacturing instructions to tools and instruments, machines and computers, facilities and training materials. Its scope in an R & D project may range from a pilot to finished production, or from human resource development to turnkey factories. All facets of technology transfer, however, have a cultural dimension. For example, two companies from different countries establish a joint venture for the transfer of unique consumer or industrial products from a First to a Third World nation. In the process their representatives communicate, but with different *cultural* understandings and systems of law, finance, education, and transportation. One entity may be from the private sector, while the other is from a government owned company, or combination of both.

The technology transfer is best accomplished when it fosters cultural synergy for all parties. For cultural factors influence project success in every phase of the transfer process—from planning (including setting goals and objectives, defining needs and criteria), to systems analysis (including examination and synthesis of alternatives, selecting optimum targets, and writing specifications), to program implementation (including work definition, scheduling, budgetings, procurement and control systems). Unless global managers cope with these cultural realities, planning is undermined, goals are fuzzy, sequencing and scheduling are unrealistic, incentives are lacking, misunderstandings abound, and corruption may flourish (Martin 1976).

Technology transfer can be applied to ancient or modern technologies, high or low technologies. Within one's own country, it can span many microcultures as scientists and entrepreneurs seek to move the knowledge beyond its initial application. But often there are cultural barriers to be overcome, and cultural issues to be considered before the transfer can be successfully made. Martin Apple (Harris 1983, 1985) discovered this as he got involved in university technology transfer through his San Francisco company, Adytum Inc. Although a former professor who has crossed into the biotechnology business, he found that it was both the "mindset" of academia and its bureaucracy that prevented the rapid translation of many university innovations and patents from the laboratory to the marketplace. The "entrepreneurial culture" is only beginning to invade the institutions of higher education, especially with the establishment of university industrial parks, incubator programs, and other such devices to bridge the gap between the academic and business worlds.

Similarly, there may be cultural barriers to overcome in the transfer of technology from government national laboratories or the department of defense to the commercial or private sector (Kuhn, 1984). NASA has had the most success in transmitting its aerospace research and technology to business and university applications (NASA Scientific and Technical Information Facility, P.O. Box 8757, BWI Airport, MD 21240, USA). Its publication *Spinoff* (1987), tells the story of how its R&D had payoff from transportation and consumer products to manufacturing and industry, including the America's Cup winning yacht (available from the U.S. Government Printing Office, Washington, D.C. 20400, U.S.A.). But technology transfer also has implications between work cultures, as with industrial and entrepreneurial types, which are quite different in perspective and practice (Sexton and Smilor, 1986). Technology venturing on a large scale, whether at home or abroad, requires innovation and risk taking beyond traditional management (Konecci and Kuhn, 1985).

Our heading uses the term "appropriate" technology transfer, meaning suitable from the viewpoint of both the type of technology and the level of development of the recipient. Kumar's research (1979, 1981) underscores the need to avoid:

1. Fostering long-term dependency on the part of the receiver of the technology.
2. Overwhelming the receiver with a technological system that is too complex and sophisticated for use and maintenance.

Instead, Dr. Krishna Kumar of Michigan State University advocates indigenization and transnational cooperation in international economic and community development. He cites the demonstrated successes of many Third World multinational and even high-technology firms in serving the markets of developing nations. Whereas a North American or European company might seek to sell and install a technology that is beyond local capabilities at this point in time, technicians from India, Singapore, and other Asian lands might recycle a legitimate technology that is new and appropriate for the indigenous people, but not "state of the art" for a First World company.

The Case of Bechtel in New Guinea

Worldwide Projects is a periodical available without charge to those in the multinational community who design, construct, and finance international projects (P.O. Box 5017, Westport, CT 06881, USA). Its pages often describe transnational undertakings that achieve or flounder over cultural and social issues. One recent illustration of the latter that appeared (August/September 1985) concerned the masterbuilder, Bechtel, and why that company pulled out of the billion-dollar Ok Tedi joint venture with MKI (Morrison-Knudsen International). An interview with their project manager, Cal Perkins, revealed the following calamities that caused the corporation's withdrawal from this Papua, New Guinea mining and community development endeavor:

1. To make the mine and plant operational atop a mountain in an isolated rain forest, complete support services had to be provided in 33 months for a people who had never before seen a Westerner (the contract called for a town of 2,500, camps for 400, power plant, airstrip, roads, hospitals, schools, etc.).
2. To add to the trials caused by rains and washouts, economic contentions with subcontractors and owners, and skyrocketing costs, the natives were in the hunting stage of development—their "primitive" or unique culture with its set of values, beliefs, and customs frustrated the construction giant (e.g., no concept of private property or modern money; no understanding of the central government, its role and regulations; the local prejudices between highlanders and lowlanders, which interfered with worker housing and training; the complexity of the multicultural workforce of 5,000, which mixed the indigenous aboriginal peoples with imported technicians from America, Canada, New Zealand, Korea, and the Philippines).
3. Various time senses of the contractors and contractees, the government and the diverse workforce. Bechtel had 33 months to meet a deadline or face financial penalties, while local road builders did not believe in working "round-the-clock"—their more leisurely approach eventually lead that contractor to bankruptcy; in fact, the native workers did not like the work schedule, so they shut the operation down by going with their bows and arrows, rocks and clubs to block plane runways, tear up telephone lines, and thoroughly frighten the expatriate personnel.

This is a mini case of the cultural issues that can affect technology transfer and project management. Combined with spending a million dollars a day, such barriers can quickly defeat a desirable program. Bechtel and MKI did do many things right on this enterprise—they did build the roads that local contractors could not finish, they did institute training programs for the locals that began with rudimentary skills for some people who had never seen a wheel before; they did cope with an 85% turnover in the native workforce and 400 inches of rain a year; and they did bring the project in on schedule. But problems of nature, economics, and logistics were compounded by cross-cultural difficulties that ranged from the natives to the Australian clients who almost daily changed the game plan.

Former McKinsey consultant, Kathleen Murphy (1983) has done an interesting analysis of such transnational partnerships. Her ground rules for this collaboration offer much insight in recommending that partners should:

1. Be willing and prepared to participate in whole or part as the project requires—that is shared, lower or no equity in lieu of contractual promises of output.
2. Be willing to consider creative options when selecting partners—be open to creating synergy with competitors, companies that have not been in the global market before, or enterprises from several nations.
3. Organize for transition points during the development phases of a project—provide a framework to anticipate many overlooked pitfalls by carefully defining tasks, requirements, risks, parameters at each stage of planning, construction, implementation.
4. Select only feasible projects for technology transfer, install project control systems that audit for excellence in performance, including adequate communications and power balance, and build on accountability procedures to all the stakeholders in the project.

After being involved in transnational technology transfer for more than twenty years and forty-five countries, the president of Eurequip, a French consulting firm, Silvere Seurat (1979) maintains that a key factor for success is training of the people involved. This is an issue addressed in our next chapter. He advocates creating a "teaching system" to mobilize human energies, especially among the locals, which considers the cultural background of the trainees; adapts the educational content and methods to the needs of the personnel, the place, and the project, both for short and long-term requirements. Seurat believes that such human resource development ensures effective technology transfer when it is conceived synergistically—namely, the system seeks synergy between necessary jobs to be performed and trained workers to perform them, between knowledge conveyed and performance desired.

We have tried to emphasize that cultural inhibitors to the transfer of technology can occur not just between countries, but within the various sectors of one's own economy.

SUMMARY

Global managers can be more culturally skillful by application of the two conceptual models discussed in this chapter. The *anthropological model* provides a framework for determining in advance where intercultural problems may occur. The *attribution model* fosters a synthesis between interactors as to meanings, inferences, or attributions during the course of verbal or nonverbal communication.

Furthermore, observing and practicing both national and international protocol facilitates human performance and cooperation, especially in development projects. Such counsel becomes even more meaningful in the context of technology transfer, whether within a nation, or across borders. (Additional insights on international business protocol are offered in various chapters of Unit III under special sections on "Tips for doing business" in a specific culture.)

11
Managing Human Resources and Cross-Cultural Training

Leonard Nadler (1980, 1984, 1986) of George Washington University characterizes human resource development (HRD) as a

> . . . series of organized activities, conducted within a specified time, and designed to produce behavioral change . . . its most common manifestations are training (learning for the present job) and education (learning for the future job).

The *Harper Dictionary of Modern Thought* describes education as the passing on of one's cultural heritage, the initiation into worthwhile ways of doing and thinking, and the fostering of individual growth. Concepts and methods of education differ by culture, and the same can be said for HRD. V. A. Miller (1979) defines "education" as learning or acquiring orderly, logical systems for processing new information, and "training" as the process for affecting change in individual human behavior as in the acquisition of limited, job-related skills.

GLOBAL HRD

Human resource development (HRD) encompasses a wide range of learning efforts from formal systems of education and training to self-instruction. The subject matter can cover everything from international business and comparative management to technical training. This chapter focuses on *cross-cultural training*, which creates awareness of cultural differences or the cultural factors affecting behavior, and develops sensitivity and skill not only in coping with such factors, but in promoting cultural synergy, i.e., cooperation and collaboration with people who are different. The Society for Intercultural Education, Training and Research (SIETAR International) actively promotes professional development in this regard through conferences, workshops, and publications. Gudykunst and Hammer (1983) systematically examine training designs used in the international preparation of teachers and students, missionaries and overseas' volunteers, business representatives, and technicians.

However, HRD efforts in cross-cultural education or training have special meaning within global management. In 1985, *The Economist*, for instance, reported on a survey of 1,300 Japanese managers and their indigeneous counter-parts in Southeast Asia, which indicated that each group had a negative opin-ion of the other. The Japanese managers thought that their local colleagues were illogical, indecisive, and inflexible, while the local managers with whom they interacted perceived the Japanese as secretive, intolerant, and inflexible. One wonders how much cross-cultural learning was included in the training of either group.

In a survey of 80 multinational companies, Rosalie Tung (1979) found that only 32% of the respondents had formalized training programs of any kind to prepare candidates for overseas work; 68% of the respondents to her question-naire had no type of training whatsoever. A decade later, when Prof. Tung (1988) surveyed 17 European and 18 Japanese multinational companies on ex-patriate practices, she found a more rigorous program for preparing candidates for overseas assignments, and concluded that their U.S. counterparts needed to provide comparable training to personnel involved in cross-cultural encoun-ters. Evidently the message is getting across because the American Manage-ment Association (P.O. Box 319, Saranac Lake, NY 12983, USA) is now spon-soring courses in "International Team Building" to discuss strategies for creating and maintaining a global network that capitalizes on cultural diversity and local strengths.

The consequences of this lack are easy to determine, with the most apparent being high attrition rates and on-the-job ineffectiveness of expatriate person-nel. Heenan and Perlmutter (1979) found that a disproportionately high per-centage of all communication between the head office and subsidiaries dealt with the problems of expatriate adaptation to overseas living (for example, buying furniture or gaining membership to a local country club). In one com-pany, this type of communication represented 75% of all transactions to the personnel department. In addition to adjustment problems related to physical aspects of the move, incidents of alcoholism, drug use, unhappy children and broken families are common among expatriates. Thus, even for those employ-ees who do not become part of the early return statistics, job performance and effectiveness may be drastically limited while working abroad.

Our research and experience indicate that performance efficiency in multinational corporations can be improved by proper human resource devel-opment of international personnel and project members. Korn/Ferry Interna-tional, an executive search company, confirmed that repatriation was a per-plexing problem for 50% of the transnational employees polled who complained of disillusionment, sense of loss, and adjustment problems in both home and office. But savvy organizations are getting the message about the multiple values of cross-cultural training. The Fortune 500 firms are beginning to include it not only in the preparation of the international personnel, but as a regular part of all management and executive development. Such corporations also appreciate its worth for female managers overseas (Adler, 1984), transna-

tional joint ventures (Paliwoda and Liebrenz, 1984), international business operations (Rugman, 1985) and marketing (Kaynak, 1984), world finance and
risk management (Agmon, 1985), and for general global performance (Dunning and Stopford, 1983; Tung, 1988).

To fully review cross-cultural training, we will employ the journalistic "six
W's" (why, what, when, where, who, and how) as headings for the sections to
follow.

THE *WHY* OF HRD AND CROSS-CULTURAL TRAINING

Cultural awareness training is not just for the employee going overseas. It
has numerous applications domestically that will increase organizational effectiveness. Findings indicate that it should be a regular part of personnel training, especially management development. The realities of a more pluralistic
society and international business make this a necessity for superindustrial organizations. The goal is to help representatives toward more appropriate, sensitive, and consistent behavior in their human interactions.

In the 1980s, companies began to move toward training for cultural diversity in the workforce (Josefowitz, 1985; Schaef, 1991). Sometimes this diversity
training in the workplace is called "bias busting"—it aims not only at understanding cultural differences, but self-acceptance and flexibility within one's
own cultural background and style (*Management Review*, December 1987,
pp. 51–54).

As we move through the decade of the 1990s, two unique HRD opportunities
are emerging. One is a growing educational and cultural exchange between the
First and Second (Communist) economic worlds, especially between the
U.S.A. and the U.S.S.R. The Soviet-bloc socialistic countries now have a great
willingness to learn Western technology and technical education. The second
trend relates to education for the space frontier, involving science, technology,
communication, habitation, commerce, and transportation. Universities and
colleges increasingly offer courses in everything from space law to satellite applications. (The International Space University (636 Beacon St., Boston, MA
02216, U.S.A.) is just one example of this educational direction.) Although the
faculty and students come from around the world, cultural synergy is promoted by summer sessions held in the U.S., France, U.S.S.R. and Japan.

It is hoped that by translating these points to the more specific area of cross-
cultural education, a positive conclusion for such training can be reached. The
first stage should be general in approach, rather than oriented to a specific culture. In other words, drawing from the fields of cultural anthropology, communication, group dynamics, and comparative management, personnel need
training to understand cultural influences on human behavior. The trainee
then applies this to differences in a variety of cultural groups and intercultural

experiences. Such basic preparation can be supplemented for employees going into specific intercultural challenges at home or abroad.

Regardless of the type of cultural awareness training undertaken, there is similarity in the general objectives for management or personnel development. Goals of these programs are:

1. To encourage greater sensitivity and more astute observations of situations and people, who are culturally different.
2. To foster greater understanding in dealing with representatives of microcultures within one's own country.
3. To improve customer and employee relations by creating awareness of cultural differences and their influence on behavior.
4. To develop more cosmopolitan organizational representatives who not only understand the concepts of culture, but can apply this knowledge to interpersonal relations and organizational culture.
5. To increase managerial effectiveness in international operations, especially with regard to cross-cultural control systems, negotiations, decision-making, customer relations, and other vital administrative processes.
6. To improve cross-cultural skills of employees on overseas' assignment, or representatives of microcultures in our own country.
7. To reduce culture shock when on foreign deployment, and to enhance the intercultural experience for employees.
8. To apply the behavioral sciences to international business and management.
9. To increase job effectiveness through training in human behavior, particularly in the area of managing cultural differences.
10. To improve employee skills as professional intercultural communicators.

The Canadian International Development Agency conducts a predeparture program for their overseas volunteers, which includes learning modules in intercultural communication and transfer of skills. Daniel Kealey of CIDA maintains that "Transfer of Skills" means more than education, teaching, or training—it implies both technical and communication competencies. In such cross-cultural situations, he believes the *how* of the communication may be as important, if not more so, as the *what*. CIDA's training aims to instill seven skills that could be offered as the objectives of all cultural awareness learning. These skills are to:

1. *Communicate respect*—to transmit, verbally and non-verbally positive regard, encouragement, and sincere interest.
2. *Be nonjudgmental*—to avoid moralistic, value-laden, evaluative statements, and to listen in such a way that the other can fully share and explain self.

3. *Personalize knowledge and perceptions*—to recognize the influence of one's own values, perceptions, opinions, and knowledge on human interaction, and to regard such as relative, rather than absolute, for more tentative communications.
4. *Display empathy*—to try and understand others from "their" point of view, to attempt to put oneself into the other's life space, and to feel as they do about the matter under consideration.
5. *Practice role flexibility*—to be able to get a task accomplished in a manner and time frame appropriate to the learner or other national, and to be flexible in the process for getting jobs done, particularly with reference to participation and group maintenance or morale.
6. *Demonstrate reciprocal concern*—to truly dialogue, take turns talking, share the interaction responsibility, and in groups, promote circular communication.
7. *Tolerate ambiguity*—to be able to cope with cultural differences, to accept a degree of frustration, and to deal with changed circumstances and people.

These skills are associated with effective managing and transferring knowledge in a different culture. To the degree that managers possess these skills, they will be effective in working in a multicultural environment.

When working in an overseas environment as a manager, one must consider the underlying values or premises of a culture in order to function effectively. Unless one appreciates existing values in a cultural situation, and their ability to influence thought and action, one's own value system may become "cultural blinders" that prevent understanding and appreciation of other cultures.

THE *WHAT* OF CULTURAL AWARENESS TRAINING

There are many approaches to the content and methodology of cultural awareness training and they can be divided as follows:

1. *Cognitive*—involves knowledge of other peoples and their culture, especially customs, values, and social institutions.
2. *Awareness*—focuses on either *self* awareness for better adjustment outside one's culture, including insight into the impact of one's native cultural conditioning, or *cultural* awareness in being sensitive to the cultural factors that influence both parties in human interaction, especially when one is a "foreigner" or "stranger." (This learning involves culture general information and being alerted to the differences in cultural systems.)
3. *Behavioral*—emphasizes learning about specific cultural behaviors and expectations in host cultures for which the trainee is being prepared;

modeling of appropriate host culture behavior, simulating host culture environment, and experiential exercises about the host culture.

4. *Interaction*—involves interaction with representatives of host or other cultures to increase awareness of the others' backgrounds, values, and learned behaviors, as well as exploring one's own culture in the same regard. (Foreign visitors and students are usually used for this purpose, or visits to subcultures within one's country or neighboring cultures.)

5. *Area Simulation*—relies on creation of a particular cultural environment or situation comparable to a host culture to which the trainee is going, even as to similar physical climate and conditions. (Cultural assimilator exercises are programmed on target cultures.)

6. *Relationship Systems*—emphasizes intercultural relations or human response in terms of a systematic approach that can be applied across culture.

7. *Language Studies*—focuses upon a specific foreign language *and* the cultures of the peoples who speak that particular language (e.g., English, Spanish, or French speaking peoples).

8. *Cross-Cultural Communication*—includes the study of communication theory in general, and of intercultural communication in particular. The focus is upon improving skills and competencies in cross-cultural interactions, both verbal and non-verbal.

9. *Confrontation/Contrast*—two related approaches involving either confronting or contrasting differences between one's own culture and that of another that may be role played or represented by a native. In such cross-cultural encounters, the trainee observes responses and evaluates behavior for improved performance. These are culture general approaches related to the previously described "awareness" and "interaction" models. Some of the training techniques include film, as well as audio or videotapes with host nationals or actors doing the role play.

U.S. military services have been most innovative in their research on large-scale intercultural training efforts. Purposes of such undertakings with enlisted personnel are: to improve race relations within military units; to improve relations between military personnel and members of the community in which they operate (communities within the nation and those in other countries); and, to improve the international and intercultural experience of the individual service-person. For more than a decade, the U.S. Navy has been a pioneer in the area of large-scale intercultural training. It now includes this training as a part of its Human Resource Management Support System, referring to it as "overseas diplomacy."

The Peace Corps also provides one of the longest and most comprehensive cross-cultural preparations for volunteers going overseas. The program is based upon a detailed task analysis of specific positions in specific locations, and an understanding of the volunteer's role in the host culture.

THE *WHEN* OF CULTURAL AWARENESS TRAINING

Various opinions exist on when it is most appropriate to provide cultural awareness input, and how long it should take. Many trainers maintain that such educational programs belong in professional schools and continuing education classes, especially for those in a "people" profession requiring diverse human interaction such as medicine or law. For graduate studies in international business, for instance, the curriculum should include some cross-cultural education, if not as a separate course, then at least as a part of comparative management.

Such training is essential for teachers in the field of bilingual education or international relations, but it could be incorporated as a regular element in any teacher preparation. In many school systems, some form of intercultural relations is a necessary component of in-service training, especially for teachers in the inner cities, or instructors of English as a second language.

The real issue, however, involves organizational representatives assigned outside their native culture for short- or long-term visits. When engaged in international relations work, service, or business, cross-cultural knowledge and skills are integral to the role requirements. Some believe cultural training should be given before going abroad, while others opt for such training only after arrival in the host culture. Still others insist that it must be a combination of before, during, and after the overseas assignment.

The length of time devoted to preparation for foreign deployment varies according to the organization and the availability of time and finances for training. Some nonprofit agencies devote a year prior to departure for such preparation, beginning with self-study and weekly meetings, and gradually accelerating the amount of time devoted to cross-cultural and related training in group settings. A year would seem desirable in the case of foreign language studies with cultural specifics accompanying the education. One major multinational corporation devotes three to six months to getting the employee and the family ready for assignments abroad.

Program planners in the Canadian International Development Agency believe timing is a critical factor. If too close to departure, trainee anxiety may block learning. Without foreign experience, the volunteers find it hard to focus on the input. Therefore, CIDA prefers to emphasize recruitment and selection for the overseas tour, and concentrate on in-country training. Whether circumstances or opinions dictate a long- or short-term approach to cross-cultural training, it is the *quality* of that training that is most important.

The "when" of training also depends on the different information needs of participants in the training. There is an interaction between the "survival" information needs (schools, doctors, housing, compensation, etc.) and the other information needs (adjusting to the new society, how to get the job done, making new friends, effective functioning in the society, etc.) The interaction is illustrated in Figure 11-1.

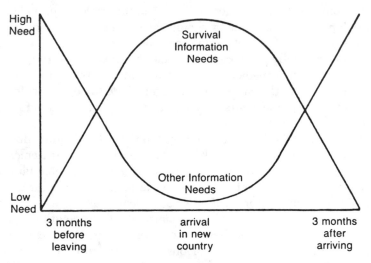

Figure 11-1. Interaction of the various needs of cross-cultural trainees.

Training for Keeps. Japanese organizations spend far more on education than their Western counterparts, and the whole concept of training is radically different. The aim is to create a lasting bond between employees and the company, rather than teach a set of transferable skills, as reflected in the following insights (Holden, 1988):

- Japanese personnel who benefit by corporate education do not use it as a competitive weapon in the labor market.
- All success in life is seen as directly linked to the learning process. Japanese learn in order to behave harmoniously in organizational groups and circles.
- Training is called the "professional ability development program" and is closely linked to organizational development—it's future oriented and may span a 42 year cycle.
- Corporate education encompasses both on- and off-the-job training. Cross-cultural communication, an obsession with the Japanese, usually is obtained through external courses.

- Japanese managers spend about 30% of their time "educating" their younger colleagues, initiating them into the lore and wisdom of an exclusive community—particularly through the induction course punctuated by ceremony that solemnizes the relationship by implicit exchange of vows and promises.
- Our recent survey of two leading Japanese banks found they spend ¥ 2m a year on training, while an electronics company with 620 employees permanently abroad and 13,000 on short-term overseas assignment invests slightly less, but half is devoted to training for international activities.

THE *WHERE* OF CULTURAL AWARENESS TRAINING

The *place* cultural awareness training occurs can influence the depth of learning and behavior change. An organization, therefore, must decide to conduct the program using its internal resources or send participants to an off-site training center, university campus, or overseas. Depending upon trainee and organizational needs, a case can be made for each position. It would, of course, be ideal to get a group away from office or plant and into a well-equipped conference center, to utilize a staff of internal and external resource personnel, and to train in the home and host culture. Realistically, time, task, and financial constraints may cause management to settle for less, unless superior facilities and staff are found within the organization or within a particular country. The involvement of the employee's family may dictate the site; or, part of the intercultural training might be conducted within the home by means of a self-instructional media program, or within an ethnic or geographic community within the home country. Thus, to train personnel for Latin America, a U.S. organization might use a location in Puerto Rico, Florida, or the Southwest. Ideally, employees involved in the international assignments should receive cross-cultural training both in the home and host culture.

THE *WHO* OF CULTURAL AWARENESS TRAINING

The issue of who should be trained can be viewed from the perspective of the cultural awareness trainer or trainee. Those in leadership positions, particularly on an international level, are most in need of cross-cultural skills. Also, there are times when total or partial family involvement is desirable. When a race relations or integration plan is introduced into an American school system, teachers, students and their families can benefit from intercultural training. When an employee is sent abroad for a long period of time, it affects spouse and children. If the family accompanies the worker, they too are subject to "culture shock," and can influence a premature return. Thus, family involvement in cross-cultural orientation can have real benefits. Some oil companies do not send the technician's family to hardship posts, but locate them in a more developed country nearby or in the home culture. The worker is rotated home to his family every few weeks. A family should be prepared to cope with the situation created by the employer which disrupts normal family life.

When there is an acquisition or take-over of one company by another, employees of both organizations would benefit by training in how to merge the organizational cultures and promote synergy between the two entities. When a foreign organization establishes a plant abroad, or purchases an existing domestic institution, personnel of both firms would learn much from intercultural training. For example, the *Los Angeles Times* (March 6, 1988, pp.1/6,IV) reports that in California the Japanese banks fare poorly in terms of return on assets. Although they have acquired some of that state's most successful banks, the Japanese seem to be hobbled by cultural differences. Obviously, among other subjects, their representatives need training on how to make risky loans within a more fiercely competitive market. And what of the American employees who now must work with and for their Japanese managers? They need to learn of the Japanese willingness to take smaller profits now for long-term objectives. Clearly, a cross-cultural component is an essential part of all management and human resource development, whether the trainees be law enforcement officers, lawyers, doctors, or business persons.

In terms of presenters, a variety of alternatives are available for live or media training in cultural awareness. Such resource persons may be professionals who understand cross-cultural education and challenges—psychologists, communications specialists, cultural anthropologists, HRD specialists—trainers and facilitators. Representatives of the host culture, foreign nationals experienced in a particular culture, and local professors with specialized, relevant knowledge can also assist with a cross-cultural program. There are consulting organizations, universities, and government agencies that specialize in cross-cultural education. The key issue is whether to utilize the organization's personnel for culture training, contract external consultants, or combine both types of resources.

When only a few persons are sent abroad in one year, it is well to mix the training class with other representatives from home culture organizations who are going to the same location. Companies working on the same project or contract in the Middle East, for instance, may engage in joint culture specific training.

Competency in the subject matter and experience in the host culture are principal factors to consider with regard to trainee and trainer.

THE *HOW* OF CULTURAL AWARENESS TRAINING

Cultural awareness training is best accomplished by a variety of methods and techniques; i.e., what best fits the situation, and what proves to be the

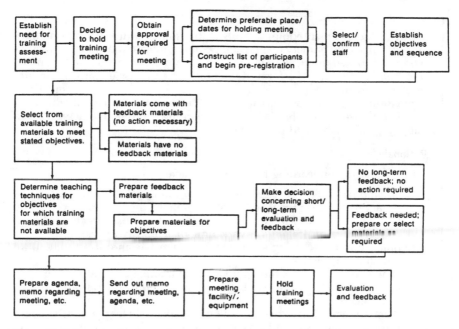

Figure 11-2. Flow path of needs assessment and planning process for cross-cultural trainees.

most effective. The methods should be the result of a needs assessment and planning process. Figure 11-2 shows a systems process for cultural training.*

Action Learning—A Synergistic Strategy

Experiential or affective learning, combined with cognitive and task educational activities, appears to be the most effective way to teach cooperation and collaboration. Furthermore, *action learning* is a viable strategy for any type of education and training, and a *systems approach* is desirable.

Orientation to Action Learning

Those in the field of human resource development must eventually get involved in training. The design, implementation, and evaluation of adult education programs for staff and clients are part of the developmental process. For these experiences to be meaningful and impactful, we suggest that the action-learning approach be utilized.

---

* Request *High-Performance Leadership, An Open System Approach* from Dr. Raymond L. Forbes, Organizational Services, Northwest Airlines, 6995 Edgebrook Place, Eden Prairie, MN 55346.

Essentially, this methodology involves the trainee in the educational process and gives the primary responsibility for learning to the student. In other words, it is based upon "learning by doing." A more formal definition of *action learning* would be—a form of training that emphasizes variety of methodology and maximum participation by the learner, usually by means of some form of group process. This approach, most appropriate in adult education, is utilized throughout this study. Learning is promoted by group data gathering, analyzing, and reporting.

Rationale

In general, action learning has these characteristics:

1. *Situational*—it is in-service education or on-the-job training that has as its target *change* in the work situation or in the person who receives the training in the work or therapy situation. It is most effective when it concentrates on training a work unit or team. By providing time for practice in the learning session, the learner has an opportunity to internalize knowledge.
2. *Experiential*—it makes the prime focus of training data gathered by participants in the learning experience or provided by them from previous experience.
3. *Plural*—it emphasizes both affective and cognitive learning; its concern is for both feelings and ideas; it should be a balance of the "I feel" and the "I think."
4. *Problem-orientation*—it deals with issues for personal and organizational change and provides practice in processes for problem-solving and decision-making; it aims for action not only in the learning process, but also in the follow-up as a result of training.
5. *Systematic*—it envisions the training effort as only a sub-system of a larger system for human resource development; it is given as part of a total program for personal and professional growth; it is viewed as an essential component for broader organization development. The systems approach can also be applied to the actual training process itself.
6. *Personalized*—although group process may be utilized, due consideration is given to individualizing the learning so as to make allowance for each trainee's unique needs, perceptions and expectations. Action-learning, furthermore, provides performance standards for the trainee by setting goals. It also offers a means for self-assessment by using feedback and group evaluation.

Action-learning is based on certain assumptions about the learner and educational methodology. As stated by Dr. Malcolm Knowles, the noted adult education specialist, these assumptions are:

1. Adults enter a learning activity with an image of themselves as self-directing, responsible grown-ups, not as immature, dependent learners. Therefore they resist situations in which they are treated with disrespect. *Implication for methodology*—if adults help to plan and conduct their own learning experiences, they will learn more than if they are passive recipients.

2. Adults enter a learning activity with more experience than youth. There-fore, they have more to contribute to the learning activity and have a broader basis of experience to relate to new learning. *Implication for methodology*—those methods which build on and make use of the ex-perience of the learners will produce the greatest learning.
3. Adults enter a learning activity with a different quality of experience and different developmental tasks than youth. *Implication for method-ology*—the appropriate organizing principle for adult learning experi-ences is developmental sequences primarily and logical subject devel-opment only secondarily.
4. Adults enter a learning activity with more immediate intentions to apply learning to life problems than youth. Therefore, adults require practical results from learning. *Implication for methodology*—adults will per-ceive learning experiences that are organized around subject topics.

The behavioral change sought in the learner as a result of the training should be in terms of:

1. Knowledge	4. Attitudes
2. Insight and understanding	5. Values
3. Skills	6. Interests

The conditions necessary for action-learning involve:

1. Recognition of trainee's needs
2. Integration of learner's and trainer's goals for learning
3. Encouragement of active role in the process of learning by learner
4. Provision for measurable criteria toward learning goals
5. Threat-free climate of acceptance and freedom
6. Competency and skill on part of the training facilitator

** From *High Performance Leadership* by P. R. Harris, Scott, Foresman, and Co., 1989.

Evaluating Cross-Cultural Training

Global managers and trainers wish to verify that there is an adequate return on investment in intercultural education and development programs. George Renwick (1979) suggests the following methods to assess program effectiveness and trainees' learning in intercultural education are:

1. Pre/post evaluation instruments with participants upon completion of training, and subsequent follow-up questionnaires (three, six, or twelve months hence).
2. Use of control groups for comparison studies on impact of training.
3. Observers to measure results during and after training sessions, and/or when trainees go into the field (observations by instruments, videotape, interviews).
4. Ratings by peers and supervisors of trainees after training is completed and they return to the job or go on overseas assignment.

METHODS OF CROSS-CULTURAL TRAINING

Cross-cultural orientation programs according to Brislin and Pedersen (1976) are "designed to teach members of one culture ways of interacting effectively, with minimal interpersonal misunderstanding, in another culture." This is a general definition and can be applied to most cross-cultural orientation or briefing programs. Specific training objectives must be developed according to specific needs and purposes of the organization. George Renwick, president of Renwick and Associates in Scottsdale, Arizona, makes the following assumptions concerning the training of persons to function effectively in another culture:

1. Individuals responsible for formulating, administrating, and evaluating policies and projects must increasingly deal with the special problems and possibilities of multicultural environments. In the private sector, managers must select, train, and coordinate the efforts of multicultural staffs to meet the complex objectives of the corporation and the demands of a culturally diverse clientele. Members of corporate staffs must anticipate, appreciate, and adjust to each others' differing values, expectations, and patterns of behavior if their efforts are to be satisfying for them and advantageous for the corporation. In the public sector, officials must anticipate, and plan to meet, the needs of multicultural constituencies.
2. The knowledge and skills essential to carrying responsibility, exercising authority, and working productively in multicultural environments can be learned, and the appropriate attitudes can be cultivated. Through proper training, perception can become more penetrating and discernment more accurate; judgments can therefore be made with more confidence. Relationships become more cooperative and therefore more conducive to the achievement of individual and organizational objectives.
3. Competence in multicultural management is learned most effectively through interaction, experimentation, and discussion within a structured, supportive, information-rich, low-risk environment.
4. Technical competence is of primary importance for international executives, managers, and others in this area. However, cross-cultural communication skills are also required.

Awareness and recognition of personal and professional failures in many international organizations have resulted in programs designed to prepare persons to interact and communicate effectively with persons from different cultures. The programs are often called cross-cultural orientation programs. These are either programs that give information (briefings) about specific countries and customs, programs that provide practice in developing specific skills (training), or a combination of briefing and training. A combination of briefing and training is most effective for managers who will be functioning in a multicultural environment (Early, 1987).

Before discussing specific methods, a couple of general guidelines would seem appropriate:

- Intercultural education should be based upon action or applied research. Sage Publications (P.O. Box 5084, Newbury Park, CA 91359) has a series of volumes on *Cross-Cultural Research and Methodology* (e.g., Brislin, Cushner, Cherrie & Young, 1986; Lonner and Berry, 1986; Bond, 1988).
- Intercultural education should make more use of adult education methodology and educational technology in presenting concepts and developing skills (refer to *Handbook of Adult and Continuing Education* by S. B. Meriam and P. M. Cunningham (1989), eds., and Ch. 4, "Advancing Human Resources Through New Technologies" in *Management in Transition* by P. R. Harris (both by Jossey Bass, Inc., 350 Sansome St., San Francisco, CA 94104, USA). With regard to the latter, teleconferencing and "distance education" show real promise for bringing together participants in a common learning experience via satellite or electronic networks.

Cross-Cultural Orientation Programs

Attempts by individuals and agencies to prepare persons for communicating and interacting across cultures have ranged from laissez-faire attitudes, "let them learn from their own experience and mistakes," to detailed and explicit training in specific skills. Technical competence and language training are, of course, prerequisite skills. But persons involved in the area are becoming convinced that these skills alone, without the interpersonal skills necessary to establish communication, are insufficient.

Most literature describing and evaluating cross-cultural training programs has been written in the past 20 years. The establishment of the Peace Corps in 1961 served as an impetus for program development at that time. Prior writings and research on cross-cultural training in the international field focused on international political relations and intercultural artistic exchange programs.

In an effort to provide a framework for the categorization of cross-cultural training programs since the Peace Corps, James Downs (1970) lists the four models of training as: the Intellectual Model; the Area Simulation Model; the Self-Awareness Model; and, a new training trend called the Cultural Awareness Model.

The *intellectual model* consists of lectures and reading about the host culture. It is assumed that an exchange of information about another culture is effective preparation for living or working in that culture.

The *area simulation model* is a culture-specific training program. It is based on the belief that an individual must be prepared and trained to enter a specific culture. It involves simulation of future experiences and practice in functioning in the new culture.

The *self-awareness model* is based on the assumption that understanding and accepting oneself is critical to understanding a person from another culture. Sensitivity training is a main component of this method.

The *cultural awareness model* assumes that for an individual to function successfully in another culture an individual must learn the principles of behavior that exist across cultures. Kraemer (1973) developed a cultural self-awareness approach to cross-cultural training that is based on the assumption that an individual's effectiveness in intercultural communication can be improved by developing the individual's cultural self-awareness—the ability to recognize cultural influences in personal values, behaviors, and cognitions. This ability, according to Kraemer, has several beneficial results: (a) it should enhance a person's skill at diagnosing difficulties in intercultural communication; (b) it should be easier to suspend judgments when confronted with behavior that appears odd; and (c) it should make individuals aware of their ignorance of other cultures and correspondingly, increase their motivation to learn about it.

The Culture Assimilator

Developed in 1971 by social scientists (Fiedler, Mitchell, and Triandis) at the University of Illinois, the culture assimilator is an area simulation program that is culture specific. Its basic goal is to prepare persons to respond to specific situations in a particular country. Culture assimilator training programs have been established for the Arab countries, Iran, Thailand, Central America, and Greece.

The culture assimilator is a programmed learning experience designed to expose members of one culture to the basic concepts, attitudes, role perceptions, customs, and values of another culture. To develop assimilators, first determine the major dimensions of social perception and cognition that are used in each culture, and the extent to which these dimensions influence responses. Themes, or culturally-determined viewpoints, are then isolated as representative generalizations about that culture. The end product is a programmed instruction simulation exercise that has the learner interpret, evaluate, and then assimilate immediate feedback. The program explains why an answer is correct or incorrect. If incorrect, the learner reviews the episode and reinterprets.

Feedback exposes the learner to major themes characterizing the two cultures, home and host. New concepts are developed from concrete incidents or assimilators. The culture assimilator can be validated by asking persons of the host culture to respond to the interaction incidents without seeing prepared alternatives.

The following example is from the Thai assimilator. It was developed after a U.S. student reported being bothered by the Thai teachers' lack of punctuality.

The student asked fellow Thai students if they were similarly disturbed. The students indicated they were, but said they would never show these feelings to their professors. The assimilator incident was refined from this episode and was written by Triandis and his colleagues at the University of Illinois.

One day a Thai administrator of middle academic rank kept two of his assistants waiting about an hour for an appointment. The assistants, although very angry, did not show it while they waited. When the administrator walked in, he acted as if he were not late. He offered no apology or explanation. After he was settled in his office, he called his assistants in; they all began working on the business for which the administrator had set the meeting.

If the incident is observed exactly as it is reported in this passage, which one of the following best describes the chief significance of the behavior of the people involved?

1. The Thai assistants were extremely skillful at concealing their true feelings.
2. The Thai administrator obviously was unaware of the fact that he was an hour late for the appointment.
3. In Thailand, subordinates are required to be polite to their superiors, no matter what happens, nor what their rank may be.
4. Since no one commented on it, the behavior indicated nothing of unusual significance to the Thais.

The first description is not entirely true, although it is characteristic of Thais to try to appear reserved under any circumstance. If the assistants were skillful at concealing their true feelings, there would be no doubt about their feelings. Also, the reference to the chief significance of the behavior of the people involved may limit it to the assistants.

Number two is a very poor choice. While the administrator behaved as if he were unaware of his tardiness after observing the hour's wait, it is possible that he was acting.

The third choice is the correct one. The information in the episode is fully used. This "deference to the boss" may be observed anywhere in the world, but it is likely to be carried to a higher degree in Thailand than in the U.S. Certain clues indicated number three— the assistants' concealed feelings, the administrator failed to apologize, no one mentioned the tardiness subsequently, the appointment was kept.

Number four is completely wrong. While the behavior reported in the passage does not seem as significant to the Thais as it might to Americans, why was nothing said about the tardiness? And why were the assistants "very angry" although they "did not show it?" Is there a more significant level of meaning for this behavior?

The culture assimilator has been subjected to more empirical study than any other training method, and several studies support its usefulness in decreasing adjustment problems. Two laboratory studies, one using the Arab assimilators and the other, the Thai assimilator, compared U.S. nationals who had been trained with the assimilator method and others who had been trained only in the geography of the country. Data from both studies indicated that assimilator training lessened interpersonal and adjustment problems between the trainees and persons of the host culture.

A field study was conducted in Honduras using the culture assimilator. Results indicated that the assimilator-trained subjects were higher on adjustment measures than a control group of subjects who had not received assimilator training.

Although these studies indicate the usefulness of the culture assimilator as a method of cross-cultural training, there are a number of problems with the approach. The program is ethnocentric in the sense that it focuses on the foreign culture and that culture's peculiar characteristics and differences. It is essential to identify the values of a culture and recognize the influence of these values when encountering a person from that culture. Other problems concern the lack of field assessment, long-range evaluation of assimilator-trained persons, and the best content for the assimilators. There is also the question of the subjects, who are probably highly motivated persons, atypical of those actually involved in an intercultural experience.

Dr. Kazuo Takaia, (ITK Inc., c/o SII International Miyata Bldg., 1-38-2 Yoyogi, Shibuyaku, Tokyo 151, Japan) has developed a computerized culture assimilator system. His research resulted from his experience as an overseas manager with Chiyoda Corporation when he observed culture friction between Japanese construction workers and the locals. His simulator on culture concepts and customs combines computers, artificial intelligence, and expert systems.

Contrast-American Method of Cross-Cultural Training

The contrast-American method is a culture-general approach rather than culture specific (e.g., the Thai assimilator). It is essentially a cultural awareness method of cross-cultural training. Stewart, Danielian, and Foster described the contrast-American method in 1969. It consists of role-playing encounters between a U.S. national and a person of another culture (this person represents a composite culture) who holds contrasting values. By interaction in the role-play, U.S. nationals develop greater awareness of their own values. The assumption underlying this method is that to function effectively in another culture, an individual must first know his own culture.

The technique was developed to simulate psychologically and culturally significant interpersonal aspects of the overseas situation in a live role-play encounter. Stewart, Danielian, and Foster outlined four steps in the simulation construction:

1. Literature describing American cultural patterns was reviewed and analyzed, and American values and assumptions were identified.
2. These dimensions were extended to derive differences of cultural characteristics that contrast with American ones.
3. A series of overseas advisory situations was then constructed to elicit spontaneous culturally derived behavior from an American trainee.
4. Role-players were trained to reflect the contrast-American values and assumptions in an emotional confrontation between the role-player and the trainee.

The following role-play situation is an example and illustrates the American desire to get the work done, while the contrast-American's desire is to preserve the status relation between the officer and the men. Following the role-play situation, the trainees receive feedback from the trainers. It demonstrates how this method brings out contrasting and often conflicting values.

> One of the scenes was designed around the topic of leadership. During one of the simulations of this scene, Captain Smith, the American role-player, tried to persuade the Contrast-American, Major Khan, to take measures to improve leadership in his battalion. Captain Smith found fault with some of the techniques utilized by some of Major Khan's second lieutenants.
>
> *American:* And I know that . . . if they are allowed to continue, the effi ciency in the duties that they're performing, or their soldiers are performing, will be reduced.
>
> *Contrast-American:* What kind of duties are they performing that are not good?
>
> *American:* They have an inability, I think, to communicate with the noncommissioned officers and to properly supervise the accomplishment of the task. They almost have the attitude that this work is the type of work that they should not take part in; they should merely stand by and watch. I know you have a big respect for General George Washington and I should point out this example. One time during the American Revolution, there was a sergeant with some artillery pieces which were stuck. He was standing by, very neat and clean in his uniform, cajoling his soldiers as they looked at him, and shouting for them to push harder to get this cannon out of the mud. General Washington rode by on his horse, noticed this situation and stopped. His rank was not showing for he had a large cape on over his uniform; it was rather cold that day and had been raining. He asked the sergeant what the problem was, and the sergeant told him, "Sir, the soldiers cannot get this cannon out of the mud." Then General Washington dismounted from his horse, walked over and assisted the soldiers in pushing the cannon out. Afterward, he walked over to the sergeant and said, "Sergeant, tell your commander that General Washington has assisted your men in pushing the cannon from the mud."

Contrast-American: Yes.

American: He was willing to assist his men and do anything that they were doing if it were really necessary.

Contrast-American: Perhaps if he were not in a disguise, not wearing a cape, if he were in his uniform of a general, he would never have dismounted the horse. He would have waited there as a general.

A problem with the contrast-American method concerns insufficient instructions to the role-players unless the players are professionals. When Stewart demonstrates this technique, he uses professional actors. When the role-players are not well trained, the technique is less effective. Another problem concerns the culture general approach and the applicability and transfer of concepts to a particular situation.

Peace Corps Training Programs

The agency most involved in preparing persons for cross-cultural living situations is the Peace Corps. Presently, the training programs are being reduced, but in 1965 the Peace Corps used 58 universities as training centers as well as several nonacademic organizations. These programs lasted an average of 11 weeks and cost $2,345 per participant. Their training programs vary and are eclectic in nature. They cannot be categorized using Downs' framework. Rather, the programs employ techniques from all models.

Peace Corps training also provides language training, training in technical skills, if necessary, and the interpersonal skills and sensitivities necessary to live and work effectively with persons whose ways may be different and, therefore, difficult to accept. Conditions essential for learning these skills are detailed, and programs are based on the assumption that the trainee will assume the major responsibility for learning. As the trainee learns from experience, the learning process should become a way of life.

Most evaluations of Peace Corps training programs are conducted after the training period, but before the trainees begin assignments in other countries. However, in order for the evaluations to be accurate, they should be performed after the trainee enters the host culture.

Prior-to-departure training should be complemented by additional training in the country of assignment. Trainees are more likely to complete their assignment if such in-country training is provided.

Self-Confrontation Training Techniques

Using videotape in therapeutic and educational situations is becoming widespread and its success is well-documented. As a cross-cultural training technique, a method called *self-confrontation*, was developed by psychologists of the Training Research Laboratory at Wright-Patterson Air Force Base. A trainee plays a role with a person from another culture in a simulated cross-cultural encounter and the situation is videotaped. Following the interaction, the encounter is played for the trainee and trainer to point out strengths and weaknesses in both the verbal and nonverbal behavior of the trainee. The trainee can observe responses and evaluate behavior for improved performance in future role-play situations and for actual performance in a different culture. This is a culture general approach, although the situations can also be specific to a particular culture. Following Downs' categories, this is essentially a self-awareness model of cross-cultural training.

This technique uses a psychological principle of stimulated-recall that is useful in rapid learning. After replaying the behavioral situation on videotape, trainees are able to relive the scene and recall their thoughts at the moment, thus permitting complete use of the psychological impact of self confrontation.

Simulation. This is a form of inductive learning that creates a situation in a classroom that is similar to the real life experience. It recreates a family, social, or job environment in a controllable form. It may be a cooperation game in elementary school, or a management game in a corporation or agency, where it may involve group dynamic exercises that promote "consensus." In training sessions, organizational leaders may be asked to engage in "the in-basket exercise," which simulates the decision-making related to handling the manager's morning mail, or "the hollow square" game, which divides the group into two teams that must develop a plan for assembling cardboard pieces that form a square with a hollow or empty center. Operators within the group must then assemble the pieces according to the plan and within a time limit. Observers then evaluate the interpersonal factors during the process and report back their findings after the exercise. The real learning occurs when the total group analyzes what happened in terms of participation, cooperation, and communication during the game, and how much such behavior is found back on the job. The educator can make up such short-term group experiences, or purchase a commercial product. Simile II (P.O. Box 910, Del Mar, Ca. 92014, USA) custom designs such simulations to meet specific client needs, and then makes them available commercially. Some examples of their products useful in training for synergy are *Starpower*, a game on the use or abuse of organizational power; *Crisis*, on international conflict; *Guns or Butter*, on international relations; *Humanus*, on change and the future; *Bafa, Bafa*, on the interactions and interchanges between culture.

Bafa, Bafa is a simulation in which participants are divided into two cultures, Alpha and Beta. After learning the "rules" of their culture, they are required to interact with members of the other culture. The Alpha culture is a warm, friendly, and patriarchal society speaking English. The Beta culture does not use English and are hard working, and their task is to accumulate as many points as possible. Once the participants in the two cultures learn the rules and the language, they are to interact with each other. Visitors to the other culture are often confused (as they are in an actual cross-cultural situation) by the strangeness of the foreign culture. This confusion often becomes frustration and hostility. In the debriefing of the simulation, participants come to realize the rationale behind the behavior they had observed during the activities. A discussion of their reactions and the specific skills that are associated with effective interactions are also discussed.

This simulation has been used in academic and business settings and in other programs in which it is important for the participants to have an experiential understanding of the meaning of culture. After playing Bafa, Bafa, according to Dr. R. Garry Shirts, its originator, participants report they have learned the following:

1. What seems logical, sensible, important and reasonable to a person in one culture may seem irrational, stupid, and unimportant to an outsider.
2. Feelings of apprehension, loneliness, lack of confidence are common when visiting another culture.
3. When people talk about other cultures, they tend to describe the differences and not the similarities.
4. Differences between cultures are generally seen as threatening and described in negative terms.
5. Personal observations and reports of other cultures should be regarded with a great deal of skepticism.
6. One should make up one's own mind about another culture and not rely on the reports and experience of others.
7. It requires experience as well as study to understand the many subtleties of another culture.
8. Understanding another culture is a continuous and not a discrete process.
9. Stereotyping is probably inevitable in the absence of frequent contact or study.
10. The feelings that people have for their own language are often not evident until they encounter another language.
11. People often feel their own language is far superior to other languages.
12. It is probably necessary to know the language of a foreign culture to understand the culture in any depth.
13. Perhaps a person can accept a culture only after he or she has been very critical or analytical of it.

Although we may construct our own simulations, ready-made ones are available, such as this publisher who issues an annual catalog—Didactic Systems (Box 475, Cranford, N.J. 07010, USA). They combine a cognitive with experiential learning in such simulation games as *Effective Supervision, Handling Conflict in Management, Managing in a Foreign Culture*, and *Women in Management*.

Computer simulations permit modeling of actual or potential situations, so that the learner interacts with the machine and may make mistakes in this manner, rather than in life experiences. Simulations of this type have been used to instruct pilot trainees about flying and MBA students about projected results of decision-making. Software can be obtained for marketing, production, and management games, such as the popular Harvard Andlinger Game, which IBM provides for its computers. Programmed instruction can also be combined through computers and word processors. *Simulations & Games* is an international journal of theory, design and research in this field (Sage Publications, 2111 West Hillcrest Dr. Newbury Park, CA 91320).

Case Studies and Critical Incidents. To avoid abuse of human energy in meaningless conflict, and to facilitate people working together effectively, the educator may create or purchase problem-solving cases of real situations or specific incidents. These may be written, video- or audio-taped, or dramatized for group analysis and learning. The Harvard case studies and methods are widely used in schools of business and training. Whether one uses long reviews of that type or shorter mini cases and critical incidents, the focus is upon real issues, concerns, experiences of people. In this way, we highlight the causes of conflict or cooperation, the sources of cultural or management problems. But always in such a way as to camouflage the identity of actual persons, corporations, or groups unless there would be no harm to revealing such information.

When the U.S. Customs had problems of prejudice and bias within its own workforce, the authors created video cassettes of situations similar to those reported by management. The critical incidents were role played to a point of climax, and then the situation was opened to Customs' officials for problem-solving and arrival at consensus on the proper and preferred action. The same technique could be done based on feedback from expatriates on critical issues they confronted successfully on overseas assignments; then the videotapes could be used in the training of those to be deployed abroad in order to promote their acculturation.

The publications in group dynamics and human relations offer descriptions of many educational methods and techniques that can be utilized to help people work together more effectively, even when there are cross-cultural differences. These range from various forms of role play and socioguidramas, to three dimensional media in which the person responds to a film/slide creation, to brainstorming and creative problem-solving. (Obtain catalog from University Associates/Learning Resources, 8517 Production Ave., San Diego, CA 92121 USA.)

Educational Media, Technology and CAT

The recent advances in media, especially film and videotape, as well as in the equipment and capabilities of communication technology, have only begun to be applied to the field of cross-cultural education and training. Consider the potential of both computer hardware and software to provide both culture general and specific information. Perhaps the following reports will help to point up some of the possibilities:

1. Federal Express has begun to use global videoconferencing as a means for worldwide corporate meeting and training of its 25,000 employees and their families who attend the sessions at 240 different sites from Brussels to Honolulu.
2. An "electronic university" has been formed through a consortium of 24 engineering schools, including MIT, Stanford, and the University of Southern California. Called the National Technological University, it offers across the nation videotape courses toward a master's degree. At the same time in LaJolla, California, Dr. James Grier Miller is developing a University of the World project that will use audio, video, computer, and other electronic instructional technology to establish a global educational network with existing schools and colleges. In the same town, Western Behavioral Science Institute already has launched a school for executive development utilizing a computer-based electronic network.
3. Laser disc video is being used by Sizzler Restaurants for the in-service training of its workers. With disc players in 400 different locations, the record-like discs contain high-resolution TV pictures and promote interactive learning. Teams of workers use break time for the training and are positive in their feedback on the method.
4. Research is underway in both Japan and the United States to produce a fifth-generation computer by the 1990s. The power of this artificial intelligence machine will be speed of processing, capacity to reason with enormous amounts of information, as well as ability to select, interpret, adapt, and update. The new computers will not require a specialized machine language, but will use conversational language, show pictures, or transmit messages by keyboard or through handwriting.

Thinking managers, educators, and trainers may be staggered by the implications of such developments for global communication and learning. Imagine how each method contributes to breaking down cultural barriers, increasing cultural understanding, and the ways they could be used for cross-cultural training.

Jean Jacques Servan Schriber (1980), director of the Paris World Centre for Personal Computing and Human Resources, says that:

Computer science is not just a field among others. It is a new language, a fresh way of learning. . . . It does away with the need for classrooms and lectures. You can immediately become active with your own computer, in effect teaching yourself.

Computer-aided training or learning has immense potential for multi-cultural education because it cuts across traditional language barriers. Research indicates that such instruction not only encourages one-to-one learning, but can save 30% of the time of more traditional methods. Angus Reynolds of Control Data Education Technology Center in Rockville, Maryland, calls CBL a "technological multiplier" because it multiplies the power of the person to serve many others who might otherwise not be served (Harris 1984). Whether in advanced or developing countries, it is a new tutor that can be employed in an interactive learning system by mixing it with video, audio, graphics, and even print. International trainers should be making greater imaginative use of it, especially for HRD and cross-cultural learning.

SUMMARY

Global managers assume responsibility for involvement in human resource management and development, including preparation of personnel for the new work culture and its technologies.

Cross-cultural training programs are designed to prepare individuals for life in another culture, and greater effectiveness with microcultures within one's native land. It is hoped that more international organizations will use the methods reviewed in the training and preparation of their personnel for overseas assignments, thereby reducing business losses and personal trauma.

Those concerned about global human resource development should seek synergistic opportunities. Joint educational and training ventures between public and private sectors, between formal and informal educational efforts, and between home and host culture enterprises can be beneficial to all parties. The complicated educational problems and challenges in this superindustrial age of transition demands such collaboration.

12
Managing for Synergy among Professionals and Technicians

Back in 1972, the Club of Rome published a pessimistic forecast of the future entitled, *Limits to Growth*. In it, the Club's founder, Aurelio Pecci, warned:

> The Eighties may yield dangerous collapses . . . unless humankind starts a new period of cooperation and solidarity. Our value systems have not kept pace with technological developments. We make poor use of democracy and planning.

We found that statement meaningful and prophetic, especially on the need for synergy and Pecci's conclusion that our times require social, political, and technological innovation. Today this Italian futurist reports that his Club has given up forecasting in order to promote world cooperation and education of the next generation. Why and how we can further such synergistic goals, especially among professionals and technicians, is the purpose of this chapter. First, consider a few examples of success and problems in this regard:

- In California a group of human resource and relocation specialists were increasingly concerned about improving intercultural awareness and skills among personnel in their various organizations as well as with their company's clients. However, various professional societies were not meeting their needs in this regard, particularly for on-going local exchanges of practical, cross-cultural strategies and techniques. Under the leadership of June Reinhart, a relocation consultant in Dean Worldwide, Huntington Beach, California, they got together to form the Pacific Area Communicator of Intercultural Affairs. Now they regularly share insights, resources, and support services on both a social, as well as a professional, basis.
- The French have been known for their individualistic and nationalistic attitudes. Their "go-it-alone" inclination also extends to technology where a recent survey of French businessmen revealed a bit of chauvinism. The respondents ranked France first in telecommunications technology, and second in aerospace and pharmaceuticals, and only a modest third in computers and chemicals (*The Economist*, Nov. 11, 1984). While it is true that

this country has made impressive gains in space, nuclear, military, and digital technologies, they can only advance in the world technology and gain a fair share of the global market by regional and international cooperation. Given cultural conditioning, is it likely that French technicians can develop synergistic relations with their colleagues from other nations? Furthermore, is the traditional French approach to technology still appropriate when so much depends upon response to the market in contrast to centralized, bureaucratic planning?

- We have all been astounded by outstanding British cinematic productions such as *Chariots of Fire* or *Ghandi*, as well as BBC presentations such as "Upstairs, Downstairs," and other great TV series. But *Learning to Dream*, James Park (1984) questions why so many English films are anemic and what is lacking in their new film renaissance. This British author blames media mediocrity on certain traditions of English education that prize balance, realism, and restraint over passion, commitment, and imagination. If his observations about British culture are accurate, why must cinema professionals in the United Kingdom collaborate if they expect to counteract this middlebrow quality, while coping with rising budgets? Such synergy seems particularly relevant when visual storytelling is in transition, and video has a voracious appetite for creative output.

- Three Thai women were fortunate in going abroad to get doctorate degrees. They now teach in three different Thai universities, and are unhappy about the low position of women on the faculty. They propose to form a network of women professors, based in Bangkok, to advance their mutual professional development and change the university environment for women. The lady professors smile as they discuss their plans, and seem serene and happy despite their work frustration. Given the Thai approach to professional relationships, which eschews unpleasantness and complaints, defers to authority, and avoids confrontation, what strategies are these professional women likely to use in order to achieve alteration of the present situation? Since the Buddhist life-style has historically been to bend with the wind, it is remarkable that these ladies are even considering collective action.

Each of these real incidents underscores the cultural dimensions involved in colleague cooperation. The Americans favor direct action when institutions fail to meet their contemporary needs. The French will learn the value of synergistic skills to stay on the cutting edge of high technology. The British filmmakers must unite to counteract inbred cultural tendencies that limit artistic expression and excellence. The Thai female professors now realize that networking can become a mechanism for change in educational traditions. In all instances, it is the *sharing* of insight and experience, of skills and strategies, that offers them all hope for achieving their potential.

Peter Corning (1983) makes a case for this theory of progress. He advocates a systems approach in which management and political scientists interact with biologists and other natural scientists. The crossing of the boundaries that have traditionally separated professionals and technicians in order to collaborate with other peers is characteristic of the new work culture. Why is this strategy so important for global managers?

William Ouchi (1984) gave one answer in arguing for an "M-form society," which results from blending Japanese-style cooperation with American-style competition, and extends to both individuals and institutions. Such an effort was made to meet the challenge of creating artificial intelligence and the fourth generation of computers, when fourteen American companies cooperated in a joint venture called Microelectronics and Computer Technology Corporation (MCC). At its Austin, Texas installation the collaborative research involves long-term programs.

> Go to work, and above all cooperate and don't hold back on one another or try to gain at the expense of another. Any success in such lopsidedness will be increasingly short-lived. These are *synergetic* rules that evolution is employing and trying to make clear to us. They are not manmade laws. They are the infinitely accommodative laws of the universe.
>
> R. Buckminister Fuller, 1969
> *Operating Manual for Spaceship Earth*

Global managers increasingly realize the validity of these insights, which apply not only to business persons and organizations, but to economies and nations. Nowhere is the latter interdependence more evident than between the U.S.A. and Japan. The economies of both countries are already closely intertwined, but the realities are resisted by trends toward "economic or technonationalism"—a syndrome of mutual suspicion and mistrust that strains relations between two allies. The sharing of technical data illustrates how friction and hard feelings can develop in this regard.

Japan's Ministry of Trade and Industry calls for competition and cooperation, such as in a research consortium like the International Superconductivity Center. However, U.S. engineers and scientists are slow in taking advantage of opportunities to work in Japanese laboratories, while the Japanese flock to American universities to pursue advanced study. One analyst explained that in the U.S. there is a "not-invented-here syndrome" which implies that if it isn't generated in an American lab, it doesn't have scientific validity, despite the fact that the Japanese have vastly increased their U.S. patent filings. Americans demonstrate formidable prowess in basic research, but this is heavily dependent on defense contracts, while the Japanese advance in research applications of commercial value. Can the East-West technological twain meet for mutual benefit? The field of space research and development is one frontier where politicians, scientists, technologists, business and financial specialists from both countries stand to gain the most by joining forces.

THE KNOWLEDGE SOCIETY

The decades ahead will be years of transition. In so-called advanced nations, more and more of humankind will be transforming an industrialized society into a metaindustrial system. It is hoped the inhabitants of preindustrial countries will use the new technology to bypass the industrial stage of human development and leap ahead into the postindustrial period. In any event, the emerging "cyberculture," or age of automation and computers, will be dominated by a marked increase in knowledge and information processing. People are becoming aware of their basic, collective *human right* to information and communication. Vocational activity will shift away from blue or white-collar designations to that of "knowledge" workers (Harris 1983, 1985, 1989).

The word "professional" is used here in the sense of one who demonstrates authority or competence in whatever he or she undertakes. Such an individual has the attitude, coupled with ability, to work for his or her own self-fulfillment and to bring to a task or occupation a thoroughness or sense of dedication in its execution. In this context this type of person professes or affirms the quality of personal thinking, effort, and spirit. The word is not meant in this analysis as membership in the traditional "learned" professions. As Christopher Evans (1979), the late innovator in microprocessors, observed:

> The erosion of the power of the established professions will be a striking feature of the second phase of the Computer Revolution. It will be marked, and perhaps more so, as the intrusion into the work of the skilled and semi-skilled. . . . The vulnerability of the professions is tied up with their special strength—the fact that they have acted as exclusive repositories and disseminators of specialist knowledge. . . . But this state of privilege can only persist as long as the special data and rules for administration remain inaccessible to the general public. Once the barriers which stand between the average person and this knowledge dissolve, the significance of the profession dwindles, the power and the status of its members shrink. Characteristically, the services which the profession originally offered become available at a very low cost.

Thus, to be a professional in our discussion, one can be an athlete, technician, or programmer, as well as an attorney, physician, or social scientist. It depends on *how* one avows self in the development and use of knowledge. It requires expertise in abstract thinking without denying intuition. Increasingly, it will involve intelligent use of computers, word processors, and data banks.

As used in this chapter, a technician is conceived as more than a technology specialist. The dictionary defines technician as a person trained or skilled in the technicalities of an art/science. During the Industrial Age, we commonly thought of technicians as people engaged in a specific aspect of a manufacturing or production process, such as a petroleum technician. But in the metaindustrial work culture, all of our occupations are becoming more technically oriented, including that of the manager. Increasingly, the technicians are those whose careers are related to new technologies—computers, robots, lasers, bio-engineering. But to be effective in such complex endeavors, synergy is required—one must be able to collaborate not just with peers, but with technicians and those from other specialities, organizations, and countries.

SYNERGISTIC COLLABORATION

Synergy has been described by *The Harper Dictionary of Modern Thought* in this interesting manner:

> The additional benefit accruing to a number of systems should they co-alesce to form a larger system. This concept reflects the classical opinion that the "whole is greater than the sum of the parts." . . . The word is also frequently used in a much looser way in discussions of corporate strategy to indicate general expectations of collaborative benefit. More generally still, the term is applied to the generation of unplanned social benefits among people who unconsciously cooperate in pursuit of their own interests and goals.

It is our thesis in this volume that all people, especially those who might be considered "professionals," should consciously cooperate for the mutual benefit of all. The very complexity of what Alvin Toffler (1980) has characterized as "The Third Wave Culture" demands such collaboration. (In terms of human development, we can adapt Toffler's terms to explain the First Wave of Change as the Agricultural Revolution, the Second Wave as the Industrial Revolution, and the current transformation or the Third Wave as the Cybercultural Revolution.)

At The First Global Conference on the Future held in Toronto, Canada (1980), some professional futurists offered the following insights about synergy:

1. Synergy means to produce more for less, while anti-synergy produces less for more.
2. Synergy produces dual or multiple effects by moving employees together in an ordered way.
3. Synergy at work now includes input from women whose contribution to management will create new institutional values and organizational cultures.

Since our beginnings as a species, we have shared information and experience, either formally or informally. Culture itself is an attempt, consciously or unconsciously, by a people to transmit to future generations their acquired wisdom and insight relative to their knowledge, beliefs, customs, traditions, morals, law, art, communication, and habits. Peers in a particular career, trade, or profession have long banded together to exchange ideas and pursue a common interest.

Some cultures are synergistic and their people are inclined toward cooperation. Others are not, and their people seem to be often in conflict with one another. The late anthropologist, Ruth Benedict, studied this phenomenon, and her research was amplified by the humanistic psychologist, Abraham Maslow, prior to his death. A summary of their insights in terms of "high synergy" and "low synergy" societies is presented below. The observations are equally valid when applied to an organization or team. Today's professionals and technicians should be *synergizers*, using information and technology to promote cooperation among disparate elements in a human system, thereby creating something better than existed by separate endeavors.

There are many cultures possessing traits that foster high synergy, and more research might help to promote such qualities on a more global basis. Americans, for example, have a penchant for organizing, as one glance at the annual

---

High-Synergy Society	Low-Synergy Society
• Emphasis is upon cooperation for mutual advantage.	• Uncooperative, very competitive culture; enhances rugged individualistic and "dog-eat-dog" attitudes.
• Conspicuous for a nonagressive social order.	• Aggressive and antagonistic behavior toward one another, leading to either psychological or physical violence toward the other.
• Social institutions promote individual and group development.	• Social arrangements selfcentered; selfishness, no collaboration, is reinforced as desired behavior.
• Social idealizes win/win, virture pays, victory for all.	• Society adheres to win/lose approach; victory over one another.
• Leadership fosters that wealth and advantage should be shared for the common good. Cooperatives are encouraged, and poverty is fought.	• Leadership encourages private or individual gain and advantage, especially by the power elite; poverty is tolerated, even ignored.
• Society seeks to utilize community resources and talents for the commonwealth and encourages development of human potential of all citizenry.	• Society permits exploitation of poor and minorities, and tolerates the siphoning of its wealth by privileged few; develops power elites and leaves undeveloped the powerless.

(continued on next page)

(continued from page 313)

• Open system of secure people who tend to be benevolent, helpful, friendly, and generous; its heros are altruistic and philanthropic.	• Closed system with insecure people who tend toward suspiciousness, ruthlessness and clannishness; idealizes the "strong man" concerned with greed and acquisition.
• Belief system, religion or philosophy is comforting and life is consoling; emphasis is on the god of love; power is to be used for benefit of whole community; individuals/groups are helped to work out hurt and humiliations.	• Belief system is frightening, punishing, terrifying; members are psychologically beaten down or humiliated by the strong; power is for personal profit; emphasis is on the god of vengeance; hatreds go deep and "blood feuds" abound; violence is the means for compensating for hurt and humiliation.
• Generally, the citizenry is psychologically healthy, and mutual reciprocity is evident in relationships; open to change; low rate of crime and mental illness.	• Generally, the citizenry tends to be defensive, jealous, and envious; mass paranoia and hostility; fears change and advocates status quo; high rate of crime and mental illness.

directory of *National Trade & Professional Associations of the United States and Canada* will demonstrate. To promote professional and scholarly exchanges one company produces a whole series of directories for every category from consultants to research centers, as well as an *Encyclopedia of Associations*. In fact, in the U.S. there is even an association of associations—the American Society of Association Executives. Occupational and professional conferences are such big business in this nation that numerous monthly magazines and annual meeting facilities directories are produced.

Many of these social institutions are experiencing "organization shock" in the post-industrial age. They are not perceived as sufficiently relevant and responsive to their constituencies so they suffer declines in membership, attendance at meetings, and support for their various programs. Huge professional associations find that dissidents form splinter groups, and many practitioners do not even bother to join. Obviously, most labor, trade, and professional associations must go through planned organizational renewal if they are to survive into the twenty-first century.

Colleagues today are seeking many innovative ways for cooperating, and some of these will be described in a later section. One development for such individuals is to move beyond the narrow confines of one's own discipline or area of activity. Thus, some professionals enter into multidisciplinary arrangements and new organizational groupings based more on mutual *interests*, rather than previous education or training. Others engage in professional activities that mix the public and private sectors, academia, and industry. The point is to avoid intellectual or professional ethnocentricity in the sharing of knowledge. This synergy of professional perspectives and skills is vital in solving complex contemporary problems. Furthermore, there must be a desire to consult with peers, not just to inform them of one's accomplishment. True professionals confer and seek feedback before making major decisions on their research investigations, writings, and pronouncements.

For effective collaboration, certain principles must be established in the professional relationship. Reciprocity and interdependence are to be encouraged, while imposition and dependency are to be avoided. Writing on transnational social science transactions, Krishna Kumar (1979) examined scholarly transactions between industrialized (IC) and less industrialized (LIC) countries. Although such professional transactions should be mutually beneficial, there is concern that in fact those from IC's may dominate their LIC counterpart, generate a system of intellectual and cultural dependency, and inhibit development of indigenous social sciences relevant in that cultural context. Symmetry should be the goal of international professional exchanges (that is, proportionate, harmonious, equality of parts to whole; correspondence in size, form, and arrangement). Asymmetry occurs when the "inflow" and the "outflow" of knowledge and expertise are not balanced, so that one may overwhelm the other. Asymmetry must be discouraged in such situations.

A cosmopolitan professional realizes that society in an LIC may be very developed in terms of cultural, social, and even economic aspects of its people's lives, despite the fact that it has not been fully industrialized. Just as raw materials can be drained away from the Third World populations to feed insatiable appetites in the First or Second World, so the "brain drain" may exhaust the human resources of the former. Many Third World scholars trained abroad suffer because all their professional reference groups and support services are outside their own countries. How many institutions and professionals from the IC's are willing to invest in the Third World infrastructure for synergistic growth of all? How else will Third World scholars within their own lands be able to transform data into knowledge because they have there adequate communication facilities and publications, computer-based data banks, and interuniversity or research centers with automated communications systems?

Robert Ayres (1979) observed:

> It is a truism that the further the world moves toward industrialization and urban living, the more interdependent it becomes. . . . This interdependence is growing inexorably, decade by decade. If every nation in the world behaved in strictly rational fashion and acted always in terms of its own best, long-term interests, the fact of growing interdependence would

persuade nations to draw together and set up international agencies with power to provide some protection against possible breakdowns of international order on which all depend.

Although nations may not comprehend this reality and take appropriate steps for changing international relations, individual professionals and their institutions can learn to act interdependently, especially in cross-cultural exchanges. Synergy seeks to remove the artificial barriers that constrain us, promoting professional relations and technical assistance that benefits the whole, rather than merely special interests. Rather than perpetuating the old cultural dependence or imperialism, this approach encourages interinstitutional collaboration, cooperative entrepreneurialism, and transnational action.

This strategy implies cultivating in professionals and technicians the competencies that will foster high, not low synergy. According to James and Margaret Craig (1979), high-synergy structures, interactions, and practices are facilitated by behaving or structuring groups in a way that maximizes coordination, information flow and continuity; gives everyone easy access to information needed for informed choices while creating a climate that builds trust and good feelings; encourages authenticity and clear intent; and fosters creativity and excellence. Obviously, we wish to avoid or delimit low-synergy behavior and organizing that concentrates power in a few and leaves the majority feeling powerless; makes open communication and cooperation difficult; and restricts information and promotes unhealthy competition, thus hampering informed choice, diminishing trust, arousing resentment, and stifling creative contribution.

Within advanced economies, the matter under discussion has taken a new twist. Instead of historic immigration of individuals, foreign corporations are coming in search of economic opportunities. Harvey Poniachek (1987) reports that 10,000 affiliates of foreign companies are operating in the United States, generating $600 billion in annual sales and employing 3 million employees who earn $75 billion a year. The U.S. Department of Commerce reveals that the United Kingdom, the Netherlands, Japan, Canada, and West Germany are among the biggest investors in these foreign-owned ventures, well over $200 billion impacting the American economy. The *Nation's Business* (April 1987, pp. 12–19) did a special feature on "The Corporate Immigrants" pointing up the synergistic implications. Such firms build new factories and shore up ailing companies, invest and loan money, provide new technologies and management techniques, while expanding American exports. The Japanese contribution to the U.S.-based enterprise emphasizes "minimize waste, maximize quality, and focus on building loyalty from satisfied customers while working through loyal employees."

Germany's Siemen Corporation operates 35 factories and 200 offices in the U.S., which employ 25,000 Americans who earn over $2 billion annually. At their Princeton, New Jersey facilities, Siemens' scientists blend knowledge with technology, envisioning themselves as "technology brokers" who manage the in-flow of ideas from around Siemens' worldwide system and channeling this information where most appropriate within their American-based firms.

COPING IN THE "TASK TEAM" ENVIRONMENT

Today professional relationships are often temporary and intense. Peers may come together on a project team, a research effort, or to write a handbook or report. It is a "bridge building process" among specialists who often come from a variety of microcultures within the fields of learning, or even within the organization. The link-up effort is even more complex when the participants are internationals from diverse macrocultures. To promote synergy in such team management, four steps are evident:

1. Bring the new person "on board" quickly by various means of reaching out, briefing, and inclusion efforts.
2. Foster intense, ad hoc work relationships, as well as possible outside social relations.
3. Disengage rapidly when the task is completed and re-assignment occurs, or another undertaking is begun.
4. Follow up on the aftermath of the professional activity and maintain limited communication with members of the prior consortium.

Dr. George Coelho, health science administrator for the U.S. National Institute of Mental Health, refers to this phenomenon as "coping issues in task environment."

This specialist in coping and adaptation believes that the management of self-esteem is involved when one enters a new professional environment or relationship. Coelho (1974) envisions different phases in the process. For example, in the initial phase of planning and initiation, he postulates three challenges for the newcomer:

1. *Gaining entry*—that is, establishing credibility with respect to leadership, objectives, instruments of agreement, use of subjects or client relations, sources of funding, sponsorship, and other institutional support systems, project clearances and blessings, and communication of results.
2. *Observing protocol*—namely, establishing the social contact and cooperative agreements in a format that recognizes the rites, etiquette, ceremonies, proprieties customary in that local cultural setting.
3. *Building rapport*—essentially, creating an auspicious climate for favorable social exchange and interpersonal interactions based on mutual respect and trust (for example in the use of instruments, interviews, simulations, or videotapes for data gathering).

Dr. Coelho believes that the competence of transnational actors in such situations can be subject to assessment, and suggests the following criteria for this purpose: How well does the professional maintain his own and other's self-esteem? Manage anxiety and tension? Maintain meaningful continuity of interpersonal relationships and social supports? Mobilize a sense of autonomy and efficacy in the face of new and complex problems?

Coelho proposes four additional phases in the life cycle of temporary group relationships. After planning and initiation, there are orientation, on-site training, activities that enhance involvement and commitment, and reentry assistance and evaluation. Joining others in a new vocational environment requires risk and self-management, as well as human creativity in adaptation. Participants are challenged to create a microculture that accommodates "doers and thinkers" despite the reality that this mix may produce tension and conflict. As Andre van Dam, director of planning for Corn Products Company, Latin America, asked:

> Can we learn to cooperate in a competitive world? Can cooperation (which thrives on consultation and participation) coexist with competition (which is deeply ingrained in human beings, groups, and nations)? . . .
>
> Admittedly, cooperation requires trade-offs between rival ideas or interests—trade-offs imply negotiation. Cooperation hinges upon the recognition of common as well as conflicting interests.

Trust among colleagues normally occurs when persons have worked together for long periods of time, and grown in respect and comfort with one another—it is earned. But in the new work culture, we often work with people in ad hoc arrangements. Gordon Shea, president of Prime Systems in Beltsville, Maryland, thinks that the trust relationship can be facilitated. He envisions trust as an organizational resource that is freely given and based upon mutual concern. Shea (1984) has not only written on this critical issue, but created a workshop for building trust in the workplace. People can learn the nature and value of trust, identify its sources, develop a trust style, assess other's trustworthiness, and achieve mutual trust relationships. Productivity is increased when trust levels are enhanced, especially between and among professionals and technicians who are responsible for a mission or task. (Readers are reminded to review the insights provided on team culture in Chapter 7 and to link that information with the following.)

ENSURING PROFESSIONAL SYNERGY

Social scientists are conducting significant research on what people can do in small groups to facilitate a meaningful experience and productive outcome. One exciting example of this occurred at the East-West Center in Honolulu,

Hawaii. In 1980, at its Culture Learning Institute, Dr. Kathleen K. Wilson spearheaded an investigation with 15 other distinguished colleagues on the factors influencing the management of International Cooperative Research and Development (ICRD) projects. Their findings have vital implications now for any professional seeking to improve human performance and collaboration. Although the researchers are examining project team effectiveness, their insights can be extrapolated to other forms of inter- and intragroup behavior, whether it is a matrix organization, product team, task force, or any work unit.

Reporting the researchers' progress to the Australian Commonwealth's Scientific and Industrial Research Organizations, Dr. Wilson reviewed the varied contexts in which international cooperative groups must operate. These external factors affect the environment within the project itself, and include such diverse elements as political, organizational, and cultural aspects, the size and scope of the endeavor, the disciplinary background of team members, and their individual characteristics, research, and development policies and problems. A summary of factors that foster or hinder professional synergy appears above. Certainly, the exhaustive listing of situations that influence a project's effectiveness points up the need for strategies to manage the many "cultural" differences existing between and among professionals attempting to work together.

As part of the new team's orientation, a discussion of such "hazards" is in order. Perhaps some guidelines can be worked out for preventing some of the situations from becoming unmanageable. Such differences in perspective can be recorded on audio cassettes during project meetings, and then used to bring new team members "on board" during the life of the project. Obviously, all these human differences will not be resolved, and many will add to the richness of the team experience. At the very least, at project start-up, a review of the effects of cultural factors and conditioning on team behavior may alert the group to some of the realities and challenges involved in professional collaboration.

The East-West research on international cooperation projects offers some criteria that can be used in recruiting, selecting, and assessing professionals. *Team member characteristics* that foster group synergy are presented on the facing page. Such benchmarks can be helpful in interviewing potential team members, choosing collaborators, and setting goals for self-improvement in organizational relations.

Finally, the ICRD researchers at the East-West Culture Learning Institute offer some indications for synergy assessment in professional cooperative efforts. They have established four criteria for evaluating project effectiveness and management competence:

1. Individual team member satisfaction.
2. Group satisfaction and morale.
3. Work progress relative to intended goal statements.
4. Social and cultural impact of the endeavor on people.

**Human Factors That Foster or Hinder
Professional Synergy Within a Project:**

- How project business is planned.
- Consideration of other problem-solving viewpoints.
- How the work should be organized.
- Approach to R & D tasks.
- Definition of R & D problems.
- Ambiguity resolution and problem formulation.
- Methods and procedures.
- Decision-making relative to recurring problems.
- Allocation of resources to team members.
- Accountability procedures relative to resource use.
- Timing and sequencing approaches.
- Determining objectives for an R & D effort.
- Affiliation and liaison with external groups and degree of formality in their work relations.
- Quantity and type of project human resources.
- Qualifications, recruitment, and selection of new members.
- New member orientation and training on the project.
- Management of responsibilities.
- Clarification of roles and relationships.

- Underutilization of workers relative to skill competencies.
- Motivating behavior and reward expectations.
- Coordination of long/short-term members.
- Agreement on degree of innovation required.
- Experience with cooperation especially relative to international R & D tasks.
- Official language(s) to use on project.
- Method of reporting everyone's involvement in the project.
- Coping with internal demands and visitors.
- Meeting face-to-face and having to resort to other forms of more impersonal communication.
- Involvement in making viewpoints known.
- Power differences because of institutional resources each brought to the project.
- Prestige, risk-taking, tolerance of uncertainty, and perceptions.
- Project leadership and/or organizational policies changing unexpectedly.
- Quality of work presented in evaluation methods.
- What constituted success in project work, and what to do when members fail to meet group expectations.

The East-West Center's ICRD researchers have also identified interpersonal skills that influence a professional group's situation and accomplishments. A summary of these *self-management competencies* is shown on the facing page.

These insights offer a compendium of the shared leadership skills that professionals should expect to contribute in the course of group collaboration. For those organizations that provide project management training or team building for their members, these are the types of competencies to be sought in the emerging "ad hocracies."

To ensure that synergy develops among professionals and technicians, consultants are creating educational programs for this purpose. *Synergy at Work* is a three-stage process for linking left/right brain skills. Designed by Rob Wall of Professional and Organization Development (P.O. Box 7641, Fremont, Ca. 94537), it enhances synergistic skills and support systems by harmonizing technical, logical, and verbal competencies associated with the left side of the brain with intuitive, humanistic, and non-verbal capacities of the right brain. To increase productive behavior, this approach attempts to connect science with art, balance resourcefulness with imagination, initiate collaborative group action. Similarly, Dr. J. Clayton Lafferty has developed synergistic training materials for management and organization development. Through Human Synergistics Inc. (39819 Plymouth Road, Plymouth, Michigan 48170), his learning instruments and simulation exercises encourage participation and feedback, problem-solving and team work.

The New York Institute for Cross-Cultural Communication (301 East 64th Street, New York, N.Y. 10021) is another example of a research and training organization that helps professionals examine how cultural assumptions and values affect their perception, and may even block their cooperation. Founded by Dr. Edgar Goldstein, a psychiatrist from Russia, its seminars and workshops sensitize educators, business negotiators, case workers, and researchers to ways for creating synergy out of cultural differences. Its efforts place special emphasis on the needs of workers who are immigrants, refugees, and minorities, as well as how to create synergy in negotiations with the Soviets.

To foster synergy among professionals and others at the local level, Art Coulter, a professor and physician at the University of North Carolina's medical school founded The Synergetic Society (1825 North Lake Shore Drive, Chapel

---

The Effective Team Member Has the Capacity for:

- Flexibility and openness to change and others' viewpoints.
- Exercising patience, perseverance, and professional security.
- Thinking in multidimensional terms and considering different sides of issues.
- Dealing with ambiguity, role shifts, and differences in personal and professional styles or social and political systems.
- Managing stress and tension well, while scheduling tasks systematically.
- Cross-cultural communication, and demonstrating sensitivity for language problems among colleagues.
- Anticipating consequences of one's own behavior.
- Dealing with unfamiliar situations and life-style changes.
- Dealing well with different organizational structures and policies.
- Gathering useful information related to future projects.

Self-Management Competencies Permit the Project Member to:

- Recognize other members' participation in ways they find rewarding.
- Avoid *unnecessary* conflicts among other team members, as well as to resolve unavoidable ones to mutual satisfaction.
- Integrate different team members skills to achieve project goals.
- Negotiate acceptable working arrangements with other team members and their organizations.
- Regard other's feelings and exercise tactfulness.
- Develop equitable benefits for other team members.
- Accept suggestions/feedback to improve his or her participation.
- Provide useful specific suggestions and appropriate feedback.
- Facilitate positive interaction among culturally different members, whether in terms of macro differences (nationally/politics), or micro differences (discipline or training).
- Accomplish required work while enjoying positive social relations with other team members.
- Build a support network for the benefit of the project team.
- Facilitate team exchanges and convert member ideas into specific tasks of accomplishment.
- Gain acceptance because of empathy expressed and sensitivity to end users.
- Encourage dissemination of project outcomes throughout its life.
- Recognize national/international differences in problem statements and procedures, so as to create appropriate project organizational responses.
- Anticipate and plan for probable difficulties in project implementation.
- Recognize discrete functions and to coordinate discrete tasks with overall project goals.
- Coordinate transitions among different kinds of activities within the project.

Hill, NC 27514). It publishes a journal entitled *Change*, has chapters in various regions, sponsors conferences and meetings, and produces cassettes on the emerging science of synergy. Such trends underscore the thesis of Peter Russell (1983) that we are on the verge of a sociocultural transformation. In the original Greek, "syn-ergos" means literally to work together. Increasingly, we seem to be realizing the interdependency of people and systems, and the positive value of collaborative action.

Finally, for global managers who wish to improve for themselves and their colleagues international management performance, Appendix E is a self-assessment of one's skills for managing abroad.

NETWORKING PHENOMENA

Intellectuals have always formed linkages and exchanges with each other within a society or field of human endeavor. What is different in recent decades is the escalation of these phenomena on a global scale, across both cultures and disciplines of knowledge. Twentieth-century advances in communication and transportation have accelerated the process on a mass scale. They also contribute to professional obsolescence, and to the need for continuous professional development in order to be relevant within a vocational activity.

One's peers within a career field provide a reference group against which individual performance can be measured, recognized, and motivated. Today, such professional colleagues may be found around the world, not just within one's own country or even within one's own field of learning. As more people study abroad, attend professional conferences overseas, or engage in career activities internationally, transnational linkages are formed.

Networking is a communication concept especially appropriate for women seeking to advance in managerial and professional careers. In San Diego, California, women in various industries and professions have formed separate networks for advancement and information purposes. Some of it is informal, like those female members of the San Diego Chamber of Commerce who formed a "downtown network." Some networks provide members with business development leads, while others gather and support women in highly visible leadership positions in business, politics, and other professions.

The potential for a new synergy among professionals through such developments is astounding. Such technology can also undermine traditional trade and professional societies, research centers, and consulting associations unless such entities renew and make use of these media possibilities. It provides a real challenge to government to sponsor public sector forums and similar opportunities for the benefit of the masses.

In these new patterns of collaboration, it is important that self-reliance is fostered in the participants and that interdependence is perceived as the basis of the network. Rudolph Rummel of the University of Hawaii reminds us that in transnational interactions, international cooperation and conflict are not necessarily irreconcilable but complementary. As he sees it, the problem with the diversity of national values, goals, ideologies, life-styles, and interests, is not to realize humanity as a single unit. Instead, synergy can be attained by developing realistic structures of mutual expectations that facilitate national interactions, while appreciating their cultural differences. Networks, in effect, represent post-industrial reference groups for professionals. They form a new microculture across the planet of people exploring for more appropriate values, attitudes, standards, beliefs, and perspectives that will be appropriate for life in the twenty-first century.

If traditional social institutions are to survive, no less develop, then they must further the mechanisms for exchanges among their membership. It begins with the identification of participants' needs and interests, often by some survey means or other form of human factor data gathering. Then an organization or association may form a personal or electronic network centered around the findings of such inquiries. SIETAR International, for example, did a computerized study of their membership in order to create an intercultural talent bank that includes professionals from many countries who speak 1,000 languages. The World Future Society, in cooperation with The Networking Group, annually surveys member resources to link up those with common interests through the medium of a yearly publication called *The Future—A Guide to Information Sources*—it lists both individuals, organizations, research projects, educational programs, publications, media, and learning materials related to future studies and research.

Networking can be a new work culture strategy for performance improvement (Harris 1985), because it creates a system of interrelated people or groups, offices or work stations, linked together personally or electronically or both, for information exchange and mutual support. Networking is a modern mechanism for coping with complexity and change in the transition to the information society. Furthermore, it is in harmony with many national cultures.

For personal networking to achieve positive contribution for its participants and society, these characteristics should be cultivated among members:

1. Free-forming and adaptive relationship in which the person is the most important feature, the boundaries are unstructured, the power and responsibility are distributed, the participants may play many roles, the balance is maintained between personal integrity and collective purpose, and the sharing of concerns and values is encouraged.
2. Willingness of those linked together to exercise initiative, take risks, be assertive, be autonomous, be informal, and be authentic in communications.
3. Ability to cope with differences, ambiguity, uncertainty, and with lack of closure.

Apart from professional and trade associations, personal networking can be accomplished through chambers of commerce and service organizations, such as the Rotary and Kiwanis clubs. Among the resources for nonelectronic networking are:

- National Association of Home Based Businesses (P.O. Box 30220, Baltimore, MD 21270, USA)
- National Business Incubation Association (114 N. Hanover St., Carlisle, PA 17013, USA)
- Professional & Technical Consultants Association (1330 Bascom Ave. Ste. D, San Jose, CA 95128, USA)
- The Network Institute (P.O. Box 66, West Newton, MA 02165, USA)

For electronic networking via computer, there is a variety of new resources, such as:

- CompuServe (5000 Arlington Blvd., Columbus, OH 43220,USA)
- Easy Net (134 N. Narbeth Ave., Narberth, PA 19072, USA)

- Electronic Networking Association, 2000 N. 15th St., Ste. 103, Arlington, VA 22201,USA)
- The Source (1616 Anderson Road, McLean, VA 22102, USA)

Teleconferencing is another form of information and insight exchange, which Norman Solomon wishes to link with computer networking through the International Business Issues Network (3891 El Camino Real, Carlsbad, CA 92008, USA). A *Catalog of Teleconferencing Resources* is available through the University of Wisconsin-Extension (Center for Interactive Programs, Lowell Hall, 610 Langdon St., Madison, WI 53703, USA).

Networks can be simply for Information exchange, as in the case of an electronic mailbox or bulletin board, or be put to more sophisticated use for peer support and professional development. For instance, the latter occurs in such networks as The Executive Committee (3737 Camio del Rio South, San Diego, CA 90018) for CEOs in small and low-tech companies, or The Southern California Technology Executive Network (12011 San Vincente Boulevard, Los Angeles, CA 90049).

At the global level executives may join the World Technology Executives Network (Suite 1185, 1900 Avenue of the Stars, Los Angeles, CA 90067, USA). Managers interested in electronic networking with each other have The Meta Network (Metasystems Design Group, 2000 North 15th St., Ste. 103, Arlington, VA 22201, USA). Those seeking legal information have LEXSIS research through Mead Data Central (P.O. Box 1830, Dayton, OII 45401, USA).

Similarly, consultants have discovered that networking can be a powerful means for keeping them "plugged into" developments in their fields. Three illustrations of this at the transnational, regional and local levels are: International Consultants Foundation (11612 Georgetown Court, Potomac, MD 20854, USA); The Consultants Network (57 West 89th Street, New York, N.Y. 10024); and the Consultants Roundtable of San Diego (311 Laurel, San Diego, CA 92101). All such efforts underscore how networking can be a powerful synergistic tool among professionals and technicians, or any type of global manager. It enables affiliates not only to keep informed and current, but to advance their careers and relationships.

INNOVATIVE COOPERATION WITH COLLEAGUES

Now that the concepts and means for promoting synergy in professional development have been reviewed, it may help to examine some creative approaches to the subject. Some wit has characterized those with knowledge and information as risk-takers, caretakers, and undertakers. It takes vision, courage, and risk to innovate. In 1931, Professor Neil Gordon of Johns Hopkins University had a brainchild for transmitting scientific information in a different way. Gordon wanted small groups of scientists to meet for summer seminars in a secluded and relaxed setting for informal, free give-and-take of knowledge. Today this innovative concept yields 100 Gordon conferences annually in seven New Hampshire schools and colleges for 12,000 professionals. Among the thinkers are many Nobel laureates who enjoy the relaxed exchange of data where there is no pressure, no publicity, and no need to publish.

When there is a coalition of people with new needs for interchange, then formal or information associations come into being. Three current examples of this are The International Organization of Women Executives, whose primary aim is to help female executives excel through continuing education; the International Association Futuribles, which reports on future studies around the world through monthly journal abstracts and European meetings, as well as joint research on practical issues, such as labor conditions and lifestyles; and *Leading Edge*, a bulletin on social transformations that offers triweekly reports on innovations and emergent patterns in all aspects of society (see Gulf Publishing Company's *Directory of Intercultural Resources* for addresses of publications and the groups mentioned here).

But what is innovation? And are there already some models of it that demonstrate synergy among professionals?

Innovation has been defined as creative idea generation, or the act of introducing something new into the established order; a change or different way of doing things from the traditional pattern. The scholars at the University of Southern California's Graduate School of Business Administration maintained that innovation should include the invention and development of new technology, as well as entrepreneurial and managerial risk-taking to improve services and productivity. Innovation, for survival and development, should be built into the operating mechanisms or policies of all postindustrial systems. All social institutions, especially government agencies and corporations, have a desperate need to encourage creative deviations from the traditional norms and practices by professionals who will instill innovation into daily operations. As these words are written the great American industrial giant is stagnant and staggering because innovation was not advocated from the boardroom to the sales room. Dr. Warren Bennis reminds us that in 1930, as today, 100 companies dominated the United States economy, but 50 years later 60 of the original group have either declined or have ceased to exist. One might take the *Fortune 500* corporations in 1986 and inquire how many will be in that category by the year 2000. Those without innovative performance certainly will not be (Kuhn, 1988).

What Peter Drucker (1980, 1985) has said for business in this regard can be applied to all human systems:

> Innovation means, first, the systematic sloughing off of yesterday. It means, next, the systematic search for innovative opportunities in the vulnerabilities of a technology, a process, a market, in the lead time of new knowledge; in the needs and wants of a market. It means willingness to organize for entrepreneurship, to creating new businesses. . . . It means, finally, the willingness to set up innovative ventures separately,

outside the existing managerial structure, to organize proper accounting concepts for the economics and control of innovation, and appropriate compensation policies for the innovators.

The new work culture values creativity and innovation, and manifests this in its support of entrepreneurial activities (Drucker 1985). Innovative management builds mechanisms for this into organizational systems, such as developing an incentive system to reward risk-taking or creating a people-oriented climate that provides employees with a sense of ownership (Diebold 1984).

The previous examples of synergy among professionals and technicians demonstrate how people from multiple disciplines and associations can be brought together cooperatively to accomplish something more than any one as an individual can achieve. Let us end this chapter with a case study of how one organization can achieve the same purposes and cross-cultural sensitivity with its own employees:

The Holiday Corporation has not only innovated in its international lodging facilities, but in a wide range of services that extend from teleconferencing to its own "university" in Olive Branch, Mississippi, for personnel development. But the Western Region of Holiday Inns under the leadership of Ronald Jeffrey, vice president, went a step further in creative human resource development of its management. In a 1985 general managers conference, the participants discussed more than financial planning, compensation, sales and marketing strategies. They also discussed organizational climate and cultural awareness. Cheryl Jordan, regional training manager, explained that the company has both a multicultural clientele and workforce. For example, the Western Region has managers representing ten countries, while the staff at their regional headquarter's hotel in San Francisco's Chinatown come from twenty-two different cultures. Thus, she is leading the effort to include cross-cultural training as a regular part of Holiday Inns' HRD efforts. To be an effective manager in this lodging chain, Jordan maintains the person must be able to manage both cultural differences and synergy, including reading body language and non-verbal communication. To excel in business services, Holiday Inn personnel must be culturally sensitive, so bonus and other incentives support such goals. Even their management conference was culturally based, featuring different foods, dress, and ceremonies from the employees' varied cultural backgrounds. Now Ms. Jordan (Holiday Inn Regional Office, 750 Kearny St. San Francisco, Ca. 94108) wants to carry this intercultural awareness message to her colleagues in the industry through the Council of Hotel and Restaurant Trainers.

SYNERGY WITH FEMALE MANAGERS AND PROFESSIONALS

Since creation, males and females have been complementary. After all, each sex possesses qualities of the other, though men have traditionally sought to camouflage their female emotions, intuitions, and personality qualities. Unfortunately, in most cultures men have raised barriers to females seeking to achieve their human potential. Although both genders often cooperate in marriage, as well as vocationally and professionally, cultural conditioning frequently prompted male leaders to delimit career choices and development for their female counterparts. However, during the past few decades, education and mass communication, as well as the feminist movement and government regulations, are combining to raise consciousness and alter the situation. The continuing progress of women in the workplace is well documented.

Despite affirmative action programs, females need to use their special talent for collaboration and networking to overcome the remaining obstacles to their advancement to management and the executive suite. The research of Morrison, White, and Van Velsor (1987) on *Breaking the Glass Ceiling* has proposed strategies for women to pursue in order to reach the top of the largest corporations.

Global business still presents unusual challenges for female professionals who function beyond their own borders, but the international business literature provides limited coverage of the unique problems and progress of female managers overseas. The following offers an overview of some of these problems and progress:

Women Managers and Professionals Abroad*

Women Managers: Professionals Abroad

The number of women managers and executives on long-term international assignments is still limited, but steadily rising. In some countries where there is a traditional culture lag with respect to the role of modern women in business, females—even foreigners—are not welcome or comfortable in the halls of commerce. In such places, women international managers sometimes face bias and prejudice. The cultures of Saudi Arabia, Italy, and Japan, for instance, have been cited as inhibiting the effectiveness of such managers. But the situation is changing, even in Japan where the Japanese leaders are more accepting of foreign business women or "gaijin" than they are of their own talented females. Many Western women hold positions of importance within Japan today, according to Madeline Porter [1], and are adapting well to the unusual business conditions there. In fact, they are more likely to experience discrimination from other Japanese women than the men who are more respectful and accepting of their presence, especially when the international female manager has competence and credentials. What the Japanese do resent is overly aggressive Westerners, male or female.

---

* By Philip R. and Dorothy L. Harris, reprinted with permission from *The Journal of Managerial Psychology,* Vol. 3:4, MCB University Press, United Kingdom, 1988.

Nancy Adler, a professor at Toronto's McGill University and an expert on the female manager overseas, recently surveyed 686 US and Canadian companies with operations abroad. She found that among their 13,388 expatriate employees, only 3% were women. In a feature for *International Management* [2] on this subject, Dr. Robert Moran commented on these findings, observing that many organizations are not giving women international assignments because the men in charge there also blame other cultures for their own prejudices and overprotectiveness of women personnel to save them from supposed difficulties abroad.

Professor Adler concludes that the barriers facing women will be reduced only when the companies perceive advantages in sending women overseas and that the numbers of expatriate female managers will increase substantially in the next decade [3]. Certainly the success of women abroad in the Peace Corps, other voluntary agencies, and academia more than demonstrates female capability and potential. When we contemplate the ability of women to function effectively overseas for the military, government and UN agencies, one asks whether the real culture lag is within multinational business itself. In her classes with graduate business students at United States International University in San Diego, one of the authors (D.L. Harris), for over a decade had approximately 80% who were of foreign background. Many of these were females and among the most competent, well-adjusted, motivated MBA or DBA students, but were limited in managerial or business experience in comparison to their male counterparts.

In her 1983 research of international personnel managers within 60 North American multinationals, Adler found that 25% of the companies had no women abroad at the time of the survey, 15% had never sent females overseas, but 72% predicted that more women would be sent in the future on overseas' assignments [4]. The excuse given for the situation by those studied was foreign prejudice towards women which limits their effectiveness and credibility; never that of their own or their company. Obviously, this is a fertile field for action research on how the situation can and is being altered, and what the problems of expatriate female managers are. Adler's studies indicate that among graduating MBAs, the males and females were equally interested in pursuing international careers, but there is still reluctance in companies actually to select women for such assignments.

Married Women Managers Abroad

For the single woman overseas who has no dependants, there is one set of challenges in international business, which has yet to be fully documented. But for the married career woman, becoming an expatriate raises unique difficulties relative to family responsibilities. In the above Adler investigation of personnel managers [4], 70% of the respondents cited the obstacles created by dual career marriages relative to international assignment; unfortunately personnel managers are not creative in seeking ways around such barriers. Too many companies show a variety of concerns when a female manager is under consideration that are treated routinely when a male manager is being selected. In all such cases, the transfer of the female manager overseas was seen as more difficult than that of posting a single woman abroad or a man married to a non-career woman.

On the positive side, 18% of the personnel managers in that last Adler survey saw an advantage in the choice of the woman as an expatriate manager—greater visibility and motivation were cited. The personnel managers did recommend that in addition to job-specific, cross-cultural, and linguistic preparation, women selected for foreign-deployment should understand and respect the host culture's views about women, act in a professional manner, work hard to get along with local staff, and establish a support network with other expatriate women. They also recognized that corporations should take responsibility in-house for changing managerial attitudes about women serving abroad, for qualifying more women for service overseas, for changing the nature of the international selection process, and for creating an overseas support system.

It is the issue of foreign support systems and networks that the authors think should gain more corporate attention. There is ample evidence that given equal opportunity, women can perform as effectively as men in international assignments—perhaps even better.

Support for Women in Foreign Posts

As we move through a transition to greater involvement of women in global management, the sponsoring organizations should initially provide special support for the woman manager who relocates with family to a foreign post. These might include:

- Counseling of the husband prior to departure and abroad on personal readjustment, as well as career and other learning opportunities at the site abroad, or if the husband remains at home while the spouse is abroad.
- Specific guidance and support services regarding care and education of dependent children overseas.
- Facilitating the establishment and conduct of an overseas women's support network within the transnational enterprise as a whole, and at the host-culture location.

Otherwise, all the other requisites for a foreign deployment system should be observed, regardless of the sex of the candidate.

The proposed women's network, both corporate-wide and at specific locales, could render many services, such as:

- Producing a directory of home and career services required by women in alien circumstances.
- Compiling information on how to cope with escalating cost-of-living in expensive foreign cities.

Tokyo, for instance, is 40% more expensive than Washington, D.C. Clothing, housing, and schooling costs can be prohibitive. Such financial considerations in Japan's capital include $6,500 to send a child to an English-speaking school for one year, and $2,000 to $4,000 a month for a two-bedroom apartment within an hour's downtown commuting distance.

Working women have always had to cope with more than their male counterparts, and this is even more complicated in the international business environment. Despite the difficulties, from the import-export business to international transportation and hotel management, competent women are succeeding in ever greater numbers. However, personnel administrators could facilitate high performance among females in the global marketplace by developing strategies in their human resource development programs which address the special needs and circumstances identified in this article [5, 6].

References

1. Porter, M., *Savvy,* April 1984, p. 78.
2. Moran, R. T., *International Management,* September 1985, p. 118.
3. Adler, N. J., *The International Executive,* Spring/Summer 1985, p.14
4. Adler, N. J., "Expecting International Success: Female Managers Overseas," *Columbia Journal of World Business,* Vol. 19, No 3, Fall 1984, pp. 79–86.
5. Harris, P. R., *Management in Transition: Transforming Managerial Practices and Organizational Strategies for a New Work Culture,* Jossey-Bass, San Francisco, 1985.
6. Harris, P. R., "Employees Abroad: Maintain the Corporate Connection," *Personnel Journal,* August 1986, pp. 107–110.
7. Adler, N. J. and Izraeli D. N. (eds.), *Women in Management Worldwide,* International Press, Yarmouth, Maine, 1989.
8. Adler, N. J., "Typology of Management Studies Involving Culture," *Journal of International Business Studies,* Fall 1983, pp. 29–47.
9. Adler, N. J., "Cultural Synergy: The Management of Cross-cultural Organizations," in Burke, W. and Goodsetins, L. D. (eds.), *Trends and Issues in OD* University Associates, San Diego, 1980, Ch. 8.

SUMMARY

Those who envision themselves as truly global, cosmopolitan managers or leaders actively create a better future through synergistic efforts with fellow professionals. The new work culture favors cooperation, not excessive competition, by people in the course of their vocational activity. This trend is evident, as well as necessary, in corporations and industries, in government and academic institutions, in non-profit agencies and unions, in trade and professional associations of all types. In an information or knowledge society, collaboration in sharing ideas and insights is the key to survival, problem solving, and growth. But high synergy behavior must be cultivated in personnel, so we need to use research findings, such as those outlined in this chapter, to facilitate teamwork and ensure professional synergy. In addition to fostering such learning in our formal education and training systems, we also should take advantage of the increasing capabilities offered to us for both personal and electronic networking.

Furthermore, the opportunities for professional collaboration will increase four-fold by the turn of the century. Within the next two decades colleagues located at various places on earth will visually communicate with each other, exchanging research reports, inventions, and graphic transmissions almost instantaneously. Information technology will permit a new synergy among thinking persons, and a mass interchange of creativity. Innovation will be valued in this process of consciousness-raising within our species.

The transformation of our traditional human society will require synergistic professionals who operate comfortably in two cultures: the industrial culture, which is disappearing, and the metaindustrial or cyberculture, which is emerging. Contemporary transnational actors must be effective bridge builders between both worlds, between the realities of the past and future.

Unit III
Cultural Specifics and Business/
Service Abroad

Managers in developing countries have unique needs for both knowledge and skills; some are of an educational nature, while others are concerned with the practical problems of managing an enterprise. Global managers can contribute much to meeting these needs* which include:

1. Economic theory—macroeconomics, developing economies, industrial and rural development.
2. Managing rural enterprises—agriculture, small business, handicrafts.
3. Entrepreneurship—in small enterprises or intrapreneurship within existing organizations, as well as in the management of cooperatives.
4. Human resource management—including knowledge of cultural understanding, languages, personnel systems, recruitment, staff development and team management.
5. Management of other resources—materials and energy conservation, including low-cost fuel technologies, land use management, inventory and control.
6. Technology understanding and utilization—selection, management, and maintenance of appropriate technology, including operative training, especially in new technologies.
7. Government relationships—understanding policies and procedures, power and politics; methods of overcoming infrastructure deficiencies and implementing change.

---

* Based largely on survey results from the International Academy of Management. *Management Education: A World View of Experience and Needs* (London: British Institute of Management, 1981).

13
Doing Business with North Americans—U.S.A./Canada

For inhabitants of other lands wishing to do business with "Americans," the experience can be quite confusing for there are many peoples who may legitimately lay claim to that title. To delimit the problem somewhat, this chapter will be concerned with the nationals and cultures north of the Rio Grande River. (Chapter 14 focuses upon living south of that river and the U.S.A.'s southern border.) In any event, it is helpful for those from elsewhere to first look at the whole "Pan American" scene, and then divide our analysis into the natives of the North American and South American continents. The main problem for foreign business persons dealing with these markets is that in both situations there are cultures that overlap and influence one another. Thus, to oversimplify or to stereotype when dealing with "Americans" can lead to difficulties, especially if one has been unduly influenced with the Hollywood film image of the typical "American."

An Ancient Stone Anchor Found Off the California Coast Indicates the Chinese Were in the Americas, 2200 B.C.

So ran the headline of a recent feature article on the latest archeological findings that implied that Asians, not Europeans, may have been the first to discover the New World. Scholars have found evidence that Phoenician merchants, Viking warriors, Irish monks, and Polynesian seafarers reached this Western Hemisphere centuries before an Italian navigator got the credit for this great feat. Of course, the Eskimos, or Inuit, as the Eskimos prefer to call themselves, of Mongolian descent, may have already crossed the Bering Sea and settled in North America long before the Phoenicians, Vikings, Irish, and Polynesians arrived.

335

North America—Profile

Population (approx.)

Canada	26 million
USA	243 million
Total	269 million

National Cultures

2 countries
2 indigenous peoples
(Eskimo/Indian)

Major Cultural Inputs

- Native North American Eskimos and Indians (nomadic aboriginals).
- European—originally Spanish/French/English and later diverse immigration from the continent.

USA
- African, including lately Haitian.
- Asian—originally Chinese, some Japanese, Polynesian, and recently Indo-Chinese.
- Mexicans and Cubans, and lately variety of other Latins.

Canada
- Ukranians and variety of Commonwealth peoples (e.g., Indians and Pakistanis, West Indies)

Socio-Political Developments

- English common law system.
- In Canada the struggle of the English/French colonial powers still affects national sense of identity and relations, and government struggles for its own constitution in British Commonwealth.
- After a revolutionary war, USA declared independence from colonial power in 1798, and expanded from East to West; eventually into the Pacific, Alaska and Puerto Rico.
- Egalitarian, democratic, individualistic, materialistic with emphasis on organization and self-development.

Land Mass (approx. sq. mi)

Canada	3.5 million
USA	3.6 million
Total	7.1 million

- Problems of race/minority relations—in Canada, it is principally the human/political rights of the French-speaking group in the dominant English society; in USA, it is principally the total rights and integration of black citizens, of slave ancestory from Africa, into the society; and Hispanics. Protests have been largely peaceful and through political/legal action for equal opportunity.
- Economically and technically advanced in post-industrial stage of development; into space exploration and development, as well as global leadership.
- Religiously pluralistic with wide variations from severe fundamentalism to major shifts to Eastern religious traditions or moving beyond religious attachments. Majority consider themselves Christian with large Jewish minority.

Education

- In the English tradition; public and privately supported institutions of higher education, with unique system of community colleges and technical institutes. In Canada, public support is provided to schools administered by religious organizations, largely Catholic. In USA there is strict separation of church and state, so there are many public elementary/secondary schools and no public support to the parochial and independent school systems. Universal education required by law usually to 12th grade, and many go on to college studies.

PAN AMERICAN MANAGEMENT PERSPECTIVES

This great land body, which extends almost from the Arctic to Cape Horn, was named "America" after another sixteenth century Italian explorer, *Amerigo* Vespucci, who was also a merchant. Trade was to be a dominant force in the discovery and development of these unknown territories between the Atlantic and Pacific Oceans. Although all the inhabitants today of the Americas have right to the title "American"—and many think of themselves as such—it was the people in that portion called the United States, who popularly appropriated the designation.

The Americas—north, central, and south—have a diversity of cultural heritages, and a synergy of sorts is being forged. It is like a huge laboratory of human relations in which a mixture of cultures from Europe, Africa, and Asia are merging. Geographically, one tends to think of North America as primarily "Anglo-Saxon" types who largely speak English. The only trouble is that Canada is bilingual with its second language of French, while the United States is moving in that direction with Spanish. For convenience, we refer to that area south of the Rio Grande River as *Latin America*, because the language there is mainly of Latin origin. Apart from numerous Indian languages, Spanish is dominant in Mexico, Central, and South America, while Portuguese is the major language of Brazil (plus Italian and Japanese to a lesser degree).

For our purpose, *Pan America* will designate that land mass of some 15 million square miles from the Arctic Ocean south to the convergence of the Atlantic/Pacific Oceans at Drakes Passage. The Americas involve approximately 30 *national* cultures, plus Eskimo and Indian cultures.

For international managers seeking to function effectively in the Pan American market, it is important that they have the "big picture" about the peoples and cultures on these two vast continents linked by that land bridge called Central America. Furthermore, for managers and other leaders from the north who do business in the southern part of the Americas, and those from Latin America who seek trade in the northern part, geoeconomic and cultural insight will facilitate the processes of business and acculturation.

To better comprehend the Pan American market, consider these realities:

Economic development. International agencies and banks generally consider the North American countries to be First World and rich in terms of annual gross domestic product per capita (GDP is $5,000 or above), whereas most of Latin America, from Mexico southward, is thought of as developing countries or Third World—only one country there (Netherlands Antilles) has a GDP of more than $5,000 per person. Despite economic progress in Latin America, economic forecasts indicate that by the end of the century, 16% of their population will still be classified as poor (i.e., GDP below $1,500 annually). This helps to explain the economic dependence of the South upon the North in the Americas, and the flow of illegal immigration northward in the search of work. It also points up the problems of these nations with the International Monetary Fund and the World Bank relative to difficulties with repayment of loans, rising inflation, and other economic woes.

Natural/material resources. Although both American continents are rich in such resources, those of the North have tended to be more developed, but the future may be in the South. For example, in terms of food production, the United Nations Food and Agricultural Organization (FAO) estimates that only one country in Latin America—Argentina—is considered a developed exporter, such as the U.S.A. and Canada. With reference to energy, the International Institute for Applied Systems Analysis divides the world into seven major energy-related regions—Region I is North America with a highly developed market economy, while Region IV is Latin America, listed as a developing region of potentially rich energy resources.

Human resources. North America has a combined population of approximately 269 million persons with a natural population increase of less than 1%. Latin America has more than 403 million inhabitants and an increase rate between 1–3%; the most populous countries at 3% or more are Mexico, Venezuela, Guatemala, Peru, and Paraguay. Obviously, unless expanding population is brought under control in the South, not only will economic growth there be affected adversely, but continuing social unrest, political and military turmoil can be expected. Yet there are human assets in Latin America waiting to be capitalized through education, and training—there are more than 36 million children under the age of six awaiting such personal and vocational development.

Sociologist Raymond Gordon (1974) notes even after extended periods of residence in Colombian homes, American guests still did not know appropriate cultural routines, and misunderstandings were often provoked. How much more might this be true in the arena of international business or economic development within the Americas? Gordon quotes the experience of the late Senator Robert Kennedy whose attempts at rousing goodwill in South America lead to some hostility. A speech in Santiago began with a neutral crowd reaction and ended with chants of "Yankee go home!" The offending words that triggered the inhospitable response was "Let us learn together" by which the Senator sought to convey an attitude of friendly equality. Unfortunately, that exact phrase had been used previously by North American politicians on Latin American territory, so according to a Chilean official, it had this special meaning:

> The phrase, "Let us learn together," would have gotten by in Italian, Swedish, or Russian. This audience assumed when an American says it, he is being a hypocrite because he is representing a government which has

repeatedly taken advantage of Latin American countries through the use of both military, political, and economic might. Often when the United States is about to put the pressure on us to do something, they make it clear that we are working together.

In this hemisphere, the interface between its northern and southern inhabitants is a contrast in opportunities and problems. The opportunities for mutual enrichment through cultural exchanges, scientific collaboration, educational and economic assistance, and efforts promoting hemispheric peace. The problems proliferate because issues like these cry out for creative solutions from Pan Americans:

1. Lack of North/South dialogue and synergistic endeavors that benefit the peoples of both continents, such as macroprojects to renew the infrastructures of societies in need, or to provide adequate food and shelter for the poor.
2. Instability in some Latin states which have yet to become nations, or who suffer from archaic political, justice and economic systems.
3. Insecurity caused by growing deviant behavior as expressed in anti-social actions such as terrorism and drug trafficking, or the expanding struggle between democratic ideals and totalitarian realities.
4. Inability to establish a meaningful North/South dialogue and collaborative exchange in the Americas, instead of exploitation and dependence.

Yet for the most part, Pan America is a free enterprise system and market of vast potential. It borders the Pacific Rim on the West, and can benefit from the trade shift from the Atlantic to the Pacific. It can become a laboratory of cooperation, and in the next chapter we will examine some of the possibilities for synergy, including joint ventures. For now, the global manager is well advised to view the whole before we go to the parts, beginning with North America.

In that context, foreign nationals from other continents should understand that the popular Latin perception of the U.S. Americans is to characterize their northern neighbors as the Yankees or "gringos." The typical Latin seems to be neutral about Canadians because they are so far north. Canadian contact with their southern neighbors beyond the U.S.A. has been limited. Many Latin Americans have a love-hate relationship about the States. They admire its equality and economic progress, and at the personal level may like many Americans; many seek to live in the U.S. because of its opportunities. But many Latins also distrust, envy, and fear "Big Brother." This is especially true for Latin countries that border or are near the U.S., such as Cuba or Mexico. Too many North Americans, on the other hand, ignore the needs and possibilities in Latin America, and do not pursue collaboration with these neighboring states and peoples; Europe or Asia gets all their attention. Even government officials tend to ignore and treat the Latin countries with benign neglect until a crisis erupts. The United States and Canada lack clear-cut Latin American policies and pro-

grams, especially of a long-term nature, that would promote mutual cooperation between north and south, as well as improved cultural understanding. It
is as if Latin Americans have yet to truly enter into the North American consciousness, while the latter seems to be in the Latin consciousness in too many
negative ways.

The U.S. has made many efforts to build better relations with its Pan American neighbors. Though such endeavors may have been premature, unsuccess-
ful, or underutilized, they contain seeds for future synergism.

NORTHERN AMERICAS' CULTURAL DEVELOPMENT—ABORIGINES

Eskimos and Indians

In the far north of the Americas are two native peoples caught in a culture
gap—the Eskimos and the Indians. Essentially nomadic hunters by tradition,
they have both been harmed and helped by the rapid advancement of "white
civilization" into their lives. With the introduction of U.S. and Canadian government health and education programs, their life expectancy and levels of
consciousness have risen. But so has their frustration, despair, and social deterioration. Some of these indigenous peoples have acculturated to the modern
way of life of their North American counterparts, have graduated from universities, and hold important posts in government or business. Others have suc-
cumbed to alcoholism, drugs, or even suicide, especially the young. Their
problems and potentials are similar on or off reservations; whether in the U.S.
state of Alaska or the Canadian Northwest Territories; whether above or below
the U.S./Canadian border.

A recent volume, *Indian Givers* discusses how the misnamed Indians of the
Americas transformed the world. Its author, Wetherford (1988) makes a con-
vincing case that the contributions of the Native Americans to our economy
and culture have been consistently underrated, if not ignored. His conclusion is
even more telling—we are allowing the Indian cultures to die away without
learning what they have to teach us.

In reality, tribal or aboriginal peoples everywhere face the same dilemma
brought on by accelerating social and technological change. Whether an Inuit
in Hudson Bay or a Navajo in northern Arizona, the confrontation with too
rapid cultural change leaves the natives bewildered, confused, and almost
overwhelmed. The rate of innovation in traditional societies is slow, while it
rises astronomically in modern societies in the midst of transition. The traditional culture is past oriented, while the modern society is future-oriented, interpreting history as progressive movement. Unfortunately, Western ethnocentrism—even among anthropologists—labeled these peoples in the hunting

stage of development as primitive and backward. A racist mentality would view such people as "underdeveloped" because of some biological inferiority. In fact, such peoples may be quite developed within their own context, and more in harmony with nature than modern persons. They seem to possess a better sense of ecology, energy conservation, food distribution, and overall happiness than many of their so-called civilized counterparts of today.

In the process of trying to enhance the native peoples of the Americas, corporate tycoons, political leaders, and welfare administrators might do well to try to understand and appreciate the values and assets in such "primitive" cultures. Then we may be in a position to create a synergy with them relative to their contribution in modern society, and how our modern systems might better meet their needs. Thus, when transnational enterprises, like giant energy corporations, move into the territories of Eskimo, Aleuts and Indian peoples, a cooperative approach that demonstrates concern for the natives is more productive for all in contrast to a destructive/exploitive strategy.

Culturally sensitive management of petrochemical companies is beginning to work with tribal leaders so that the Indians can develop their own energy companies with technical training and assistance. Similarly, Eskimos are being assisted in establishing cooperatives so that they may develop their own economic units in the fishing industry. The U.S. government and courts have been ruling favorably about honoring old treaties and making financial restitution for lands stolen from the Indians. Under new government policies the native peoples are being urged and trained to provide management leadership in agencies that affect their lives, such as the Bureau of Indian Affairs and Public Health Service. They are even provided assistance through the Small Business Administration to start up their own minority enterprises.

The Eskimos and Indians of North America have paid a high price for acculturation. Many of their peoples suffer mental and physical, as well as economic, handicaps that range from alcoholism to suicide. But with cooperation and collaboration by their fellow citizens, these proud and resourceful peoples can be developed to help themselves and create a new place in the superindustrial age.

This discussion focuses on the tribal peoples not just because they are among the most neglected inhabitants of North America—that is the problem of aboriginals in most countries from Australia to India—but also because the vast natural resources of Alaska and Northern Canada, as well as on the Indian reservations, are now attracting the attention of multinational corporations and even high-technology companies. Joseph DiStefano, professor of business at The University of Western Ontario, has published some interesting observations about "Managing in Other Cultures" (*The Business Quarterly*, Autumn 1972). Among the "do's and don'ts" that he provides are two reproduced here because they center upon issues of "doing business with Eskimos:"

Making Decisions with Cultural Sensitivity

DON'T assume away the problems. Most case studies reveal the same pattern. Managers are so attracted by the potential of the cross-cultural venture that they are blind to the problems. A good example comes from the Canadian rail system in their efforts to build a line in the North. The company had total command of the technology; it knew the demanding environmental conditions and put a well-intentioned and sensitive manager in charge of a project to hire Eskimos to help build and subsequently maintain the line. Undoubtedly motivated by expected mutual advantages to both the company and the Eskimos, the firm failed to consider culturally related problems which quickly surfaced when the Eskimos and their families were brought to the training center and then put to work on the line. When hunting season arrived, men disappeared into the bush. Trained as engineers, the Eskimos found it difficult to keep the trains on schedule. When they got tired, they simply stopped the long trains on the single track and slept. This was their view of normal behavior which didn't take into account delaying other trains. When the company sought remedies, Eskimos misinformed their supervisors (when their friends were present, but corrected the information when their friends left the employ of the firm). The results of these and other problems were increased costs, hostility from other minority groups working on location, and the eventual loss of all but 3 of the 80 Eskimos that the company hoped to retain as permanent employees.

DO include cultural problems in estimating costs and developing preventive measures. Companies used to operating cross-culturally are often prone to being seduced by their previous expertise into ignoring this warning, especially when introducing a change in a situation where they have long experience. A firm with experience in the Arctic predating Confederation provides an illustration. Based on their excellent experience in hiring Eskimo clerks and identifying significant potential savings (for example, in transportation), the company decided to employ the Eskimos in retail managerial positions in their home communities. Soon the pressures of strong family relationships were in evidence. One manager, bowing to this pressure, extended credit to customers in excess of their earnings for several years in the future. With a sense of futility after realizing his plight, he permitted customers to purchase whatever and whenever they wanted and kept sketchy records on cigarette packs, old envelopes, etc. Other managers responded in the other extreme by inflating prices, extending no credit and being miserly in their fur pricing. One man was reported to be incredibly tight. There was a file for sale in his store priced at two fox skins. When the customer only had one skin to offer, the manager broke the file in half! In order to insulate himself from family pressures, he over-protected his store, and his relatives and neighbors lived in fear of him.

Albeit extreme examples, these incidents highlight the need to anticipate cultural problems. But, as these cases show, experience doesn't necessarily provide *pre*cognition. An ad hoc inventory of past problems isn't the same as a conceptual scheme or framework that suggests problems that are likely to occur. For example, in the case just cited the policy change might have been examined for the effects of the Eskimo's notions of family values and their interplay with the economic system.

American Indians

There are approximately 1.4 million American Indians in the U.S. of whom over half are on reservations. The average annual income is below poverty level and their unemployment rate is the highest in the country.

When America was discovered, there were probably less than one million Indians living in what is now the U.S. These Indians were scattered and their tribal organizations were unrelated. Columbus wrote of the Indians, "They are a loving people. . . . They love their neighbors as themselves, and their speech is the sweetest and gentlest in the world." Many early colonists intermarried with Indians and this was motivated largely by social and cultural factors. For example, an Indian wife was an asset to a fur trader in teaching him the language and customs of the tribe from which he bought furs. In early New England, however, Indian women had little use in the trading and farming communities and intermarriage was rare.

The U.S. government, which came into existence with the adoption of the Constitution, began its relationship with Indians by considering the various tribes as national entities and negotiated with them for land. An imperialist relationship with the Indians was thus begun. One of the early debates in the Colorado legislature was concerning bounties for the "destruction of Indians and skunks." The remark of a U.S. general in 1869, "The only good Indians I ever saw were dead," is an expression known to most Americans and conveys an implicit attitude about the conflict.

One of the negative images that many have of American Indians is that they are a savage group of hostile persons who are uncivilized. In books describing Indian and white relationships, when Indians killed settlers, it was a "massacre," but the settlers did not massacre, they only "fought" or "battled" the Indians. When Americans think of colonialism, it generally means things like the British in India but not Americans in Georgia.

Who is the Indian? An Indian is an individual whose origins can be found in the indigenous peoples of America. What are some cultural differences between Indian culture and the mainstream American culture? Faherty in the *American Indian* points out three fundamental differences, but there are many.

In the mainstream culture, time is to be "used, saved, and spent." People are paid for their time. Indians generally view time as a continuum that is related to the rising and setting of the sun and to the changes in the seasons.

In the mainstream culture, decision-making is based on authority. Some people have authority to make decisions and others do not. Authority in Indian cultures is more horizontal than vertical because of the necessity of reaching unanimity on a decision before any action will be taken.

Most Americans live pretty much for the future. We ask our children what they want to be when they grow up. In contrast, Indian children are not asked the same question, because they already are—they are children and they do not have to wait to be.

Understanding the Indian way of life provides us with a challenge and an opportunity. We can learn to develop skills and to work with Indians without destroying their dignity and allow them to change at their own pace.

Within the continental United States, many of the native Americans have passed into the mainstream culture. For those who still live on government reservations, painful progress is made to gain greater control over their own administration of their own affairs, whether this be in schools and services, or within the Federal Bureau of Indian Affairs. With recent financial settlements through the Courts over abrogated treaty rights and lost lands, some tribes have established modern corporations to manage their natural resources and to enter into joint ventures with major companies for economic development purposes, even in the field of high technology on the reservations. North American Indians never had the white man's sense of private property, and tribal culture thought in terms of collective responsibility for the preservation of the land and nature's gifts. Today the modern ecology and nature movements are catching up to the aboriginal's concern for the environment.

Foreign observers of the North American scene are reminded that aboriginal tribes moved in the past back and forth across the borders that now separate the U.S.A. from its northern neighbor, Canada. So let us now turn our attention to those other citizens of this part of the hemisphere—the Canadians. Almost half a million of them are classified as of native ancestry, and three quarters live on reservations. These are grouped by their government in four categories—status Indians (registered formally under the Indian Act); non-status Indians who have not registered with the government; Metis (descendents of mixed aboriginals and European ancestry); and Intuits, a distinct cultural group who generally live north of the tree line and mostly speak their own language (Inuktitut). A 1985 change in Canadian law has caused a dramatic rise in Indian population figures, for the count of the natives will now include Indian women who marry Canadians of non-Indian ancestry.

CANADA

Canada is a bilingual and multicultural country, whose more than 26.4 million people live in 10 provinces, 2 federal districts, and the Northwest Territories (which comprise a third of Canada), and the Yukon Territory in the Far North.

Canada is a nation in the midst of an identity crisis between its two major cultural heritages—English and French—and with a powerful southern neighbor, the U.S.A. When the matter is resolved and the process of national maturation is completed, Canada may either become a world superpower, or split into a new geographical realignment. Although a referendum a decade ago rejected separatism, the national identity crises of Canada is again revealed in a recent Gallup Poll *(Los Angeles Times,* August 16, 1989, p. 2)—28% of its citizens still believe French-speaking Quebec should become an independent country, 27% of the respondents were English-speaking. Futurists speculate that if Quebec were ever to become independent, then in time the western Canadian provinces might align themselves with the western U.S. states to create a separate political entity or some new regionalism, while the northeast provinces might do the same with the northeast states. Meanwhile, the country is legally governed under The Constitution Act (Bracken 1985).

Although Canada was established as a political entity in 1807 through the British North American Act, only recently has the House of Parliament in the United Kingdom voted to amend it so the Canadian constitution could be brought home and "patriated."

Foreign multinational managers seeking to do business in Canada or form joint ventures with Canadians should better understand this country's vast resources and potential, and complex ethnic groups.

Throughout Canada, the family is the center of society, and homes are often passed along from one generation to another. Nowhere is this more true than in the central province of Quebec, the heart of French Canada. If you have some insights into Latin Europe, you may better comprehend the French-Canadian. (See Chapter 16 for culture specifics on the French.) It is a culture that is somewhat unsynergistic and very individualistic. People tend to be more reserved until you get to know them well. As a minority in Canada, the citizens of French heritage feel they have been discriminated against and a separatist movement was launched. This human rights struggle has raised the consciousness of both groups in the country, and has increased the legal privileges of the French-speaking in employment and other social arenas. Remember, French sovereignty existed in this part of Canada since Cartier landed in 1534 until 1763 when "New France" was ceded to Britain. The Roman Catholic tradition dominates, though some schools are operated by Protestants. The major industries are mining, forestry, hydroelectricity and agriculture.

As the task of a nation building toward unity proceeds, Canadians are more aware of their rich cultural diversity and natural resources. The country's economic wealth is centered in forests, petroleum, natural gas, and iron ore. Sprawling democratic Canada has one of the world's highest standards of living and its people are very industrious. From a management standpoint, workers are very punctual, but the fun-loving French Canadians are more easy-going and less time-conscious. Operating a bilingual business is a challenge, but then French-speaking citizens can be an advantage in international commerce. The English spoken in Canada is slightly different from the American version (e.g., British pronunciations, Scottish diphthong sounds like "about"). Proud of their country, sensitive about their relations with the U.S. and comparisons to it, fiercely independent while self-deprecating as a people, Canadians resent being lumped together with the other "Americans" below the 49th parallel. Despite that and the U.S. media/economic dominance, the relations between North Americans is generally good and friendly. There is tremendous potential for synergy between the northern neighboring countries who in many ways are more alike than different.

For those doing business in Canada, it is wise to remember that they are not culturally "just like" their counterparts in the United States. Normally, Canadians are open and friendly, but conservative—more so in the Atlantic and Ontario regions than in the Western provinces; more reserved than their neighbors to the South, Canadians tend to observe formalities and rules of etiquette that might be overlooked in the U.S.A.

Patriotic, law-abiding, proud of their dual heritage, Canadians also realize that their nation is vast—the second largest country in the world after the U.S.S.R. Therefore, they resent being patronized or a "slick salesman" approach. With a strong economy, high levels of education and health services, Canadians are confident of their future and welcome both foreign business and immigration. Fortunately, the separatist movement is receding and political stability currently reigns. Remember that Canada is very cosmopolitan; in addition to its main cultural heritage of English and French, there are strong ethnic groups of German, Scandinavian, Asian, Dutch, Ukranian, Polish, and Italian minorities that often retain customs of their mother countries. It is an interesting cultural mosaic. Recall, too, that the government operates on the model of the British parliamentary system under a Prime Minister, the Armed Forces have been streamlined into a single defense organization, and it does not have a free-market economy for Canada fears foreign domination of its economy. As a part of the British Commonwealth system, many peoples of those countries, such as India and Pakistan, have relocated to Canada and become its citizens. The latest cultural enhancement to the Canadian west coast is coming from Asia. Apart from Indo-Chinese refugees and Japanese investors, the biggest influx is from Hong Kong residents with Commonwealth passports who fear the oncoming take-over of that former colony by the People's Republic of China. These are talented, largely affluent, Chinese entrepreneurs who will invest much in their new country.

UNITED STATES OF AMERICA

That is the official title, and the citizens refer to themselves as "Americans," while many others call them "Yanks" or "Yankees," a nickname that originally referred to the inhabitants of the New England or northeastern States. The nation consists of the mainland—the central portion of the North American continent, or 48 States; the state of Alaska in the northwestern tip of the hemisphere; the state of Hawaii, which is located west of the mainland in the Pacific Ocean; and the District of Columbia with its federal capital of Washington. The Commonwealth of Puerto Rico will be discussed, along with the Virgin Island Territory in the Hispanic America. Since the end of WWII, the U.S.A. has administered 11 trust territories in the South Pacific over which it has gradually been relinquishing control. Between 1975 and 1980, accords were negotiated with the native islanders to establish the Commonwealths of the northern Marianas, the Marshall Islands, and the Federated States of Micronesia; and the Republic of Palau. The 1980 census indicates a population of 226.5 million people, with a 17% increase of black Americans to 26.5 million. There are 1 million American Indians and 3.5 million Asian and Pacific Islanders. This federal republic will probably have 250 million people by the year 2000.

The U.S. is a multicultural society on the way to becoming bilingual. Although the American version of English is spoken with a variety of dialects (18 or more), Spanish is emerging as a second language. American speech is as varied as the country's geography and climate, which is temperate on the coasts, subtropical in the south with extensive deserts and widely different seasons/rainfalls. The part that western Europeans find most difficult to comprehend is the immense size and difference of the mainland. The fourth largest nation in the world, the U.S.A. has been thought of popularly as a "melting pot" of diverse cultures. It is true that it is a land of immigrants—from the time of colonists (English/French/Spanish), plus the African slave and nineteenth century European influx, to the present waves of refugees from IndoChina, Cuba, and Haiti. The population is largely white, Anglo-Saxon, but the significant, growing minorities of Hispanics, blacks, and Asians as well as the native American Indians, are rapidly changing that configuration.

A free enterprise economic system prevails, and the nation's industrial/agricultural/technological leadership in the world market is awesome but under challenge. A quick overview of the culture might reveal these generalizations, subject to many differences among people and in specific places:

1. *Goal and achievement oriented*—Americans think they can accomplish just about anything, given enough time, money, and technology.
2. *Highly organized and institutionalistic*—Americans prefer a society that is strong institutionally, secure, and tidy or well kept.
3. *Freedom-loving and self-reliant*—Americans fought a revolution and subsequent wars to preserve their concept of democracy, so they resent too much control or interference, especially by government or external forces. They believe an ideal that all persons are created equal; though they sometimes fail to live that ideal fully, they strive through law to promote equal opportunity and to confront their own racism or prejudice.

They also idealize the self-made person who rises from poverty and adversity, and think they can influence and create their future. Control of one's destiny is popularly expressed as "doing your own thing." Americans think, for the most part, that with determination and initiative, one can achieve whatever he or she sets out to do and thus fulfill that individual's human potential.

4. *Work oriented and efficient*—Americans possess a strong work ethic, though they are learning in the present generation to enjoy leisure time constructively. They are very time conscious and efficient in doing things. They tinker with gadgets and technological systems, always searching for easier, better, more efficient ways of accomplishment.

5. *Friendly and informal*—Americans rejected the traditional privileges of royalty and class, but do defer to those with affluence and power. Although informal in greeting and dress, they are a noncontact culture (e.g., avoid embracing in public usually) and maintain certain physical/psychological distance with others (e.g., about two feet).

6. *Competitive and aggressive*—Americans in play or business generally are so oriented because of their drives to achieve and succeed. This is partially traced to their heritage of having to overcome a wilderness and hostile elements in their environment.

7. *Values in transition*—Traditional American values of family loyalty, respect and care of the aged, marriage and the nuclear family, patriotism, material acquisition, forthrightness, and the like are undergoing profound reevaluation and the people search for new meanings.

8. *Generosity*—Although Americans seemingly emphasize material values, they are sharing people as has been demonstrated in the Marshall Fund, foreign aid programs, refugee assistance, and their willingness at home and abroad to espouse a good cause and to help neighbors in need. They tend to be altruistic and some would say naive as a people.

In terms of U.S. social institutions, three are worth noting here. Education is viewed as a means of self-development, so participation in the process and within the classroom is encouraged—it is mandatory until age 16 and 97% finish at least elementary school, so the literacy rate is fairly high. There is a public (largely free of cost) and private school system up through the university level of education; the latter are either independent or religious affiliated schools. The average family is nuclear, consisting of only parents and children, if there are any. More than half of American women work outside the home, and females have considerable and improving opportunity for personal and professional growth, guaranteed by law. The home has been matriarchal and child-oriented, though today there are many single-parent families and childless couples by choice. The society is youth oriented, and usually cares for the elderly outside the home in institutions. It is experimenting with new family arrangements from couples living together without the legal sanction to group communes. Politically, the government operates on the Constitution of 1787 and the Bill of Rights, which provides a three-branch approach of checks and balances. Currently, there are increasing problems of disillusionment in political leaders, corruption in public offices, and a push toward decentralization or the confederation of states concept (e.g., emphasis on states rights and less government regulation over individual lives).

The Americans too are in the midst of profound social change, and even an identity crisis. Among the factors contributing to this maturation challenge are:

1. The lessening of world leadership and influence forces a reassessment of the national self-image. After much success in its war abroad, Korea and Vietnam proved to be costly and questionable conflicts that mass media brought into American homes. In addition to inflation and economic setbacks, American confidence was also undermined by the hostage crisis in Iran and Beirut. All of this coupled with assassinations of the country's leaders in the 1960s led to an undermining of the national will, organized public protests, and the need now to reexpress national goals. In the 1980s, America's economy is robust, patriotism is high, entrepreneurialism and high technology ventures flourish, and the people are optimistic about space developments both for commerce and defense, in spite of the space shuttle, *Challenger*, disaster. However, these Americans are also frustrated by terrorism and the limits it places on the use of the country's power and military.
2. Latinization of the U.S. is affecting the character of the country and its communication. (This is discussed later in this chapter.)
3. Transition into a post-industrial society is happening first and faster in the U.S. than in most other countries because of scientific and technological advances. The values and life-styles brought on by the industrial stage of development are being reexamined and new replacements sought for more effective coping in cyberculture. (Chapter 7 described this in some detail under the heading metaindustrial work culture.)

The impact of such contemporary trends depends on where you are in America, for there are considerable regional differences and subcultures. For example, the clear-cut distinctions since the Civil War between Northerners and Southerners are eroding, as many northern Yankees move south to the "sun belt" for jobs, retirement, or improved quality of life. Above all, Americans are a very mobile people—geographically and organizationally. There is also a big difference between eastern and western life-styles and attitudes: the eastern U.S. is thought to be more establishment, conservative in thinking, over-organized and deteriorating; the western U.S. is seen as more casual, innovative, and flexible.

One aspect for foreign readers to note is that Americans are becoming less isolationist and provincial in their thinking and actions. Mass travel abroad, international communications and business, more foreign students and visitors have affected American perceptions. Furthermore, the impact of foreigners is currently considerable—more outsiders are being transferred to the U.S. for business or professional purposes, and more foreign capital is being heavily invested here. (Corporate acquisitions and property purchases by Canadians, Japanese, Europeans, Middle Easterners and South Africans are considerable, and have even caused some fear and backlash.) Foreign tourism in the U.S. has increased dramatically. The influx of refugees and legal and illegal immigrants has strained existing social systems. But Americans are generally of a cooperative spirit, so they are open to international influences in their society, and usually support endeavors that will promote regional or world synergy. The presence of the United Nations headquarters in New York City is symbolic of this.

CULTURAL ASPECTS OF THE UNITED STATES

What is America? Is there a mainstream culture shared by the "average" American? Did the melting pot theory work in practice? Is the United States a pluralistic society? Is it a multicultural society? What is America?

This chapter assumes that there is a mainstream culture (macroculture) and many minority groups (microcultures) functioning either within or on the periphery of the macroculture. The following list, taken from Stewart and others, is a summary of what can be called U.S. mainstream cultural assumptions and values. The main categories are the mode of activity, social relationships, motivation, the perception of the world, and the perception of self.

I. Definition of Activity
    1. How do people approach activity?
       • concern with "doing," progress, change external environment
       • optimistic, striving
    2. What is the desirable pace of life?
       • fast, busy
       • driving
    3. How important are goals in planning?
       • stress means, procedures, techniques
    4. What are important goals in life?
       • material goals
       • comfort and absence of pain
       • activity
    5. Where does responsibility for decisions lie?
       • responsibility lies with each individual
    6. At what level do people live?
       • operational, goals evaluated in terms of consequence

7. On what basis do people evaluate?
   - utility (Does it work?)
8. Who should make decisions?
   - the people affected
9. What is the nature of problem-solving?
   - planning behavior
   - anticipates consequences
10. What is the nature of learning?
    - learner is active (student-centered learning)

II. Definition of Social Relations

1. How are roles defined?
   - attained
   - loosely
   - generally
2. How do people relate to others whose status is different?
   - stress equality
   - minimize differences
   - stress informality and spontaneity
3. How are sex roles defined?
   - similar, overlapping
   - sex equality
   - friends of both sexes
   - less legitimized
4. What are members' rights and duties in a group?
   - assumes limited liability
   - joins group to seek own goals
   - active members can influence group
5. How do people judge others?
   - specific abilities of interests
   - task-centered
   - fragmentary involvement
6. What is the meaning of friendship?
   - social friendship (short commitment, friends shared)
7. What is the nature of social reciprocity?
   - real only
   - nonbinding (Dutch treat)
   - equal (Dutch treat)
8. How do people regard friendly aggression in social interaction?
   - acceptable, interesting, fun

III. Motivation

1. What is motivating force?
   - achievement

2. How is person-person competition evaluated?
   - as constructive, healthy

IV. Perception of the World (World View)

1. What is the (natural) World like?
   - physical
   - mechanical
2. How does the world operate?
   - in a rational, learnable, controllable manner
   - chance and probability
3. What is the nature of man?
   - apart from nature or from any hierarchy
   - impermanent, not fixed, changeable
4. What are the relationships between man and nature?
   - good is unlimited
   - man should modify nature for his ends
   - good health and material comforts expected and desired
5. What is the nature of truth? goodness?
   - tentative (working-type)
   - relative to circumstances
   - experience analyzed in separate components dichotomies
6. How is time defined? Valued?
   - future (anticipation)
   - precise units
   - limited resource
   - lineal
7. What is the nature of property?
   - private ownership important as extension of self

V. Perception of the Self and the Individual

1. In what sort of terms is self defined?
   - diffuse, changing terms
   - flexible behavior
2. Where does a person's identity seem to be?
   - within the self (achievement)
3. Nature of the individual
   - separate aspects (intent, thought, act, biographical background)
4. On whom should a person place reliance?
   - self
   - impersonal organizations
5. What kind of person is valued and respected? What qualities?
   - youthful (vigorous)
6. What is the basis of social control?
   - persuasion, appeal to the individual
   - guilt

The dominant mode of activity in mainstream American society is "doing." Americans have a preoccupation with time, organization, and the use of resources so that everything has to have a purpose that is measurable. "Getting things done" is an American characteristic. In our social relationships we assume that everyone is equal and this removes the need for elaborate forms of social address. Our social relationships are characterized by informality and social reciprocities are much less clearly defined. Mainstream Americans are motivated by achievements and accomplishments. Our identity and, to a certain extent, our self-worth is measured by what we achieve. We also assume that the world is material rather than spiritual and man's purpose is to overcome or conquer the forces of nature. Mainstream Americans also see themselves as individual and unique. Is this an accurate description of ourselves? Like most descriptions it is probably partially accurate.

In attempting to understand ourselves, it is useful to listen to and hear what aspects of our life and culture are puzzling to other people. John Fieg and Lenore Yaffee (1977) suggest the following areas of concern for foreign visitors to the United States. They are presented to serve as a further reflection on aspects of mainstream U.S. culture.

Pace of Life. Visitors from a variety of African, Asian, and Latin American countries are amazed and often somewhat distressed at the rapid pace of American life and the accompanying emphasis on punctuality and efficiency.

Friendship. Because Americans are generally gregarious on first meeting someone, visitors often mistake this strong "come-on" for the beginning of a deep reciprocal friendship. This is because in many societies there is much more initial reserve in interpersonal relations, particularly with strangers. For many visitors, the American comes on too strong too soon and then fails to follow up with the implicitly promised friendship.

Service and Egalitarianism. The sense of egalitarianism on the part of American waiters, taxi drivers, bellboys, etc., causes them to perform their services in a brusque, businesslike manner, without the cordial (and from the American point of view, fawning) manner that many visitors are accustomed to at home. The visitor often compounds his problem by giving what the American service person perceives as an order from on high, thereby causing the service to become even more surly.

Emotional Expressiveness. Americans seem to stand near the center of an emotional spectrum that extends out to embrace the effervescent Latins at one extreme and the cooly subdued Southeast Asians at the other. While we appear unemotional and cold to the Latins, we may appear hyperbolic and impulsive to the Asians.

Individualism, Freedom, and Privacy. Some visitors are deeply impressed by the individual freedom, particularly in the political arena, that an American enjoys. Others are appalled, however, by what they sometimes call "too much freedom" in terms of excessive individualism, and cite lack of gun control laws as an example of what they mean.

Self-reliance and the Nuclear Family. Visitors have ambivalent feelings about the self-reliant American nuclear family. Some are impressed by the males' handling of household chores and the children's independent assertiveness. Others see the American pattern as abrasive, somewhat chaotic, and lacking the strong extended family supports to which they are accustomed.

Informality and Morality. Because many visitors come from societies that stress neat, formal, and (by American standards) conservative clothing styles, they are sometimes shocked by what they view as Americans' slovenly way of dressing. Often they tend to equate this informality with immorality, and they are persuaded that America is on the way to moral ruin when they observe provocative clothing styles and public displays of affection. Currently, the U.S. is in the midst of strained public and legal debate over ethical and moral issues related to birth control, abortion, genetic technology, euthanasia, and the death penalty (e.g., life control).

Crime. Reports have reached the four corners of the world about the high crime rate in American cities. Many new arrivals are thus highly concerned for their personal safety, although some are surprised and somewhat encouraged to find that the violence level is not as high as they had anticipated. We have tried to allay the fears of the visitors and at the same time to caution them about the very real danger of crime—to strike in their minds some kind of balance between incapacitating dread and complete abandon. As in urban areas anywhere in the world, the wise traveler avoids certain areas of a city at any time, travels if possible in groups, and checks with reliable locals on safe procedures, especially on airport security and the carrying of valuables.

Global problems of substance abuse presently plague America. The rapid growth of alchoholism, drug and gambling addiction, women and child abuse is seen as symptomatic of "future shock" and a major contributor to crime and violent behavior. In 1989, drug abuse alone was costing the U.S. private sector $100 billion annually. Indicative of the breakdown in social order is the "National War on Drugs," the rise in the use of guns and automatic weapons, the increase in urban gangs (especially among minorities and disenfranchised peoples), and expanding homeless citizens (many of whom are mentally ill). At the same time, "white collar crime" and corruption in public office is also increasing. Yet, economic and budget constraints have lead to a lessening of expenditures on social services and prisoner rehabilitation. Traditional inhibitors of violent and deviant behavior—the church, family, school, and social taboos—are weakening as the society experiences trauma while transitioning to another way of life and another century.

Tipping, Taxes, and "Sales." To many visitors to the U.S.A., tipping appears to be giving something extra for what the waiter is already paid to do, and the failure to include the sales tax in the stated price of an article is sometimes construed as a trap for the unwary. They also want to know how they can distinguish a genuine "sale" from a phony.

Race Relations. Comments from international visitors concerning the current racial situation in the U.S. mirror the confused, conflicting views expressed by Americans. Sharp attacks on lingering racial discrimination are mingled with expressions of surprise that race relations is not as big a problem as some visitors had been led to believe.

Teacher-Student Relations. Coming from cultures where the teacher is near the top of the social hierarchy, many visitors are stunned by the slouching, "disrespectful" demeanor of the students and the easy, often flippant, interchange between the teacher and students in the U.S. Many, however, come to appreciate the freedom of expression that exists in American schools. Generally, inadequate selection, training, and compensation of educators in the U.S. contribute to lessening the importance of education and those who teach, despite the critical role in a democracy of the learning process to provide an informed public.

Lack of Knowledge about Their Countries. Particularly disheartening to many visitors is the American's lack of knowledge of and interest in their home countries and cultures. This attitude has developed because of our longstanding geographical isolation coupled with the immigrant experience, in which to become a full-fledged member of the "New-World" one had to cast aside the customs and culture of the homeland.

Philip Slater (1970) has suggested that three human desires are profoundly frustrated by the American culture:

1. The desire for *community*—the wish to live in trust and fraternal cooperation with one's fellows in a total and visible collective entity.
2. The desire for *engagement*—the wish to come directly to grips with social and interpersonal problems and to confront on equal terms an environment that is not composed of ego-extensions.
3. The desire for *dependence*—the wish to share responsibility for the control of one's impulses and the direction of one's life.

Slater is referring to mainstream Americans. In some microcultures in the U.S., these frustrated human desires in the mainstream culture are more strongly present.

On July 8, 1985, *Time,* a national magazine, did a special issue on "Immigrants, the Changing Face of America." It noted that in 1984, 600,000 immigrants came legally, and perhaps an equal number illegally. (In 1990, experts estimate 8 million illegal aliens.) Why do so many come seeking to live permanently in the USA? Among the answers offered by the newcomers of diverse national origin, social class or ideology, this quotation from the story summarizes their reasoning:

> "What binds Americans to one another, regardless of ethnicity or religion, is an American civic culture," says Brandeis Professor Fuchs. "It is the basis for the *unum* in *E pluribus unum*. It is a complex of ideals, behaviors, institutions, symbols and heroes connected by American history and its great documents, the Declaration of Independence, the Bill of Rights, the Gettysburg Address. It is backed by a civil religion giving transcendent significance to those ideals. And it is the basis for accepting ethnic diversity while protecting individual rights. An American can be as ethnic as he or she wishes in private actions, but in public actions, the rules of the civic culture are binding."

There is a unique symbiosis because the U.S.A. shares a border with Mexico of 1,939 miles. This First/Third world mix has created what *Time* (July 8, 1985) dubs a "third country." It is most evident in 700 twin plant projects by which Fortune 500 companies set up joint ventures or subsidiaries inside the Mexican border, mixing American and Mexican managers in cities like San-Diego-Tijuana, or Juarez, in Texas and in Mexico. White collar workers of both countries interface both on the job and socially in such projects that dot the Rio Grande River and valley from Tijuana to Matamoros or from San Diego to Brownsville on the Gulf of Mexico. The residents who straddle this border, including Mexcali, Nogales, Laredo, form a new economic zone, are more affluent, more tolerant of each other, and mutually reliant in the pursuit of a decent living. Anthropologists call it, "The Americanization of Mexico and the Mexicanization of Americans" as culturally different neighbors learn to become friend and create synergy.

MICROCULTURES OF THE UNITED STATES

Walter Lippman introduced the term "stereotype" in his book on public opinion over 50 years ago. He used the word in the sense of a rigid and standardized picture that people have of others. To demonstrate the diversity in the group called "Americans," we began this chapter with a discussion of two U.S. microcultures—Eskimos and Indians. Now consider two more American microcultures:

- Blacks or African-Americans
- Latinos or Hispanics (Chicanos and Puerto Ricans)

Answer the following questions about each of these groups:

1. What is their communication style (nonverbal as well as verbal)?
2. What clothing do they wear at work?
3. What kind of people are they?
4. What are their work habits and attitudes?
5. What is their sense of time?
6. What kinds of food do they enjoy?
7. What other customs, traditions or behaviors are you aware of?

The chances are we were able to respond to each of these questions to a certain extent. We may have ideas about each of these cultures even though we may never have met anyone from that cultural group. In many ways you would probably conclude they are different from mainstream Americans.

In order to develop authentic and effective relationships with persons from these subcultures, it is important to not only accept and overlook, so to speak, racial differences but to be aware of, fully accept, value, and appreciate these differences. The following brief descriptions are intended to be starting points in this challenge.

Other minority cultures or groups of people living in the United States, such as Chinese-Americans, Japanese-Americans, Jews, as well as persons who are handicapped and senior citizens, to name but a few, could also be considered. Each of these groups has aspects of their lives and priorities or values that differ in part from mainstream America. To work effectively with such peoples, it is necessary to be aware of and respect uniqueness in all dimensions.

The material presented for these microcultures does not follow a particular format. Rather, certain themes or aspects of their cultures are indicated in a summary fashion.

Black Americans

The United States of America has been largely a white society. But as Jesse Jackson's "Rainbow Coalition" demonstrated in the 1984 Presidential election, times are changing—the skin color of the U.S. population is being enriched. We know of French, Italian, and Spanish explorers of the U.S., but historians told us little of the Africans who not only assisted in the discovery of "America," but fought in its revolution and helped to tame its western frontier. Because most Africans were brought to this country against their will and then misused as slaves, their contribution to the building of the nation, like their human rights, tended to be ignored by the mainstream of the population. Originally called Negroes or worse, those dark skinned Americans prefer today to be designated simply as "black," or African-Americans.

A Civil War was fought to liberate their ancestors and give them full citizenship, but for their descendents, the struggle for Civil Rights and equal opportunity under the law still goes on for black Americans. Despite the accomplishments of black colleges and universities, as well as black entertainers and athletes, the process of integration into the mainstream for this microculture has been slow. However, in the past few decades, the black middle and upper class has grown dramatically, while black teenage unemployment, black single mothers on welfare, and black deaths from violence within their own communities have also risen. The consciousness of mainstream America regarding its black brothers and sisters has risen, so there is hope that by the 21st century, blacks in America will experience the full benefits of this democracy. Although as a people we are impressed by the feats of black astronauts, politicans, and executives, there is much to be done together if all our black citizens are to share in the American dream.

During the past forty years, barriers within the military services to the advancement of African-Americans have been withdrawn so that now a black, Gen. Colin L. Powell, heads the Armed Forces Joint Chiefs of Staff. Although black studies have been introduced into the mainstream university curriculum and 32 black colleges are still in existence, the overall percentage of African-Americans pursuing higher education is declining and the United Negro College Fund reports that most of their institutions and students are economically hard-pressed. Despite emphasis on black pride and ethnic beauty, despite the valiant leadership of black women and clergy to protect and promote family life in their community, the long-term impact of slavery and social injustice on the lower-class African-American family has been devastating! A landmark 588-page study, *A Common Destiny: Blacks and American Society* (Jaynes & Williams, eds., 1989) confirms these observations. That National Research Council report concludes that the economic status of blacks relative to whites has, on the average, stagnated or declined. The United States has a long way to go toward improving race relations and education before its black citizens totally enjoy equal treatment and opportunity.

Much research has been conducted on the verbal and nonverbal communication patterns, values, and many aspects of black American life and culture. It has been demonstrated that many blacks speak a dialect of English that differs from many other dialects of English. The prides or important aspects of their lives also differ in many respects from the majority white culture and from other groups in the United States. Andrea L. Rich (1974) portrays many of the dynamics and factors involved in interaction situations between blacks and whites. Her book presents a framework to analyze the factors that are present when black Americans and white Americans interact and communicate with one another. Failure to recognize the distinctiveness of black culture and communication, Thomas Kochman (1977, 1981) observes, has caused the misunderstanding, even conflict, between the races.

In an attempt to develop authentic relationships between blacks and whites, Bertam Lee and Warren Schmidt list assumptions and behaviors that blacks and whites make about each other that hinder or facilitate authentic relations:

Assumptions that *Block* Authentic Relations

Assumptions Whites Make:	Assumptions Blacks Make:
—Color is unimportant in interpersonal relations.	—All whites are alike.
—Blacks will always welcome and appreciate inclusion in white society.	—There are no "soul brothers" among whites.
	—Honkies have all the power.
—Open recognition of color may embarrass blacks.	—Whites are always trying to use blacks.
—Blacks are trying to use whites.	—Whites are united in their attitude toward blacks.
—Blacks can be stereotyped.	—All whites are racists.
—White society is superior to black society.	—Whites are not really trying to understand the situation of the blacks.
—"Liberal" whites are free of racism.	
—All blacks are alike in their attitudes and behavior.	—Whitey's got to deal on black terms.
—Blacks are oversensitive.	—Silence is the sign of hostility.
—Blacks must be controlled	—Whites cannot and will not change except by force.
	—The only way to gain attention is through confrontation.
	—All whites are deceptive.
	—All whites will let you down in the "crunch."

Assumptions that *Facilitate* Authentic Relations

Assumptions Whites Make:	Assumptions Blacks Make:
—People count as individuals.	—Openness is healthy.
—Blacks are human, with individual feelings, aspirations, and attitudes.	—Interdependence is needed between blacks and whites.
	—People count as individuals.
—Blacks have a heritage of which they are proud.	—Negotiation and collaboration are possible strategies.
—Interdependence is needed between whites and blacks.	—Whites are human beings and, whether they should or not, do have their own hang-ups.
—Blacks are angry.	
—Whites cannot fully understand what it means to be black.	—Some whites can help and "do their own thing."

(continued on next page)

Assumptions that *Facilitate* Authentic Relations (continued)

Assumptions Whites Make:	Assumptions Blacks Make:
—Whiteness/blackness is a real difference but not the basis on which to determine behavior. —Most blacks can handle whites' authentic behavior and feelings. —Blacks want a responsible society. —Blacks are capable of managerial maturity. —I may be part of the problem.	—Some whites have "soul."

Behaviors that *Block* Authentic Relations

Behaviors of Whites:	Behaviors of Blacks:
—Interruptions. —Condescending behavior. —Offering help where not needed or wanted. —Avoidance of contact (eye-to-eye and physical). —Verbal focus on black behavior rather than white behavior. —Insisting on playing games according to white rules. —Showing annoyance at black behavior that differs from their own. —Expressions of too-easy acceptance and friendship. —Talking about, rather than to, blacks who are present.	—Confrontation too early and too harshly. —Rejection of honest expressions of acceptance and friendship. —Pushing whites into such a defensive posture that learning and re-examination is impossible. —Failure to keep a commitment and then offering no explanation. —"In group" joking, laughing at whites in black culture language. —Giving answers blacks think whites want to hear. —Using confrontation as the primary relationship style. —Isolationism.

Behaviors that *Facilitate* Authentic Relations

Behaviors of Whites:	Behaviors of Blacks:
—Directness and openness in expressing feelings. —Assisting other white brothers to understand and confront feelings. —Supporting self-initiated moves of black people. —Listening without interrupting.	—Showing interest in understanding white's point of view. —Acknowledging that there are some committed whites. —Acting as if "we have some power," and don't need to prove it.

Behaviors that *Facilitate* Authentic Relations (continued)

Behaviors of Whites:	Behaviors of Blacks:
—Demonstration of interest in learning about black perceptions, culture, etc.	—Allowing whites to experience unaware areas of racism.
—Staying with and working through difficult confrontations.	—Openness.
—Taking a risk (e.g., being first to confront the differences).	—Expression of real feelings.
—Assuming responsibility for examining one's motives.	—Dealing with whites where they are.
	—Meeting whites half-way.
	—Treating whites on one-to-one basis.
	—Telling it like it is.
	—Realistic goal-sharing.
	Showing pride in their heritage.

Insights into such behaviors and assumptions are as useful to Britons and South Africans as they are to Americans.

It is important for us to recognize the attitudes and assumptions we make of other groups, in this case, assumptions whites and blacks make of each other. These assumptions usually are unconscious and without our awareness. The importance of our behavior—particularly nonverbal behavior that blacks and whites demonstrate to each other—is apparent in the adage: "Your actions speak so loudly, I can hardly hear what you say."

Sometimes foreign visitors or global managers from other countries find it easier to communicate with black Americans than do their fellow white Americans. The French, particularly, have never made a big issue of color and with their long history in Africa, have always been open to black Americans. Perhaps this helps to explain why black jazz musicians, dancers, and other artists have always been so comfortable in that culture.

The following case study considers intracultural relations in terms of Americans normally overlooked in analyses of this very pluralistic culture. The first part focuses upon two organizational microcultures, the American university and a government agency. The second examines relations between stateside Americans and those in their commonwealth or territories and the third poses questions about "typical" Americans.

Case Study: Mixed Americans at University International

Scenario

- The troubled dean on campus
- The disturbed customs official
- The questions to be resolved

The Troubled Dean on Campus

Dr. Joseph Polito, dean of students at University International, did not expect to open up a "can of worms" when he sponsored the special forum to facilitate the adjustment of new students to their San Diego campus. The city had become quite a cosmopolitan community since it grew beyond its border and Navy-town days. Because of the many transfers of Americans from the University's Mexico City and Hawaii campuses, he intended to foster their adjustment by this forum for "Very Special Americans." The idea had been simple—representatives of the various American subcultures would tell something about their group, and what challenges and problems they experienced since coming to California.

Thus, Lolita Lipwe from American Samoa told the audience that her homeland consisted of 7 islands, 76 square miles, and a population of 30,000. Her brother, Tali, also pointed out that their home was 2,300 miles from Hawaii, had its capital on Pago Pago, and shared its locale with 9 other islands called Western Samoa. The latter area was independent, and although they shared a common culture and language, it had a much simpler and lower living standard. Both Lipwes were fiercely loyal to the United States and its system, and remarked, "We are U.S. nationals, carry U.S. passports, and have free movement on the U.S. mainland."

Then Tiser Guerro, another kind of American, told of his native Guam and how they had become Americanized when their island became a major staging area of the U.S. Armed Forces in WWII. A big smile rose on his flat, round, dark tan face, when he said that like all Polynesians, their ancestry included aboriginal peoples, Orientals, Spaniards, and now Americans. He liked California because of its climate and the fact that a large community of Guamanians resided in Los Angeles where he could visit them every weekend.

Manuel Ortez, a Chicano, said that he had been born in "occupied California" and that his forefathers once had a land grant in Rancho Santa Fe nearby. His hobby was Mayan art and history, and he reminded everyone that his people had a flourishing civilization before Cortez landed in 1519. He spoke with vehemence as he described the long struggle of his ancestors to throw off the Spanish and French yoke, only to lose part of their lands to the Republics of California and Texas. Although proud of his heritage and its contributions to the development of the American West, he identified himself now as an American of Mexican extraction.

Loly Gomez said that her father was born in the Philippines when it was still under American control, that he fought in the American Navy all during the occupation of their homeland by the Japanese, and finally retired from the service in San Diego. She was proud of the large Filipino-American community in the city and told how their "Association" conducted folk dances in nearby Balboa Park on Sundays.

After a parade of sharing by these unique Americans, the forum began to cause Dean Polito some trouble when there was near unanimous agreement that they generally had problems when they crossed the border south into Mexico.

The students liked to surf along the coast of Baja California, and congregate on weekends in Ensenada, Mexico. That western port city was only sixty miles south of the campus and Americans were not required a special visa or tourist cards for short visits there. The complaints centered around how they were treated by U.S. Customs officials as they came back and forth through the port of entry at San Ysidro. The Mexican-Americans complained they were treated like migrant workers and asked to show "green" work identification cards.

The Americans from the Trust Territories said the inspectors were nice but made them feel like Mexicans and always demanded a passport. A Filipino-American girl claimed that when she crossed back into the States at the Tecate entry, a male inspector made an insulting remark suggesting she was a prostitute coming over; she had reported the incident. One of the Nisei said she had gotten into trouble when she tried to bring up some relatives from Ensenada to show them the campus. The whole series of incidents prompted Dr. Polito to request an interview with the district director of the U.S. Customs.

The Disturbed Customs Official

Benjamin Fine was upset when he got the dean's telephone call. Now he sat in a large office in the downtown federal building looking out over the harbor and awaiting Dr. Polito's arrival. He had been transferred recently to Southern California after many years of service in the New York District, and he was still undergoing mild cultural shock relative to the California scene and the organization's culture. He now directed one of the busiest ports of entry into the United States. The millions of people who crossed back and forth from San Diego to Tijuana through the San Ysidro gates on the Mexican border were staggering.

His understaffed and overworked personnel were subject to enormous pressures from tourists, drug traffickers, and illegal aliens. The traffic build-up at peak hours and holidays caused monumental back-ups, and the whole inspection and processing system needed to be revised. The traveling public often projected their frustrations on his dedicated employees. He could understand why his tired workers might react negatively to some of these college students. However, to assess the dean's complaints accurately, he had invited Jose Tellez, his director of border operations, to join him. Tellez was a well-educated, widely traveled, experienced customs officer—and a Mexican-American. He should be able to provide real insight into the situation.

"O.K., Joe, you have read of these documented complaints from the University International students and checked it out, what is your opinion? The dean tells me that more than half their student body is made up of foreign students, but there are some problems between them and us because of passports. The problem seems to be with the American students who look like Mexicans."

"Well, Mr. Fine, you should know that already the Hispanic population is 8% in the United States, and growing. So apart from these Pacific Island peoples who are Americans and might be mistaken for Mexican, there are millions of Mexican-Americans legally in this country. My point is that our staff needs some training in managing cultural differences, so they can be more effective in cross-cultural communications. This goes whether they are interacting with foreigners or with Americans who are of different cultural backgrounds. Your predecessor did a good job pushing language training, especially in Spanish, among our personnel. Now we need to follow up with training in cultural awareness."

"You may be right, Joe, because they get little input on such subjects in their basic training at the Customs Academy. I see another value internally. The workforce in this San Diego district has changed radically in the last fifteen years as I study the records. It has grown from 75 to 400 officers. It used to be white males, usually of an Anglo and military background. Now we have 21% minority and 16% women employees with new emphasis on Equal Employment Opportunity. I know there has been a very small group of hard-core opponents to our Affirmative Action efforts in the district, and they have even opposed minorities being promoted into supervision. Perhaps the time has come for some new organizational norms of behavior on this score, and the training in cultural sensitivy might help."

"Another thing, Chief, that complaint of the Nisei kid is not with our office but with the U.S. Border Patrol. She visited her Japanese-Mexican relatives in Ensenada, and tried to bring them back to visit the campus without the proper papers. That's why the guys on the "Big Green Team" (Border Patrol) stopped them. The public is always mixing us up with the people from Immigration and Naturalization, or the Border Patrol."

Ben Fine mused to himself that if that proposed Border Management Agency ever comes into being and elements of the three federal agencies converge into a new organization, then they all will need professional development in managing cultural differences. His train of thought was interrupted when his secretary buzzed to inform them that the dean had just arrived.

Questions to Be Resolved

1. Do you have a stereotype of a "typical" American that excludes consideration of many special microcultures in their society?
2. What are the implications for you in this case for growing pluralism in American society?
3. Certain occupations and professions imply a role responsibility to gain intercultural skills, for example, customs officials should be "professional intercultural communicators." In your role, what responsibility do you have for cross-cultural understanding?
4. Consider the information obtained in this case relative to regional/organizational culture. What are the implications of Fine's transfer from East to West? Why would the joining of three federal agencies—organizational cultures—be a challenge?

5. Who are the Americans from the Trust Territories? (Note: the situation is fluid with the emergence of The Federated States of Micronesia, plus the Marshall Islands, both groups are in the process of gaining a semi-independence from the U.S.A. American Samoa and Guam are still under American sovereignity and citizenship. With the ongoing trade and military shift to the Pacific Basin, the Pacific Island groups are of increasing strategic importance to the United States.)

HISPANIC AMERICANS

As a bridge into the next chapter on Latin America, we end this discussion on U.S. culture by examining its Hispanic microculture. "Hispanic" is a convenient term for considering those in this country of Latin American origin.

From the viewpoint of cultural differences and synergy, one of the more fascinating developments in the U.S. during this century has been the rapid and rising Latin growth and influence in the country. After wars and treaties, the Spanish seemingly gave up their claims, principally along the southern borders of the U.S. from east to west. Culturally, however, the Spanish influence in Florida, Nevada, Arizona, California and Texas has always been most significant, principally by way of Cuba, Puerto Rico, and Mexico. Now the very face of America and many of its major cities are being vastly changed by the Hispanic peoples in their midst. The 1980 U.S. census revealed that of the minority population of 16.8%, 61% were of "Spanish" origin. Table 13-1 provides a breakdown of estimated figures; 1990's census may reflect increases.

Table 13-1
Estimating Hispanic-American Population in the USA—1985

Chicanos (Mexican Americans)	7 + million
Puerto Ricans	3 + million
Cubans	1 million
Other Latin Americans (Dominicans, Colombians, Ecuadorians, etc.)	3 million
Illegal aliens of Latin origins, principally undocumented Mexicans	8 million
Projected Hispanic total	22 + million
Forecast Year 2000	30 + million

U.S. States in which Hispanics concentrate:	% of State Population:
— Texas & California	51%
— New Mexico	36%
— Florida	25%
— Arizona	16%

Miscellaneous:
Cities where concentrated:
Los Angeles, New York, Miami, Hartford, Denver, San Diego
Median age—23 years; Average household—54% —4 + persons

It has been predicted that Hispanic Americans will become the largest minority in the U.S. before the turn of the century. Raul Yzaguirre, director of the National Council of La Raza (The Race), an umbrella organization for Hispanic-Americans, maintains the 1990s will be their decade. Just on numbers alone a valid argument can be made to support his thesis. By the turn of this century, Hispanics are expected to comprise 15% of the U.S. population, and advance rapidly into and beyond the middle class. And it should be noted that the "numbers" do not necessarily reflect an accurate count of the number of Hispanics in the U.S. because many such people are either overlooked in the census taking, or avoid being included for fear of legal actions. Also, the 1980 census did not include Cuban refugees. The Hispanic population is largely Roman Catholic, and therefore, generally does not believe in birth control, so it is evident what the outcome will be in the future relative to changes in numbers relative to the "Anglo" citizenry and the traditional Protestant American culture.

The Hispanics are a people who are only beginning to organize to gain political power and representation. One of their goals will be bilingualism in the American society, and they already have achieved some success with bilingual public education.

The Hispanics were on this mainland for centuries before the U.S.A. became a nation. Today they bring distinctive flavor and diversity to the American cultural mainstream. Strong regard for family and kinship in a patriarchal society is the first contrast. Other contributions to note are: gentleness and considerateness, especially with regard to women; lively, colorful music, art, and food; industrious entrepreneurs and hard-working laborers; large Spanish-language media capabilities and influence; and many other such Latin qualities to be described in the rest of this chapter on Latin America. Latinos offer the United States an amalgam of buoyancy, sensuousness, and flair that will either enrich the nation, or cause a schizophrenia with those of "Anglo-Saxon" heritage.

This Hispanic expansion is not just in the southwest or southeast, but throughout the U.S. with major concentrations in urban areas such as Miami, New York, Chicago, and Los Angeles. The exploding ethnic population of that largest California city, which was settled by Spanish colonists 200 years ago, is radically changing that area. Latinos, combined with Koreans, Chinese, Filipinos, and other foreign minority groups have now become the majority in that city, and downtown Los Angeles on a weekend is a babel of foreign languages and skin complexions. Considering that 20% of the voters in Los Angeles and 30% of the city's school enrollment is Hispanic, the future of the "City of the Angels" is evident. At the other end of the country in the East, Florida struggles to absorb its latest influx of refugees from Cuba and Haiti. Miami is fast emerging as Latin America's "capital." Not only have the Latin American divisions of multinational corporations chosen it for its headquarters, but Venezuelans, Chileans, Peruvians, and Argentinians have discovered it as a shopping haven. Despite the social unrest caused by more than 700,000 Cuban refugees descending on Dade County, Latin American trade and tourists have ignited a commercial boom. Miami is already more than 50% Hispanic and the bilingual signs everywhere are symbolic of a changing community, a harbinger for the whole country. Increasingly, throughout the U.S., advertising and marketing are being customized for and directed toward the Hispanic population.

One small indicator of how the internal character of America is being altered was seen when the U.S. Equal Employment Opportunity Commission proposed that employers not require bilingual workers to speak only English on the job unless businesss necessity dictated otherwise. Such guidelines will assist the more than 10.6 million people in the U.S. who speak Spanish as their primary language.

These Hispanic developments in North America have enormous implications for managers who do business in or with the U.S., and offer tremendous opportunities to promote new synergies. In fact, the whole blending of the American and Latin cultures on the U.S. mainland is an unconscious model of synergy. Two other such paradigms of cooperation can be cited in San Diego, California. Increasing trade with its adjoining urban metropolis of Tijuana has prompted San Diego business leaders to join with their Mexican counterparts in developing a Mexican-American trade center, and participating in their World Trade Association. Why? Because 79% of San Diego imports are from Mexico, and 90% of its exports go to Mexico. Perhaps trade along the international borders can become a major force for more synergistic efforts by these two great national neighbors.

The other synergistic model is the "Program in United States-Mexican Studies" at the University of California-San Diego. Dr. A. Wayne Cornelius has brought together leaders from both countries in the creation of a center for research, training, and public service activities between Mexico and the U.S. The scholarly effort will address problems and interactions between the two peoples, develop a library and data bank, and promote interdisciplinary, international seminars on public issues of mutual concern. It is a long-term program in international collaboration that will bring about an exchange of information and practitioners. Furthermore, at the same UCSD campus is located the Institute of the Americas (10111 North Torrey Pines Road, La Jolla, CA 92037, USA). This is an independent, inter-American organization centered on issues and shared problems confronting countries in the Western Hemisphere. The Institute sponsors research, conferences, publications and dialogue among governments, business, press, youth, and other sectors, particularly with reference to Latin America. Both the Center and the Institute programs focus on the mutual border between the United States and Mexico, where each year 192 million people cross legally, but disorder occurs by countless other millions who are forced by economic hardship to cross illegally (Pastor & Castaneda, 1989).

Before closing this section on North America by forecasting its future, it might be advisable to look beyond the horizon for U.S. Latinos. Robert Anson (1980) reminds us that Hispanics comprise a varied tapestry reflecting Spanish,

Indian, mulatto, and Afro-American heritages, and today comprise a substantial proportion of the U.S. population.

Chicanos

Mexican-Americans, the largest population bloc among U.S. Hispanics, are also known as "Chicanos," a popular designation for the group. The Chicano presence permeates the Southwest. In the U.S., there are approximately 7.2 million Chicanos who are concentrated in Arizona, California, Colorado, New Mexico, and Texas. In Texas, one of four persons is Chicano and in California one in five. Recent changes in U.S. immigration law have resulted in an increase in Mexican-Americans.

For those in business who wish to understand "La Raza"—literally "The Race," "The People" of Mexican heritage living in the United States—it might be helpful to learn more about the Mexican culture. Below is a description of American and Mexican managers in contrasting positions. The Chicano manager is a mixture of both traditions. The excerpt is by Dr. Ward M. Kelly (1978):

> One of the most noticeable American traits is individuality. But despite the oft-heard value he places on independence of mind and speech, he is paradoxically oriented to the group—he is a team worker. This observation must strike a foreign observer as being incompatible; but Americans are pragmatic, at least to the extent that they place a considerable value on workability, even at the expense of individual expression. Team players are allowed to be individuals, but certainly not at the expense of the team meeting its goals.
>
> Mexican managers, by contrast, have nothing in their cultural baggage which promotes team play. While the American tends to balance his need for individual expression against the needs of the team, the Mexican usually does not show the same balance. There is a strong need to be individualistic in the Mexican manager, a need which is not diminished by the team's needs for unanimity of action. It is prompted by his attitude toward the delegation of authority. If the Mexican manager delegates, he allows his subordinates to relegate him to a group limbo by restricting his opportunity to act as a singular entity. Hence, authority is tightly gripped, lest the boundaries to exercise his authority and thereby his individuality are circumscribed by his underlings.

The word "Chicano" is a relatively new term and is more accepted by young Mexican-Americans than by their elders who often reject the word and associate it with radicals. There is much diversity in the Mexican-American community. Many are highly educated and found in all businesses, professions and governmental posts throughout the U.S. Others work in the agricultural, assembly, food packaging, and other industries along the Mexican/U.S. border.

Some Chicanos are among America's lowest paid workers, and nearly 20% live below the poverty level. In 1983, the median family income for Hispanic-Americans was $16,960 compared to $25,760 for white Americans who are not Hispanic. (The *Instructor's Guide* discusses Puerto Ricans in more detail.)

SUMMARY

Back in the 19th Century a Frenchman, Alexis de Tocqueville, wrote about "Democracy in America." He discovered what he called *habits of the heart*, which form the American character and sustain free institutions—family life, religious convictions, and participation in local politics. That expression inspired the title of a recent book by a group of professors, Bellah et al. (1985), which examined individualism and commitment in American life. They conclude that rampant individualism within American culture may threaten freedom itself, especially when individual achievement is attained at the expense of the community that provides support, re-inforcement, and moral meaning for the individual. Furthermore, within North American society, competition is almost a cultural imperative, but pure selfishness, Bellah argues, does not result in the common good. Yet, he sees new community forces at work within America, such as our modern corporations' becoming more personal and participatory, contributing to the renewal of this society and the creation of a new work culture. Perhaps that is why we began this chapter within the context of Pan American management as a means for attaining synergy in our interactions within this hemisphere and with those of other nationalities. To get the big picture, we contrasted both North and Latin America in terms of population, geography, culture, as well as socio-political and educational developments, in addition to economic, natural, material and human resources.

For the benefit of the foreign business person or visitor, as well as the new emigré, we have examined here the macrocultures and microcultures of North America. We started with analysis of the native American culture—the Eskimos and Indians, peoples still experiencing the impacts of modernization. Then we examined the multicultural society of Canada with its dominant British and French influences on both culture and language. Finally, we reviewed the diverse make-up of the United States and its territories, as well as the major forces shaping its culture.

To highlight the complexity of doing business with "Americans"—the term popularly but incorrectly ascribed to U.S. citizens—various subcultures were studied from black Americans to brown-toned Pacific Islanders. As a bridge into the next chapter, we ended with an overview of Hispanic America, the fastest growing minority whose Spanish language is widely spoken throughout the nation. Although our focus was upon Mexican-Americans or Chicanos, Cuban-Americans and other immigrants here from Latin America, the aim of the discussion throughout was that foreigners should not stereotype Americans as simply Anglo-Saxons, for the heterogeneous population and life-style in this democracy has attracted residents from every corner of the world. Whether in marketing or interacting with North Americans, global managers would be well advised to differentiate which "Americans" their communications are directed to, and then customize their approach accordingly.

It is also wise to remember that Americans are a very mobile people, even within their own homeland. In 1985, for instance, a census report announced that one-fifth of the U.S. population relocated. These Americans were seeking opportunity, a better life; many moved from rural to urban areas in pursuit of better jobs or wages.

To help foreign visitors or immigrants cope better with diverse American culture and quirks, a former South African, Leon Snaid has prepared six hours of audio cassettes. Entitled *The Newcomer's Guide to Living in the U.S.A.*, the discussions deal with American education, business practices, customs, recreation, consumer buying, practicalities, and resources. Snaid, president of International Business Seminars (5060 Via Papei, San Diego, CA 92122), said that newcomers face three major adjustment challenges in the U.S.: loss of identity and personal networks; misperceptions about America and Americans; and limited applicability here of their experience from their home countries. He thinks that American movies and television contribute much to the foreigners' misunderstandings about the country.

Another author, Joel Kotkin (1988) suggests that the United States can capitalize on its ethnic diversity and entrepreneurial skills within the Pacific Rim with its growing economic opportunity. In *The Third Century: America's Resurgence in the Asian Era*, he contends that Los Angeles will inevitably ascend as a multiracial, world-class metropolis. Serious global investment is taking place in Southern California on a vast scale. With Spanish and Korean already as its second and third languages in Los Angeles, new immigration is seen as the transforming force in this urban area with ties to almost every race and region. Through the year 2010, the Southern California Association of Governments projects an average of 110,000 immigrants annually for the Southland, which extends through San Diego to the Mexican border! Some have suggested that Los Angeles is on its way to becoming the capitol of the Third World, while other writers maintain that the mold of a *new American culture* is being set here—a collage of co-existing, disparate ones (*Los Angeles Times Magazine*, January 15, 1989).

As a marketing psychologist, Dr. Henry Adams-Esquivel advocates transnational marketing. Given the implications of the previous information, it is no wonder that his company, Market Development, Inc. of San Diego, concentrates on strategies to reach the Hispanic market by *Fortune 1000* clients. The next chapter will further underscore this significance.

14
Doing Business With Latin Americans—
Mexico, Central & South America

In 1983, a mummy was accidentally uncovered in Arica, Chile, and may be the oldest remains of the human species yet discovered. Scientists claim that the Atacama Desert mummy is more than 7,800 years old, making it about 2,600 years older than its nearest Egyptian counterpart. That ancient seaside settler, along with 95 other mummified people of the Chinchorro culture, were aboriginal hunters and fishermen in what may be the earliest of Latin American settlements. In a 1985 interview at the nearby University of Tarpaca, Dr. Marvin J. Allison, a U.S. pathologist, mused that the burial system indicated a well developed social structure. Until now, scholars thought that mongoloid Asian peoples migrated some 30,000 years ago from Alaska down the West Coast of the Americas. But Allison contends that they could not have moved quickly enough to reach the Southern Hemisphere by the date of the earliest Chinchorro settlement. Thus, archeologists are unsure from where those early inhabitants came. One anthropologist, Silvia Quevdo of Chile's Museum of Natural Science, maintains that the Chinchorro's knowledge of anatomy was superior to that exhibited by mummies in Egypt. In any event, we will begin our examination of the diverse cultures in the southern parts of Pan America with their aboriginal descendents, the so-called "Indians." We do this, as in the last chapter, because today's global managers and technologists frequently impinge upon such primitive peoples in the name of economic development.

LATIN AMERICA'S INDIANS

Today, Indians make up a high proportion of the populations of many Latin countries, such as in Mexico and Bolivia. In some parts of the southern hemisphere the Indians have made more progress integrating into modern civilization than in other nations. For example, their conditions in Brazil are comparable to the U.S.A. in the mid 19th century—the warriors have a running battle going for survival against the settlers and the federal Indian agency; in 1984, the press reported that for the first time the Indians won a battle without bloodshed when the government recognized the Caiapo tribe's rights to sacred hunting grounds. Agencies like the World Bank are now demanding inclusion of programs that protect the rights of 200,000 aborigines before they will fund economic development projects in the Amazon region. In Central America, on the other hand, Indians try to survive the ravages and clutches of civil and guerrilla warfare. The Indians are caught between the forces of both left and right, Communists or the oligarchy. Sometimes the rebels seek haven or recruits among the Indians, and then the government troops destroy the Indian villages. In Nicaragua, for instance, the Miskito Indians have their own guerrillas fighting against the leftist Sandinista government, demanding only secure land rights and autonomy for the indigeneous peoples. In Honduras, the Misuras had aligned themselves with the Contra forces who were backed by the American administration in their battle with the Sandinistas. The Indians are caught in the middle of various revolutionary struggles and drug wars currently taking place throughout Latin America.

Latin America—Profile

Population

404 million people

National Cultures

24 countries
1 commonwealth (PR)
(12 island countries
   of West Indies ?)
Variety of Indian cultures

Major Cultural Inputs

- Native Indians (descended from ancient, highly developed civilizations of Incas/Aztecs).
- European—in most countries largely Spanish with lesser influences of Germans and Italians, except in Brazil where dominant input was Portuguese; some English input.
- African.
- Asian—ancient Polynesian influence, and some Japanese input in Mexico and Brazil.

Socio-Political Developments

- Napoleonic Code of laws.
- Feudalistic societies of Spain/Portugal imposed by conquerors on developed Indian civilizations.

Land Mass

8 million square miles

- French/Austrian royality/empire imposed on Mexico; the latter was center of revolutions in 1821, 1824, 1838 which impacted on South America.
- Family oriented with authority centered in the father and often extended to the "father of the nation" a strong dictator.
- Universities and republics from the 19th century with great dependence on military institutions/control.
- Problems of social class integration—although there was much intermarriage of the races, the powerful elites from an economic/social/political standpoint control and dominate the poor, often peasants of Indian heritage. The disenfranchised have moved beyond political/military protest for social justice to terrorism as a means for changing the status quo.
- Economically and technically developing, and in the process of moving from the agricultural and through the industrial

---

Latin America—Profile (continued)

Socio-Political Developments (cont).

stage of development; energy discoveries and development in Mexico can dramatically forge a new relationship with its neighbors.

- Although significant growth in spiritualism and Protestantism, the Roman Catholic tradition is still dominant, but undergoing profound role change—instead of traditional support for the oligarchy, many clergy providing leadership in a revolution for social justice

Education

- In the European tradition, especially Spain/Portugal/France. Ancient and traditional university education with emphasis on the humanities, especially studies in law, medicine, and engineering. Colegios are more numerous then American secondary schools and offer the equivalent of junior college. Upper classes tend to send their offspring to private schools and universities, often conducted by the orders of the Catholic Church. Although literacy is increasing many in the population overall do not receive more than a very few years of primary education, notable exceptions in the larger countries which provide more education. Rigorous examination competition for university entrance. Technical education also on the increase and use of mass media.

MEXICO AND CENTRAL AMERICA'S CULTURAL DEVELOPMENT

Going south of the Rio Grande River from the United States one enters the Third World and Latin America with over 340 million people. This is also true moving southeast of Florida, but there one encounters in the Caribbean Sea area a series of small nations that represent a curious mix of British-French cultures. Considering that some of these West Indies occasionally changed hands between Britain and France, an unusual cultural synergy has occurred which goes beyond a langauge interchange between French and English. Among eight major nations in the mid-continent and fourteen adjoining island states to the west, we will begin with the largest and most powerful.

Mexico

Situated on the Pacific Rim and extending eastward to the Gulf, Mexico is a land of contrast and promise. Over 761,000 square miles in land mass, this country has an expanding population of more than 70 million people. Its diverse peoples have increased a hundredfold in the past forty years. Lacking an effective birth control philosophy or program, Mexico's total population seems to have doubled between 1968 and 1988. Half of that burgeoning population lives in the central highlands, which constitutes half of the country's total cropland. With an annual population increase of more than 3%, this nation is expected to have 100 million people by the year 2000. This has enormous social and business implications not only for Mexico, but especially for the "Norte Americanos." With 31 states in the United States of Mexico, 14 million people are concentrated in the Federal District capital of Mexico City. Like many developing countries, the young greatly outnumber the old, and the life expectancy is 65 years, contrasted to 73 years in the U.S. Other interesting population trends are:

1. Thirteen percent are of Indian pure blood ancestry, 10% of European heritage, 75% mixed.
2. Increasing urbanization—80%.
3. Decreasing infant mortality, but still a death rate of 70 per 1000 (in contrast to 13 per 1000 in the U.S.).
4. Rising literacy rate—now 84% of the population, plus a rising educational level (in 1980, 15 million in elementary school, 4 million in secondary level, and 800,000 in higher education).
5. Rising income per capita ($2,100 annually in 1980 per person average), but still 18 million underprivileged people, largely in rural areas.
6. Inadequate diet, medical care, housing and social security still plague the nation.
7. *A Los Angeles Times* (August 21, 1989) poll in Mexico on its most important problems revealed these interesting priorities: 45%—unemployment; foreign debt—38%; corruption—23%; pollution—21%; inflation 19%; crime—10%, but what actually is the biggest problem, population growth, was perceived by only 9%.
8. The poll also revealed that more than 4.7 million of the 85 million Mexicans believe they are likely to move north in the next year! In addition to the multitude who have previously made this transfer legally, Jorge Bustamante, a Mexican immigration expert, estimates 1.7 million Mexicans are still living illegally in the U.S. despite the impact of new American immigration reforms (Langley, 1988); American estimates are much higher!

As the decade of the '90s unfolds, several major realities must be considered by those planning to work or do business in Mexico. There is a crushing external debt (per capita, $1,253 in 1988) that the current federal administration is only now addressing. Pluralism is just beginning to enter the political and religious scene—the dominant one party and one religion system is opening up.

One fourth the size of the U.S., Mexico has a topography that features desert, tropical, mountainous and temperate regions with equal parts divided by the Tropic of Cancer. The lofty central plains are the main agricultural region, but only 24 million hectares of the agricultural land is cultivated. In the next five years, it is anticipated that another 3.3 million additional hectares will be developed. Although predominately an agricultural nation, Mexico is rapidly industrializing and is a leading exporter of metals, especially silver. In addition to spectacular growth in manufacturing and tourism, Mexico's hope for a better economic future lies in its recent discoveries and developments in oil and gas. Its energy supplies may rival those of Saudi Arabia. Mexico has a proven oil reserve of 40 billion barrels, and a potential of 220 billion barrels.

This is altering Mexico's whole relationship with the U.S., which has been somewhat stormy since the Americans invaded the country in 1846. After the war Mexico ceded almost half of its original territory to the U.S. by the Treaty of Guadalupe (this included Texas, California, Arizona, New Mexico, and part of Utah/Colorado). No border on earth separates two more widely divergent standards of living between two nations. Despite conflicts over illegal immigration, trade and drug smuggling, the American and Mexican peoples are generally friendly, and the prospects for Mexican and American synergy are promising.

From a business perspective, multinational managers should understand that:

- The nineteenth century in Mexico was marked by political unrest, the twentieth century by economic progress, and the country may really come into its own promise and potential in the twenty-first century.
- Discovered by Hernan Cortez in 1519, Mexico revolted against Spanish rule and achieved independence in 1821. It defeated French influence and interference by 1876, and survived a series of revolutions, achieving political and economic stability by 1940. One political party has dominated since 1930. The federal government consists of an executive, legislative, and judicial branch, and the military does not play a significant role in governance. Government seized and nationalized all Roman Catholic Church properties and reduced the power of that religious organization by anti-clerical laws (culturally, the people are still influenced by Roman Catholic morality and spirituality).
- The structure of capital and labor is somewhat different here from other countries in Latin America. The old, landed oligarchy has lost a major share of its property and power. A large rural bourgeoisie has grown among a large group of small landowners who today provide the capital for industrial and financial development. There is a growing salaried middle class, some of whom also cultivate their own land. An agrarian revolution has created a new type of peasant class, benefiting by government land distribution policies, or becoming a major source of U.S. agricultural manpower, as well as the Mexican industrialized workforce. Relative to returns for capital and labor, two thirds go to the corporation and only one third to the employees.
- The large public sector and public corporations contribute 44% of total investment, and is part of the state's power. State-owned companies imple-

ment public policy to generate jobs, goods and services, and an ability to negotiate with other nations or their corporations. The power of the state is limited by its single market orientation toward the U.S., which accounts for two-thirds of its imports and exports. Mexico is America's fourth largest trading partner, and its attempts to sell more in the north are blocked to a degree by obsolete, protectionist U.S. trade policies, regulations, and unions. Its new energy strength could force a change in that economic relationship.

- In the '70s, multinational corporations in Mexico (95% American controlled) provided 93% of the payments for imports of technology; and in the '80s, 80% of the technology employed is still foreign. Multinational corporations occasionally obtain slightly lower but safer profits on their investments in Mexico than they do in other Latin American countries. By 1980, the growth rates of public and private investment increased by 18%. Trade balances, employment, family planning, consumer price index, worker wages, and other indicators of economic well-being all continue to be troubling issues for Mexico. Frequent devaluation of the peso and high inflation (65% in 1985), as well as declining oil prices cause much hardship there.

Many of these insights result from a report by Pabloe Gonzalez Casanova (1980) which is still largely valid today. He reminds us that Mexico is a country in major transition, seeking to broaden its social and democratic basis, to control tensions between the evolving middle class and the disadvantaged masses, and to contain radical and revolutionary forces within the society.

The Mexicans are a relaxed, hospitable, and warm people who may relate more to their Indian than Spanish heritage. They are proud, patriotic and family oriented, and very hard working. Emotional, with a leisurely sense of time, they are generally comfortable with themselves and others, and are very person oriented. With Mexicans, as elsewhere in Latin America, it is wise for external business persons to take time for conversation and socialization. Subsequent sections in this chapter will deal with the cultural dimensions and challenges of doing business in Latin America which generally are applicable to this nation.

Relative to communications, specifically, between Mexicans and their immediate northern neighbors, their former president, Porfirio Diaz, made this classic observation: "Poor Mexico, so far from God, and so near the United States." John Condon has provided some clues that we summarize here for our readers; he expanded upon these insights with George Renwick (1980) in another publication cited at the end of this chapter in a special resource section (*InterAct: Guidelines for Mexicans and North Americans*). To avoid culture-based misunderstandings, remember:

- Mexican images and ideals are not only drawn from their "Indian" heritage, but from Europe (e.g., concepts of freedom and democracy come from France); their views and approach to their Latin neighbors is quite different from North American (e.g., attitudes currently toward controversies in Central America).

- "Pelado" or the plucked one may express the essence of the national character (e.g., Mexicans often view themselves as at the bottom of the pecking order like a child before a parent or conquistador, so their cultural themes express self-doubt, frustration, and a tragic outlook on life). As a defense against feelings of inferiority, many will act child-like.
- Although the uniqueness of the individual is valued and provides inner dignity, it is not necessarily evident through actions or achievements; slights against personal dignity are regarded as a grave provocation (e.g., Mexicans are confortable talking about inner qualities like soul or spirit, and may look at North Americans as insensitive because they avoid such subjects).
- "Respect" or respeto in Mexico is an emotionally charged word bound up with values of equality, fair play, and democratic spirit, and may involve in a relationship, pressures of power, possible threat, and love-hate affections.
- In conversations, Mexicans tend to maximize differences between persons due to sex, status, or age in contrast to North Americans who often minimize them (e.g., they defer to one of higher authority, and may say what they think the person wants to hear; reality for them is not just objective but interpersonal, so they may reply in a way that makes the receiver happy although it may not be the fact.
- Mexicans live with a sense of death, celebrate it in their holidays or feast-days, even with disguises, toys, confections, song and dance. It is treated as a bosom friend or exotic personage, joked about and played with (yet in many Latin countries, even dying is a luxury many inhabitants cannot afford; in Mexico a third class burial can be the equivalent of three annual wages). [Readers may wish to relate these observations to those cited in the last chapter for Hispanic Americans and Table 13-1 (right-hand column).]

Eva Kras (1989) covers many important and specific management issues faced by U.S. and Mexican managers as they work together.

Central America's States

On the western side of the Caribbean Sea is a land bridge between the northern and southern continents of the Americas, which also fronts on the Pacific Ocean. The seven nations located between Mexico and Colombia are usually referred to as Central America—all but Belize are primarily Latin in culture.

If ever there was a need and case for synergy, it is in these Central American states. The nineteenth century federation called the United Provinces of Central America may have been premature, but it provided a cooperative model for the future—if not politically, at least economically. Only by collaboration, such as in Europe's Common Market, can this block of countries overcome their chronic poverty, illiteracy, violence. Perhaps where political and military power-types have failed, local business leaders and multinational managers may succeed in raising the standards and quality of living for the populace. Sandwiched between North and South America, this area cries out for synergistic solutions and contributions from both the Anglo-Latin cultures.

Central America has been described as "the land of the smoking gun," where terrorism and turmoil imperil hopes for moderate reform. Unfortunately, too often in the past these "banana republics" became comic-opera fiefdoms of U.S. commerce, especially United Fruit Company. Despite bustling capitals, the 20 + million people in this strife-torn and suffering region are, for the main part, gentle peasants who have been exploited too long. This strategic land mass is a glaring challenge to the more affluent in the Americas to right the unequal distribution of wealth and land, a festering source of political instability. As General Wallace Nutting reminds us, "All of Central America could easily radicalize, and a very substantial wedge would be driven between north and south." But consider another scenario under the aegis of the industrialized Pan American countries in which: educational technology is used to provide mass education and literacy; cooperatives are formed on a massive scale to include the peasants into a better way of life; scientific and technological know-how is shared to improve the economies, the health services, and development of the region; and social justice is brought to all levels of society.

Panama, conceivably, which has never considered itself part of Central America but has experienced the regional strife, might become a laboratory, along with Costa Rica, to create demonstration models that would influence the other states to join in a regional entity for self-improvement. Efforts by such new governments, as in Nicaragua, to liquidate over $1.5 billion in war debts by ambitious reforms from agrarian redistribution of a literacy campaign should be encouraged. Application of new techniques to promote social peace and reduce internal political violence, as in El Salvador and Guatemala, should become the concern of Pan American social scientists. Simplistic, anti-communist and military approaches will not solve the region's problems and tap its vast undeveloped human and natural resources. In contrast to North American bribery and support of corrupt officials, Mexico and Venezuela have provided an example of synergistic magnanimity by concerned neighbors: these major oil producers agreed to provide regional importers with a 30% credit. Perhaps Latin American commercial leaders are in the best position to assist Central America?

SOUTH AMERICA'S CULTURAL DEVELOPMENT

As the multinational manager flies over the twelve countries that compose the southern continent of the Americas, he or she is struck by the immensity of this land mass and the potential resources down below, especially in Brazil and

Argentina. Nine of these Latin peoples have, in addition to their ancient Indian heritages, a Spanish cultural base, and one nation each has Portuguese, French, or Dutch cultural inputs. All but Surinam share the Roman Catholic cultural tradition. Most have been enriched by African cultural influxes. Centered between the Atlantic and Pacific Oceans, South America has been a multicultural cauldron for mixing Asian, East Indian, as well as European and African, cultures in a curious synergy.

South America is a place where we can simultaneously be amazed at the beauty of the pre-Columbian art and civilization, or the very modern and colorful art works and high-rise architecture; and be appalled by the poverty of the masses and the great wealth of the few, by the violence and terrorism and by the dominance of a powerful military or dictator. We can be encouraged by the progress in education and literacy, improvements in health services and population control, changing images and aspirations of South Americans. The World Bank helps to counteract economic deterioration by inflation, rising unemployment and energy costs.

Despite the great diversity in Latin America, there are common themes and patterns. After the development of fairly sophisticated Indian civilizations, there was a period of European colonization and exploitation from the fifteenth through eighteenth centuries, followed by wars of independence and attempts at federation during the nineteenth century. Since the early twentieth century, Latin American nations have been engaged in internal and external conflicts. Yet, the last half of this century has seen relative peace between the nations of Central and South America, and significant economic progress.

These countries also share another factor—a Roman Catholic cultural tradition that not only pervades their history, but ways of life and thinking. The Spanish and Portuguese explorers and conquerors brought the missionaries with them to convert and "civilize" the pagan inhabitants. Accompanying the military from South America up through North America were Franciscans, Dominicans, and Jesuits. At first, the clergy protected the Indians and helped through their missions to educate the indigenous populations. Their agricultural and trading centers became the great cities of South, Central, and North America. With the passage of time and increase in wealth, the Church became part of the establishment, despite the notable successes of priest revolutionaries, like Father Miguel Hidalgo, who espoused the causes of nationalism of the peasants. As a major land owner itself, the Church has not only supported the oligarchy, but opposed population control, divorce, and social change. But recently, in opposition to the continuation of feudal conditions and serfdom for peasants, a group of socially-minded clergy have provided Latin leadership.

With the encouragement of Pope John XXIII's Second Vatican Council in the 1960s, the promotion of social justice became a Roman Catholic priority in Latin America. A series of episcopal conferences confirmed the efforts, while Latin bishops such as Leonidas Proaño of Ecuador, the martyred Oscar Romero of El Savador, and Dom Helder Camarra of Brazil, became forces for change in their dioceses and nations. Some priests and religious leaders became militant and even joined the guerrillas or Marxists. Others suffered harassment, beatings, torture, and death in their defense of the poor and human rights. Bishop Proaño stated their case in these dramatic words:

> Exploitation, oppression, and repression of one group by another is socially sinful. God created the world for all, not just a few landowners or large corporations. It is therefore our duty in the Church to protest such conditions and develop a conscious awareness of the causes of oppression among the poor, encouraging them to unite and develop their own political solutions and leaders.

The growth of the militant theology and activities in the Latin American Church caused Pope John-Paul in his visits to the Western Hemisphere in 1980, to protest social inequities, and yet warn the clergy of the need to concentrate on their spiritual mission. In any event, no modern manager operating in Latin America can afford to ignore the Church as a cultural force. One author (Harris) has personally witnessed in Venezuela a decade of positive effects of a movement called "Faith and Happiness" which brought about a synergy on behalf of community development by religious organizations and executives. Cooperation and collaboration for social improvement in Latin America can be significantly advanced when business cooperates with institutions for human development.

Richard Rodriquez examined the conversions underway in Latin America from Catholic to Protestant beliefs (*Los Angeles Times*, August 13, 1989). The new brand of Christianity on the rise is "Evangelico," principally Pentecostal, with a fundamentalist view of scriptural teachings. In the 20th century, Protestants have now risen to 50 million on that continent. With a conversion rate of 400 per hour, demographers predict Latin American will be evangelical before the end of the 21st century! The "born again" movement matches the transition toward industrialization and urbanization. The religious cultural shift is away from the more tolerant, feminine orientation with its tragic sense of life and death, toward self-reform, spiritual empowerment, and taking responsibility for improving your own life now, not just in the hereafter. Rodriquez reports that a powerful tool for this religious revolution is satellite television beamed southward from what is left of Protestant America's "Bible Belt." Four hundred years of authoritarian Christianity may be overturned in a single generation, and Latin peoples will never be the same again!

The great Latin American liberator, Simón Bolívar, envisioned hemisphere solidarity 150 years ago. Consider his plea for Latin synergistic contributions:

> We are a small race of men; we possess a world apart, surrounded by wide seas, which is new in almost all the arts and sciences, although to some extent old in the uses of civil society.

. . . Racing ahead to coming ages, my imagination looks at future centuries and observes there, with admiration and wonder, the prosperity, splendor, and way of life this vast region has received. I feel carried away, and I seem to see this region in the heart of the universe, extending out over its long coasts, among those oceans that nature has separated, and that our country joins together with extended and wide channels. I see it serving as a link, a center, an emporium of the human family. I see it sending to all corners of the globe the treasures harbored in its mountains of silver and gold. I see it distributing health and life to suffering men of the old universe through its divine plants. I see it communicating its precious secrets to the wise men who do not know how superior the sum of its culture and the riches that nature has lavished upon it are. I see it seated on the throne of Liberty grasping the scepter of Justice, crowned by Glory, showing the old world the majesty of the modern world.

LATIN AMERICAN CULTURAL THEMES

Global managers realize that all the countries and peoples south of the U.S. border are **not** basically the same. Communication and business practice has to be adapted to local circumstances. As we indicated in the last chapter, those who understand Hispanic Americans, especially Puerto Ricans, will have an advantage in doing business in Latin America, as will those who take the trouble to learn Spanish or Portuguese. Some of the cultural characteristics previously described for such groups within the U.S.A., will be reinforced and expanded upon here. Perhaps the place to begin is by reviewing Table 14-2 which contrasts the North and Latin American business approaches from a cultural perspective.

This continent of Central and South America is made up of many nations and cultures. The Spanish heritage and language dominates except in Brazil where the Portuguese language and culture reigns supreme. Other European influences (German, Irish, Italian), as well as African influence, are evident across the Americas. Some countries, such as Colombia and Mexico, have strong manifestations of ancient Indian cultures. In addition to the social and cultural insights already provided about Hispanic Americans and Mexicans, we reinforce the message with the following guidelines to facilitate business, professional, and personal interaction. (The authors acknowledge that many of these insights came from the *Update Series* or overseas' briefing materials prepared by Allison Lanier and published by the Intercultural Press of Yarmouth, Maine):

Social Customs

Shaking Hands. This is the same as in Europe. If there are several people in the room enter with a little bow and then go around to each person and shake their hands. The "hi everybody" is considered rude and brash. "So long, see you tomorrow" is equally poor.

The *abrazo* (embrace) is a common greeting, but don't use this unless you know the person and your relationship justifies it.

Pleasantries. Nobody rushes into business. As a foreign businessman take your time and ask about your colleague's family's health, or make a few compliments about the weather. The local sports team is a good beginning point of conversation.

Thank-you notes. Use these often after any courtesy that is shown to you and send promptly. Flowers are often presented as a thank you.

Time. Latin Americans are often late according to North American standards but expect North Americans to be on time. Their offices close about 6 and dinner usually begins at 8. As a guest never arrive exactly on time.

Party Traditions. The old tradition is for women to congregate on one side of the room and for men to be on the other but this is changing.

If you visit a Brazilian's home, cafezinho (demi tasse) will be served you and you should do the same for guests in your home.

For large formal affairs, invitations are written by hand. Flowers are often sent before a large affair. At a smaller party you should take them to your host or hostess.

Women. South American countries are conservative for the most part. It wasn't long ago that women did not go out without a chaperone. Visiting females should be careful not to be noisy or conspicuous in any way and drink only light drinks.

As a foreigner be prepared for Latin men to flirt with all wives, but men should be careful not to flatter or flirt with a South American wife. Also be aware that a Latin may have a public wife (legal) and a private wife (mistress).

Privacy. There are closed doors, fences and high walls around their home. Wait, knock, and wait to be invited in. Don't drop in on neighbors. This is not a custom.

What About Questions? North Americans begin getting to know people by asking a lot of questions. However, it is safer to talk about local things. Questions are often interpreted as prying.

Space. Latin speaking distance is closer than North American speaking distance. They may also break our "bubble" without saying "excuse me." Instead of handshakes men often embrace.

Class and Status. People may not be served on a first come, first served basis. Their place in society may determine the order of preference.

Doing Business. The pace in Latin America is traditionally slow especially when negotiations are under way. Decisions are made at the top. Brazilians, for example, do not like quick, infrequent visits. They like relationships that continue. This implies a long term commitment to Brazil.

Deals are never concluded over the telephone, usually not even by letter, but in person.

Don't call anyone by his or her first name unless the person has made it clear they are ready for it. When in doubt, be formal.

Dress conservatively and use calling cards of good quality and in the local language.

Themes and Patterns

Themes are basic orientations which are shared by many or most of the people. They are beginning points for understanding, and sometimes form a pattern of behavior.

Personalismo. For the most part, a Latin's concerns are his family, his personal friends, his hobbies, his political party, possibly athletics such as the local bullfight, but transcending all these is his concern for *himself*. So to reach a Latin, relate everything to him in those terms: himself, his family, his town, his country and above all his personal pride. To be successful, everything should be personalized for the male.

Mañana Concept. It means to a Latin American an indefinite future. Here is an example from Liebman: A small bookkeeper will willingly promise to have ready for you something at a particular time. He knows he will not have it ready at that time. Why does he promise? A prominent Mexican psychiatrist offers the following explanation:

1. The promiser may die before the time promised and thus be relieved of the obligation.
2. The recipient of the promise may die and thus not require fulfillment of the promise.
3. The customer may renege on the contract and thus end the transaction.
4. Others whose work had priority may cancel their orders and thereby fulfillment may be possible.
5. The promisee may wait to inquire until the day following the day promised for delivery. This allows an extra day. An explanation of sickness or emergency can absolve the delay and a new date can be set.
6. Who knows? A miracle may happen and the work can be completed.

Meanwhile, you are happy. This is important. To make people happy is to exercise power.

Machismo. It means "maleness" and is an attitude that men have towards women. The macho is aggressive and sometimes insensitive and machismo represents power. Machismo is made up of virility, zest for action, daring, competitiveness, and the will to conquer. How is it translated into daily business life? A man must demonstrate forcefulness, self-confidence, visible courage, and leadership with a flourish. The machismo concept is implanted early in childhood and is impressed in both sexes. Yet, the female may actually control the home, children, and husband.

Desires to Get Rich Quick—Fatalism. There is instability in many Latin American economies and as a result there is a boom or bust attitude. Many desire to make it rich by speculation, manipulation or gambling. As a result, businessmen are not as interested in stable growth as U.S. businessmen.

Wagley, in the *Latin American Traditions*, says that for Latin Americans wealth comes and goes—you can be rich today and poor tomorrow and vice versa.

Related to this is the Latin American tendency to let *chance guide their destiny*. Most are convinced that outside forces govern their lives.

They are willing to "accept the inevitable" Don Quixote who followed his quest whether or not it appeared hopeless seems like a foolish man to many Americans. To most Latin Americans he is heroic. He was "bowing to fate," "taking what comes" and "resigned to the inevitable."

Good Manners and Dignity. Latin Americans are much like Europeans in this respect. They are more formal, and more elaborate. They shake hands on meeting and departing. Helping in the home is something a Latin American would not do because such a task would lower their dignity. In Latin America, the work one does is directly related to the social class one is in.

One is born "high" or "low." Latin Americans are by and large stratified societies. Aristocratic values plus late industrialization and strong central governments have combined to create an imbalance in manpower needs of South America and the supply. Seventy percent of South American workers have no industrial skills at all. In the remaining thirty percent there is an over supply of professional and white collar workers and an acute shortage of managers.

In the more advanced Latin American nations, such as Venezuela, all this is changing.

Latin Americans are born with a sense of place but the two class society (very rich and very poor) is giving way to a growing middle class.

Hospitality. Latin Americans are warm, friendly and hospitable. They like to talk, and want to know about a visitor's family and your interests.

Authoritarianism. There are signs of respect in both tone of voice and manner that denote grades of inferiority and superiority in a hierarchical society. It is present in the rich who believe that the poor are poor and that the rich are rich because God ordained it that way.

The *caudillo*, owner-manager, is master in his own domain. He has power and authority, and believes that the poor want a strongman who can give orders. The caudillo will jump when someone stronger pulls his string.

The *patron* is the man of power or wealth who sustains loyalty from those of lesser status. He can be the employer, the politico, the landowner and in other cases the money lender or merchant. Decisions are therefore difficult. They have to be made by the one in authority, and the Catholic priest or bishop often had a role in this in the past.

Authoritarianism does not allow for questioning. The *patron* knows everything and is all powerful. To play these roles, one has to be respectful in a subservient position.

Latin America is going through a social revolution in which agricultural and traditional societies are giving way to modern industrial nations. The impact of Roman Catholicism is strong in the Latin cultures but lessening as a force in the daily lives of people especially in the urban areas. The profound social and economic changes underway are altering many of the above customs and influences, especially among the younger generation. World communications, international exchanges, and contemporary realities are transforming Latin America. Its multinational managers are sophisticated in the ways of international business practice, and may not illustrate, at least on the surface, the typical social or cultural characteristics of the region.

Professor Raymond L. Gordon, author of *Living in Latin America* (1976), offers these conclusions from his research that may help to improve cross-cultural communications throughout the Americas:

1. *Syllogistic nature of meaning*—be alert to covert assumptions which may act as the context for interpreting the meaning of an overt message from another of a different cultural background. The message is only the raw material for interpretation, and one should attempt to consider the silent assumptions.
2. *Situation-associated assumptions*—link particular assumptions for interpretation with a situation, not just with words, gestures, or voice tone used in the message sending. The concept of situation, whether speaking Spanish or Portuguese, or operating through an interpreter, is to seek out the objectives of the situation; the time and space patterns of the activities involved; the roles of actors in the situation; the rules govening the interaction in that local Latin situation. The word "familia," for example, connotes much more to a Latin American than the American sense of family.
3. *Dissonant cross-cultural assumptions*—occurs in communications if the sender tries to impose his or her cultural assumptions upon the foreign assumptions behind the interaction. The problem in U.S.-Canadian interfaces is that both too often assume they are quite similar, whereas the subtle cultural differences may escape each other. North American bankers or Catholics can make many misassumptions about their Latin American counterparts.
4. *Values, conflict and communication*—the real difficulties in cross-cultural communications may be occurring because value systems are in conflict. While northern and southern Americans at a Pan American conference, for instance, may be in agreement on general goals, the conflict might be anticipated in the means to achieve such goals. That is, the time, place, division of labor, sequence of actions and other factors. When one is not open to consideration of the other's values, then emotions may rise and disagreements increase.
5. *Trivial actions and profound effects*—in cross-cultural negotiations, the seemingly trivial aspects may lead to an accumulation of

misunderstandings that have profound impact upon the relationship. North Americans, for example, when guests in a Latin home
or office may overlook mundane details to their own detriment and
a fruitful intercultural encounter. If one does not have sensitivity in
"small matters," it can lead to misinterpretation of intent or motives.

6. *Making allowances for foreigners*—although members of a host culture may make normal allowances for guests' alien behavior, some
of the foreigner's behavior may not be forgiven for the native does
not comprehend the other's context and reason for such unacceptable actions. More often the North American gets into difficulty by
not making allowances with self because of foreign status, as well as
not attempting to conform to behavior norms of a given situation.

7. *Vicious circle effect*—minor communication breakdowns can esca-
late and be exacerbated so that the natives make judgments about
the visitor's desires and motivations which may indeed be false, and
create negative images in the mind of the host. This may lead to social isolation of the foreigner, making it more difficult for the visitor
to understand the host culture and people. To move behind a superficial level of communication, this vicious circle must somehow be
broken by the foreigner or he/she becomes a prisoner of isolation.

8. *Blind leading the blind*—amateur observers of a foreign culture
may provide ethnocentric distortions of reality produced by systematic misinterpretation of the cross-cultural experience. Thus, a business person from North America about to be assigned in Latin
America may seek out a colleague for input about the culture because that other person had already done business there. A manager
should check out the feedback of a single colleague with objective
data (e.g., books and reports) and then only make tentative judgments before living in the host culture for some time.

For successful Pan American exchanges and collaboration, Professor Gordon's research indicates that each party in the cross-cultural encounter *must
learn:* (a) to recognize symptoms of miscommunication in oneself and the
other; (b) to separate fact, interpretation, and conclusion; (c) to derive silent
assumptions about major premises in the interpretive process from the foreigner's minor premises and conclusions; and (d) to request information from the
host country citizen in such a way as not to bias or inhibit the response.

CHALLENGES FOR PAN AMERICAN COOPERATION

The prospects for Pan American synergy in the twenty-first century are
bright. The last half of the twentieth century has seen some remarkable
progress in the Americas. First, there has been relative peace between the nations of this Western Hemisphere, despite internal upheavals within various

Latin states. World War II brought military cooperation among many countries of these two continents against a common external threat.

There have also been some noble efforts toward economic cooperation that lay the groundwork for real collaboration in the future. It takes time for such diverse cultures to learn the value and skills of joint endeavors. But the ground for synergy has been broken in such undertakings as the Organization of American States, the North Atlantic Treaty Organization, the Central American Common Market, the Andean Pact, the Alliance for Progress, and the Latin American Free Trade Association. One hopeful sign relative to United States involvement in such activities is the shift away from unilateral foreign aid to sharing of resources through multilateral institutions, such as the World Bank and the Inter-American Development Bank. Lately, the concerns of the various American nations have shifted more to the social arena with the establishment of such entities as the Inter-American Commission on Human Rights.

To resolve some of the serious inequities and exploitations within Pan America during this complex period of social transition demands collaboration among the people of this hemisphere. Numerous organizations in the private sector have made substantial contributions, but the natural and human resources in Pan America are enormous and the potential for improvement of the human condition in this area of the planet is staggering. It requires cosmopolitan leaders with vision who can set goals that capture the imagination of all Americans, north and south, and then energize them to actions toward mutual social and economic development. John F. Kennedy was such a leader when he joined with other Latin statesmen in signing an agreement at Punta del Este in 1961, which launched the Alliance for Progress.

In 1970, The Peterson Report offered unique guidance relative to inter-American affairs; namely, not to impose one's cultural values or institutions upon another state, but to have as development objectives "the building of self-reliant and healthy societies . . . an expanding world economy from which all will benefit, and improved prospects for global peace." Señor Plaza reminded North Americans of Latin America's importance to the United States and Canada as a multi billion-dollar market for goods and services, a source of raw materials for North American industry, an arena for private investment which yields high returns, and as a strategic site for defense and the advancement of human welfare and security. Such pragmatic reasons should stir investments in their southern neighbors by Canadian and Yankee traders, as well as their governments. But it will take more than altruistic assistance by such groups as the Canadian International Development Agency or the U.S. Peace Corps. The challenge in Latin America is to provide management development and systems, as well as to support self-help. France and Japan recognize this and have made significant investments in the region.

Those with vision will set goals to close the Pan American poverty gap within the next fifty years. Those who look beyond the horizon appreciate the wisdom of a Raul Prebish when he reminded North America of the interest and commitment we should have in Latin America, "the inevitable corollary is a systematic long-term effort in which the scale of the means is in reasonable proportion to the magnitude of the end pursued."

In a 1980 *Los Angeles Times* interview the then chief of OAS, an Argentine diplomat named Alejandro Orfila, noted that the principal issues facing the Americas is a fairer distribution of wealth to break up patterns of the past:

> Concentration of wealth must be mobilized, in a democratic way, to serve the majority of people. Neighbors need to help neighbors in resolving conflict, as when the OAS provided observers to reduce the crisis of near warfare between El Salvador and Honduras in 1976. That was a typical example of helpful presence without interference . . .
>
> With reference to the gap between rightists landowners and leftist politicians and peasants, Nicaragua's recent experience has had an impact in Latin America. The violence of the revolution there was something nobody wants to repeat. People in their right minds are not going to come up with a solution that destroys everything.

The OAS secretary general reminded us that underlying all of Latin America's difficulties is the need for integral development in the areas of education, health care, and opportunities for self-development. Orfila emphasized the interdependence of North and Latin America, and the need of one part of the hemisphere for the other. He is encouraged that economic development is now horizontal in the Americas, and not just vertical. He commended the industrialized nations of the south, such as Brazil and Argentina, or oil producers like Venezuela and Mexico, for contributing to the welfare of their neighbors. In addition to the economic power of that big four, he pointed to the organizing progress of the Andean Group of five—Bolivia, Colombia, Ecuador, Peru, and Venezuela—in forming a common market. Orfila believes that one of the big recent changes in the hemisphere has been the recognition by all member states—democracies and nondemocracies—that they must deal with each other and strive for understanding.

This opinion was confirmed on December 18, 1980 when eight Latin countries issued the "Declaration of Santa María" marking the 150th anniversary of the death of Simón Bolívar. Along with the Spanish government and the representatives of the Andean group nations, other signatories included Costa Rica and El Salvador. The 1,200-word document pointed out that "a new and vigorous effort to cooperate is indispensable" to create the conditions for a more social and economic order. The chief executives agreed that there would be no intervention in other nations' internal affairs, in the unity of peoples, or the sovereign will of citizens.

One reason for optimism about the future of relationships in the Americas is the accomplishments and prospects of the Pan American Development Foundation. It is a nonprofit, private voluntary agency established in 1962 through leading citizens of the Americas and the General Secretariat of the OAS. Its objective is to help the lowest-income people in Latin America and the Caribbean to participate productively in the socioeconomic and cultural development of their societies. PADF activates the involvement of the local private sector, especially the business community, through the formation of national development foundations in the various countries.

"Synergizing" the Pan American potential presents a macromanagement challenge:

1. To better manage the national resources of all states in the hemisphere by more effective collaboration of public and private sectors in each country, and between north/south regional relations.
2. To manage the transfer of technology and information for mutual development of North and Latin American peoples.
3. To contribute to economic and social development of Latin America through the exercise of corporate social responsibility by multinational enterprises on both continents.

We are not only suggesting a more effective trilateral partnership between business, labor, and government in the Americas, but we are proposing that transnational corporations throughout Pan America apply their management skills in developing human and natural resources in the hemisphere. Here are some possible scenarios for synergy and the exercise of corporate social responsibility:

1. Multinational companies within the "big four" countries of Latin America form joint ventures with their smaller and less fortunate neighbors to develop those countries' resources, especially for entrepreneurial, high technology ventures.
2. Canadian and U.S. multinational corporations operating in Latin America set up major training and health centers in the vicinity of their facilities, not just for their own employees, but for the benefit of the community nearby.
3. Establishment of a Pan American job or Peace Corps movement for youth to become involved in hemispheric development projects, as a means of promoting a skill exchange and combatting youth unemployment.
4. Promotion of Pan American human resource development and population control goals and plans for the 1990s—a joint endeavor of foundations, corporation, and government agencies with specific targets for the turn of the century.
5. Feasibility studies for regional development projects on a macroengineering or economic scale that would direct the energies of people in the Americas outward toward economic and social improvement, especially for involvement of the military in such endeavors in place of warfare (e.g., Army Corps of Engineers type programs).
6. Pan American joint studies and action task forces to deal with hemispheric problems of great magnitude, such as:

(a) population management and control;
(b) debt reduction and inflation control;
(c) substance abuse, and control of the illegal drug traffic;
(d) capitalization of human assets, transfer of workers, and prevention of illegal immigration;
(e) improvement of public administration and strengthening of democratic institutions by strategies for better public service—education of official personnel and their practice of operational skills, modernization of the criminal justice systems.

Lest the reader think that such positive undertakings are fanciful, let us conclude with a few demonstration models of trans-American synergy:

• The Itaipu Construction Project—Scheduled for completion in 1988, the Itaipu Dam is under construction and will have an energy producing capacity of 12.6 million kilowatts. The most powerful dam in the world straddles the Paranā River between Brazil and Paraguay and is a joint venture of both governments. The $11 billion project will provide power for further industrialization in both nations. Under the coordination of two MNCs, the contractors are Morrison-Knudsen of the U.S.A. and Electroconsult SpA of Italy. The 15 stories high dam requires 17,000 Brazilian and 11,000 Paraguayan workers. When finished, this macro project should enable Brazil to generate enough electricity that it can reduce its oil consumption and import by 100,000 barrels a day! It will also become a famous tourist attraction like the nearby Iguacu Falls which helps with the water flow.

• Ecuador, graced with virgin jungles, fertile mountains, and miles of ocean shores, keeps uncovering its natural treasures. In the last century, it was pearls, cacao, coffee, and bananas. Now it is oil and sea harvesting. It has opened its doors to vast reserves of oil, to industrial potential, and to 70 million consumers in the five member countries of the Andean Pact. Furthermore, with the help of American entrepreneurs, it is going into shrimp farming in a big way. The Andean Pact, plus the International Monetary Fund, have opened new development horizons for its own citizens and neighbors.

• Canada has made a major commitment to Caribbean development. The nation will increase cooperation in trade to CARICOM and raise Canadian economic and technical assistance to the regions. Canadian high commissioner to Ghana, John Graham recently observed:

> We are aware that if Canada cannot come to an understanding on the contentious and difficult North-South issues with the Caribbean, we will have great difficulty building bridges with other parts of the Third World.

- The Organization of American States has launched data gathering studies on the extent of the illegal drug menace in Latin America and the social ills it spawns. An OAS conference for all member nations will present the findings in 1986, and a regional fund is being developed to eradicate the abuses of drugs which is having a destabilizing effect on the Latin nations.

In some ways, the old Spanish administrators provided some potential models for the economic integration and regional cooperation that will be the highlight of the Americas in the twenty-first century. Thomas Mooney reminds us that the Spanish captain-general who lived in Guatemala City over three centuries ago administered a region extending from the southern Mexican border to what is now the northern Panamanian frontier. From other great Latin American centers like Lima and Mexico City, the Spanish promoted regional and international trade. In conjunction with the nineteenth century independence movements, visionaries such as Simón Bolívar, promoted cooperative entities, such as Gran Colombia, which may be harbingers of tomorrow's collaborative schemes, if not politically, at least socially and economically. The signs of the future are already evident in undertakings, such as the Organization of American States, the Central American Common Market (CACM), Caribbean Common Market (CARICOM), the Latin American Free Trade Association (LAFTA), the Andean Pact (ANCOM), and other emerging attempts at synergy in this hemisphere. Many such efforts under the stimulus of the U.S. government were perceived as "imperialistic." Perhaps the time has come to take the north-south issue of cooperation in the Americas out of the political arena. Perhaps transnational managers operating in the international marketplaces of North/Central/South America may offer the innovative leadership necessary to develop the potential of our two continents?

SUMMARY

In the last two chapters, we have sought to provide global managers a kaleidoscopic view of the Western Hemisphere in terms of its diverse national cultures and their development, as well as their problems and opportunities for synergy. Our realistic appraisal has analyzed human and natural resources from the Alaskan state in the far north to the Patogonia state in the far south, covering unique peoples from Eskimo hunters to Argentinian sheepherders. To improve the quality of life for all the hemisphere's inhabitants, effective and ecologically controlled utilization of resources on these twin continents is a *major management challenge*. Trained and experienced managers in transnational enterprises throughout the Americas may be able to accomplish in the decades ahead what politicians, dictators, revolutionaries, and soldiers have failed to accomplish in the past centuries—Pan American cooperation and collaboration in the common good.

In Chapter 14, our focus has been on doing business with the peoples and cultures of Latin America. In addition to the aboriginal peoples of this southern hemisphere, the so-called Indians, our first stop south of the Rio Grande River was Mexico. Our analysis provided an overview of the historical, political and social developments in this country with special emphasis on clues for improving interactions with its 14 million citizens.

Since most of these countries are Spanish in cultural background—except Brazil which is principally Portuguese, our next section emphasized Latin American cultural themes. Contrasts were made with North America business practice, as well as some of the principal social customs in the region. Our discussion ended with highlights of the principal challenges for Pan American synergy, along with some key culture specific resources for global managers. With greater cultural sensitivity and skill exercised toward Latin America—its peoples, problems, and promise—multinational leaders can contribute much to developing the potential there.

15
Doing Business with Asians— Japan/China/India/Pacific Basin

The dictionary defines Asia as a continent bounded by Europe, the Arctic, Pacific, and Indian Oceans. Sometimes referred to as the Far East, its almost 2 billion inhabitants are dispersed over 16 million square miles of this planet. It is an area of increasing importance to global managers as a trade shift occurs from the Atlantic to the Pacific. The emerging markets of this Pacific Basin are discussed in more detail in Chapter 19. One world leader referred to the next century as "The Century of the Pacific"; if that forecast is somewhat valid, then the information about to be shared takes on more meaning.

"Asian" refers to a wide diversity of peoples and cultures—largely Oriental in character, but including many types from Caucasian to Polynesian. For practical purposes, this chapter and the next three on cultural specifics are limited to a representative sampling of nations. Each section begins with a profile that offers a quick overview of the country, a commentary of timely quotations to illustrate themes and trends at the time of this writing, and finally a summary of cultural characteristics. We hope the insights will enable international managers and technicians to be more effective when doing business with the representatives of the target culture.

Previously, we cited the culture contrast method as a means of learning about a human group that is different from us. We are grateful to Schnitzer, Liebranz, and Kubin (1985) for assembling the perfect introduction to our topic in the form of Table 15-1, which we adapted. Remember, Table 15-1 describes *general* tendencies in each culture and there are many exceptions.

JAPAN

Commentary

The changing patterns of current political and economic change in Japan may be appreciated somewhat in these random excerpts from the media on the contemporary Japan scene. Specifically with regard to business, this commentary from our public press provokes interesting images.

Table 15-1
A Comparison of Cultural Differences

East Asian Countries	United States of America
• Equity is more important than wealth.	• Wealth is more important than equity.
• Saving and conserving resources is highly valued.	• Consumption is highly valued, awareness for conservation is growing.
• Group is the most important part of society and is emphasized for motivation.	• Individual is the most important part of society and the person is emphasized for motivation, although team emphasis is growing.
• Cohesive and strong families and ties often extend to distant relatives—even the nation and its leaders. Relationship society with strong network of social ties.	• Nuclear and mobile family. Experimentation with new home/housing/commune living communities of non-relatives. Fluid society that de-emphasizes strong, social ties.
• Highly disciplined and motivated work-force/societies.	• Decline in the "protestant work ethic" and hierarchy.
• Education is an investment in the prestige and economic wellbeing of the family.	• Education is an investment in personal development/success.
• Protocol, rank, and status is importance.	• Informality and competence is important.
• Personal conflicts are to be avoided—e.g., few lawyers.	• Conflict is energy, to be managed—many lawyers.
• Public service is a moral responsibility.	• Distrust of big government and bureaucracy.

Japan—Profile

Population	122,000,000
Ethnic Groups	Japanese (99.4%) Other, mostly Korean (0.6%)
Religions	Shinto and Buddhist, 16% belong to other faiths
Education	99% Literacy
Land	143,000 square miles
Government	Constitutional Monarchy
Political Parties	Liberal Democratic (LDP) Japan Socialist (JSP) Democratic Socialist (DSP) Japan Communist (JCP) Clean Government (CGP) New Liberal Club (NLC) Social Democratic Federation (SDF)
Per Capita Income	1983 US$ 11,300
Exports to U.S.	1984—$235,085 million
Imports from U.S.	1984—$51,206 million

"Japan Perplexes the World"

These four words are the first words of the book *The Enigma of Japanese Power* by Karel van Wolferen, a European journalist who has worked in Japan more than twenty-five years. His premise is that Japan does not work as it appears—he discusses many fictions in depth—and there is even more reason for foreigners to be concerned about the economic power of the Japanese than most realize.

> *A.P.* (Tokyo) April 15, 1985—"Chrysler, Japanese automaker in deal"—Chrysler Chairman Lee Iacocca and Mitsubishi President Toyoo Tate signed a memorandum of understanding today on forming a joint venture, to be equally owned by the two companies, to produce a new small car in a Midwestern state, Mitsubishi said in a statement.

> *Business Week*, March 4, 1985—"Japan's Secret Economic Weapon: Exploited Women"—Frequently, women workers are forced into menial jobs with low pay and little chance for promotion. Some 25%, or 5 million of them, are euphemistically classified as part-timers—largely service industry employees who work up to 48 hours a week for an average $2.40 an hour and few fringe benefits. The influx of such workers has helped reduce women's pay as a percentage of men's to 52% from 56% in 1978. Japan has no law requiring equal pay for equal work.

> *Los Angeles Times*, July 30, 1989—"Standing Out in Japan"—Women have begun to crack the traditional male-dominated corporate culture but the going can be tough. A handful of women executives in Japan are slowly making their way up in the Japanese corporate world, and most head their own businesses. Many prefer working for foreign firms because they offer better opportunities. Japanese companies only recently lifted discriminatory hiring practices against women and now allow them to take management track jobs. Japanese women face formidable challenges working in Japan's closed and clubby business circles where much business is generated by personal relationships and transacted after-hours over drinks.

> *TIME*, August 7, 1989—"Takako Doi: An Unmarried Woman"—In a land where unmarried women are considered somehow incomplete, Doi remains steadfastly single. But the leader of Japan's Socialist Party has used her differences to advantage. It was 20 years ago that she abruptly decided to stand up to her country's male-dominated political culture. A constitutional lawyer and former mayor of her hometown, Kobe, she is now leader of the opposition within the Japanese government. In light of recent scandals within the ruling Liberal Democratic Party, she is a potential prime minister.

World Monitor, November 1988—"Orient Express"—There are cultural factors, which we can measure but not fully understand, that contribute to growth in Asian societies. For example, the level of total personal savings is very high—in 1985, 30% or more of the GNP in virtually all of the East and Southeastern Asian countries (with Singapore leading at 42% and Japan next at 32%). By contrast, the United States total savings rate was 11%.

Because Japan is going through profound economic and social change within a generation, its cultural specifics must be viewed in that context (Hall and Hall, 1987; DeMente, 1987). As one American trader remarked, "If you have not done business in Japan within the last five years, you do not know the situation because it is so dynamic." Regularly reading a publication like *Business Tokyo* (Keizaika Pacific, Inc., 21515 Hawthorne Blvd., Suite 820, Torrance, CA 90503) may help to keep one somewhat up-to-date.

Japanese markets are indeed hard, but not impossible to crack, as McDonald's, Coca-Cola, and IBM have demonstrated. Informal protection, in the form of close linkages between supplier and customer, is a handicap to outsiders. As *The Economist* (December 12, 1987) observed:

- The Japanese are not a rational people in the sense economists use that term—they will sacrifice their interests as consumers for the nation as a whole; they will make spending decisions on the basis of who is selling, not on the basis of what is sold; in short, they would rather pay more for something than less for it.
- The Japanese are prone to value quality and reliability to a degree that Westerners find hard to understand, and then insist on high standards of after-sales service. They also place a premium on long-term relations with customers and suppliers, or trustworthiness.
- The Japanese society is more "cartelized" than America, so that people at the same level in different organizations know each other from school days and are comfortable doing business with one another—with a minimum of explanation and a maximum of cooperation.

Yet, realities of their participation in the international market are causing changes in such cultural preferences, especially among the new generation.

Correspondent Paul Maidment described Japan's new place in the world as, "rich in pocket, confused at heart" (*The Economist* December 5, 1987). The economy has started to switch from a high-powered export machine to meet domestic demand. Astute observers of the Japanese contemporary scene are watching the generational changes impacting national vision and political expression. Author Daniel Burstein predicts that in the 1990s, Japan will be a global economic superpower on a par with America (*U.S. News and World Report*, September 26, 1988). Kumar's research (1988) on how cognition and decision-making influence U.S. and Japanese negotiations indicates differing cultural standards trigger differing emotions that affect each party's approach to the interaction.

Cultural Characteristics of Business in Japan

Perhaps the old saying, "East is East, and West is West, and never the twain shall meet," should be revised. To those of the West, the Orient has seemed inscrutable, disconcerting, charming, and mysterious. But Asia is a polyglot of nations and cultures, so it is difficult to generalize about its diverse peoples and their mindsets. For North Americans perched on the Pacific rim, Japan is the epitome of the Far East and its seeming enigmas.

To Americans, in particular, the Japanese may seem a paradox and source of both confusion and wonderment. They have read the history of the feudal society, which lasted until the nineteenth century when Commodore Perry's voyage helped to open Japan to the West. Typically, Americans have a series of changing images about the Japanese people and culture. The images can be grouped around stages. One is pre-World War II, when the Japanese were admired for their ambitious effort to catch up to European and American industrialization. At this stage and the next, many Americans viewed Japanese diplomatic endeavors as devious.

During World War II, the image shifted as Americans were abashed by the daring Japanese attack upon the citadel of Pearl Harbor, forced grudgingly to admire the fighting prowess of these "little yellow men" lampooned by the U.S. media, and puzzled by continued loyalty to their Emperor even in defeat. Finally, in the present post-war period, Americans find it hard to believe that these victims of atomic devastation and military occupation could bounce back, produce an economic miracle, and become a leading superindustrial nation.

The following cultural insights apply to doing business in Japan:

Language and Communication

1. Indirect and vague is more acceptable, than direct and specific references—ambiguous terminology is preferred.
2. Sentences frequently are left unfinished so that other person may conclude in his own mind.
3. Conversation transpires within ill-defined and shadowy context, never quite definite so as not to preclude personal interpretation.
4. The language is capable of delicate nuances of states of mind and relationships—while rich in imagination, it can be clumsy for science and business.
5. There are layers of soft language with various degrees of courtesy and respect. The female is especially affected by this; "plain" or "coarse" language is considered improper for her.

6. The listener makes little noises of tentative suggestion, understanding, and encouragement—"hai" may mean more than "yes" and imply, "I'm listening," or, "I understand."
7. There is a formal politeness for official negotiation and ordinary business communication, while an informal approach may be used while socializing. Frequently, while entertaining, the real business and political deals are concluded.

Tips for Business Interactions with the Japanese

1. Saving face and achieving harmony are more important factors in business dealings for the Japanese than achieving higher sales and profits.
2. Third party introductions are important. They prefer this indirect approach whereby you use a go-between or arbitrator who may be involved until the conclusion of the negotiation.
3. Whomever you approach in the organization, do so at the highest level; the first person contacted is also involved throughout the negotiation.
4. Avoid direct communication on money; leave this to the go-between or lower echelon staff.
5. Never put a Japanese in a position where he must admit failure or impotency.
6. Avoid praise of your product or services; let your literature or go-between do that.
7. Use business cards with your titles, preferably in both Japanese and English.
8. The logical, cognitive, or intellectual approach to them is insufficient; the emotional level of communication is considered important (e.g., as in dealing with a known business associate vs. a stranger).
9. Formality prevails in senior staff meetings with interpreters present. The more important the meeting, the more senior executives present.
10. Wait patiently for meetings to move beyond preliminary tea and inconsequential talk.

Dress and Appearance

1. Neat, orderly, and conservative for managers; ordinary workers and students frequently wear a distinctive uniform and even a company pin, which managers also may sport (holdover from feudal days when a kimono carried a lord's symbol). Western dress is fashionable for the modern Japanese for external wear, but ancient, classical dress is frequently preferred in the privacy of the home (e.g., kimono and zoris); Western formal dress is used for important state occasions.

2. Traditional native dress is sexless and often neutral in color, with women sometimes tending toward flowery patterns.
3. Younger Japanese tend toward "mod" clothes and hair styles; appear to be physically larger than their parents because of dietary changes since World War II.
4. Colors have different significance in Japanese culture (e.g., white for sorrow, black for joy).

Food and Eating Habits

1. Eating is more ritualistic, communal, and time consuming. The interaction is considered more important than the food.
2. Tokyo is said to have a restaurant, bar, or cabaret for every 110 members of the population; fast food establishments are increasing.
3. Traditional diet emphasizes rice and fish, tempura pan and style of cooking, chop sticks.
4. The youth tend toward popular Western foods and accoutrements for eating.
5. Avoid bringing your wife to a business dinner, even if a Japanese host invites her out of politeness.
6. Learning to drink alcohol in public without offense is one of the important accomplishments that a young Japanese would-be executive must learn.

Time and Age Consciousness

1. Japanese tend to resist pressure on deadline or delivery dates—supposed agreement on a date may have been only to achieve harmony.
2. They are punctual yet they expect you to wait for group decisions that take time.
3. In negotiating a licensing agreement, it may take three years for a decision, but once made, the Japanese may be ready to go into production within a few weeks (unless this point of decision is followed by quick action, the Japanese may criticize the Westerner for "endless delay and procrastination").
4. Respect seniority and the elderly.
5. Young managers, recruited from the universities after stiff examinations, are expected to stay with a company until they are forty-five years of age, conforming, doing what's expected of them, and showing respect and deference. Then the crucial decision is made as to whether the forty-five year-old manager is to become a company director; if he makes it, he can stay beyond the normal Western retirement age and may work into his 80s. The remainder of the managerial group not so selected become de-

partment or subsidiary directors and are expected to retire at fifty-five, though even then they can be retained in a temporary capacity.

Reward and Recognition

1. There is a tendency away from individual reward, and recognition to the group or organization.
2. Great emphasis is placed on security, as well as a social need for "belonging."
3. Money, if passed to a Japanese businessman, should be in an envelope.
4. For social visiting, the guest is frequently given a present or small gift, such as a hand towel beautifully wrapped; however, on the next exchange of visit, you are expected to offer a gift in kind.
5. Personal relationships score high with them and future relationships depend on how you respond in the first encounter.
6. Cut and dry relationships with business contacts are inadequate and must be supplemented by a social relationship for maximum effect. This is usually entertaining the client for a "night on the town," but not at his home; part of the Japanese manager's reward is a generous budget for entertaining. When away from home—for example, in this country, the Japanese businessman expects to be entertained lavishly by his host (theater tickets, et al), but repays this kindness manyfold.

Relationships

1. Cohesive and crowded in a California-size nation—this accounts for rituals of bowing, politeness, etc. in crowded, urban areas.
2. Familial and group oriented, instead of individualistic.
3. Youth epitomize the culture in change—energetic, productive, yet anxious for change; gaining a new sense of "I/my/me-ness" while the pattern for other is "we-ness."
4. Group leadership regarded more than individual initiative—tendency toward clannishness based on family or group connections, know your place and be comfortable with it.
5. Drive toward agglomeration, combines, clustering of organizational relationships.
6. Sense of order, propriety, and appropriate behavior between inferiors and superiors (with women generally considered inferior to men); ancient "boss/henchmen" relationship maintained in new forms.
7. International relationships—close emotional and economic ties to U.S. but suspicious of aggressive Americans; fear China, yet emotionally allied and identify with the Chinese.

8. In business relationships, there are two Japans—officialdom and the intellectuals (e.g., politicians and businessmen). In both, decisions tend to be by group mulling for consensus, give and take inconclusiveness, and the traditional authority pyramid.
9. Symbiotic relationship between government and business—cozy but not constricting.
10. Social and self control disguise highly emotional quality of Japanese character and relationships; mesh of binding social relationships weakening and hard to comprehend.
11. Even riots, especially among the more rebellious youths, can be orderly, well-conducted public events staged within a mutually accepted framework of a dangerous game.
12. In context of social relations, Japanese tend to be clean, polite, and disciplined; but publicly with strangers, can be pushy and inconsiderate (e.g., the tourist).
13. Sensitive to what others think or expect of the individual and have a sharp sense of right and wrong; yet find it difficult to deal with the unexpected and strange (so may laugh inappropriately).
14. The general gap between the generations is very wide. In business, it is somewhat bridged for the young manager who is assigned an elder "godfather" or "guru" (to use our terminology) who is an upper middle manager, fifty-five years old or more, is rarely the young man's direct superior, is expected to know him, meet regularly and be available for advice and counsel, and to assist in transfers and discipline, when necessary. This respected elder manager is always consulted on promotions and other personnel matters concerning that young person's career. He is the human contact for the organization with the young manager, the listener and guide who provides a significant human relationship.

Attitudes and Beliefs

1. The Japanese character is diverse with a sense of poetry and of the ephemeral; there is a concern for the transitory, inconclusive qualities of life, for nature, and its observation. It is actively curious, energetic and quick, with a sense of delicacy and wistfulness.
2. These great lovers of success are extremely adaptable—basically, they do not resist change, and are open to automation and new technology.
3. Fundamentally, the Japanese have little concern for theology or philosophy, and seemingly substitute the family in this regard. Although realists, they are like their island homeland—a floating world that changes course.
4. The dominant religious thrust is the convergence of Shintoism and Buddhism (married Shinto, buried Buddhist). Christianity has made limited

impact. The crusading Soka Gakkai sect is also a political party that fights inequalities of the social structure, while enshrining the idealistic, self-denial, and the espousal of the underdog.

Business Attitudes

1. Increasing concern for acquisition of second generation management skill, not simply technical, knowledge of products, or manufacturing, but sophisticated management theory and concepts transferred to the Japanese environment. This is forcing changes in the way of dealing with foreigners. A more competitive climate is developing for foreigners that permits direct investment.
2. The following are myths to be dispelled in dealing with the Japanese business organization:

   - Your company has more know-how and they must learn from us, not vice versa.
   - The on-the-job training of American managers abroad can be combined with their simultaneous roles as trainers of our Japanese staff.
   - The American "Asian expert" is the best person to handle our company relations with Japan.
   - To overcome our lack of knowledge of the Japanese language, all we need is an interpreter to get on with building our Japanese subsidiary and developing amicable rapport with other Japanese companies and government agencies.
   - The best place to recruit capable Japanese managers for our subsidiary in Japan is in the United States among Japanese now studying or seeking jobs.
   - To transfer Japanese to the home office in the U.S. for management training and study tours will allow for sufficient transfer of our management practices into their situation.
   - The Japanese need our management skills, so the best way to transplant them is by direct investment.

3. In some companies, a Japanese management recruit is sent to a company training institute for orientation in spiritual awareness, consciousness, and company pride. Even laborers are sometimes sent to Buddhist temples for several days of Zen meditation, interspersed with lectures on religion and company policy.
4. The typical Japanese company attitude is for total employee involvement in return for company gymnasium facilities, free medical care, commuting allowances, subsidized lunches, cut rate groceries, bachelor quarters, and sometimes help from their marriage brokers and counselors.

Values and Standards

1. The Japanese personality generally is self-confident and flexible, demonstrating a sense of order, propriety, and appropriate behavior; there is a tendency toward diligence and thrift, balanced by a fun-loving approach which, at times, seems almost frivolous and extravagant.
2. In outlook the Japanese are cautious and given to stalling tactics, as well as insular manifested by the ingroup tendency.
3. The Japanese value social and self-control; but the rigid, ossified class system by which each man has his place as superior or inferior (women) is disappearing.
4. Today's Japanese value peace and economic progress, ensured somewhat by the fact that only 1% of the nation's gross national product is devoted to defense spending.
5. This culture highly regards new ideas and technologies, swallowing them up until they are Japanized (internalized) after careful, detailed examination; there is a subtle shift of emphasis from copying to creating underway.
6. The Japanese are changing their image of themselves as a people—from being in a dark, world closet looking out to Asian leaders in the international community with the attitude, "ours is never the best, so search for improvement."
7. Japanese society values training and education, especially of the young. It also values a spirit of intensity and craftsmanship—manifest in a quality of deep penetration into work and a pride in work, no matter how humble.
8. Japanese value congenial, known surroundings and seek to create an atmosphere of well-focused energy and disciplined good cheer.
9. A basic standard of Japanese life is work and play hard—work particularly for the good of the family or company family, and maintain controlled competition and cooperation in the process.
10. The yen is mightier than the sword.
11. The Japanese fear foreign military involvement.
12. The radical, revolutionary portion of Japanese youth have an entirely different set of values from the majority—they can be vicious and violent, yet espouse a spirit of self-denial, self-correction, self-dedication to what they consider a high cause.
13. Even criminal gangs (à la Mafia) will publicly apologize in press conferences to the public when they cause too much violence and disruption in society.
14. Generally, the Japanese are moved to heroically inspired deeds, rather than charity or noblesse oblige.

15. The goals of Japanese society seems to be steady employment, corporate growth, product superiority, and national economic welfare, which is considered more important than profits; the goals of the individual seem to be "more" for the organization and for self, in that order.
16. Corporate social responsibility is a standard built into the Japanese system: increasingly Japanese companies are giving a percentage of profits to promote education, social welfare, and culture.
17. Another organizational standard is to provide psychological security in the job, in return for loyalty to the company; there is a concept of mutual obligation between employer and employee. Strikes are only beginning to creep into the work culture.
18. The seniority standard is slowly giving way to merit promotion.
19. The Japanese value decision by consensus. Before action is taken, much time is spent on defining the question. They decide first if there is a need for a decision and what it is all about. The focus is upon what the decision is really about, not what it should be; once agreement is reached, then the Japanese move with great speed to the action stage. Referral of the question is made to the appropriate people, in effect indicating top management's answer to the question. The system forces the Japanese to make *big decisions*, and to avoid the Western tendency toward small decisions that are easy to make (minutia). For example, instead of making a decision on a particular joint venture, the Japanese might consider the direction the business should go, and this joint venture is then only a small aspect of the larger issue. By emphasizing the importance of understanding alternative solutions, the Japanese seem to avoid becoming prisoners of their own preconceived answers.
20. The Japanese standard of lifetime employment is not as simple as it seems:

    • Not all workers are considered permanent. A substantial body of employees (perhaps 20%) are not subject to this job security. Some positions are hired and paid for by the hour; women are generally considered in the temporary work category, and some who retire at fifty-five may be kept on in that temporary capacity: adjustments in work force can be readily made among these "temporaries."
    • Pay as a rule is on the basis of seniority and doubles every fifteen years.
    • Retirement is a two-year salary, severance bonus, usually at fifty-five. Western pension plans are beginning to come into companies slowly and are low in benefits.
    • Permanent employees who leave an employer will have a very difficult time being permanent again for another employer.

- The whole concept of permanent employment is left over from feudal arrangements of the past, and is now being undermined by superindustrial developments.

21. Another standard of Japanese work life seems to be *continuous training*:

    - It is performance focused in contrast to our promotion focus; in scope, it involves training not only in one's own job, but in all jobs at one's level.
    - The emphasis is on productivity and the real burden of training is on the learner—"What have we learned to do the job better?"
    - On the whole, they believe the older worker is more productive, and output per man hour is invariably higher in a plant with an older work population.
    - The industrial engineer teaches how to improve one's own productivity and process.
    - Generally, there are no craft unions or skills in Japanese industry and little mobility among blue collar workers; what mobility exists is among office workers and professionals.
    - Education is seen as a preparation for life, rather than life itself; those with "graduate education" are generally too old to start in the Japanese work system, and when employed they come in as specialists.

Synergy with the Japanese

The Japanese are a remarkable and unique people. Their subtle, complex culture, in particular, illustrates the differences and diversity of oriental cultures, in general. It points up why Western business leaders would benefit by training in cultural awareness and area studies if they expect to succeed in their business and social relations when operating in the Far East. As Den Fujita, president of McDonald's Company of Japan, reminded us: "American exporters should study the cultural aspects of Japan more carefully. You must send first-class Americans, experts, to Japan. Before you start production, you must learn Japanese culture and what Japanese are like. Then you can export in huge quantities!" The words of this Japanese hamburger king are also valid in reverse—Asians who expect to succeed in business abroad should be equally well informed about the cultures in which they do business. Finally, remember this section has only touched upon the tip of the iceberg—whatever one thinks he or she knows about the Japanese, must be continuously reexamined and scrutinized for Japan has a dynamic, changing culture.

The Japanese have well learned and successfully applied many lessons from Americans. As U.S. managers seek to renew their country's industrial base, to recapture lost technological markets, and to reverse foreign debt burdens, it is fitting for them to also study the Japanese and engage in joint ventures for the mutual benefit of both peoples (Condon and Kurata, 1987; Barnland, 1987).

PEOPLE'S REPUBLIC OF CHINA

People's Republic of China—Profile

Population 1,080,000,000
Ethnic Groups .... Han Chinese 93.3%
Religions .... Officially atheist, but also Muslims, Buddhists, Lamaists, Christians (Confucian philosophy still a force in the culture.)
Education .... 5 years compulsory
Literacy—over 75%
Land .... 3.7 million square miles
Government .... People's Republic, a Communist State
Political Parties .... Chinese Communist (CCP)
8 Minor Parties, including People's Liberation Army or Loose Coalitions
Per Capita Income .... 1985 US$ 310
Exports to U.S. .... $3,046 million
Imports from U.S. .... $4,800 million

Commentary

The New Yorker, November 19, 1984—By linking our country with the world market, expanding foreign trade, importing advanced technology, utilizing foreign capital, and entering into different forms of international economic and technological cooperation, we can use our strong points to make up for our weak points . . . We must abandon once and for all the idea of self-sufficiency.

Premier Zhao Ziyang

Forbes, July 29, 1985—"The China Guanxi: Thinking About a Joint Venture in China"—Dozens of U.S. corporations are setting up shop in China. Pity the lawyers who draft those joint venture contracts, however. They aren't easy. There's very little case law to rely upon.

Nick Gilbert

The Los Angeles Times, April 4, 1982—"China's Modernization Meeting a Major Barrier: Resistance to Language Reform"—For perhaps 6,000 years, the written Chinese language evolved to express the most complex ideas and has united the Chinese people. But despite its beauty, subtlety, and antiquity, increasingly it is an obstacle to modernization. The language does not absorb new ideas readily and new characters are rarely invented. As a geneticist at the Chinese Academy of Science described the situation, "We are being held prisoners by our language. There is an information explosion in the world that we cannot cope with in our language as it is now."

Michael Parks

New Management, Fall 1988—"What Americans Need to Know About Doing Business in China"—Eight years of economic reform in China have produced an achievement that the people of its powerful neighbor may find puzzling—the gross national product has more than doubled . . . (There is) emergence of township enterprises, more flexible measures from the Chinese government, a new generation of Chinese entrepreneurs, economic reform of state enterprises, more foreign investment in light industry, technology trade requiring training courses, business opportunities for foreign banks, and an improved climate of investment. After all, China is energetically developing a commodity-based economy for a hundred years to come.

Zhuge Lin, University of International Business and Economics, Beijing

Los Angeles Times, June 18, 1989—"No Turning Back for China"—The turmoil in China has changed that nation's business scene dramatically. Recent political developments have shaken—and in some cases crushed—the confidence many U.S. companies have had in their ability to prosper in the massive Chinese market. And as questions are raised about whether business will return to normal after the unrest subsides, projects are being put on hold. For the long term, however, prospects for U.S. business in China remain bright. Now that economic reforms have unleashed rising expectations among the Chinese people, there is no turning back from economic progress—even if the Chinese government continues its pattern of taking two steps forward and one step backward. . . . In the past, American firms have struggled because they haven't understood the "yin" and "yang" of selling to China. Viewing the process of selling to China as an interplay of negative and positive elements that grow out of each other is essential to success in business there. A series of decisions, first liberalizing and then restricting foreign trade, has characterized business with China in the past and confused U.S. companies, but things will continue that way regardless of who is in power.

Wesley J. Johnston, University of Southern California, Los Angeles

Los Angeles Times, June 25, 1989—"The Shattered Dream" Special Report—For centuries before Christ, a succession of emperors had ruled China with the power of the sword. Deng Xiaoping had appeared to try a new way. For the better part of a decade, the 84-year-old Deng, China's supreme leader, had permitted a measure of economic freedom. For many Chinese students, that was not enough. They massed in Tian An Men Square in central Beijing, chanting slogans for democracy, demanding a free press, erecting an imitation Statue of Liberty [protest period there began with a strike on April 24 and ended with Army suppression on June 5, 1989]. . . . But the shock waves from the Chinese demonstrations will reverberate for years both inside China and throughout the world. For many in China, the spring of 1989 shattered whatever faith they retained in the ruling Communist Party and its leaders.

Cultural Characteristics of Business in the PRC

On January 1, 1979, full diplomatic relations between the People's Republic of China (PRC) and the United States of America were established. Deputy Prime Minister Teng Hsiao-ping of the PRC came to the U.S. the last week of January. On March 1, 1979, embassies of the U.S. and the PRC opened in Peking and Washington, respectively. The first U.S. ambassador to the PRC was Leonard Woodcock, former United Auto Workers' president. Since that time a great deal of water has flowed along the Yangtze River and the number of U.S. business people and others visiting mainland China has steadily increased. Visitors now report luxury goods, such as color televisions, are being marketed on the streets of the major cities, and the message is clear to all Chinese: "Work hard and these things can belong to everyone." China is attempting to respond to problems of low productivity, obsolete technology, and other issues affecting their desires to increase the average monthly wage from $40.00 to over $1,000 per year by the year 2000. Previous economic systems that did not work because of ineffective decision-making, and the inadequate training of managers, technicians, and laborers are being changed to incorporate aspects of a free market economy. Mainland Chinese are now appealing to overseas Chinese to assist in revitalizing the "mother land." Despite the bad memories about foreigners from the old days of the Boxer Rebellion, in 1986 the "welcome mat" is still out for the more than 1,000 foreign companies who have opened offices there.

As this third edition is released in 1990, it is difficult to forecast the future of international trade with China. By blocking political and social reforms with violence and propaganda, the octogenarian Central Committee has alienated their younger generations of citizens and the world business community. *The Economist* (June 24, 1989) reports widespread reductions in productivity, in foreign aid and loans, and in international credit ratings. That publication predicts worse to come, for only Asian capitalists and the West can supply the technology, expertise, and hard-currency markets to turn China in the next 50 years from an underdeveloped to a moderately developed nation. Although in 1972 there was zero trade between China and the U.S.A., by 1988 America was the biggest foreign investor in China—$3.1 billion in 408 enterprises. In the short term, foreign companies have found it difficult to make money in the PRC, and with the current regressive situation, it is doubtful that international investment will be immediately increased there.

Only the Hong Kong Chinese, with their advantage of family links, shared currency, and language, have prospered in the PRC, and now they are uncertain of their future. Outside the mainland, free enterprise has flourished in the overseas Chinese community, especially in Singapore and Taiwan (Leppert, 1986).

Background Briefing

One of China's most predominant characteristics is its tradition of isolation. It is one of the oldest advanced civilizations in this world, and more than 2,300 years ago China enclosed itself behind the Great Wall and forced traders and merchants to remain outside these walls in order to conduct business. This same general attitude of isolation is present today. It is also necessary to remember that in spite of the relationships with Western people and other countries, China is a communist country where the teachings of Mao were aimed at completely reforming the social and moral life of the people. It is very often difficult to know who is responsible for making the final decision in business transactions as a result of the emphasis on equality. All Chinese are generally dressed alike with the only distinction of upper class rank being the existence of four pockets instead of two pockets stitched on the jacket. This is changing.

The Chinese have always held themselves in high esteem. The name of their country translates as "middle kingdom" for they saw themselves, their country, and culture as the center of human civilization. They expected that all other peoples and nations would pay tribute and homage to the Chinese. This situation continued until modern times, when the Chinese met head on with Europeans and Americans who did not understand this attitude and did not accept it as a condition for working and doing business with them. Global managers must place the present rejuvenation of China within a larger context.

The long history of Western imperialism in China is one of great humiliation for the Chinese. In 1949, following the establishment of the People's Republic of China, the Chinese Communist party attempted to change basic attitudes, values, and behavior of the Chinese people. The purpose of Mao Tse-tung and his reformers was to give the country the new direction and build from a traditional feudalistic society to a modern socialistic society.

A fundamental tool in effecting these changes in basic Chinese values was the development of a people's democracy where each and every individual in the country from peasant farmer to high government official would take a part in decision making at all levels on a regular basis. To accomplish this, work crews, communities, factory organizations, and schools were organized into study teams as a part of the daily business to investigate the socialistic principles upon which the government was established. In attempting to make these changes, four major areas were identified as obstacles to overcome:

1. The reduction of the difference in economic and political development of urban and rural areas.
2. The reduction of economic and political inequality between the industrial and peasant workers.
3. The reduction of inequality between manual laborers and the elite.
4. The reduction of inequality between the sexes.

The Chinese became even more involved in the politics of the nation during two major events in their history since 1949. These are the Great Leap Forward in the late 1950s and the Cultural Revolution of the late 1960s. During these two periods, economic efficiency and social order were forsaken as the country embarked on major new programs that were designed to eliminate "revisionist" elements and to illustrate to the people the significant importance of their role. By mid 1985, China's top leader, Deng Xiaoping* inaugurated campaigns for modernization and economic reform, even encouraging entrepreneurialism and replacement of senior party leaders with a younger generation. The events of June 1989 have been referred to by many as the great leap backward.

Negotiating Business

The Chinese rank among the toughest negotiators in the world. In addition, China is probably one of the most difficult countries for an outsider to understand and adapt to. Lucian Pye (1982) makes the following points from discussions with American negotiators in China:

1. They place emphasis on trust and mutual connections.
2. The Chinese stick to their word.
3. They are interested in long-range benefits.

---

* Pinyin—On January 1, 1979, China adopted officially the "pinyin" system of writing Chinese characters in the Latin alphabet. This is a system of romanization invented by the Chinese that has been widely used for years in China on street signs, as well as in elementary Chinese textbooks. Pinyin is now to replace the familiar Wade-Giles romanization system. The following are examples of the Wade-Giles and pinyin systems:

Wade-Giles	Pinyin
Peking	Beijing
Kwangchow/Canton	Guangzhou
Mao Tse-tung	Mao Zedong
Teng Hsiao-ping	Deng Xiaoping
Hua Kuo-feng	Hua Geofeng
Chou En-lai	Zhou Enlai

4. They respond well to foreign representatives who say they "specialize" in the PRC.
5. They are sensitive to national slights and still addicted to propagandistic slogans and codes.
6. Many Americans are convinced that the Chinese consciously use such slow down techniques as bargaining ploys because they believe they can exploit a natural American tendency for impatience.
7. In the first encounters the Chinese usually seem to be bound by their traditional non-legalistic practices.
8. The American business person comes to appreciate the fact he will be able to operate only at the tolerance of the Chinese and that it will be very easy for him to do the wrong thing once he gets to China.
9. The fact that the Chinese seem to have a compelling need to dwell on the subject of friendship convinced many American businessmen that reciprocity in this spirit was a prerequisite for doing business with China.
10. Once the Chinese decide upon who and what is the best, they show great steadfastness.
11. Businessmen also report that the Chinese sometimes put pressure on them when discussing the final concrete arrangements by suggesting that they have broken the spirit of friendship in which the business relationship was originally established.
12. In negotiations with the Chinese, nothing should be considered final until it has been actually realized.
13. The Chinese make such obviously self-serving demands that one immediately expects they must have some scheme afoot because otherwise they could not be taken seriously.
14. So as not to lose face, the Chinese prefer to negotiate through an intermediary.
15. Initially, a business meeting is devoted to pleasantries—serving tea, chit chat, fencing, waiting for the right opening to begin serious discussions.
16. Several American businessmen felt that a key early signal of the intensity of Chinese interest in doing business with them was the caliber of the Chinese assigned to their sessions.
17. The Chinese posture becomes rigid whenever they feel their own goals are being compromised.

Technical competence is the primary criterion for the representatives according to experienced travelers to the PRC. Many American companies that have visited China during the past few years have had to leave China midway through a visit and return later with more technically seasoned engineers.

Business Courtesies

When a foreign visitor has an appointment with a Chinese official, one will generally be introduced and offered some tea and cigarettes. The offering of a cigarette in the PRC has become a common expression of hospitality. Prior to your entrance, your Chinese host will be briefed on who you are and why you are there. There may be initiated polite questions about your trip and the U.S., generally in the area of pleasantries, and perhaps even about your family. If your call is merely a courtesy call, it may not go beyond this. If this is more than a courtesy call, it would be appropriate to begin discussion of a business nature at this time. The Chinese host will generally indicate when it is time for a person to leave.

It is also important to reciprocate invitations if they are given by the PRC. For example, if a banquet is given in the honor of the American team, they should reciprocate by giving a banquet for the Chinese team. Small company souvenirs or American picture books often make good presents, but expensive gifts should not be given.

Some business cautions—the Chinese are sensitive about foreigners' comments on Chinese politics. Even a joke about the late Chairman Mao, or any of their other political leaders, is extremely *inappropriate*. It is suggested that it is best to listen, ask questions related to your particular business for being in the PRC, and leave it at that.

The Chinese are punctual, and you should arrive promptly on time for each meeting.

The Chinese do not like to be touched or slapped on the back or even to shake hands. A slight bow and a brief shake of the hands is more appropriate.

In China, the family name is always mentioned first. For example, Teng Hsiao-ping should be addressed as Mr. Teng. During one's stay in the PRC, a visitor could be invited to a dinner in a restaurant by the organization that is sponsoring the visit. The guest should arrive on time or even perhaps a little early. The host would normally toast the guest at an early stage of the meal with the guest reciprocating after a short interval. During the meal, alcoholic beverages should not be consumed until a toast has been made. It is a custom to toast other persons at the table throughout the meal. At the end of the dinner, the guest of honor makes the first move to depart. The usual procedure is to leave shortly after the meal is finished. Most dinner parties usually end by 8:30 or 9:00 in the evening.

It is customary to use business cards in the PRC, and it is recommended that one side be printed in Chinese. However, business cards from the Chinese to Americans may not be given in return. Americans or foreign businessmen traveling to Peking via Hong Kong can easily have these cards printed in a matter of hours in that city.

The Chinese generally believe that foreign businessmen will be highly qualified technically in their specific areas of expertise. The Chinese businessmen do not have a need to show their intellectual expertise or to make an impression on the foreign guest. The foreigner or foreign businessman who is worthy and a true professional will have discreet but lavish attention showered on him while he is in China.

The Chinese businessman traditionally places much emphasis on proper etiquette. It is recommended that the qualities that foreign businessmen possess going to the PRC have are *dignity, reserve, patience, persistence,* and a *sensitivity to and respect for Chinese customs and temperament.*

The Chinese generally give preference to companies with long standing relationships with state trading companies. Newcomers and new business organizations have to adjust to the Chinese style of making contracts, negotiating, and arranging for contracts.

One should also attempt to be a good guest and listen politely to talks on Mao and the great progress China has made during the last several years. The Chinese are known as tough bargainers but they are also known as being reputable and honorable.

Very often, several visits to the PRC are necessary to consummate any business transaction. The foreign businessman should realize this. It has been found by many American businessmen that three, four, and five business negotiating sessions are often required in order to finalize the negotiations.

Traders coming to sell products in China must be prepared to spend a much longer time than *buyers,* and may find themselves waiting for appointments day after day. This is when one must exhibit patience, and perseverance, as well as a sensitivity to Chinese customs and way of doing business.

Guidelines for Doing Business in the PRC

1. The foreign businessman should avoid attempting to encourage the people from China to increase their productivity on the basis of "getting ahead."
2. The foreign businessman should not focus on the individual Chinese person, but rather on the group of individuals who are working for a particular goal. If a Chinese individual is singled out as possessing unique qualities, this could very well embarrass the person.
3. The visitor should also behave in a noncondescending manner. The people from the PRC have had their experience in the past with Western imperialism and superiority.
4. Generally, in discussions with Chinese people, the foreigner should avoid "self centered" conversation in which the "I" is excessively used. The Chi-

nese view with contempt the individual who strives to display personal attributes, as Chinese are much more oriented to the group.

5. The Chinese are somewhat more reticent, retiring, reserved, or shy when compared with North Americans. They avoid open displays of affection and the speaking distance between two people in nonintimate relationships is greater than in the West.

6. The Chinese are not a "touching" society, and in this respect, they are very similar to North Americans; nor do they appreciate loud, boisterous behavior. A foreign businessman may find himself in difficulty if he is overly aggressive and loud.

John Frankenstein writing in the *Asian Wall Street Journal* (August 26, 1985) summed it up best:

> Business savvy and cultural sensitivity are needed for success and preparing a manager adequately for his stay in China could make the difference between merely servicing and succeeding.

Finally, it is wise for global managers to remember that in all developing nations—from Asia to Africa, Westerners should never denigrate traditional beliefs and practices that are still fundamental to the culture. Avoid references and jokes about superstition, spirits, seances, voodoo, whatever. Third World villagers, especially where agnostic Confucianism dominates, tend to believe in magic, demons, evil spirits, and exorcism. It is often a part of political and social life, as in Indonesia where mystic tendencies cause government officials to check with their gurus and astrologers before making decisions.

OTHER PACIFIC BASIN COUNTRIES

The Pacific Rim has a diversity of peoples and cultures in various stages of economic and technological development. A fourth of mankind lives in the rapidly developing People's Republic of China. The potential of Indonesia is mind-boggling. As one views Asia and its management, can we afford to overlook Australia? But the East is so large in terms of geography, human and natural resources, and disparate business practices that total coverage is beyond the scope of this unit. So, this section examines several Asian peoples and apologizes to other ancient cultures and areas that space limitations force us to exclude. But the insights shared in this representative sample of the East will help global managers to be more sensitive and appreciative of their Asian counterparts, so that greater collaboration and cooperation may be fostered through international commerce.

Nearly two billion people in Asia, about half the human race, are experiencing dramatic changes in their lives. The Chinese are attempting to modernize their country, while Japan is learning to live with the successes of modernization. Secretary of State George Schultz on February 21, 1985, in San Francisco, expressed his opinion of the importance of this region:

> In the Pacific today there is a new reality, though the world may not yet fully comprehend it. In economic development, in the growth of free institutions, and in growing global influence, the Pacific region has rapidly emerged as a leading force on the world stage. Its economic dynamism has become a model for the developing world and offers a unique and attractive vision of the future.
>
> Perhaps even more important, there is a new trend toward wider cooperation among many East Asian nations. A sense of Pacific community is emerging. We see an expanding practice of regional consultations, a developing sense of common interests, and a desire to cooperate on a widening range of economic issues.

Victor Hao Li, president of the East-West Center, thinks the Pacific Era or Asian Century is arriving fast. In an article on the "The New Orient Express" (*World Monitor*, November 1988), he provides some documentation:

- East and Southeast Asia now share one-fifth of the gross world products, and their leaders are asserting traditional cultural values and ways while questioning Western models.
- Newly Industrialized Countries (NICs) there have a per capita income between $2–7,000, citing Taiwan's foreign exchange as the second largest in the world ($75 billion); South Korea, an economic powerhouse, exports automobiles, computers, and electronic equipment and has established a worldwide reputation for quality; Singapore and Hong Kong have not only made surprising economic gains, but are very modern urban communities.
- ASEAN (Association of Southeast Asian Nations)—4 resource-rich nations have per capita income between $500–2,000 and are still industrializing: Indonesia has become self-sufficient in rice production; India has a rising middle class of 150 million; Philippines output of goods and services has grown 5.6% and inflation dropped below 10%; Malaysia and Thailand experience steady economic growth, including tourism. Australia and New Zealand have per capita incomes exceeding $7,000 (as does Japan), and are integral parts of the Asia/Pacific community.
- The Fourth World in the South Asian region are economically undeveloped nations with under $400 per capita annual incomes—Pakistan, Bangladesh, Sri Lanka, Nepal, Bhutan, Maldives, North Korea, Vietnam, Cambodia, and Burma.

The problem in the last four is the direction of the military dictatorships, as epitomized in Burma. Renamed "Myanma" by cohorts of General Ne Win after 27 years of his misrule, including the broad-based National League for Democracy under the leadership of Su Kyi, the country is systematically suppressed by totalitarian tactics. Otherwise, the Pacific/Asian area is promising.

SOUTH KOREA

South Korea—Profile

Population	42,772,956
Ethnic Groups	Korean Small Chinese Minority
Religions	Buddhism, strong Confucian tradition, Shamanism, Chondokyo, Christianity
Education	Six years compulsory Literacy over 90%
Land	38,000 square miles
Government	Republic
Political Parties	Democratic Justice (DJP) Democratic Korea (DKP) Korean National Citizens (KNCP) New Korea Democratic (NKDP) Several small parties
Per Capita Income	US$ 2,800
Exports to U.S.	$13.88 billion
Imports from U.S.	$6.537 billion

Commentary

New York Times, April 11, 1985—"Korean Companies in the U.S."— This carefully cultivated image of the friendly, caring company of one happy family typifies the Korean management style. But the friendship is not for nothing. It is intended to keep unions at bay, and to foster a loyalty and enthusiasm in the work force that will generate more televisions per hour than American mangement can.

Nicholas Kristof

The Economist, June 24, 1989—"The Cunning Learning of South Korea"—Foreigners are still mystified by Korean business: how it works, why its firms are so vast, and the secret of its success . . . In Korea, it is the all-too-visible hand of government that helped promising firms by offering the monopoly power, with cheap and sometimes more-than-free credit, and with the opportunity to buy up bankrupt businesses for a song. In the process the government created vast, diversified business conglomerates called "chaebol" . . . The sales of the five biggest account for more than half of South Korea's $160 billion GNP . . . What counts is managing labor more efficiently. . . . No wonder (South) Korea is suffering a rash of bitter strikes. Now that politics has turned democratic, can its big business continue to be run by despots?

Cultural Characteristics of Business in South Korea

Asia, or the Far East, is puzzling and generally difficult for most Western businesspeople to understand. Until recently, Japan was the market and the country most well known. With the normalization of diplomatic relations between the United States and the People's Republic of China, much work and study have been conducted in that area. But Korea was virtually unknown to the rest of the world until the great struggle and war in the 1950s. At that time, it became a focus of world attention in a clash between the East and the West. Korea became a battleground of communist and democratic ideologies. Thus, today it is a divided country, with the U.N. maintaining a buffer zone of peace between the communistic system of the North and a somewhat democratic, but totalitarian military regime of the South.

But, South Korea's economic transformation is the wonder of the world, and some see its future role as comparable to Japan (Kang, 1989; Amsden, 1989.) Its quality products and energetic workers are exported around the globe, along with eager-to-learn technicians. South Korea has renewed its cities and is building satellite cities south of Seoul, as well as renewing the country's west coast. While northern relatives stagnate under totalitarianism, this dynamic society produced first-class Olympic games and facilities in 1988. It has managed a relatively peaceful election transition toward a more democratic government. Its population is restless for more democracy, improved working conditions and benefits, and progress toward national reunification with the North. Student radicals continue to promote mass disturbances over such issues, including the removal of U.S. troops and bases. The Korea Development Institute reports that the country, like Taiwan, is restructuring toward a domestic-driven economy, especially with citizens having more disposable income. With the increase of families earning annual incomes of $18,000 or more, there is a growing demand for domestic goods and services, along with the desire for improved housing and tourism abroad. (U.S. sales there increased 46% in 1988). Yet, most South Koreans feel they have sacrificed too long, live in relative poverty, and complain of inequities. The workforce there is no longer docile and cheap. The Bank of Korea reports 75–85% growth in exports from 1980–88, adding to a 12% national growth rate for the past three years. Doing business there requires great care and sensitivity (De Mente, 1988; Leppert, 1987).

Religion

The underlying ethic of Korea is Shamanism, but the people have also been strongly influenced by Buddhism and Confucianism. Shamanism is the religion of ancient Koreans for whom the elements of earth, mountains, rivers, etc. were sacred. Shamanism was introduced in Korea in the fourth century and has the longest history among the organized religions in Korea. Confucianism also has been a strong force, and the most influential of the newer native Korean religions is Ch-ondo-gyo, which was founded in the mid-nineteenth century on the belief that every person represents heaven. As author Richard Critchfield reminds us (*Los Angeles Times*, June 1, 1980):

> The tenets of Confucianism still provide the inner compass to Korean minds; it is a heritage based upon long centuries of inculcation, and to ignore it is as futile as to ignore Islamic tradition in the Middle East.

Christianity was introduced in Korea in 1783 by Korean diplomatic delegates who came into contact with the Bible in China.

Cultural Concepts

A vital concept to understand in Korea is *kibun*, which is one of the most important factors influencing the conduct and the relationship with others. The word literally means inner feelings. It one's *kibun* is good, then one functions smoothly and with ease and feels like a million dollars. If one's *kibun* is upset or bad, then things may come to a complete halt, and one feels depressed. The word has no true English equivalent, but "mood" is close. In interpersonal relationships, keeping the *kibun* in good order often takes precedence over all other considerations.

In business functions, businessmen try to operate in a manner that will enhance the *kibun* of both persons. To damage the *kibun* may effectively cut off relationships and create an enemy. One does not tend to do business with a person who has damaged one's *kibun*. Much of the disturbance of *kibun* in interpersonal relationships has to do with lower class persons disturbing higher class persons. Thus, for example, a teacher can scold a student in the class and no individual feels hurt or no one's *kibun* is especially disturbed.

Proper interpersonal relationships are all important among Koreans, and there is little concept of equality in relationships among Koreans. Relationships tend to be almost entirely vertical rather than horizontal, and each person is in a relatively higher or lower position. It is essential for one to know the levels of society and to know one's place in the scheme of things. In relationships, it is often necessary to appear to lower oneself in selfless humility and give honor to other people. A well-respected Korean often assumes an attitude of self-negation and self-effacement in social and business contacts. To put oneself forward is considered proud arrogance and worthy of scorn.

Protocol is extremely important to Koreans. When meeting others, if you do not appreciate one's actual position and give it due recognition, then one might as well withdraw on some pretext and try to avoid future contacts with those who have misjudged one's true status. A representative of another person or group at a meeting is treated with even more care than that person or group because the substitute may be sensitive to slights either real or imagined and report it back to his colleagues. This is very difficult for Westerners to understand, but a Korean who fails to observe the basic rules of social exchange is considered by other Koreans to not even be a person—he is an "unperson." Foreigners to a certain extent and in a certain sense are considered by Koreans as unpersons. Koreans show very little concern for an unperson's feelings, his comfort, or whether he lives or dies. In short, such an unperson is not worthy of much consideration. When relationships are broken among Koreans, some people tend to resort to violence, but every effort must be made to remain within the framework of polite relationships.

Deference or Respect to Elders

Elders in Korean society are always honored, respected, pampered, appeased. To engender the anger of an elder means serious damage, because his age allows him to influence the opinions of others, regardless of the right or wrong of the situation. In the presence of an elder, one remains at attention and one does not even smoke or drink. Like children, elders must be given special delicacies at meals, and their every wish and desire is catered to whenever possible. The custom and manner in which elderly people are sometimes sent to old persons homes in the United States is extremely barbarous and shocking to the Koreans. Every home in Korea, no matter how poor, allocates the best room in the house to the honored grandfather or grandmother. Again the words of Richard Critchfield say it best:

> It would be difficult to exaggerate the influence of Confucian thought in South Korea's 36,000 villages, where customs of hierarchy, harmony and communal obligations flow from the adage, "Filial piety is the basis of all conduct." Sons are subordinate to fathers, younger brothers to elder brothers, wives to husbands and everyone to the state.

Etiquette

Koreans are considered by others to be among the most naturally polite people in the world when the proper rules of etiquette are followed. In personal relationships with strangers or associates, Koreans tend to be very strict in observing the rules of etiquette. To touch another person physically is considered an affront to his person, unless there is a well established bond of close friendship or childhood ties.

In modern Korean society many businessmen now shake hands as a sign that they are modernized. However, they will very often bow at the same time that they shake a person's hand. To slap someone on the back or to put one's arms around a casual acquaintance or to be too familiar with someone in public is a serious breach that may effectively cool future relations.

To embarrass someone by making a joke at his expense is highly resented even if done by a foreigner who does not understand the customs.

After a few drinks, businessmen often become very affectionate, but at the same time apologize for being a bit drunk. The next day they will tell their colleagues that they are sorry for imposing one's good nature while being a little tipsy.

When appearing in public to speak, perform, or whatever, one bows first towards the audience and then towards the chairman of the meeting. Businesspeople should learn the proper bowing procedures and etiquette of Koreans. Korean businessmen do not seem to worry about keeping time, being on time, beginning on time, or leaving on time to the same extent that Western businessmen do. However, this is changing now and there is more of a tendency to follow the same time schedule as in the West.

Introductions. It is not the custom among the Koreans to introduce one person to another. Instead, one would say to another, "I have never seen you before" or "I am seeing you for the first time." The other person repeats the same thing, and then usually the elder of the two persons in age or rank says, "Let us introduce ourselves." Each person then steps back a little, bows from the waist, states his own name. They are then formally introduced. Names are stated in a low, humble voice that cannot be heard accurately, and then calling cards are exchanged. One may learn the new person's name and position at leisure. Do not say, "Sorry, I did not get your name. Would you tell me again?" Calling cards are very necessary in Korea and should be used by foreign or Western businesspeople at all times.

The use of names in Korea has an entirely different connotation than in most Western countries. To the Confucian, using a name is presumptuous and impolite, as a name is something to be honored and respected and it should not be used casually. In Shamanism, to write a name calls up the spirit world and is considered bad luck. One's name, whether it is written or spoken, has its own mystique, and is that person's personal property. To call someone directly by his name is an affront in most social circumstances.

In Korea there are relatively few surnames, thus there appears to most Westerners to be an inordinate number of Kim's and Park's. When a Western businessperson uses a Korean's name to his face, one can usually observe a slight wince around the eyes of a Korean. It is almost always there. A Korean is addressed by his title, position, trade, profession, or some other honorific title such as teacher. As opposed to our U.S. training of saying, "Good morning, Mr. Kim," a polite good morning is better or "Good morning, teacher" is acceptable. Many Koreans work and live next to each other for years without even knowing their full names. The president of Korea is referred to by high officials as "excellency," even in his absence, because it is considered too familiar to use such a high person's name in conversation. A Korean's name is usually made up of three characters—the family's surname is placed first, and then the given name, which is made up of two characters. It is used by all members of the same generation. By knowing this name, a person's generation in the family tree can be recognized.

Privacy and Propriety. Privacy is a luxury that few can afford in Korea, and Koreans have learned to make imaginary walls about themselves. A visitor calling on a person on a hot day may find this person in his undershirt with his feet on his desk, fanning himself. The visitor coughs to announce his arrival, but he does not knock. This person does not "see" the person he has come to visit, nor does this person "see" the visitor until he has risen, put on his shirt, coat, tie and adjusted himself. Then they "see" each other and begin the formality of greeting. To have privacy, a Korean withdraws behind an imaginary curtain and undresses, or does what he has to do, not seeing or being seen by those who, by the literal Western eye, are in plain view. It is considered discourteous to violate this screen of privacy once it is drawn about a person. A discreet cough is intended to notify the person behind the screen that an interruption is impending.

Table manners are based on making the guest feel comfortable. The attitude of a servant is proper for a host with his guest. At meals, the hostess is at the lowest place, the farthest from the place of honor, and often will not even eat in the presence of a guest. Before beginning to eat, the host will often make a formal welcome speech stating the purpose of the gathering and paying his respects to his guest. Often food is served on small individual tables, each with many side dishes of food, a bowl of soup, and a bowl of rice. One removes the top off the dish of the hot rice and places it on the floor under his place at the table. Korean food tends to be highly seasoned with red pepper, thus a careful sip of the soup is advisable before taking a large mouthful. To lay the chopsticks or spoon on the table is to indicate that you have finished eating. To put them on the top of a dish or bowl means that you are merely resting. A guest may show his appreciation for the meal by slurping his soup or smacking his lips. Guests are not expected to clean their plates, and to leave nothing indicates that you are still hungry and embarrasses the host by implying that he has not prepared enough food. The host will continue to urge his guest to eat more, but a firm refusal is respected. A good healthy belch after a meal is a sign that one has eaten well and enjoyed it.

Gift Giving. Koreans give gifts on many occasions, and the appropriate etiquette surrounding the giving of gifts is often a problem to Western businesspeople. In this context, every gift expects something in return, and one rarely gives an expensive gift without a purpose. The purpose may be to establish an obligation, to gain a certain advantage, or merely to create an atmosphere in which the recipient will be more pliable to the request of the donor. To return a gift is considered an affront, but in some instances it may be better to return the gift than to accept it with no intention of doing a favor in return. Some Koreans have a special ability to work their way into the affection of foreigners and form personal relationships that may later prove embarrassing and/or difficult to handle when some impossible or very often illegal and unlawful request is made. In Korean, "yes" may merely mean "I heard you," and not agreement or intention of complying. To say "no" is an affront and could hurt the feelings, and thus is poor etiquette. Many Koreans often say "yes" to each other and to foreigners and then go their own way doing quite the opposite with little sense of breaking a promise or agreement.

Business Attitudes

In business, flattery is a way of life, and without subtle flattery, business would come to a halt. One must begin on the periphery in business relationships and gradually zero in on the main business in narrowing circles. To begin directly a discussion of some delicate business matter or new business venture is considered by Koreans to be the height of stupidity and dooms the project to almost certain failure. Impatience to a Korean is a major fault. A highly skilled businessman moves with deliberation, dignity, and studied motions, and senses the impressions and nuances being sent to him by the other businessman.

To Korean businessmen, Western business persons often appear to make contracts on the assumptions that all the factors will remain indefinitely the same. They take a gamble that society will allow them to complete the agreed conditions of the contract. In Korea a written contract is sometimes of little value, though this is currently changing. It may be only a paper contract, and there may be no understanding that it will be kept if the conditions at the time it was made should change. A change in the economy, the political situation, or personal reasons of one of the contractors may invalidate the completion of the contract without any sense of misdeed.

Since there are many similarities between Korean and other Oriental cultures, cross-cultural skills that are effective in this society have application elsewhere. For example, there is a large minority population of Koreans in Los Angeles and their native language is the third largest spoken in that California city. In many ways Korean is also a synergistic culture, except for the political division of the peninsula. Fortunately, North and South Korea have begun a positive dialogue to permit further exchanges among divided families; this may eventually lead to improvement in their political relationships.

PHILIPPINES

Philippines—Profile

Population	57.36 million
Ethnic Groups	Christian Malay 91.5%, Muslim Malay 4%, Chinese 1.5%, Other 3.0% (Polynesian and Spanish cultural influences.)
Religions	Roman Catholic 83%, Protestant 9%, Muslim 5%, Buddhist 3%
Education	6 Years Compulsory (7–12) Literacy about 88%
Land	116,000 square miles
Government	Republic
Political Parties	Marcos's New Society (KBL), Unido, Liberals, Nacionalistas, PDP, Laban, Mindanao Alliance and Pusyon Visaya (Prom. Reg.)
Per Capita Income	1983 US$ 600
Exports to U.S.	$2,160 million
Imports from U.S.	$1,766.4 million

Commentary

New York Times, August 28, 1984—"The American Influence in the Philippines"—In addition to the country's fixation with foreign goods and status symbols, especially American ones, political, cultural and material expectations in the Philippines seem to be measured against the American standard. For many Filipinos, their country is found to be wanting, and their reaction is to try to move to the U.S., "This is a developing country with Madison Avenue taste."

New York Times, June 6, 1985—"Huge Number of Filipinos Migrating to the U.S."—With immigration accelerating, so is the "brain-drain" from the Philippines to the U.S. A study by the Center of Policy and Development of the University of the Philippines concluded that the savings in the cost of education that the U.S. gains each year from the migration to American of Filipino scientists, engineers and other professionals, is more than Washington's annual economic aid to the Philippines. Accordingly, the study concludes that the brain-drain constitutes a "reverse foreign aid paid by the Philippines."

Steve Lohr

World Monitor, November 1988—Twenty years ago, the Philippines had the greatest promise among Southeast Asian nations. But the later Marcos years spread an oppressive gloom over the political and economic landscape, from which the country has not yet recovered. Despite these problems, inflation has dropped, the output of goods and services increases, and investment from the outside is growing.

Victor Hao Li

Cultural Characteristics of Business in the Philippines

Geography, Government, and People

In this multicultural society, Tagalog is the principal language, but English is widely spoken because of Western influences, primarily U.S.

Hospitality, friendliness, and sincerity are prominent aspects of the Filipino culture. An ambience filled with gaiety is the result of over 400 years of the Spanish influence. Filipinos are predominantly of Malay stock, with Chinese and American cultural influences. The Philippines' 700 islands cover approximately 115,000 square miles in the South China Sea. The eleven largest islands comprise over 95% of the total land area and population, with Luzon being the largest island, and Mindanao being the second largest. Although Manila, located on Luzon, is the most well-known area, Quezon City was declared the capital of the Philippines in 1948. However, most government activity still remains in Manila.

Great contrasts in terrain and climate exist throughout the Philippines. Northern Luzon is mountainous, the southern islands are comparatively dry, while other parts are dense jungle areas. In addition, throughout the islands there are a number of volcanoes. The Philippines are located within the tropic zone with the low areas having a warm, humid climate and only slight variations from the average temperature of 80 degrees Fahrenheit. The monsoon season lasts from June to November, and periodic typhoons pass over the island causing immense floods and damage to crops and homes.

The military government of President Ferdinand E. Marcos remained in power until early 1986, when Corazon Aquino became president. The president is the head of state and together with the prime minister is elected from the membership of the National Assembly. The prime minister appoints his cabinet and initiates most legislation. The traditional parties in the Philippines are the Liberal, and the Nacionalista, and also a small Communist group which has essentially operated independently.

The foreign policy of the Philippines is based on a close alliance with the United States and in cooperation with many other Asian countries. The United States, the Philippines, and six other countries signed the Manila Pact in 1954, which established the Southeast Asia Treaty Organization, or SEATO.

Western business people have generally reported that the Filipino government is inefficient and that having contacts in high places of government is essential in cutting through the bureaucratic red tape. The people basically work on the "mañana" system, since they seldom complete things on time despite deadlines. However, in their own fashion, things do get done. "Almost, but not quite" is the foreigner's conclusion.

More international businesses appear to be returning to the Philippines as President Aquino consolidates her political base. The Philippines' commitment to free enterprise and friendly relations with Western nations exists even with the recent establishment of relations with many Communist nations in the past years.

The Philippines' economy is based on agriculture, forestry, and fishing, which employ more than half of the total labor force and account for more than 50% of all exports. The agricultural sector consists of the production of food crops essentially for domestic consumption (rice and corn), and cash crops for export. The country's major exports are sugar, copra, copra meal, coconut oil, pineapple, tobacco, and abaca. The Philippines is also one of the world's leading producers of wood and wood products. Although fishing contributes to the Philippines' economy, the fertile fishing area has not been developed to its full potential. The Philippines are rich in mineral resources with nickel, copper, and other mineral deposits among the largest in the world. However, only a small portion of these have been surveyed and exploited. Government programs have recently been initiated to strengthen the industrial development and have included protective import duties and taxes. Until 1970, the U.S. was a leading trading partner of the Philippines. However, trade with Japan has now surpassed that of the U.S. because of considerable tourist and business investments.

The Philippines' population has doubled since it received independence from the United States in 1946. With a population numbering approximately 46 million, the Philippines has one of the highest birth rates in the world. Manila, the largest city on the islands, has a population of around 2 million persons, and Quezon City, the capital, has nearly a million inhabitants. People have come to the Philippines from many Southeast Asian countries, such as Indonesia, Malaysia, and China. The blend of these cultures has formed the Filipino race. The most significant alien ethnic group residing in the Philippines are the Chinese who have played an important role in commerce since the nineteenth century, when they first came to the Philippines to trade. With a million and a half Moslem Filipinos on the island, Moslem practices are also prevalent.

The present culture strongly reflects Hispanic influence. The education system was influenced by the presence and the relationship of the Philippines to the United States from 1898 to 1946. Education is highly valued and a family will make great sacrifices in order to educate the children. The literacy rate is approximately 85% and nearly one-fourth of the nation's budget is spent on education. However, the goal of compulsory education has not yet been realized completely because of the lack of facilities and qualified teachers.

The standard of living in the Philippines varies, with only a few families owning a large percentage of the rural and urban real estate. These wealthy few control profitable businesses and the universities, and they live in luxury. Reform, especially in land ownership progresses slowly.

The Filipinos are a conforming people who rarely create disturbances. Thus, they are willing to go along with conditions rather than trying to change them. Their belief in *pakiksama*, which literally means the ability to get along with people, emphasizes the Filipino attitude of submission as opposed to disturbing those around them with whom they might disagree. Confrontation is avoided. Consequently, the true feelings of the Filipinos are often hidden behind an agreeing façade, and the foreign business person in the Philippines should attempt to read these hidden signals that are given him.

Cultural Concepts

Filipinos generate warmth and friendliness. The everyday greeting for acquaintances and friends is a handshake greeting for men and women, and occasionally a light pat on the back for men. Older people should be shown respect and should always be allowed to take the lead. Filipinos place great importance on the family. The well-being of the family supersedes every other desire, therefore questions concerning the family are very important. The Filipino does not strive to accumulate money and power for his own sake, but rather in order to better his family position. Large extended families, including cousins and friends, reflect the great interdependence of the family in the Philippines.

Hiya or shame is an important social force for Filipinos, and the idea is instilled in their children at an early age. To accuse a person of not having this *hiya* trait is a gross insult because it indicates that a person is unable to feel shame as well as all other emotions. Therefore, it is very important never to criticize another person in public or in front of his friends because it shames him, and is thus the greatest of insults.

The negative ramifications of *hiya* are that the Filipinos avoid change, innovation, or competition simply because if the result is failure, it would cause him to shame his family. Consequently, the Filipino family and the Filipino businessperson will "save face" at any cost.

The Filipinos are a very fatalistic people. An everyday saying in Tagalog is "bahala na," which translates either as "accept what comes and bear it with hope and patience," or "God wills it." Success in the mind of the Filipino is often a function of fate rather than individual merit, and therefore, most people are content in their social position only because they feel fate has placed them there. Expressions such as "never mind," "it doesn't matter," or "it was my fate" are common reactions to problems such as typhoons, epidemics, and crop failures. Another demonstration of their belief in fate is that the Filipinos frequently gamble and play games of chance.

The Filipinos also have some ancient beliefs with regard to spirits and ghosts. At times, the Filipino will use the excuse of these phantoms when he fails to keep an appointment or a promise, which is difficult for Western people to understand.

Due to the Spanish influence, the Filipinos are a somewhat emotional people, and very sensitive. They are loyal friends and demand the same kind of loyalty in return. This aspect is reflected in social situations, as well as business interactions. They are reluctant to share or to do business with a person unless there is a mutual sincerity. This has been a great obstacle in the past, as Filipinos have described American businessmen as being overly aggressive and insensitive to feelings.

The Filipinos are hospitable and enjoy entertaining. When accepting invitations, one should inquire if the starting time is "American time" or "Filipino time." In the case of American time, one should arrive at the hour requested. However, if the arrival time is on Filipino time, it is not necessary to arrive until an hour or two later than requested.

For those Filipinos with a Spanish cultural background, many of the insights from Chapter 14 may also be applicable with such groups within this multicultural community.

For example, the concept of individualism is valued by the Filipinos. If a foreign businessman fails to treat a Filipino as an individual, the foreigner will be refused help. It is important to take time to talk with adults and children and not be judgmental. The Filipinos will make every effort to maintain their reputation as being a hospitable people. In return, foreign business people should be polite and respectful towards the Filipinos.

Another influence brought to the Philippines by the Spanish is the machismo attitude. Many married Filipino men may keep a *casa chica*, or concubine, which is generally accepted by their wives. However, this attitude has been changing with the development of human rights and the women's liberation movement. The Philippines prides itself on being one of the few Asian countries with a large percentage of women in government and politics.

Nonverbal Communication

There are several nonverbal communication techniques used in the Philippines, and the following are some examples that can be helpful in a business context. The raising of the eyebrows indicates an affirmative reply, namely a "yes." A jerk of the head downward means no, while a jerk upward means "yes." Like the Japanese, the Filipinos rarely say "no" as we do. They resist confrontation and may say "yes" verbally while putting their head downward, namely a nonverbal signal for "no." To indicate "come here" one would extend the hand out with the palm down moving the fingers in and out as in a scratching motion. When calling a waiter or a waitress in the Philippines, it is customary to hiss in order to get service. Filipino women use fans in this tropical climate and have developed a nonverbal gesture system using various fan movements to signal messages.

Religion

The Philippines is the only predominantly Christian country in the Far East primarily due to the Spanish influence. Over 90% of all Filipinos are Roman Catholic, which affects their culture and daily activities. There are several phrases in Tagalog that incorporate Catholic traditions that are used every day. For example, if someone indicates that he or she is frightened, one would say to that person in Tagalog, "May the Blessed Virgin Mary protect you." At the turn of the century, there was a significant Filipino resentment against the foreign domination of the Catholic Church, which led to a group of native Filipino priests splitting off and forming the Philippine Independent Church, now the second largest church in the islands.

A significant minority striving for human and religious rights is the one and a half million Filipinos who are Moslems. In southern areas of the islands, Islamic practices and militants dominate.

The Idea of Right and Wrong

Although the concepts of morality and ethics are much the same in the Philippines as in the United States, there are certain contrasts. According to American tradition, also present in these islands, right and wrong behavior reflects the relationship between an individual and the Almighty God. Theoretically, punishment or rewards are according to divine judgment. The individual may see certain behavior as sinful, and thus feel guilty if he has sinned. To most Filipinos, however, religion is less specifically related to daily behavior. What is "correct" behavior is more likely to be defined by tradition and related to the family and other reciprocal obligations. Failure to measure up in terms of family expectations and traditions produces feelings of shame.

As in most developing nations, including the Philippines, corruption is prevalent in the public services, government, and business. It is not uncommon for many complications in business and government bureaucracy to be speedily resolved by the payment of a favor. Such practices are the result of long historical and cultural development, rooted in the Spanish tradition in the Philippines.

The Filipinos have produced an extraordinary synergy among their diverse cultural groups. They are a people open to cooperation and collaboration with outsiders. There is also much internal dissension due to lack of political freedom, class inequities, and active guerrilla movements (e.g., Communist and Moslem extremists).

INDONESIA

Indonesia—Profile

Population	170.2 million
Ethnic Groups	Majority Malay Stock, 45% Javanese, 14% Sudanese, 7.5% Madurese, 7.5% Coastal Malays, 26% Other
Religions	Muslim 88%, Protestant 6%, Roman Catholic 3%, Hindu 2%, Other 1%
Education	Compulsory (7–12 Yrs. old) Literacy 64%
Land	736,000 square miles
Government	Republic
Political Parties	Golkar, Indonesia Democracy, United Development
Per Capita Income	1984 US$ 530
Exports to U.S.	1984—$3,000 million
Imports from U.S.	1984—$1,700 million

Commentary

New York Times, May 26, 1985—"Indonesians Try to Sort Out a Path for the Future"—Indonesians have certain advantages, foreign diplomats and other expatriate residents say. The national language, Bahasa Indonesia, a form of Malay, was adopted in the late 1920's and it has been a unifying force.

"We are a society coming from many tribes," the Balinese actor-director Ikranagara said in an interview in his Jakarta home. "Indonesians are lucky."

Wall Street Journal, April 11, 1984—"Hard Times on Indonesia's 'Gold Coast'"—Officials say they are counting on the strong family and religious ties of the population, nine out of 10 of whom are Moslem, to keep the modernization process from destroying Balikpapan.

Financial Times, January 20, 1984—"Indonesia's Tough Withdrawal from 'Oil Drug'"—President Suharto's reputation for caution and realism nevertheless remains untarnished. He has again shown himself willing to back the assessments of the "Berkeley mafia," the California trained technocrats who advise him, and who have demanded a curbing of Indonesia's addiction to the "oil drug."

Chris Sherwell

Asian Bulletin, April 1989—The Associated Press quoted civilian sources as saying that Indonesian troops in southern Sumatra had killed more than 100 Muslim radicals. . . . The state philosophy *Pancasila* stipulates that Indonesians should believe in one God, but falls short of making Islam the state religion. (The ideology also has principles of humanitarianism, national unity, consensus democracy, and justice.) Some army officers say privately that they believe Islamic fundamentalism could be one of the most serious problems threatening stability inside this multi-ethnic country. While most of 176 million people are Muslims, there has been a tradition of religious diversity and tolerance.

National Geographic, "Indonesia", January 1989—The number of people underemployed is 40 percent. Some two million new workers enter the labor force each year, far more than the new jobs available. About 50 percent of the population is under the age of 20. . . . By some estimates as much as a fourth of Jakarta is without housing. Many residents eke out a sub-rosa existence in slums like "bongharan" (rubble). . . . But Bali is also Indonesia's tourist mecca, attracting a third of the nation's foreign visitors. In 1988, 400,000 visitors spent an equivalent of $250 million on this one island. . . . About half of Java's people are farmers. Eight out of ten own land, in most cases not enough—or barely enough to live on. . . . 700,000 Indonesian families have been relocated through the government's transmigration program from overcrowded regions of Java, Madura, Bali, and Lombok to some 600 outer-island settlements.

Arthur Zich

Cultural Characteristics of Business in Indonesia

Geography and Government

"Bkinneka tunggal Ika" translated "unity through diversity" is the national motto of Indonesia. This nation of islands represents a rich variety of local customs and traditions found among its diverse people.

Indonesia is an archipelago situated across the equator between the continents of Asia and Australia. It is the largest archipelago in the world, with 13,677 islands of which 6,044 are inhabited. It stretches 3,330 miles from east to west, and 1,300 miles from north to south. There are four main island groups in Indonesia. The Greater Sunda Islands are composed of Java, which has population of 80 million, Sumatra which is the sixth largest island in the world, and two other large islands. The other three groups of islands include the Lesser Sunda Islands, the Malukus, and West Irian.

With the present population estimated at approximately 170 million, Indonesia is the fifth most populous country in the world, exceeded only by mainland China, India, the U.S.S.R., and the U.S.A.

Although Indonesia is primarily an agricultural land, it is not self-sufficient in food. Approximately 8% of the land in Indonesia is cultivated and most of this area is on Java, where the population is extremely concentrated. There are many small farms on Java, but the farming methods are old and very time consuming. Thus, farm life is generally hard and not profitable.

Over 60% of the national income of Indonesia is derived from oil. Recent significant oil finds have prompted estimates that the country has about 90% of the known and proven oil reserves in Southeast Asia. These reserves are of very high quality and are extremely low in sulfur.

Formerly known as the Dutch East Indies, Indonesia remained the territory of the Netherlands until 1942 when it was occupied by the Japanese. Although Indonesia gained its independence in 1945, it continued to struggle with intermittent guerrilla warfare until 1949 in order to gain total independence from the Dutch. In 1949, the Dutch transferred sovereignty of nearly all of the land of the Dutch East Indies except West Irian, which is now known as the Netherlands New Guinea. The new country became known as the Republic of Indonesia in 1950, and in 1963 West Irian also became part of the nation. General Suharto, a leader of the counter-coup, was formally made President of Indonesia in 1966.

Suharto's "new order" remains a strongly centralized government based on the Constitution of 1945, which was amended in 1950. As President, he is subordinate, as well as responsible, to the People's Assembly, although this assembly, consisting of 1920 members, is basically a ceremonial body that elects the President, approves his programs, and meets every five years to organize the election. The House of Representatives is made up of 460 representatives who meet annually. Three hundred sixty of these 460 seats are elected on a proportional system, and the other 100 persons are appointed by a coalition of different parties and functional groups. In Indonesia, there are a total of 27 provinces. Voting in Indonesia is the right of anyone over 17 years of age or who is married regardless of the age of the person.

In 1920, an Indonesian Communist Party was formed and in 1927, Sukarno and his followers formed the Indonesia National Party. For many years, these groups have struggled for life and growth.

In Indonesia, there has been and continues to be a long tradition of government corruption, which has been labeled "speed money" and means basically that which gets things done. Since 1970, the government has spent enormous time and energy in attempting to reduce corruption in high places, although how much has been is questionable. In addition, there has been considerable unrest in Indonesia, but the hopes have been that these energies could be channeled into constructive directions.

Indonesia is the largest Islamic land in the world. Indonesians mix Hindu and Moslem prayers and allow various kinds of religious beliefs to meld with the ideas of the prophet Mohammed. Generally, people do not strictly adhere to the rules of the Koran, rather the village law or *Adat* prevails in Indonesian rural and urban areas. Even though Indonesia is a Moslem country, women have never been veiled, nor have they been secluded like other Moslem women in the Middle East. On many of the islands, women vote and hold leadership positions. However, in spite of the fact that women have been guaranteed full and complete rights, Indonesia is a male-dominated country. Education of women is a problem with women comprising only 30% of the students at the university or college level. Thus, with this disparity in education, the Indonesian woman's position is behind that of her male counterpart.

Cultural Concepts

The family is the basic unit of Indonesian life. It is a highly complex system with many interlocking relationships in the vast network of an extended family system. For most Indonesians, the family is the first priority. There are many young people in Indonesia, with nearly 70% of the total population under 30 years of age. The customary law or *Adat* permits polygamy, but it is not practiced by many persons. In December, 1973, a bill was passed requiring free consent for girls with the minimum age of 16 and for boys with the minimum age of 19 in the sharing of property acquired in marriage. In the case of divorce, the children are often assigned to the custody of both parents, and in court, men desiring to practice polygamy must still prove that all of their wives will receive equal treatment.

A basic concept in Indonesian daily life both in a social and a business context is the importance of avoiding making someone feel *malu*. The word literally means ashamed or embarrassed. Criticizing or contradicting a person in front of others will cause you to lose face with the group and the person will feel *malu* as a result of your action.

Also important to Indonesians are the concepts of unity and conformity. They do not strive, as many Americans do, to become individualistic.

Behavior Modes

A common courtesy that should be respected is not raising one's voice or demonstrating externally intense emotions. Head-on confrontations are embarrassing to most Indonesians. Thus, they prefer to talk indirectly and ambiguously about areas of difference until common ground can be found. *Sembah* is the art of paying respect to one's superiors who are generally persons of higher rank or position either by birth, by economic status, or by age. One form of demonstrating *sembah* is by not questioning one's superiors.

In Indonesia, there is a subtle but very hierarchical approach to interpersonal relationships that is related not only to family and to the village, but also to the larger community and to the government. Leadership is very paternalistic and consensus is the mode followed by all persons. Young persons defer to old people, though in the cities this is changing somewhat. Indonesians are known for their friendly hospitality.

It is suggested that foreigners working in Indonesia never refuse an offer for food or drink, but at the same time, it is customary not to finish it completely.

Gestures and Greetings

There are certain gestures that should be avoided while in Indonesia. For example, never touch the head of an Indonesian as it is thought to be the place where the spirit resides. Kissing and embracing in public should also be avoided because it is considered rude and coarse. In addition, personal questions should not be asked as this may be interpreted by Indonesians as probing into territory that is none of one's business. The use of the left hand for eating or for passing of gifts should be avoided because it is considered the unclean hand. Pointing is also considered rude in Indonesia, and therefore should be avoided. Handshaking has become customary in Jakarta among Westernized Indonesians. However, in general, there is no physical contact. The traditional greeting is a bow with the hands together, a nodding of the head and a gracious smile.

Business Interactions

Indonesians are extremely indirect in business contexts. Therefore, it is very important to circumvent a subject before the critical issues are mentioned. Everything is negotiated in Indonesia, and the people love to bargain. With the exception of the major department stores, there are few fixed prices. Once a person is respected as a bargainer, a merchant will offer far more reasonable prices.

Indonesians do not like to be pressured or hurried. Time in the United States can be wasted, spent, utilized, and saved. In contrast, time in Indonesia is viewed as a limitless pool. There is a phrase in Indonesia describing this concept that translates as "rubber time," so that time stretches or shrinks and is therefore very flexible.

The national language of Indonesia, Bahasa Indonesia, was officially adopted in 1928. At the time of this decision, Bahasa Indonesia was a regional language spoken by only 5% of the total population of Indonesia. In order to achieve a higher ideal of the unity of the Indonesian people, the major sub-races such as Javanese (47%), Sudanese (14%), and others pushed aside their regional feelings and adopted the idea of a common language.

Corruption and bribery may pose difficulties for foreign business persons in this developing country.

MALAYSIA

Commentary

New York Times, February 17, 1985—"Oranges Stir Tensions for Malaysia's Chinese"—It has been nearly 15 years since Malaysia, a former British colony, began trying to improve national self-sufficiency and general living standards on the one hand, while giving a greater share of the national wealth to "bumiputras"—ethnic Malays and indigenous tribal and aboriginal people.

Wall Street Journal, April 10, 1984—"Malaysia Promotes Idea of Big Families to Spur Economy"—Going against the world-wide trend, Malaysia has decided to deemphasize family planning and to encourage families to have up to five children as the country seeks to multiply its population almost five-fold by the end of the century.

John Berthelsen

Malaysia—Profile	
Population	16.53 million
Ethnic Groups	Malay 50%, Chinese 36%, Indian 10%, Other 4%
Religions	Muslim, Buddhists and Hindu
Education	Compulsory 7 Years (6–13 Years)—Literacy 75%
Land	50,700 square miles
Government	Constitutional Monarchy
Political Parties	Main parties are: National Front (UMNO), Democratic Action (DAP), Islamic (PAS)
Per Capita Income	1983 US$ 2,050
Exports to U.S.	$2,976 million
Imports from U.S.	$2,373 million

Foreign Times, April 5, 1983—"Malaysia Puts End to British Trade Row"—Dr. Mahathir Mohamed, the Malaysian Prime Minister, has formally announced the end of the "buy British last" policy, saying that in the future, British goods would be treated on an equal basis as those of their competitors.

The Malaysian leader later expanded on the reasons behind the directive, saying Britain had taken Malaysia for granted, and had been insensitive to Malaysian aspirations, in particular over the New Economic Policy, which aims to buy back Malaysian assets to increase Malay ownership to 30% by 1990.

Wong Sulong

Cultural Characteristics of Business in Malaysia

Geography, Government and People

The Federation of Malaysia, consisting of 13 states, was formed in 1963 at the end of the British rule. Eleven of the states are part of peninsular Malaysia and the two states of Sabah and Sarawak are separated by 400 miles of the South China Sea. The land is approximately 90% forested and both the peninsula and the states of Sabah and Sarawak are characterized by flat coastal plains rising to steep mountain ranges. Malaysia's major exports are rubber, tin, palm oil, timber, and petroleum; the major imports are machinery, transportation equipment, and consumer goods.

Kuala Lumpur is the capital of Malaysia and is the location of the federal parliament and the prime minister. In addition, each of the 13 state governments have parliaments and prime ministers and 9 have sultans. The present government policy promotes Malay participation in business and the dispersal of industry to less developed areas. The government is a parliamentary democracy under a constitutional monarchy.

Cultural Concepts

Courtesy, etiquette, gentleness, and good manners are hallmarks of the Malay culture.

A fundamental concept surrounding the ethical system of the Malay people revolves around the concept of *Budi*, which illustrates the ideal behavior expected of a Malay. Its basic rules are respect and courtesy, especially towards elders, and affection and love for one's parents, as well as a pleasant disposition and harmony in the family, the neighborhood, and in the society as a whole. There are two forms of *Budi*: *Adab*, which means that the individual has a responsibility to show courtesy at all times; and *Rukun*, which means that the individual must act to obtain harmony either in a family or in society.

Malays do not seem to value the pursuit of wealth for its own sake. They do, however, believe in hard work and self-reliance. Life is viewed as a passing thing, and family and friends take precedence over self-centered interests, such as the accumulation of profit and materialism. The Malays' love for children is reflected in the gentle and tender manner in which they raise them.

Gestures and Greetings

There are several forms of nonverbal communication that one might use while in Malaysia that could easily be misconstrued or insulting to the Malay people. Therefore, familiarity with greetings and certain gestures to avoid could lead to a more successful business trip. The following are a few examples. In meeting a Malay, the elder person should be mentioned before the younger, the more important before the less important, and the woman before the man. In rural areas, it is customary for men and women to shake hands with each other. When meeting a man, a Malay woman may *salaam*, which is bowing very low while placing the right palm on the forehead, and then covering their hands with cloth. However, men and women in the cities generally shake hands if they believe that a person is unaware of the social etiquette pertaining to handshaking. The traditional Malay greeting resembles a handshake with both hands but without the grasp. The man offers both hands to his friend, lightly touches his friend's outstretched hands, and then brings his hands to his breast. This simply means that "I greet you from my heart."

In Malaysia, instead of pointing to a place, object, or person with the right index finger, which is considered impolite, it is more common to point with the thumb of the right hand with the fingers folded under. In calling for a taxi, one uses the fingers of the right hand, moving them together with the palm facing down in a waving or "come here" gesture, which is opposite to the typical American beckoning of a taxi. A gesture to avoid is patting a child on the head. The head is considered to be the center of the intellectual and sacred power, and is therefore holy and should not be touched.

Values and Attitudes of Malayans

The following contrasts are intended to be especially helpful to the business person working in Malaysia. It will cover a number of basic considerations and cultural contrasts in attitudes towards work, motivation, leadership, planning, as well as a number of basic differences between American and Malay society and way of life. Many of these ideas were derived from a cultural analysis prepared by George W. Renwick (1977).

Religion. Islam is the predominant religion in Malaysia and exerts a great influence not only on the method of worship but the Malays' whole way of life. Therefore, any foreign business representative hoping to function effectively in this environment should have an understanding of Islam, as it is very important in order to obtain a total picture of Malay culture. Whereas Americans' religious practices are generally confined to Sundays, Malays' religious concerns seem to be on a more profound daily basis. The Malays stress the importance of their belief about God and the hereafter in their language.

A person is guided by the prescriptions of the Koran, which spells out and details rules of behavior that include all social and business activities. As Muslims, they are expected to recite the creed, "There is no God but Allah, and Muhammad is his Prophet," and they must pray five times a day and worship Allah as the only true God. Providing charity, helping the needy, fasting during the month of Ramadan, and if possible, making a trip to Mecca are additional practices that the Muslim Malays are expected to follow. They should also refrain from eating pork or drinking alcoholic beverages. In the main portion of the Mosque, the Muslim place of worship, Malay women sit apart from the men and are not allowed at any time to mix casually or to eat with them.

Tradition. The Malays deeply respect traditional customs but, in some cases, these customs do not complement their religion. In these instances, the practices of Islam have been adapted to fit more effectively with the traditional customs. These traditional practices and beliefs are called *Adat*, the Malay word for custom. The importance of these *Adat* are illustrated by their proverb, "Let the child perish but not the *Adat*."

Nature and Human Nature. Man is considered basically good by the Malays, which is somewhat different from the Protestant ethic and the concept of original sin in Western Christianity. Throughout the history of the United States, an underlying belief has been that man can overcome nature. Mastery and control over nature is even becoming more evident in view of how America is attempting to deal with the shortages of fuel, water, and food. In the Islamic faith, the Malay position concerning man's relationship to nature is one of being subject to or living in harmony with nature. At times, a Malay feels subject to the elements because of his fatalistic attitude and belief of the supremacy of God's will. A Malay also believes that he is part of the natural world, which reflects his belief in animism—the notion that plants and animals have a spiritual dimension.

A Malay pays little attention to what has happened in the past and regards the future as both vague and unpredictable. Planning for the future or hoping that the future will be better than either the present or the past is simply not their way of life. Americans, who are seldom completely satisfied with the present and have little respect for the past, place a high value on change and feel most comfortable in looking towards the future.

Individualism and ambition also offer significant contrasts between the two cultures. Whereas individualistic talents and characteristics are held in high regard in America, the Malay places the utmost importance on relationships with relatives, friends, and colleagues.

In the United States, ambition generally means to strive for worldly success, financial and social. There is generally a lack of such ambition in Malaysia, which could be attributed to a variety of causes. In the past, the chances of a Malay succeeding in worldly terms were very small and did not depend on the efforts of the individual Malay. Furthermore, if in fact he did succeed, there were laws that prohibited the accumulation of wealth by Malay peasants. A third reason for this lack of ambition is that from the perspective of the Islamic faith, there is a strong sense of fatalism as indicated by the common expressions such as "God willing" or "If God wants me to be something I will, if not, God's will be done." These factors favor a lack of motivation for worldly success, which is replaced by a motivation to develop deep and lasting relationships with friends and relatives. Therefore, Malays have traditionally felt that in receiving material success, they might lose the highly valued respect of their family and friends.

In contrast to the American tendency to change the environment and concentrate most energy in working to get ahead, a Malay's energies are directed in many areas. Furthermore, the hot and humid climate in Malaysia is a drain on energy; thus, little attempt is made to alter the environment.

Trust, Respect, and Leadership. Trust for a Malay is fundamental to a successful interpersonal relationship regardless of the nationality of the person with whom he is interacting. A person's capability for loyalty, commitment, and companionship are the key characteristics upon which the Malay generally bases his trust. On the other hand, an American bases his or her trust on a person's capacity for performance, level of expertise, and position in the social structure. For Malays, the process for developing trust is more internal and personal whereas for Americans, the emphasis is on external and professional aspects. For an American respect must be earned, but for Malays, it comes with a person's status.

There also exists a subtle difference between Americans and Malayans concerning the interaction of formality and respect. Malays show respect initially through formalities, however, as a relationship progresses, formalities are slowly dropped until an informal atmosphere is reached. Americans also start out formally, but the progression to a less formal situation occurs much more rapidly. The slower transformation from formality to informality often confuses Americans who are unaware of the differing progression. Although an American generally respects a very aggressive person who demonstrates that he can get what he wants, the Malay respects a compromising person who shows that he is willing "to give and take." In Malay negotiations the person who compromises is the most respected person and will often receive more than he anticipated.

When a Malay meets a stranger, he not only evaluates the person but also his background, family, and social position. An American generally evaluates a person in terms of his accomplishments. Therefore, the American might not pay the Malayan the respect that the Malay feels that he deserves, due to this difference in orientation. These attitudes reflect the fact that America is a very "doing" oriented society, whereas the Malay is oriented toward "being" or "existing."

In U.S. organizations and institutions status is usually attributed to someone demonstrating leadership capabilities. In Malaysia, the process is somewhat reversed. Malays are born into a certain social position or status, and if the status is very high or important, then they are expected to demonstrate leadership capabilities. Americans and Malays base good leadership on different personal qualifications. To be aggressive and confident are basic to the American concept of leadership. For a Malay, the most important quality of a leader is confidence and the ability to understand people. A leader in Malaysia is also expected to be religiously devout, humble, sincere, and tactful. One's position in Malay society is also important. Even if a person is not worthy of respect, his position might demand that he receive it. A Malay feels most comfortable in a heirarchical structure with a clearly defined role, and emphasis is on room for growth in interpersonal relationships.

Work Ethic. Since the Industrial Revolution, the Protestant work ethic has been a mainstay of American achievement in business, as well as other areas. Idleness has been looked upon as the work of the devil. The distinction between action and idleness is not as clearly delineated in Malay culture and language. Work is viewed as one of many activities by the Malays. A large percentage of the time in a Malay's life is spent developing deeper relationships with family and friends in ways that would appear as idle time to many Americans. This contrast is clearly illustrated by the differing perspectives of how the elderly are viewed in Malaysia and in America. When a person reaches old age in the United States, the fact that he can no longer work generates the feeling that he is no longer useful, whereas in Malaysia, an elderly person is regarded as a wise counselor who plays an important role in society.

The concept of promotion is another aspect of the working environment that differs between the Malay and American culture. A Malay would never take the initiative to request a promotion for himself. When a Malay receives a promotion, it is when his superior respects and thinks very highly of him, and this is of utmost importance to the Malay.

Malaysia is composed mainly of fishing and farming villages with only a few large cities. This factor has important ramifications concerning the educational and technical abilities of the Malay people in contrast with Americans, who are for the most part, raised and socialized in an urban environment. In the past the Malay found it unnecessary to learn about business or to specialize in one field. In general, the Malays do not go up to college and those who do often major in liberal arts as opposed to business or engineering. American business people in working with Malayans often complain about this lack of specialization and technical sophistication.

Politics and Power. Of fundamental importance to anyone working in Malaysia is an understanding of the pluralism among the Malays and Chinese. In order to succeed in Malaysia, one must understand some of the differences and difficulties between the two cultures. Traditionally, the Malay has not been involved in the economic sector of the economy. As mentioned earlier, he has farmed, fished, and earned only enough to support his family. In Malay society there was an occupational void which was largely filled by the Chinese, who eventually gained virtual control over the economic sector of Malaysia. The political situation was reasonably stable until 1969 when there was serious rioting. A high-tension level between the Malays and the Chinese was touched off by election results that favored the Malays. Since then, the government has taken a very pro-Malay stand.

A twenty-year development plan, which favored the Malays, was initiated in 1970. The plan contained two principal economic objectives. First was to check the dominance of Chinese economic control by requiring a definite percent of the labor force to be Malay at all levels of business. Second, the plan stated that the foreign share of the Malay market would be reduced from 60% to 30% by 1990. Due to the general lack of interest in business by the Malays, it has been difficult to reach the designated percentages and, in spite of the efforts towards modernization and education, the results have not been completely satisfactory. Another barrier is the strength of the Malay traditional values: the government cannot force people to change these values. Concerning the second point, even though there will be a decrease in the Malay market allocated to foreign investors, there is still room for expansion of the present foreign-controlled market.

The fact that a near balance of power exists between Malays and Chinese requires close cooperation between the two cultures. However, due to the differences in customs, culture, and values, there has been a great deal of tension between the two groups. As a result, the climate in Malaysia is unstable. An atmosphere of mistrust and feeling of exploitation has led to a defensive stance and negative perceptions and expectations of each group. The unpleasant balance of power between the Malays and the Chinese seems to be more permanent than in other multi-cultural societies, due to the strong cultural differences; for example, the Chinese Buddhist background versus the Islamic practices of the Malays.

An additional cultural obstacle that hinders the American understanding of the Malay-Chinese relations stems from the fact that the American comes from a low-context culture. When communicating, the American uses and expects explicit messages. For the American, it is the words that convey meaning and information. Malays and Chinese, however, have grown up in a high-context culture, where they depend more on non-verbal means of communication than on verbal messages. Unlike many Americans, persons from high-context cultures usually depend on a traditional structure that resists change or modification, and such persons tend to be group-oriented, rather than individual-oriented.

Foreign business persons coming to Malaysia are challenged to apply synergistic skills to their relationships. This will foster not only cooperation between themselves and the Malays, but will contribute to collaboration among the country's diverse inhabitants.

INDIA

India—Profile

Population	816,828,360
Ethnic Groups	72% Indo Aryan, 25% Dravidian, 3% Mongoloid/Other
Religions	Hindu, Muslim, Christian, Sikh, Buddhist, Jains
Languages	15 major languages with English as link
Education	36% literacy
Land	2,973,190 square km
Government	Federal Republic
Political Parties	Congress (I), Lok Dal, Janata, Communist (CPI), (AIADMK), others
Per Capita Income	US$ 250
Exports to U.S.	$2,273.35 million
Imports from U.S.	$1,684.09 million

Commentary

In India, Winter 1988. Rajeev Ghandi has opened the door for American businesses. The U.S. has become India's largest trading partner with a two-way trade of $4 billion annually. . . . Well-managed, private-sector companies, the ones most likely to attract foreign partners, have superb profitability records. . . . There is a highly-developed legal system, based on British law. (Insurance, banking, business, government administration, transportation, and education are also formed on the English model and practice.). . . . The Indian stock market is nearly a century old, though five of its 14 exchanges opened within the last six years, and there has been a five-fold rise in activity since 1980. . . . The quality of training varies from institution to institution, but top engineering schools provide world-class education. American-style management education in India is now a quarter-century old (the two pioneering institutes were set up in collaboration with Harvard and MIT). Knowledge workers are already the key forces in the service sector, and they are fast acquiring that role in the manufacturing sector as well. . . . One more factor makes India attractive for foreign investment: the abundance of technically skilled labor and highly trained (and English proficient) professionals. . . . During the last two years, Indian companies have entered into nearly 1000 new foreign collaborations, and nearly 20% of these have been with American firms. . . . Yet there are severe problems in doing business with socialist countries—political control, massive bureaucracies, centralized planning, considerations for services performed, infrastructure limitations, and scarcity of basic resources. . . . All and all, there are diverse and substantial opportunities for synergistic cooperation. . . .

Nirmal Sethia

Time, April 3, 1989—"The Awakening of an Asian Power"—. . . the sleepy giant of the subcontinent is determinedly transforming itself into a regional superpower. . . . The 1989–90 budget froze defense spending at $8.5 billion, though some estimate the actual figure to be as high as $11 billion . . . the common perception, particularly in the West, is that India remains a backward nation mired in superstition and squalor. In fact, alongside the impoverished land of beggars and cardboard shacks, there has risen a high-tech, post-industrial state led by an army of self-confident and efficient engineers, scientists, and military officers.

Ross H. Munro

Cultural Characteristics of Business in India

Geography, Government, and People*

Through the organized efforts of Mahatma Gandhi and other Indians infused with a sense of nationalism, British rule ended in August 1947. In January 1950, the Indian Constitution was promulgated, and the country became a sovereign democratic republic.

The government of India is based on the British parliamentary system with a bicameral legislature and executive and judicial branches. India is governed by a president who is advised by a council of ministers led by the prime minister (appointed by the president). The ministers and prime minister are responsible

---

* Adapted with permission from *Venturing Abroad in Asia* by Robert T. Moran International Management.

to the House of People, the Lok Sabha, which is elected by universal adult franchise.

The government owns and runs many enterprises, such as the airlines, railroads, insurance industry, power facilities, and irrigation projects. The government also has the controlling power in the production of metals, steel, chemicals, and engineering equipment. Eighty-five percent of the nation's banking assets are government controlled.

Money supply is managed by the Reserve Bank of India, which is the country's central bank. The unit of currency is the rupee. The Reserve Bank acts as banker to the government, the commercial banks, and some of the financial institutions. The banking system is deeply involved in the industrialization of the country through financing of both fixed assets as well as working capital.

Commercial banks may be classified into four categories: 1) The State Bank of India and its subsidiaries, 2) nationalized banks, 3) foreign banks, and 4) non-nationalized Indian scheduled banks.

Tighter control over the money supply is likely as the government attempts to hold down prices and curb inflation. India's economy is very weather-dependent as 50% of the country's national income is derived from agriculture and allied activities. The weather also affects the health of the laborers.

In terms of business, the public sector banks, namely the State Bank of India and nationalized banks, occupy a dominating position. The State Bank of India is the biggest commercial bank in the country, and it also carries out some of the functions of the Reserve Bank of India. Some of the larger banks also provide merchant banking service.

Since 1950, India's economy has been directed by a series of five-year plans that set goals and allocate resources. Major areas addressed by the plans include electric power generation, irrigation, gas and oil exploration and production.

The industrial economy of India has a public sector and a private sector. The public sector companies are government-run industrial and commercial undertakings, while the private sector is composed of profit-oriented business organizations run increasingly by professional managers. The country has made rapid industrial growth in recent years with capabilities increasing in almost every sphere of industry. Exports have become much more diversified from just agricultural products to textiles, tea, iron ore, spices, and light engineering products.

Foreign trade has become an important part of the Indian economy. Imports include fuel, petroleum (two thirds of crude oil needs are imported), fertilizers, iron and steel, chemicals, machinery, transportation equipment, paper, and gemstones.

There are positive aspects to doing business in India. English is the major language, and there is a large pool of managerial, skilled and semi-skilled labor. There is also a good and developed capital market and a large domestic market.

The main focus of Indian trade policy is on export promotion and import substitution. Over the years the U.S.A. has been the largest supplier to India. The U.K. and the U.S.A. have been the largest buyers of Indian exports.

India's foreign trade policy is generally restrictive. Approval for investment is very selective and is granted on a case-by-case basis. The government updates its trading policy annually and publishes statements accordingly. Corruption, bribes, or payments for "fixing" exist in everyday life and are something that must be dealt with and accepted to get things accomplished.

At times, Hindus may appear hypocritical and dishonest by employing many standards from their way of living. The Indians see themselves as responsible or irresponsible in regard to necessity.

In India, business is based on personal contacts and it is crucial to know the right person in order to get contracts.

India is bounded northwest by Pakistan; north by China, Tibet, Nepal and Bhutan; east by Burma; southeast, south, and southwest by the Indian Ocean.

India is rich in coal, hydroelectrical power potentials, industrial raw materials (iron and manganese), and manpower. Like their resources, economic development has occurred in only a few isolated sectors of the economy which many attribute to the constraints of tradition and culture.

There is not enough work for all their people, so poverty is prevalent. With an adult population of 326 million and official urban unemployment rate of 15 million, the last thing India needs is labor-saving modern equipment. Over the last twenty years, India has implemented intensive population control programs, but none were successful. The high birth rate has been attributed to early marriage, the emphasis placed on bearing sons by the Hindu religion, the security of having children to take care of parents in old age, and the low level of education achieved by the rural masses.

Climate and culture contribute to the high incidence of disease and influence the patterns of work. The hot weather season brings constant dust, which results in various infections and eye irritations and also limits the outdoor physical activity. The cold, damp, rainy season brings on colds, malaria, and rheumatism. Their practice of vegetarianism contributes to malnutrition and protein deficiencies. The people of India have a general syndrome known as "weakness" brought on by their constant exposure to epidemic diseases such as cholera and typhus, and the malnutrition factor. This syndrome is usually seen more frequently among the wealthy and educated.

India has a great variety of languages, customs, beliefs, and cultures, almost all of which are difficult for a westerner to comprehend.

Although the Hindu woman's legal position has greatly improved over the years, she is still bound by ancient traditions of behavior that emphasize her absolute dedication, submission, and obedience to her husband and his wishes.

This may not be so strictly adhered to in the big cities and westernized circles where women are increasing in the workforce, especially in the professions (doctors, engineers, lawyers) and in government.

Her status in the household is low until she has given birth to a male child. Female children are seen as a burden and future debt due to the dowry paid at marriage to the husband's family.

Family and friends have an importance far beyond that to which the West is accustomed. Extended family living is strived for.

A friend's role is to "sense" a person's need and to do something about it. To speak one's mind is a sign of friendship.

Astrologers play an important role in India, as the people believe that nothing is accidental and the universe and all living components have a fundamental order.

Social Customs

Social freedom between the sexes is not appreciated very much in India. A stranger should not speak to a woman if he is not acquainted with her or her family.

A stranger will not be expected to help a woman out of a car, boat, etc. as her husband might resent it.

For a young woman to take the hand of a man who is not her husband is objectionable.

Bold, emancipated women may dare to indulge in dancing with their husbands, but to dance with anyone who is not her husband would be improper.

Use of first name for address should be, as mentioned before, avoided. It is customary to add to the names of the Hindus the affix "ji" as a mark of respect. For instance, Ravi in polite speech becomes Raviji. Here Ravi is the first name but, by adding affix "ji," you are calling the person with respect and, in this instance, use of first name will not be improper.

In Bengal, mister is replaced by "Babu." Thus, Ravi Babu = Mr. Ravi.

In most parts of India, in correspondence or invitation cards, the classic Sanskrit prefix "Shriman" for men and "Shrimati" for women used.

The method of greeting depends upon the social status of the persons meeting. A son greets his father usually by bowing down and touching his feet.

An American businessman in India will be considered an equal and, among equals, the usual method used will be to press one's palms together in front of the chest and say "namaste" meaning "greetings to you."

Among the other classes of people, educated in western style, shaking hands is acceptable.

Hindu women who have been educated usually would not mind shaking hands with men when introduced. However, it is safer not to extend one's hand to a Hindu woman until she takes the initiative and extends her hand first. It is safer to stick with "namaste." This actually is the universal form of greeting in India.

Indian food varies from province to province. Hindus in most cases are vegetarians and beef is prohibited for a Hindu. Meat of other kinds is eaten by the Hindus. Tandoori chicken from the north is one of the most popular chicken dishes in India.

Among respectable Hindus, the drinking of alcoholic beverages of any kind is considered most degrading. It can be said that traditional Hindus are a nation of water drinkers. While entertaining at home, it is purely with non-alcoholic beverages like tea, coffee, etc.

Western food is available in all the good hotels. A variety of desserts made out of fruits or milk are also available. Betel leaf (pan in Hindi) is usually taken after a meal to aid the digestion and freshen one's mouth.

Hospitality is universal in India. The duty of entertaining guests is laid down in religion as of prime importance. A well mannered Hindu will not eat without asking his guest to join him. It is said that satisfaction of a guest will assuredly bring the housekeeper wealth, reputation, long life, and a place in heaven.

One is not required to take any gift if invited for supper but, if one did, it would be accepted graciously.

Do not be surprised if you have your meal only with your business partner and not the whole family. Wives and children usually help from the kitchen to make sure that the guest is treated well.

At homes, eating without knives and forks and spoon is not uncommon. People eat with their hands at home.

If dining with the whole family, wait until everybody is at the table before you start eating. Let the host start eating first before you do or start when you are asked to go ahead.

Do not get upset if your host asks you several times to have some more food. Simply refuse politely if you don't want more. It is Indian custom to ask repeatedly to make sure their guest does not get up hungry from the table.

Indian businessmen, in many situations, wear "dhotis." The "dhoti" is a single piece of white cloth about five yards long and three to four feet broad. It is passed round the waist up to half its length, and the other half is drawn between the legs and tucked at the waist. For the upper part of the body they wear long shirts. Due to hot climate most of the year, long overcoats are worn only on special occasions. Sikhs from Punjab wear turbans, which have a religious significance.

Well-to-do Hindus who wish to appear aristocratic wear long coats like the Rajahs. The long coat, known as "sherwani" has been standardized and is the dress recognized by the government of India for official and ceremonial wear.

The dress of a Hindu woman, businesswomen or else, is sari and blouse. The Hindu lady is extremely loyal to her sari. While most of the modernized Hindu males have adopted the European costume in their outdoor life, Hindu women have kept the sari. The modern sari compares favorably with fashionable clothes of western women.

For American businessmen visiting India, shirt, trousers, tie, and suit will be proper attire. The Indian climate is hot; therefore, a very light suit in winter is recommended. If a person is in the north during winter, he will find it a little cooler and, again, a light sweater and a jacket will be sufficient.

Women in public places should avoid wearing shorts or revealing dresses, as it draws unneeded attraction.

The dominant religion in India is Hinduism, which is more than a religion— it is a complete rule of life. India also has Muslims, Parsees, Jains, Buddhists, Sikhs, Christians, and Jews. Hinduism represents approximately 87% of the population. The customs and manners of the Hindus are strongly influenced by religion. Hinduism advocates the *caste system*, which rigidly separates the social classes in which privileges or disabilities are transmitted by inheritance. Although caste discrimination is illegal, in practice it pervades the culture.

Hinduism involves a variety of beliefs, practices, and gods. The rules of Hinduism may be interpreted in many ways, depending on the community.

Non-Verbal Communication and Social Tips

- Grasping one's own ears expresses repentance or sincerity.
- A toss of the head means "yes."
- Beckoning is done with the palm turned down; pointing is often done with the chin.
- Backslapping is not a sign of affection.
- The namaste gesture can be used to signal you've had enough food.
- Use the namaste—palms together, nod of the head—to greet people.
- American men should not touch women in public, nor talk to a lone woman in public.
- The left hand is considered unclean. Use the right hand for eating with the fingers or for giving or accepting things.
- Do not lick postage stamps.
- Be on time.
- Eat willingly with your hand if the occasion calls for it.
- Don't ask personal questions until you become close to someone.
- Use titles such as doctor and professor.
- Whistling is considered impolite.
- Public displays of affection are inappropriate.
- Bargain for goods and services.

One important thing to remember when going to India: the Indians are very tolerant and will completely accept the fact that you are unfamiliar with their customs and procedures. There is no need to conform to Indian behavior.

Finally, remember that India has 15 major language groups and myriad dialects. Among the educated and business people, the British form of English is the linking language, although Hindi and Tamil are official government languages.

SUMMARY

Asia is a demonstration model of the complexity and multidimensional aspects of culture. Unfortunately, we were only able to briefly review these cultural variations for doing business in Japan, China, South Korea, Philippines, Indonesia, Malaysia, and India. Perhaps it is enough to convince global managers of the important distinctions that exist between the people of this region and ourselves in critical matters like physical appearance, language, religion, family, social attitudes, and other assumptions that influence business practice and relationships. The new market opportunities in the Pacific Basin alone should motivate us to seek culture specific information whether we are dealing with Australians who are seemingly similar or with Thais who are so obviously different.

The emerging importance of Asia in general and Japan as its leader was underscored by Sheridan Tatsuno (1986). In *The Technology Strategy*, this California consultant predicts that through its advances in high technology, Japan may control the twenty-first century. The six strategies the Japanese government is pursuing in this regard are: transformation of key capital cities into twenty technopolises; parallel-track research-and-development projects; strategic international alliances; telecommunications networking; venture capital and venture businesses; and selective import promotion. Now link that insight with our norms of the new work culture in Chapter 7. It may help to justify why global managers look to the Orient for new learning, as well as new partners and joint ventures.

16
Doing Business With Europeans

Europe is a continent divided into two geopolitical spheres, so business practices will vary according to whether the capitalist or socialist system is used. The apparent demise of communism has the potential of simplifying the situation, but in the foreseeable future it will complicate matters by adding more nations and cultures to an already highly diverse mixture of peoples. Thus, it is difficult to generalize about Europe.

Europe is a dynamic and very exciting place to do business in the 1990s! The winds of economic, social and political change are sweeping throughout the whole continent, both in its western and eastern portions. Travelers, traders, and those planning to relocate there should seek out the very latest sources of information, some of which are listed in this chapter. To penetrate that tariff-free, single market of consumers (more than the U.S. and Japan combined), foreign companies are being invited to base their headquarters or facilities in the United Kingdom (Britain Bureau, British Consulate General, 845 Third Ave., N. Y. 10022, USA), or in Italy, one of the seven leading industrialized nations (SDA Bocconi, Via Bocconi, 8-20136, Milano, Italia), or even in the international finance and diplomatic paradise of Switzerland (Office of Economic Development, State of Vaud, c/o International Marketing & Communications Consultants, Suite 200, 5095 Murphy Canyon Rd., San Diego, CA 92123, USA).

Since 1957, the European Community (EC) member nations have striven together to improve their standard of living, and to foster closer relations among their countries. Beginning in 1993 a formal agreement allows goods, people, services, information, and capital to move freely among the EC states. Currently, the twelve members consist of Belgium, Denmark, France, Germany, Greece, Ireland, Italy, Luxembourg, the Netherlands, Portugal, Spain, and the United Kingdom. While customs duties have already been removed in this internal market, legislative changes will eliminate existing trade barriers. The *ideal* is that by January 1993, three barriers will have been removed:

- Physical—cross-border delays from customs controls and paperwork.
- Technical—differing national standards and regulations, conflicting business laws, and protected public procurements.
- Fiscal—differing tax rates and excise duties.

That ideal may take time to implement everywhere in the Community, but EC directives are committed to:

- Free flow of goods, once they have cleared customs in the EC, as if national boundaries did not exist.
- Free movement of workers, so that citizens of one state may seek employment in another without discrimination relative to type of job, remunerations, or other employment conditions.
- Freedom of establishment, so a citizen or business from one state has the right to locate and conduct business elsewhere in the Community.
- Freedom to provide services to persons throughout the EC.

The efforts toward European integration and standardization may eventually lead to greater political and currency unification. For a more complete description of the provisions for fair competition, protections (consumer, worker, environment), and common external policy, we refer readers to the complimentary publications, *1992—Your Passport to Europe; EEC Focus,* a quarterly review; and *World* magazine (KFMG Peat Marwick, Three Chestnut Ridge Road, Montvale, NJ 07645, USA).

Some of the benefits of the new EC policies include—

Industry

- Direct cost savings from removal of internal border controls.
- Increased competition.
- Economies of scale in production.
- Greater expenditures on research and development.

Economy

- Lower prices.
- Increased consumer demand.
- Decreased unemployment.
- Increased growth throughout the EC.

The EC Commission predicts benefits to the EC that will include a rise in gross domestic product of 4.5%, a 6% decrease in price levels, and the creation of 2 million new jobs over the first six years.

To take advantage of the single market opportunities, global corporations are establishing EC-based companies, and the Japanese are most prominent in this

---

* Reprinted with permission from KFMG Peat Marwick newsletter, *European Community—1992,* March 1988, p. 3.

strategy. Many foreign enterprises are acquiring or merging with European industrial units, and the cross-cultural challenges increase at both the national and corporate levels. Foreign managers assigned to Europe will have to be more competitive, as well as better trained and culturally sensitive. And the trade flows both ways, creating a global interdependence. In 1987, for instance the 12 EC nations invested $158 million in the U.S.A.

In the European Economic Community (EEC) headquartered in Belgium, the big three markets are Great Britain, France, and Germany, so we have selected these target cultures for analysis as a representative sample: the first because it is the "mother country" of all English-speaking nations, and the third because it is the center of French cultural influences throughout the world and the home of many international agencies, such as UNESCO.

EUROPEAN MANAGEMENT SYNERGY

Western Europe slowly moves beyond national borders and cultures toward regional cooperation. Although the EEC is still in its childhood and the European Parliament is in its infancy, the barriers to the exchange of people, information, and trade are being removed and a new European identity is coming into being. Nowhere is this collaboration more evident than in the field of management. Managers readily cross national boundaries not only on mutual business, but for professional development together. The three great management learning centers have multicultural participants—INSEAD (Fontainebleu, France), International Management Institute (Geneva, Switzerland), and Management Centre Europe (Brussels, Belgium). Furthermore, the European managers attend courses and workshops in each other's universities, and read one another's management journals and business publications. They also take advantage of numerous international conferences held in Europe, such as when the "knights of high technology" gathered recently at Leeds Castle, U.K.—that is, twenty-five leaders of the global communication systems industry. Management consultants are also multilingual and multicultural in their European practice.

Perhaps the transnational aspects of European management is best demonstrated in matters of partnerships, joint ventures, and acquisitions. Chapter 6 illustrated this with the Airbus Industrie consortium and the Dutch N. V. Phillips company, as well as in the case of the French-based multinational, Schlumberger.

The Republic of Ireland not only boasts of its 200 British industries, and many new American and European firms, but of the young, well-educated work force available for service throughout the Common Market countries. The "internationalization" of European "manpower" has been progressing throughout this century, as will be documented by the International Labour Office in Geneva. This is caused by more than the growth of the multinational corporation. Labor migration under "guest worker" programs became a means for European countries to augment their own work force and to relieve chronic unemployment in labor exporting countries. Since WWII, an estimated 30 million workers—mostly from underdeveloped countries in southern Europe and North Africa—flowed into northern Europe. European business people have always excelled at multilingual skills. However, these trends are some of the reasons why cross-cultural training is increasing within European management development.

But it is not only business that seeks to benefit from the $6.5 trillion gross national product of the EC nations. Legal and illegal immigration into Western Europe has soared. A multicultural Europe is absorbing from 10-15 million foreigners, so that the EC countries are being forced to become more multiracial, multinational, and multireligious. Apart from the world's refugees and asylum-seekers, many of the unlawful entries are smuggled into Spain from North Africa.

Commenting on the unsettling phenomenon of large-scale, non-European resettlement into the Community, the *Los Angeles Times* (February 6, 1989) observed:

- By 1995, every second child born in Brussels, the self-proclaimed capital of Europe, will be Arab.
- Twice as many Britons speak Urdu, Punjabi, or Gujarati as Welsh, the native language of Wales in the U.K.
- 700,000 Arabs in France will be eligible to vote in the next presidential election.
- Three of West Berlin's television stations now broadcast in Turkish.
- Road signs now appear in Spain in Arabic to accommodate the one million Moroccans who vacation there in the summer.

Such changes can alter a society's image of itself in Western Europe, undermine the socialistic welfare states, and unravel the social and religious traditions of centuries.

Global managers seeking to understand the new situation, will benefit by reading *Europeans* (Kramer, 1988). Other sources of European insight include:

- *Journal of European Business*, targets coverage of the new market. Contact Frost & Sullivan, 106 Fulton St., New York, NY 10038, USA.
- *International Management*, Europe's business magazine published by Reed Business Publishing Ltd., Oakfield House, Room 105, Perrymount Road, Haywards Heath, West Sussex, RH163DH UK (tel. 0444 441212).
- *The Economist*, a respected, London-based news weekly magazine, in conjunction with Prentice Hall Press, now offers Business Traveler's Guides. These in-depth analyses of a country's economy, politics, and business practices, plus maps and service directory are available for Britain

and other nations. Contact: *The Economist,* P.O. Box 904, Farmingdale, NY 11737, USA (1-800-628-0677). In addition, the *Financial Times* is a thorough source of current information.

- A 1986 doctoral dissertation of United States International University by Azzedine Mezbache reports a comparative study of *American and French Managers' Self-Perceived Abilities for Effective Functioning in Another Culture.* Available from University Microfilm International. For a summary, contact: Dr. A. Mezbache, Intercultural Resources Group, 10696 Arboretum Place, San Diego, CA 92131.
- *Undiscovered Europe,* a travel book, is available free with a subscription to *International Living,* a newsletter. Contact: William Bonner, Publisher, Agora, Inc., 824 E. Baltimore St., Baltimore, MD 21202 (1-800-223-1982, ext. 400).
- *European Affairs,* Elsevier Publication, P.O. Box 470, 1000 AL Amsterdam, The Netherlands.

For further information, consult the software databank available from Gulf Publishing—Directory of Intercultural Resources (1/800-231-6275).

ENGLAND

England—Profile	
Population	56.93 million
Ethnic Groups	British, (Anglo-Saxons) West Indian, Indian, Pakistani, and some Middle Easterners.
Religions	Church of England Roman Catholic Presbyterian
Education	12 Years Compulsory Literacy 99%
Land	94,226 square miles
Government	Constitutional Monarchy
Political Parties	Conservative, Labour, Liberal, Social Democratic, Communist, Scottish National, Official Unionist, Democratic Unionist, Social Democratic
Per Capita Income	US $8,930
Exports to U.S.	$18,708 million
Imports from U.S.	$19,130 million

CULTURAL CHARACTERISTICS OF BUSINESS IN THE UNITED KINGDOM

The English language has almost become a universal means of communication, especially in business and international travel. It is a tribute to the world domination once engineered by a hearty race of Anglo-Saxon-Celts living on two small islands off the eastern coast of Europe. Even though the sun is setting on the British Empire, their global influence in the past, and to some extent in the present, is staggering to conceive. Not only their language, but their customs, laws, and life-styles penetrated remote corners of the planet and held sway over several continents from North America to Asia. While the United States is indebted to many nations for its cultural heritage, the English-Irish-Scotch combination provided the main thrust to its society. Through the unique format of the British Commonwealth of Nations, the United Kingdom with its royal family and social institutions impacted on most races and many cultures. The British were even the stimulant for the export of Irish immigrants, missionaries, politicians, and prisoners throughout the world. There are leaders today in Australia and Argentina, as well as Africa and the Americas, of Irish heritage whose ancestors left "Hibernia" with British encouragement. Furthermore, the British spearheaded the European effort in both World Wars I and II.

Today, the British have been forced to retreat, in many ways to the confines of their island kingdom. And they have been followed by the multicultured inhabitants of the commonwealth who used their privilege of British passport to resettle in the "mother country." Added to this influx from the "colonies," are the transfers of many affluent Middle Easterners to England seeking property, education, health services, and recreation. It would appear that the phenomenon of the medieval crusades has been reversed. In any event, what was once a largely white, homogeneous society is becoming quite heterogeneous. Furthermore, the United Kingdom is not so united at the moment as Scotch and Welsh separatists seek their own national parliaments, Ulster is racked by armed struggles between Catholic and Protestant extremists, and the heart of Great Britain itself is rendered asunder by the terrorism of I.R.A. extremists, as well as racial riots among immigrant groups. Yet, despite this unrest the British still go about business in a very civilized, unflappable way. After all, this courageous people did withstand Nazi bombings and blitz almost fifty years ago. They are rebounding today as they did then.

The material in this section is presented using the case study method for analysis, learning, and application:

Case Study: Americans in Great Britain

Scenario—
- Background of the characters
- Briefing of the boss
- Critical incidents
- Issues for analysis

Background of the Characters

Jeff Donovan was born in Ebbensburg, Pennsylvania, U.S.A. in 1932, attended the local parochial schools and graduated with a B.B.A. in finance from St. Francis College, Loretto, Pa. His graduate studies included a Master's degree in management from Pennsylvania State University, and attendance at the Executive Institute of the Wharton School of Business, University of Pennsylvania on a corporate scholarship.

Jeff is now a transatlantic commuter and an employee of Easting, Inc. Two years ago he was appointed the corporate executive liaison officer for the British Isles, responsible for supervising the company's subsidiary there, Aquaphone, Ltd. He was quite satisfied with his rise in the new-style aristocracy of American business. He would jet four times a year to London and stay at the Claridge Hotel in some splendor. He was especially excited by the employee rallies that he addressed at Fairfield Hall, Croydon. He liked this peculiar British practice, which gave him an opportunity to provide the personnel with a pep talk so that he could counteract the cynicism in workers, a blight across so much of British industrial thinking. He hoped to instill enthusiasm, the lack of which is the biggest curse of their industry. Jeff was not only competent but highly motivated in the spirit that the "business of America is business." Up until now he seemed to have been reasonably successful on this assignment. He seemed to get along well with the man-on-the-spot in England who reported directly to him—Dudley Letts-Jones. In fact, whenever Dudley visited corporate headquarters in Pittsburgh, Jeff and his wife made a point of entertaining their guests at the Rolling Hills Country Club where they were members. Jeff was surprised that it took Dudley two years to invite him to his gentlemen's club.

Dudley Letts-Jones was born in Calcutta, India, in 1920, the son of an English colonel and a British Viscount's daughter. In early childhood, the family returned to England where he was raised in the Royal Mews—his father had become the Royal Equerry. Later he attended the public school at Eton and graduated from Cambridge with a degree in the social sciences. During World War II, he commanded a battery of antiaircraft guns in the Battle of Britain. He belongs to the Church of England and the Conservative Party, as well as to the exclusive Imperial Club in London.

After special studies in management and technology in one of the new redbrick universities, Dudley had drifted into industry with the help of some old school buddies. He was a natural leader and soon moved into executive positions. At the time Easting acquired Aquaphone, Ltd., Dudley was a managing director and the American multinational eventually confirmed him as president of their subsidiary. His wife, Dolores, was not too happy over these developments. She jokingly reminded him that his first duty was to home and family, and warned that she might be forced to act like Mrs. Terese Patten. That lady blithely accused Avon, an American-owned firm, of enticing her 33-year-old husband away from her; she had threatened to sue the corporation because her executive husband was overly influenced by a sales policy that demands all his time and attention, so that he was "married to the job."

Dudley was typically British-generous, enterprising, inventive, loyal to the Crown and with an instinct to compromise. A perfect English gentleman, at times, he appeared to conceal character under a veneer of dandyism. On occasion, his high-pitched nasal mumblings were useful for evading precise conversation on delicate issues. However, recently Dudley was beginning to get really frustrated. He felt financially constrained by the devaluation of the pound and the taxes of a Socialist-welfare government. He had to sell his weekend country house, couldn't take the usual family vacations to the Continent or Bermuda, and was hesitant to replace his aging Bentley. His absolute assurance had been shaken. The advantages of the past for his class had eroded.

Angus McKay was born in Dundee, a bleak town on the beautiful Tayside—a city of jute, jam, and journalism. He was the son of a craftsman and attended state schools until eventually he became a mechanic's apprentice. His early employers were impressed by his self-reliance, persistence, and brains. During World War II, he served with the Royal Highlanders and rose to the rank of sergeant major with decorations. As a boy he had worked summers as a caddie at St. Andrew's, the home of golf, and met there a wealthy member of his own clan. Upon his return from the service, that gentleman advised Angus to study engineering, and loaned the funds so that he could graduate from the University of Edinburgh.

After working for a series of English firms in Scotland in minor management and technical positions, he got his first big career break when Easting took over the company with which he was employed. Now he is general manager of the Aquaphone plant in Leith and reports directly to Dudley-Letts Jones. He welcomes the periodic visits of Jeff Donovan for he says he "likes to work for Yanks—they're just like Scotsmen." Besides he has American relatives who work in the factories of New England and the coal mines of Pennsylvania.

Angus welcomes the American invasion of Scotland because he believes the London government has given exclusive advantage to English concerns, and neglected the development of Scottish industry. Before the American take-over, he complained of having to make do with obsolescent equipment in cramped conditions. He thinks Jeff has done a good job of replacing nineteenth-century ideas, pay rates, and equipment. He has urged Easting to take advantage of the favorable treatment afforded to them in Scotland, and points out that they are not restricted in locating new factories. Labor and rent are cheap and plentiful, and local authorities most accommodating. Already the Scottish Council for Development and Industry has been most helpful to Aquaphone, Ltd.

With the introduction of American management know-how and advanced technology, production has soared to over 200 million pound sterling. Angus notes that as of last year Americans owned 95% of the office machine industry, 92% of the household appliances trade, and 66% of the computer output in

Scotland. And this bothers him a bit. He is still a fierce Scottish nationalist and wonders if they are exchanging one master for another. He knows that the profits he helps to earn go largely back to the U.S. and that their position is vulnerable to changes in American commercial policies, research, and development.

Briefing of the Boss

Jeff would never forget the day he got the assignment to Great Britain. His boss called him into his office and began the conversation in a unique way: "The English have a great tradition of service to the empire; they choose their very best young men for an overseas posting to broaden their experience before returning home to a major career assignment. Jeff, I am giving you such an opportunity in the field of international business in the British Isles." Then, he described how he had served in Britain during the war when the English were at their "finest hour." He proceeded to share some remarkable insights about the British which served Jeff well in his business relations over the past two years. As he recalled the highlights of that momentous communication, Jeff had found the following points to be most significant:

- Don't ever assume that the British are just like us because we *seem* to speak the same language and seem to *share* a common heritage. Centuries of civilization and empire building have given them an inner pride and composure. Yes, their current position in the world's economic and geopolitical scene has diminished, but they still have their network of commonwealth nations, and exercise considerable global influence. We have a lot to learn from the British experience in international affairs.
- Furthermore, you must learn to respect the accomplishments of British technology. When they founded the thirteen colonies here, they were already pioneering the Industrial Revolution. We benefited from their technological advances from then to now, most recently from radar to atomic power. Yes, Britain is suffering today from financial reverses, but the British as a people respond best to adversity, as World War II demonstrated. North Sea oil, tourism, and other developments may yet create a situation in which we more than welcome their friendship.
- Remember, the United Kingdom is a polyglot of ancient cultural influences—Angles, Saxons, Normans, Vikings, Celts, Picts, Romans, and others. Today this so-called homogeneous isle is becoming more pluralistic with the influx of immigrants from the commonwealth nations—East and West Indians, Arabs, Africans, Orientals. Nationalism is being manifested in Scotland, Wales, and North Ireland, sometimes with bloody or devastating economic results. Even the languages of these small islands range from standard English to Cockney, Scottish, Yorkshire, Norfolk, and Welsh versions. You have to be sensitive to such forces when you do business in the United Kingdom and rid yourself of the John Bull stereotype.

- It is a country of paradoxes, and if you are going to be successful there, you have to understand what makes the British tick. To get inside their life-space or mindset, you have to analyze their national character, culture, and current environment. Normally, you will find them reserved, polite, and often friendly, but don't take them for granted. For all their simulated modesty, the British can be tough and blandly ruthless when necessary. They are masters at intelligence gathering, political blackmail, and chicanery, as a reading of the book *Intrepid* will illustrate. Despite how quaint and eccentric they may appear to you at times, don't sell them short. They are a game people who built an empire with a handful of men and women. Although England and Wales are only the size of Alabama, and the population density is close to the size of France, the British once ruled 14 million square miles and more than 500 million souls. I remember reading once: "Because their Union Jack once flew over a good portion of the globe, the people have an empire ethos that gave real meaning to those who served it."

- As one of Irish ancestry, you may scowl "very noble" as you recall the other side of their colonialism and their plunder. You may decry the patronizing manner of imperial splendor and their rank consciousness, but the previous quotation gets to the heart of this people's idealism. It explains their effortless superiority in world affairs, and their inward, invisible grace as a people. It produced a tradition of public service and an education and class system that was dedicated to the needs of the Empire. It also spawned a credo that natural leaders, not low-born self-made men and women, should rule among the multitude.

These are some of the underlying forces that influence the people you are about to do business with in Britain. We are a free-ranging land and people who have never experienced the feudal system. Such ancient experiences even affect modern British labor relations in a very staid society that is slow to change. There, a militant trade unionism has developed to combat the class system curtailments of the workers. It arose with the Industrial Revolution, which devalued the ancient crafts and replaced them with factory work. It even led to a radical socialism that advocates the public ownership of production, distribution, and exchanges, challenging the whole free enterprise system. Truculence and a bloody-minded reluctance to toil for the "boss class" added to the natural conservatism of British labor. It produced a class-war outlook in which profit is regarded as a dirty word and productivity is not popular currency. So tread carefully in matters of labor relations, lest you stir up deep passions. Don't think you can just translate your experience on the American labor scene to the United Kingdom.

The making of money is not an overwhelming preoccupation of the British worker, and toil is not taken as seriously there as in America. They value free time, and are content with fewer possessions (at least they were before the advent of our mass media, consumer advertising blitz). They are careful to preserve status and convention on the work scene, even with regard to tea and the pace of work. The American view of money making and profits, efficiency and cost effectiveness, has been almost thought to be irreconcilable with the British approach.

Our whole approach to search for management talent, for example, puzzles the British who formerly waited for such candidates to apply to the company, or to surface through old school ties. It is apathy not snobbery that affects such recruitment in England, and you are going to have to introduce American management recruitment, assessment, and development into our new subsidiary, as well as a system of job evaluation.

Finally, our corporate policy is one of tactfulness and identification with a host country abroad in which we operate. We seek to adapt our company policies and ways to meet the legitimate concerns and grievances of indigenous people beyond our borders and in whose nation we operate. In the case of the United Kingdom, I do not think we can presume upon the traditional special relationship of past AngloAmerican friendship and cooperation. It springs not from formal arrangements, but from numerous personal contacts, generations of shared experiences and dangers, common traditions and perspectives. Yet, the flow of U.S. capital has caused a growing British dependency and inferiority complex. You must be alert to the reality that if American businessmen in the British Isles do not handle our relations there deftly, we could drive the English into a European economic bloc that competes with us, but permits them to regain their self-respect. Furthermore, in 1975 the problem then was the pound; in a few years our relations may reverse themselves because of a dollar devaluation!"

Critical Incidents in London and Edinburgh

As he flew British Airways back to New York, Jeff was uneasy. Those parting words of his boss some two years previously were coming back to haunt him. He thought he had the United Kingdom situation well in hand. With the changes he had introduced, Aquaphone, Ltd., had increased sales and profits, better working conditions, and avoided significant labor strife. Yet, something had happened on his latest visits to London and Edinburgh that disturbed him and had portent for his corporation's relations with its subsidiary.

It started first with Dudley Letts-Jones. This English executive had always been most proper and gentlemanly with him. He seemed to accept and adequately implement the management changes Jeff proposed, and even came up with some worthwhile innovations of his own. Dudley did not illustrate some of the lackadaisical outlook of some of his British colleagues. The issue that surfaced his feelings was the matter of *overstaffing*. Jeff felt that Aquaphone could manage with fewer production workers, fewer researchers, and fewer maintenance personnel. In fact, he had proposed to Dudley goals for reducing personnel in each category by one fifth, one third, and forty percent, respectively. He was surprised when Dudley balked at his obvious attempts to promote improved cost effectiveness and efficiency.

The Englishman fumed, and said, "Three percent of our top management here have quit in the last few months to work for British-owned firms. They are irked by decisions like this that are made in Pittsburgh without regard or insight into our unique situation."

Jeff suspected that he did not make matters better when he pointed out that the interests of shareholders demanded such economies. In fact, he may have made the situation worse when he paraphrased Bill Keafer, vice-president of Warner Electric Clutch and Brake of Illinois, who had contrasted the performance of American and British workers: "With the same machinery the American turns out three times as much as his British counterpart. Even though we pay our workers twice as much as yours, even though we are four thousand miles from Europe and we're just two hundred years old, we each make the same product and undersell you all over the continent. Do you wonder why Britain is going bust?"

Dudley had silently accepted this rebuff and the new proposals on staffing. Yet, Jeff was startled a few days later when Dudley finally invited him to be his guest for lunch at the Imperial Club. He wondered how long it would take for him to be admitted to the inner sanctuary of the English gentlemen. Dudley has greeted him graciously there and the lunch proceeds with aplomb. After a hearty meal of chops and ale, it dawned on Jeff that Dudley was still upset. In fact, it became obvious that his English partner was slightly tipsy. Jeff should have suspected the worst when Dudley suggested they retire to the rear of the gameroom for some port. Settled in comfortable leather chairs, Dudley fortified himself with quite a few glasses before this outburst ensued:

> "Do you realize, Donovan, that since 1850 the U.S. has brought over 200,000 of our patents to produce products that you then sell to us. Furthermore, you hire away to America or in your companies here our best brains among our professions, scientists, and technicians. Even our most talented actors and actresses have flown away to your tax haven!
>
> The past two bloody World Wars have put us in your debt. It drained the core of my country's strength and manpower. While we fought to preserve democracy in Western Europe and even the Pacific, as well as Africa and the Middle East, we also squandered in these bloody struggles the patrimony that twelve generations or more of Englishmen had built. I know you Yanks came into both conflicts to help us, but our expenditure in proportion to population, in terms of lives and money, was many times that of your country. Britain may have seemed to have been a major force in defeating Germany in both wars, but America emerged as the real victor in both conflicts. We mortgaged most of our possessions in the Western Hemisphere to stop the Nazis. While the wealth of our nation de-

clined, yours went up. While the cream of our male leaders and even our civilian population were devastated, yours were relatively untouched. While our factories deteriorated, our gold pledged for loans during World War II, your American traders prospered and your nation left rich beyond your dreams. When we were compelled in 1940 to deposit our securities with the U.S.A. for a loan to survive, other European nations got similar aid in the postwar years under the Marshall Plan for nothing."

Jeff had been startled by this line of talk from Dudley and wondered about the point of it. Yet, it was uttered with a quiet intensity and feeling that he had never before sensed in his British colleague. It could not just be written off as the effect of too much alcohol. Especially, when Dudley had continued:

> "During my lifetime, England has lost a territorial empire, while America has gained a commercial empire. I have watched my country decline drastically in natural resources and productivity, while we pursued an insane internationalism. How do you think I feel when I witness Arabs and other foreigners like yourself buying up the British Isles! I almost resent having to be employed by an American-owned subsidiary!!! Many of your American business chaps over here are vulgar, noisy, and brash. Your high pressure salesmanship is causing Britons to buy what they don't need and can't afford."

The conversation was loaded with implication, and Jeff did not quite know how to deal with it, or where to begin. He tried to be empathetic and agreed that some Americans were pushy, but then got back to his favorite theme of industriousness. He suggested that the British economy was improving and people could afford more if his countrymen got over its obsession with "full employment." Americans and Germans, he countered, face up to such realities as depression and overmanning. He cited the 1960 Fawley Agreement, which abolished the mate system (three watching mates to every five craftsmen), cut overtime drastically, lowered the hours of the working week to forty, increased worker pay, introduced incentive payments, and doubled productivity. This Esso-inspired management action raised the status of manual workers, diminishing the gap between white and blue collar workers. It also demonstrated his point that British workers can and do work happily in U.S.-owned plants. But Dudley ignored his input, and continued on a larger theme:

> "Jolly good, I don't mind you in your country defending your way of life and doing business, but don't impose your way of life on us in Great Britain and then get upset with us if we try to preserve our way of life. You set policies in the U.S., and then expect British plants to follow instructions based on American experience and requirements. I loathe the absolute conviction of your corporate headquarters on the absolute virtuousness of their policies and the perfectness of their products. You treat us like a branch factory. There are a lot of us who feel that American execu-

tives like yourself are here mainly to watch over us. In fact, the whole form of the American take-over of business here begins to look like 'commercial apartheid.' What bugs me is that some of our own young technologists almost take the line, 'God bless the Yanks and his relations, and keep us in our proper stations.' Many of our business and government leaders have a sickening anxiety to please the Americans."

Jeff was taken back by the new direction of Dudley's responses. He has always tried hard to be fair and just in his relations with his British counterpart. Was he responsible for this ventilation of pent-up emotion? But Dudley was not finished:

"Your firms force us into a dependency relationship. The power is firmly in American corporate headquarters, so that no matter how competent or effective we may be here in Britain, we have little input into your corporation policy and finance plans that affect our business here. We often have to make parts for American products which our government then contracts to buy, such as aircraft. To make matters worse, in some of the American subsidiaries, Britons are being replaced in key positions by Americans and we are not even allowed to be shareholders. You hog all the capital! As things are now going Britain is becoming a U.S. industrial satellite. I would like to see my country next July declare a Declaration of Economic Independence from the U.S.A., or else apply to become the 51st State! With more than 1600 firms here, you have old John Bull in a bind. Maybe with growing U.S. currency devaluation and inflation problems at home, your attitude will change."

And thus ended the tirade. Jeff thanked Dudley for his candor, said he would report back to headquarters on its implications, and get back to him to explore if anything could be done, at least by Easting, to improve their British relations.

But Jeff's troubles were not over on this United Kingdom jaunt. For when he took the Edinburgh Express up to visit the Leith plant, he hoped to relax with the genial Scot, Angus McKay, and get in a few rounds of golf. Their first few meetings went well, and by the third day when they shared a pleasant salmon dinner, Jeff thought all was in order. But then the very next morning, Angus got to the issue of expansion of research and development. He started on it quite bluntly, despite a lilting Scottish burr:

"It sticks in my gullet that because of the War, American research and development flourished, while ours declined, putting your firms in a position to follow-up and exploit many of our patents. If we are going to have a genuine business association, our people need the opportunity to develop their research capabilities. Right now most of the significant investigations and studies are being done in Pittsburgh. But you don't pick our brains enough here, so that we have an interchange of ideas and an intermixing of effort in every phase of activity, especially research and development. If we are to have a cooperative technology and relationship, there needs to be mechanisms for more cross-fertilization. I have some bright lads here who are bogged down in production, and I can offer little scope to utilize their research competencies. Now, don't get me wrong, Mr. Donovan, I am not complaining. But I think it is to Aquaphone's advantage to keep such talent here before some other American firm woos them to the States. You Americans have done much to build up the economy of Scotland, which we appreciate. Looking forward to the day when we get our own Parliament and are responsible for our own Scottish affairs, we are very grateful that twice as many American firms have invested here as in England. I am just proposing a new direction for Aquaphone's further expenditures in Leith."

Jeff thanked him for his suggestion and asked Angus to prepare a detailed memorandum on his idea for research and development expansion, along with costs and personnel to be involved. He promised to push it in Pittsburgh, but had private reservations on how receptive top management would be to this particular proposal. Then he flew home to ponder the new challenge he was facing in the British Isles.

Issues for Analysis

1. Contrast the life space of the three principal characters in this critical incident and examine how their cultural values affected their perceptions and communications.
2. Review the briefing of the boss for what information it provides to you on the British character, culture, and way of doing business.
3. Review the critical incident in London with Dudley. List some of the learnings you received which help you to better understand why he reacted as he did. If you were Jeff, how would you report the situation to headquarters and what would you recommend?
4. Review the critical incident outside of Edinburgh with Angus. Is it a real issue for many American firms? If you were Jeff, how would you handle it and what would you recommend? As you reread Angus' background and the incident, what are the implications of Scottish nationalism for Americans doing business there? How would you deal with such issues, whether there or in Wales or North Ireland? It is a real problem in the late 80's?
5. As you go back over this case, what applications could you make to your own situation when doing business in Britain? (Do consider the differences in British people, the social class system, the national inferiority feelings, the constraints on American executives who are not on the scene for long time periods, as well as the limitations of their own cultural backgrounds, etc.) Are there other implications from this case about doing business in Europe?

6. Does this case provide any clues on these current problems in Britain?

   • social class unrest and conflict
   • obsolete social institutions and legislation
   • labor conflict with frequent strikes and high unemployment
   • progress through joining the European Common market and strengthening foreign exports
   • differences in British/American perspectives during communications.

FRANCE

France—Profile

Population 56,000,000
Ethnic Groups .... Celtic and Latin Teutonic, Slavic, North African, Indochinese, Basque
Religions .... Roman Catholic 90%, Protestant 2%, Jewish 1%, Muslim 1%, Unaffiliated 6%
Education .... Compulsory ages 6–16 Literacy 99%
Land .... 213,000 square miles
Government .... Republic
Political Parties .... Socialist (PS), Communist (PCF), Left Radical (MRG), François Republic (RPR), Union for French Democracy Republicans (PR), Center for Social Democrats (CDS), Radical (RAD)
Per Capita Income .... 1983—$9,500
Exports to U.S. .... $12,200 million
Imports from U.S. .... $13,700 million

Commentary

France Magazine, Bicentennial Issue, Spring 1989—Shaking off decades of outmoded practices dating from Louis XIV and Napoleon, pressing to assume the natural leadership role they see for themselves in a united Europe, the French are becoming more predictable and more valuable partners. . . . The modernization of France's economic spirit is being fueled by the modernization of its economic system, which for decades prided itself on producing rigidly trained, rigidly thinking bureaucrats. . . . Business is viewed now as a human adventure. The ranks of the entrepreneurs continue to grow as they increasingly gain social acceptance. . . . Despite all the changes, Frenchmen are doing their best to retain a certain French style, especially in important matters, like clothes.

Philip Revzin

National Geographic, July 1989—"France Celebrates Its Bicentennial—France provided the technical know-how and political impetus for the European Space Agency to develop the Ariane rocket. These are marketed by Arianespace, the world's first commercial space transport company. When Ariane 4 is launched from French Guiana, it carries parts supplied by 11 of the 13 member nations of the ESA. . . . With the work only half done on the "Chunnel" under the English Channel, money is already crossing. In 1987, English investors bought 50 pieces of property near the French end of the Eurotunnel. In 1988, they bought 550. . . . When the Eurotunnel opens in 1993, shuttles will make the run between the terminals at Folkestone and Coquelle in about 35 minutes, high-speed trains from London to Paris in about three hours. With the French TGV trains from Paris carrying passengers at 168 miles an hour or more, they branch out not only all over France, but will connect someday with a high-speed, trans- Europe rail network. . . . France is shaping her destiny with technological advances from the world's second largest nuclear system, to 18% of the world's airliner market with her Airbus Industrie partners, to SPOT imaging satellites, to Numeris digital telephone system, to the Minitel computer that France Telecom provides free for 4.4 million subscribers, to the French computer programming language ADA which even the Pentagon adopted. All signs that when it comes to amour, cuisine, wine—and now technology—56 million Frenchmen could be right.

Cultural Characteristics of Business in France

. . . the French constitute the most brilliant and the most dangerous nation in Europe and the best qualified in turn to become an object of admiration, hatred, pity or terror, but never of indifference.

Alexis de Toqueville

Idealism

The French tend to believe that the basic truths on which life is based derive from principles and immutable or universal laws. They are concerned with the essence of values. The motto of the French Republic is "Liberty, Equality and Fraternity." To the French, values such as these should transcend everything else in life. They behave in an individualistic manner. "Chacun defend son beef-steak" (everyone protects his own steak). Sometimes they are frustrated. They find it hard to live by these ideals in everyday life, yet the hunger for these altruistic ideals is still present and deeply ingrained in most French people.

Social Structure and Status

Social classes are very important in France. The French social classes are: the aristocracy, the upper bourgeoisie, the upper-middle bourgeoisie, the middle, the lower-middle, and lower classes (blue-collar workers, peasants). Social classes categorize people according to their professional activities (teachers, doctors, lawyers, craftsmen, foremen, and peasants), as well as, their political opinions (conservative, left-oriented).

Social interactions are thus affected by these social stereotypes. It is extremely hard for a French individual to be rid of social stereotypes. They affect personal identity. Unlike an American who can theoretically attain the highest levels of social consideration by working hard and being professionally successful, a Frenchman finds it difficult to do so. If professionally successful, a Frenchman can expect to climb one or two stages of the social ladder in a lifetime, but often nothing more.

The French are very status conscious. Social status in France depends on one's social origins. Outward signs of social status are the level of education, a beautiful house with a well-designed, tasteful façade (not a gaudy one), knowledge of literature and fine arts, and the social origins of one's ancestors.

Cooperation and Competition

The French are not basically oriented towards competition. To them, the word competition has a very narrow meaning—practicing a sport at the highest level of international excellency. For example, for the French, only superstar athletes such as Greg LeMonde, Carl Lewis, or Joe Montana are involved in competition.

The average Frenchman does not feel affected by competition. This attitude can be dangerous. For example, in a 1978 New Year's Eve television speech, President Giscard d'Estaing tried to educate the French and make them face the fact that competition really should affect their lives. He said competition is not just what the French soccer team experiences during the Soccer World Cup. The economic welfare of the French people actually depends on how competitive French goods are on international markets. He tried to awaken the French to the notion of competition, so that they would motivate themselves to work harder and be more productive.

A consequence of these different attitudes is that when Americans interact with French people, they may manifest their competitive drive. The French may interpret their American interlocutors as being antagonistic, ruthless, and power-hungry. They may feel threatened, and overreact or withdraw from the discussion.

Personal Characteristics

French people are friendly, humorous, and sardonic. Americans may also be friendly, but they are so friendly that they are seldom sardonic. Americans need to be liked. French people do not. Americans tend to like people who agree with them. French people are more likely to be interested in a person who disagrees with them. Because they want to be liked, Americans try to impress others. On the other hand, the French are very hard to impress, and impatient with those who try. A Frenchman, when trying to get a sense of a person, looks for qualities within the person and for personality. An American looks at the person's achievements. Frenchmen tend to gain recognition and to develop their identity by thinking and acting against others, while Americans increase their self-esteem by acting in accord with the actions and expectations of others. French people are more inner-oriented, and base behavior and evaluations upon feelings, preferences, and expectations.

Trust and Respect

A Frenchman trusts a person according to inner evaluation of the personality. An American trusts a person according to past achievements and upon other people's recognition, and ranking of that person.

French people tend to respect an individual according to character. Americans tend to respect an individual according to professional accomplishments. Because social stereotypes are so vivid, an average Frenchman cannot earn respect from members of other social classes merely through work accomplishments and performance.

In *Cultural Misunderstandings—The French-American Experience*, Carroll (1988) reports on a foreign student living with a French family who closed the door to his bedroom after dinner. He did not understand that closed doors are considered rude and that the visitor was expected to socialize with the family. Furthermore, when their shutters to the outside are closed, this is not a sign of the "distrustfulness of the French," but a desire for privacy from the passer-by.

Style of Conversation

Many Americans use superlatives like most, best, and largest. The reason may be the importance of competition as a social value for the Americans, along with the importance of quantified measurements in assessing standards of excellency. American conversations usually include numerous pronouns such as "I" or "my." French interlocutors seldom put themselves forward or try to make themselves look good in conversations. If they accidentally do, they will usually add, "Je ne cherche pas à me vanter mais . . ." ("I do not want to boast but . . . "). Boasting is often considered a weakness, a sign of self-satisfaction and immaturity. In conversations with French people, Americans may ask their French counterparts questions about themselves. The French will probably shun such questions, and orient the conversation towards more general subjects. To them, it is not proper to show characteristics of self-centeredness.

The French often criticize institutions, conditions, and people they live with. A conversation where disagreements are exchanged can be considered stimulating by a Frenchman, while an American will likely be embarrassed. It is not uncommon to see two Frenchmen arguing with each other, their faces reddened with what seems to be anger, exchanging lively, heated, and irreconcilable arguments. Then later, they shake hands and comment, "That was a good discussion. We should do it again sometime!" The French tend to think that such arguments are interesting and stimulating. It is also a meaningful outlet for tension.

Humor

Americans and French enjoy and appreciate humor. However, the French tend to use humor in more numerous situations than Americans do. They also often add a touch of cynicism to their humor, and may not hesitate to make fun of institutions and people.

Consistency and Contradictions

Americans prefer consistency and predictability, and expect role-conforming in their relationships. The French on the other hand abound in contradictions and are not overly disturbed by them. They profess lofty ideals of fraternity and equality, but at times show characteristics of utmost individualism and selfish materialism. For example, the things that occasionally seem to matter most are owning a little car, a little house, and cashing in on one's little retirement pension. On the political scene, they seem continuously restless, verbally criticizing the government and capitalism, yet are basically conservative. They have supported a conservative government for the last 20 years.

Attitudes Toward Work

Attitudes of the French toward work depend on whether they are employed in the public sector or in the private sector. In the French bureaucracy and in public concerns, there is little incentive to be productive. Quotas are rarely assigned, and it is virtually impossible to lay-off or dismiss employees on the basis of job performance.

In the private sector, the situation is different. It is true that French workers do not respect the work ethic as much as many American counterparts do. They are usually not motivated by competition or the desire to emulate fellow-workers. They frown on working overtime and have the longest vacations in the world (between four to five weeks a year). However, they usually work hard in their allotted working time. French workers have the reputation of being productive. Part of the explanation for such productiveness may lie in the French tradition of craftsmanship. A large proportion of the French work force has been traditionally employed in small, independent businesses where there is widespread respect for a job well-done. Many Frenchmen take pride in work that is done well because traditionally they have not been employed in huge, impersonal industrial concerns. They often have a direct stake in the work they are doing, and are usually concerned with quality.

Authority

French companies contain many social reference groups that are mutually exclusive. Tight reins of authority are needed to ensure adequate job performance. The lesser emphasis on delegation of responsibility limits accountability and contributes to a more rigid organization structure. As a consequence, decision-making is more centralized in French companies, and it may take longer before decisions are reached and applied. This may be a source of frustration for American executives (especially lower- and middle-management executives) who are working with French executives from a comparative management level. Americans may resent the amount of time that is necessary before their recommendations are considered and dealt with by top-management. Americans are accustomed to executives having a higher degree of responsibility. The flow of communication is improved if American executives have direct access to two or three top executives of a French company. This is where the actual decision-making power is.

The highest executives of large French companies also differ from their American counterparts in their conception of authority. The top two men of a French company are accountable to a lesser extent than their American counterparts. It takes poor performance for them to be challenged in their functions by a board of directors or by subordinates. Patterns of authority are more stable in French industry. Therefore, because they do not need to justify their actions to the same extent, the very top French executives tend to be more autocratic in their managerial style.

Executive functions, also, have more overtones of social leadership. For example, one often depicts industry leaders, such as Mr. Dreyfus, the head of Renault, or Mr. Michelin, the head of the tire company, as ruling their empires in the same way as Napoleon ruled his. In their professional activities, these very top industry executives are autocratic leaders of men, but in addition, they have a high social, and even political, status.

It is interesting to compare French and American business magazine interviews of executives. Along with professional experiences and activities, top

French executives usually mention details concerning their personal lives such as former professors who had an impact on them, enriching social and personal experiences, books that influenced their outlook on life, and what their convictions on political and social issues are. On the other hand, top American executives will more likely emphasize the progression of their career in terms of professional achievements.

Organizational Structure and Decision-Making

The organizational structure of French companies tends to be more rigid than that of American companies. The French put less emphasis on control of individual performance. The Americans, on the other hand, tend to favor a flexible organizational structure with greater delegation of responsibility, and greater control of individual performance.

Americans attach much importance to achievement. Therefore, decision-making in U.S. companies occurs at levels where the results allow managers to reach quantifiable goals.

The decision-making process is more centralized in French companies. Important decisions are made by only the top executives.

Walter Ulmer, president of the Center for Creative Leadership, recently addressed a Human Resources Forum in Monte Carlo, making this astute observation about the experience: "My sensing of the French audience reaction to my main theme of empowerment and responsibility building was that it was recognized as clearly desirable, but that few senior French managers were into listening or decentralizing in practice."

Motivation

Most Americans put high value on professional accomplishments. Their self-esteem derives largely from these accomplishments, and so does their social status. They are motivated to work hard in order to earn money, particularly in light of the fact that there is little job security and social security in America. As a result, most Americans are very ambitious and expend considerable energy in their work.

However, there is a major difference between the motivations of Americans and French people concerning work. Although the French appreciate the Americans' industriousness and devotion to their work, they do not believe it is worthwhile. To the French the *qualitè de la vie* (quality of life) is what matters. In the present French government, there is even a Minister in charge of the quality of life. The French attach a great importance to freetime and vacations, and are seldom willing to sacrifice the enjoyment of life out of dedication to work.

Conflict

Americans do not like conflict, especially interpersonal conflict. They feel uncomfortable, and are concerned about what others think when they are involved in conflict. Because most Americans are pragmatic, they think of conflict as a hindrance to achieving goals.

However, the French, partly because they live in a more closed society with relatively little social mobility, are used to conflict. They are aware that some positions are irreconcilable, and that people must live with these irreconcilable opinions. They, therefore, tend not to mind conflict, and sometimes enjoy it. They even respect others who carry it off with style and get results. The French are also less concerned about negative reactions from those with whom they are in conflict.

Dr. Azzedine Mezbache (1986) discovered that French managers reported difficulties in adjusting to life in other countries. In a study of 31 French managers from 16 French companies, he reported problems caused by emphasis in the French culture on pride in their past cultural heritage, causing them to be too critical of people who do not benefit from that same cultural tradition. In their self-descriptions, the French managers felt handicapped by their conditioning to a formal way of thinking, and by lack of actual knowledge of other cultures.

Tips for Working in France

- A firm and pumping handshake is considered uncultured. A French handshake is a quick shake with some pressure in the grip.
- A French woman offers her hand first.
- Punctuality in business and social invitation is important. If invited to a person's home for a social occasion, it is polite to bring a gift of flowers, but not roses or chrysanthemums.
- At mealtime a French person enjoys pleasant conversation, but not personal questions or the subject of money.
- Snapping the fingers of both hands and slapping an open palm over a closed fist have vulgar meanings.
- Great importance is placed on neatness and taste.

General Tips for Doing Business in Europe

The U.S. Department of Commerce and the World Trade Association of San Diego recently sponsored a conference on "When doing business in Europe, do as the Europeans do!" Some of the recommendations from these discussions:

- Consider locating an office or plant in Europe so as to have more direct access to customers and suppliers. Remember there are more than 280 million consumers in the EEC alone.
- Customer service is the key to success. The standards of Europe in this regard are not up to that of the United States, especially in matters of rapid repairs and home service.
- Publish price lists in terms of local currency, not U.S. dollars.
- Deploy Americans to Europe on the basis of a two-year minimum commitment to stay there and establish meaningful customer relations; the staying power of expatriate personnel is a subtle indicator—whenever possible, hire locals and then train them.
- Lease AV/office equipment and typewriters in Europe because of the power situation there.
- Ensure that sales personnel know their products and tell the truth—Europeans are sophisticated buyers of foreign merchandise.
- Europeans gauge the forethought and commitment of a foreign firm by the way it treats its sales representatives. They perceive the sales person as a key role to be judged on long-term performance; select such representatives *very carefully*.
- Europeans do not like change, so it is important for the foreign company to project stability and long-range commitment; yet they are attracted to "new" products, processes, and services.
- When able to properly serve the primary market in Europe, remember geographic distances are not great. Assess the secondary markets (Spain and Portugal, Yugoslavia and Greece, and the Eastern European countries), and respond carefully to all inquiries from such areas (e.g., telexes and letters).
- Beside cultural, language, and political differences in Europe, be prepared to cope with technical differences (e.g., length of stationery and forms that do not fit standard copying machines, ink that does not reproduce well, strange abbreviations).
- European nomenclature and honorific titles are to be observed in oral and written communication (especially, spellings in English that differ between British and American versions).
- Europeans value personal contacts and mementos, so the token gift may create a favorable impression or participation in a trade fair which is part of centuries-old tradition.

Perhaps this story told at this international trade conference by Gerald Kahl, vice-president of Kahlsico International, best illustrates the last point and the business differences between North Americans and Europeans:

> Several years ago we sold an inexpensive instrument to a chemist in Bulgaria. It wasn't a large or expensive purchase, but every year he goes on vacation to a Black Sea resort, he sends us a postcard with this message—"All is well and the instrument is working very nicely."

Federal Republic of Germany

Germany—Profile

Population	78,000,000
Ethnic Groups	German, Danish, Turkish minorities
Religions	Roman Catholic, Protestant, others
Education	99% Literacy
Land	286,108 square km
Government	Federal Republic of West/East Germany
Political Parties	Christian Democratic Union (CDU), Christian Social Union (CSU), Free Democratic (FDP), Social Democratic (SPD), Communist (DKP), Greens
Per Capita Income	$14,890 (Deutschemark)
Exports to U.S.	$25,806.92 million (West Germany)
Imports from U.S.	$16,716.18 million (1988)

The July 2, 1990 treaty that integrated East Germany (German Democratic Republic) into the Federal Republic of Germany commited both East/West Germany to a free market economy and democratic federal system with an open flow of people, goods, services, capital and information throughout the United States. East Germany adopted the West Germany monetary, tax, and economic policies, while the latter will help in reconstruction.

"Where were you the day the Wall came down."

Business Week, November 27, 1989

For Europeans the day November 9, 1989 was a date that will live long in their memories. The elimination of the Berlin Wall is a new starting point marking the end of an era. We present this information on the Federal Republic of Germany and some paragraphs on Eastern Europe, realizing that the political and economic situation is changing very rapidly. Cultural values, mindsets, as well as customs, and courtesies however, do not change quickly and endure even when political events change.

Geography, Government, and People

Located in the northern part of Europe, the Federal Republic of Germany was composed of ten states and West Berlin. It occupied an area of approximately 96,000 square miles with a population estimated at 62,000,000. Northern Germany is relatively flat, however, the elevation rises gradually in the south. The climate is considered temperate. East Germany had a population of 16 million living in 41,828 square miles.

Germans have a reputation for being industrious, hard working, reserved, and perhaps even cold. They are meticulous and exact, and often very militaristic in the preciseness of their actions. On the other hand, some of the world's greatest composers, writers, and philosophers are products of a German heritage.

The Germans are not an outward people; they tend to be very private. Though their daily routine brings them into close contact with many different people, they are close to only a very few. The German language has a key to understanding this. The Germans make a strong distinction between an acquaintance (Bekannte) and a friend (Freund). The German will only use Freund when he really means it, otherwise it is a Bekannte. Close family ties are also cherished.

Germans tend to be very exact. Bus, train, and plane schedules all run on schedule. The manager's day is also well planned. The Germans are not a spontaneous people. Their attitude is to organize the time allotted for something to its greatest efficiency, rather than take an attitude of wait and see what happens.

West Germany had existed in its present form since 1949—the Federal Republic was only a part of an earlier and far more extensive Germany. The basic legislation establishing the present form of government is the Grundgesetz (basic law) of 1949, which established a constitutional federal democracy in Germany. After the Second World War, the Allied forces divided Germany into two countries. The capital was also moved from Berlin to Bonn during this period. It was felt it would be difficult to have Berlin continue to serve as the capital, because it was not only a divided city, but also it was completely surrounded by the communist East Zone, the German Democratic Republic (East Germany). In 1990, the two Germanies were reunified, and Berlin will probably again become the common capital.

There are two main governing bodies in Germany, the Bundestag (Parliament) and the Bundesrat (Federal Council). The Bundestag, the larger of the two, comprises elected representatives from the ten states, including West Berlin, and possesses legislative power. The Bundestag consists of 496 deputies, plus 22 representatives from West Berlin, who are elected for a 4-year term. The Bundesrat consists of 41 members, who have nonvoting status, although it can exercise the veto power in matters concerning Laender (the 10 states) interests. Germany has a president; however, the position is of honor and formality, not one of power. The real power lies in the office of chancellor (Bundeskanzler). The chancellor is either the leading representative of the party with a majority of seats in the Bundestag, or the leader of the largest party in a coalition government.

The Christian Democratic Union, the major party, operates with the Christian Socialist Union. Although each party maintains its own structure, the two form a common caucus in the Bundestag and do not run opposing campaigns. The CDU/CSU is generally conservative on economic and social policy.

The SDP is the second major party in West Germany and stresses social programs. In foreign policy, it emphasizes ties with the Atlantic alliance but seeks improved relations with Eastern Europe. The SDP has a powerful base in the larger cities and industrialized Laender.

Though some of Germany's past can be seen in the old cities and buildings, much of Germany is very modern. This is especially true of the major cities and industrial areas, which were almost destroyed during WWII. Germany has risen from the rubble to become the third largest industrial giant in the Western world, following the U.S. and Japan. Germany is the largest exporter in the world.

There are three items that heavily influence the structure of business in Germany today. These points are the European Economic Community (EEC), co-determination, and government involvement. Germany is one of the original members of the EEC. Much of German business practices and laws are directly tied to the regulations and directives from the EEC.

The principle of collective good is important in the idea of co-determination (Mitbestimmung). Co-determination allows for worker input into the management of the firm. Any firm with more than five employees should have a worker's council (Betriebsrat) that represents the employees and helps them solve various grievances with the firm's management. Any coal or steel firm of more than 2,000 workers is required to have 50% of the company's supervisory board composed of workers. There is also a specially chosen labor representative to represent labor on the management board of the company. This all illustrates an attempt to include a most important part of the economic structure, the worker.

Unions are very strong and provide workers with many more rights than some foreign counterparts. For example, they can become involved in decisions on dismissal. The process of co-determination gives management and workers the opportunity to work together to shape or define the firm's goals, objectives, and responsibilities. Employees are represented in five trade unions of professional organizations: German Trades Union Federation, German Salaried Staff Union, Christian Trade Union Federation, German Civil Servant's Federation, and the Union of Executive Employees.

The Germans are among the highest paid workers in the world and enjoy a high standard of living. They are able to afford the luxuries and extras of life. An important part of this concept is the vast welfare state, which supports the German worker. This includes liberal pensions, bonuses, medical and dental care, and five to six weeks of paid vacation. Though taxes are heavy, this system has relieved the typical German from many financial worries.

Germany is committed to a free enterprise economy, but government and business work very closely together. The former communist system of East Germany is being transformed into an economy where there is more voluntary participation of business with government in planning the economy. This means there is much closer work in trying to decide what is best for Germany as a whole. There is greater cooperation and understanding.

Another important factor in the economy is the extent of government control/participation in industry. The state holds control or equity participation in hundreds of firms. In the public service arena, the railroads and the postal system are totally state controlled. The state also owns a trade monopoly in alcohol.

An area that is perhaps the fastest growing in Germany, as well as throughout Europe, is joint government and private business ventures. This means a partnership between private business and firms controlled by the government. With denationalization ongoing, this increase in joint partnership ventures is another indication of "collective interest" being an important part of the German business and economic community.

Trade plays a very important role in the German economy to sustain growth and the German standard of living because sufficient natural resources are very limited. By far the largest percentage of trade is within the EEC, although West Germany had extensive trade relations with East Germany, which is now being integrated into a greater Germany.

Social Customs

Germans are very knowledgeable and capable business people. They pride themselves on having quality products to offer on the world markets. They are formal in their business dealings, not only with foreigners, but among themselves as well. For the foreigner it is best to be conservative and subdued, unless you are given the indication to be more informal. The Germans do not like loud people, especially in business. They have no respect for the pushy, brassy, or loud business executive. To them such behavior reflects a weakness in the person or company.

In Germany, you must be very careful of what you say. This means either in print or verbally. If the other party can show that something was promised or intimated, even though a contract wasn't signed, you can still be held liable for that promise. This is a reason why the Germans tend to be so exact in their dealings and somewhat more distant in their business relationships.

The handshake is an important part of the German greeting. They shake hands often, not only on the first greeting of the day, but also at the conclusion of a conversation. Firm handshakes are preferred. Generally the older person, or the person of higher authority, will extend the hand first. The woman extends her hand first, unless the man holds a higher position. A verbal response also accompanies the handshake.

Men should bow slightly. This is mostly a slight bow from the shoulders and neck as the man leans forward a little as he greets the other person. If one is entering a room filled with many people, the person should proceed around the room shaking everyone's hands. Again, a friendly "good morning" or "good day" is appropriate.

In Germany, there are two forms of address, the polite and the familiar. The familiar form "du," similar to "thou" in English, is used only for relatives, very close friends, children, and animals. The polite form "Sie" is used on all other occasions, including the business environment. Any foreigner addressing a German should use the polite form. Many Germans have known each other for years and still use the polite form. A German may initiate the usage of the "du" form, although this is a rare occurrence.

Not only should you use the polite form of speech, but you should also refrain from using first names; "Herr" and "Frau" are more appropriate. In addition, women should always be called "Frau" regardless of their marital status.

The Germans are title conscious and proper etiquette requires addressing them by their title. Also, those who have attained their Ph.D. are addressed by the term "doktor"; i.e., "Herr Doktor Schmidt" or "Frau Doktor Braun." Women are called by their first names. The wife of Georg Meyer will not be Frau Georg Meyer, but rather Frau Ursula Meyer. A friend or associate should introduce the newcomer to the group, as Germans prefer third-party introductions.

In some countries, it is quite common to entertain a client; perhaps dinner at a fashionable restaurant. In Germany, particularly with large corporations dealing in multimillion dollar contracts, the superiors will not allow their subordinates to accept the invitation. Many German firms would consider this to be a conflict of interest and one could easily lose his objectivity—"Verpflichtungen." A good rule to follow is to conduct business during business hours.

The Germans like to discuss things and enjoy a good topic of discussion. Religion, politics, sexual trends, and nuclear power are freely discussed, but topics relating to one's private life should be avoided. One should use good judgment in weighing the situation, but generally the Germans enjoy a good conversation on any of the important topics of the day.

The Germans are generally restrained in their body movements. They do not wave their arms and hands a lot as in other cultures. It is impolite to talk to someone with your hands in your pockets. It is also considered rude to sit with the bottom of your shoes facing another person. For this reason, German men cross their legs at the knees, rather than with an ankle on the other knee. Most body movements could best be characterized as conservative. Whether sitting or standing, it is generally in a more upright and rigid position.

German is the official language in Germany, although in border areas, other languages are spoken more often. There are hundreds of dialects and local variations spoken throughout the countryside, although dialects are generally only spoken in less formal situations with friends. Hochdeutsch, or the "high" German, is found in all magazines, newspapers, television, etc. In a business context, your counterpart will avoid the usage of dialects. English is the major foreign language taught in Germany. Most business people are conversant in English.

The Roman Catholic Church (45%) and the German Protestant Church (45%) account for 90% of all religious affiliations. Other denominations are grouped together in what the Germans call Sekte (sects). Church activity in general has dropped over the years.

Both churches are very powerful and influential in Germany. There is not the clear separation of church and state as in the U.S. or other European countries. Among the new minorities are "guest workers" from Turkey and Italy.

Social Tips

- Guests usually stand when the host enters the room and remain standing until he offers them a seat again.
- References to baseball, basketball, or American football are usually not completely understood.
- Don't talk with your hands in your pockets.
- Don't prop your leg or legs on desks, chairs, or tables.
- A handshake is the most common form of greeting, but it should be firm only with men.
- Remember to shake hands!
- Chew gum only in private.
- Don't point at your head.
- Use cosmetics and jewelry sparingly.

EASTERN/CENTRAL EUROPE

Time has finally run out for Communism. But its edifice has not yet crumbled. May we not be crushed beneath its rubble instead of gaining liberty.

Alexander I. Solzhenitsyn
Rebuilding Russia, *July 1990*

Among the disappearing institutions to which Solzhenitsyn refers was the East Bloc or COMECON, which once included in this economic "alliance," the Soviet Union and its satellite nations (see Figure 16-1 for population breakdown). Predictably, the former Union of Soviet Socialist Republics (U.S.S.R.) outweighed the other countries, accounting for two thirds of the total market and absorbing the resources of member states who were also bound by military allegiance to its Warsaw Pact. Freed of the Communist yoke, the nearly 380 + million behind the Iron Curtain said "goodbye" to such arrangements, and turned westward for capital, resources, and training. Although the newly liberated nations of Eastern and Central Europe will look to develop markets in Western Europe, North and South America, Asia and Africa, their principal trading partners are likely to be each other and the emerging "Commonwealth of Independent States" (C.I.S.).

After decades under rigid Communist control, East Germany (now united with West Germany), Poland, Czechoslovakia, Hungary, the disintegrating Yugoslavia, Romania, Bulgaria, and Albania, as well as the C.I.S. itself, are in the midst of slow, painful, traumatic changes toward greater democratic reforms and market economies. In the process, all these victims of centralized socialistic planning are left with exhausted labor reserves and high unemployment, ill-prepared and unproductive workers, out-of-date machinery and plants. In addition to severe shortages of food and consumer goods, these nations are devastated by a frightful legacy of environmental pollution, ecological and economic ruins, as well as a collapsing infrastructure. The failed totalitarian utopia and ideology left them a damaged citizenry on the verge of social collapse. Zbigniew Brzezinski, former U.S. Presidential adviser, reminds us not to mourn the passing of this empire called "evil" because it produced more deaths than any other country, through purges, exile, mass deportation, genocide, and state terrorism. No wonder its citizens became cynical, and rejected the "dictatorship of the proletariat."

Figure 16-1. Central/Eastern Europe populations, in millions. (Source: ILO, IMF)

Much has happened in "Eurasia" during the last two editions of this book, and in the next sections we will describe the "way it was for the last 70 years— a system of "top-down" control over society's entire structure by a single bureaucratized party called the "nomenklatura." For that was the environment in this vast area which still affects "mindset" of this generation even after the demise of the Soviet Union and the onset of the second Russian Revolution.

Now the whole political, social, and business situation is in profound transition. Representatives there from free-enterprise nations and companies are more welcome, but they face a whole new series of challenges and opportunities. The eight countries adjoining and somewhat aligned to the Soviet Union are being pressured by their citizenry to move from totalitarianism to more pluralism. The pace of change in these lands differs from Hungary and Poland, which are in the vanguard, to Albania, which still clings to the hard-line Communist approach. One of the major forces unraveling the post World War II status quo is the reform movement underway in the Soviet Union, led by former President Mikhail S. Gorbachev with his approach of "glasnost," or openness, and "perestroika," or restructuring of a deterministic society. The underlying reasons for the alterations are economic—authoritarian government with its centralized planning and administration is not working, and the economies of all nine nations are in severe trouble. Reforming Communist societies economically, however, has led their peoples increasingly to demand political reforms—mainly toward more democratization and nationalization (as in the case of the Baltic and other "independent" states within the former U.S.S.R.).

However, the essential problem for the 431.8 million people in Eastern Europe's nine nations is *cultural conditioning*. Having been conditioned for decades to a totalitarian system run by a Communist elite, the workers are not easily coaxed into making individual decisions and participating, into exercising initiative and imagination. Even when given freedom, creativity has been long stifled by mindless conformity. In a special survey of Eastern Europe, *The Economist* (August 12, 1989) observed that the people cannot be expected immediately to display energy and enterprise:

> Reforming governments pass laws to encourage the growth of the private sector, but depressingly few new private businessmen step forward. The governments announce the break-up of the huge old loss-making state conglomerates, and tell the smaller new units to compete with each other; but most managers go on doing exactly what they did before.
>
> Not many human beings actually enjoy taking risks, trying unfamiliar things, working late rather than going home early. Almost everybody of working age in Eastern Europe has spent a life in a job which demands little except casual obedience. When a system based on the issuing of orders suddenly barks "Make up your own minds!" it is not surprising that the first reaction is a stunned apathy. . . . The liberation is coming, but it will take time, it will suffer zig-zags, and it will often be incomplete.

Eastern Europe's Changing Business Culture

The East European market is basically open for agricultural products, new industrial, electronic and chemical products. The future may be for consumer products and high technologies, as well as significant foreign aid.

In the recent past the Communist Party of the East European countries dominated the countries' political and economic life. All major government and economic decision-making posts were filled by party members. The guiding party doctrine of democratic centralism ensured that decisions taken at the top were not questioned by the lower echelons. This led to a situation in which a few people at the peak of the pyramid made almost every significant decision and local initiative was practically nonexistent.

The export and import monopoly of the Ministry of Foreign Trade and its foreign trade organizations prevented industrial ministries and producing enterprises from having any meaningful contact with world market demand and supply. The main idea governing the institution of a state monopoly was to prevent capitalist countries from influencing the course of economic activities in the East European countries. Now, western investment and trade are sought.

One other organization very helpful for newcomers in East European countries is the Chamber of Commerce and Industry. This organization is not directly involved in foreign trade deals, but carries out numerous functions aimed at promoting East European foreign trade. This organization can set up contacts with officials in the Foreign Trade Organization and in other organizations. The national Chamber of Commerce coordinates the activities of the Chambers of Commerce from all branch offices in large cities throughout each country. Among the main functions of the Chamber of Commerce is developing contacts with foreign business organizations. In order to promote trade and economic relations with particular countries, several joint chambers of commerce have been set up. They invite and act as a host to foreign commercial delegations visiting the country and send their own delegations abroad. They help arrange foreign exhibitions in the particular country and organize participation of their own countries in international trade fairs abroad. The Chamber handles operations involved in patenting foreign inventions in East European countries and East European countries' inventions abroad, as well as the registration of trademarks in East Europe.

Until the current reforms, it should be noted that members of these Eastern Europe Chambers were members of the Communist Party, and some used it as a cover for government intelligence organizations. Now the system is under transformation, which may go on for decades. The trends, depending on where you are in Eastern Europe, are toward reviving the private sector, so that business people cannot only own property, but get access to labor, capital, machinery and raw materials. Increasingly, managers and executives are being permitted direct negotiation with foreign business representatives and investors. In opening up the huge, inefficient public sector, governments have undertaken a number of reform experiments, such as:

- Demonopolization and down-sizing to hundreds of smaller production entities.
- Production subsidies, like those given to consumers, but to losing state companies.
- Legislative changes making it easier to transform state-owned to private or cooperative-owned enterprises.
- Price setting by the market instead of the government.
- Creation of a more flexible and open banking system that lends money on the basis of fiscal soundness instead of planner's whim.
- Innovations to attract Western investment and credit, and foster joint ventures (e.g., Western debt-holders permitted to cancel part of their foreign debt holdings in return for equity share in state firms).

The slow shift is seemingly away from ideology and the planned economy toward a non-capitalist market economy—production, price, and the like come from the market, not government, but the factories responding to the orders are somehow communally owned and democratically managed by a board of experts. Many Eastern European countries, such as Poland and Russia itself, are attempting to transfer ownership of state properties to share-owning workers. Property ownership is a key concept undergoing redefinition. To comprehend why these reforms are happening, read *Central and Eastern Europe: The Opening Curtain* edited by William Griffith (1989), and subscribe to the publications on doing business with Eastern Europe by Business International Ltd. (40 Duke St. London, W1A 1DW, UK).

Global managers with vision see new market possibilities in Eastern Europe, and seek to develop links there with representatives from governments, parties, unions, businesses, churches, environmentalists, and students. Aware of the cultural and intellectual heritage of the region, as well as its potential, they network and encourage entrepreneurs, provide training and services, promote diversification and outside investment. Exchanges of managers and students between free enterprise nations and organizations with counterparts in Eastern Europe is fostered. Trade and education can be powerful means to facilitating reform, and the countries to start with are Hungary and Poland as these media reports demonstrate. From the *Los Angeles Times*, August 27, 1989:

> But for those accustomed to operating in a market economy, even the simplest tasks can become daunting in socialist Hungary which suffers from the calcification brought on by more than 40 years of central planning. "It's like hacking your way through jungle with a machete to get things done," says Charles Rudd, president of Interconcepts, a firm based in Concord, California, that is setting up joint ventures here in computer software and desk-top publishing. But Rudd and a growing number of American business people say they intend to keep hacking, lured by the

potential for long-term profits. Although Hungary's 10.6 million people constitute a small market, their purchasing power of about $7,520 annual income is much higher than the Chinese. . . . Hungary is viewed as a gateway to the rest of Eastern Europe. The U. S. Embassy in Budapest says in return for investment, quality control, overseas marketing skills, and management experience from abroad, Hungary offers tax breaks, repatriation of profits in hard currency, and other advantages.

Levi Strauss Company of Budapest, a $1 million joint venture with several Hungarian state-owned firms, epitomizes the new opportunities. The jean-makers from San Francisco retain 51% of the company and enjoy a 5-year tax holiday, as well as control of production and marketing. Having built a modern factory in southern Hungary, 700,000 pairs of jeans are produced and sold within the country. Employees get paid double the local pay scale and have more incentives to be productive. Transcultural success!

After the devastations of WWII, Poland has suffered through 45 years of Communist mismanagement of its political and economic systems. In 1989, the opposition union, Solidarity, was permitted to join the government and now controls key ministries until the first free election can be held in 1993. The coalition hopes to revitalize their country by fostering decentralization desubsidization, privatization, and productivity. To counteract the ruling class of privileged party bureaucrats in place, the reformers appeal for massive Western assistance, investment, and joint ventures, which feature a mix of generous terms and innovative marketing. It is a turning point—Poland may set the pace for the de-communization of Eastern Europe and the return of true democracy. A cultural revolution is underway, as well as an ideological reformation in which the concept of "socialism" is being redefined and reapplied.

The 1990s provide a rare chance to produce cultural synergy and peaceful prosperity in this region. For those bold enough to participate in the improvement process, consult the Eastern European Trade Directory (International Trade Press, P.O. Box 14101, San Francisco, CA. 94114,USA).

Making Distinctions Between Peoples and Systems

For effective international trade and relations, global managers must distinguish between a people and culture that one may admire, and a political and economic ideology or systems that one may abhor. The myriad cultures of Eastern Europe from Poland through Russia have produced admirable civilizations and talented citizens. Although one may prefer an open, free enterprise system over a closed, totalitarian form, a cosmopolitan still seeks synergy and peaceful relations with the inhabitants of the latter, especially those who have been victimized by such systems and now have been liberated. Stereotyping all Communists is not only ethnocentric, it is not good for business.

A case in point was the late Armand Hammer, a physician who became chairman of Occidental Petroleum Corporation in Los Angeles. Probably no Western business person did more to develop large-scale economic cooperation between the United States and Marxist countries. A classic entrepreneur who first went to the Soviet Union in 1921 with medical relief, that intercultural experience helped to transform him into an importer and exporter who in the process became a multimillionaire. After 60 years of dealing with Communist leaders from V. I. Lenin of the Soviet Union to Deng Xiaoping of the Peoples Republic of China, Hammer had high praise for the leaders personally, as well as for their peoples and their national achievements. But in an interview with the *Los Angeles Times* (April 5, 1982), he confessed that socialism as an economic system simply fails to deliver:

> I think that socialism will be replaced in time by more private ventures. . . . because communism just doesn't work. What will emerge, I would not call capitalism, but a hybrid, a mix of government undertakings and private enterprise.

This seems to already have started in mainland China, where Hammer observed as he finalized a $230-million long-term surface-coal development project:

> We can do business with every country by keeping out of politics and rendering a service. Let history decide which ideological system is best for people.

How prophetic was Hammer as the culture of free enterprise takes root not only in Russia and its neighboring republics, but as the 20th century draws to a close, in all of Asia, even the People's Republic of China is moving in this direction. The old, passive and submissive mentality of populations formerly under totalitarian regimes is dying as inhabitants regain their dignity and enthusiasm for work. Listen to these words of Alexander Kislov, deputy governor of the Penza region (1.5 million persons) in liberated Russia:

> We were raised as parasites. You were always waiting for kindness from your boss, waiting for the raise or job or for products to appear on store shelves, but you did nothing to make it happen. . . . People are maturing and realizing their fate is in their own hands. . . . People are starting to understand that under the reforms, you'll have less money, but you'll have a chance to get rich.

To acculturate the peoples of Eastern Europe to real democracy and a market economy is a massive re-education challenge. George Soros has made the case for this in his remarkable book, *Underwriting Democracy* (New York: Free Press, 1991). Through his private Soros Foundation, this billionaire funds practical projects in this region and China by dissenters, journalists, educators, and entrepreneurs seeking to bolster battered economies in their transition from socialism to free enterprise systems. In 1991, at the start of the infamous Soviet coup, his foundation gave photocopiers to Russian President Boris Yeltsin and helped print fliers to rally Moscow citizens to support the embattled reformers behind the barricades at the Federation's "White House." Since then, this founder of the mutual Quantum Fund spends 80% of his time traveling to urge, cajole, and influence leaders and policy to stop spiraling chaos and economic collapse of the Commonwealth republics and their Eastern Bloc neighbors through a new type "Marshall Plan" with a central bank to further credit and trade in the region (*USA Today*, Nov. 14, 1991, p. 88).

Lewis Perelman and John Berenyt (*Wall Street Journal*, Oct. 14, 1991) maintain that academic initiatives, including those of the U.S. Treasury secretary and the International Monetary Fund, make a mistake by focusing upon education of the old Soviet managerial elite. Instead the emphasis should be upon broadly cultivating entrepreneurial job skills, as well as basic market and consumer literacy among the masses of people victimized under the former Communist empire. They advocate the following for former Soviet bloc countries, temporarily impoverished as they come out of their "dark age":

- Economic re-education of whole workforces as was done by General Electric at Hunary's Tungstram plants to cut costs and improve productivity.
- Encourage distance education by telecommunication as done by the National Technological University of Fort Collins, Colorado, instead of relying on traditional scholastic methods bound by buildings and transportation of students. . . .
- Enhance commercial enterprise to discount sales of products and services needed in Eastern Europe for re-learning about capitalism and how it works, rather than depend on the grant approach.

Instead of charity and philanthropy for these emerging democracies, Perelman and Berenyt advocate seeking lucrative market opportunities for prodigiuos learning in Eastern and Central Europe like franchise business with training, such as McDonald's Hamburger University. They suggest that the Commonwealth itself devote part of their foreign sales of oil and gold to this reeducation process.

RUSSIA AND THE COMMONWEALTH OF INDEPENDENT STATES (C.I.S.)

Commentary

The Economist, Dec. 1988, — "The Soviet Political Earthquake Continues."—The surprising thing in a country with 140 different national groups, is that conflicts were so well hidden for so long. *Glasnost* has changed that. Apart from the feuding Azerbijanis and Armenians, a more peaceful challenge is coming from three Baltic republics, Estonia, Latvia, and Lithuania. Georgians have been demonstrating for more in-

---

Former Soviet Union*—Profile

Population .... 288 million
Ethnic Groups .... Russian 52%
                             Ukranian 16%
                             100 Ethnic Groups 32%
Religions .... Russian Orthodox 18%,
                             Atheist 70%, Muslim 9%,
                             Other 3%
Education .... Compulsory 10 years (from age 7 on)
                             Literacy 99.8%
Land .... 8,649,540 square miles (includes ocean waters)
Government .... Communist Socialist State, currently being replaced by Commonwealth of Independent States
Political Parties .... None
Per Capita Income $6,763
Exports to U.S. .... $543 million
Imports from U.S. .... $2,900 million

*Based on 1990 statistics.

---

dependence from Moscow. Where might trouble strike next? The Soviet Union has more than 50 million Muslims out of a total population of 290 million. . . . Loyalties tend to be to local clans, rather than to national republics, created as recently as 1920. . . . Yet tensions had reached a high pitch earlier this year in the central Asian republics for the Communist parties of Uzbekistan and Tajikistan hastily to exchange delegations and promise to improve cultural links. . . . But recently grumbles have been heard, rebroadcast for listeners abroad by Radio Kiev, that Russians living in other republics enjoy far more rights and privileges than other minority nationalities do. If ever the Soviet Union's non-Russians do join forces, Mr. Gorbachev would have a fight on his hands. But there is even bigger worry: the possibility of a nationalist backlash from the Russians, who are about half the Soviet population.

The Economist, April 22, 1989—"On the Banks of the Volga"—Russia is trying to create a banking system virtually from scratch. Before last year the state-owned Gosbank had a monopoly. No more. Gosbank has been split in six and a new law has created about 80 cooperative and so-called "joint stock" banks. . . . Russia's domestic banking system is primitive. . . . Yet the boom in joint ventures and the success of cooperatives show that there is a flickering entrepreneurial instinct in Russia. A proper banking system is the very least that is needed to fan it into a flame. . . . By the end of 1988 there were over 200 joint ventures. New rules let a foreign partner hold a controlling share of equity. As many as 750 new joint ventures could be registered in 1989, according to OkanEcon, a Russia-watching consultancy, taking the total to almost 1000. In all, companies from non-communist countries had invested some $440 million in

Russian joint ventures by the end of 1988, the biggest chunks from West Germany (15%) and Italy (14%).

Los Angeles Times, January 7, 1992—"Sudden Death"—The year's most momentous story was the rapid collapse of the Soviet Union, which seemed to implode and disappear into a black hole of history in less than five months. By the end of 1991, the 74-year-old Soviet superpower had ceased to exist. Rising from the ruins was the Commonwealth of Independent States led by Russian Federation President Boris N. Yeltsin. Meanwhile, former Soviet President Mikhail S. Gorbachev was a man without a job.

Characteristics of C.I.S. Business Culture

The struggle between would-be democrats and hard-line ultraconservative communists climaxed at the opening of this decade of the '90s with the dissolution of the U.S.S.R. What is emerging is a Commonwealth of Independent States (C.I.S.), which Zbigniew Brzezenski believes is a cover for genuine national diversity that will be characterized for a generation by cooperation, conflict, and confusion. The Commonwealth under the leadership of Yeltsin's Russia has Minsk, not Moscow, as its capitol. In early 1992, the C.I.S. encompasses 11 of the 15 principal republics. With economies still closely integrated to their old oppressors, the three Baltic states of Latvia, Lithuania, and Estonia have declared their separate independence, and seek Western investment and trade as they create a common market. Georgia has also asserted its independence, but not yet signed up for the Commonwealth because of internal strife.

The old Soviet Union stretched from the Gulf of Finland to the Pacific with a total of 31 autonomous republics and regions containing 450 million people, 112 recognized languages, and 5 different alphabets! Imagine the complexity of doing business today in this arena without centralized government services from Moscow, and local governments unused to wielding authority!

To appreciate the new difficulties in doing business here, consider: (1) the *Great Soviet Encyclopedia,* among other reference works, is being delayed because of the instability of the situation, as reflected in the uncertainty of using the term "Soviet"; (2) there are at least nine territories within the new Russian Federation that may or may not continue as autonomous regions; (3) the significant ethnic diversity in these localities.

Instability and Transformation

Some immediate problems facing the Commonwealth are:

- Accelerating disintegration of the economy and need for new economic systems and enterprises.
- Deepening crises in food/consumer goods production and distribution, as well as housing.

- Breakdowns in fuel and transportation systems.
- Extensive job dislocation and rising unemployment.
- Devaluation of the ruble and development of separate currencies in some republics.
- Collapse of socialism as an ideology and the need for a new philosophical underpinning and viable political framework.
- Political fragmentation and power-seeking by the republics.
- Resurgent nationalism and ethnic conflicts with possibilities for misuse of huge Soviet arsenal, including nuclear weapons.

The transition to a market system within the Commonwealth and among its neighboring republics has many positives to capitalize upon, such as:

- Incredible human resources of literate peoples with a millennium of unique traditions and contributions to the arts and sciences from the music and the ballet to space technology and physics.
- Vast natural and material resources, much of which is yet to be developed.
- Sound educational system that provides high-level instruction in mathematics and sciences.
- Co-dependent economies that foster cooperative alliances, as in a compact signed among five Central Asian republics of Kazakhstan, Kirghizia, Tadzhikistan, Turkmenia, and Uzbekistan.
- Growing interest in preserving and protecting the environment, and preventing disasters like nuclear accidents.
- Widespread movement toward divesting state industries to private enterprise, and state landholdings to private ownership.
- Majority of the population demonstrating for conservative public decisions made in a democratic way, desiring order and discipline, but not totalitarianism.
- Increasing interest in protecting individual and human rights, while moving in the direction of democracy and economic pragmatism.
- Resurgence of religion and religious tolerance.
- Expanding entrepreneurialism, even among academics and scientists.

The objectives of the C.I.S. founded on December 8, 1991 are summarized as follows (*Business Week*, December 23, 1991, p. 42):

- Repeal all Soviet laws and assume powers of old regime.
- Launch radical economic reforms, including freeing most prices.
- Keep the ruble, but allow new currencies.
- Set up European community-style free trade.
- Create joint control of nuclear weapons.
- Fulfill all Soviet foreign treaties and debt obligations.

In addition to the Russian Federation, the other key Commonwealth player is the ancient Ukraine with its beautiful capital of Kiev. This major republic encompasses a land mass of 233,100 square miles with 52 million inhabitants.

Native Ukrainians make up 74% of that population, with 21% ethnic Russian. Although entirely dependent upon Russia for oil, gasoline, and natural gas, this new country is known as the "breadbasket" for producing in the previous Soviet Union, 56% of its corn; 54% of its sugar beets; 25% of its wheat; 21% of its milk and meat; and 26% of its potatoes. The Ukraine also provides 47% of its iron, 23% of its coal, and 30% of its chemical industry equipment. The importance of this republic in the new economic alliance is evident not only in these statistics, but in the fact that it manufactured a fourth of the U.S.S.R.'s agricultural machinery and construction equipment.

Trade and Business Opportunities

Breaking into the Soviet market has always taken an enormous amount of perseverance and hard work by foreign firms. The emergence of the C.I.S. may ease that process, but it is important to remember that those organizations that succeeded in the "old" Soviet system did not wait for occasional sales or one-shot deals—they developed long-range strategies and did not approach the market half-heartedly.

Although the C.I.S. can offer foreign companies and universities much in terms of scientific, technical, and engineering talent, as well as processes, its greatest need from the West and Japan is for capital investment, plus management systems and development. A good case in point is KamAZ, an auto and truck manufacturing giant founded in 1060 at Kama in Central Russia which developed hundreds of subsidiaries in the Ukraine, Kazakhstan, and Bashkiria. During the "detente" period of the '70s, it benefited from a multinational consortium of American, West German, French, and Italian firms which provided millions of dollars worth of equipment and 1,000 foreign experts. By the '80s, production of rugged, sophisticated trucks and engines had risen to 250,000 units annually. But with the Communist state pocketing the profits, no modernization, and an acute shortage of equipment, the huge enterprise with 170,000 employees and a "company city" of 500,000, began to suffer from deterioration. In 1989, "perestroika" led to more privatization as workers approved lease-holding and empowered management to negotiate for them to take over the state-owned business. Under the innovative leadership of its general manager, Nikolai Beth, a joint stock company was established with shares purchases by its own personnel and 1,200 other plans and organizations. In the '90s, the KamAZ products are winning prizes at international rallys and competitions, but the worker-owners link their higher living standards and social protection with growth of production and quality improvement. Their corporate future depends upon penetrating foreign markets with their reliable, heavy-duty trucks, as sales in Saudi Arabia, Senegal, and Egypt prove. For that to happen, KamAZ seeks international partners in trading firms and automotive firms throughout the world (FAX: 7-095/271-31-34). The saga of the transformation and requirements of this one Russian business is both symbolic of what is happening throughout the republics in the C.I.S., and the opportunities for cultural synergy by businesses from mature market economies.

In the past few years more than 1,300 joint venture agreements were entered into by Western and Russian companies and institutions. Corporate giants have proven that successful projects could be accomplished even with the old regime, as Pepsico, Coca Cola, Dow Chemical, Marriott, and American Express have demonstrated. Most suffered from the Soviet bureaucracy and their regulations, but some, like McDonald's, are achieving superbly. If fledgling democracy and free enterprise are to prosper in the Commonwealth, then Western and Japanese business innovators must reach out and take risks for long-term technological and commercial undertakings, such as the following:

- KMPG-Peat Marwick formed a joint venture in 1991 with Moscow's Institute of Post Graduate Management Training in Construction, the Civil Engineering Institute, and Perestroika Joint Venture. Together they established the International Construction Management Center (I.C.M.C.) to provide management training and technical assistance to 40,000 Commonwealth managers in construction and related industries. This was accomplished after KMPG had established a successful presence in nearby Eastern European countries. The I.C.M.C. also hopes to link Western businesses, suppliers, financiers, and governments to construction opportunities in the area (Tel: 212/909-5091).
- Novogorod Business School is the second to be opened with the help of the Soviet-U.S. Society of Business Training. Set up in 1991 in the ancient town of Novogorod in northwestern Russia, the two-year, American-style curriculum includes two months of education in the U.S.A. so that graduates may receive an M.B.A. from Portland University in Oregon. The first such school has already been situated in Khabarovsk.
- Center for U.S.A.-U.S.S.R. Initiative, which presumably will undergo a name change like the above S.U.S.S.B.T., is working with the Foundation for Social Invention in Russia to promote exchanges of Moscow business people to establish contacts with their counterparts on the East Coast of America.

Negotiating Style and Protocol

During the transition from centralized planning to market economies within the C.I.S., foreigners can expect much confusion, frustration, and uncertainty. However, most of the inhabitants are anxious to find international partners and learn about Western business practices. No longer having to answer to a centralized government and wanting to move as quickly as possible toward "free enterprise," C.I.S. business negotiators may be more flexible and accommodating than their Soviet predecessors. The following insights should provide valuable guidelines when conducting business with the C.I.S.

Russian officials expect to conduct business with only the highest-ranking executives. On the initial visit, the Western firm is advised to send its top personnel to ensure a favorable first impression. Any person representing a Western company in the C.I.S. should be at least a regional or East European manager. Russians are not impressed by "representatives." Final negotiations on larger deals should be handled by a top executive to demonstrate to the Russians the importance the Western firm is placing on this business. The chairperson or deputy chairperson might even consider entering the negotiations at some decisive stage.

The Russians are renowned for their negotiating skill. One tactic is to stall for time if they think they can get a better deal. These days, time is no longer their ally, but one should be aware of the Russians' propensity for delay, haggling, and perhaps the casual involvement of many authorities.

There are two stages to negotiating with the Russians. During the first stage, they try to get as many competitive offers as possible, and play one supplier against another before making a final decision. Nothing may happen for a while after the Western firm has submitted its bid. Then, the Russians may notify the firm that it is still interested and resume negotiations. Potential suppliers are expected to provide detailed technical explanations of their products, so that the Russians can evaluate precisely what is being offered.

Having collected several competitive offers, the Russians are adept at creating competition among the suppliers. Quotations from competitors are revealed to force bidding suppliers to cut their prices. But it is often the case that the quotations cited by the Russians are for a product of much lower quality.

The second phase of negotiations begins when the supplier has been chosen. This phase is usually shorter than the first one, but it still takes time to settle all the various points in the final contract.

Russian negotiators often negotiate with the weakest competitor first. After concessions are obtained from the weakest, the other companies are notified they also must accept them.

Another maneuver used by Russian negotiators is to first fix the final price the supplier is willing to take for its product. Once this price is firmly fixed, the Russians may make additional demands for such extra services as free training of technicians or equipment maintenance, that were not originally included in the producer description and price. Experienced companies make it a standing rule to begin contract talks by discussing the articles of the purchasing agreement before any discussion begins on final price.

It should also be made clear at the beginning on which points the supplier is willing to make concessions and on which it is not. The longer an executive postpones talking about demands that are of major importance to his/her company, the more forcefully the Russians may oppose them later.

Each agreement made with the Russians should stand on its own accord. Granting a price discount or making concessions to the Russians to win future business simply does not work. A common Russian tactic is to ask for a bulk price for a product, and then to apply the lower price-per-unit from the bulk price to a smaller lot. It is implied, and sometimes even promised verbally, that more purchases will follow. However, the Russians will honor only written agreements.

It is important to let the Russians know exactly where your firm stands on all issues. The Russians do not respect negotiators who make too large of concessions, because they think the firm's position is padded to grant them for special effect. The firm should be prepared to stand by its position, and to drop negotiations and cut its losses if necessary. This will impress the Russians far more than slowly acquiescing to their demands.

Although the "old" Soviet system may no longer exist, attitudes and cultural perceptions are much more resilient. Remember these people are very protocol conscious. Here are some cultural clues that may advance synergistic relations:

1. *Consumers* are only beginning to get accustomed to higher quality for higher prices. In addition to a plentiful and consistent supply of quality food, they seek modern conveniences and entertainment. Having been subjected to substandard clothing and outdated styles, they hunger for Western adornments that are colorful, stylish, and practical in their climate. However, business dress is conservative (e.g., suit and tie).

2. *Business contacts*—new Commonwealth and individual republic ministries are gradually taking over the functions of the Ministry of Foreign Trade. The latter's renamed Russian Market Institute can provide useful data and quotations. Instead of cultivating the Foreign Trade Officers as in the past, outsiders will have to network and seek direct contacts with new factory owners and entrepreneurs. Emerging there and in the U.S., are consulting firms to facilitate business activites in Eastern Europe, including the C.I.S. (e.g., The Keith Group, 8070 La Jolla Shores Dr. #264, La Jolla, CA 92037; Tel: 619/454-6885).

3. *Currency challenges*—innovative ways must be developed to convert the volatile ruble and other new monetary units into international hard currency, such as by barter, exchange of services, or third-country transfer.

4. *Attention to details*—because of the Soviet cultural conditioning for the past seven decades, visitors can expect local officials to give much attention to such matters as seating arrangements and invitations, business cards printed in both Cyrillic and one's own language or English, whether the representative is a top executive, and the caliber of a technical presentation both in writing and orally. Continuity is an important factor, so the visiting team should designate one person as project manager or spokesman in all business dealings. Remember that these peoples are trying to overcome prior totalitarian conditioning to be dependent and compliant to authority, not to exercise personal responsibility or initiative.

5. *Communication* is facilitated when the foreigner can speak the local lan-

guage, but many Russians, Ukrainians, and other republic representatives are comfortable speaking in English or German, while the elite may prefer French. The use of interpreters has both positives (like in clarifying meaning or building interpersonal relations) and negatives (perceptual slanting by the translator or lack of technical understanding). Orally, Russians may greet foreigners with "gospodin" (citizen) or "gospozha" (citizenness), and ask acquaintances for their "imya" (first name) or "ochestvo" (patronymic). The later is formed by adding "-vitch" or "ova" to the person's father's name as a token admission of familiarity. Normally, custom uses first names for close friends and family.

6. *Time sense* is quite different here, and the locals dislike the quick tempo of Western business or the attitude that time is money. They use the slower tempo to good advantage, especially in negotiations or business socializing. The inhabitants here quote old Russian proverbs like, 'If you travel for a day, take bread for a week,' or "Patience and work, and everything will work out." Part of this stoicism and slowness is due to inadequate telecommunications and transportation which modern technological advance, like the facsimile machines, which save time and facilitate communication within a colossus of a country!

7. *National psyche*—Russians have long suffered from a sense of inferiority (for which they overcompensate); in the days of the aristocracy, the Czar's court turned to everything French to show how civilized and sophisticated they were. Having been often cut off from outside contacts, the Russians also have manifested xenophobia periodically. Totalitariansim made many citizens feel like prisoners in their own society. The younger generation is more educated, more open, and more cosmopolitan, as well as more disillusioned and cynical.

With new freedoms and opportunity to practice democracy, as well as to suffer its pitfalls, the millions in the Commonwealth of Independent States are changing rapidly. What has been said in this section today, may prove to be invalid tomorrow. During the transformation underway, the only certainties in this vast area are change and diversity.

Body Language

To the Western observer, the Russian may appear stiff and dull. Gestures are usually kept to a minimum, and expressions may seem blank and uninterested. Smiles are rare, except between people who are very close. This is the public image Russians seem to convey. In private, Russians are much more expressive and the modest reserve they project in public breaks down under more personal surroundings.

Russian officials can be very generous hosts, with food and beverage. Dinners are long and elaborate, and toasts are frequently and heartily made to good business relationships and mutual friendships. The visiting foreign executive should be prepared to encounter some friendly "imbibing competition," stemming from the Russian prowess for drinking.

Tips for Succeeding with C.I.S. Negotiations

- Be conscious of the emphasis the Russians place on dealing with high-ranking executives.
- Russians will enter all negotiations well prepared, so it is advisable to be accompanied by at least one member of your technical personnel.
- Continuity is an important factor, so one person should be identified as the project manager throughout all negotiations.
- Be prepared to devote a lot of senior executive time, because of the chaotic situation and lingering bureaucracy.
- Take advantage of the many cultural opportunities and historical sites—then praise your hosts when you enjoy such experiences.

SUMMARY

The San Diego Union, (May 18, 1990)—VIENNA, Austria—A top economic advisor to Soviet President Mikhail S. Gorbachev yesterday said that all economic reforms in his country have failed and appealed to Western economists, businesses and governments for help.

"We have come to a very profound conclusion that without the cooperation of the West, we simply can't build a market economy," said Shatalin, the only economist on the Presidential Council that has been working on Gorbachev's reforms. "I'm sure the president also shares this position."

Although cultures and business practices change, we have provided sufficient information for the global manager to be more effective in Europe, both East and West. Culture-specific insights about England, France, Germany, Russia, and the new Commonwealth of Independent States are but a sampling of that continent's complex cultural groupings and national entities. Such material may help us to avoid the trap of overgeneralized assumptions about Europeans, so as to create more synergistic relationships there with management and other leaders in industry and commerce. The clues shared here with readers are but the initial step in developing a personal file of business intelligence about countries and cultures in which one is expected to perform well; such information should be continually verified for validity in specific times and places, as well as with different individuals and organizations.

17
Doing Business With Middle Easterners

Most cultures in the Middle East are traditional and Moslem, and caught in the midst of conflict and change. Israel, although largely Jewish, must learn to cooperate with its Christian and Arab minorities, as well as its fellow Semites in neighboring lands. Lebanon may not make it into the 21st century as a national entity unless it can produce synergy between its Christian and Islamic factions. Iran must bring together its own diverse populations, while learning to live in peace with its neighbors. It is a prime example of what happens when national leaders do not plan change, and try to bring a people along too fast from the agricultural to industrial stage of development. The repercussion is revolution, which not only plunges its Persian adherents into turmoil, but affects the world outside. The returned American hostages understand that reality now. Their ordeal might have been avoided if First World America had been more culturally sensitive to Third World Iran and its religious past.

Perhaps no country is more fearful of such "progress" than Saudi Arabia. The anomaly is that while this country has invested billions of oil revenue dollars to create an infrastructure and industry in a tribal nomadic society, which is faithful to Islam and copes with change, there is considerable opposition to such modernization (as was expressed by armed religious followers who, in 1980, took over the Great Mosque in Mecca). Although fears are expressed that Saudi Arabia is vulnerable to the same kinds of forces that operated in Iran, the policy in Saudi Arabia of rapid economic growth and continued development is pursued.

How technology changes a country's environment is difficult to judge over a short period of time. But we must be aware of the needs of other cultural groups and retain cultural values and pride in the ancient culture while, at the same time, introducing appropriate technology. The following "culture specific" examples from several countries in the Middle East suggest what some of these cultural synergistic challenges are.

We regret that we are unable to cover all the remarkable peoples of the area, but the target culture presented will offer insights that can be applied elsewhere in the region. Remember, too, not all Middle Easterners are Arab, although such cultural characteristics not only dominate here, but in Islamic nations and states from Indonesia to Egypt, and Moslem minorities from the Southern Philippines to Detroit, Michigan.

AMERICANS IN THE MIDDLE EAST

Approximately 40% of the world's oil is being produced in the Middle East and Arab Africa, and about 70% of all proven oil reserves are located there. These figures clearly illustrate the necessity of cooperation and synergy between the Western world and the Arab world.

When Jack Grey (1975) asked foreign managers what bothered them about working with Americans, their answers indicated why U.S. business people have difficulty working in an intercultural situation. The answers, which clustered around six responses, serve as a warning to any representative of an advanced technological culture seeking to be effective in a more traditional culture, such as in Arab countries:

1. *Americans display feelings of superiority; they know the answers to everything.* It is not enough to give; it is how you give that is important. Giving, and leaving the impression that you can easily afford it, is not making a favorable impression on the receivers of your help. Feelings of inferiority and superiority occur. And nobody likes to feel inferior.

2. *Americans want to take credit for what is accomplished in joint efforts.* If one thinks he is superior, it will be difficult for him to recognize the input of the others, whom he perceives as being inferior. Since Americans are extremely geared to competition, performance, and fast-track careers, it is not surprising to see some of them using this universal tactic. But already having the "American image" it is not forgiven, where it might be for the local man.

3. *Americans are frequently unable or unwilling to respect and adjust to local customs and cultures.* The American way of cutting meat is considered by the Europeans as primitive and is the subject of a lot of jokes. Eating with only a fork is considered as being impolite. The way most Americans treat wine and flowers make the French talk about "massacre and barbarianism."

4. *Americans fail to innovate in terms of the needs of the local culture.* The U.S. is, in comparison with most countries, more advanced in technology. The danger exists that the American manager (or consultant) will look for innovations based on the American situation, whereas the overseas employee is looking more for a less sophisticated solution. A lot of innovations are inspired by American situations and are therefore welcomed with reservation if not with hostility.

5. *Americans refuse to work through the normal administrative channels of the country.* Local management sometimes has a tough job in making the

U.S. manager understand that he has to respect the legal and contractual stipulations as well as the local existing administrative procedures.

6. *Americans tend to lose their democratic ways of working and acting when on a foreign assignment.* The most surprising tendency is that some foreign (American) managers want to instill fear in their local subordinates. They think it is a successful management style. Even if it would be in terms of results (getting the sales or production targets), the image they leave after their departure is a serious handicap for their (foreign) colleagues taking over.

How much of this constructive criticism would apply also to managers of other foreign nationalities when in the Middle East?

The Arabs possess a common culture that has united them by religious and historical factors. Their life is interdependent and many of its elements are inseparable as each aspect of life depends on another. The Western world has been cognizant of the Arab world for centuries, but the Arabs have often been approached with suspicion. Equality, trust, mutual respect, and admiration have not been characteristics of the relationship.

The presence of Aramco in Saudi Arabia is an example of cooperation and the fruitful interaction of diverse groups of people. The first agreement was signed between the Saudi Arabian Government and Standard Oil Company of California in 1933. Since that time the original terms of the agreement have been successfully renegotiated several times to the benefit of Americans and Arabs, and now the company is largely under local control.

In discussing Iranians, who are not Arabs, we would like to refer to the ABC News three-hour presentation "America Held Hostage: The Secret Negotiations," originally shown on January 22, 1981, shortly after the hostages were released. The program's reporter, Pierre Salinger, concluded that the United States spent more than a year trying to negotiate the hostages' release with Iranian officials who were powerless to end the crisis. Salinger stated there were large "cultural gaps" and errors and misunderstandings on both sides. The executive producer of the program, Robert Fry, said:

> . . . We (U.S. negotiators) approached the crisis with a Western mindset. We dealt with government officials. What better people to deal with? But in Iran, it's the religious leaders who are the political power. It's impossible to realize the turmoil that surrounded the circumstances, the nibbling away, and the erosion of the political climate in Iran.

Had the U.S. negotiators more fully understood the cultural aspects of the crisis, communication might have been facilitated and the crisis cooled. A manager on international assignment should at least be able to answer the following questions concerning the country or culture in which he or she is working:

1. Do you know the names and responsibilities of the persons you will be meeting?
2. Will these persons be able to make the decisions related to your assignment?
3. What do you know of their background?
4. How would you describe the political process?
5. What are the interest groups and how do they express their concerns?
6. Is there a state religion? How many religions are there?
7. How does religion influence the people?
8. What are some differences between your religious beliefs and the beliefs of this religion?
9. What is the relationship between this country and the U.S.? Presently, in the past ten years, and before that time? What is the projection of their future attitude?
10. Are Americans liked, disliked, and for what reasons?
11. What is your attitude toward the people? Do you feel superior? Inferior?
12. Do you know any effective ways to persuade?
13. What else do you think you should know about this culture in which you will be a "foreigner"?

Now having raised these questions, consider the following authentic incidents and how knowing the answers to the above inquiries could alter diplomatic or business relations when operating in the Middle East:

- Middle Easterners, as in other cultures, prefer to act through trusted third parties—the Iranian hostage impasse achieved a solution when the U.S. enlisted the Moroccans as intermediaries in the negotiations.
- Middle Easterners prefer oral and aural communications—this applies to business meetings, learning by audio cassettes, to direct encounters with the Syrians or PLO members.
- Middle Easterners revere in their humor the figure of "Goha," the lovable, eccentric, optimistic, generous "fool" who is also perceived as clever and conniving, outwitting others. He is the Walter Mitty of the Arab world and is the way Egyptians see themselves for they like to joke about themselves in the midst of adversity, thus maintaining their sanity despite difficulties.
- Middle Easterners have been influenced by the Bedouin lifestyle from Bahrain to Jordan, despite the decline of this desert tribal culture with rapid modernization and oil wealth. Scholars are not sure how long its characteristics will survive—restlessness and mobility, generosity and visitor hospitality up to three days to offset the harshness of the environment, gallantry and courage, patience and endurance.

- Middle Easterners consider coffee to be more than a beverage—strong and black, it is the ultimate sign of hospitality and cordiality in a region where graciousness is a way of life.
- Middle Easterners extend their sociability to business meetings where the first encounter is only to get acquainted and schedule-keeping is loose. They resent American representatives who are accustomed to no-nonsense, "cut-the-small-talk" management style.

The Middle East is a region in the midst of profound social, political, and economic or cultural transition. This acceleration in the twentieth century has lead to violence and wars, as well as hopeful signs. Among the latter is the rapid building of an infrastructure that necessitated the importing of 3 million Asian workers. It may be seen in the plans for economic integration of the six Persian Gulf countries through a new Cooperation Council including Saudi Arabia, Kuwait, United Arab Emirates, Oman, Qatar, and Bahrain. The slow regional progress toward synergy may also be perceived with the introduction in some Israeli schools of an experimental course called "Living Together," which explores the needs of its 700,000 minority Arab citizens.

However, the primary success story in the Middle East is undoubtedly Saudi Arabia, so it is the first target culture we "put under our microscope" for analysis. It is the "rags-to-riches" story of this century for a whole kingdom—the transformation in just decades of one of the world's most conservative lifestyles, where religion and law are one. But sudden wealth, input and construction of everything from modern shopping malls and apartments to super airport and universities implies a dynamic situation that can undermine tradition. Everything to be described here about doing business with the Saudis is subject to change. For example, the sudden expansion has caused their government in the last decade to shift from using trusted Moslem middlemen or agents to issuing "requests for proposals." *Worldwide Projects* (April–May 1983) describes the "new ball game" there resulting in stiffer competition and new laws and regulations affecting foreign commerce. These emerging consultancy rules have to do with licensing, turnkey operations, partnerships, boycott, financial capability and taxation. The cyclical rise and decline in OPEC and oil revenues has also reduced Saudi spending and slowed its rapid development.

Perhaps the most dramatic symbol of change in the lives of these former desert "camel herders" is the Saudi prince catapulted into space as a mission specialist. The first Arab to come home from the stars is Sultan ibn Salman al Saud. After earning an American degree in mass communication, he helped to launch the telecommunication satellite owned by the Arab League. The young astronaut is the "personification of the Islamic renaissance" after his voyage on the NASA space shuttle, *Discovery*. As he spoke to King Fahd from outerspace, he felt like his "country that has been developing from a primitive society at 2000 mph" for the past thirty years. The experience in orbit also transformed his perceptions—as he hurdled around the Earth at awesome speed, the Saudi first sought out his homeland, then the Middle East with all its current troubles, and then he realized the cosmic dimensions of our planet as a global village. Understandably, he no longer believes in passports and visas.

SAUDI ARABIA

Saudi Arabia—Profile

Population	9.75 million
Ethnic Groups	Arab 90%
	Afro-Asian 10%
Religions	Islam—100% Muslim
Education	12 Years
	Literacy 52%
Land	830,000 square miles
Government	Monarchy with Council of Ministers
Political Parties	None
Per Capita Income	$8,860
Exports to U.S.	$3,200 million
Imports from U.S.	$3,500 million

Commentary

Christian Science Monitor, February 27, 1984—"Saudi Contrasts: High-Rises and Veiled Women"—First-time visitors—and especially those who return after some time away—find the images of Saudi Arabia a startling study in contrasts. It is almost as if someone had pressed the country's fast-forward switch, and accelerated Saudi Arabia from the 14th to the 20th century with a few stops in between.

Along the eight-lane highway to the brand new and highly modernistic $3.2 billion King Khalid airport, herds of camels wander and graze. Before Saudi Arabian Airlines jumbo jets begin their takeoff roll, a recorded passage from the Koran is played for the passengers' benefit. And because men and women may not work together under the Saudi interpretation of Islamic law, the efficient and cheery flight attendants are Jordanian, Egyptian, and Pakistani.

Brad Knickerbocker

New York Times, April 13, 1985—"Saudi Women Start to Peek from Behind the Veil"—Islam, and the particularly strict Saudi interpretation of it, imposes several restrictions on women. Saudi women are not allowed to drive cars, work with men, or travel or live abroad without a male member of the family. When they leave their homes, they must cover their heads, arms and legs, and the vast majority cover their faces with veils of black gauze or chiffon.

Elaine Sciolino

The Arabian Sun, June 1989 (published by the Aramco Services Company)—Fifty years ago, King Abd al-Aziz Al Saud, the founder of Saudi Arabia, stood in Ras Tanura and prepared to release the nation's first tanker shipment of crude oil to the world. . . . Oil production would total 4 million barrels a day for 1939, the first full year of production. . . . Today Saudi Aramco manages more than a quarter of the Earth's crude oil. The Aramco work force which in 1939 totaled about 3,600, stands at 44,000 in 1989. Since 1938, the company has produced more than 1.8 billion barrels of crude oil. Saud opened the valve on the Kingdom's and Aramco's future.

Cultural Characteristics of Business in the Arab World

A midwestern banker is invited by an Arab sheik to meet him at the Dorchester Hotel in London. The banker arrives in London and waits to meet the sheik. After two days he is told to fly to Riyadh in Saudi Arabia, which he does. He waits. After three days in Riyadh, he meets the sheik and the beginning of what was to become a very beneficial business relationship between the two persons and their organizations began. The American's experience may have been unique but he demonstrated one of the fundamental qualities for doing business in Saudi Arabia—patience.

"There is no god but Allah and Mohammed is his messenger." This is written on the Saudi Arabian national flag in stylized Arabic script. Saudi Arabians of all professions and at all social levels reaffirm this statement and all its implications. In spite of a rapid introduction into Saudi Arabia of technology and machinery, there will not be a rapid departure from traditional religious values. However, like most Arab cultures in profound transition, for Saudi Arabia modernization causes painful choices between the old and the new. With the acceleration of change, Saudis encounter some social and political problems while the oil pipes still produce billions of dollars.

Among the modern institutions of higher education established recently within the kingdom is King Fahd University of Petroleum and Minerals in Dhahran. Dr. Mohammed I. At-Twaijri (1988) has conducted studies that compared American and Saudi Arabian cultural behavior in a high tech industry, particularly focusing on purchasing agents with reference to environmental interdependence and uncertainty. In comparison with their American counterparts, analysis of the Saudi managers in such projects revealed their dissatisfaction with salary received, as well as with opportunities for decision-making and organizational advancement. Confirming the trend toward "Westernization" of Middle East managers, these Saudi managers indicated less orientation toward paternalism. Obviously, the more exposure to Western education and multinational management, the less likely the indigeneous manager is to behave entirely according to the traditional cultural patterns described in this chapter.

Business Customs and Protocol

Arab businessmen are not all the same, but are differentiated by sub-cultural indentities, hostilities, attitudes, and rivalries. Nevertheless, there are some common traits among Arabs. An Arab is any individual whose mother tongue is Arabic, considers himself Arab, and has some heritage that may in any way be traced to Saudi Arabia. Not all Arabs are Moslems, nor are all Moslems Arabs. There are Arabs who are Christian and there are Moslems who are Russian, Chinese, Iranian, or American. Besides religion, it is the Arabic language that serves primarily as the basis of Arab culture. Arabs are often considered to be a people of excess, a people of extremities, a people of great emotion.

Arabs tend to be warm, hospitable, friendly, and courteous. By tradition, Arabs are expected to extend hospitality for up to three days to a guest. Arabs also seem to have the reputation of being either completely sincere and trustworthy or totally insincere and sly. The best salespeople in the world are supposed to be either the Jews or the Arabs. They are proud of their culture, their religion, and heritage. The glories of ancient Arab civilization, mathematical and scientific achievements, Arabic language and poetry are often the topics of many conversations among Arabs. They accept the fact that these were the highlights of their past, and are aware of the disunity they have among themselves today. Arabs are known to be very emotional and sentimental. They have a strong sense of justice and get morally outraged by historical events and any individual's behavior that goes against their sense of justice.

Arab society honors honor, and its concept of shame is foreign to the Western mind. As a result of tribal influences and values, Arab society demands a high degree of conformity which in turn confers a strong authoritarian tone. Honor, social prestige, and a secure place in society are brought about when conformity is achieved. When one fails to conform, this is considered to be damning and leads to a degree of shame. In Arab attitudes, shame has a further dimension; it is caused by not only committing an act against the accepted system of values, but having outsiders discover that act. Arabs do not worry only about their acts, but about how their acts will reflect on their families, clans, tribes, and countries.

There is a proverb in Arabic which is translated as: "a concealed sin is two-thirds forgiven." When responding to the common inquiry of courtesy "How are things?" an Arab may reply, "Mastur al-hal," idiomatically meaning "we're all right," but having the literal translation "the condition is covered." Muslims often pray to Allah for "protection, for hiding of acts from the others." Shame must be avoided; and if it strikes, then it must be hidden; and if it is to be exposed, then it must be avenged. Honor must always be restored, at all costs.

The issue of shame is very important in order to understand the Arab society. The fear of it is so powerful because the identification between the individual and the group is much closer than it is in the Western cultures. An individual committing an act that brings him shame, loses power and influence; and by the same token his family suffers as well, perhaps to the point of destruction.

Social pressure in Arab society is significant. It is public opinion that judges, praises, or condemns the behavior of the individual.

Business Tips for Saudi Arabia

To an Arab, commerce is a most blessed career. For a Moslem, Mohammed the Prophet was a man of commerce and married a lady of commerce. Thus business, trade between people, is highly respected. Arab businessmen have reputations for being sound and shrewd, as well as knowledgeable in the field of making money.

Connections is a key-word in conducting business. Well-connected people find their progress is made much faster. Connections in the Middle East are vital to gain access to public and private decision makers, and to maintain good relations.

Negotiating and the bargaining process are also normal and commonplace in conducting Arab business. Bargaining is a Middle Eastern art, and the visiting businessman must be prepared for some old-fashioned "haggling." Establishing a personal rapport, mutual trust, and respect are essentially the most important factors leading to a successful business relationship. The Arab businessman does business with the "man," not with the "company," or the "contract."

Decision Making

Decisions are usually not made by correspondence or telephone. A company's personal presence must be a prerequisite for doing business in Saudi Arabia.

Decision-making power usually rests with the top man in the company. The decision-maker relies heavily on personal impressions, trust, and rapport.

Use of Time

"Bukra insha Allah," a favorite expression for the traditional Arab, is an extremely difficult concept for Westerners to understand and accept. It simply means "tomorrow if God wills," an expression assuring the fatalistic approach to time. Business travelers who try to force the Arabs to conform to their time will be frustrated and will end up returning home earlier than anticipated. The flow of life in the Arab world is related to the Arab time concept. Being on time for appointments or keeping appointments is unusual. It is never good to be early for an appointment, in contrast to what the Americans view as being good. This sense of time is changing among modern Arab business leaders, as they move beyond the culture of their tribal, nomadic past.

Who controls time? A Western belief is that one controls his own time. Arabs believe that their time is controlled, to a certain extent, by an outside force— namely Allah. When scheduling time, the Arab will usually use the expression—"insha Allah," "if Allah wills." This indicates that the power of time is actually in the hands of Allah and, therefore, the Arabs become very fatalistic in their view of life. It is interesting to note how little control an Arab individual has over himself, his god controls his time and his life; his society controls his actions and behavior. Most Arabs are not clockwatchers, nor are they planners of time. One may commit himself to an advance date, and he may forget about it entirely as time comes, and in no way will he feel guilty about it. Why should he? He has no control over it anyway.

"Bukra insha Allah" basically indicates to the Westerner that the Arab is telling him that the thing to be done will be accomplished as soon as possible, given other conditions about which the individual may be presently unaware of, which may interfere with its accomplishments.

Greetings, Business Customs, and Courtesies

The Arabs use elaborate and ritualized forms of greetings and leavetakings. Knowledge of these formalities and protocol are essential for the foreign businessman visiting Saudi Arabia.

The foreign business representative may have a long wait before seeing one's host, as the Arab sense of time is much more leisurely. The meeting may not be private, and often in a group setting. Once having met the host, interruptions may be frequent, constant visitors are usually arriving, messengers being sent and received. It is very rude to show impatience or to fail to respond to social preliminaries. The visitor will always be offered a refreshment as a sign of hospitality, and this offer should always be accepted.

Business cards are essential, and are usually presented upon the first meeting. This gesture usually results in an exchange of cards. Business cards should be presented in English on one side, with Arabic on the other. The Arabic side of the business card should face up in every presentation to an Arab businessman.

A meeting concludes with an offer of coffee or tea. Such an activity is a normal sign indicating that the meeting has ended, and that future meetings should then be arranged.

Titles are not in general use on the Arabian Peninsula, except for royal families, ministers, and high-level military officers. At the conclusion of the first or second visit, one might present a modest gift. A novelty or souvenir item from the visitor's home country would be quite suitable.

In short, the first business visit and initial transactions of commerce should be approached as a leisurely "getting to know each other" process. Conversation may not get to business for several days, and it is considered rude for the visiting businessperson to press the issue.

In regard to Arab generosity, a visitor must take care not to overly praise or admire anything that his host owns, because the host may feel obliged to give it to the admirer. This is a tradition, and one may diplomatically decline the gesture. However, it is wiser to initially take care not to express too much admiration of any object one's host owns.

Also very important to recognize is that the system of hospitality is based on mutuality. An invitation must be returned; an equal gift must be offered in return. The offer of hospitality to visit an Arab's home must be accepted. Today you may be the guest, but tomorrow you must play the host, according to social customs and courtesies.

Arabs are generally very status and rank conscious. Take care to acknowledge and pay deference to the senior man first. Another important thing to remember for any visitor to Saudi Arabia is to never berate or criticize a person publicly. You will make him lose "face" and you will also be looked down upon for doing this. Don't show any signs of condescension towards others. Mutual respect is expected at all times.

The right hand is for public matters, the left hand for private. Be careful of your hand gestures! Do not accept or give anything with the left hand, the "toilet" hand. Particularly, do not eat with the left hand.

Also, placing hands on the hips may appear to be a challenging gesture to an Arab. Consider your gestures before making them.

Bodily functions such as sneezing, nose-blowing, etc., are all downplayed. The ritual burping after a big meal is no longer considered acceptable in polite circles.

Exposing the soles of your feet to those present is very rude.

To express a point, the Arabs will use much bodily contact in their conversations (i.e., tapping a person gently, resting a hand on the other's shoulder or knee, etc.). However, the Western "backslapping" is considered rude and rather vulgar by most Arabs.

Styles of Communication

The Arab style of communication is always courteous and hospitable, whether socially or in business. An extremely noisy, boisterous style of communication on the part of the visiting businessman is not looked upon favorably.

A businessman should note that social courtesies and social invitations do not mean that a business deal has been concluded. These social gestures are merely displays of personal hospitality, and a necessary social gesture and common courtesy.

For social contact and entertainment, Arab person-to-person contact is quite ritualistic and private. The use of first names should be initiated by the Arab host.

Most social customs are based on the Arab male-dominated society. Women are usually not part of the business or entertainment scene for traditional Muslim Arabs. Modern foreign women will find a traditional Arab culture, such as in Saudi Arabia, difficult but not impossible. Whether there on business or as expatriate spouses, such females will not only have to develop inner resources and local support networks, but also take advantage nearby European and Asian resources.

Topics of Conversation

Topics of a general nature can be discussed readily. It is wise to follow your host's lead in this respect, and to show agreement and harmony in conversation. The Arabs have a high-context language; language and conversation are important.

Often, when a foreigner views two Arabs speaking together, the observer may believe they are engaged in an argument because of the wide gestures, raised voices, and animated facial expressions. This is probably not the case. They are most likely engaged in some lively discussion concerning business or politics.

There are some important subjects that one would be wise to *avoid*, most of which are considered an invasion of your host's privacy:

- AVOID bringing up subjects of business before getting "to know" your host. This is considered rude.
- AVOID any questions or comments on a man's wife or any female children over the age of twelve. This is also taboo.
- AVOID any colloquial questions that could be misunderstood and taken wrongly by the Arab host.
- AVOID swear words, because they are the supreme of bad taste. Off-color jokes are also not appreciated.
- AVOID pursuing the subjects of politics or religion.
- AVOID any discussion of Israel; this is not an acceptable topic generally for most Arabs.

Body Language

Contrary to the Oriental reservedness, emotional displays are commonplace among Arabs. Arabs stand much closer together when talking than do Westerners. Eye contact is also much more intense than Westerners are usually comfortable with. However, when an Arab businessman meets a stranger for the first time, he may avert his eye contact because he does not yet know that person.

The Arab handshake may appear limp when compared with a hearty Western handshake. In fact, the Arabs do not generally like the hard-pumping Western handshake.

Kissing on the cheeks is also commonplace when men greet each other or when women greet each other. Also, handholding among men friends walking together is a common sight. Much more bodily contact is made between Arab men than between Western men.

Some Arab gestures and expressions may be quite confusing to a Westerner. There is much nonverbal communication in the Arab culture. This includes much talking with the hands, and a profusion of facial expressions. A raising of the eyebrows, or a clicking of one's tongue (or a combined response of the above) signifies a negative response. A positive response is usually given nonverbally by a side nod of the head.

SYNERGY: THE HOPE OF THE MIDDLE EAST

The new relationship being established between Israel and Egypt is an example of what can happen when persons develop and apply problem-solving skills in resolving long-time conflicts. Simply sitting down, talking, and trying to understand each other better was not what brought Israel and Egypt as far as they have come. A mediator of stature was necessary. Analyzing the conflict, exploring each side's perspectives, and developing new solutions are important. Mediators to international conflicts attempt to create the conditions to accomplish this analysis and problem-solving. Nations cannot be treated as individuals, but individuals with a common heritage share much in common, and these common perceptions can be explored and understood.

The Middle East is but a short jet hop to Europe, and the interchange of people from both continents has vastly increased, for business and pleasure. Arabs fly regularly to Europe to study, invest, engage in commerce, seek medical assistance, or vacation. Many reside permanently or temporarily on that continent, especially in the UK. On the other hand, Europeans go to the Middle East for new markets and as tourists. The potential for synergy is there if the Europeans and Arabs learn to understand each other's cultural differences and historical developments, respect one another, and consciously search for cooperative endeavors for mutual benefit.

Thousands of Middle Eastern youth have been educated abroad in American, Canadian, and European (including the Eastern bloc) universities. The choice will be for them to decide how to create synergy between that learning and their own cultural traditions. They have the opportunity to promote peace and prosperity not only in their region, but the world.

SUMMARY

Although the business boom is currently over because of declining petroleum prices, global organizations—their managers and technicians—will continue to seek commercial opportunities in the Middle East, especially in those areas with a peaceful environment. The area needs Western educational, technical, and financial expertise to develop a modern infrastructure. But this can only achieve synergistic success if Pan American, European, and Asian representatives are sensitive to the Islamic renaissance underway and respect Moslem tradition while its adherents struggle, sometimes violently, to integrate such with the realities of economic and social development for the modern world.

Since Arab culture dominates this region, our analysis has focused upon this aspect of Middle Eastern society with acknowledgement of the Jewish and Christian presence and contribution there, even those of whom see themselves as Arabic. Of the many states in the areas from Abu Dhabi to Egypt to Qatar, we choose Saudi Arabia as most representative of the cultural transition underway. Thus, our review of business customs and protocol, as well as communication styles and conversational topics, must be viewed in the context of a dynamic process subject to change.

18
Doing Business with Africans

When North and South America was largely inhabited by aboriginals, ancient civilizations flourished in Africa from white Carthage in the North to black empires in the South. Africa is a land of 11,700,000 square miles, lying south of Europe and the Mediterranean Sea and extending downward to the Cape of Good Hope between the Atlantic Ocean of the west and the Indian Ocean on its east. It is a large continent of contrasts with many cultures and nations whose names change, and whose population of 250 million plus people constantly expands. The great majority of its inhabitants struggle to move beyond the constraining effects of colonialism, tribalism, and poverty. From an economic perspective and with the exception of South Africa, it is largely the Third World of developing nations with bloated public sectors and weak private sectors. The political and financial instability of twentieth century emerging countries in Africa is understandable in light of the nineteenth century exploitation by European masters, particularly the educational deprivation of the masses and failure to adequately develop personnel for the administrative infrastructure (Gutkind and Wallerstein 1985).

The global managers' awareness of Africa is not of the diversity and generosity of its people, their eagerness to learn and their hard-working ways; nor of the continent's immense resources and natural beauty. Instead, mass media captivates us with horror stories of famine, struggles with apartheid, unrest, and corruption. The success stories of African foreign students, business enterprises, and green revolution are overlooked in the spectacular reporting on disasters, like drought and civil wars, which help to spawn the continent's 5 million refugees. When doing business in Africa, one deals with diversity that can best be illustrated in three countries of that huge continent. First, consider Egypt which is one of the many Islamic nations of the area. Peace has enabled it to gear up for rebuilding its exhausted economy at a real growth rate for the past five years of 8–10%. The present administration is emphasizing production-oriented enterprises and building construction, largely as a result of $2 billion in foreign aid from democratic countries. It seeks joint venture partners.

Next, look at the Ivory Coast, one of the nations on that continent that had an influx of French cultural influences. Caution is the watchword as a five-year economic plan for the 80s is implemented, aiming for a 7% growth rate from 1985 onward. After previous rapid expansion, the nation is in a financial bind and looks toward private investment ventures. The government is divesting itself of public corporations, and agriculture continues to be the most important sector; projected government expenditure for development currently is about $8 billion.

The major cultural considerations in this chapter will involve black Africa, where our target culture is Nigeria, one of the more economically progressive countries on the continent and illustrative of that English-speaking group that formerly were under British control and belong to its commonwealth alliance. Alas, space limitations do not permit us to get into the many other fascinating national groups that previously experienced the impact of English, French, German, or Portuguese colonial imperialism. The point of Africa's complexity has been made. Only two countries in black Africa (Liberia and Ethiopia) were never colonized, so most Africans are just now recovering from the effects of the colonialists who wrongfully taught them that their African cultures were shameful and they should act like white men.

Although the masses fought for independence from colonial rulers, too often the latter has been substituted by self-interested elitists, a class of military and political "leaders" who have little affinity for the people or their progress. Only five countries in black Africa (Botswana, Djibouti, Gambia, Burkina Faso and Nigeria, which again has given up civilian for military rule) meet the criteria for a free nation set by Freedom House, a New York-based human rights organization. The Organization for African Unity (OAU) remains more a hope than an effective force today—a continental defense force does not exist. Instead, black Africa is economically and militarily dependent on outside powers, both from the East and West. With a high foreign external debt, many black African nations have become international welfare states living on foreign aid.

Observers on the contemporary African scene point to four broad areas for hopeful progress:

1. Regional cooperation (only 4% of black African nations trade with their counterparts); rural development (less emphasis on urban development and more on agricultural production).
2. Effective leadership (replacement by second generation leaders who are better educated, more competent, more foresighted, and more aware of international interdependence). This will require cultural change so that Africans become more goal oriented, and less fatalistic.
3. Rural development (less emphasis on urban development and more on rural opportunity and agricultural production).
4. Population control (traditional large families that enlarge tribal power bases have to be regulated, while social security provisions are made for the aged). Only then can tough problems be solved in black Africa related

to infant mortality, illiteracy, income ($365 a year average), and political instability.

Africa covers 20% of the world's land mass and has 10% of its people—800 million by the year 2000. Yes, it has problems—such as in an Information Age, 60% of those Africans will be illiterate—but nothing North-South dialogue and collaboration could not resolve. For Africa is a potentially rich continent— it now produces 40% of the world's hydroelectric power and 15% of its oil; it contains 35% of the world's uranium outside the Eastern block and is the largest supplier of diamonds.

GENERAL INSIGHTS FOR AFRICAN BUSINESS SYNERGY

One would hope that international business might succeed where Western politicians and soldiers have failed in the development of Africa and its markets. Before the high dollar valuation, one-fifth of American goods were sold abroad and 20% of the U.S. trading partners were in 42 developing countries—Africa plays a growing part in that mercantile system with Nigeria being our second largest exporter of oil. But Africa accounts for only 2.5% of U.S. exports, and approximately two-thirds of that goes to Nigeria and South Africa, excluding massive relief aid. As Europe suffers a market decline in Africa, the continent represents opportunity to U.S. traders. But the Africans, after decades of complaining in the UN about the U.S., are wary.

A. A. Ajakiye, the consulate general of Nigeria, put it this way in a conference of World Econoculture (*San Diego Business Journal*, May 25, 1981):

> When you say multinationals, we say "we can't cope." But sometimes we have no choice. There are some fields in which we must deal with multinationals (corporations). The multinationals have loyalty to no flag. Their economies are not consistent with the economies of developing countries. We would prefer to enter into joint ventures with smaller firms.

Ajakiye maintained that MNC's have no stake in transfer of technology and view the Third World only as a cheap labor pool. Perhaps this explains why Africa is turning for technical assistance to India. It is running Nigeria's railways and teaching the locals how to manage a rail network. Perhaps another Third World nation is more sensitive to the needs for appropriate technology transfer, and not overwhelming the indigenous peoples with too sophisticated technologies and systems.

Other avenues for improved trade relations in Africa are:

- Seek information about African business conditions and cultures from voluntary agencies with sound experience in Asia—such as the Peace Corps,

Canadian International Development Agency, British Voluntary Service Overseas, or even the foundations and church groups from abroad. For example, Canadian University Service Overseas has a successful track record in Africa, and could supply useful intelligence and personnel counsel on regions in which they have managed projects—such as Biafra, Sierra Leone, and the United Republic of Tanzania.

- Send trade missions of related business groups to Africa and arrange for them to meet with high-level contacts. Trade shows are not the way to enter the African market since there is no middle class in most of the countries there.
- Utilize the services of the African-American Chamber of Commerce headquartered in Los Angeles, and recruit American business representatives from among the 120 land grant universities in the U.S. that are predominantly black with students of African heritage.
- Obtain explicit clarification from African host governments of any guarantees to be received, expropriation risks, tax or duty breaks, whether the structure should be a branch or local corporation, taxes on corporation and its properties, labor regulations and currency practices.

Scott Kennedy of the City University of New York believes that in order to encourage business enterprises in Africa for profit and social welfare, a synergy must be created between the African nations and the African-American communities, such as establishing banks for this specific purpose.

Cultural Characteristics of Business in Africa

The Family

The basic unit of African society is the family, which includes the nuclear family and the extended family or tribe. In traditional African society, the tribe is the ultimate community. No unit has more importance in society. There may be some loose confederations, but they are temporary and limited in scope. In political terms, the tribe is the equivalent of a nation. It does not have fixed boundaries, but on its sanction rests the law (customary law like the English Common Law). All wars were fought on the tribe's behalf, and the division between "them" and "us" lay in tribal boundaries.

In some ways, the tribe is more than a nation. In Europe and America, ethical and moral standards are not given by national sanctions, but rest on religious and cultural traditions common to the whole continent. But in traditional Africa, except for areas under Islamic control, the tribe provides the guidelines for accepted behavior. The tribe bears a moral connotation and provides an emotional security. It is also a source of social and moral sanctions as well as political and physical security. It provides its members with rules governing responsibilities, explanations of the responsibilities, and guidelines for organizing the society, and hence, the culture. The following quotations from *Business International Research Report* suggest the importance of the tribe:

> The basic sociological unit in Africa is the tribe, which inhabits one village or a series of villages, or (in the case of nomadic tribes) is widely scattered. A feeling common throughout Africa is the sense of tribal responsibility and brotherhood. When tribal members go to the cities for jobs or education, their enhanced stature brings the responsibility of assisting tribal brothers. This obligation often imposes a burden on the successful member far in excess of his income.
>
> In such a situation, the successful African is unlikely to resist the pressures of his society. He is thus forced to augment his income, often by means regarded by foreigners as theft and corruption. In the Western sense, it may be. In the African context it is not.

The presence of tribalism may be giving way, but its importance cannot be ignored. The article "Nigeria," *Atlantic* (December 1976) states:

> Tribalism is a major factor in who gets what job, especially in the civil service, even though jobs in an office seldom go to members of the boss's tribe, as they used to. Some businessmen refuse to hire members of their own tribe because they think it encourages demands for favors and militates against good performance, and younger men fight tribalism harder than the older generation. But tribalism is also a major factor in the rebirth of Nigerian politics. In each of the seven states I visited, people spoke only of their own tribe's candidates for leadership and predicted that the national parties would be alliances of tribal leaders.

The tribe is broken down into different kinship lines. The concept of kinship is important to understanding African societies. It constitutes the primary basis for an individual's rights, duties, rules of residence, marriage, inheritance, and succession.

Kinship refers to blood relationships between individuals, and is used to describe relationships in a narrow, as well as a broad sense. Parents and their children are a special kind of kin group. The social significance of kinship covers a wide social field in most African societies. In Western culture, its significance usually does not extend beyond the nuclear family, but in the African culture, it embraces a network of people including those that left the village for the urban areas.

The family—father, mother, children—is the ultimate basis of the tribe. But the tribal and family unit organization is being disrupted by changes in the economic organizational structure. The economic organization has tied reward to individual effort, and developed road, rail, water, and air communication networks that have increased the range and speed of contact, and therefore, the rate of intercultural contact and change. The reorganization has also brought tribes together as territorial units, thereby increasing opportunities for migration from one area to another and weakening family bonds.

As this new-found mobilization moves more people to the large urban areas, they try to maintain some family ties. This involves a responsibility to support family members still in the villages. It also affects Africans' business relationships with managers from abroad in terms of hiring practices and the need for extra income to support those at home. Earnings from business transactions are often used for this purpose.

Trust and Friendship

Trust and confidence are essential elements needed for successful enterprise in Africa. It is very important to get to know co-workers as individuals before getting down to actual business activities. Friendship comes first. Often, a friendship continues after specific business activities end. Socializing outside of the office is common. It is under those relaxed conditions that managers talk politics, sports, and sometimes business.

Contrast this with American businessmen who are interested primarily in getting the job done. There is some socialization outside the office, but only for business purposes. As soon as the job is done or the contract fulfilled, the U.S. manager moves on to other things. A friendship that develops outside of the office and continues for an extended period of time is unique. The prior *Business International Research Report* states that:

> No amount of capital, know-how, goodwill, or energy will guarantee success for multinational corporations if they cannot win the trust and confidence of the governments and people with whom they deal . . . such trust and confidence is sadly lacking in Africa today.

In Africa, interpersonal relationships are also based upon sincerity. African societies are warm and friendly. People generally assume that everyone is a friend until proven otherwise. When Africans smile, it means they like you. When smiles are not seen, it is a clear sign of hate and distrust.

Africans believe strongly in friendship and once a person is accepted as a friend, the person automatically becomes a member of the family. A friend can pop into a friend's place anytime. In African societies, formal invitations and appointment making are not common. Friends are readily prepared to entertain fellow friends anytime.

One of the most important factors to remember when doing business in Africa is the concept of friendship before business. Normally before a meeting begins, there is general talk about events that have little or nothing to do with the business at hand. This can go on for some time. If the meeting involves the coming together of people who have never met, but who are trying to strike a deal (an African and a foreigner), the African will try to reach out for friendship first.

Essentially, the African culture is still friendly and warm to strangers. Making real friends in Africa is an easy task. In addition, friendship and trust must come before an African enters a business deal. A close bond must develop between the two people involved. If an African tries to reach out but receives a cold response, he may become alert and suspicious, and lose interest in the deal.

Time

The way an individual views the concept of time has a major impact on any business situation. If two businessmen enter a situation with complementary goals, abilities, and needs, a successful arrangement can be thwarted if each has different ideas about time. The U.S. manager tends to be inflexible when it comes to time. Everything is done according to a schedule with little or no deviation. Meetings must begin on time and end on time. The entire day is segmented into time slots, and the American becomes uneasy or nervous if the schedule is interrupted or if little is accomplished.

In Africa, time is viewed as flexible, not rigid or segmented. People come first, then time. Anyone in a hurry is viewed with suspicion and distrust. Since trust is very important, individuals who follow inflexible time schedules will have little success. The African wants to sit and talk—get to know the person before discussing business.

In the larger cities of Africa, the concept of time is changing. Punctuality is becoming more important. Contact with Western businessmen has brought an increasing awareness and acceptance of the segmentation of time and its consequent inflexibility. But away from the capital city, time is still viewed in a relaxed and easy-going manner. Businessmen in outlying areas like to talk politics and hear the latest news when city people come to visit.

Time is not seen as a limited commodity. What cannot be done today can always be accomplished tomorrow. Among friends, people who know one another, meetings are not held promptly. People may arrive several hours late. Many times foreigners misinterpret this as laziness, untrustworthiness, lack of seriousness in doing business, or even lack of interest in the venture. However, lateness in meetings is seen as very much a part of life. It is understood among friends that even though everybody agrees to meet at a given time, they will not actually gather until much later. This lateness has become known as "African time." However, when Africans are dealing with foreigners, they normally try to be on time out of respect for the non-Africans' concept of time.

Corruption

Corruption in Africa is often a result of tribal responsibilities that individuals carry with them when leaving the village for a job or schooling in the city. The enhanced stature of city life brings a responsibility of assisting tribal brothers.

This obligation often imposes a financial burden on the successful member far in excess of income. The worker is unlikely to resist the pressures of society, and is thus forced to augment income, often by means regarded by foreigners as corrupt. However, to the African, it is not. As long as great disparities in income and standards of living continue, the bribe system is also likely to continue as it has in many countries. In Africa, extra income is swiftly distributed through the extended family system to remote relations living in remote places. The tradition of sharing continues even as individuals move away from their tribal origins.

One of the greatest problems in Nigeria, for example, is the corruption in government on all levels. General Obasanjo recently declared: "It is gross and destructive indiscipline on the part of any society to accommodate cheating by any member of that society. It is alien to our African traditional society." In the same address, he publicly admitted that "it is a matter for regret that most public servants tend to subdue their political discipline in the face of personal aggrandizement." The following mini case is an example:

> The company, Jones & Smith Food Company, is located in the capital of a large African country. However, they want to expand their headquarters to another state capital. To do this, they need approval from the federal government and the state government. The company sent in a written application a few months ago, but did not get any response.
>
> The manager of the project went several times to the Federal Ministry of Trade and Economic Development but was always told to come back the next day. Mr. Jones became frustrated and mad at the clerks and officials involved. However, in the process of the argument, one of them said, "This is not America. It's Africa. If you want anything done on time, you've got to give a bribe. Kind of like a gratuity tendered before, rather than after a service is performed."
>
> Mr. Jones, who is not accustomed to such practices, angrily stormed out of the office. In the car, he narrated the incident to the driver who advised him to give the "gratuity" or have the proposal denied.
>
> In emergency meeting, the company's board of directors decided to offer the gratuity. To the company's surprise, the proposal was approved the next day.

But back in Jones' home culture a board of directors may frown upon such payments, and home country laws may consider such bribes illegal.

Task Orientation

If a foreigner appears too task-oriented, the African counterpart interprets it as planned foul play. If hurried through business negotiations, the African suspects cheating. In addition, Africans might brand the task-oriented approach of Americans as a demonstration of their superiority complex. They may even associate Americans with the previous British colonial masters. Some natives believe that European imperialists kept Africans down, humiliated and ridiculed, and exploited Africa's resources. If that happens, there is very little chance for the business deal to succeed if contemporary foreigners get lumped with the mistakes of their predecessors.

Respect for Authority

Age is another important factor to consider in Africa. It is believed that the older one gets, the wiser one becomes—life has seasoned the individual with varied experiences. Hence, in Africa, age is an asset. The older the person, the more respect the person receives from the community, and especially from the young. Thus, if an American is considerably younger than the African, the latter will have little confidence in the American. However, if sincerity, respect, and empathy are shown, the American will receive a positive response. Respect for elders tends to be the key harmony in African cultures.

Young people may not oppose the opinion of elderly people. They may not agree, but they must respect the opinion. In some cases, especially in rural areas, young people are not expected to offer opinions in meetings. The informal and formal interpersonal relationships in Africa are based on cultural norms of various African societies.

Business and Common Courtesies

Business is normally discussed in the office or in a bar or restaurant—always outside the home. When an African is the host of such meetings, he will pay for everyone. If an American is the host, the American should pay.

Home matters are not discussed in business meetings. What happens in the home is considered private.

When invited to someone's home for a meal, do not discuss business. All business is done outside the home, and men are expected to be away from home on business matters much of the time.

As indicated earlier, age commands respect. Age and wisdom are seen as the same, and the norms of the elders must be followed in order to ensure smooth business dealings.

In general, Africans are in transition from their traditional cultures based on a rural, agricultural, and tribal way of life. Rapidly, they are moving toward an urban lifestyle that is based upon industrial and technological development.

Los Angeles Times, January 8, 1989—"For Chinese, Sophisticated Africans Are Contradictions in Cultural Terms" (excerpted report by Edward A. Gargan)—

A West African businessman who was in China last year trying to arrange a coca-processing deal found himself shunted from ministry to ministry. Although he is internationally prominent in the coca business, he never managed to sign a contract with the Chinese. In the end, he blamed his failure to clinch the deal on what he described as entrenched racism. The Chinese, he said, cannot grapple with a well-dressed, sophisticated African who knows more about something than they do, is richer than they are, and is negotiating the way white investors do. . . .

In fact, China's post-revolutionary history has exhibited deeply etched patterns of institutionalized racism toward the 7% of the country's population not ethnically Han. . . . Many Chinese speak contemptuously of Tibetans, employing language echoing unself-conscious racism heard three decades ago in the United States. . . . Offically, of course, there is no racism in China. . . . African students, almost all of whom are male, have discovered this most acutely when they attempt to spend time with Chinese women students. . . . Several months ago an East African diplomat in his Beijing apartment, spoke despairingly of Chinese attitudes toward Africans. . . . This perception clashes with a Chinese foreign policy that proclaims solidarity with developing countries, particularly in Africa. Chinese technicians and engineers have worked in Africa for decades. . . . There are now 1,500 African students studying in China at Chinese expense. . . . Yet African students were targets of violence there because they were different, because they were not Chinese, because they were black.

From an interview reported in *World Issues* between two political science professors, Gerald L. Bender and Otis L. Graham (Oct./Nov. '78), on the subject of superpowers involvement in Africa:

Graham: If Americans want to know how best to be effective at helping Africans, what kind of people should we be sending, with what sort of outlook and techniques?. . . .
Bender: The Chinese and Cubans are effective there for different reasons. The Chinese stay away from the Africans when their work is done for the day. The Cubans mix with the people without any of the cultural and racial arrogance that one often sees in the representatives from developed societies, like the U.S., the Soviet Union, Hungary, Czechoslovakia, Bulgaria, and others. For example, Cuban engineers on a project do not say, "Go do this, go do that." Instead, they will take somebody actually by the hand—the Cuban is not afraid to hold a black hand—and he will walk with the African, explaining in a very patient, nonarrogant way what has to be done and how to do it. . . . I don't think socialism explains that Cuban attitude. I think it is because Cuba is not a highly developed, or

racist, society. Americans tend to be much more sensitive to African feelings than Eastern Europe or Russian technicians are. . . . Basically, the Peace Corps has been successful because—and this is what I observed in Cubans—there is motivation. Call it ideological motivation, call it altruism, call it internationalism. But it is there.

NIGERIA

Nigeria—Profile	
Population	112 million
Ethnic Groups	250 Tribal Groups (three largest are Hausa-Fulani, Ibo, and Yoruba = 65%)
Religions	Muslim 47%, Christian 39%, Indigenous African Beliefs 18%
Education	Six years compulsory 25–35% Literacy
Land	356,700 square miles
Government	Military
Political Parties	None
Per Capita Income	$760
Exports to U.S.	$3,400 million
Imports from U.S.	$325 million

Commentary

Christian Science Monitor, February 15, 1984—"Financially Pinched Nigerians Lose Some Patience with Expatriates in their Midst"—In what is often considered Africa's most African city, they are scarcely visible in the crowded market areas of Lagos.

But in the late afternoons and on weekends they swarm in their air-conditioned cars into the mahogany-paneled Ikoyi Club, and from there onto its squash and tennis courts and its oasis of green fairways.

They are the expatriates—the big businessmen, the construction engineers, the agricultural experts, educators, and technocrats—who streamed into Nigeria when it was sloshing in oil money.

David Winder

Foreign Times, September 3, 1984—"Two Senior Nigerian Leaders Suspended"—Two of the most senior Nigerian traditional rulers, Alhaji Ado Bayero, the Emir of Kano, and Oba (chief) Okunade Sijuwabe, the Oni of Ife, have been suspended from their offices for six months following their visits last month to Israel.

Newsweek, September 9, 1985—"Nigeria Replays a Coup"—Last week, the military shoved Buhari out, installing Major General Ibrahim Babangida in his place . . . Nigeria's economic mess will be harder to fix . . . the worldwide drop in oil prices, and years of administrative mismanagement and corruption.

Everything discussed in general about African culture comes into sharp focus within the context of one of black Africa's most advanced nations, economically—Nigeria.

Cultural Characteristics of Business in Nigeria

Social Structure

In Nigeria the family dominates the social structure. Nigerian tradition places emphasis on one's lineage through the male head of the household. In non-Moslem sections, these familial connections form vast networks that serve as a foundation for one's social identity. Marriage is seen as a way of producing more children to contribute to this lineage or network. Sterility is ground for divorce!

Three forms of marriage exist in Nigeria. Among Christians and non-Moslems, unlimited polygamy is customary. Wives are acquired through the payment of a bride price to the bride's parents. Moslem custom differs in that the number of wives is usually limited to four. The Western Christian marriage is relatively uncommon in rural areas, although they are occurring with increased frequency in the cities.

Women play a vigorous role in this society, although domestic authority always rests seemingly with the husband. There is a network of marketing and trading in commodities that occurs throughout the country. This is the exclusive province of women, who run their own businesses the way they see fit.

The stratification of Nigerian society varies with region. In northern Nigeria, rank is more important than it is in the south. In the east, some egalitarian tradition exists, while in the west there is a distinct aristocracy.

Groups and Relationships

Among the many tribes, the major ones are:

1. The Hausa, who are very religious. They are practicing Muslims and usually take a long time to make a decision.
2. The Yoruba, who are festive, party people. They love to be wined and dined. They are outgoing, not secretive about their business activities and have the "eat, drink, and be merry" philosophy of life.
3. The Ibo, who understand business customs and the value of money. They are excellent merchants and extremely resourceful. The Ibos are hard working and conscientious, and expect a professional image of a Westerner.

In the country as a whole, the nature of competitiveness of the industry determines how business is conducted. In the construction industry, for example, there is high competitiveness and no time for small talk.

At state and federal meetings, protocol must be observed. Extreme politeness, respect for authorities and a slower pace is normal. If an authority doesn't answer your question, it may mean they don't know the answer and do not want to be embarrassed.

An American business person should establish a Nigerian counterpart, first of all. One needs expertise in how to deal with the Nigerian business community. Such a local resource will prove invaluable in translating later what was said during a meeting. Even though the official language is English, the Nigerian accent can be difficult to understand. A native can become insulted when the foreigner does not comprehend their local version of English, often British in origin.

It takes a long time to become established in the Nigerian business community and it's who one knows that will make a difference. Connections are important and should be cultivated.

In investing in Nigeria, start at the state government level instead of the federal government level. Each state operates differently, but all want and need business, and consequently are very receptive. The state officials can greatly facilitate business formalities.

Since choosing a Nigerian counterpart or representative is crucial to the business success, the U.S. Embassy's Commercial Officer can be of help. References should be carefully checked and choosing someone with influential contacts is important.

All significant business is conducted face to face. Therefore, projecting a refined, confident image will prove to be an asset as a business visitor in Nigeria.

Business Tips

Three important business attitudes exist in Nigeria:

1. *Old family business tradition:* One does not share information because everyone else is a competitor. (This traditional attitude has often been reinforced by subsequent European influences.)
2. *New U.S. training:* Free flow of information; share; communicate; trade knowledge. (Many young Nigerian businessmen are U.S.-trained.)
3. *Moslem attitudes:* Predestination rather than free will; reliance on precedent; mistrust of innovation; unwillingness to take risks; learning by rote rather than by experiments or problem-solving.

To facilitate business interactions with Nigerians:

1. Be formal and respectful.
2. Don't be suspicious and openly check on something.

3. Be trustworthy—deliver when and what is promised.
4. Relax, slow down—Nigeria is not on the same time schedule as the U.S.
5. Don't be overly sensitive to criticism or advice. Maybe one can learn something from the locals.
6. American skills are technical, not cultural. Learn about the people—take an interest in and try to experience the culture.
7. Don't try too hard and "go African." Remain professional.
8. Patience is the key to successful business in Nigeria.

It will almost always be necessary to deal, in some capacity, with Nigerian government officials. Considering the number of recent coups, the exact person one wants to see is not always available. When a meeting is granted, whether with the desired official or someone else, there are important practices to be aware of. First of all, any significant business transaction is always conducted in person. Any attempt to conduct business either over the telephone or by mail is seen as considering the matter as trivial and unimportant. When visiting a colleague's office, tea, coffee, or other refreshments are always available and offered. These refreshments should not be refused, as this may be taken as offensive. Also, refreshments must always be available when the colleague comes to visit the foreign businessman's office. Along these same lines, a visiting business person will often be invited to a colleague's home for a meal. Once again, if at all possible, the invitation should not be refused.

When conducting negotiations with a Nigerian, dress is very significant, as it reflects one's attitude towards the importance of the meeting. The tone of such meetings is generally friendly and respectful. Notice should be taken of titles to be sure the appropriate ones are used correctly. Nigerians don't look well on those who make promises that can't be kept. For this reason, it is better to be realistic when promising delivery dates or price specifications.

Age is highly respected in Nigeria and often associated with wisdom. Therefore, to maximize chances of success, an older person should be sent to meet with prospective business persons, as this will show a certain amount of respect for Nigeria's emphasis on age.

It is not unusual for a Nigerian worker to try to involve his foreign manager or supervisor in politics. It is much better to not get involved in these politics, as sides will undoubtedly be chosen and one's authority will be minimized, and an air of hostility and tension will be apparent.

Decision Making

Decision making in middle level management is based on a centralized system and delegation of authority is almost nonexistent. Nigerians cling to authority and are dependent on supervision. A manager must command a decision from subordinates or they will put it off indefinitely. Because age is important in the Nigerian society, a "fast-tracked" young Nigerian manager giving instructions to an older subordinate worker may find difficulties being respected. Again, a Westerner, regardless of age, should hold high respect for elders.

The extended family concept applies to the Nigerian manager at a higher level position. He feels obligated to find jobs for his family and will not hesitate to "pull-strings" to employ members of his family. If the Nigerian is very powerful, there is nothing a foreign businessman can do to stop this practice. This decision-making process based on family responsibilities can be very frustrating to an American business representative who is conditioned to merit selections and promotions.

Communication Tips

There are certain words that should not be used by a Westerner in Nigeria, such as "native," "hut," "jungle," "witchcraft," and "costume." The connotation behind these expressions tends to be that Africa is still a dark backward area where people still run around half-dressed, throwing spears, with rings in their noses. Nigeria, as is true with many other parts of Africa, has made great strides in development and is proud of their advancement. Therefore, it is best to remember that a hut is a home and a costume is really clothing. Nigerians want to be friends with foreign visitors and they are proud to have them in their homes. They will go to great lengths to be a friend, but they do not want to be condescended to or patronized.

Concept of Time

The concept of time in Nigeria can be summed up as unlimited. Lagos, the center of business, is a huge metropolis that is very congested and often full of huge traffic jams called "go slows." These can hold you up for several hours. Consequently, late appointments are common and usually anticipated, and telephone service is poor and unreliable.

Time is, therefore, not of the utmost importance to most Nigerians. As a matter of fact, time is viewed as being unlimited. As such, punctuality is not very prevalent. Work is important to the Nigerians, but so is their leisure. Sports are a big favorite way to spend time. Those that are most popular with the Nigerians are football, boxing, and horse racing. Hockey, tennis, cricket, polo, golf, rugby, table tennis, and softball are also played.

Greetings

Upon meeting a Nigerian business associate, the greeting is Westernized but formal. A simple "Good morning Mister Opala, how are you?" is accepted as proper and asking personal questions about his family is common practice.

Once you've established some degree of familiarity, you can use a first name basis if the Nigerian initiates it. Always shake hands when greeting someone, no matter how busy they seem. It is extremely rude not to acknowledge a person when entering the room or shake his hand. A typical situation for an American businessman unfolds as follows: he enters a room, shakes hands, is then formally introduced, shakes hands again, is announced as the new senior accountant, shakes hands again, prepares to leave the room, and shakes hands good-bye.

Forms of Address

Nigerians distinguish the levels of familiarity between one another by their forms of address. Friends will call one another by their first names. Parents are addressed as mother, father, or mom and dad. However, older brothers and sisters are very rarely addressed by their first names. An older brother is addressed as N'da Sam and an older sister as N'se Sarah, which means "my senior Sam" or "my senior Sarah." This is simply a sign of respect towards seniority and age. The expressions "sir" and "ma'am" are always used when speaking to a business person, government official, someone older, or someone in a position of authority.

Social Customs

Nigerians are a proud and self-confident people. Much of this confidence comes from a knowledge that their country is a leader in Africa, in many ways. They are very extroverted, friendly, and talkative. Nigerians are known also for their hospitality. Strangers are taken in, fed, lodged for as long as the guest desires. Consequently, it is possible to make many more long-lasting relationships that are less superficial than in some other cultures. Once a friend is made, both parties can expect a great deal from the other one and will be insulted if one's friend doesn't come to the other in times of trouble.

When a friend, acquaintance, or relative becomes ill, it is customary for that person to receive many, many visitors. Anyone who even remotely knows the sick person will come to visit. It is the Nigerian way of saying, "I want to know for myself how you're feeling." The courtesy is expected to be reciprocated when a friend becomes ill.

When two people are considering marriage, there is a proper procedure that must be followed. The first step is for the prospective groom to send an intermediary to the woman's home to present the idea of marriage to her parents. Gifts are sent to the woman and then the man himself comes to the woman's parents to discuss the notion. So far, nothing has been said to the woman about the pending marriage. If everything is in order with the prospective bride's family, the woman then goes to live with the man's family to make sure this is where she wants to live. If so, the marriage can occur. Society enters into the decision as far as if the people feel the woman will fit in. The dowry involved in the marriage is not a fixed amount. It is an insurance against maltreatment for the woman. It is not until the wife dies and is buried in her natal land that the dowry is paid to her husband, if she has been treated well.

Most Nigerian cultures are patriarchal. In some areas, particularly the rural ones, polygamy is still prevalent. However, in urban areas, it is much more common to find one-man, one-woman marriages. Marriage age is becoming more of an economic decision. Couples wait until they have an education and can afford a marriage.

Nigeria is a "right-handed" society. As in many cultures, the left hand is unclean, as it is the "toilet hand." It is extremely impolite to extend the left hand to others or to eat with it, even if the person is left-handed.

Although mentioned before, it is important to re-emphasize the importance of age in Nigeria. There is a profound respect for one's elders. Older people are not placed in nursing homes when they become ill. They are taken in by their families, looked after, and revered. The importance of the elderly seems to lie in their capability to pass on family history and tradition. Although Nigeria is growing quickly and becoming more modernized, traditions are still very important to the people, as can be evidenced by the fact that local customs still play a very significant role in Nigerian life. One such ritual, that is quickly disappearing, is found strictly in the western portion of the country and has to do with tribal marks. When a child reaches the age of two or three years, he or she has the appropriate tribal marks burned into his face, very similar to the branding process. These marks reflect tribes or family. When one sees the marks, it is not necessary to ask what the person's last name is or from what tribe he comes. It is said that if the child cannot withstand the pain during the ceremony, as there is no anesthesia, he or she is not worthy of that family or tribe. The whole process is very unhygienic and dangerous, and seems to be dying out gradually.

Intermarriage between tribes currently is very rare in Nigeria. It is more common for a Nigerian to marry a foreigner than out of his tribe for another tribe member. There is still a great deal of rivalry between the tribes and the intent seems to be to try and keep them pure. However, if such an intertribal marriage should occur, oddly enough, the stranger will be treated almost royally by the other members of the other tribe. The reason for this is that the non-tribe's member is viewed as having made a supreme sacrifice by giving up his/her tribe and their traditions and adopting those of the spouse, as they almost always do in this situation.

The custom of eating with one's hands is practiced in Nigeria. If there is a big festival, or even in a private home, where there are foreign visitors not used to this custom, allowances are made and silverware is often provided them. However, an honest effort will be greatly appreciated. Before eating, a communal bucket is passed around for everyone to wash their hands, prior to the beginning of the meal. Once again, it is important to use only the right hand.

Family ties and kinship are very, very strong in Nigeria. Family members remain extremely close throughout their entire lives. It is not unusual for family members to expect a relative to either find or create a job for them once this relative is employed.

As in all of Africa, the role of women in Nigeria is changing with modernization. Females have always performed the major laboring tasks from farming to road building. Now with increased education and opportunity, they are moving up in commerce and industry, as well as in government and the professions. Perhaps the Nigerian women achieving positions of leadership and influence in the political and economic arena, will also set the example for the liberation of women elsewhere on the continent. That was one of the objectives of the meetings and reports at the 1985 Women's Year Conference sponsored by the United Nations in Kenya, Africa.

SUMMARY

Global managers appreciate both the potential of Africa's human and natural resources, and the struggles of its Third World nations seeking to move beyond the effects of colonialism. Synergistic partnerships, such as joint ventures, can do much to contribute to the development of the area and its peoples. The chapter underscored this significance and contemporary realities, especially by in-depth analysis of one promising black African culture, Nigeria.

When comparing the American and African cultures and how they affect the business environment, it is necessary to understand that the U.S. is a low-context culture. It is technologically oriented with emphasis on individual achievement rather than group participation. In the communication process, a low-context culture places meaning in the exact verbal description of an event. Individuals in such a culture rely on the spoken word. This is typified by the common statement, "say what you mean."

Africa's culture is high-context. In the communication process, much of the meaning is not from the words, but is internalized in the person. Meaning comes from the environment and is looked for in the relationship between the ideas expressed in the communication process. High-context cultures tend to be more human oriented than low-context cultures. The extended family fits into the high-context culture.

Businessmen from Africa and the U.S. can profitably work together if they accept the differences between them and work to create an atmosphere of non-judgmental acceptance. On the part of the American, it means slowing down; not being tied to a time schedule.

19
High Performance in Global Markets

Human performance is dependent on culture and the attitudes it engenders, particularly toward work and the future. The hunting culture, now found only in isolated locations, focused upon survival through the skill of the hunter in the pursuit of game and food. It was appropriate to a past time of the world, despite isolated aboriginal tribes who still manage to sustain themselves by superb performance in this manner. For the mainstream of civilization, the agricultural work culture followed, and today lingers on in many lands—long hours devoted to the tilling of the soil and the herding of flocks. Labor intensive and family oriented, such rural living led to the growth of civilization as we know it. Tribal cultures flourished in both these initial stages of human development, but represented a less developed way of life appropriate only to that point in time long since past. Pockets of obsolete tribal cultures are even today in famine-struck Africa, in the Middle East and Afghanistan conflicts, and in remote parts of Asia and Latin America.

With the rise of the industrial culture, humankind advanced to another stage of its development. Then over the past few hundred years, machines, factories, and urbanization influenced the worker's life-style. Industrialization brought unions and safety emphasis, social legislation and security, equal employment oportunity and career development. It also provided workers with more time for education and recreation, for actualizing human potential. Obviously, there were detriments and dangers inherent in each of these previous work environments. All this was discussed in Chapters 1 and 7 so as to enable global managers to put their current efforts into a larger context.

Now we have the opportunity to create the new work culture—the metaindustrial society with its emphasis on information processing and servicing others. We can exercise leadership in the design of the mainstream work culture that will permeate the twenty-first century; a leadership that will transform the dying industrial culture.

In this emerging world culture, electronic communication technologies are converging, uniting, and educating us. Joseph Pelton (1981), the former director of INTELSAT, calls this *telepower* through the "global electronic machine"—the linking of optical and electrical technologies that now allows 3 billion people to see and hear about planetary events. This new capacity to share information and knowledge across traditional boundaries is the catalyst for the globalization of trade and culture, of the economy and market. When further empowered with artificial intelligence, Pelton believes such telepower technologies can advance the species, or even divide and control us. Computers, first digital and now neural, are the powerful tools that modern men and women use to further transcultural communication. These extensions of the human brain can aid in both design and manufacturing; combined with graphics, they free up human integrating sciences with other learnings. Caltech physicist Carver Mead indicates that today's real leaders are those who master ideas and technologies, not land and material resources—they use the global network of telecommunications to liberate human creativity (Gilder, 1989). But to use such technological advances effectively, new cross-cultural competencies are required, as when innovations in information systems necessitate the crossing the borders of functions and departments, as well as disciplines and nations. To fully comprehend the significance of this phenomenon, we must understand the connection between culture and high performance as human beings.

Throughout this book we have underscored the pervasiveness of culture in impacting our lives in general, as well as management and work practice in particular. Some cultures inhibit people, constrain their creativity and intellectual activities. From the viewpoint of work performance, they box in the mind, trap the spirit, and promote passive acceptance of divine will. Such cultures burden human aspirations and efforts with ritualism, legalism, defeatism, and even fatalism. With an over-concern for the past, they confine all hope for a better life to a murky future in the heavens or through reincarnation. These cultures exclude whole segments of their populations because they are *different*, whether their prescriptions are against ethnic or religious minorities, youth, or women. In such cultures, females, for example, are not permitted to be free and independent human beings; their minds, voices, and desires are locked inside social prisons; their lives are dedicated to the service of males and their families—women's personal rights are minimal, their contributions to the advancements of society and themselves are aborted. These cultures feed on suspicion and hatred of those who are different, encouraging an outlook that is ethnocentric and xenophobic. Violence, destruction, corruption, ignorance, and submission are the norms that are fostered within such groups, tribes, organizations, or countries. In these unsynergistic societies, teamwork or team management is unworkable for trust is difficult. International business persons and travelers are aware of such cultures; they may deserve our tolerance, but not our respect for what they do to the human spirit. They are social systems suffering culture lag from the upward movement of the human species. For the most part, such cultures refuse to change or adapt. Today, they contribute little to human emergence and enlightenment.

Yet, even within so-called advanced cultures, there can be pockets of regression. Bigotry and intolerance can assert itself in universities that are supposed to be centers of knowledge and understanding. Students pursuing higher education, but complacent in their insensitivity and ignorance, can be plagued by prejudice as long as they feel parents, professors, and politicans find such misguided attitudes acceptable (Susan Tifft, *Time*, January 23, 1989). Within affluent societies, churches, as well as whole communities, can discourage or prohibit interracial or intercultural marriages (Romano, 1988). As civilization progresses and consciousness is raised, the cultural inhibitors on human performance and happiness normally are reduced or eliminated.

In contrast, there are on this planet human cultures that enhance people, stimulate their creativity, and challenge their intellectual activities From the viewpoint of work performance, they encourage open-mindedness and trust, foster strong morale and group achievement, and promote participation by all. Such cultures inspire and support human aspirations and endeavors, rewarding those who strive for excellence and do their best to improve the present conditions. These self-actualizing cultures seek to provide equal opportunity and to use talent. These more appropriate cultures for our post-industrial times, reinforce the norms of human resource development, high performance and competence, innovation, and entrepreneurialism. Such synergistic cultures encourage a cosmopolitan outlook, cooperation, and collaboration with others, information and knowledge sharing for the common good. Individual and team action is centered upon the planning of change, the accomplishment of goals, the pursuit of dreams. These dynamic, forward-looking cultures advance the human condition on Earth, and explore the prospects for further developments in outer space.

For global managers who would improve human performance and provide transformational leadership, the choice of which cultures to support and advocate is clear, whether in this world or in the high frontier. Perhaps the place to begin the cultivation of such a metaindustrial work culture is in our own group or team, our own organization or community (Tichy and Devanna, 1986; Belcher, 1987; Harris, 1989; Nanus, 1990; Bennis, 1991).

IMPROVING INTERNATIONAL PERFORMANCE

Astute observers on the contemporary scene are well aware that modern society is in transition, and that it is impacting both work and management performance (Harris 1985). The traumas are evident in social, economic, and work life. Examining the cycles and patterns of economic upswings and downswings, Gerhard Mensch, a German economist, observed in the 1970s that basic innovations increase dramatically during periods of transitions from one era to another. We live in such a period, and witness the innovations in information, silicon, solar, and space technologies that are causing a decline in traditional industries and pointing the way to tomorrow's work culture. Global managers with vision capitalize upon the ongoing changes—that is, they exercise leadership. Bennis and Nanus (1985) remind us that "managers do things right; leaders do the right things." What are some of the trends of which cosmopolitan leaders are aware, and what are some of the right things they do to increase human performance in the international marketplace?

Professionals at *The Economist* (June 29, 1985) provided a concise summary of business trends that require managing for change:

1. *Globalization* of economies and markets, which causes international companies to produce standardized products for worldwide markets, rather than local markets. Coca-Cola, Mars Candy, Sony, and Toyota follow this tact.
2. *Diversification* to maintain coherence, corporate strategies prefer to diversify within their industry so as to attain better integration and synergy. Merrill Lynch thus transforms itself into a financial services company, while UAL (United Airlines and Westin Hotels) takes over Hertz to create a fly-drive-eat-sleep travel business.
3. *Corporate culture* to develop a high performing organizational culture, foster innovation and intrapreneurship, as well as a more diversified work force. This is being done successfully at General Electric, Citibank, Procter & Gamble, Siemens in West Germany and GKN in Britain among others.
4. *New technologies* to revitalize mature industries, inject high technology applications to the production of low tech goods and services. Japan's Mitsubishi adds value by putting computers to work in the navigation of the ships they build; General Motors utilizes its mass production skills in high-tech industries it acquires, like aerospace, while employing more automation and robotics in automobile manufacturing with new materials.
5. *Environmental scanning* to keep on the cutting edge of new developments and competition, using business intelligence and information gathering methods to improve forecasting for strategic analysis and planning. Thus, Security Pacific National Bank has a Futures Research Division, Jaguar gathers and uses data about its principal rivals (BMW and Mercedes-Benz).
6. *Tracking Third World developments* to spot opportunities for new markets and joint ventures in the nearly developed or underdeveloped nations, corporate strategists keep informed of trends and requirements in such regions. Thus, multinational corporations seek growth possibilities for foreign investment and partnerships in India, China and ASEAN countries, attuning themselves to local needs and concerns.

Underlying all five trends in this report is the need for *cultural sensitivity and synergy* if improved performance and profitability is to be achieved, whether the issue is world or work culture, national or organizational culture. It is the pervasive message throughout the chapters in this book.

In the context of such changes as reported, global managers then examine how the ongoing technological revolution and its new tools can become a means toward enhanced human performance. Castells (1985) found a complex interaction between high-tech growth and urban demographic changes leading to developments of new industrial space, a transformation of services and communication, and innovative social use of new technologies. It has been amply demonstrated, for example, that fewer human workers using automation and robotics can produce more and often of better quality at less cost.

But there are also other ways to increase organizational performance. M. E. Porter (1985) details how corporations can create and sustain superior performance in the second of two volumes on how companies can analyze and improve their competitive position. If one added a cultural synergy dimension to that writer's advice, then a enterprise would have a global edge with its goods and services relative to strategies for harnessing interrelationships among related industries or diversified business units, for identifying differentiation among buyers from various nations or ethnic groups.

Similarly, Davis, and Cluterbuck (1984) provide insight on what made for success within twenty-five top performing British firms. Their research and interviews revealed eight major organizational behaviors that contributed to market leadership and high profitability. Many of their findings confirm the message of our pages on the new work culture, particularly in the opening unit. For example, an adaptive management style that encouraged participative leadership and more autonomy through decentralized profit centers; market orientation that maintains close, good relations with both customers and suppliers; company culture that provides innovative and involving controls; strategies that include zero basing and reputation for integrity.

Some of these findings confirm the analysis of Peters and Waterman (1982) on excellent companies in North America. Tom Peters (1985) went on to write a sequel on his passion for excellent performance. In a *U.S. News and World Report* (July 15, 1985) interview, he added these astute observations on transnational corporate performance:

> The major failure of American business is seeing the employee as part of the problem, instead of as part of the solution. . . . Another shortcoming is that Americans are really poor internationalists. We don't speak other people's languages, an indicator that we don't take the international world seriously. . . . The average American would blame 85% of the problem [re: difficult international markets] on external forces; my hypothesis is that only half the problem is external and the rest is inter-

nal, self-imposed by management. And our business schools don't focus on international management skills.

Peters then went on to show how top performing U.S. multinationals take a long-time to develop relationships in foreign markets, often without profits there for a dozen years.

In the course of a doctoral dissertation at United States International University, Moon-ik Song (1983) concluded that the Peter and Waterman model and findings for studying excellent companies can be applied cross-culturally. His research on outstanding Korean-American businesses was similar to U.S. counterparts in a bias for action, staying close to the customer, seeking productivity through its personnel, simple in organizational form with lean staffs, flexible in business controls, managed by superordinate goals and diversification. The Korean companies were culturally different and dissimilar in terms of autonomy and entrepreneurship since they did not encourage risk-taking; were execution rather than planning oriented; placed more emphasis on personality than production-related factors in hiring and limited business expansion into known areas. The doctor of business administration research program, when under USIU Professor Dorothy L. Harris, had also extended the Peters and Waters' paradigm to other macrocultures, such as excellent companies in Thailand, and to organizational microcultures, such as the military and hospitals. (Such studies are available through University Microfilms International, 300 N. Zeeb Road, Ann Arbor, MI 48106, U.S.A.)

Both in popular and academic business literature, there is a growing body of information to guide global managers on intercultural performance improvements.

SYNERGISTIC ROLE OF GLOBAL MANAGERS

The first unit in this book explored the emergence of organizational leaders as intercultural communicators, change agents, and cultural transmitters. Specifically, we examined the role of the multinational manager in changing organizational, work and team cultures.

Thus, the modern global manager must be sensitive to the broader implication of his or her actions and decisions upon organizational and world cultures. Furthermore, such leaders need both a sense of history and of the future, so that they may share their visions, as well as their sense of responsibility, with their fellow employees, regardless of what country or community in which they may be located.

The second unit of this text focused attention upon cultural factors that influence behavior and decision making both for the multinational manager and the persons with whom he or she interacts. Chapters 8 and 9 provided insights into ways of analyzing and understanding a foreign culture. Information was shared to indicate how culturally-conditioned assumptions, values, attitudes, and practices of key personnel, such as sales representatives, buyers, and overseas managers, can influence the success or failure of intercultural business relations.

We reviewed the phenomenon of culture shock, which can restrict or enhance the international experience, depending on how the individual responds to its challenge. The concept was linked to the more fundamental issue of identity crises, heightened in a cross-cultural exchange, and this was related to other life traumas that challenge people to change (e.g., role crises, reentry shock).

When a corporation, association, or agency goes outside its parent culture into that of another "foreign" country, a two-way action takes place. First, the other culture impacts upon the organization and its representatives. There is a broadening of perspective, attitude about the foreign people change, adaptations are made to the way they do business. This influence can be both positive and negative. On the plus side the transnational organization may learn new managerial or technical practices, as well as different values and goals. For example, global managers who do business in Japan can benefit if they will take the time to study in depth Japanese business operations—the Japanese economic system is possibly the most successful in the world.

The point is that the transnational enterprise can gain many constructive inputs from the host culture and people, if expatriate management will listen and learn. On the minus side, the multinational corporation, for example, may find itself pressured to conform to local unwritten norms of questionable behavior that can range from bribery and corruption on the one hand, to racism and class distinction on the other.

The transnational actor also has an impact upon the indigenous culture, the effects of which can be healthy or adverse upon the native society or economy. The issue is sensitive in terms of developed and less developed countries, or information-rich versus information-poor peoples. Not every endeavor of advanced countries and their representatives is a benefit to the consuming nation. Colonialism in some less developed areas of the world has been replaced by corporate imperialism or economic exploitation. There are naïve multinational executives who think what is good for their corporation, is automatically good for the nation in which they operate. Like the missionary "do-gooders" of the past, they point to what they are doing for these less fortunate peoples of underdeveloped lands—they bring jobs, technical know-how, training, and capital. Some scholars point with pride to the gradual affluence and industrialization that advanced, technological societies bring by their presence in Third and Fourth World nations. The late futurist Herman Kahn maintained that while the rate of growth in these areas will not be as spectacular as in the First and Second Worlds, it will be significant in raising the inhabitants above existing poverty levels, and will help to close the gap between the rich and poor nations.

When one considers the impact of these transnational enterprises (TNE), it is wise to remember that they are not limited to the West or capitalistic organizations. It has been estimated that the Soviet Union and Eastern European socialist nations have more than 700 trading and manufacturing concerns abroad—about two thirds are located in developed countries (DC's), while the remaining were in less developed countries (LDC's).

Interesting studies have been conducted at the Center for Cultural and Technical Interchange Between East and West in Honolulu on transnational organizations and networks. The East-West Center project was under the leadershp of Krishna Kumar (1980, 1981), now at the University of Michigan. One focus was on promotion by the TNE of a consumption-oriented value-system through effective advertising and marketing strategies in host LDC's. In the process, the TNE may raise the level of knowledge and skills among the locals, but the training imparted is used primarily by the TNE's themselves, not widely diffused in the country, and may not profit indigenous sectors of the economy. Perhaps this extract from Kumar's insightful research contributes something to reader enlightenment on the issue of interventions in other cultures, and their side effects. The investigators sought to answer the questions: (a) What are the ways in which TNE's can affect societies and cultures? (b) What are the major elements of social structures and processes that are likely to be affected by them? (c) What are their consequences for the cultural systems of the LDC's? The researchers identified three modes of TNE's impact:

> First, it has been suggested that TNE's directly produce and diffuse certain elements of cultural systems. In this connection, consider the role of communication by TNE's, especially those involved in television, book publishing, news dissemination, and advertising deserve special mention. They do not only disseminate news, information and the arts, but also a set of beliefs and values. . . . they affect the structures and functioning of local organizations. . . . often influence life-styles and values. . . .
>
> Second, TNE's transfer social and mechanical technologies to host nations. . . . that these effects are likely to be significant in most cases. Technological innovations can influence family, community, social classes, ethnic relationships, economic disparities, knowledge and beliefs of the people. Moreover, the products and services made available by the TNE's can affect consumption patterns, social interactions, symbolic systems and the like. Finally, TNE's can exert pressure on host governments for following certain social and cultural policies.

Kumar emphasizes that such ideas are only working hypotheses needing empirical testing on the basis of cross-national, multidisciplinary involvement. Regardless of whether one agrees with the researchers' hypothesis and tentative findings, their thinking should stimulate global managers' thinking. Transnational enterprises, their decisions and actions, impact a host culture and its people. That was the whole point of Chapter 5 on change makers.

As late as the 1970s, half of the multinational corporations were owned by the U.S.; now foreign companies have reversed such ownership and expanded their investment in America (10% of total assets in 1988).

In a series on economic nationalism for the *Los Angeles Times* (Aug. 8, 1989), Tom Redburn reminds readers that differences between "us" and "them" blurs in the global economy. "Made in America" no longer means what it once did, for a single product increasingly may be manufactured in many countries because of economic integration. The reality is:

- Transnational corporations are loosening their ties with their homelands and ignoring national borders.
- Television manufacturing is thriving again in the U.S. but largely under ownership by 20 foreign companies.
- International joint ventures in automobile manufacturing make it difficult to pin a national label on a particular car—Ford Motors owns 25% of Mazda and will join its Japanese partner to produce vehicles in Europe.
- Prosperity does not depend on where corporation headquarters is located, but on the knowledge and skill of those who work here, regardless of whose name and nationality is on a building.

Instead of passing obsolete protectionist legislation, *the role of government should be to ensure* (a) its citizens receive the education and training necessary for advanced technologies, so workers may perform competently; and (b) adequate investment in research and development.

Increasing Leadership Effectiveness with Cross-Cultural Skills

Our second unit examines how the performance of global managers and their leadership could become more effective through cross-cultural understanding and skills. Various chapters (8/9) have pointed out how culture confirms our sense of identity, but this can be threatened by any type of transitional experience.

We expect that this volume will enable its readers to use their energies in intercultural relations, or international business, to improve communication and cooperation between and among people. In the U.S., for example, there has been a rise in the "new ethnicity." Social philosopher, Michael Novak, explains this as a movement of *self-knowledge* on the part of members of third and fourth generation of southern and eastern European immigrants here. Novak contends that in a broader sense, the new ethnicity includes a renewed self-consciousness on the part of many other American ethnic groups, be they Irish, Norwegian, Swede, German, Chinese, Japanese, or Italian. With 22 million Hispanic Americans now constituting a major segment of the U.S. population, it is understandable why those Americans with Mexican, Cuban, Puerto Rican, or some other Latin origin, are not only seeking new expression of identity, but also political-social power in the society. The consciousness-raising pride in heritage and accomplishment has been especially evident among the native Indians and black Americans in the U.S. during the last half of this century.

Writing in *The Center Magazine* (July/August 1974), Novak observed:

> The new ethnicity entails, first, a growing sense of discomfort with the sense of identity one is supposed to have—universalist, "melted," "like everyone else"; then a growing appreciation for . . . their historical roots; a growing self-confidence and social power; a sense of being discriminated against, condescended to, or carelessly misapprehended; a growing disaffection regarding those to whom one has always been taught to defer; and a sense of injustice regarding the response of liberal spokesmen to conflicts among various ethnic groups. . . . There is, in a word, an inner conflict between one's felt personal power: a sense of outraged truth, justice, and equity.

This quotation captures the essence of what we tried to convey in Chapter 9's discussion of identity crisis and culture shock. It also expresses what a modern woman, or for that matter a "gay" person, often experiences in trying to liberate her- or himself from culturally-conditioned, prescribed roles. As society becomes more pluralistic, and cultures become more "open," people become more aware of both dissimilarities and similarities between themselves and others. They also demand the freedom to be themselves, regardless of cultural context. Minorities of all types seek acceptance and tolerance, rather than discrimination and prejudice. Becoming more culturally sensitive fosters a living environment in which internal dignity, as well as equity of treatment, can coexist. A sense of one's separateness, one's uniqueness, one's ethnic or racial background, need not hamper an individual from becoming a multicultural cosmopolitan. Rather, it may enhance the contribution of a new infusion of diversity toward a *common culture*. Michael Novak explains that this world culture "struggling to be born is a creature of multicultural beauty, dazzling, free, a higher and richer form of life. It was fashioned in the painful darkness of the melting pot and now, at the appointed time, it awakens."

When people are unsure of themselves, uncertain of who they are, and are upset by the transition to a new way of life or work, their performance is affected. Accelerating change threatens our images of self and role. People need assistance in conjuring up new perception of themselves, both individually and institutionally. This is where organizational leaders can help personnel bridge the gap between where technology is and where culture, in general, lags, contributing to identity crises for many persons on this planet. We thought we knew who we are, but the old absolutes give way, and we are uncertain. We are people in transition, caught between disappearing and emerging cultures.

Not only is the self-concept for many in doubt or inadequate, but traditional *role* images in society are being undermined. What is a woman, a black, a teacher, a manager, a parent? We thought we knew, but again rapid change makes us unsure, causing us to redefine our roles. Nowhere, for instance, is such crisis more pronounced than with the Arab women today. Contrast the upper-class, educated, well-traveled Arab female in chic clothes with her Islamic sister in the peasant class—uninformed to a large extent and with a life wholly centered around her family and village. Both represent strikingly different roles in a Moslem world turned upside down.

Similar representations may be made of *organizations,* because human systems—collections of people—also suffer identity crises. Caught between a disappearing bureaucracy and an emerging "ad-hocracy," the institution may experience down turns in sales, poor morale, membership reductions, bankruptcy threats, obsolescence of product lines and services, and increasing frustration with unresponsive management. Organizations, then, are challenged to go through planned renewal and to reproject their public images.

So too with *nations*. When the social fabric unravels or wavers, there are national identities in crisis. Three such examples are: the U.S. which lost "face" in Vietnam and had its diplomats seized as hostages in Iran; Great Britain, which lost its empire and nearly went bankrupt as a nation; and Japan whose very economic and technological progress threatens its traditional culture. Whether one goes to Canada, Pakistan, or China, the peoples of various countries seek to rediscover their collective selves in the post-national period.

Finally, Homo sapiens struggles with an identity crisis for the *species*. We thought we were earthbound, but now we have launched out into the universe. What are the limits of human potential? Is our real home out there? Cosmopolitan leaders can help in promoting synergy between past and future conceptions of ourselves, which so powerfully influence our behavior and accomplishments.

William Christopher (1980) suggests that business itself has an identity problem in the emerging superindustrial age:

> If we have no concept of what we are as a business enterprise, our journey into the future will be haphazard . . . If our actions, adjustments, and reactions derive from a philosophy in tune with the world around us, we will find some kind of identity . . . that is consciously articulated and made central to every action taken everywhere in the organization. . . .

Christopher suggests that this search for a more relevant identity seek answers to such questions as What business are we in? What are we as an organization? What should we become? We would add two more: Who are our customers? and Where are our markets? Many corporations are afraid to enter into the world marketplace, cope with its diverse customs and import/export regulations, and to do business beyond their own borders. Personnel should be trained for high performance in a global economy.

Human response to cultural change and contact with differences, as the late Herman Kahn reminded us, can be constructive or pathological, nonviolent or violent, rational or apocalyptic. Cultural exchange, Octavio Paz observed, requires experiencing the other and that is the essence of change. It alters our psyche, our outlook, and causes some loss of our own cultural beliefs. The paradox is that it may also stimulate a gain or an enlargement of one's perceptions and performance in the adoption of new cultural patterns. Cultural, like biological, evolution demands adaptations for survival and development. Although cultural change is multicausal, "metaindustrial humans" not only create it at the most rapid rate in history, but are also learning to plan and manage change. Culture is a human product subject to alteration and improvement. We are, therefore, discovering innovative ways to improve our performance, even within the new realities of outer space. As we continue to unravel who we really are and become more comfortable with our "selves," then our performance increases and our potential begins to be realized.

As a case in point, our second unit on international business also analyzes what a transnational enterprise should do when preparing their representatives and dependents for foreign deployment. It includes some form of *cultural awareness training*, which is also valid for managers of minorities within the home culture. In fact, our premise is that such *general culture training should become an integral part of all professional or management development.* In Chapter 11 we reviewed the scope and content of such human resource development, including some additional information on methods and techniques for such a learning experience. For multinational organizations involved in the world marketplace, constantly exchanging personnel from one nation to another, a foreign deployment policy and system was recommended.

In other words, the organization has a responsibility to help its people cope with cultural differences. This makes good sense from the viewpoint of economic and social policy, as well as public relations. Without such information and insight, productivity, job effectiveness, sales, and community relations are undermined.

Janette Turner Hospital (1989) reminds us that in the last few decades an ever-increasing number of people find themselves moving between and among several or more cultures within a lifespan. This dislocation may occur for political, economic, educational, or professional necessity. Thus, the issue of cross-cultural malaise and trauma keeps surfacing in short stories and novels, while the research literature on the subject expands. One cultural anthropologist claims it takes two generations to make the transition from one culture to another and that those in transit can experience problems after years of apparently successful adaptation.

Therefore, the second unit ended with Chapter 12 discussing a key element in the emerging work culture. That is, the concept of synergy and how it can be developed among professionals and technicians to improve their performance. The following provides a summary of specific strategies some companies are pursuing to improve expatriate employee performance.

Improving Expatriate Employee Performance

Selection. David Jackson, industrial psychologist, and Ross Lawrence, engineer, have developed a method for quantitatively choosing the right person for two-year assignments in Jeddah, Saudi Arabia. The test proved that success for the expatriate employee was due to key personality qualities—high-energy involvement; experimenting attitude; self-sufficient resourcefulness; maturity; self-assurance; planning competence; imagination; and self-control. The results indicate the less personally sensitive and conforming the individual, the better chances to achieve abroad.

Appraisal. Increases in compensation and other rewards should be tied into better performance, according to Walton Winder, vice-president in the New York consulting firm of Towers, Perrin, Forster & Crosby. Formal evaluation systems for personnel at home or abroad should replace automatic raises. A Sibson survey of 875 companies confirmed the trend, especially with bonus-incentive or pay raise merit plans. Some firms are also deducting pay from underachievers. The work culture has to reward people for extra effort, assuring that pay is for productivity and not politics.

Training. Top performers can be used for problem-solving and behavior models, according to La Jolla, California consultants Bruce Qualset and Philip R. Harris. Through the medium of Performance Management Workshops, their research has demonstrated that high achieving personnel can be brought together for both recognition and input on critical organizational issues. When such sessions are videotaped, the information not only provides management feedback, but the tapes can be used in training others. In this way, Harris International uses high performing expatriate managers and technicians for the orientation of candidates before foreign assignments.

Realistically when operating in the world marketplace, corporations have to modify the performance criteria dictated by their home culture. For example, Dwight Foster of Peat Marwick's executive search division, reports that Japanese companies are missing a key point in looking for Americans to run their U.S. operations (*Forbes*, July 20, 1985). While the Japanese perceive company stability and growth to be pivotal factors in attracting personnel, according to a recent survey, American prospects want money, responsibility, and a chance to run the show. They were also fearful of being unable to adjust to the Japanese management mystique, a factor that Japanese respondents tended to downgrade.

Cultural bias at work can also cause whole segments of personnel to be underemployed, so that their full performance potential is never achieved. The U.N. Nairobi conference in 1985 on the status of women reported that while women represented 50% of the world population and one-third of the official labor force, they perform nearly two-thirds of all working hours, receive only one-tenth of the world income, and own less than 1% of the world property. Obviously, global human energies will never be fully channeled and performance potential realized until competence, not gender, becomes the norm for work behavior, recognition and reward.

Although peak performance is associated in the West with recognition, incentives, and responsibility, there are many other factors that contribute to improved international productivity by global managers. (See Appendix E.)

Cultural Specifics for Performance Effectiveness

Our third unit got into cultural details that make for excellence in business and service abroad, or with foreign nationals or minorities within the home culture. These last seven chapters comprise the largest segment of this cross-cultural management series. Six global regions were selected for analysis in terms of North and Latin America, Asia, Europe, Middle East, and Africa. More than ten specific cultures and their peoples were analyzed, so that global managers will be more effective in their commercial or social interchanges with them. The expectation is that readers will take the insights and information from this cultural sampling, and extrapolate to the many other nationals in these areas and elsewhere. Furthermore, readers may be thus motivated to make additional inquiry by using the resources suggested in the final unit of this volume.

EFFECTIVE GLOBAL LEADERSHIP

First, in his or her exercise of leadership, the global manager must continually update and broaden his or her understanding of culture and its impact on our lives. Although there may be no valid management theories that can be universally applied across all cultures, there are many principles and practices of leadership that can be adapted to various countries despite cultural differences. Professor Andre Laurent has been collecting data at INSEAD on a variety of European managers. Laurent discovered that despite the fact that French managers strongly disbelieve in matrix organization because it seemingly violates unity of command, one French multinational corporation subsidiary had a long history of successful team management. Thus, despite the cultural differences in managerial approaches, it is possible to produce cultural synergy in the pragmatic operations of management.

Another example of how cross-cultural research within international management may help improve cosmopolitan leadership has been provided by Professor Teruyki Kume. His investigations at the Department of Foreign Studies, Nanzan University in Nagoya, Japan have centered on one aspect of the management process—decision making. Since more than 200 Japanese plants have been established in the United States, Kume's research examined the ways Japanese managers in these factories introduced their approaches to decision making, and under what conditions American managers would favorably adopt Japanese styles of choice making. It is an excellent illustration of synergistic research at a time when much of the management literature in America emphasizes the value of group decision making. Kume found, however, that American cultural factors, such as individualism and self-reliance, tend to inhibit the transfer of the Japanese style:

> Namely, Americans tend to control, dominate, and compete in various group situations, causing a conflict with the Japanese approaches. Their tendency to specialize in certain areas and their sense of urgency are also likely to inhibit them from using the Japanese style of intense horizontal and vertical coordination. The Japanese, whose major motives are security and safety, tend to be more cautious and thorough in their analysis of problems that require solutions. In contrast, the Americans, whose major motives are achievement and accomplishment, are more likely to be quick and impulsive in making decisions. Not being apprehensive about making the wrong decisions, they are willing to live with the outcome. Contrary to "common sense" expectations, it was found that the Japanese are more egalitarian than Americans who are more hierarchal at least in the process of decision-making.

We believe that such findings from intercultural management research, while insightful, also offer managers a mirror image of their national approaches to leadership for comparative analysis. Foreign managers are forced to rethink their positions when they realize that the success of Japanese decision making is based on a management philosophy that fully recognizes every member of the organization as an important person who can help the company achieve its goals most effectively. Such leadership practice is culturally conditioned.

Dr. Farid Elashmawi (1991) reports on his research into global joint ventures. This international consultant from Tech-Trans (111 West St. John St. #724, San Jose, CA 95113, USA) focuses upon clashes within multicultural work environments, such as in establishing a plant overseas. These offshore enterprises require the hiring, training, and management of local in-country personnel of differing cultural and technical backgrounds. He identifies cultural clashes arising from language and nonverbal communication, time and space orientation, decision-making and information systems, conduct of meetings and training, as well as motivation.

For effective global leadership, the transnational manager must also be able to think big and think ahead. Therefore, one must have the capacity to envision the increasing interdependence of all facets of human life. The late statesman, Adlai Stevenson, demonstrated this sense of leadership in his activities with such words as these:

> We travel together, passengers on a little spaceship, dependent on its vulnerable reserves of air and soil; all committed for our safety to its security and peace; preserved from annihilation only by the care, the work and the love we give our fragile craft. We cannot maintain it half fortunate, half miserable; half confident, half despairing; half slave of the ancient enemies of man, half free in a liberation of resources undreamed of until this day. No craft, no crew can safely travel with such vast contradictions.

D. L. Hawk, formerly of Center for Creative Leadership (Greensboro, North Carolina 27402, USA) underscored the same theme more recently. Writing in the Center's newsletter about "Leadership 2000," Hawk reminded us that participation in an interdependent world system is required even though goals are diverse, power is dispersed and conflict is inevitable. He cited these examples of synergistic possibilities:

> When a common purpose can be found, then diverse interests of individual parties can be subsumed . . . and smaller goals can be accomplished within the framework of that larger purpose. Chrysler Corporation's bailout by a coalition of government and banks is an example of how a superordinate goal overcame the parochial interests of individual bankers . . . When superordinate goals are found, they minimize the disruptions of the ripples of change. Basic agreement on purpose and direction reduce conflict, and produce a center of gravity to hold a group together. Such a center of gravity allows groups to act quasi-independently within their interdependent relationships.
>
> In addition, leaders of the future will need to be able to show people how to work with and for others without sacrificing their individuality, betraying their values, or silencing their consciences. To provide clear leadership, leaders will need to act independently . . . yet collectively . . . So, effective leaders of the future will build coalitions, influence others skillfully; and solve problems with consensual, not compromised, solutions.

Perhaps the founder of the American organization, *Common Cause* put our point on this matter best. John Gardiner stated:

> Leaders have a significant role in creating a state of mind that is society . . . they can conceive and articulate goals that lift people out of their

petty preoccupations, carry them above the conflicts that tear society apart, and unite them in the pursuit of objectives worthy of their best efforts.

The cosmopolitan manager in global enterprises is now in a position of influence not only to provide such vision for his or her own organization, but for the world community. Such sensitive executives have a rare opportunity to contribute to the creation of cyberculture, the new post-industrial way of life, as well as to design the new meta-industrial organization culture.

In any event, it is culture that has a powerful influence in giving a people identity. Culture is the collective meaning a people put into their unique life-space. It is the pattern of attitudes, beliefs, customs, traditions that generally express the way the average person in that place think and behave. When a people isolate themselves and communicate only with one another, they delimit their capacity to cope with diversity and the challenges of an increasingly "global village." Such an approach is contrary to the mainstream trend wherein the human family worldwide is seemingly creating a new planetary culture based on the refinement of its diverse cultures. The growth and rapid diffusion of communication and technology has been the catalyst in this process.

Leaders must become more transnational and transcultural in their thinking, planning, and involvement. Medieval or industrial-age mindsets on the part of executives and top administrators are inappropriate. As the old cultural structures disintegrate and we struggle to create contemporary substitutes, true "leaders" keep their minds-eye on the post-technological culture yet to come into being. Such a person was R. Buckminster Fuller, who understood that the greatest revolutions in human history are now underway, and he envisioned it as a "geosocial revolution." For Fuller the twentieth century has been a turning point in which unplanned, human inadvertencies in weaponry development have lead to technological spinoffs that could vastly improve the human condition. Fuller points out that the standard of living for average workers in advanced societies has risen from less than 1% for all humanity to 44% within the first two thirds of this century. Because of advances in scientific industrialization, world leaders now can extend that success model to all of humanity.

An inspiring vision is present in the U.S. Declaration of Independence with its emphasis on individual human rights and dignity, and the national goal for government to guard such rights, while ensuring the growth and development of the human person. Perhaps the time has come for world leaders to declare a new "Declaration of Interdependence." Dr. Warren Schmidt sketched a beginning for such a document in his award-winning film, "Is It Right to Be Always Right?":

> All persons are created equal, but each should be permitted to develop in
> a unique way;

> All persons are endowed with certain inalienable rights, but each must
> assume inevitable responsibilities for the happiness of all depends upon
> the commitment of each to support both quality and difference . . .

When such a declaration is completed and acted upon, then adversaries may discover their common beliefs and realize also that "you may be right and I may be wrong." Awareness of our interdependence and need for one another may become the principle by which we can shape our future together.

To conclude this section on global leadership, we turn to Dr. Charles Tavel, Chairman of the Committee on Industrial Innovation in the Organization for Economic Cooperation and Development, who maintains that this "third industrial age" calls for a *strategist*. In complex, interrelated, and interdependent activities, such a person is the brain, the synthesizer who assigns everything to its proper place. Tavel feels that this is one organizational function that cannot be assigned to a group of people, but that the executive strategist must make decisions and take responsibility for them. That strategist not only formulates but implements strategy relative to organizational structures and processes, task assignment, performance and motivation/reward. Furthermore, the corporate or government strategist is a generalist who can promote teamwork among specialists. Tavel believes the character of the strategist implies determination, originality, and commitment to personal and professional accomplishment.

To these observations, we add Peter Drucker's comment that one needs strategies for tomorrow that anticipate the areas in which the greatest changes are likely to occur. Drucker (1980) speaks of developing strategies that enable a business or public service institution to take advantage of the unforseen and unforseeable:

> Planning tries to optimize tomorrow the trends of today. Strategy aims
> to exploit the new and different opportunities of tomorrow.

Readers would be well advised to get on the mailing list for the above IC² seminar announcements, newsletter and publications (2815 San Gabriel, Austin, TX 78705-3594, USA). Request a free subscription to *Leading-edge Technologies,* a report issued three times a year on worldwide developments in high technology. Recent book titles from the Institute include: *Technology Companies and the Global Martketplace; Entrepreneurial Management; Pacific Cooperation & Development.*

SYNERGY THROUGH WORLD TRADE AND DEVELOPMENT

Down through the ages there have always been people characterized as having a "trading culture." Perhaps if we developed an international trading culture, the world economy and the human condition would be the better for it,

and there would be less poverty and war. Cooperative international development would rule out rich nations exploiting poor ones, or technologically advanced peoples draining the resources of less developed members of the human
family to support their own wastefulness. Furthermore, it has always been understood that business flourishes when there is political and economic stability.
As we move into the twenty-first century, prosperity can only be achieved by a
trilateral synergy between business in the form of the transnational corporation, and the home/host governments. Orville Freeman, when at the Business
International Corporation, addressed that theme in another way relative to
"Global Opportunities for Business." He proposed a new synergy between the
industrialized countries mostly in the Northern hemisphere with their management and technological skills, the OPEC nations with their financial power
from oil, and the Third World peoples (mostly in the Southern hemisphere)
with their natural and human resources, as well as consumer needs. To bridge
this "North/South" gap, Freeman called for a global "Marshall" type plan on a
planetary scale for which the multinational corporations would provide the
initiative and infrastructure. Tens of thousands of people in Third World countries are already being developed in business, technology, and management under MNC auspices. The very cost of sending American managers abroad, for
instance, has stimulated the training of Third World indigenous managers.

If synergies such as have been previously suggested could be fostered, then
we might begin to grapple more effectively with the earth's poverty/population
problems. Addressing the 141-nation International Monetary Fund at the turn
of the decade, Robert S. McNamara reminded his audience that one-quarter of
the world's population lives in countries where the per capita income does not
exceed $200 a year. Stepping down as chairman of the World Bank, he spoke of
a sustained attack on poverty as a continuing social responsibility and an economic imperative. During his term of office, McNamara focused on world cooperation to improve the human condition. In the distribution of $12 billion in
international loans, he proved that cooperation can be effective.

Culture also seems to affect high technology exporters and their share of the
world market. Europe, seemingly, is unable to capture and retain these new
markets, despite its scientific breakthroughs. According to Bruno Lam-
borghini, director of economic research at Olivetti, "The problem in Europe is
not lack of technical and scientific knowledge. It is the incapacity of European
industry to transfer this knowledge into new products and enterprises" (*U.S.
News & World Report*, May 27, 1985). This would appear to be partially a
cultural problem. Ray Leonard of U.K.'s Manchester Institute of Science and
Technology argues that European firms view technological innovation as a
danger with problems, rather than an opportunity, whereas the Americans and
Japanese intuitively see the benefits of new technology. Unless such cultural
handicaps are countered, Europe may not take full advantage of some of the
emerging markets to be described next.

Twin Plant Synergy

To contain labor costs, advanced industrialized societies moved overseas in the last three decades to develop partnerships with locals in opening up plants linked to homeland facilities. Some of the high tech computer manufacturers in Silicon Valley, for instance, established chip manufacturing plants in new industrial parks of Taiwan or Singapore. But as these countries progressed economically and workers demanded more compensation or benefits, the offshore enterprises shifted closer to home. A prime example is the *maquiladora* strategy functioning inside Mexico, adjacent to the border with the United States, where laborers are plentiful and less expensive. Today there are over 1,500 such plants operating within the Mexican border region from the Gulf of Mexico to the Pacific Ocean. Many of these Mexican plants would have a U.S. "twin" operation in Texas, Arizona, Nevada, or California. Five hundred of them are in the Tijuana area, south of San Diego, California, employing 60,000 Mexicans.

Maquiladora is an old Mexican term for "production sharing." This innovative program provides an exception to the local law requiring 50% ownership by Mexicans—in such twin plants, restricted to the coastal or border region where construction and operational costs are less than the U.S., the property, buildings and equipment can be 100% foreign-owned by use of a Mexican trust to handle assets and company negotiations. Rudy Fernandez, a director of international services for Touche Ross (1633 Broadway, New York, N.Y. 10019-6754, USA), notes that the tax advantages are described in their free monograph *Mexico Tax & Investment Profile* (1988). Border industrialization encourages manufacturers to assemble products in Mexico and then ship them out, usually to the North American market without the typical duty charges. The synergy occurs by helping the less developed economy through capital investment, job creation, skill development, and technology transfer. Furthermore, Mexican foreign debt may be reduced by "equity swaps" (purchase of debt for 50 cents on the dollar and conversion in peso for investment only in Mexico). Apart from reduction in immigration pressure from Mexicans and stabilizing the political/economic situation in a neighboring country, the advantage to the United States is that no duty is paid on the raw materials, equipment, and technology shipped down to the twin plant, as long as 80% of the products produced are exported. Foreign managers and technicians in Mexico are issued special living and/or work permits for the maquila industry.

The program originated under special provisions of both Mexican and United States law, so that U.S. charges duty only on the value added to the American-made components of goods assembled in Mexico. To gain entry in the U.S. market via Mexico, many other nations, such as Japan, Korea, and Germany, are opening up maquiladora plants and a tricultural environment evolves. A report worth obtaining is *Maquiladoras: Economic Impact and For-*

eign Investment Opportunities—Japanese Maquilas: A Special Case (Bureau of Business Research, University of Texas, c/o IC2, 2815 San Gabriel, Austin, TX 78705, USA). In 1989, for example, the Japanese owned 23 maquila plants in Tijuana, Baja California. Just north at a new U.S. Custom's border crossing in Otay Mesa, there is a high tech industrial park where many of the twin counterpart facilities are located (Otay International Center, 701 B St., Suite 720, San Diego, CA 92101, USA).

Synergy in Market Frontiers

Sensitive leaders, whether in business or industry, government or education, project ahead and seek to begin now to satisfy emerging human needs. There are qualities that metaindustrial managers cultivate, which help us to identify and capitalize upon these growing markets of the future. In Chapter 7, we described some of these characteristics so necessary in the new work culture.*
Apart from synergy, which we have amply discussed, here are three characteristics that are essential for anticipating tomorrow's markets today:

1. *Openness* to new ideas, possibilities, processes and peoples.
2. *Innovation* in solving problems, meeting challenges, and dealing with people.
3. *Creative risk-taking,* so that we dare to try out new markets, to experiment, to probe the unknown.

When authentic leaders employ such creative approaches to management, marketing, and research, then we optimize human capabilities and realize more of our potential (Kaynak, et al, 1984).

It is impossible within the scope of this book to report on all of these future markets, which range from biotechnology to recreation. However, because of their cultural challenges, we summarize the research and thoughts from one of the authors (Harris 1983) on one marketing target of opportunity—the trade shift underway to the Pacific Rim. Global managers would do well to explore this prospect for cultural and economic leadership, as well as profitability:

Pacific Rim Ventures. The new technologies will turn the Pacific Ocean into a lake of commercial exchange. Bounded by Canada, America, and Mexico on the east, and by Australia/New Zealand, Japan, China, Indonesia, and Malaysia on the west, the Pacific's key trading cities will be Hong Kong, Singapore, Tokyo, and possibly Sydney, Manila, Vancouver, Los Angeles, and San Diego.

---

* An *Inventory of Transformation Management Skills* by P. R. Harris is available from Management Research Systems/Talico, Co., 2320 S. Third St., #5, Jacksonville Beach, FL 32250.

Derek Davies, editor of the influential newsmagazine *Far Eastern Economic Review*, observed in a recent interview: "The 21st Century is the Pacific Century. I believe the United States has been blind to this. This place is growing and Europe isn't. This place is more important economically than Europe." According to Davies, Hong Kong is the financial center of the entire geographic area, more active than Tokyo and less regulated than Singapore. He believes that the world's center of economic gravity is shifting to the Trans-Pacific, and he expects a 600 percent expansion of trade, with the Peoples Republic of China to be the focal point. It certainly should be a central endeavor of the metaindustrial work culture, and will pull Micronesia and other Polynesian peoples into the twenty-first century.

Indicators of this promising market are evident in many recent publications:

> *Los Angeles Times* (January 23, 1989)—As the numbers of Asian consumer electronics manufacturers setting up plants in Tijuana continues to grow, so does the roster of U.S. legal and accounting firms trying to grab some of the potentially lucrative multinational business. . . . Perhaps more important, the firms say they provide a buffer between clashing cultures. . . . Luce, Forward, Hamilton & Scripps, one of San Diego's oldest law firms, helped to form the Pacific Rim Advisory Council in 1987, a network of firms representing 1,850 lawyers around the Pacific, the United States, and Canada.

> *The Economist* (January 19, 1985)—Among the fast-growing, noncommunist economies in the Pacific region are the Association of South East Asian Nations (ASEAN).

> *Los Angeles Times* (December 30, 1991)—"Most Asian Nations Are Avoiding Recession"—The newly industrialized economies of Taiwan, South Korea, Hong Kong, and Singapore are likely to continue to see modest growth next year as they spend more on roads and bridges, and buy more, especially from within the region.

Pac Rim—2010. An undated special report of the Futures Research Division of Security Pacific National Bank in Los Angeles observes:

> The positive forces for economic growth and opportunity in this region are large market and varied workforce, abundant raw materials and food supplies, advanced technology created in/by/for the Pacific region, and a developing cultural synergism. We foresee these factors overcoming negative forces in the area such as nationalistic and protectionist sentiments, economic warfare or trade barriers, technological espionage, and other temporary problems.

Then-editors, Hank Koehn and Roger Selbert envisioned that by 2010, the Pacific Basin will be a vast, powerful, interconnected economic and cultural community of 4.5 billion people, over half the world's poulation and 60% of its consumers.

The common theme in such reporting is that the Pacific Ocean is becoming a "highway" that links the countries that rim this waterbody, and that a regional synergy is being forged. The economic synergy centers around abundant markets, human and material resources, enhancing the cultural synergy aided by advanced communications, including information, transportation, and entertainment systems. Its citizens are developing a growing consciousness of community shaped by technology, trade and history.

The reality of all this is appreciated by the U.S. Department of Commerce whose assistant secretary, William Morris, recently told businesspeople that Los Angeles could not become a hub of Pacific trade unless they begin to meet foreign competition, which has cut the U.S. share of the Pacific market down to 33 percent in 1981. He lamented that Taiwan, South Korea, and Hong Kong have followed the Japanese lead into major consumer markets. Richard King, president of King International, reported that trade between Los Angeles and the Pacific Basin amounted to $44 billion in 1981 and should double in the next year. California traditionally has done well in the area by exporting products of aerospace, transportation, metals, chemicals, and instrumentation, but it is agribusiness development and expertise that will be most in demand in Southeast Asia. It is predicted that there will also be a big market for high-technology products and services.

In 1980, at the International Management Seminar of the Pacific Basin Economic Council, futurist Herman Kahn confirmed, "The center of dynamism that used to be in the Mediterranean, and which then moved to northwest Europe and to the North Atlantic, is moving to the Pacific Basin." The full potential of the region can be realized only through cooperation. In the same year, William Kintner, former ambassador to Thailand and president of the Foreign Policy Research Institute, put it another way in a forum on the same theme: The spread of European Western civilization was due primarily to the development of modern science there and nowhere else. Its technology has become a prime mover, bringing peoples of the world into closer contact, as well as being a force for changing political arrangements in the international community. In turn, the United States became the chief instrument of Pacific Basin exchanges and a principal force in the creation of ASEAN. Now new actors, chiefly Japan and China, are promoting social heterogeneity. The spread of both American and Japanese technology could increase the interconnectedness of the region, especially in the area of communications. Trade, tourism, cultural and scientific exchanges, and government and institutional meetings should promote cooperation in the Pacific community.

The countries on the western rim of the Pacific Basin are coming alive to the potential of this unique area. Taiwan's economic planners, for instance, have already launched their own multibillion-dollar, high-technology version of Silicon Valley. They are shifting their economy from labor-intensive to high-technology production. In the Hsinchu Science-Based Industrial Park, 21 companies have put $21 million into development and production, and 12 of these are affiliated with American companies. Their aim by 1990 is 200 firms doing $1 billion in sales and that the endeavor will raise the technological level of all their industry. At the other end of the rim, Canon USA is broadening its push into the American camera market and is typical of the West-East flow of Asian technology. This producer of cameras and copiers uses electronics and optics technology, primarily through robots, and puts 6 percent of sales into R&D annually.

Asian-American business and technological synergy are demonstrated in the success story of H. P. Hwang. A Korean educated in the United States, he revolutionized one part of the American electronics industry and is now worth $100 million. Hwang's Televideo Systems, Inc., of Sunnyvale, California, surged to the forefront of cathode-ray terminal manufacturing. Sales for his CRT's for office and home reached $35 million in fiscal 1981. Hwang has forged a successful business merger between his native and adopted lands. Information technology will link the farflung Pacific peoples together in peace and prosperity.

Within each of the Asian nations, there are specialized markets waiting to be discovered. For example, the senior citizen population is exploding worldwide, but in Japan this is happening at a swifter pace. Some American businesses are already targeting the Japanese elderly who increasingly are living their final years outside the three-generation family. With 14.8% of Japan's 120 million people 65 or older, the potential is incredible. So Beverley Enterprises of Pasadena joined with Shimizu Construction of Tokyo to build retirement housing which is culturally oriented (e.g., pool-like baths). Obviously, this market niche can be expanded to nursing homes, health care and other specialized services.

Atlantic Rim Enterprises

Despite the mania about the Pacific markets, many firms see Europe as their best hope in the near future, especially because of the changes underway (Chapter 16). In its Western countries, that continent has a concentration of some of the most advanced economies and highest living standards in the world. Combined by the EEC agreement of 1992, their economic muscle rivals that of the United States with which they share important cultural and historic ties. The Europeans were the first to invest in the "New World," and the legacy continues for their financial stake in America dwarfs that of Asia—since 1988, Europeans have purchased 319 U.S. firms worth $45.1 billion.

The trade routes to Europe go from both America's East and West Coasts. A 1988 study of the California State World Trade Commission revealed that Europe as a key market for California exports had been underestimated—$1/3$ of that state's goods and services are shipped across the Atlantic Ocean, while under half go to Asia (*Los Angeles Times*, April 30, 1989). Nationally, the U.S. Department of Commerce reports $86.8 billion worth of exports to Western Europe for 1988. No wonder the European community's creation of a genuinely common market is also attracting Asian investors and exporters. Ford aerospace executive, Kenneth Hollander, observes: "U.S. companies that don't show interest in what is going on in Europe right now are going to be left out." For business in Europe is a new game requiring organizational consolidations and streamlining, altered regulations and distribution systems, language translations and communication technologies, financial and marketing transformations. Furthermore, as previously indicated, Eastern Europe is also in transition, and there are new opportunities to trade there and to form joint ventures within formerly Second World socialist countries.

Global Opportunities

Throughout these chapters, we have been referring to an ongoing process of globalization, whether in terms of management, markets, or economics. It is evident in all industries, trades, professions, and fields, even music. In a Public Broadcasting television special on the phenomenon (September 29, 1989), the MacNeil-Lehrer Report noted the homogenization of world culture by "pop culture" versus cultural diversity. Among the principal forces contributing to this global consciousness, even with reference to the planet's ecology and environment, are advances in transportation and especially communication. Both product and service corporations are discovering that they take advantage of economies of scale with a global, not local, market. Joseph N. Pelton describes how the global electronic machine in communications is redefining work and world economies by functioning on a 168-hour workweek throughout the year (*The Futurist*, Sept.-Oct. 1989). Converging technologies are not only displacing workers by automation and robotics, but Pelton sees them creating a new type of global worker—"electronic immigrants" who move their minds, not their bodies, over great distances. Thus, these telecommuters can be recruited and trained in relatively cheaper labor markets—like the Caribbean, the Philippines, India, or China. Cross-cultural issues arise in the assessment, development and management of such remote personnel, as well as in their input into computer programming, word processing, and telemarketing.

Unchecked, Pelton fears "telecolonies" of these immigrants whose local finance and politics are controlled by overseas capital. On the positive side, Pelton points to telepower techniques in education, health, and social services that can care for rural and remote areas at lower cost. He cites the tele-education innovations by the University of the South Pacific and the University of the

West Indies with reference to teleconferencing, data sharing, and the like. This director of the Advanced Telecommunications Center at the University of Colorado (Boulder, CO 80309, USA) thinks telepower is designing a new fate for our species by interlocking global consciousness.

The chief executive officer of the American Management Association, Thomas R. Horton, believes that to win in the global market, everyone must learn to think in a global context, and that communications is key to creating such awareness, so as to benefit from the ideas and efforts of people within the global village. For this purpose, the United States is developing a new electronic superhighway for high performance data transmissions, and the world is creating a new cultural norm that all new technology be designed to enhance consciousness. To keep abreast of technology applications in global business, request the *PRTM Insight* newsletter and special publications of High Technology and Manufacturing Practices, KPMG Peat Marwick (303 East Wacker Drive, Chicago, IL 60601, USA).

SUMMARY

High performance in the new work culture requires individual and institutional cooperation because of the complexity of our times and the explosion of information. Whether in nations, regions, organizations, or teams, this necessitates the cultivation of a synergistic culture. With the globalization of knowledge, economies, and markets, cross-cultural competence becomes essential. Such skills help us in coping with changing transnational corporate and work environments, with environmental scanning and forecasting, with understanding of foreign and emerging markets, especially in the Third World.

Global managers can exercise a synergistic role in this process and improve their international performance through greater effectiveness with cultural differences. Manifold opportunities to apply such insight exist with ethnic and minority groups at home, especially in management and marketing; with the selection, preparation, support and evaluation of expatriate personnel; with a cosmopolitan approach to business development abroad. In an interdependent world, metaindustrial executives are expected to exercise such collaborative leadership not only in improving the human condition, but the performance of the planet's citizens.

World trade is both a learning laboratory and a mechanism for doing this. Peaceful and cooperative free enterprise on an international basis contributes not only to global economic development, but can reduce the North/South gap in terms of poverty and population. The export/import exchange, particularly of information and new technologies, fosters political and social stability, as well as human resource development. Among the healthy related trends in this regard is the growth of multinational cooperatives, joint ventures, and entrepreneurial activities.

Tomorrow's market frontiers, both global and interplanetary, are being probed today by innovators. One such market, the Pacific Basin, was discussed here and at the end of Chapter 15. Another is the emerging market of space industrialization (Harris, 1992). Observing the 500th anniversary of Columbus' voyage in 1992, we too are exploring another New World. Open, creative risk-takers and top performers are needed now to confront the new market and cultural challenges.

Epilogue

In the cultural model, the purpose of development changes and is measured by more than economic growth. . . . Now development is also to be judged by the effect it has on people in terms of changes in their life-style, their attitudes, their health, their level of education, their power to choose for themselves the kind of life-style they want to lead, and their relationship with their environment.

Development cooperation must first start with understanding people:

- Whose beliefs we may not share, but must respect.
- Whose cultures and societies may demand different patterns of economic and social development.
- Who may refuse to accept our own beliefs and assumptions.
- Who may or may not share our own views on equitable distribution of wealth within their national borders.
- Who may not have forgotten hundreds of years of colonial domination, and may be suspicious of our motives even when we believe our intentions are pure.
- Who may be struggling to free themselves from some part of their cultural past. *

Culture is the key to comprehending human behavior and civilizations. It is the application to local circumstances of our capacity to adapt to the rhythm of sun, moon, and tides; to the realities of nature's offerings in terms of geography, climate, and creature life. To survive, we adopt themes, patterns, and practices of living within the metronomic structures of day and night, heat and cold, food and water. For our species, the process began when our ancestors climbed down from the trees and walked upright, and continues as astronauts alter earth culture to fit the challenges of outer space. To improve human performance and the quality of life, analyze and alter the cultures of your teams and groups, organizations and nations.

---

* From an address on "The Intercultural Dialogue: Cornerstone of Development" presented to the Annual Conference of the Society for Intercultural, Education, Training and Research International on March 12, 1981 by Marcel Masse, President of the Canadian International Development Agency.

Unit IV
Management Resources and Services for Global Professionals

Appendix A
"So, You're Going Abroad" Survey*

Part I   — Pre-deployment Area Questionnaire
Part II — Overseas Position and Company Policies Inventory
Part III — International Living Questionnaire
Part IV — Rating Scale on Successful Expatriate Qualities
Part V   — Family Pre-departure Checklist

Instructions

This survey is intended for use by a global manager who is planning to go abroad on an extensive foreign assignment. The assumption is that there will be a sponsoring organization, such as a multinational corporation, voluntary agency, international foundation, or government organization. It provides comprehensive coverage of key issues to be confronted, and the information to be obtained prior to departure abroad. Should the potential expatriate have dependents or family that will be accompanying him or her overseas, then they should be involved in the relocation preparation. Sometimes the sponsoring organization will provide professional assistance for this purpose, or at least pay for the expenses involved when manager and family have to have recourse to external resources for this foreign deployment consultation.

The administration of this survey is best accomplished over a six-month period. Part I, for example, on area and cultural information might be completed some months in advance of deployment. Part II involving corporate relocation negotiation should be completed several months before departure. Part III contains questions on international living that the family should explore together at least two months before going overseas. Part IV and V are a final review that should be completed by the final month in the planning process. The contents

* Based largely on the research of Robert T. Moran, Ph.D., that was incorporated in a copyrighted booklet (1980), *So You're Going Abroad—Are You Prepared?* which is available for quantity use from Intercultural Communications, Inc. (Minneapolis, MN. 55414, U.S.A.). This revised survey format was edited by Philip R. Harris, Ph.D. Individual contributions of others have been acknowledged. The authors particularly wish to cite the work of the late John M. Hoffman, an esteemed colleague, who founded Family Relocations Services, Inc., on whose board they served.

of Chapters 8, 9, and 10 should be particularly helpful for these specific preparations. Many parts of this survey will also prove useful to the manager or technician going abroad on a short-term assignment or business trip.

PART 1—PRE-DEPLOYMENT AREA QUESTIONNAIRE

• Name of target country/culture _____

The following questions will be useful in your preparation for an overseas living or working experience. These questions are not intended to cover every situation, but will serve as a basis for gathering information which will assist your successful entry into another culture. After you have checked the appropriate reply in the box at the right column, put in the correct information in the space provided. If you do not know the answer, search out the information.

General Considerations

	YES	NO
1. Do you have a clear idea of the purpose of your trip or assignment?	( )	( )
2. Do you know the names and responsibilities of the people you will be meeting?	( )	( )
3. Will these people you meet be in a position to make decisions relative to your assignment?	( )	( )
4. Do you know anything about their background?	( )	( )

5. There are many prominent contemporary and historical people of whom the country is proud. Can you name one of each?

	Contemporary	Historical
Leadership/Celebrities	( )	( )
A Politician	( )	( )
A Poet	( )	( )
A Philosopher/Intellectual	( )	( )
A Musician	( )	( )
A Writer	( )	( )
An Actor/Actress	( )	( )
A Radio/TV Broadcaster	( )	( )
An Inventor	( )	( )
A Religious Leader	( )	( )
An Artist	( )	( )
A Sports Figure/Athlete	( )	( )
A Business/Corporate Leader	( )	( )

Politics

		YES	NO
6.	Can you identify current, prominent political leaders and their titles?	( )	( )
7.	Do you know the names of the political parties and their beliefs, functions, and symbols?	( )	( )
8.	Are you able to describe the political process or system of government?	( )	( )
9.	Do you know the name of the parliament or legislature?	( )	( )
10.	Do you know if there is a form of chief executive in the country?	( )	( )
11.	Do you know how political power is delegated?	( )	( )
12.	Do you know who the "interest groups" are and how they express their concerns?	( )	( )
13.	Is the payment of special fees (bribery) a part of the business system?	( )	( )
14.	Are women allowed to vote and hold public office?	( )	( )
15.	Is politics an appropriate topic for conversation?	( )	( )

The Country

		YES	NO
16.	Do you know the geopolitical divisions of this country? Is the country divided into states, provinces, counties or some other way? How many? Name them.	( )	( )
17.	Can you name the principal cities?	( )	( )
	The population?	( )	( )
	The main industries?	( )	( )
18.	Are you familiar with the country's basic culture and history? Date of independence? Relationship to other countries?	( )	( )

Non-Verbal Communication

(65% of the meaning of a message is communicated non-verbally)

		YES	NO
19.	Are you aware of non-verbal forms of communications in your native land?	( )	( )

20. Are there any non-verbal behavior patterns you use   ( ) ( )
    which may be interpreted as "offensive" in this country
    (e.g., the A-O.K. gesture is obscene in Brazil)?

21. Can you anticipate some possible miscommunication   ( ) ( )
    problems? If so, identify a few here:

22. Are you aware of the host culture's non-verbal behavior ( ) ( )
    or communication pattern?

23. Do you know when it is appropriate to cry? Or to   ( ) ( )
    express other emotions?

24. Do you know what the appropriate speaking distance is ( ) ( )
    between persons who are getting to know each other in
    a social context? In a business context?

Daily Life

	YES	NO

25. Do you know what some routine courtesies are that you ( ) ( )
    should observe?

26. Do you know how people greet each other? Foreigners? ( ) ( )

27. Do you know how people say "good-bye"?   ( ) ( )

28. Do you know if gift-giving is a custom? (What kind of ( ) ( )
    gift is appropriate for what particular occasion? Are
    gifts opened in the presence of the giver or later in
    privacy?)

29. Do colors connotate certain meanings? (What about the ( ) ( )
    color of flowers? Is there a particular significance to a
    certain number of flowers?)

30. Are you familiar with their work practices? (How many ( ) ( )
    days per week do people work? What days? What
    hours? Are business and social conversations mixed?)

31. Is alcohol permitted? (What about non-alcoholic   ( ) ( )
    beverages and their place in the business and social
    environment?)

32. Do you know their recreational or leisure-time   ( ) ( )
    practices? (How do classes or groups of people spend
    their free time?)

33. Do you know where you will find the   ( ) ( )
    intellectual/social/recreational stimulation that you
    need?

34. Are you familiar with the media situation? (Is television ( ) ( )
available? Movies? If so, what kinds of each? What
kind of newspapers and magazines will be available to
you and in what languages?)

Religion

	YES	NO
35. Is there a state religion? (Are other religions tolerated? If so, how many religions are there and what are some of the major beliefs and practices?)	( )	( )
36. Do you know how religion influences the people?	( )	( )
37. Do you know what the religious holidays are?	( )	( )
38. Do you know what some differences are between your religious beliefs and the beliefs of the religion(s) of the host country?	( )	( )

Social Structure

	YES	NO
39. Do you know what the class or caste divisions are?	( )	( )
40. Do you know if people generally employ servants? (And what their place is?)	( )	( )
41. Is discrimination recognizable in the social structure? (If so, against whom?)	( )	( )
42. Does dress reflect social or economic status?	( )	( )
43. Do you know what the nature of social mobility is? Are people in the host culture able to move up in social class?	( )	( )
44. Has the experience of colonialism or foreign domination affected class structure? (Or the attitude toward foreigners?)	( )	( )
45. Is there intergroup friction? (If so, is it serious enough as to be a danger to your family? What precautions would then be necessary?)	( )	( )
46. Do you know what the major occupations of people are?	( )	( )
47. Do you know what the size of the average family is?	( )	( )
48. Is there an "extended" family? (If so, what are the roles of the various members?)	( )	( )

49. Is family planning widely practiced? (Are there   ( )   ( )
    government policies on population control?)

50. Do you know the pattern of social roles and   ( )   ( )
    relationships? (What qualities constitute a good
    husband? Wife? Daughter? Son? Grandparent?
    Businessman? Businesswoman? Foreign Businessman?
    Foreign Businesswoman? Guest? Neighbor?)

51. Is the "group" more important than any "individual"   ( )   ( )
    member of that group?

53. Do you know to whom people go for advice regarding   ( )   ( )
    their different problems?

Education

	YES	NO
54. Do you know the educational level and practices there? (Is education free? Compulsory? How many years of attendance is required?)	( )	( )
55. Are you able to compare their educational system to yours? (What are some advantages and disadvantages?)	( )	( )
56. Do you know how the discipline of children is administered at school? (At home? By whom? What implications does this have for adult behavior?)	( )	( )

Roles of Men and Women

	YES	NO
57. Are female and male children equally desired?	( )	( )
58. Do they share equally? (Are they delegated similar responsibilities?)	( )	( )
59. Are there differences between male and female roles in business? (Do women have positions in all areas of responsibility?)	( )	( )

Business Customs

	YES	NO
60. Do you know what the most important elements of success are? (e.g., salary? title? power? etc.)	( )	( )
61. Is there a strong "task orientation"? (e.g., work is more important than relationships)	( )	( )

62. Do you know what some of the dominant business values are? (e.g., competition, etc.)   ( ) ( )

63. Do you know what determines whether you will succeed or fail in business?   ( ) ( )

64. Do you know if it is customary to invite business colleagues to your home? (Will such an invitation be reciprocated? Are thank you notes to be written after a dinner invitation? For other occasions?)   ( ) ( )

65. Do you know the time customs for appointments? (Should you be "on time" or "late" for a business or social occasion? Should invitations be specific as to time and day or general?)   ( ) ( )

66. Do you know in what situations you behave formally or informally?   ( ) ( )

67. Do you know how you expose an error to a colleague?   ( ) ( )

68. Do you know how a reward is given? (Is an increase in pay an incentive to work harder?)   ( ) ( )

69. Do you know how people are motivated in the host culture?   ( ) ( )

70. Do you know ways to persuade effectively in this culture?   ( ) ( )

Food

	YES	NO
71. Do you know what kinds of food are eaten and any health hazards for you?	( )	( )
72. Are you expected to eat all foods?	( )	( )
73. Will you be expected to drink the local beverage?	( )	( )
74. Are you familiar with their dining practices? (Is cooking considered an art?)	( )	( )
75. What rules govern dining at a restaurant? (What determines who pays?)	( )	( )

Mass Communication

	YES	NO
76. Are you familiar with their mass communication policies? (Which newspapers are most popular? Is censorship practiced?)	( )	( )

77. Are books of all subject matters generally available?   ( ) ( )
78. Do you know what the government's attitude toward   ( ) ( )
    the media is? (Is freedom of public expression carefully
    controlled?)

Health

	YES	NO

79. Do you know what medical facilities are available?   ( ) ( )
    (What is their state in terms of modern medical
    practice?)
80. Do you know what preventive measures are necessary   ( ) ( )
    to maintain good health? (Have you checked with
    professionals yet on what injections and health practices
    you must observe in the host culture? For example, is it
    a malaria area?)

Humor

	YES	NO

81. Do you know what kind of humor is understood and   ( ) ( )
    appreciated?
82. Do you know what the elements of a good story or tale   ( ) ( )
    are in this culture?
83. Is odd behavior considered amusing?   ( ) ( )

Their Attitude Toward You

	YES	NO

84. Do you know currently what is the relationship   ( ) ( )
    between this country and yours? (At present? In the
    past 10 years? Expected to be in the next 5 years?)
85. Are people of your nationality liked? (If generally   ( ) ( )
    disliked in this culture, what are some reasons?)
86. Is there a large expatriate group? (Do they live in a   ( ) ( )
    "ghetto" or self-contained colony?)
87. Do you know generally what your host's attitude will   ( ) ( )
    be towards you?
88. Are you aware of what your attitude toward the host   ( ) ( )
    people will be? (Do you feel superior? Inferior?)
89. Have you identified what concerns you most and least   ( ) ( )
    about this assignment?

90. When you experience "culture shock" will you recognize the symptoms? ( ) ( )

91. When you return home, do you think you will have changed? ( ) ( )

92. To better prepare for this cross-cultural experience, what other important questions should you consider?

Action Plans

When you have reflected on these questions and searched for the answers, you are now better prepared to effectively work with people who have a different history customs, and values from your own.

Review the items in the 92 inquiries that were checked no. Then outline a specific series of tasks or activities for yourself that will better qualify for this overseas assignment (for example, what would be considered an adequate lifestyle or program for you and your family to follow in the host culture so as to maintain mental and physical fitness?).

(NOTE: if your company or organization does not supply the assistance of relocation services, you may wish to inquire externally about such consultants.)

PART II—OVERSEAS POSITION AND COMPANY POLICIES

Some basic information about the position and company policies is needed so the family can reasonably measure the advantages and disadvantages of the international assignment. The following list is a general outline of questions that should be answered with your company. Space is provided for notes to facilitate review with your family. This section was contributed by the late John M. Hoffman.

The Position?

What it is: _____

Objectives and goals: _____

Reporting relationships: _____

Overseas: _____

With the U.S.: _____

Estimated length of assignment: _____

Future career possibilities: _____

Other: _____

Compensation & Benefit Policy?

Salary: _____

Status of home country programs: _____

Special allowances: _____

Housing: _____

Schooling: _____

Living costs: _____

Transportation in the new country: _____

Vacation and home leave: _____

Taxes: _____

Repatriation assistance: _____

Other: _____

Preparation Required for the Assignment?

Professional training: _____

Language training: _____

Cultural orientation: _____

Introductory trip: _____

Other: _____

Relocation Policy?

Home country residence and personal property: _____

Travel allowances: _____

Shipping and storage: _____

Relocation assistance overseas: _____

Other: _____

Travel Preparations?

Tentative departure dates: _____

Visa requirements: _____

Medical exams for family: _____

Other: _____

Special needs your family may have. It's better to be up front with special needs rather than bring them up at a later date. For example, if you are a two-career family and your spouse needs job hunting assistance abroad; or, if you have a physically or mentally handicapped dependent, and need special assistance for travel and living abroad for that child. Such matters should be part of your negotiations. In all of the previous items which require a financial expenditure, who pays? Does corporate relocation policy provide compensation for such expenditures?

In discussions or negotiations with company representatives, often from the personnel department or human resources, bear in mind the following considerations.

Negotiation Considerations

- In the past, it was common to negotiate individual compensation and benefit programs. Today, most companies are standardizing these programs.
- How well you do financially overseas will depend on how well you manage your income. Cost of living allowances are usually calculated on the cost of a mixture of local and imported products. The ability to shop wisely, with a high level of local products, will save money and probably permit you to live well within the allowances.
- Depending on your income, all, or part, of your salary may be exempted from your home country income taxes. You will, however, be subject to the tax laws of the country of assignment. If this is a low tax country, taxes will be minimal or nil. If it is a high tax country, your liability could be substantial. To solve this problem most companies establish tax equalization or tax protection programs for their expatriate employees. Be sure to understand your company's tax policy.

- Buying a home in a soft currency country for a short term assignment usually leads to troubles and financial loss. For almost all overseas assignments, rental housing is the answer.
- Work and residence visas are becoming harder to get. Many countries take three months or more to process applications, so start as soon as possible.
- High costs cause many companies to set limitations on the amount of personal effects an employee can take overseas. The average cost of relocating a family of four to and from an international assignment is $125,000.
- Because of the high costs of maintaining Americans abroad, many companies are replacing Americans overseas with nationals of other countries.
- Given issues of inflation and taxation, it is wise to consult an accountant familiar with international business finances, or the free Price Waterhouse Information Guide on *U.S. Citizens Abroad* and *U.S. Expatriate Compensation*, 1251 Ave. of the Americas, N.Y., N.Y. 10019, USA.
- Given the state of civil unrest and terrorism on the international front, a new factor to be included may be security precautions to prevent kidnappings and other violence against global managers and their families.

PART III—INTERNATIONAL LIVING QUESTIONNAIRE

Specialists in relocation have determined that global managers and their families should seek satisfactory answers to these sixteen questions before undertaking an international assignment:

1. How will living abroad affect this family, both as a group and individually?
2. What adjustment problems will the adults and children likely have, and will they be able to cope with them?
3. What assistance is likely to be available to help us get started in the new country and strange environment?
4. Will this move advance our personal and professional development (e.g., career(s))?
5. Will we be safe, and what security precautions are essential?
6. Will we be affected by anti-Americanism? (If so, what strategies should then be employed as citizen ambassadors?)
7. What about our home and personal property while we are abroad?
8. What is our life-style likely to be like in this different environment?
9. How will we socialize abroad (e.g., make friends)?
10. What about our children's education?
11. Is it likely that both spouses will be able to work abroad? (If not, what are the alternatives for the other's career?)
12. What about our health and family emergencies while abroad?
13. What about culture shock and its impact on our lives?
14. How will the local nations respond to us?

15. Can we take or acquire pets abroad? (If we take them, then what are the procedures and regulations at the foreign site?)
16. What are the best, basic preparations that we can take to ensure success in this international assignment?

PART IV—RATING SCALE ON SUCCESSFUL EXPATRIATE QUALITIES*

Directions:

The following list of qualities have been identified in the management literature as being associated with success in an overseas environment. Consider the list and rate the degree to which you possess each quality on a scale of 1 (low), 3 (moderate), or 5 (high). Also ask a colleague to rate you. This will give you an overview of some of your strengths and liabilities and your likelihood of success.

Qualities	Self Rating	Colleague Rating
Technical skill/competence for assignment		
Resourcefulness/resilience		
Comprehension of complex relationships		
Adaptability/flexibility		
Emotional stability		
Ability to deal with ambiguity/uncertainty/differences		
Desire to work overseas and with people who are different		
Adaptability of your spouse and family		
Willingness of your spouse to live abroad		
Stability of marriage and family life		
Management skills applicable to another culture		
Administrative skills suitable for another culture		
Communication skills in another culture		
Successful domestic career performance		
Language ability for host culture		
Cultural empathy/sensitivity		
Cultural specific knowledge		
Interest in host culture		
Ability to get along with host nationals		
Tolerance of others' views, especially when they differ from your own		
Sensitivity to attitudes and feelings of others		
Good health and wellness		

---

* Adapted from a list developed by Paul W. Russell and Terry L. Dickinson from the management literature on the subject of Overseas Success and Adaptation.

List below your personal qualities which may cause difficulty for you in your overseas assignment.

_____

_____

List below practical steps to overcome or counteract such difficulties.

_____

_____

List below your personal strengths for an international assignment.

_____

_____

List specific steps you can take to capitalize upon these personal assets.

_____

_____

PART V—FAMILY PRE-DEPARTURE CHECKLIST

The following checklist has been modified from materials prepared by Robert T. Moran and Helen L. McNulty, Intercultural Communications, Inc., Minneapolis, Minnesota. Each item should be considered and when completed or prepared check (✔) the item. A space is included for other items you may wish to include.

Item	Check (✔) When Completed
Obtain passport	_____
Passport for spouse	_____
Passport for each accompanying child	_____
Visas (if required)	_____
Medical examination (review itinerary and immunizations to prevent diseases)	_____
Copies of any important records required abroad	_____
Prescriptions for medicines	_____
Each person's blood type for family	_____
Inquire about gamma globulin and other travel shots	_____
Inquire about the antibiotic "doxycycline" to thwart diarrhea (bring an antacid medication with you)	_____
Copies of eyeglass prescriptions	_____
Extra pair of glasses	_____

Dental appointments for each family member (consider
    fluoride treatments for children and emergency dental
    medication)   _____
Veterinarian for required shots and certificates if taking a
    pet   _____
Legal appointment so that each adult member of the family
    should have an up-to-date will. Arrange to draw up
    power of attorney to relative/friend at home   _____
Appointment with travel agent to plan round-trip itinerary:
    Reservations   _____
Review overseas and domestic tax needs with accountant   _____
Appointment with a personal banking consultant to discuss
    your financial needs   _____
Place important records, power of attorney, etc., in your
    safety deposit box   _____
Notify the children's teachers of departure date   _____
Request sufficient grade reports, test results, teacher
    evaluations, samples of work, etc.   _____
Arrange for adequate insurance for household effects   _____
Get appropriate health insurance coverage   _____
Remember to fill out change of address cards that you can
    get from the local post office   _____
With a personal shopper in a department store, plan for
    future needs of your family (items to be shipped or
    carried which may not be available abroad)   _____
Check absentee voting procedure and register   _____
Obtain an international driver's license from American
    Automobile Association   _____
Give notice of your moving date to all utility
    companies—gas, oil, water, electricity, telephone   _____
Keep records of official expenses involved in the move   _____
Pick up transportation tickets and confirm reservations   _____

Appendix B
Questionnaire on Cross-Cultural Management*

In the statements that follow, please circle the number that accurately represents the extent to which you agree with either the statement on the left or the statement on the right:

Circle 1—if you *agree strongly* with the statement on the left
   2—if you *agree* with the statement on the left
   3—if you are somewhat indifferent, but tend to agree more with the statement on the left
   4—if you are somewhat indifferent, but tend to agree more with the statement on the right
   5—if you *agree* with the statement on the right
   6—if you *agree strongly* with the statement on the right

Circle only *one* number for each question.

---

* Designed by George W. Renwick and Stephen H. Rhinesmith as *An Exercise in Cultural Analysis for Managers* (Intercultural Press, Inc., P.O. Box 768, Yarmouth, ME 04096, U.S.A.). Reprinted with permission.

Planning, Evaluating, Innovating

Harmony. When planning, evaluating and innovating there should be an attempt to take into consideration the way things are and to initiate change only within the context of the social order and the order which nature has established in the universe.

1 2 3 4 5 6

Control. Individuals and organizations should constantly set goals, plan actions to accomplish goals, develop means to evaluate progress toward these goals, and initiate changes when old ways cannot meet new demands.

Past. Plans should be based upon, and evaluated in terms of, the customs and traditions of the organization and society. Innovation and change are justified only to the degree that precedent can be found in the past for the new action.

1 2 3 4 5 6

Future. Plans should be based upon, and evaluated in terms of, the projected future benefit to be gained from a specific activity. Innovation and change are justified in terms of future payoffs with little regard for customs and traditions.

Abstract. Plans should be made and evaluated in terms of general, abstract, social, and moral values that are used as the yardstick for measuring man's activities in his personal life and in organizations. Innovation and change must be justified in terms of these social and moral values.

1 2 3 4 5 6

Concrete. Plans should be made and evaluated in terms of concrete, quantifiable results that can be measured and compared against other individual and organizational performance to determine competitiveness and effectiveness.

Limited Good. Plans should be based upon the recognition that the resources necessary for, as well as the benefits to be gained from, individual or organizational activity are *limited*; i.e., these resources and benefits exist in finite quantity and cannot be obtained without "taking an equal amount of good" from others.

1 2 3 4 5 6

Unlimited Good. Plans should be based upon the recognition that the resource necessary for, as well as the benefits to be gained from, individual and organizational activity are *unlimited*; i.e., these resources and benefits exist in infinite quantity and can be obtained by everyone to the extent that they are willing to seek, develop and utilize them.

Wisdom. The older personnel in the organization should be given as much or more respect than the younger ones. The older personnel, because of their experience and perspective, should be trusted and relied upon for advice, sound planning and direction.

1   2   3   4   5   6

Energy. More attention should be paid to the younger personnel in an organization than to the older personnel. Because they know more about current problems and modern techniques of dealing with them, the younger personnel should be relied upon for dynamic planning and direction.

Organizing and Controlling

Collectivity. Organizational structure and controls should emphasize group and organizational needs with little concern for the individual. A high degree of organizational control should be maintained in order to maximize organizational solidarity against any potentially disruptive individuals. Emphasis should be upon organizational loyalty and years of service.

1   2   3   4   5   6

Individualism. Organizational structure and controls should emphasize individual growth and development within the organization. There should be high concern for job satisfaction. If necessary, organizational structures and controls may be altered to meet individual need preferences and interests. Emphasis should be upon individual freedom.

Dependence. Authority and responsibility should be centralized. Organizational structure should be tightly organized and controlled, and should require high conformity and adherence to a strict set of rules and regulations in order to ensure individual conformity.

1   2   3   4   5   6

Independence. Authority and responsibility should be decentralized. Organizational structure should be loose, and should require little control over individual performance. Emphasis should be upon self-reliance and upon individual accountability for decision and results.

Recruiting, Selecting, Rewarding

Affiliation. Strong emphasis should be placed on recruiting and selecting persons who are compatible with persons already in the organization. Rewards should be given in the form of personal praise and support with emphasis upon loyalty and personal leadership.

1 2 3 4 5 6

Achievement. Emphasis should be placed on recruiting and selecting persons who have unique accomplishments and are highly skilled in areas of organizational need. Persons should be rewarded with more challenging and complex tasks and greater responsibility which motivates them to work against inner standards of excellence.

Ascription. Social and family background should be stressed in recruiting and selecting personnel. Rewards should be given to those related to family, caste or social connections.

1 2 3 4 5 6

Achievement. Unusual competence, accomplishments, and highly developed skills necessary to the organization should be sought in recruiting and selecting personnel. Rewards should be given to those who perform best under competitive conditions.

Leadership

External. Because of man's dislike for work, he must be coerced, controlled, directed or threatened with punishment to get him to put forth adequate effort toward achieving organizational objectives.

1 2 3 4 5 6

Internal. The threat of punishment and external control are not the only means of getting people to work toward organizational objectives. Men will exercise self-direction and self-control toward achieving objectives to which they are committed.

Communication

One-Way. Information should flow down through the hierarchy of the organization in the form of orders and directives which are not questioned by subordinates.

1　2　3　4　5　6

Two-Way. Information should flow both up and down through the organization with subordinates suggesting alternatives to their superiors and testing alternatives in order to arrive at the best decision.

Indirect. When one has opinions and complaints to express, it is best to join with others and let representatives present the views.

1　2　3　4　5　6

Direct. Opinions and demands should be presented to one's superiors in person. An individual should be known to hold the views he does and should accept responsibility for them.

Interpersonal Relations

Hierarchical. Protocol and codes to regulate interpersonal relations are extremely important; persons must observe a strict separation between different levels in the hierarchy.

1　2　3　4　5　6

Egalitarian. While a pattern of relating to one another across authority levels and different functions exists, it should be flexible; persons should be encouraged to alter formal relationships when necessary to meet the needs of the situation.

Relationship Between Work and Social Life

Integrated. Little distinction should be made between social relationships and work relationships. Friendships should easily cross the line between work and social life.

1　2　3　4　5　6

Separated. There should be much concern for separation of work and social relations. Care should be taken to avoid "conflicts of interests" and to avoid personal obligations that might affect job performance.

Problem-solving

Abstract. Problem-solving should be approached from the perspective of a system of theories and principles. As problems arise, they should be classified under well-known principles and the solution is automatically indicated. The Managerial challenge lies in the proper classification of problems as they arise.

1 2 3 4 5 6

Concrete. Problem-solving should be approached from a concrete perspective with emphasis upon a cost-benefit analysis of alternative solutions. The managerial challenge lies in formulating the alternative solution and choosing among them based upon their future operational consequences.

Decision-making

Being. The primary concern should be expression. Criteria for decision-making should be based upon the degree to which the results will allow the manager to express his or her personality.

1 2 3 4 5 6

Doing. The primary concern should be achievement. Criteria for decision-making should be based upon the degree to which the results will allow the manager to achieve goals that are measurable and valued by society.

Negotiating

Autocratic. Negotiating strategies should be based upon management's assumption that subordinates have little to contribute to organizational decisions and no right to make demands on management or the organization.

1 2 3 4 5 6

Collaborative. Negotiating strategies should be based upon management's assumption that subordinates share equal interests, organizational goals and success; they should be consulted on major organizational decisions in order to reach a total organizational consensus.

Managing Conflict

Smoothing. Organizational and interpersonal conflict may be recognized, but there should be little attempt to carry through an analysis of the conflict for management or resolution. Conflicts, if concentrated upon and dealt with directly, are seldom resolved to anyone's satisfaction.

1   2   3   4   5   6

Confrontation. Organizational and interpersonal conflicts should be identified and dealt with directly. Their causes should be diagnosed and plans should be made for their management or disolution. All problems can be overcome with concerted effort on the part of the individuals involved.

Training

Cognitive. Training should take place in highly structured situations in which the supervisor or instructor explains facts and theories which the trainee should know; the trainee should listen and attempt to remember what he is taught.

1   2   3   4   5   6

Experiential. Training should involve actual experience. One learns from experience through reflection, generalization and further testing in order to determine what lesson or principles are are transferable to other cases or situations. The trainee takes much responsibility for his own learning, depending upon his particular needs and interests.

Note: Analyze the profile which emerges on your managerial perspectives based upon the above data, and ascertain the significance of cultural influences upon your leadership philosophy.

Appendix C
Intercultural Relations Inventory*

Introduction:

This inventory is best used in conjunction with the model presented in Chapter 8 for analyzing a culture, whether it be macro or micro. The facilitator may wish to use it in one of three ways. First, with global managers or technicians who are going abroad on a foreign assignment. The culture contrast exercise permits the respondent to compare a host culture with his or her home culture on nine major dimensions, and then to analyze what problems may occur as a result of the cultural differences (Part 1). For example, it could be used by a North American company to study the culture of a foreign subsidiary or joint venture. Secondly, in a domestic situation, a manager may compare his or her cultural background with that of subordinates (Part 2). This is especially helpful for male managers of women, or a supervisor of a minority or ethnic group. Thirdly, these forms can be adapted for personnel at home who are being managed by a foreigner, or who have a foreigner on a project team (as frequently happens in the high technology firms).

Although the inventory is filled out on an individual basis, it is best used as a learning experience in a small group situation. By using an overhead projector, blackboard, or flip chart, members of a training team can summarize their individual perceptions of the two cultures being analyzed, and try to come to some consensus, stimulating them to seek more specific cultural information.

PART 1—INTERCULTURAL RELATIONS INVENTORY FOR AN AMERICAN ABROAD

Situation: You are a representative of an American corporation abroad. You are in the process of developing a contract with a representative of a company in another nation to produce your product or services for that country. Your firm is to provide the basic guidelines and parts for your copyrighted product/

* © Philip R. Harris/Harris International, 1984. Short version available in quantity from Management Research Systems/Talico, Co.

service, the assembly and delivery is to be done by your foreign counterpart for his people. Assume that the other country is (a) in Latin America, such as Mexico or Brazil; or (b) in Asia, such as Japan or Indonesia; or (c) in Europe, such as France or Hungary.

Directions: (1) In about five minutes note your observations on the items below in view of the situation presented. (2) Share your insights with your group members and try to arrive at some consensus.

Indicate here the national or cultural Group whose behavior you will be comparing _____.

Contrast your culture with the other in terms of the categories below. List briefly some of the characteristics of each to be considered in this new business relationship. Use back side of this form if necessary.

Foreign/Host Culture

1. Communication style (non-verbal and verbal, as well as the language of business):

   _____

   _____

2. Food and diet:

   _____

   _____

3. Clothing (especially business dress):

   _____

   _____

4. Time sense:

   _____

   _____

5. Values and business ethics:

   _____

   _____

6. Work habits and practices:

   _____

   _____

7. Attitudes/practices with "minority" workers:

   _____

   _____

8. Family and marriage:

   _____

   _____

9. Other customs, traditions and beliefs:

_____

_____

10. What problems or challenges do you see in this business relationship because of some of the differences which you have noted above?

_____

_____

American/Home Culture

1. Communication style (non-verbal and verbal, as well as the language of
business):

_____

_____

2. Food and diet:

_____

_____

3. Clothing (especially business dress):

_____

_____

4. Time sense:

_____

_____

5. Values and business ethics:

_____

_____

6. Work habits and practices:

_____

_____

7. Attitudes/practices with "minority" workers (sex, class, caste, color,
etc.):

_____

_____

8. Family and marriage:

_____

_____

9. Other customs, traditions and beliefs:

_____

_____

10. What problems or challenges do you see in this business relationship because of some of the differences which you have noted above?

_____

_____

PART 2—INTERCULTURAL SUPERVISOR/WORKER RELATIONS
INVENTORY

Situation: Choose either A or B for your reporting. You are a Supervisor of (a) A minority group member from any ethnic group you wish to select (black, Chicano, Oriental, Filipino, etc.) or (b) A young worker under 21 years of age.

Directions: This exercise requires three steps: (1) Note your observations on the items below in view of the situation presented by filling in the blank spaces with appropriate information. (2) Share these data with your fellow group members and try to arrive at some consensus with your combined observations. (3) Report your group findings on newsprint paper with the marking pencils provided to your group.

This person represents a "micro" culture within another society; his/her background, attitudes, and perceptions are different from yours. Try to place yourself in his/her "life space" or "private world" and report how he/she may act or feel in regard to the categories described below. Try to record the *differences* in viewpoint you might expect from this worker; the first column below should be used for this purpose. When you have finished inserting your observations about *his/her* outlook, then use the column (Supervisor's Cultural Background) to list the contrasting viewpoint which *you* hold that may affect your relationship.

Indicate your selection as to *which group* you have selected in A/B for your observations:

Worker is _____

Micro Culture Background
(his/her)

1. Communication style (non-verbal, as well as verbal including special jargon):

   _____
   _____

2. Food and diet:

   _____
   _____

3. Clothing and appearance at business or work (hair, beards, etc.):

   _____
   _____

4. Sense of time/attention span:

   _____
   _____

5. Values and business ethics:

_____

_____

6. Work habits and attitudes:

_____

_____

7. Attitude toward majority/other minorities:

_____

_____

8. Family and marriage practices/relationships:

_____

_____

9. Other customs, traditions or beliefs which may affect the relationship:

_____

_____

10. Finally, what problems or challenges do you see in your work relationship with this person because of some of the differences which you have identified?

    a. _____

    _____

    b. _____

    _____

Supervisor's Cultural Background
(you)

1. Communication style (non-verbal, as well as verbal including special jargon):

_____

_____

2. Food and diet:

_____

_____

3. Clothing and appearance at business or work (hair, beards, etc.):

_____

_____

4. Sense of time/attention span:

_____

_____

5. Values and business ethics:

_____

_____

6. Work habits and attitudes:

_____

_____

7. Attitude toward majority/other minorities:

_____

_____

8. Family and marriage practices/relationships:

_____

_____

9. Other customs, traditions or beliefs which may affect the relationship:

_____

_____

10. What about educational or information differences between you and this worker?

_____

_____

In analyzing cultural diversity in the workforce, consider the following issues:

- Primary and secondary language of the worker? For example, is English a second language, and if so, what is its impact on organizational communications? Does competency in English, or lack of it affect staff meetings, written descriptions, customer relations? Should the organization's career development programs make more provisions for more training in English or foreign language skills, especially for those serving in an area where a different language predominates?
- Does a multicultural work environment require revision of one's opinions and approaches to leadership, management, employee relations? For example, in the twin plant operations along either side of the southern border of the U.S.A., four cultures and managerial approaches are frequently interacting—American, Mexican, Japanese, and German.
- Coping with a small amount of bigots or racists in a workforce may require drastic managerial decision-making. It can range from surveys of employee attitudes to bias busting through training to discharge of those who harrass minorities.
- Cultural differences in perspective between supervisors and employees may also relate to the new work culture that is emerging. This post-industrial work environment involves providing employees and work units with more autonomy and participation, more information and better communications, more informal and synergistic relationships, more creative and high performing norms, more technical orientation and emphasis on research/development skills, more automation and robotics for improved productivity, more opportunity for improved quality of work life and intrapreneurship.

Appendix D
Organizational Culture Survey*

Instructions

This questionnaire should be as complete and authentic as possible. It provides you with an opportunity for: (a) giving feedback *anonymously* to foster your organization's development, (b) for evaluating its key management, including yourself; and (c) for understanding better your organizational environment, whether at home or abroad.

There are 6 major sections to this inquiry, and a total of 100 items seeking your opinion. A maximum of 50 minutes should be allowed for thoughtful completion of this inventory. Please consider your answers carefully for each point. Your first effort at responding should reflect your spontaneous reactions and thoughts on how you view your organizations culture from your position. If time permits, review your replies, and make changes if necessary.

Please check the appropriate categories that best depict your response to the inquiry. Where necessary, *fill in* the information requested.

This analysis will be for the total organization ( )

or for the subsystem of which you are a part ( )
(e.g. division, department, subsidiary)

The majority of questions are to be answered by checking one column in a 7-point scale with the lowest evaluations on the left or low side of the continuum, average in the middle area, and higher assessments on the right side. The exceptions are questions #23, 68, 69-81, which require a checking of the appropriate category provided.

* © Philip R. Harris/Harris International, 1984. Available in quantity from Talico, Inc. 2320 S. Third St., Ste. #7, Jacksonville Beach, FL 32250.

Organizational Diagnosis

On this scale of *lowest* (1) to *highest* (7), circle your rating of your organization's effectiveness or ineffectiveness on the following items. On question 23, simply mark the appropriate category for your response.

Over-all Analysis   **Effectiveness**

1. The goals/objectives of this organization are clearly defined and regularly reviewed.   1 2 3 4 5 6 7

2. Managers and supervisors at all levels have the opportunity to participate in this process of setting goals/objectives.   1 2 3 4 5 6 7

3. The organization has mechanisms for periodic evaluation of its achievement of goals/objectives.   1 2 3 4 5 6 7

4. Key management devotes adequate time to advanced, dynamic planning, and involves subordinates in the process as appropriate.   1 2 3 4 5 6 7

5. Key management in this organization supports high achievers among employees.   1 2 3 4 5 6 7

6. Management regularly reviews the assignment of roles and responsibilities, as well as the delegation of authority for performance.   1 2 3 4 5 6 7

7. Key managers ensure that adequate personnel development and training is available for employees to carry out assigned tasks.   1 2 3 4 5 6 7

8. Management has an adequate system for regular and meaningful performance evaluation of employees.   1 2 3 4 5 6 7

9. The organization emphasizes cooperation as an operational norm.   1 2 3 4 5 6 7

10. The organization demonstrates commitment to providing satisfactory service to its clients/customers.   1 2 3 4 5 6 7

11. The organization utilizes well, the human energies of its work force.   1 2 3 4 5 6 7

12. The organization rewards personnel on the basis of merit and performance, encouraging competence.   1 2 3 4 5 6 7

13. The work climate encourages employees to do their best and perform well.   1 2 3 4 5 6 7

14. The atmosphere in the organization encourages people to be open and candid with management.   1 2 3 4 5 6 7
15. The organization treats employees equally, regardless of their sex or race.   1 2 3 4 5 6 7

Organization Communication

16. Are you satisfied with the present state of organizational communications?   1 2 3 4 5 6 7
17. Do you think the communication between management and yourself is adequate?   1 2 3 4 5 6 7
18. Do you believe that organizational communications between the central headquarter's staff and field personnel are satisfactory?   1 2 3 4 5 6 7
19. Do you believe that in your area of responsibility, communication is satisfactory between you and your subordinates?   1 2 3 4 5 6 7
20. Do you think there is adequate written communication in the organization?   1 2 3 4 5 6 7
21. Do you think there is adequate oral and group communication?   1 2 3 4 5 6 7
22. Are you satisfied that adequate communication is provided about organizational changes?   1 2 3 4 5 6 7
23. Is your communication with various levels of management around you *largely*

            downward ( )
               upward ( )
               circular ( )

Management Team Evaluation

In terms of upper level management, the emphasis as I evaluate it is:

24. Clear organizational objectives and targets.   1 2 3 4 5 6 7
25. Confidence in themselves and their subordinates.   1 2 3 4 5 6 7
26. Providing a leadership model for subordinates.   1 2 3 4 5 6 7
27. Continuous, planned organizational renewal.   1 2 3 4 5 6 7
28. High productivity standards.   1 2 3 4 5 6 7
29. High service standards.   1 2 3 4 5 6 7

30. Experimenting with new ideas and approaches.   1 2 3 4 5 6 7
31. Encouragement of human resource development.   1 2 3 4 5 6 7
32. Coordination and cooperation in and among the organizational work units.   1 2 3 4 5 6 7
33. Conducting meaningful and productive meetings.   1 2 3 4 5 6 7
34. Confronting conflict directly and settling disagreements rather than avoiding or ignoring it.   1 2 3 4 5 6 7
35. Promoting creative thinkers and innovative performers.   1 2 3 4 5 6 7
36. Always *trying* to do things better.   1 2 3 4 5 6 7
37. Equal employment opportunity and affirmative action.   1 2 3 4 5 6 7
38. Creating a motivating environment for employees.   1 2 3 4 5 6 7
39. Open, authentic communications with each other, and their subordinates.   1 2 3 4 5 6 7
40. Seeking suggestions and ideas from employees and the public (feedback).   1 2 3 4 5 6 7
41. Clarifying organizational roles and responsibilities so there is no confusion or overlap.   1 2 3 4 5 6 7
42. Team work and collaboration within and among upper level management.   1 2 3 4 5 6 7
43. Effective concern for training subordinates to perform competently.   1 2 3 4 5 6 7
44. Willingness to consider innovations proposed to increase organizational effectiveness.   1 2 3 4 5 6 7
45. Sharing of power, authority, and decision-making with lower level management.   1 2 3 4 5 6 7
46. Policies and procedures which counteract absenteeism, slackness, and uproductivity.   1 2 3 4 5 6 7
47. Management of responsibility on the part of employees they supervise.   1 2 3 4 5 6 7
48. Problem-solving and confronting issues.   1 2 3 4 5 6 7
49. Constantly improving working conditions, both physical and psychological.   1 2 3 4 5 6 7
50. Consistency in organizational policies and procedures.   1 2 3 4 5 6 7

Work Group Assessment

Please answer this section in terms of the work group you manage. That is, respond in terms of personnel who report to you or for whom you are responsible.

51. The atmosphere and interpersonal relations in my group are friendly and cooperative.   1 2 3 4 5 6 7

52. The members encourage one another's best efforts, reinforcing successful behavior.   1 2 3 4 5 6 7

53. The group organizes and problem solves effectively.   1 2 3 4 5 6 7

54. The members maintain adequate standards of performance.   1 2 3 4 5 6 7

55. The group is open to and ready for organizational changes.   1 2 3 4 5 6 7

56. The members work effectively as a team.   1 2 3 4 5 6 7

57. The group communicates well within our work unit.   1 2 3 4 5 6 7

58. The group communicates satisfactorily with other work units.   1 2 3 4 5 6 7

59. The members provide group input and may participate in the management process as appropriate.   1 2 3 4 5 6 7

60. The group makes effective use of available equipment and resources (both material and human.)   1 2 3 4 5 6 7

61. The members generally demonstrate pride in themselves and in their work.   1 2 3 4 5 6 7

62. The group actively seeks to utilize the skills and abilities of its members.   1 2 3 4 5 6 7

63. The members do not feel constrained by rules, regulations, and red tape in accomplishing their work.   1 2 3 4 5 6 7

64. The group is dynamic in its approaches and activities, that is, the work environment "turns people on."   1 2 3 4 5 6 7

65. The members of this group are not characterized by conformity and dependency.   1 2 3 4 5 6 7

66. The group has a record of consistent accomplishment in the organization.   1 2 3 4 5 6 7
67. The members in my work group generally
exercise responsibility and achievement.   1 2 3 4 5 6 7

Managerial Self-Perception

68. As a leader in this organization, check the words or word combinations that best describe your management approach:

( ) idealistic   ( ) realistic
( ) innovative   ( ) pragmatic
( ) cooperative   ( ) individualistic
( ) task oriented   ( ) sensitive
( ) change maker   ( ) change reactor
( ) hard-nosed   ( ) imaginative
( ) inspiring   ( ) participative
( ) traditional   ( ) futuristic

Managerial Self-Perception (check appropriate category)

	Rarely	Sometimes	Usually
69. Do you seek out and use improved work methods?			
70. Does your managerial performance demonstrate sufficient skill in • administration • human relations • obtaining results?			
71. Do you reinforce and support positive behavior and performance in your subordinates?			
72. Do you actively encourage your subordinates to make the most of their potential?			
73. Are you willing to take reasonable risks in the management of your work units?			
74. Do you take responsibility to ensure that the employees you manage make their best contribution toward achieving organizational goals and production targets?			
75. Do your key subordinates really know where you stand on controversial organizational issues?			

Rarely | Sometimes | Usually

76. Do you demonstrate by example personal standards of competency and productivity?

77. Are you generally objective, friendly but business-like in dealing with employees?

78. Are you doing something specific for your own personal and professional development?

79. Do you take responsibility to seek change in organizational norms, values, and standards when these are not relevant and in need of updating?

80. Please read back to yourself the above twelve statements. In light of the demands of modern management and employee expectations, how would you rate the above evaluations of your leadership role? Please check one: Inadequate ( ) Adequate ( ).

81. A study by Michael Maccoby describes the new post-industrial organizational leader in this way: A gamesman, "in contrast to the jungle-fighter industrialist of the past, is driven not to build or to preside over empires, but to organize winning teams. Unlike the security-seeking organization man, he is excited by the chance to cut deals and to gamble." The author also states that such new leaders in top management are more cooperative and less hardened than the classical autocrats, as well as less dependent than the typical bureaucrats. This sociologist suggests that the new leader is more detached and emotionally inaccessable than his predecessors, yet troubled that his work develops his head but not his heart.
How does this description of the emerging executive fit you? (check one)
This is comparable to the way I am/feel ( ).
I do not identify with this new type of manager ( ).

Organizational Relations

Please check the category that best describes the present situation for you.

82. Employees generally trust top management.   1 2 3 4 5 6 7

83. Employees usually "level" in their communications with management, providing authentic feedback.   1 2 3 4 5 6 7

84. Employees usually are open and authentic in their work relations.   1 2 3 4 5 6 7

85. If employees have a conflict or disagreement with management, they usually work it out directly, or seek mediation.   1 2 3 4 5 6 7

86. When employees receive administrative directives or decisions with which they do not agree they usually conform without dissent.   1 2 3 4 5 6 7

87. Older managers are threatened by younger, competent staff members or subordinates who may have more knowledge, information, or education.   1 2 3 4 5 6 7

88. Managers are able to interact effectively with minority and female peers or subordinates.   1 2 3 4 5 6 7

89. Managers really try to be fair and just with employees, using competency only as their evaluative criteria of performance.   1 2 3 4 5 6 7

90. Many managers have generally "retired" on the job, and are indifferent to needs for organizational renewal.   1 2 3 4 5 6 7

91. Employees have opportunities to clarify changing roles and relationships.   1 2 3 4 5 6 7

92. Is organization concerned about the needs of people as well as getting the task done?   1 2 3 4 5 6 7

93. Organization encourages and assists employees in the development of community relations.   1 2 3 4 5 6 7

Organizational Changes

94. The organization is able to adapt as to the dramatic shifts and changes underway in society and the larger culture.   1 2 3 4 5 6 7

95. The organization is able to handle the new demands made upon it as a result of the changes in top administration and management emphasis. 1 2 3 4 5 6 7

96. The organization does seek adequate input from employees on those changes that affect them, or they are to implement.   1 2 3 4 5 6 7

97. The organization is able to deal effectively with the new kind of person coming into your workforce and management.   1 2 3 4 5 6 7

98. The organization has changed its management priorities and approaches with regard to scarce resources, as well as environmental and ecological concerns.   1 2 3 4 5 6 7

99. The organization is innovative in finding ways to improve the institutional environment.   1 2 3 4 5 6 7

100. The organization is cosmopolitan (versus domestic), attuned to the global marketplace, pluralistic in both its attitudes and personnel.   1 2 3 4 5 6 7

Note: Please recognize that cultural factors influenced the way the above questions were constructed, and the way in which you responded. However, this evaluation can provide insight into your organizational culture in terms of Western perspective and future trend criteria.

References

Adams, J. D. (ed.) *Transforming Work.* San Diego: Miles River Press/University Associates, 1984.

Addo, H. *Transforming the World Economy: Nine Critical Essays on the New International Economic Order.* Boulder, CO: Westview Press, 1985.

Adler, N. and Izraeli, D. N. (eds.) *Women in Management Worldwide.* Yarmouth, ME: Intercultural Press/Sharpe, 1988.

Adler, N. J. *International Dimensions of Organizational Behavior.* Boston: Kent Publishing Company, 1985.

Adler, N. J. "Expecting International Success: Female Managers Overseas," *Columbia Journal of World Business* 19, No. 3, Fall 1984, 79–86.

Adler, N. J. "Typology of Management Studies Involving Culture." *Journal of International Business Studies,* Fall 1983, 29–47.

Agmon, T. *Political Economy and Risk in World Financial Markets.* Lexington, MA: Lexington Books, 1985.

Allen, R. F. and Kraft, C. "Transformations that Last: A Cultural Approach," in *Transforming Work,* J. D. Adams (ed.) San Diego: Miles River Press/University Associates, 1984.

Almaney, A. J. and Alwan, A. J. *Communicating with Arabs: A Handbook for the Business Executive.* Prospect Heights, IL: Waveland Press, 1982.

Amsalem, M. *Technology Crossing Borders: The Choice, Transfer and Management of International Technology Flows.* Boston, Harvard Business School Press, 1984.

Amsden, A. *Asia's Next Giant: Late Industrialization in South Korea.* Cambridge, UK: Oxford University Press, 1989.

Ansoff, H. I. *Implanting Strategic Management.* Englewood Cliffs, N.J.: Prentice-Hall, 1984.

Anthony, R. and Roe, G. *Educators' Passport to International Jobs.* Yarmouth, ME: Intercultural Press/Peterson Guides, 1984.

Aoki, M. Y. and Dandess, M. B. *As the Japanese See It: Past and Present.* Honolulu: University of Hawaii Press, 1981.

Asante, M. K. and Gudykunst, W. B. (eds.) *Handbook of Intercultural Communications,* Newbury Park, CA: Sage Publications, 1989 (annual).

Athen, G. *American Ways.* Yarmouth, ME: Intercultural Press, 1988.

At-Twaijri, M. I. "Empirical Analysis of the Effects of Environmental Interdependence and Uncertainty on Purchasing: A Cross-cultural Study." *Industrial Marketing Purchasing,* Vol. 3:1, Bradford, UK: MCB University Press, 1988.

Atwater, D. F. (ed.) *Communication and the Afro-American Journal of Black Studies.* Beverly Hills, CA: Sage Publications, 1989 (annual).

Axtell, R. E. (ed.) *Dos and Taboos Around the World: A Guide to International Behavior*. New York, NY: John Wiley & Sons, 1987.

Ayres, R. U. *The Next Industrial Revolution*. Cambridge, MA: Ballinger Publishing, 1984.

Azar, E. E. *International Interactions—A Transnational Multidisciplinary Journal*. New York: Gordon & Breach Science Publishers, Vol. 13, 1985.

Auletta, K. *Art of Corporate Success*. New York: Putnam, 1984.

Austin, C. N. *Cross-Cultural Re-entry: An Annotated Bibliography*. Yarmouth, ME: Intercultural Press, 1985.

Bagley, E. K. *Beyond Conglomerate: The Impact of the Supercorporation on the Future of Life and Business*. New York: AMACOM, 1985.

Baranson, J. *North-South Technology Transfer*. Mt. Airy, MD: Lomond Publications, 1981.

Barnett, R. J. and Muller, R. E. *Global Reach: The Power of the Multinational Corporation*. New York: Simon and Schuster, 1974.

Barnlund, D. C. *Public and Private Self in Japan and the United States*. Yarmouth, ME: Intercultural Press/Simul Press, 1987.

Bass, B. M., et al. *Assessment of Managers: An International Comparison*. New York: Macmillan Publishing, 1979.

Baugh, J. G. "A Study of Decision-Making Within Matrix Organizations." Unpublished doctoral disseration, United States International University, San Diego, 1981 (available through University Microfilms, Ann Arbor, MI. 48106).

Belcher, J. G. *Productivity PLUS + : How Today's Best Run Companies Are Gaining the Competitive Edge*. Houston: Gulf Publishing, 1987.

Bellah, R. N., et al. *Habits of the Heart: Individualism and Commitment in American Life*. Berkley, CA: University of California Press, 1985.

Beliaev, B., Mullen, T. and Punnett, B. J. "Understanding Cultural Environment: U.S.-U.S.S.R. Trade Negotiations," *California Management Review*, No. 2, Winter 1985: 100–112.

Bennis, W. *Why Leaders Can't Lead*. San Francisco, CA: Jossey-Bass, 1991.

Bennis, W. and Nanus, B. *Leaders: The Strategies for Taking Charge*. New York: Harper & Row, 1985.

Bernstein, R. *From the Center of the Earth: The Search for Truth About China*. Denver, CO: Little Books & Co., 1982.

Bolman, L. G. and Deal, T. E. *Modern Approaches to Understanding and Managing Organizations*. San Francisco: Jossey-Bass, 1984, Ch. 9.

Bond, M. H. (ed.), *The Cross-cultural Challenge to Social Psychology*. Newbury Park, CA: Sage Publications, 1988.

Botkin, J., Dimancescu, D. and Stata, R. *Global Stakes: The Future of High Technology in America*. Cambridge, MA: Ballinger/Harper & Row, 1982.

Brackel, A. (ed.) *People and Organizations Interacting*. New York: John Wiley, 1985.

Bracken, S. *Canadian Almanac and Directory*. Toronto: Copp Clark Pittman, 1985.

Bradford, D. L. and Cohen, A. R. *Managing for Excellence: The Guide to Developing High Performance in Contemporary Organizations*. New York: John Wiley, 1984.

Brigham Young University, *Culturgram—1988 Edition*. Provo, UT: BYU Publication Services, 1988.

Brigham Young University, "Coming Home Again," *Infogram*. Provo, UT: BYU Language Research Ct., 1980.

Brislin, R. W., Cushner, K., Cherrie, C. and Yong, M. *Intercultural Interactions: A Practical Guide*. Newbury Park, CA: Sage Publications, 1986.

Brooks, E. and Odiorne, G. S. *Managing by Negotiations*. New York: McGraw-Hill Books, 1985.

Brown, L. R. *State of the World*. Washington, D.C.: Worldwatch Institute, 1986.

Buckley, R. *Japan Today*. New York: Cambridge University Press, 1985.

Buening, C. R. *Communications on the Job*. Indianapolis: Bobbs-Merrill, 1975.

Buono, A. F. and Bowditch, J. L. *The Human Side of Acquisitions and Mergers— Managing Collisions Between People, Cultures, and Organizations*. San Francisco, CA: Jossey-Bass Pub., 1989.

Butterfield, F. *China: Alive in the Bitter Sea*. New York: N.Y. Times Books, 1982.

Campbell, J. (ed.) *Myths, Dreams and Religion*. Camp Hill, PA: Quality Paperbacks, 1990.

Carroll, R. *Cultural Misunderstandings: The French American Experience*. Chicago, IL: The University of Chicago Press, 1987.

Casewell, C. W. *Foreign Jobs: The Most Popular Countries*. Yarmouth, ME: Intercultural Press, 1985.

Casse, P. and Deol, S. *Managing Intercultural Negotiations*. Yarmouth, ME: Intercultural Press/ SIETAR International, 1985.

Casse, P. *Training for the Multicultural Manager*. Yarmouth, ME: SIETAR/Intercultural Press, 1982.

Casse, P. *Training for the Cross-cultural Mind*. Yarmouth, ME: SIETAR/Intercultural Press, 1979.

Castelis, M. *High Technology, Space & Society*. Beverly Hills, CA: Sage Publishing, 1985.

Catoline, J. E. *Managing Across Cultures*. Merrimack, NH: Digital Equipment Corporation, 1983. (This brochure and a free subscription to *The Consultant*, International Edition, can be obtained from Digital Equipment Corporation, Merrimack, NH 03054, USA).

Cetron, M., Pagano, A. and Port, O. *The Future of American Business: The U.S. in World Competition*. New York: McGraw-Hill, 1985.

Certo, S. C., Applebaum, S. H. *Principles of Modern Management: A Canadian Perspective*. Dubuque, IA: W. C. Brown Co., 1983.

Chapman, E. N. *Winning at Human Relations*. Los Altos, CA: Crisp Publications, 1989.

Charnes, K. and Cooper, W. W. *Creative and Innovative Management*. Cambridge, MA: Ballinger/Harper & Row, 1984.

Che, Wai-kin *The Modern Chinese Family*. Palo Alto, CA. R & E Research Associates (936 Industrial Avenue), 1979.

Cherry, C. *World Communication: Threat or Promise?* New York: John Wiley, 1978.

Chesnow, N. *The World Class Executive: A Guide to Negotiating in Other Cultures*. New York: Rawson Associates, 1984. (Available from Intercultural Press, Yarmouth, ME 04096.)

Christopher, R. C. *The Japanese Mind: The Goliath Explained*. New York: Linden Press/Simon & Schuster, 1983.

Christopher, W. C. *Management for the 1980s*. Englewood Cliffs, N.J.: Prentice Hall, 1980.

Cline, W. R. *Exports of Manufacturers from Developing Countries*. Washington, D.C.: The Brookings Institution, 1984.

Cohen, M. *Volunteer: The Comprehensive Guide to Voluntary Service in the U.S. and Abroad*. Yarmouth, ME: Intercultural Press, 1985.

Condon, J. and Kurata, K. *In Search of What's Japanese about Japan*. Yarmouth, ME: Intercultural Press/Charles E. Tuttle Co., 1987.

Condon, J. C. *With Respect to the Japanese: A Guide for Americans*. Yarmouth, ME: Intercultural Press, 1984.

Condon, J. *Good Neighbors: Communicating with the Mexicans*. Yarmouth, ME: Intercultural Press, 1985.

Connors, M. M., Harrison, A. A., and Akins, F. R. *Living Aloft—Human Requirements for Extended Spaceflight*. Washington, D.C.: U. S. Government Printing Office, 1985 (NASA SP-483).

Copeland, L. and Griggs, L. *Going International: How to Make Friends and Deal Effectively in the Global Marketplace*. New York: Random House, 1985.

Corning, P. A. *The Synergism Hypothesis*, New York: McGraw-Hill, 1983.

Cornish, E. (ed.) *The Future: A Guide to Information Sources* (Annual). Bethesda, MD: World Future Society, 1989.

Corporate Handbook to International Economic Organizations and Terms, New York: United States Council for International Business, 1985.

Craig, J. *Multinational Cooperatives: An Alternative for World Development*. Saskatoon, Saskatchewan (Canada): Western Producers Prairie Books, 1976.

Crocker, J. (ed.) *After Affirmative Action: Barriers to Occupational Advancement for Women and Minorities*. Beverly Hills, CA: Sage Publications, 1984 (annual).

Crouch, C. and Heller, F. A. (eds.) *International Yearbook of Organizational Democracy*, Vol. 1, 1983; Vol. 2, 1984 (Eds.-Wilpert, B. and Sorge, A.). New York: John Wiley (annual).

Dasen, P. R., Berry, J. W. and Sartorius, N. *Health and Cross-cultural Psychology*. Newbury Park, CA: Sage Pulications, 1988.

Davidson, F. P. and Cox, J. S. *MACRO: A Clear Vision of How Science and Technology Will Shape Our Future*. New York: W. Morrow, 1983.

Davis, S. M. and Lawrence, P. R. *Matrix*. Reading, MA: Addison-Wesley, 1977.

DeChardin, P. T. *The Future of Man*. New York: Harper & Row, 1969.

Delphos, W. A. *Washington's Best Kept Secrets: A U.S. Guide to International Business*. New York: John Wiley, 1983.

Deal, T. E. and Kennedy, A. A. *Corporate Cultures*. Reading, MA: Addison-Wesley, 1982.

DeMente, B. *Korean Etiquette and Ethics in Business*. Yarmouth, ME: Intercultural Press/National Textbook, 1988.

DeMente, B. *Made in Japan—The Methods, Motivations, and Culture of the Japanese and Their Influence on U. S. Business*. Yarmouth, ME: Intercultural Press/National Textbook, 1987.

Desatnick, R. *The Business of Human Resource Management*. New York: John Wiley, 1983.

Deutsch, M. F. *Doing Business with the Japanese*. New York: New American Library, 1983.

Dickens, J. and F. *The Black Manager: Making it in the Corporate World*. New York: AMACOM, 1984.

Diebold, J. *Making the Future Work* New York: Simon & Schuster, 1984.

Dillard, J. M. *Multicultural Counseling*. Chicago: Nelson-Hall, 1983.

Dodd, C. H. *Dynamics of Intercultural Communication*. Dubuque, IA: W. C. Brown Publishers, 1982.

Dougherty, D. E. *From Technical Professional to Corporate Manager: A Guide to Career Transition*. New York, John Wiley, 1984.

Drucker, P. E. *The New Realities,* New York, NY: Harper & Row, 1989.

Drucker, P. E. *Innovation and Entrepreneurship*. New York: Harper & Row, 1985.

Drucker, P. E. *Managing in Turbulent Times*. New York: Harper & Row, 1980.

Drucker, P. E. *People and Performance*. New York: Harper's College Press, 1977.

Duignan, P. and Gann, L. H. *The United States and Africa: a History*. New York: Cambridge University Press, 1984.

Dunning, J. and Stopford, J. *Multinational: Company Performance and Global Trends*. Hants, U.K.: Globe Book Service Ltd., 1983.

Dyer, W. G. *Cultural Change in Family Firms*. San Francisco, CA: Jossey-Bass Publishers, 1986.

Dyer, W. G. *Strategies for Managing Change*. Reading, MA: Addison-Wesley, 1985.

Dyer, W. G. *Team Building*. Reading, MA: Addison-Wesley, 1987.

Earley, P. C. "Intercultural Training for Managers: A Comparison of Documentary and Interpersonal Methods." *The Academy of Management Journal*. 1987, Vol. 30, No. 4, pp. 685–698.

Ebrey, P. B. *Chinese Civilization and Society: A Source Book*. New York: Free Press/ Macmillan, 1981.

Elashmawi, F. and Harris, P. R. *Global Joint Ventures—Managing in the Multicultural Environment*. Houston, TX: Gulf Publishing Co., 1991 (proposed).

Ely, J. B. "A New Japanese/American Dynamic," Chapter V of a forthcoming book to be published in 1986 (for information, contact Communications Media Consultants, 16620 S. Shenandoah Ave., Cerritos, CA 90701).

England, G. W., Megandhi, A. R. and Wilpert, B. *Organizational Functionings in a Cross-cultural Perspective*. Kent, OH: Kent State University Press, 1979.

Eitington, J. E. *The Winning Trainer*. Houston: Gulf Publishing, 1984.

Epstein, C. F. *Deceptive Distinctions: Sex, Gender, and Social Order*. New Haven, CT: Yale University Press, 1989.

Evans, C. *The Micro Millenium*. New York: The Viking Press, 1979.

Ferguson, H. *Tomorrow's Global Executive*. Homewood, IL: Dow Jones-Irwin, 198.

Fernandez, J. P. *Racism and Sexism in Corporate Life: Changing Values of American Business*. Lexington, MA: Lexington Books/D.C. Heath, 1981.

Fernea, E. W. and R. A. *The Arab World: Personal Encounters*. New York: Doubleday, 1985.

Fiedler, F., Mitchell, T. and Triandis, A. "The Culture Assimilator: An Approach to Cross-cultural Training." *Journal of Applied Psychology*, 1971: 55, 95–102.

Fieg, J. P. *Thais and North Americans*. Yarmouth, ME: Intercultural Press, 1989.

Fieg, J. P. and Yaffee, L. E. *Adjusting to the U.S.A.: Orientation for International Students*. Washington, D.C.: Meridian House International, 1977.

Finch, E. R. and Moore, A. L. *Astrobusiness: A Guide to Commerce and Law in Outer Space*. New York: Praeger/CBS Educational & Professional Publishers, 1984.

Finney, B. R. and Jones, E. M. *Interstellar Migration and the Human Experience.* Berkley, CA: University of California Press, 1985.

Fisher, G. *Mindsets—The Role of Culture and Perception.* Yarmouth, ME: Intercultural Press, 1988.

Fisher, G. *International Negotiation: A Cross-Cultural Perspective.* Yarmouth, ME: Intercultural Press, 1980.

Fisher, R. and Ury, W. *Getting to Yes: Negotiating Agreement Without Giving In.* Boston: Houghton Mifflin, 1981.

French, W. L. and Bell, C. H. *Organization Development: Behavioral Science Interventions for Organizational Improvement.* Englewood Cliffs, N.J.: Prentice Hall, 1984.

Fombrun, C., Tichy, N. M. and Devanna, M. A. *Strategic Human Resource Management.* New York: John Wiley, 1985.

Foster, T. *High-Tech Society—The Story of the Information Technology Revolution.* Cambridge, MA: MIT Press, 1987.

Fuentes, A. and Ehreneich, B. *Women in the Global Factory.* Boston: Institute for New Communications/Southend Press, 1983.

Fuqua, P. and Wilson, J. V. *Terrorism—The Executives Guide to Survival.* Houston: Gulf Publishing, 1978.

Furnham, A. and Bochner, S. *Culture Shock: Psychological Reactions to Unfamiliar Environments.* New York: Methuen (29 W. 35th St., NY 10001), 1987.

Gardiner, H. S. *Soviet Foreign Trade: The Decision Process.* Hingham, MA: Kluwer Academic Press, 1983.

Gardiner, J. H. (ed.) *Technology and the Future of U.S. Industry in World Competition.* Indianapolis: White River Press, 1985.

Gelderman, C. A. *How to Survive in Style in England.* Yarmouth, ME: Intercultural Press, 1985.

Gelderman-Curtis, C. and Niks-Corkum, R. *Inside Information: Living in Holland, A Practical Guide.* Yarmouth, ME: Intercultural Press, 1979.

Gibbon, C. F. and Jackson, B. B. *The Information Imperative—Managing the Impact of Information Technology on Businesses and People.* Lexington, MA: Lexington/D.C. Heath, 1987.

Gibney, F. *Japan: The Fragile Superpower.* Tokyo: Chas. E. Tuttle Co., 1975.

Gilder, G. *Into the Quantum Era of Microcosm: Economics and Technology.* New York, NY: Simon & Schuster, 1989.

Giordano, J. A. and Shea, M. S. *Safety and Health Abroad.* Yarmouth, ME: Intercultural Press, 1985.

Glenn, E. and G. *Man and Mankind: Conflict and Communication Between Cultures.* Norwood, N.J.: Ablex Publishing, 1983.

Glover, G. and Shames, G. W. *World-Class Services.* Yarmouth, ME: Intercultural Press, 1989.

Gmelch, W. H. and Miskin, W. H. *Productivity Teams: Beyond Quality Circles.* New York: John Wiley, 1984.

Godet, M. *The Crisis in Forecasting and the Emergence of the "Prospective" Approach.* Elmsford, N.Y.: Pergamon, 1979.

Goldman, N. *Space Commerce.* Cambridge, MA: Ballinger/Harper & Row, 1984.

Goldstein, S. M. *China Briefing.* Boulder, CO: Westview Press, 1985.

Goodman, J. *American Genesis*. New York: Summit Books, 1981.

Goodman, L. J. and Associates, *Change in Organizations*. San Francisco: Jossey-Bass, 1982.

Gordon, R. *Living in Latin America*. Skokie, IL: National Textbook, 1976. (Available Intercultural Press, Yarmouth, ME. 04096.)

Ghosh, P. K. (ed.) *Developing Latin America: A Modernization Perspective*. Westport, CT: Greenwood Press, 1984.

Graham, J. and Herberger, R. "Negotiators Abroad-Don't Shoot from the Hip," *Harvard Business Review*, July–August, 1983.

Graham, J. L. and Yoshihiro, S. *Smart Bargaining: Doing Business with the Japanese*. Cambridge, MA: Ballinger/Harper & Row, 1984.

Griffith, W. E. (ed.) *Central and Eastern Europe: The Opening Curtain* Boulder, CO: Westview Press, Inc. 1989.

Grieff, B. S. and Munter, P. E. *Tradeoffs: Executives, Family and Organizational Life*. New York: New American Life, 1980.

Grunwald, J. and Flamm, K. *The Global Factory: Foreign Assembly in International Trade*. Washington, D.C.: The Brookings Institution, 1985.

Gudykunst, W. and Hammer, "Basic Training Design: Approaches to Intercultural Training" in D. Landis and R. Brislin (eds.) *Handbook of Intercultural Training* Elmsford, N.Y., Pergamon Press, 1983.

Gudykunst, W. and Kim, Y. Y. (eds.) *Method for Intercultural Communication Research*. Beverly Hills, CA: Sage Publications, 1984 (annual).

Gudykunst, W. and Young, Y. *Communicating with Strangers: An Approach to Intercultural Communications*. Reading, MA: Addison-Wesley, 1984.

Gudykunst, W. B., Stewart, L. P., and Ting-Toomey, S. (eds.) *Communication, Culture, and Organizational Processes*. Newbury Park, CA: Sage Publications, 1985.

Gudykunst, W. B. *Intercultural Communication Theory: Current Perspectives*. Beverly Hills, CA: Sage Publications, 1983.

(The) Guidebook on Trading with the People's Republic of China. London: Graham and Trotman, Ltd., 1985.

Gunn, T. G. *Manufacturing for Competitive Advantage—Becoming A World Class Manufacturer*. Cambridge, MA: Ballinger/Harper & Row, 1987.

Gutek, B. A. *Sex and the Workplace*. San Francisco: Jossey-Bass, 1985.

Gutkind, P. C. and Wallerstein, I. (eds.) *Political Economy of Contemporary Africa*. Beverly Hills, CA: Sage Publications, 1985.

Hall, E. T. *The Basic Works of Edward T. Hall*—Vol. 1, *The Silent Language*; Vol. 2, *The Hidden Dimension*; Vol. 3, *Beyond Culture*; *The Dance of Life*. New York, NY: Bantam/Doubleday, 1989.

Hall, E. T. and Hall, M. R. *Hidden Differences—Doing Business with the Japanese*. Garden City, NY: Anchor/Doubleday, 1987.

Hall, E. T. and Hall, M. R. *Understanding Cultural Differences: Keys to Success in West Germany, France, and the United States*. Yarmouth, ME: Intercultural Press, 1990.

Hall, R. H. (ed.) *Work and Occupations: An International Sociological Journal*. Beverly Hills, CA: Sage Publications, 1985.

Hamner, W. C. and Organ, D. W. *Organizational Behavior*. Dallas: Business Publications/Irwin-Dorsey, 1978.

Hampton, G. M. (ed.) *Marketing Aspects of International Business*. Hingham, MA: Kluwer Academic Press, 1983.

Harman, W. *Global Mind Change*. Indianapolis, IN: Knowledge Systems, Inc., 1988.

Harris, P. R. *Living and Working in Space—Human Behavior, Culture and Organization*. Chichester, UK: Ellis Horwood Ltd. (USA—West Nyack, NY: Prentice Hall), 1992.

Harris, P. R. "Human Futures on the High Frontier." *Futures Research Quarterly*, Vol. 32, Summer 1987, pp. 53-81.

Harris, P. R. "The New World of Creative Work." Ch. 61 (pages 555–566) in Kuhn, 1988.

Harris, P. R. *High Performance Leadership*. Glenview, IL: Scott, Foresman & Co., 1989.

Harris, P. R. *Management in Transition: Transforming Managerial Practices and Organizational Strategies for a New Work Culture*. San Francisco: Jossey-Bass, 1985.

Harris, P. R. "Management Challenges in a New Space Era" and "The Influence of Culture on Space Development." In M. F. McKay (ed.) *Space Resources: Technological Springboard to the 21st Century*. Houston: NASA/Johnson Space Center, 1990.

Harris, P. R. "Living on the Moon. Will Humans Develop an Unearthly Culture?" *The Futurist*, April 1985, pp. 30–35.

Harris, P. R. (ed.) *Global Strategies for Human Resource Development*. Washington, D.C.: American Society for Training & Development, 1984.

Harris P. R. and Malin, G. (ed.) *Innovations in Global Consultation*. Washington, D.C.: International Consultants Foundation, 1980.

Harrison, P. A. *Behaving Brazilian: A Comparison of Brazilian and North American Social Behavior*. Yarmouth, ME: Intercultural Press, 1985.

Harrison, A. A., Clearwater, Y. A., McKay, C. (eds.) *The Human Experience in Antarctica: Applications to Life in Space*. New York, NY: Springer Publications, 1990.

Haynes, M. E. *Effective Meeting Skills*. Los Altos, CA: Crisp Publications, 1988.

Heenan, D. A. and Perlmutter, H. V. *Multinational Organizational Development*. Reading, MA: Addison-Wesley, 1979.

Hersey, P. and Blanchard, K. H. *Management of Organization Behavior: Utilizing Human Resources*. Englewood Cliffs, N.J.: Prentice-Hall, 1982.

Hiltz, S. R. and Turoff, M. *The Network Nation*. Reading, MA: Addison-Wesley, 1978.

Hofheinz, R. and Calder, K. R. *The Eastasia Edge*. New York: Basic Books, 1982.

Hofstede, G. *Cultures Consequences: International Differences in Work-Related Values*. Beverly Hills, CA: Sage Publishing, 1984.

Holden, N. *Executive Development*, Vol. 1, Bradford U.K., MCB University Press, Aug. 1988, pp. 43–45.

Hoopes, D. S. *Global Guide to International Education*. Yarmouth, ME: Intercultural Press, 1985.

Hoopes, D. S. and Ventura, O. (eds.) *Intercultural Sourcebook: Cross-cultural Training Methodologies*. Yarmouth, ME: Intercultural Press, 1984.

Hospital, J. T. *Dislocations*. Baton Rouge, LA: Louisiana State University Press, 1989.

Hsu, F. L. K. *Americans and Chinese—Passage to Differences*. Honolulu, HI: University of Hawaii Press, 1981.

Illman, P. *Selecting and Developing Overseas Managers.* New York: AMACOM, 1976.

Jablin, F. M., Putnam, L. L., Roberts, K. H. and Porter, L. W. *Handbook of Organizational Communications.* Newbury Park, CA: Sage Publications, 1987.

Jandt, F. E. *Win-Win Negotiations: Turning Conflict into Agreement.* New York: John Wiley, 1985.

Jaynes, G. D. and Williams, R. M. (eds.), *A Common Destiny: Blacks and American Society.* Washington, D.C.: National Research Council, 1989.

Jenkins, R. *Transnational Corporations and Industrial Transformation in Latin America.* London: Macmillan, 1984.

Josefowitz, N. *You're the Boss! A Guide to Managing People with Understanding and Effectiveness.* New York, NY: Warner Books, 1987.

Kahn, H. and Pepper, T. *The Japanese Challenge.* New York: Crowell Co., 1979.

Kakabadse, A. and Parker, C. (eds.) *Power, Politics, and Organizations.* New York: John Wiley, 1984.

Kang, T. P. *Is Korea the Next Japan?.* New York, NY: Free Press, 1989.

Kanter, R. M. *The Change Masters.* New York Simon and Schuster, 1983.

Kaplan F. M. and Dekeijaer, A. J. *The China Guidebook-1982-83.* Boston: Houghton-Mifflin, 1983.

Kaplan, R. E., Lombardi, M M. and Mazigve, M. *A Mirror for Management Using Simulations to Develop Management Teams.* Greensboro, NC: Center for Creative Leadership, 1983.

Kapp, R. A. (ed.) *Communicating with China.* Yarmouth, ME: Intercultural Press, 1983.

Kardiner, A. and Linton, R. *The Psychological Frontiers of Society.* Westport, CT: Greenwood Press, 1981.

Kast, F. and Rosenzweig, J. *Organization and Management: A Systems and Contemporary Approach,* 4th Edition. New York: McGraw-Hill, 1985.

Kaynak, E. (ed.) *International Marketing Management.* New York: Praeger Publishers, 1984.

Kerr, J. and Slocum, J. W. "Managing Corporate Culture Through Reward Systems." *Academy of Management Executive.* May 1987, Vol. 1, No. 2, pp. 99–108.

Kilmann, R. H., Covin, T. J. and Assoc., *Corporate Transformation: Revitalizing Organizations for a Competitive World.* San Francisco, CA: Jossey-Bass, 1987.

Kilmann, R. H., et al. *Gaining Control of Corporate Culture.* San Francisco: Jossey-Bass, 1985.

Kimberly, J. R. and Quinn, R. E. (eds.) *Managing Organizational Transitions.* Homewood, IL: Irwin/Dow-Jones, 1984.

King, N. and Huff, K. *Host Family Survival Kit-A Guide for American Host Families.* Yarmouth, ME: Intercultural Press, 1985.

Kline, J. M. *International Codes and Multinational Business.* Westport, CT: Quorum Books, 1985.

Knapp, M. L. and Miller, G. R. (eds.) *Handbook of Interpersonal Communication.* Beverly Hills, CA: Sage Publications, 1985.

Kochman, T. *Black and White-Styles in Conflict.* Chicago: University of Chicago Press, 1981.

Kochman, T. (ed.) *Rappin' and Stylin' Out—Communication in Urban Black America*. Chicago: University of Illinois Press, 1977.

Kohl, L. R. and Tyler, V. L., (eds.) *A Select Guide to Area Studies Resources*. Provo, UT: BYU Publications Services, 1988.

Kohl, L. R. *Survival Kit for Overseas Living*. Yarmouth, ME: Intercultural Press, 1979.

Konecci, E. B. and Kuhn, R. L., (eds.) *Technology Venturing—American Innovation and Risk-Taking*. New York, NY: CBS/Praeger, 1985.

Korn, L., quote from *Los Angeles Times*, January 20, 1982, p. J2.

Koslow, D. R. and Salen, E. *Crossing Cultures in Mental Health* Washington, DC: SIETAR International, 1989.

Kozmetsky, G. *Transformational Management*. Cambridge, MA: Ballinger/Harper & Row, 1985.

Kramer, J. *Europeans*. New York, NY: Farrar, Straus & Giroux, 1988.

Kras, E. *Management in Two Cultures: Bridging the Gap Between U.S. and Mexican Managers*. Yarmouth, ME: Intercultural Press, 1989.

Kraselsky, B. (ed.) *Space Commerce—An Industry Assessment*, U.S. Dept. of Commerce, Washington, D.C., 1988.

Kravetz, D. J. *The Human Resources Revolution*. San Francisco, CA: Jossey-Bass Publishers, 1988.

Kritz, M. M. (ed.) *Global Trends in Migration Theory and Research on International Population Movements*. Staten Island, N.Y.: Center for Migration Studies, 1981.

Kroeber, A. L. and Kluckholm, C. *Culture: A Critical Review of Concepts and Definitions*. New York: Random House/Vintage Books, 1985.

Kuhn, R. (ed.) *Commercializing Defense Related Technology*. New York: Praeger, 1984.

Kuhn, R. L. (ed.) *Handbook for Creative and Innovative Managers*. New York: McGraw-Hill, 1988.

Kumar, K. and McLeod, M. G. (eds.) *Multinationals from Developing Countries*. Lexington, MA: Lexington Books/D.C. Heath, 1981.

Kumar, K. (ed.) *Bonds without Bondage: Explorations in Transcultural Interactions*. Honolulu: East-West Center/University Press of Hawaii, 1979.

Kumar, Rajesh, *Affect, Cognition, and Decision-Making in Negotiations: An Experimental Analysis of U.S. and Japanese Business Negotiations*, Ph.D. dissertation, New York: New York University Library, 1988 (available through University Microfilm International, Ann Arbor, Michigan 48106).

Lamb, D. *The Arabs: Journey Beyond the Mirage*. New York, NY: Random House, 1987.

Landis, D. and Brislin, R. W., *Handbook of Intercultural Training* (Vols. I/II/III). Elmsford, N.Y.: Pergamon Press, 1983.

Lanier, A. R. *Living in the U.S.A.* Yarmouth, ME: Intercultural Press, 1988.

Larwood, L., Stromberg, A. H. and Gutek, B. A. *Women and Work: An Annual Review*. Beverly Hills, CA: Sage Publications, 1985.

Lauffer, A. *Careers, Colleagues and Conflicts: Understanding Gender, Race and Ethnicity in the Workplace*. Newbury Park, Sage Publications, 1985.

Lee, E. *The American in Saudi Arabia*. Yarmouth, ME: Intercultural Press, 1983.

Leppert, P. *How to Do Business with Chinese—A Taiwan Handbook for Executives.* Yarmouth, ME: Intercultural Press, 1986.

Leppert, P. *Doing Business with Koreans—A Handbook for Executives.* Yarmouth, ME: Intercultural Press/Patton Pacific Press, 1987.

Lewicki, R. J. and Litterer, J. A. *Negotiation: Readings, Exercises and Cases.* Homewood, IL: Richard D. Irwin, 1985.

Lewis, T. and Jungman, R. *On Being Foreign: Culture Shock in Short Fiction—An International Anthology.* Yarmouth, ME: Intercultural Press, 1986.

Lifton, R. J. *Home from the War: Vietnam Veterans, Neither Victims nor Executors.* New York: Touchstone Press, 1984.

Lipnack, J. and Stamps, J. *Networking.* New York: Doubleday, 1982.

Lodge, G. and Walton, R. "The American Corporation and Its New Relationships," *California Management Review*, Spring 1984, pp. 9–24.

Logsdon, T. *Space Inc.—Your Guide to Investing in Space Exploration.* New York, NY: Crown Publishers, 1988.

London, M. *Developing Managers.* San Francisco: Jossey-Bass, 1985.

Lonner, W. J. and Berry, J. W. *Field Methods in Cross-cultural Research.* Newbury Park, CA: Sage Publications, 1986.

McFarland, D. E. *The Managerial Imperative: The Age of Macromanagement.* Cambridge, MA: Ballinger Publishing, 1985.

McKay, D. and M. F. (eds.) *Space Resources: Technological Springboards into the 21st Century.* Houston: NASA/Johnson Space Center, 1990

McKay, V. *Moving Abroad: A Guide to International Living.* Yarmouth, ME: Intercultural Press, 1984.

McManus, M. L. and Hergert, M. L. *Surviving Merge & Acquisition* Glenview, IL: Scott, Foresman, 1988.

McNulty, N. G. (ed.) *Management Development Programs: The World's Best.* North Holland, NY: McNulty Associates, 1981.

Maccoby, M. *The Leader: A New Face for American Management.* New York: Simon and Schuster, 1981.

MacLeod, R. *China Inc.: How to Do Business with the Chinese.* New York, NY: Bantam Books, 1988.

Maddux, R. B. *Team Building: An Exercise in Leadership.* Los Altos, CA: Crisp Publications Inc., 1988.

Maddux, R. B. and Maddux, D. *Ethics in Business—A Guide to Managers.* Los Altos, CA: Crisp Publications, Inc., 1989.

Maddux, R. B. *Successful Negotiation.* Los Altos, Crisp Publications, Inc., 1988.

Mandle, J. R. *Patterns of Caribbean Development.* New York: Gordon & Breach, 1982. (Vol. II of series.)

March, R. M. *The Japanese Negotiator—Subtlety and Strategy Beyond Western Logic.* Yarmouth, ME: Intercultural Press/Kodansha International, 1988.

Marshall, J. *Women Managers: Travelers in a Male World.* New York: John Wiley, 1984.

Marshall, T. *The Whole World Guide to Language Learning.* Yarmouth, ME: Intercultural Press, 1989.

Masuda, Y. *The Information Society as a Postindustrial Society.* Bethesda, MD: World Future Society, 1981.

Mathews, E. *Culture Clash*. Yarmouth, ME.: Intercultural Press, 1982.

Mazzeo, D. (ed.) *African Regional Organizations*. New York: Cambridge University Press.

Melody, W. H., Salter, L. R. and Heyer, P. (eds.) *Culture, Communication and Dependency*. Norwood, N.J.: Ablex Publishing, 1983.

Mensch, G. and Niehaus, R. J. (eds.) *Work, Organization, and Technological Change*. New York: Plenum, 1982.

Mesbache, A. "American and French Managers' Self-Perceived Abilities for Effective Functioning in Another Culture: A Comparative Study," unpublished doctoral dissertation. San Diego, CA: United States International University, 1986. Available through University Microfilms International.

Middle East and North Africa, 1984–1985. Detroit: Gale Research Co., 1985.

Miller, B. and Sugiyama, N. *Mitsubishi-U.S.A.* Queens, NY: Business Research Institute/St. John's University, 1982.

Miller, J. G. *Living Systems*. New York: McGraw-Hill, 1978.

Miller, V. A. *The Guidebook for International Trainers in Business and Industry*. New York: Van Nostrand Reinhold, 1979.

Mills, P. *Managing the Service Organization: A Post-Industrial Perspective*. Cambridge, MA: Ballinger Publishing, 1985.

Minsep, F. *The Business Traveler's Handbook—How to Get Along with People in 100 Countries*. Englewood Cliffs, NJ: Prentice Hall, 1983.

Montana, P. J. *Managing Terrorism Strategies for the Corporate Executive*. Riverside, CA: Global Risk Assessment Inc., 1983.

Moon-ik Song, *Successful Korean Businesses in the United States—a Study of Excellence*. San Diego: Unpublished doctoral dissertation, School of Business and Management, U.S. International University, 1983. (Available from University Microfilm International, Ann Arbor, MI.)

Moran, R. T. *Venturing Abroad in Asia*. New York, NY: McGraw-Hill, 1988.

Moran, R. T. "Cross-Cultural Contact," *International Management*, May 1985.

Moran, R. T. *Getting Your Yen's Worth: How to Negotiate with Japan, Inc.* Houston: Gulf Publishing, 1985.

Moran R. T. and Harris, P. R. *Managing Cultural Synergy*. Houston: Gulf Publishing, 1982.

Moran, R. T. "Japanese Participative Management or How Ringi Seido Can Do the Work for You," *Advanced Management Journal*, Summer, 1979.

Moran, R. T. and Stripp, W. G. *Dynamics of Successful International Business Negotiations*. Houston, TX: Gulf Publishing, 1991.

Morishima, M. *Why Has Japan Succeeded? Western Technology and the Japanese Ethos*. New York: Cambridge University Press, 1982.

Morris, D. *Manwatching: A Fieldguide to Human Behavior*. London, U.K.: Jonathon Cope, 1978.

Morrison, A. M., White, R. P., Van Velsor, E. (eds.) *Breaking the Glass Ceiling—Can Women Reach the Top of America's Corporations?* Reading, MA: Addison-Wesley Publishing, 1987.

Morrison, A. M., McCall, M., and Lombardo, M. M. *The Lessons of Experience—How Successful Executives Develop on the Job*. Lexington, MA: D. C. Heath/Lexington, 1988.

Moskowitz, M. *The Global Marketplace—102 of the Most Influential Companies Outside America.* New York, NY: Macmillan Publishing, 1989.

Mumford, S. J. "Overseas Adjustment as Measured by a Mixed Standard Scale," paper presented at the meeting of the Western Psychological Association, Sacramento, Calif., 1975.

Murphy, K. J. *Macroproject Development in the Third World: An Analysis of Transnational Partnerships.* Boulder, CO: Westview Press, 1983.

Nadler, L. (ed.) *The Handbook of Human Resource Development.* New York: John Wiley, 1984.

Nadler, L. *Corporate Human Resources.* New York: Van Nostrand Reinhold, 1980.

Nadler, L. and Nadler, Z. *The Conference Book.* Houston: Gulf Publishing, 1977.

Nadler, L., Nadler, Z., and Fetteroll, E. (eds.) *The Trainer's Resources.* Amherst, MA: Human Resource Development Press, 1986.

Naisbit, J. *Megatrends.* New York: Warner Communications, 1982.

Nanus, B. *The Leader's Edge.* Chicago, IL: Contemporary Books, Inc., 1990.

Nash, M. *Managing Organizational Performance.* San Francisco: Jossey Bass, 1983

Nath, R. *Comparative Management—A Regional View.* Cambridge, MA: Ballinger/ Harper & Row, 1987.

Nath, R. (ed.) *Comparative Management—A Regional View.* Cambridge, MA: Ballinger Publishing/Harper & Row, 1987.

National Commission on Space. *Pioneering the Space Frontier.* New York: Bantam Books, 1986.

Nawwab, I. I., Speers, P. C., and Hoyt, P. F. *Aramco and Its World—Arabia and the Middle East.* Houston, TX: Aramco Services Co. 1981.

Nordenstreng, K. and Schillen, H. I. *National Sovereignty and International Communication.* Norwood, NJ: Ablex Publications, 1983.

Nydell, M. K. *Understanding Arabs—A Guide for Westerners.* Yarmouth, ME: Intercultural Press, 1987.

Nydrop, R. F., et al. *Area Handbook for Saudi Arabia.* Washington, D.C.: Government Printing Office, 1977.

O'Neill, G. *The High Frontier—Human Colonies in Space.* Princeton, NJ: Space Studies Institute, 1989.

O'Neill, G. *The Technology Edge.* New York: Simon & Schuster, 1984.

Odiorne, G. S. *Strategic Management of Human Resources.* San Francisco: Jossey-Bass, 1984.

Orr, D. W. and Soroos, M. S. *The Global Predicament: Ecological Perspectives on World Order.* Chapel Hill, NC: University of North Carolina Press, 1979.

Ouchi, W. *The M-Form Society.* Reading, MA: Addison-Wesley, 1984.

Overseas Assignment Directory Service. White Plains, N.Y.: Knowledge Industry Publishing, 1985.

Ouichi, W. G. and Jaeger, A. M. "Made in America Under Japanese Management," *Harvard Business Review* Vol. 52, No. 5, pp. 61–69, 1974.

Paliwoda, S. J. and Liebrenz, M. L. "Expectations and Results of Contractual Joint Ventures by U.S. and U.K. MNCs in Eastern Europe," *European Journal of Marketing,* Vol. 18, No. 3, 1984:51–66.

Palmer, B. C. and Palmer, K. P. *The Successful Meeting Master Guide.* New York: AMACOM, 1984.

Pascale, R. *The Art of Japanese Management.* New York: Warner Books, 1981: "Fitting New Employees into the Company Cultures," *Fortune*, May 28, 1983: 40.

Pastor, R. A. and Castaneda, J. G. *Limits to Friendship: The United States and Mexico.* New York, NY: Alfred A. Knof, 1989.

Payer, L. *Medicine and Culture Varieties of Treatment in the United States, England, West Germany, and France.* New York, NY: Henry Holt, 1988.

Pedersen, Paul B., Draguns, J., Lonner, W., and Trimbler, J. E. *Counseling Across Cultures.* Honolulu, HI: University of Hawaii Press, 1989.

Pedersen, P. *A Handbook for Developing Multicultural Awareness.* Alexandria, VA: American Association for Counseling and Development, 1988.

Pegels, C. C. *Japan vs. the West.* Hingham, MA: Kluwer Academic Press, 1984.

Pelton, J. N. *Global Talk.* Boulder, CO: Advanced Telecommunications Research Center, University of Colorado.

Peters, T. J. and Austin, N. *Passion for Excellence.* New York: Random House, 1985.

Peters, T. J. and Waterman, R. H. *In Search of Excellence.* New York: Harper & Row, 1982.

Piet-Pelon, N. and Hornby, B. *In Another Dimension: A Guide for Women who Live Overseas.* Yarmouth, ME: Intercultural Press, 1985.

Piradov, A. S., "Creating a World Space Organization," *Space Policy*, May 1988, pp. 112–114.

Pitman, W. IN: Cornish, E. (ed.) *Through the 80s: Thinking Globally, Acting Locally.* Bethesda, MD: World Future Society, 1980.

Poniachek, H. A. *Direct Foreign Investment in the United States.* Lexington, MA: D.C. Heath/Lexington, 1987.

Porter, M. E. *Competitive Advantage: Creating and Sustaining Superior Performance.* New York: Free Press/Macmillan, 1985.

Pryce-Jones, D. *The Closed Circle—An Interpretation of the Arabs.* New York, NY: Burlingame Book/Harper & Row, 1988.

Purvis, A. C., (ed.), *Writing Across Languages & Cultures.* Newbury Park, CA: Sage Publications, 1988.

Pye, L. *Asian Power and Politics.* Cambridge MA: Harvard University Press, 1985.

Pye, L. *Chinese Commercial Negotiating Style.* Cambridge, MA: Oelgeschlager, Gunn & Hain Publishers, 1982.

Ramsey, P. G. *Teaching and Learning in a Diverse World—Multicultural Education for Young Children.* New York, NY: Teachers' College Press/Columbia University, 1987.

Raymond, D. J. and Eliot, S. V. *Grow Your Roots Anywhere Anytime.* Ridgefield, CT: Peter H. Wyden Publisher, 1980.

Reardon, K. *International Business Gift Giving Customs.* Janesville, WI: A Parker Pen Co., 1981.

Redden, W. W. *Culture Shock Inventory-Manual.* Fredericton, N.B., Canada: Organizational Tests Ltd., 1975. (Also available from International Publications Ltd., Melbourne House, Parliament St., Hamilton 5-31, Bermuda.)

Reischauer, E. O. *The Japanese.* Cambridge, MA: Harvard University Press, 1977.

Renwick, G. W. and Smart, R. *Australians and North Americans Interact.* Yarmouth, ME: Intercultural Press, 1990.

Renwick, G. W. *Malays and Americans: Definite Differences, Unique Opportunities.* Yarmouth, ME: Intercultural Press, 1986.

Rhinesmith, S. H. *Cultural Organizational Analysis*. Cambridge, MA: McBer & Company, 1971.

Richmond, Y. *U.S.-Soviet Cultural Exchanges, 1958-1986*. Boulder, CO: Westview Press, Inc. 1987.

Riddle, D. I. and Lanham, Z. D. "Internationalizing Written Business English," *The Journal for International Business*. Spring, 1985.

Ride, S. K. *Leadership and America's Future in Space*. Washington, D.C.: U. S. Government Printing Office, 1987.

Riggs, H. E. *Managing High Tech Companies*. Belmont, CA: Wadsworth, 1984.

Romano, D. *Intercultural Marriage—Promises and Pitfalls*. Yarmouth, ME: Intercultural Press, 1988.

Rosow, J. M. "Adapting Japanese Management to American Organizations," *Training and Development Journal*, September 1982, p. 9.

Rossman, M. L. *The International Businesswoman*. New York, NY: CBS Books/ Praeger, 1986.

Rowland, D. *Japanese Business Etiquette*. New York, NY: Warner Books, 1985.

Ruben, B. *Handbook of Intercultural Skills*, Vol. 1. Pergamon Press, New York, 1983.

Rugman, A. M. *International Business Firm and Environment*. New York: McGraw-Hill, 1985.

Ruprecht, M. M. and Wagoner, K. R. *Managing Office Automation*. New York: John Wiley, 1984.

Russell, P. *The Global Brain*. Los Angeles, J. P. Tarcher, 1983.

Sakmar, T. P., Gardiner, P. and Peterson, G. N. *Health Guide for International Travelers*. Yarmouth, ME: Intercultural Press, 1986.

Salk, J. *Anatomy of Reality*. New York: Columbia University Press, 1983.

Samovar, L. A. and Porter, R. E. *Intercultural Communication: A Reader*. Belmont, CA: Wadsworth Publishing, 1988.

Sapir, E. "Conceptual Categories in Primitive Languages," *Science* 74: 578, 1929.

Schaef, A. W. *Women's Reality and Emerging Female Systems in the White Male Society*. Minneapolis, MN: Winston Press, 1981.

Schein, E. W. H. *Organizational Culture and Leadership*. San Francisco: Jossey-Bass, 1985.

Schmidt, K. *Business Customs and Protocol Services*. Menlo Park, CA: SRI International, 1984.

Schnitzer, M. C., Liebrenz, M. L., and Kubin, K. K. *International Business*. Cincinnati: Sputh-Western Publishing, 1985.

Schuman, H. *Making It Abroad—The International Guide to Job Hunting*. Somerset, NJ: John Wiley & Sons, 1988.

Scott, B. *The Skills of Negotiating*. New York: John Wiley, 1982.

Scott, C. and Jaffe, D. *Managing Organizational Change*. Los Altos, CA: Crisp Publications Inc., 1988.

Sears, W. H. *Back in Working Order: How American Institutions Can Win the Productivity Battle*. Glenview, IL: Scott, Foresman, 1983.

Servan-Schrieber, J-J, *The World Challenge*. New York: Simon & Schuster, 1980.

Sethi, S. P., Nobuaki, N. and Swanson, C. L. *The False Promise of the Japanese Miracle*. Boston: Pitman Publishing, 1984.

Sexton D. L. and Smilor, R. W. (eds.) *The Art and Science of Entrepreneurship*. Cambridge, MA: Ballinger Publishing, 1985.

Seurat, S. *Technology Transfer—A Realistic Approach.* Houston: Gulf Publishing, 1979.

Shaevitz, M. *The Superwoman Syndrome.* New York: Warner Communications, 1984.

Shea, G. F. *Practical Ethics.* New York, NY: American Management Association/Publications Division, 1988.

Shea, G. F. *Managing a Difficult or Hostile Audience.* Englewood Cliffs, NJ: Prentice-Hall, 1984.

Shea, G. F. *Building Trust in the Workplace.* New York: American Management Associations (AMA Management Briefings) 1984.

Sheehy, G. *Passages: Predictable Crises of Adult Life.* New York: E. P. Dutton, 1976.

Sheffield, C. and Rosin, C. *Space Careers.* New York: William Morrow, 1984.

Sheppard, C. S. and Carrol, D. C. *Working in the Twenty-first Century.* New York: John Wiley, 1980.

Sherman, B. *The New Revolution: The Impact of Computers on Society.* New York: John Wiley, 1985.

Sherwood, J. "Creating Work Cultures with Competitive Advantages," *Organizational Dynamics*, Winter 1988, pp. 5–26.

Shilling, M. *Update Belgium.* Yarmouth, ME: Intercultural Press, 1989.

Shilling, N. *Bakra Insha Allah! Business, Living, and Travel in the Arab World.* New York: Inter-Crescent Publishing, 1978.

Shipler, D. K. *Russia: Broken Idols, Solemn Dreams.* New York, NY: Times Books, 1989.

Simon, D. F. *The China Venture: Corporate America Encounters the People's Republic of China.* Glenview, IL: Scott, Foresman, Co., 1988.

Simons, G. F. *Working Together—How to Become More Effective in a Multicultural Organization.* Los Altos, CA: Crisp Publications Inc., 1989.

Simons, G. F. *Bridging Gender Diversity.* Los Altos, CA: Crisp Publications Inc., 1990.

Simons, G. F., Colin, C. V., and Harris, P. R. *The Transcultural Manager—Strategies for Empowering the Multicultural Workforce.* Houston, TX: Gulf Publishing, 1992 (proposed).

Sinetar, M. "Relo Shock," *Personnel Journal*, May 1986 pp. 45–49.

Slack, J. D. and Fejes, F. *The Ideology of the Information Age.* Norwood, N.J.: Ablex Publishing, 1981.

Smilor, R. W. and Kuhn, R. L. *Corporate Creativity: Robust Companies and the Entrepreneurial Spirit.* New York: Praeger Publishers/CBS Inc., 1984.

Smith, M. *Western Europe and the United States.* Winchester, MA: George Allen & Unwin, Inc., 1984.

Snowdon, S. *The Global Edge How Your Company Can Win in the International Marketplace.* New York, NY: Simon & Schuster, 1986.

Stepford, J. M. (ed.) *The World Directory of Multinational Enterprises.* Detroit: Gale Publishing, 1983.

Stewart, M. *The Age of Interdependence: Economic Policy in a Shrinking World.* Cambridge, MA: MIT Press, 1984.

Stobaugh, R. and Wells, L. T. (eds.) *Technology Crossing Borders.* Boston: Harvard Business School Press, 1984.

Strassman, P. A. *The Information Payoff: The Transformation of Work in an Electronic Age.* New York: Free Press/Macmillan, 1985.

Szalai, A. and Petrelia, R. (eds.) *Cross-National Comparative Survey Research.* New York: Pergamon Press, 1977 (231-278).

Tager, M. J. *Transforming Stress Into Power.* Los Altos, CA: Crisp Publications Inc., 1988.

Tatsuno, S. *The Technology Strategy: Japan, High-Technology, and Control of the Twenty-first Century.* Englewood Cliffs, NJ: Prentice-Hall, 1986.

Taylor, T. W. *American Indian Policy.* Mt. Airy, MD: Lomond Publications, 1983.

Terpstra, V. *International Dimensions of Marketing.* Yarmouth, ME: Intercultural Press, 1988.

Terpstra, V. and David, K. *The Cultural Environment of International Business.* Cincinnati: South-Western Publishing, 1985.

Terry, E. *The Executive Guide to China.* Riverside, CA: Globe Risk Assessment, Inc., 1984.

Thurow, L. C. (ed.) *The Management Challenge: Japanese Views.* Cambridge, MA: MIT Press, 1985.

Tichy, N. *Managing Strategic Change: Technical, Political and Cultural Dynamics* New York: John Wiley, 1985.

Tichy, N. M. and Devanna, M. A. *The Transformational Leader.* New York: John Wiley, 1986.

Ting, W. *Business and Technological Dynamics in Newly Industrialized Asia.* Westport, CT: Quorum Books, 1985.

Toffler, A. *The Adaptive Corporation.* New York: McGraw-Hill, 1985.

Toffler, A. *The Third Wave.* New York: William Morrow, 1980.

Toffler, A. *Future Shock.* New York: Random House, 1970.

Torbiorn, I. *Living Abroad: Personal Adjustment and Personnel Policy in the Overseas Setting.* New York: John Wiley, 1982.

Triandis, H. C. and Lambert, W. W. (eds.) *Handbook of Cross-Cultural Psychology: Perspectives,* Vol.I–IV. Boston: Allyn and Bacon, 1980–81.

Triandis, H. C. (ed.) *Variations in Black and White Perceptions of the Social Environment.* Urbana, IL: University of Illinois Press, 1976.

Tung, R. L. *The New Expatriates—Managing Human Resources Abroad.* Cambridge, MA: Ballinger/Harper & Row, 1988.

Tung, R. L. "Selection and Training Procedures of U.S., European, and Japanese Multinationals. *California Management Review,* Fall 1982, Vol. 25, 57–70; "Selection and Training of Personnel for Overseas Assignments." *Columbia Journal of World Business.* Spring 1981 Vol. 16, 68–78.

Tung, R. L. *The New Expatriates: Managing Human Resources Abroad.* Cambridge, MA: Ballinger/Harper & Row, 1987.

Tyler, V. L. *Intercultural Interacting.* Provo, UT: BYU David M. Kennedy Center for International Studies, 1987.

Unterman, I. "Negotiation and Cross-cultural Communication" in *International Negotiation* edited by D. H. Bendhmane and J. W. McDonald. Washington, DC: Foreign Service Institute, U.S. Department of State, 1984.

Van Dljk, T. A. *Communicating Racism: Ethnic Prejudice in Thought and Talk.* Newbury Park, CA: Sage Publications, 1987.

Van Horn, M. *Pacific Rim Trade: The Definitive Guide to Exporting and Investment*. New York, NY: AMACOM, 1989.

Van Wolfern, K. *The Enigma of Japanese Power*. New York, NY: Alfred A. Knof, 1989.

Vetter, C. T. *Citizens Ambassadors Guidelines for Responding to Questions about America*. Provo. UT: BYU David M. Kennedy Center for International Studies, 1983.

Vogel, E. F. *Japan as Number One: Lessons for America*. Cambridge, MA: Harvard University Press, 1979.

Vreeland, N. *Area Handbook for Malaysia*. Washington, D.C.: Government Printing Office, 1977.

Walker, J. and Ambrex, M. (eds.) *The Business Travelers Handbook: A Guide to Europe; a Guide to the Middle East: A Guide to Latin America: A Guide to Africa*. New York: Facts on File Publications, 1981.

Wallerstein, I. (ed.) *The Struggle for Liberation in Southern Africa*. Beverly Hills, CA: Sage Publications, 1984.

Ward, T. *Living Overseas: A Book of Preparations*. New York: The Free Press/Macmillan, 1984.

Ways, M. *The Future of Business: Global Issues in the '80s and '90s*. Elmsford, N.Y.: Pergamon Press, 1979.

Wang, G. and Dissanayake, W. *Continuity and Change in Communications Systems: A Cross-cultural Perspective*. Norwood, NJ: Ablex, 1982.

Weatherford, J. *Indian Givers: How the Indians of the Americas Transformed the World*. New York, NY: Crown Publishers, 1988.

Webber, R. A. *Culture and Management*. Homewood, IL: Richard D. Irwin, 1969.

Weinshall, T. D. (ed.) *Culture and Management: Selected Readings*. New York: Penguin Books, 1977.

Weiss, S. E. and Stripp, W. *Negotiation with Foreign Business Persons: An Introduction for Americans with Propositions on Six Cultures*. New York University/Faculty of Business Administration, February 1985.

Whorf, B. L. *Collected paper on Metalinguistics*. Washington, D.C., Dept. of State, Foreign Service Institute, 1952.

Wilkens, A. L. *Developing Corporate Character—How to Successfully Change an Organization Without Destroying It*. San Francisco, CA: Jossey-Bass, 1989.

Williams, F. and Dordick, H. S. *The Executives' Guide to Information Technology*. New York: John Wiley, 1983.

Witham, L. *Malaysia: A Foreigner's Guide*. Yarmouth, ME: Intercultural Press/Hornbill Books, 1988.

Win, D. *International Careers*. Yarmouth, ME: Intercultural Press/Williamson, 1986.

Woodward, H. and Buchholz, S. *Aftershock—Helping People through Organizational Change*. Somerset, NJ: John Wiley & Sons, 1987.

Workman, S. *Bringing Up Children Overseas*. New York: Basic Books, 1977.

Wurzel, J. *Towards Multiculturals: Readings in Multicultural Education*. Yarmouth, ME: Intercultural Press, 1988.

Wriston, W. B., "The World Corporation—New Weight in an Old Balance," *Sloan Management Review*, Winter 1974.

Yoshino, M. Y. *Japan's Multinational Enterprises*. Cambridge MA: Harvard University Press, 1976.

Yun Kim. Y. and Gudykunst, W. B. (eds.) *Cross-cultural Adaptation*. Newbury Park, CA: Sage Publications, 1988.

Yun Kim, Y. and Gudykunst W. B. (eds.) *Theories in Intercultural Communication*. Newbury Park, CA: Sage Publications, 1988.

Zeira, Y. and Harari, E. "Structural Sources of Personnel Problems in Multinational Corporations: Third Country Nationals," *Omega*, Vol. 5, No. 2, 1977.

Zimmerman, M. *How to Do Business with the Japanese: A Strategy for Success*. New York: Random House, 1985.

Author Index

Subject Index

population trends in, 374
socio-political status, 373–378
Meyers, Judith, 224
Miami, Florida, and Latin American
population, 360–361
Microcultures, 206, 213, 216–217, 350
U.S., 356–365
Microelectronics and Computer
Technology Corporation, 310
Middle Easterners
communication with, 50–53
doing business with, 495–508
Midlands Bank of London, 14
Migration, and cross-cultural matters,
201
Military subcultures, 207, 208
Miskito Indians, 372
Misura Indians, 372
Mitchell, Scott, 245
Mitsubishi, 116–117, 261, 530
Models, for cross-cultural training
programs, 297–298
Mooney, Thomas, 391
Morality, 354
Philippines, 428–429
U.S., 354
Morgan Guaranty & Trust, 162
Morris, William, 549
Morrison Knudsen International, 246,
280, 390
Morton, Jack, 180
Multicultural management concepts,
102
Multicultural skills, 104–106
Multicultural training, 283–307
Multicultural understanding, 78–90
Multinational acquisitions, 159
Multinational corporations, in Mexico,
376

N

Nadler, Leonard, 133
Napoleonic Code, 260
National Association of Foreign Student
Advisors, 244

National Association of Home Based
Businesses, 324
National Business Incubation
Association, 324
National character, concept of, 263
National Foreign Trade Council, 26
Naval Overseas Duty Support Program,
246
Negotiating, 55–70
face-to-face behavior, 66–67
guidelines, 57–58
international, 61–62
skills, 58
decision-making and, 57
self-assessment of, 69–74
style, 69–74
in China, 410–411
in Soviet Union, 489–491
in U.S., 60–61
variables of, 57–58
Negotiation, ethics and, 67–69
Negotiators, skills of successful, 64–67
Neoricans, 222
Networking, 301
phenomena, 322–325
women and, 323
Networking Group, the, 324
Network Institute, 324
"New ethnicity," 535
New Guinea, and Bechtel, 279–280
New York Institute for Cross-Cultural
Communication, 321
Nicaragua, 378
Nigeria
business in, 520–526
business tips, 521–523
communication tips, 523
culture specifics, 520–526
decision making, 522–523
family, 513
forms of address, 524
greetings, 523–524
profile, 518
religion, 521
social customs, 524–526
social structure, 520

About the Authors

Philip R. Harris received his M.S. and Ph.D. from Fordham University. President of Harris International in LaJolla, California, he is a licensed management and organizational psychologist. As an international management consultant, he has successfully served over 180 multinational corporations, government agencies, associations, and educational institutions. His clients include Westinghouse Electric, Control Data Corporation, N.A.S.A., and the U.S. Department of Labor and Navy. A former college dean and vice-president, Dr. Harris was a Fulbright professor to India, as well as visiting professor at Pennsylvania State University, Temple University, and Sophia University, Tokyo. Dr. Harris is author/editor of numerous articles and books in the fields of education and management, and served as senior research associate for the California Space Institute, University of California—San Diego. Currently he is senior scientist with Netrologic, Inc. of San Diego, and serves as a research consultant for California's Law Enforcement Command College. He is also on the advisory boards of *European Business Review* (UK) and the Institute Security and Cooperation in Outer Space (Washington, DC).

Robert T. Moran, who received his M.A. and Ph.D. from the University of Minnesota, is a psychologist and an organizational management consultant whose specialties include cross-cultural training, program development and global human resource development. As an international consultant, he has worked with thousands of managers and executives who travel abroad and families moving overseas. Dr. Moran has designed and conducted programs and seminars for the American Management Associations, Control Data Corporation, Chase Manhattan Bank, N.A. Esso Eastern, Inc., J. I. Case, Exxon Chemical Asia Pacific, Volvo, FMC, Arthur Andersen and Company, the United Nations, and more than 100 other business organizations. Dr. Moran is director of the program in cross-cultural communication and professor of international studies at the American Graduate School of International Management, Glendale, Arizona. He is also a columnist for *International Management* (UK).